Art and
Architecture in
the Service
of Politics

Art and Architecture in the Service of Politics

edited by
Henry A. Millon and
Linda Nochlin

The MIT Press
Cambridge, Massachusetts,
and London, England

This book was set in VIP Optima by The
Composing Room of Michigan, printed and
bound by Halliday Lithograph Corporation in
the United States of America

Library of Congress Cataloging in Publication Data
Main entry under title:

Art and architecture in the service of politics

    Includes bibliographical references and index.
    1. Politics in art. 2. Art and revolutions
I. Millon, Henry A. II. Nochlin, Linda.
N8236.P5177   701   78-1311
ISBN 0-262-13137-4

$\cancel{B}$ 4-10-80

Contents

Introduction

What effect has politics had upon art? This was the basic question animating the editors of this volume of essays in their initial enterprise. The answers, as might be expected, were neither simple nor concise. As a group, these studies provide a great deal of new information and many new ideas about a controversial area. Yet as a whole this book may seem to provoke as many questions as it answers— and this, we believe, is all to the good.

The authors of the articles originally prepared their papers for a two-stage colloquium held at MIT under the sponsorship of the Department of Architecture in December 1972 and February 1974 and revised them for publication after these critical discussion sessions. It was the stated purpose of the colloquium to examine the effects of political intention on works of art in the broadest kind of historical context and from a multiplicity of viewpoints. The areas to be investigated included painting and graphics, sculpture and film (although the latter was eventually omitted), and architecture and city planning. Art historians of varying backgrounds and viewpoints, united only by an interest in the interaction of art and politics in previous work, were called on to prepare papers in their particular realms of expertise. The historical periods under investigation ranged from the Middle Ages to the present day. Approaches and methodology varied significantly, ranging from what might be called "traditional-empirical" to "Marxist-critical," with many shades between; a good deal of the discussion time of the colloquium was, in fact, given over to examination of the ideological assumptions, overt or hidden, controlling the ways various participants dealt with their particular subjects.

Interpretations of the subject of this book vary considerably, as does the methodology of the various authors. Yet one stipulation has provided, and continues to provide, a firm center uniting all the essays: each of the authors was requested to deal with a work or works of art clearly dedicated to a previously stipulated political purpose, rather than with artworks to which political implications had accrued over time or which had vaguely socially significant subject matter.

The aim of this volume, like that of the colloquium from which it arose, was in no sense a complete coverage of the field of art and politics, if, indeed, any such field even exists. The intention was rather to examine interesting, significant, or at times unexpected or controversial instances in which art has indeed served political aims,—instances in which artistic intentions and political strategies have intersected. In many cases as in suffragette posters, fascist city planning, or the art produced by the late leftist régime in Chile, the political intentions may be vividly present on the surface of the works in question. However, at times the political intentions animating the artists or architects in question must be searched out, painstakingly recaptured, and contexts of political intention reconstructed. In still other instances, the political intentions or the stipulated program of the work, although by no means completely hidden, may seem at the outset to be veiled in ambiguity: conflicting ideologies may indeed make some artworks visual palimpsests, in which latent and manifest content give off apparently contradictory political and psychological messages.

Certainly, political purpose in art and architecture, although far from being a major interest of art historians[1], has not been totally neglected, especially in recent years.[2] Yet rarely has the issue of art and architecture in the service of politics been dealt with on an expansive scale and at the same time focused sharply on a quite specific notion of what is meant by the interaction of the aesthetic and the political. Precisely this combination of breadth and stringency, at least in part, constitutes the novelty of this collection of essays—essays that are the final product of, although they hardly exhaust, the lively and critical discussions of the colloquium itself.

Although each of the studies in this volume is a finished and substantial examination of a specific instance in which artworks have been shaped by political purposes and therefore in a sense may be said to constitute a last word in its particular domain, it is to be hoped that the collection as a whole may serve to generate further questions, substantive or methodological, and suggest further areas of investigation or interpretation.

One might wish to consider, for example, not merely the ways politics may affect the work of art, but in what sense an artwork may itself constitute a political act or statement, rather than being conceived of merely as the result of a political intention. This is perhaps obvious in the case of a pageant or a building program but less immediately evident in works of high art, in which art historians and critics have had quite different interests at stake in their interpretations or analyses. What, from this vantage point, is the position of completely abstract works whose creators had definite political goals or doctrines in view? One might think especially of artists associated with the Russian revolution. And what, on the other hand, of the tendency of the public or some fraction of it to see political meaning—revolutionary or counterrevolutionary threat—in works of abstract art, often created without any such overt, or even covert, political intention? Martin Dies, for example, saw advanced twentieth-century art as "subversive" or "communistic" at the same time that Stalin condemned it as symptomatic of bourgeois decadence, while the Nazis reviled it as both Bolshevik *and* decadent at the same time.

One might also ask what is implied by referring to certain artworks or types of art as "propaganda," or, more frequently, as "mere" propaganda. What biases or judgments are often concealed beneath this generally pejorative term? Is an artwork that makes a deliberate effort to spread doctrines, ideas, arguments, facts, or allegations in order to further one's cause or damage an opposing cause (to paraphrase the dictionary definition of propaganda), by definition bad or inferior art? Are propaganda and quality necessarily mutually exclusive? How much political deliberateness is possible for good art? One might examine the premises upon which the mutual exclusiveness of art and propaganda is based and see that they themselves have a basis in ideology, rather than being rooted in objective fact or natural aesthetic law. If the intention to convince, characteristic of propaganda, is necessarily antithetical to those properties identifiable as art, then quite a few medieval, Renaissance, and baroque works must be stricken from the lists. Does the passage of time tend to dim the propagandistic thrust of the original art statement?

Are there specific formal qualities or types of imagery peculiar to political art? If there is a distinctive type of political art language, is it different in different contexts and in different periods? Is it meaningful to trace the fate of a particular political image through varying historical periods? What is the political implication of the metamorphosis of certain politically charged icons? Is the art used to further politically reactionary causes different in kind from contemporary art sponsored by liberal or radical positions, or are there sometimes striking resemblances? How, and under what circumstances, has political radicalism been equated with formal innovation?

One might consider for which groups or class interests particular works of art are created. Are more subtle definitions and differentiations than those generally employed by art historians necessary to determine the precise political context within which certain works came into being? Are the traditional methods of art history adequate for a discussion of the deeper relations existing between artworks and ideology generally, artworks and political ideology specifically, or do these traditional methods tend to veil such connections with a kind of softening neutralism which is itself an ideological position?

How is a new revolutionary or emergent political group consciousness formulated in art? It would have been useful to have some discussion of black politically focused art, both here and in the African nations, Puerto Rican art, the art of certain radical feminist groups, and the art of contemporary China. Do such groups tend to invent new art languages, do they simply take over available languages, or do they transform existing languages in order to serve new purposes, thereby creating new styles? Is there an interaction among the various media in the creation-transformation of these new languages?

Finally, in the context of a discussion of the relation of politics to art it is important to consider the crucial borderline that seems to separate the realm of private sensibility from public demonstration in nineteenth- and twentieth-century art. Why, since the middle of the nineteenth century at least, has there been such a strong tendency to associate public and collective, hence, political, experience with the aesthetically shoddy, banal, and shopworn (sometimes subsumed under the term *kitsch*) and private and personal experience with the highest achievements in art? To what extent does this division coincide with the actuality of art and experience during the last 150 years, and to what extent is it part of the ideology controlling our conception of it?

Notes

1
That art (and perhaps art history and criticism) can be politically dangerous to the status quo has always been recognized by art historians. Its potential revolutionary value has been attested to from the time of Plato's *Republic* to the suppression of certain forms of art (and of art history and criticism) by governments, fascist and socialist, in our own age. Art (art history and criticism) may also support an existing regime, as the chapters by Catlin, Butler, Kunzle, Kostof, Schroeter, and Millon demonstrate.

2
For some recent examinations of this issue from a variety of vantage points concerned mainly with the art of the nineteenth and twentieth centuries, see the following:

Albert Boime, "The Second Republic's Contest for the Figure of the Republic," *Art Bulletin,* 53 (1971): 68–83; T. J. Clark, *The Absolute Bourgeois: Artists and Politics in France, 1848–1851* (London, 1973); idem, *Image of the People: Gustave Courbet and the Second French Republic, 1848–1851* (London, 1973); Francis Haskell, "The Manufacture of the Past in Nineteenth-Century Painting," *Past and Present* 53 (Nov. 1971): 109–120; Eugenia W. Herbert, *The Artist and Social Reform: France and Belgium, 1885–1898* (New Haven, 1961); Robert L. Herbert, *David, Voltaire, 'Brutus' and the French Revolution: An Essay in Art and Politics* (New York, 1972); Robert L. Herbert and Eugenia W. Herbert, "Artists and Anarchism: Unpublished Letters of Pissarro, Signac, and Others: I," *Burlington Magazine,* 102 (1960): 473–482; 2:517–522; Ruble Kaufmann, "Francois Gérard's 'Entry of Henry IV into Paris': The Iconography of Constitutional Monarchy," *Burlington Magazine,* 117 (1975): 790–802; Robert Rosenblum, "Painting During the Bourbon Restoration, 1814–1830" in *French Painting 1774–1830: The Age of Revolution* (exhibition catalog), Réunion des Musées Nationaux, Paris; Institute of Fine Arts, Detroit; Metropolitan Museum of Art (New York, 1975).

Art In Revolution: Soviet Art and Design since 1917 (exhibition catalog), Hayward Gallery (London, 26 February to 18 April, 1971); Carol Duncan, "Neutralizing 'The Age of Revolution'," *Artforum* 14 (Dec. 1975): 36–45; A. Higgins, "Art and politics in the Russian Revolution," *Studio,* 180 (Nov./Dec. 1970): 164–167, 224–227; Manvela Hoelterhoff, "Arts of the Third Reich: Documents of Oppression," *Artforum* 14 (Dec. 1975): 55–62; Max Kozloff, "American Painting During the Cold War," *Artforum,* 11 (May 1973): 43–54; Barbara Miller Lane, *Architecture and politics in Germany, 1918–1945* (Cambridge, Mass., 1968); Linda Nochlin, "The Paterson Strike Pageant of 1913," *Art in America* (May–June 1974), pp. 64–68; Susan Sontag, "Introductory Essay," *The Art of Revolution* (New York, 1970); R. Taylor, *The word in stone, the role of architecture in the National Socialist ideology* (Berkeley, 1974); Audrey Topping, "The Rent Collection Courtyard," *Art in America* (May–June, 1974), pp. 69–83; Peter Walch, "Images of the Chinese People," *Artforum* 14 (Dec. 1975): 63–64.

In addition, while they do not deal specifically with the relation of individual art works and political intentions, the following more general surveys are useful in approaching the issue under discussion:

Jean Cassou, et al., *Art and Confrontation: The Arts in an Age of Change,* trans. N. Foxell (Greenwich, Conn., 1968); Donald Drew Egbert, *Social Radicalism and the Arts: Western Europe (New York, 1970);* Nicos Hadjinicolaou, *Histoire de l'art et lutte des classes* (Paris, 1974); Mikel Dufrenne, *Art et politique,* (Paris, 1974).

Art and
Architecture in
the Service
of Politics

1
Constantinian Politics and the Atrium Church

Richard Stapleford

To Richard Krautheimer

Architecture through its political content can influence the course of events and at the same time determine historical attitudes that obscure the alternate paths history might have taken. The standard Christian basilica is a case in point. Its appearance is integrally bound up with Constantine's program to Christianize the Roman state, yet the ubiquitousness of the Christian basilica down through history has obscured its original meaning and thus its true role in the emperor's plans. Removal of the layers of meaning accrued through subsequent centuries, however, reveals with startling clarity the revolutionary character of Constantine's decision and demonstrates more convincingly perhaps than any document that the emperor was not only forming a new imperial organization but establishing a pattern of priorities destined to control the shaping of history even into our century.

Most studies of the origin of Christian church architecture have considered the basilica as a form independent of the other elements in the church complex, quite justifiably since some of Constantine's churches consisted, as far as we know, of only a basilica.[1] A substantial number of the most important churches, however, were complexes composed of propylaeum, atrium, and basilica. Since the separate parts of Roman architectural complexes are never independent in meaning from each other but add to and deepen the content of the whole composition, a consideration of the atrium should lead to a further enrichment of our understanding of the meaning of the Constantinian basilica complex and of Constantine's intentions in imposing this form on Christian architecture.[2]

Unfortunately, not one Constantinian atrium has survived intact, so in order to reconstruct accurately the form and use of the atrium, we are forced to rely on documentary and archeological information. Such evidence, however, is often quite illuminating. The Cathedral of Tyre, for instance, has vanished without a trace but Eusebius has left us a passage which describes both the form and function of an Early Christian atrium. That passage is worth quoting in full.

The outer enclosure he made strong with the wall surrounding the whole, so that it might be a most secure defence thereof; while he spread out a porch, great and raised aloft, towards the rays of the rising sun, and even to those standing far outside the sacred precincts supplied no scanty view of that which is within; thus, one might say, turning the gaze, even of strangers to the faith, towards the first entrances, so that none might hastily pass by without first having his soul mightily struck. . . . Now he hath not permitted him that passeth inside the gates to tread forth with unhallowed and unwashen feet upon the holy places within; but hath left a space exceeding large between the temple and the first entrances, and adorned it all around with four transverse colonnades, fencing the place into a kind of quadrangular figure, with pillars raised on every side, and filling the spaces between them with wooden barriers of lattice-work rising to a convenient height; and in the midst thereof he hath left an open space where men can see the sky, thus providing it with air bright and open to the rays of light. And here he hath placed symbols of sacred purifications, by erecting fountains right opposite the temple, whose copious streams of flowing water supply cleansing to those who are advancing within the sacred precincts. And this is the first stopping-place for those that enter; supplying at once adornment and splendour to the whole, and a place of sojourn suited to such as are still in need of their first instructions. (Eusebius *Ecclesiastical History* 10. 4. 37–40 trans. K. Lake, Loeb Classical Library)

In short, the atrium is, Eusebius says, a very large quadrangular area situated between the porch and the church proper, open to the sky and surrounded on four sides by colonnades. Conveniences for washing, apparently in the side facing the basilica facade, and areas for catechumens to gather were provided within. To be sure, the term *atrium* is not used by Eusebius. In fact, he is exceptionally elusive in his terminology and uses no more precise a word than τετραγωνον, but his description leaves no doubt that he is referring to that element of the church complex that we commonly call the atrium.[3]

Several of Constantine's churches had atria corresponding to Eusebius's description while several others had variant forms or none at all. Following is a summary of the current state of knowledge concerning the atrium in those Constantinian churches relevant to our discussion.[4]

Catalog

S. Giovanni Laterano in Rome (Fig. 1), the Basilica Constantiniana, which was Constantine's first Christian foundation and therefore of seminal importance for his later churches, has never been shown to have had an atrium; not the slightest fragment of indubitable authenticity has been found, in spite of the fact that the area in front of the church has always been relatively free of later structures. In fact, one of the two principal ancient roads leading from the Porta Asinaria cuts across the area immediately in front of the church, bisecting the presumed place of an atrium.[5] The basilica, however, was only one element of what must have been an exceptionally extensive palace. Remains of baths and other ancient structures have been discovered all around the site. Moreover, Constantine also had a baptistery built, apparently as part of the same complex and strongly oriented toward the basilica by means of a monumental pronaos. Excavations of 1876–1877 revealed remains of previous structures between the apse of the basilica and the freestanding baptistery some 50 m northwest and enabled the excavators to reconstruct the outlines of a court connecting the two structures.[6] The recent excavations of 1964–1966 (as

yet unpublished) have revealed remains of Constantinian columns and painted rooms embedded in the walls of the baptistery chapels and representing perhaps other architectural elements fronting on this hypothetical court. The Constantinian basilica may not have had an atrium in the conventional sense, then, but it apparently did have an enclosed area behind open to the sky and perhaps flanked by rooms linking two important buildings in the complex.

S. Paolo fuori-le-mura, begun by Constantine in about 326, seems to have been a surprisingly modest commission in light of the magnificence of his reconstruction of that other apostle's tomb in Rome, St. Peter's. It was replaced in the last decades of the fourth century, but a segment of the Constantinian apse foundation was discovered in excavations in the nineteenth century permitting a hypothetical reconstruction of a rather small church with its facade close to the Via Ostiense—too close, it would seem, to allow room for an atrium.[7]

The basilica of St. Peter's (Fig. 2) did have an atrium—at least by 397, when it is mentioned and praised by Paulinus of Nola (*Patrologia Latina*, 61, cols. 213, 215). While no conclusive proof that this atrium was of Constantinian date can be adduced, the great weight of evidence indicates that it was.[8] It seems to have been columned, and it had a fountain in the middle, thus comparing favorably with Eusebius's cathedral of Tyre.

After ca. 330, Constantine began no new architectural projects in Rome but confined his energies to buildings in the Holy Land and Constantinople.[9] The greatest of his projects was, of course, his Church of the Holy Sepulchre (Figs. 3, 4, 5), begun in 328 and consecrated in 335. Though the present site preserves none of the majestic work of Constantine's architects, its basic outlines as well as a fair idea of the details of the structure can be reconstructed by means of Eusebius's description and of the comments of Etheria, a pilgrim of ca. 385.[10] Eusebius describes in detail the two courtyards of the complex. First, the courtyard behind the basilica:

The next object of his attention [after the sepulcher] was a space of ground of great extent, and open to the pure air of heaven. This he adorned with a pavement of finely polished stone and enclosed it on three sides with porticoes of great length. For at the side opposite to the cave, which was the eastern side, the church itself was erected.

Now the atrium proper:

. . . In the next place [after the "church itself"] he enclosed the atrium which occupied the space leading to the entrances in front of the church. This comprehended first the court, then the porticoes on each side, and, lastly, the gates of the court. After these in the midst of the open marketplace, the general entrance gates, which were of exquisite workmanship, afforded to passersby on the outside a view of the interior which could not fail to inspire astonishment. (*Life of Constantine*, 2. 35–36, 39)

1
S. Giovanni Laterano, Rome. Plan by
C. Rainaldi, ca. 1645.

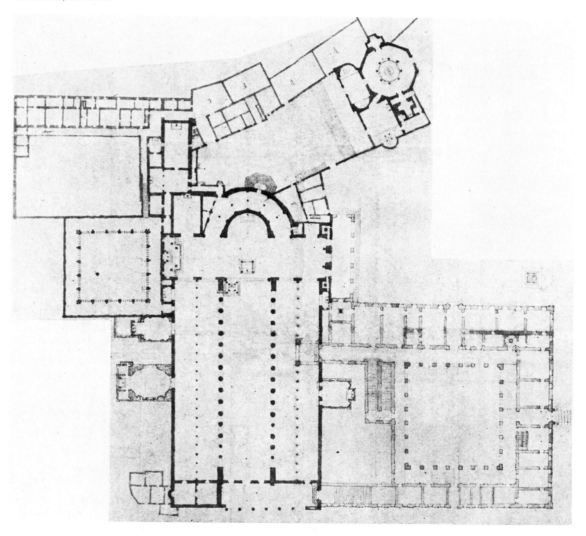

2
Old St. Peter's, Rome. Exterior reconstruction. (Conant, *Early Medieval Architecture,* pl. III)

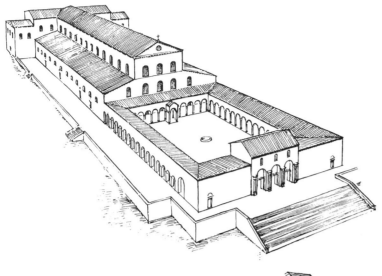

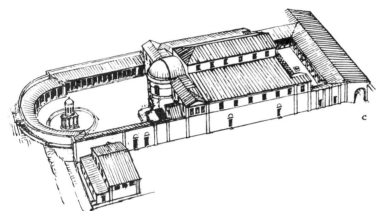

3
Holy Sepulchre, Jerusalem. Exterior reconstruction. (Conant, in *Speculum,* 1956, pl. III)
4
Holy Sepulchre, Jerusalem. Plan. (Conant, in *Speculum,* 1956, pl. IV)

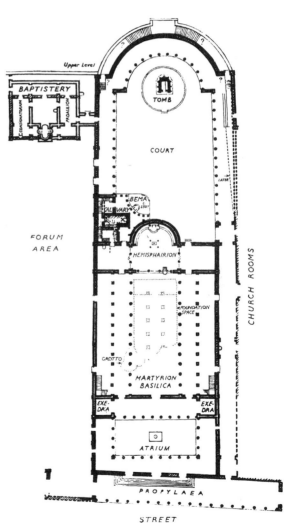

5
Holy Sepulchre, Jerusalem. Recon-
struction of rear courtyard. (Conant, in
Speculum, 1956, pl. VIII)

The reconstruction is quite clear: A monumental propylaeum gave onto an open peristyle at the bottom of which was the entrance facade of the basilica, apparently also columned. Behind the basilica was another court surrounded on three sides by columns and containing the two memoriae of the site, Golgotha and the Holy Sepulchre itself. By the end of the century when Etheria saw the complex, both memoriae had been given independent buildings—the sepulcher an elaborate rotunda and the hill apparently a small double-entranced structure of some sort—but they remained enclosed in the Constantinian courtyard, "a court of great size and some beauty [in which] all the people assembled in such numbers there is no thoroughfare" (*Pilgrimage of Etheria,* 76). Etheria states further that this large rear courtyard was the assembly area before service (thus if ritual ablutions were necessary they would be performed there) and that the same area was the place where the catechumens remained while the faithful entered the anastasis rotunda. These two functions are exactly those ascribed to the atria of Tyre and of St. Peter's by Eusebius and Paulinus, respectively. Thus a problem: if the rear courtyard of the Holy Sepulchre served a function identical to that of the atrium, why did the architect bother to include the atrium preceding the basilica? Clearly, the atrium preceding the facade must have had a special significance beyond its utilitarian function as a gathering place or its ritual function as the place of personal ablution.

The basilica on the Mount of Olives, the Eleona (Fig. 6), seen by the Bordeaux pilgrim in 333 and identified by him and Eusebius as an imperial commission, was excavated in 1910.[11] Pére Vincent's reconstruction is pure fantasy in certain details (for example, the polygonal apse), but the existence of an atrium and a monumental entrance seems to be clearly proved. Again details of the atrium's structure are impossible to determine, but its size was ca. 25 m by 21 m, and it was of an area equal to that of the basilica.

The Church of the Nativity at Bethlehem (Fig. 7), though rebuilt entirely after Justinian, is mentioned by Eusebius as having been built by Constantine and was seen by the Bordeaux pilgrim in 333. Here too archaeologists have discovered the remains of Constantine's atrium, and it can be reconstructed as having been an almost square colonnaded peristyle preceded by a deep open forecourt.[12]

Constantine had a basilica built also at Mambre (Fig. 8), where the three angels appeared to Abraham, a site already sacred to Jews for centuries.[13] The structure as excavated was quite strange: it consisted of a precinct wall (ca. 65 m by 50 m) preceding a small squat basilica flanked by two small courts. No evidence of a peristyle was found, and the excavators concluded that the forecourt was a sort of sacred enclosure for the holy oak and spring. The court then differs from a true atrium by its lack of a peristyle, by its rather overwhelming size in relation to the church itself, and perhaps by the lack of a strong entrance axis created by a monumental entrance opposite the church facade. Its function as a sheltering area for a venerated site recalls that of the second courtyard at the Holy Sepulchre.[14]

At Constantinople the emperor built the Church of the Holy Apostles, which was to include his tomb. Eusebius tells us that the building "was surrounded by an open area of great extent, the four sides of which were terminated by porticoes which enclosed the area and the church itself. Adjoining these porticoes were ranges of stately chambers, with baths and promenades, and besides many apartments adapted to the use of those who had charge of the place" (Eusebius *V.C.* 3. 58). Thus still another use is introduced for the peristyle—it surrounds an area in the middle of which stands the church building including the emperor's tomb.[15]

This use of the peristyle is exactly paralleled in another Constantinian building, the Golden Octagon in Antioch: "... [in Antioch] as the head of that portion of the empire, he consecrated to the service of God a church of unparalleled size and beauty. The entire building was encompassed by an enclosure of great extent within which the church itself rose to a vast elevation, being of octagonal form" (Eusebius *V.C.* 3. 50).[16]

Hagia Sophia (Figs. 9, 10), the cathedral of Constantinople, seems to have been begun between 335 and 337 and was apparently preceded by an atrium of rather shallow depth but extending the width of the church. This atrium was reconstructed by Theodosius II; hence the excavations of A. M. Schneider revealed very little of the Constantinian structure. It was in all likelihood a colonnaded forecourt with an imposing entrance opposite the facade of the basilica.[17]

Finally, in order to flesh out the picture of Constantinian atria, churches in other parts of the empire should be mentioned. The double basilica of Trier (Figs. 11, 12), dating ca. 326, after 340 was preceded by a genuine atrium. The double basilica of Aquileia, however, though of similar date (314–325), seems to have had no atrium.[19] The basilica of St. Reparatus at Orléansville (completed by 324) in North Africa likewise had no atrium.[20]

Analysis

Several different uses of enclosed courtyards can be distinguished, then, among Constantinian churches, and it is useful to analyze these variants in order to determine as nearly as possible what special role the

6

Eleona Basilica, Jerusalem. Plan and
elevation. (Vincent and Abel,
Jérusalem nouvelle, Paris, 1925)

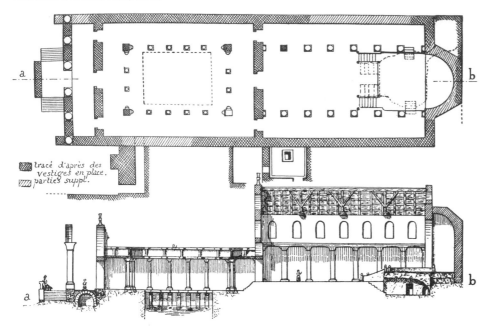

7

Church of the Nativity, Bethlehem.
Isometric reconstruction.
(Krautheimer, *ECB Arch.,* fig. 15)

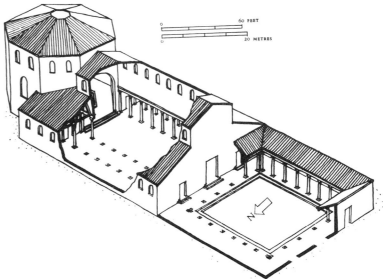

8
Basilica of Abraham, Mambre. Exterior reconstruction and plan.
(*R.A.C.*, 1929, fig. 16)

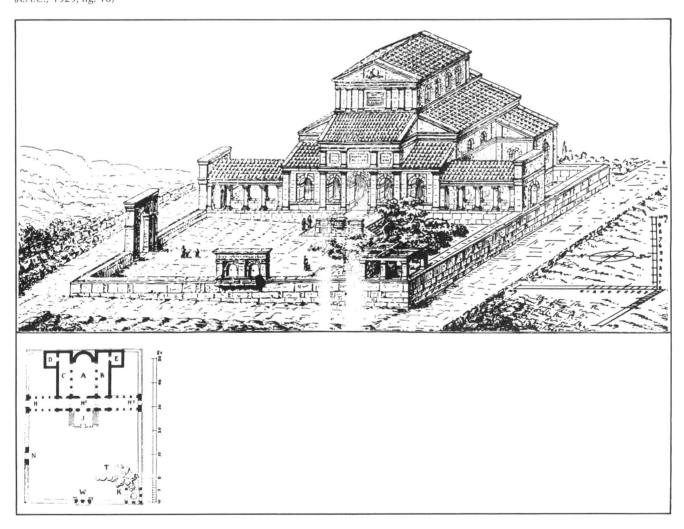

9
Hagia Sophia, Constantinople. Reconstructed plan. (*Istanbuler* Mit-
teilungen, 1965, fig. 4)

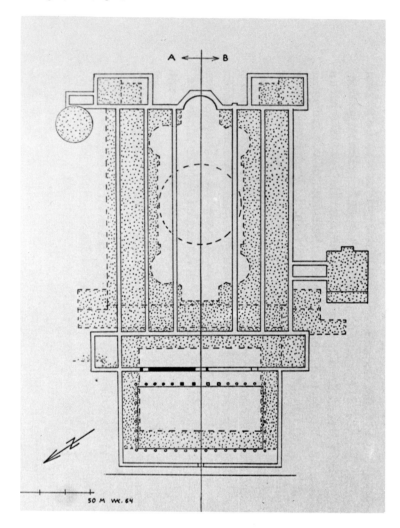

10
Hagia Sophia, Constantinople. Recon-
struction of fastigium. A.M. Schneider,
(*Archeol. Anz.*, 1935, fig. 2)

11
Double basilica, Trier. Plan. (*Germania,* 1951, fig. 2)

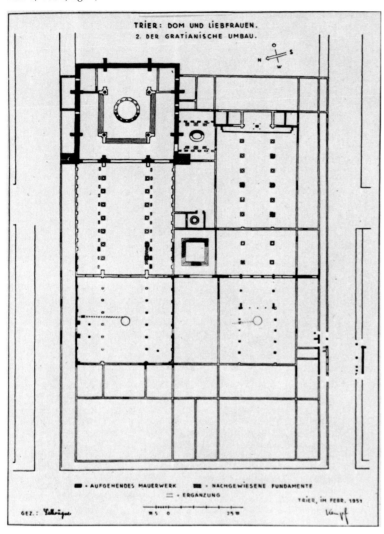

TRIER: DOM UND LIEBFRAUEN.
2. DER GRATIANISCHE UMBAU.

■ = AUFGEHENDES MAUERWERK   ▦ = NACHGEWIESENE FUNDAMENTE
═ = ERGÄNZUNG

TRIER, IM FEBR. 1951

GEZ.:

12
North basilica, Trier. Isometric.
(Krautheimer, *ECB Arch.,* fig. 23)

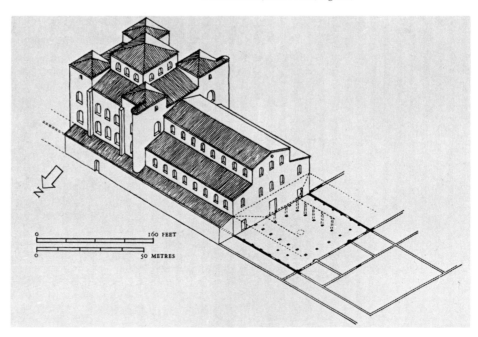

160 FEET

50 METRES

atrium took within the complex. What are traditionally recognized as genuine atria existed at Tyre, St. Peter's, Trier, the Holy Sepulchre, Eleona, Bethlehem, and Hagia Sophia in Constantinople. All these atria share certain features: they occupy a large open area between a monumental entrance and the church facade, and they are surrounded by columned porticoes. The worshipper, moreover, was forced to pass into and through them as a necessary first experience before he could enter the church proper; thus they become a kind of monumental vestibule both to the complex and to the religious experience.

Variant usages of courtyards in church complexes help to clarify the special nature of the true atrium. The church at Mamre, for instance, included a large open courtyard before the church building, but here the function of the courtyard was to surround the sacred precinct containing the oak and springs of Abraham. The basilica, rather small and with a facade occupying substantially less than a whole side of the courtyard, could not have been said to be the inevitable completion of either the architectural or the spiritual experience. On the contrary, it was merely one element in a series of sacred elements enclosed within the precinct wall. We should not be surprised then that the different function of the courtyard produced different architectural forms. Most notably, the civilizing effect of the all-around portico was replaced by the sense of simple enclosure of the plain precinct wall; the strong axiality of the atrium with its single monumental entrance opposite the church facade was diluted by the three entrances at Mamre, the principal one apparently in the lateral wall and not opposite the facade. Clearly, then, an atrium was a special feature in both form and function to Constantine's architects; just any forecourt preceding a church was not an atrium.

Another instructive variant usage of the porticoed courtyard occurred at the Holy Sepulchre and at S. Giovanni Laterano. In the former the rear courtyard described by Eusebius and Erithria was an intermediate assembly area between and surrounding the venerated sites. The architect must have considered true atria more than merely utilitarian assembly areas since he included in the same complex a monumental entrance and atrium preceding the basilica facade. In comparable fashion, at S. Giovanni the courtyard, set obliquely between the back of the basilica and the baptistery, whatever its details, was architecturally an intermediate area and by virtue of its oblique angle and its position behind the basilica did not provide the axiality and vestibule character of the true atrium.

Finally, at Antioch and at the Church of the Holy Apostles at Constantinople, Constantine's architects used the porticoed courtyard to set off a whole precinct in the middle of which rose the church proper. The expansion of the area *around* the building rather than up to it would have basically altered the essential vestibule function of the atrium, that is, as an intermediate architectural experience culminating inevitably in the church. Equivalent uses of the portico to enclose a sacred precinct with the object of veneration isolated in the middle are common enough in late antique architecture: for example, the mausoleum of Romulus on the Via Appia and the mausoleum of Diocletian at Spalato.[27] Both are, incidentally, tombs to shelter imperial bodies, and Constantine's Holy Apostles was also intended to be his mausoleum. But Antioch seems never to have been intended for use as a mausoleum, so the all-encompassing portico apparently did not have exclusively funeral connotations. Indeed, the ancient descriptions of these buildings with periboli are more reminiscent of the great imperial thermae than anything else.

Given the assumption that an omission can be as telling as an inclusion, the exclusion of atria from St. Paul's in Rome, Orléansville, and Aquileia is perhaps significant. The three churches are alike in that all three are modest, probably inexpensive, and small (Orléansville was only ca. 15 m by 27 m; St. Paul's was perhaps equivalent; and Aquileia, though larger, 32 m by 74 m, was still dwarfed by the imperial double basilica at Trier, 150 m by 105 m). Ostentation is absent from the three plans, and nowhere in them can we sense the expansive rhetoric of imperial architecture present in all of the other examples. They are utterly simple and utilitarian. Because of its exclusion here, then, the atrium can perhaps be seen as a rhetorical device and not a formal necessity—and this point will prove to be especially important.

Might the atrium be, however, merely a convenient response to liturgical demands? After all, Eusebius, Etheria, and Paulinus all describe how the atrium was used liturgically—for ablutions and for the isolation of catechumens. But as has been pointed out previously, the Holy Sepulchre satisfied these needs with its second courtyard; yet the architects still felt compelled to add the atrium. Moreover, the very fact that some churches were not equipped with atria suggests that the atrium was not a liturgical necessity.[22] In architecture function is never sufficient excuse for form, and nowhere is that truism more clearly demonstrated than in the unexpected choice by Constantine's architects of basilica and atrium for Christian sanctuaries.

Secular Parallels

The problem of the meaning of the atrium can be illuminated, perhaps, by determining where in contemporary secular architecture can be found atria paralleling the use and form of those in Constantinian churches. Several examples can be reconstructed, and all of them, strikingly enough, are in imperial semipublic audience hall complexes. No less a building than Constantine's throne room in the Great Palace at Constantinople, the so-called Magnaura, was, according to ancient sources, a colonnaded hall preceded by an atriumlike forecourt.[23] Another imperial audience hall of Constantine, that at Trier (Fig. 13), was preceded by a long narthex with a monumental entrance and apparently a forecourt.[24] The palace of Diocletian at Split (Fig. 14), though a castrum in its basic plan, has the significant addition of a long colonnaded courtyard leading up to a monumental arched fastigium through which the emperor appeared to the people. Behind this fastigium was a rotunda giving onto a long basilica-like hall.[25] Though the function of this hall cannot be definitely determined, the preceding colonnaded courtyard and the monumental entrance in combination with the basilica form suggest an analogy with Constantine's audience halls at Constantinople and Trier. The fastigium, then, would have been a monumental frame for the emperor when he made official public appearances to the citizens gathered in the courtyard, and the rotunda would have been a sort of vestibule (like a church narthex) before entry into the sacred presence of the emperor. As if to verify this analysis, another Diocletianic structure, the castrum at Palmyra (Fig. 15), uses the same axially disposed sequence of propylaeum, peristyle, vestibule, and basilica.[26]

Another approximately contemporary imperial structure that contained a large audience basilica was the villa at Piazza Armerina (Fig. 16). Aside from its extraordinary plan, the villa is interesting in our context for its unusual inclusion of a peristyle courtyard (irregular area at the lower right in the plan) entered through a monumental entrance containing fountains. True, this "atrium" by no means gives onto the imperial basilica, which is situated rather far from it; it is nevertheless comparable in that it serves as a monumental porticoed entrance court to an imperial architectural complex culminating in an audience basilica.[27]

The funeral complex, including the mausoleum of Galerius in Salonica, later converted to the Church of St. George, was entered through a large, richly decorated triumphal arch. Then the worshipper passed along a long colonnaded area that opened into a courtyard within which was the rotunda of the mausoleum. Though the form of the complex is not identical to the previous ones, the sequence of experiences was: monumental propylaeum and porticoed open area leading to the object of veneration—in this case not the enthroned emperor but the entombed emperor.[28]

These examples of "atria" (if such they may be called) are all imperial and are all parts of architectural complexes intended to effect the highly ceremonial function of the emperor's personal apparition to his subjects.

But how strong is this architectural tradition? Is it a Diocletianic invention or can it be traced back in imperial architecture? Birgitta Tamm in a recent book has attempted to define the special functions and forms of imperial private and semipublic domestic architecture in the first centuries B.C. and A.D.[29] Miss Tamm's conclusion is that during the first century of the empire there grew up out of Republican standard forms architectural types that were intended to represent to the populace the elevated nature of the emperor and his special relation to them. Thus where Augustus was wont to receive the common people in the atrium (here the Roman meaning) of his house, by the time of Nero the "vestibulum" of his Golden House was an enormous peristyle with the famous colossus rising up in the middle of the court and visible from all over the city (Fig. 17).[30] Indeed Vitruvius shares the view that is clearly behind this development of an iconography of imperial architectural entrances: "For persons of high rank who hold office and magistracies, and those whose duty it is to serve the state, we must provide princely vestibules [vestibulia regalia alta], lofty halls and spacious peristyles [atria et peristylia amplissima], plantations and broad avenues finished in a majestic manner" (De re aedificatoria VI. 5. 2).

The imperial fora (Fig. 18), which are themselves quintessential expressions of the complex and increasingly ritualized relationship between the emperor and the people,[31] are all great enclosed peristyles entered through a monumental gate and focusing on a central object of veneration.[32] (The Forum of Vespasian is an exception to this last qualification, but its exact use remains a mystery.) Considering the Roman predilection for bilateral symmetry and axial complexes, however, these fora with their dependent peristyles need not be considered necessarily the result of the aforementioned development. Numerous more modest complexes testify to this: the Library of Hadrian at Athens, a Hadrianic public building and portico at Side, the forum at Augusta Raurica, the sanctuary complex at Baalbek, the Pantheon complex, and many theaters with their adjacent peristyles, to name only a few. Even the great imperial bath complexes are entered through monumental entrances, are bilaterally symmetrical, and have huge peristyles connected. This minimum list of portico complexes makes it perfectly clear, then, that the key element in the atrium is not its form, which was if anything even more common than that of the basilica, but the function of the form within the complex and the rich web of specific associations it invoked in the mind of the worshipper.

13

Aula Palatina, Trier. Exterior reconstruction. (Reusch, *Freuchristliche
Zeugnisse,* fig. 144)

14

Palace of Diocletian, Split. Peristyle
court.

15
Diocletian camp, Palmyra. Plan.
(*Palmyra*, pl. 10)

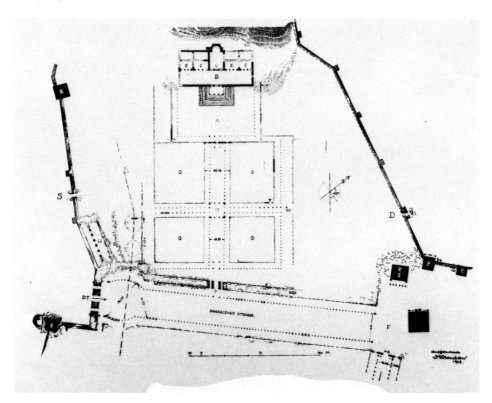

16
Imperial villa, Piazza Armerina.
Isometric.

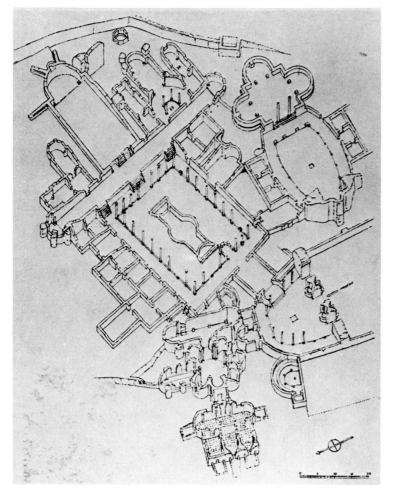

17
Villa of Nero, Rome. Plan. (J. B. Ward
Perkins, Antiquity, 1956, fig.1)

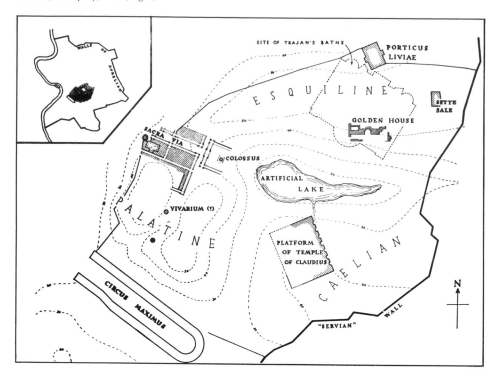

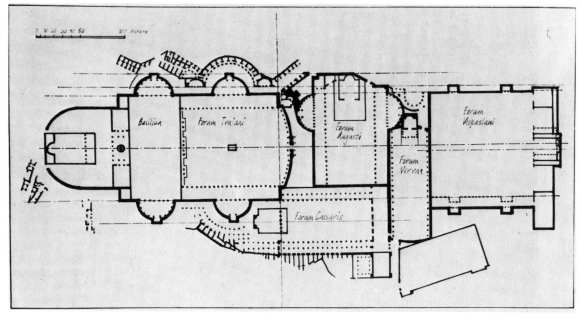

18
Imperial fora, Rome. Plan. (von
Blanckenhagen, *JSAH,* XIII, 1954,
fig. 2)

Conclusion

The atrium, as Constantine's architects saw it, was a prelude, a vestibule, depending for its meaning on the dominant facade and entrance of the basilica sanctuary. Though its basic components, the peristyle surrounding an open court, had been commonplace in ancient architecture for centuries, the specific combination of these components with a full basilica facade opposite a monumental propylaeum was highly charged with the significance of imperial panoply by virtue of its having been traditionally the basic architectural setting for appearances of the emperor to the people. With the increasing ritualization of the divine nature of the emperor culminating in the Tetrarch emperors, the architecture of imperial public appearances became comparably increasingly stylized and charged with meaning.

The Constantinian atrium in the final analysis must be seen to be an unexpected and eccentric choice, deriving from the iconography not of religious architecture but of imperial semipublic domestic architecture. If Constantine had not identified his personal imperial aspirations so intimately with the Christian religion, perhaps he would not have chosen such clearly imperial prerogatives for Christian architecture. But by doing so he invested Christianity from the start with the most intense degree of architectural rhetoric available—a rhetoric calculated to call to the mind of the faithful and the curious alike preprogrammed images of majesty and cosmic power. [33]

The sudden elevation of Christianity from a somewhat troublesome, loosely organized religious fraternity to a powerful arm of the State is one of the most surprising and portentous events in Western history. The archeological evidence just adduced supports the contention that Constantine was motivated less by pure devotion than by an accurate sense of the empire's problems and an intuitive grasp of appropriate solutions. He sensed a spiritual bankruptcy in the empire and, in what can only be called a revolutionary move, gradually but with clear purpose adopted a new state religion. This revolution he effected by superimposing imperial forms on Christianity's images and imperial rights and powers on its organization. [34]

Perhaps the cataclysms that shook the Church under Constantine and his successors, usually considered the inevitable growing pains of a young church, might more profitably be seen as the result of the calculated imperial decision to force the Church into the mold of the State: the great heresies, for instance, which rent the Church and the Roman world during the fourth and fifth centuries, might

have had little more than local effect had not Constantine by means of his ecumenical conventions insisted on dogmatic unanimity. It can be argued, after all, that while consistent legislative policy is appropriate for a secular government, a religion based on an ethical system and a few common mysteries, and professed by a great disparity of peoples, is ill served by a rigid dogma imposed from a central administration.

Whatever might have happened to Christianity had Constantine not alloyed it with the State is a matter of idle speculation, but that the Church acquired from Constantine the aims and ambitions as well as the forms of the State is indisputable. It is no accident that the awe-inspiring pomp of Roman imperial liturgy is still alive, not in the ceremonies of modern governments but in the elaborate rituals in which the Pope appears to the public. The archeological evidence concerning the meaning of the Constantinian basilica and atrium complex clarifies, perhaps even more than the documents, the revolutionary character of Constantine's plans for the Church. For better or worse we have lived in the shadow of Constantine's decision; and as long as the Church shaped or participated in the actions and destinies of nations, it did so according to the priorities established in that decision.

Notes

My thanks to Alfred Frazer for reading an early draft of this paper and making valuable suggestions.

1
Richard Krautheimer in a brilliant paper ("The Beginning of Early Christian Architecture," *The Review of Religions,* 3 (1939): 127–148) clarified our knowledge of Constantinian architecture by separating fact from legend and establishing a morphology of meaning for the basilica. He was followed by the important paper of J. B. Ward Perkins ("Constantine and the Origins of the Christian Basilica," *Papers of the British School at Rome,* 22 new series 9, 1954, 60 ff.), which further refined our knowledge. Subsequent studies have more or less depended on the direction of inquiry established by these two articles.

2
Following the preparation of this paper, an exhaustive and excellent article on this subject was published by Suzanne Spain Alexander: "Studies in Constantinian Church Architecture," *Rivista di Archeologia Cristiana* 47 (1971): 281–330 and 49 (1973): 33–44 (hereafter cited as Alexander, "Studies"). Ms. Alexander meticulously unravels the skein of documentary and archeological material concerning the topographical position of Constantinian churches and particularly the role of the atrium. Our conclusions, arrived at independently, are in the best of relationships, not identical but complementary. I am indebted to Ms. Alexander for generously making available to me a manuscript copy of part 2 of her article before its publication.

3
The word is an unfortunate one because it inevitably invites comparison between the Christian basilica complex and the Roman atrium house. In fact, neither functional nor formal relationships between the two can be sustained.

Krautheimer in *Early Christian and Byzantine Architecture* (Harmondsworth, 1965), p. 317, n. 20, derives the Christian usage of *atrium* from the Greek *aithrion* (an area under the open sky). This sensible solution relieves the architectural historian from having to rebut in detail the atrium-house to atrium-church derivation. See, for example, G. Dix, *The Shape of the Liturgy,* (London, 1945), pp. 22–23).

4

A complete list of Constantinian churches, including those for which we have no information about whether an atrium existed, may be found in Alexander, "Studies." My list is confined to those churches we can determine had atria or courtyards or definitely did not. Other relevant studies include Krautheimer, *Early Christian and Byzantine Architecture,* (Harmondsworth, 1965), (hereafter cited as Krautheimer, *ECB Arch.*); Krautheimer, "The Constantinian Basilica," (*Dumbarton Oaks Papers,* 21, 1967): 117 ff.; G. T. Armstrong, "A Catalogue of Constantinian Churches," (*Gesta,* 6, 1967): 1 ff.

5

A. M. Colini (*Storia e topografia del Celio nell'antichità,* Rome, 1944) provides an excellent summary of excavations in the Lateran area including an analysis of the road structure in antiquity. Rodolfo Lanciani (*Forma Urbis Romae,* Rome, 1900) reconstructs S. Giovanni with an atrium for no discernible reason.

6

See G. B. Giovenale, *Il battistero lateranense* (Rome, 1929).

7

Paolo Belloni, who excavated the scanty Constantinian remains, reconstructed a compact basilica atrium complex giving directly onto the Via Ostiense (*Sulla grandezza e disposizione della primitiva Basilica Ostiense,* Rome, 1853). He miscalculated the apse diameter, however, as E. Kirschbaum correctly points out (*The Tombs of Peter and Paul,* New York, 1959, pp. 176–177), so that the basilica must have been wider and longer and probably would have had insufficient room between the facade and the Via Ostiense for an atrium.

8

See particularly Alfred Frazer, "A Graphic Reconstruction of Old St. Peter's," unpublished M.A. thesis, Institute of Fine Arts, N.Y.U., pp. 25–27. Also Alexander, "Studies," pp. 292–295.

9

Krautheimer, *ECB Arch.,* pp. 17–44, 63.

10

For reconstructions of the Holy Sepulchre see K. J. Conant, *Speculum* 31 (1956): 1 ff., and Krautheimer, *ECB Arch.,* pp. 39–40 and pp. 319–320, n. 45.

11

L. H. Vincent and F.-M. Abel, *Jerusalem Nouvelle* (Paris, 1914), II.

12

See Krautheimer, *ECB Arc.,* pp. 38–39, and I. H. Harvey, "Recent Discoveries," *Archeologia,* 87 (1937): 7–17.

13

Was Eutropia's letter describing the "heathen idols" formerly set up at the site an early example of Christian anti-Semitism? Eusebius, *Life of Constantine* III: 53.

14

E. Mader, *Mambre* (Freiburg, 1957).

15

Krautheimer, *ECB Arch.,* pp. 46–47.

16

Krautheimer, *ECB Arch.,* pp. 52–53; W. Dynes, "The First Christian Palace—Church Type," *Marsyas,* 11 (1962–64): 1 ff.; G. Downey, *History of Antioch* (Princeton, 1966), p. 342.

17

A. M. Schneider, *Die Grabung in Westhof d. Sophienkirche* (Berlin, 1941); also Krautheimer, *ECB Arch.,* pp. 317–318, n. 2.

18

T. Kempf, *Neue Ausgrabungen in Deutschland* (Berlin, 1958), pp. 368 ff.

19

Krautheimer, *ECB Arch.,* 22–23.

20

S. Gsell (*Monuments,* II: 263 ff.) seems to suggest that the church fronted on a street.

21

Luigi Crema, *L'Architettura romana, Enciclopedia classica,* sezione III, volume 12, tomo 1 (Turin, 1959), pp. 612 ff., 628. (Hereafter, Crema, *L'Architettura romana*).

22

The best explorations of ancient liturgy are G. Dix, *The Shape of the Liturgy* (Westminster, 1945); J. A. Jungmann, *The Mass of the Roman Rite* (New York, 1951); and B. Steuart, *The Development of Christian Worship* (London, 1953). None reveals even the slightest liturgical necessity for an atrium.

23

E. Dyggve, *Ravennatum Palatum Sacrum* (Copenhagen, 1941). See also Ward Perkins, "Constantine and the Origin of the Christian Basilica" (*PBSR,* 1954), 75.

24

Crema, *L'Architettura romana,* 612 ff.; W. Reusch and H. Mylius, *Trierer Zeitschrift,* 18 (1949): 194 ff.

25

J. and T. Marasović, *Diocletian Palace,* (Zagreb, 1968); also A. Boethius and J. B. Ward Perkins, *Etruscan and Roman Architecture* (Baltimore, 1970), pp. 524–527.

26

Crema, *L'Architettura romana,* 620, 624.

27

Boethius and Ward Perkins, *Etruscan and Roman Architecture,* pp. 529–533; also recently C. Ampolo et al., "La Villa del casale a Piazza Armerina," *Melanges de l'Ecole Française de Rome,* 83 (1971).

28

Boethius and Ward Perkins, *Etruscan and Roman Architecture,* 522–524; also Crema, *L'Architettura romana,* 599.

29

B. Tamm, *Auditorium and Palatium* (Stockholm, 1963).

30

Ibid., pp. 94 ff.

31

See, for example, P. Zanker in *Archäologischer Anzeiger,* fasc. 4, 1970, pp. 499–544.

32

For the fora see Crema (*L'Architettura romana*) passim; Boethius and Ward Perkins, *Etruscan and Roman Architecture,* esp. pp. 228–244; and P. von Blanckenhagen, "The Imperial Fora," *JSAH* (1955), pp. 21–26.

33

Compare similar conclusions about the nature of Constantinian architecture in Krautheimer, *ECB Arch.,* 43, p. 322, n. 23.

Discussions of Constantine's relation to Christianity are numerous. Some of the more provocative and relevant to our discussion are A. Alföldi, *The Conversion of Constantine and Pagan Rome,* (Oxford, 1948); A. H. M. Jones, *Constantine and the Conversion of Europe* (London, 1948); W. H. C. Frend, *Martyrdom and Persecution in the Early Church* (New York, 1967); N. H. Baynes, *Constantine the Great and the Christian Church (Proceedings of the British Academy, XV)* (London, 1929).

2
Chivalric Declaration: The Palazzo Ducale in Urbino as a Political Statement

C. W. Westfall

"The influence of patronage on art," Geoffrey Scott informed us in 1924, "is easily misstated. Art may be brought to the service of the state and its rulers, but the most that rulers can do towards determining the *essence* of an art is to impose upon it a distinctively courtly character and the coherence which comes of a strongly centralized organization. We should, for instance, misconstrue the inmost nature of Augustan art, or of the art of Louis XIV, if we were to ignore this factor. But nothing similar is true of the Renaissance city-state. Here the conditions were merely such as to give free play to an architecture which, intrinsically, in its character as an art, remained independent of them."[1]

For Scott, architecture was an art of pure taste indebted only to the impulse of an idealist aesthetic. Like any other art, it was to be treated as a purely visual phenomenon. It was made by the men Jacob Burckhardt had found in the Renaissance, the "first born of modern men." Like Cézanne, they were themselves virtually the sole agents of artistic creation. To consider the relationship between the artist and his work was to exhaust the art historian's task.

Although Scott considered the state and politics irrelevant to art, Burckhardt had not. He contended that "the majority of Italian states were in their internal constitution works of art—that is, the fruit of reflection and careful adaptation."[2] But he had isolated statesmanship and politics from other cultural activities and had ignored the political content of official patronage in the arts. Still, an art of pure form, whose political content was unrelated to aesthetic quality, had served Burckhardt as an index of the cultural achievement of a Renaissance court. He had paved the way for Scott.

To insulate content from form as Burckhardt and Scott did requires that one hold three beliefs. The first is that the sole role of the past was to produce the glorious present, a belief enshrined in the contemporary historiography of current practice. Ernst Gombrich has recently unmasked the Hegelian— and Burckhardtian—exegetical procedure that flows from this belief and has suggested that art historians begin to ask important new questions.[3]

The second belief is that the issues of good and evil that stirred the politics of the past are no longer relevant to the issues of the present. Does it really make a difference whether the Borgia poisoned all those people? Yes, it does. We study good people and just regimes, and avoid those that are morally suspect or politically corrupt. A recent book on Renaissance Ferrara notes that it is the first study by an American devoted to a Renaissance tyrant court "which," the author suggests, "is attributable in part to . . . republican preferences of Western European and particularly American historians, especially after the global conflicts of this century." Of course Florence is a pleasant place to pursue scholarship, as he notes.[4] But Florence was also the leading Renaissance republic, and it defined Renaissance republican ideology. What, then, of Rome, Naples, Milan, and a host of smaller states where there was an active princely alternative to republican politics? These states are largely neglected. To understand them, and to understand their republican antagonists, one must turn to Rome, the source of princely ideology, the center of the world where politics (the good) and religion (the true) were manipulated by popes operating a princely regime in a cosmopolitan city. Art historians ignore this. They know Rome mostly because popes who tended to be tyrannical despots placed art (the beautiful) in the hands of Fra Angelico, Melozzo di Forli, Pinturicchio, Raphael, Michelangelo, and Bramante. Americans, who defer to Jefferson and suspect Hamilton and who commute from a semblance of Broadacres City to the central city and shun the Ville Radieuse, naturally find the politics of Rome and its popes distasteful. Perhaps the issues of good and evil during the Renaissance are not so unconnected to the deeper beliefs of modern "objective" historians after all.

The third belief sustains an idealistic aesthetic and a phenomenological inquiry into artistic quality. Sometime between the Renaissance and the late nineteenth century, the fundamental bonds between the good, the true, and the beautiful were ruptured, and atomistic studies of politics, religion, and art became possible. When art became valuable nearly exclusively for its visual qualities, art history became only a little more than a list of attributions while it slipped to much less than a history of man. The technique of iconological interpretation helped to broaden the inquiry, but this very special methodology is embedded in beliefs that are clearly dated.

It has supported only one major interpretation of architecture, which began with Rudolf Wittkower's direct question: "If this [Ruskin's and Scott's] customary interpretation of Renaissance architecture as a profane style (and as an architecture of pure visual form) is correct, then what would be the *essential* difference between the eclecticism of the fifteenth and sixteenth centuries and that of the nineteenth century?" Wittkower answered, "In contrast to nineteenth-century classical architecture, Renaissance architecture, like every great style of the past, was based on a hierarchy of values culminating in the absolute values of sacred architecture. . . . The forms of the Renaissance church have symbolical value or, at least, . . . they are charged with a particular meaning which the pure [visual] forms as such do not contain."[5] Wittkower seems to state:

"Renaissance ecclesiastical architecture was religious architecture, which made it beautiful, and it was rendered by symbolical forms, which allowed it to reveal the true." Thus, he seems to commit what Scott called the "ethical fallacy." But he avoided that fallacy because his value judgments depended upon the special role played by symbolical forms as opposed to pure visual forms. His argument gave special value to what Erwin Panofsky called "essential tendencies of the human mind," which are rendered in symbolical forms that have their own history.[6] Wittkower believed that the symbolical forms revealing religious tendencies are superior to the pure visual forms that gave Ruskin moral qualms and Scott aesthetic pleasure, and that this is universally the case ("like every great style of the past").

Scott did indeed err by finding goodness and truth in the beauty that preceded them, but Wittkower erred by believing that beauty could only be found by discovering symbolical forms charged with particular meanings. These meanings were locked into the view of man promulgated by the Warburg Institute, and if one rejects that view with its history of style, history of types, and history of cultural symptoms or symbols in general, as Panofsky outlined it, he must reject Wittkower's judgments.

Nevertheless, Wittkower's scholarly procedure is essential if one is to raise the study of architecture above mere phenomenology. He proposed that "both the theory and the practice of Renaissance architects are unambiguous" in revealing the role of certain forms to convey certain values within a hierarchy of values.[7] This suggests that Scott can be upended: The influence of patronage on art is easily misstated. Art was brought to the service of the state and its rulers, and the essence of that art is in its distinctively courtly character.

This study will attempt to remove the Palazzo Ducale in Urbino from isolation and insert it within the hierarchy of values held during the Renaissance. Because this study is in the form of an exploration, it cannot arrive at definitive conclusions, but it might suggest questions that are too often ignored. The palace will be considered a visual statement that describes the character of Federigo da Montefeltro, the prince who built it. In all, it will be juxtaposed with contemporary biographies that will reveal Federigo's character and will indicate whether he was a benevolent prince or a malevolent tyrant. That was the relevant Renaissance question, and it has universal significance. As Leon Battista Alberti put it on the basis of sound juristic opinion, one needs to know whether the prince is guided by justice and integrity as he rules over willing subjects, or only by his own interests so that he "may be able to continue his dominion over them, let them be ever so uneasy under it."[8]

Federigo (1422–1482) became the subject of biographers late in the fifteenth century, after his character had been formed and his fame assured. Before midcentury chaotic conditions afflicted central and north Italy, but during the second half of the century states became more stable and the many grand and petty princes began to attract courtiers adept in literary forms appropriate to their great and noble subjects.

Their biographies descended from ancient and late medieval prototypes that stressed the virtues and occupations appropriate to the office of the subject. Unlike modern biographies, they do not discuss psychological motivation, personality, or resolved or unresolved problems of the inner character. Instead, they dwell upon common and traditional themes. Federigo's biographies demonstrate that he exemplified the highest standards expected of a man in the two roles he played, those of governor and chivalric knight, by citing abundant examples of typical and expected activities.[9] Of course, Federigo excelled in them all. Six of Federigo's biographers knew him directly—Pierantonio Paltroni,[10] Vespasiano da Bisticci,[11] Francesco Filelfo,[12] Giovanni Santi,[13] Antonio Porcellio de' Pandoni,[14] and Antonio di Francesco (Feltresco) Merchatello.[15] Another, Girolamo Muzio, wrote early in the sixteenth century,[16] and another, Bernardino Baldi, who also wrote about Federigo's palace, worked at the end of that century.[17]

For Federigo as governor and chivalric knight, noble or at least appropriate birth was important, but actions that justified his playing the role were more important, although not essential. Thus, Paltroni, Federigo's chancellor who knew him very well, could hedge: "Whether he was the son of Count Guido Guidantonio da Montefeltro or his nephew, the son of Bernardino of the house of Ubaldini, either way it is manifest that the said Count Federigo was born of an exceedingly outstanding line and of the most generous blood."[18] But because Guidantonio had a younger but legitimate son, Federigo was turned out to become a soldier, as later he would do to his own bastards.

His accident of birth determined his upbringing. The tiny Federigo was placed in the court of Bartolomeo Brancaleoni's widow in Imola until 1433. Next, after a year and a half in Venice as a political hostage securing his father's pledge to the Venetian pope, Federigo went for two years to the Gonzaga court in Mantua, where he studied with Vetterino da Feltro.[19] In Venice he had been tutored in prudence and eloquence; in Mantua he pursued "letters and studies in *humanità*." He was then allowed to return to Urbino, "exercising the person of a knight, arms, sword play and similar maneuvers." In Urbino he continued to develop his "intelligence and perspicacious ability . . . in governing the state."[20]

The young man was now ready for active combat. After outstanding success in the field, where he captured and governed Pesaro, the townspeople in Urbino murdered his half brother, Oddantonio, the town's new governor. Federigo's life changed abruptly. He hastened home to claim the Montefeltro patrimony but found the gates locked against him. "And," relates Paltroni, "although the will of the citizens was universally good toward count Federigo, they however would not allow him into the city until he swore a solemn oath: he obligated himself not to take notice of the things that had happened during the recent events, and having done that, they admitted him. By voice and by united consent of everyone, they declared him *signore*."[21]

He also signed an accord with the citizens showing that he was expected to be a prince but would not be allowed to be a tyrant.[22] The biographies stress that he was more solicitous of the citizens' well-being than was common, a judgment confirmed by the tranquility of Urbino during his tenure. Federigo was now established as governor and *signore* (lord), one of his two offices.

The townspeople had made Federigo de facto signore, but only the pope could establish him in his other office, that of chivalric knight, and give him de jure legitimacy in the Montefeltro patrimony. In addition to Urbino, this included the lands and other cities the family had traditionally dominated in the Marches. Because Pope Eugenius IV had conferred the title of duke on Oddantonio uniquely, he made Federigo Count of Montefeltro and Casteldurante. Later popes confirmed him in those titles[23] and gave him more titles and vicarate jurisdictions as they rewarded him for his successes as chivalric knight.

The biographers dwell with obvious relish on Federigo's activities as a knight within the chivalric hierarchy. From mid-century he is described as an invincible condottiere who was faithful to his employer. In 1454 Nicholas V made him Captain General of the Lega Italica. Pius II depended upon Federigo in his ongoing battle against Sigismondo Malatesta and planned for his service in the crusade against the Turks, which was frustrated by the pope's death. Federigo's difficulties with Paul II, which strained but never ruptured their feudal bonds, were dissolved by that pope's death in 1471. No pope could have valued Federigo more than Sixtus IV. In 1474 Sixtus installed Federigo as permanent Gonfaloniere della Chiesa, a post he had held briefly under Paul. Sixtus also made him a Knight of St. Peter, gave him the Golden Rose, raised him to Duke of Urbino, and arranged a marriage between Federigo's daughter Giovanna and the papal nephew Giovanni della Rovere. Giovanni had studied war under Federigo and would be the father of the first della Rovere Duke of Urbino, the successor of Federigo's own son. Federigo now reached the acme of knightly honor. As an Englishman noted, "His justice, clemency, liberality, made hym everywhere famous, and did equalize and adorn his victores with peace. The arming sword which hee wore had this inscription, Son quella che difende la ragione, no ti fidar s'il cor ti manca."[24] Edward IV inducted him as a Knight of the Garter in 1474, the same year the King of Naples enrolled him as a Knight of the Ermine. In 1479 Sixtus honored him with the gift of the papal sword and hat. The construction of the palace coincides with the increasing importance he had assumed in the chivalric peacekeeping activities of the stabilized papacy that had begun with Nicholas V's Lega Italica, and it was financed by the fees they paid for his sword and his trust until his death in 1482.

Biographers cited specific examples of Federigo's actions in order to embellish his character as governor and chivalric hero with the appropriate virtues, organizing them into three categories. Paltroni's introduction is exemplary:

It appeared that the life of this excellent prince is to be compared and equated with the life of any of the more worthy and notable ancients in any of the great generations. For the things he did so outstandingly in handling arms he merits the greatest fame and eternal memory, as he does for his singular *sapienza* (wisdom) in ruling and governing, not only in his campaigns and his own state, but also in many great states of the greatest signori and magistrates to which he gave care and thought, and for being learned in *scienza* (knowledge), eloquence, liberality, benevolence, and clemency, and for the splendid court and for magnificent and splendid buildings.[25]

Paltroni's three themes are typical. One compares Federigo's abilities and actions to those of ancient heroes, a Renaissance commonplace that need not be discussed. A second rehearses his specifically chivalric virtues, a popular theme because it provides engaging narrative material. The third uses the common *topos* of arms and letters to reveal the instruments Federigo used in acting in his two major roles.

In discussing Federigo's specifically chivalric virtues, Paltroni stresses the principal ones of magnificence, trustworthiness, and control of earthly concerns. In addition, Federigo is always prudent, industrious, intelligent, and honorable, and he is always concerned that his reputation and his trust remain unblemished by deceit.

As Baldi put it later, "he made his principal profession out of the *virtù* of *fede* (trust),"[26] and as Giovanni Santi said of the fourteen-year-old soldier, with the gifts of heaven and reason "he joined Prudence with Strength to strive for glory."[27]

Paltroni also used Federigo's appearance, constitution, and temperament to portray his chivalric character. Federigo was "very agile and strong, very resistant to the cold and to heat, hunger, thirst, sleepiness, and fatigue. . . . He was jocular, affable, most liberal," and ambitious from youth. He was "without *superbia* (pride) and wrath such that he was never seen to be agitated if not by mental activity and industry, and unless it gave him the impetus to overcome and to win." Finally, "He was most sober, and in his language and in all other things he was most courteous, except that his lust and love of women overcame and conquered him. He was generally loved and he generally loved and desired." But this was, Paltroni quickly reminds us, when he was in the "flower of his youth, and his virtù and ability at arms together with his favor with fortune and his prosperity made him very appealing." While young and recovering from some wounds in Urbino, "he ruled and governed most copiously the most delicate and most delicious women."[28] This connection of governing and loving is not capricious. Paltroni is saying that although Federigo was not yet a legitimate governor of a state, he was already governing his estate in an orderly and knightly manner. Muzio connected loving and governing by saying that following "the desire of his father he was married and joined his wife, and took the government of the state and of other lands that *il Padre* had given him."[29] This conceit will find architectual representation in the Urbino palace, as we shall see, as did magnificence and the other chivalric virtues found in the decorative program and in other products of Federigo's patronage that will not be discussed here.[30]

Paltroni's biography, largely an unstructured chronological narrative, stands in sharp contrast to Vespasiano da Bisticci's. The Florentine's has the clarity of type others sought to achieve, presenting Federigo as the perfect embodiment of each of the typical activities pursued by men of Federigo's type. Placed as the first in a series devoted to military leaders, it declares, "Of all the abilities one is able to attribute to a most outstanding man, we begin with military discipline, the greatest expertise in the Latin language, learning in philosophy, and having the greatest knowledge of sacred writing and of history. He was not only a most able governor in military matters, but marvelous in governing in the broadest scope."[31]

In developing this catalog of abilities, Vespasiano constantly compares Federigo to ancient examples. He narrates many of his military exploits, largely following Paltroni, and leaves out none of the chivalric virtues. Prudence is cited most often, followed by faith—meaning trust in one's word—and by reputation and honor, with reason, justice, good sense, and force sprinkled in.

Following his presentation of the chivalric knight and man of arms, Vespasiano turns to Federigo's learning. This was an instrumental virtue; knowing ancient examples allowed Federigo to conduct his campaigns better and to govern better. But it was also a good in itself. "He was careful to keep intellect and virtue to the front, and to learn some new thing every day."[32] He was learned in theology, philosophy, poetry, and history. Turning again to the use of learning, Vespasiano observes that "one may see in all of the buildings he caused to be made the grand order and the measure of every element as he had supervised it, and especially in his palace, of which in this age there is no more worthy building, so well is it done, and where there are so many fine things here and there."[33] His architects followed his intentions and the *misure* (measure) he gave, and he explained the manner of construction. Vespasiano makes it clear that Federigo directed both the general designing procedure and the actual construction process, and that these abilities demonstrated his learning. Architecture is followed by Federigo's involvement in geometry, arithmetic, music, sculpture, and painting. A brief description of the palace's *studiolo* (small study), the tapestries, and the patronage of men of letters that had filled his library with all of the most worthy books, including "all the books on architecture,"[34] is included as further evidence of his well-developed intellect.

Next and last, governing. Vespasiano pointed out that just as letters had been joined to arms, so too were they joined to governing. His recitation of Federigo's virtues in governing began by his saying, "First, in order that his rule might be conjoined with religion, he was before all things most devout and observant in his religious duties; for without this, and without a good example to others by his life, his rule would never have endured."[35] His observance included piety, alms, clemency, and mercy, as well as the rich endowment of religious houses and faithful attendance to the needs of the religious. Furthermore, as governor he observed the laws, gave good counsel, was accessible to his subjects, made peace between them, remained discrete and decorous, and provided a worthy example for imitation. Finally, he was prudent and trustworthy, just as he was in his military regime.

Federigo's character, then, was composed of his two offices, one attached to the governing of Urbino and his larger patrimony, and the other concerned with actions undertaken in the larger chivalric hierarchy headed by the pope and in governing his patrimony, a papal fief. He embodied three primary attributes attendant on those offices—a hero of ancient stripe, an outstanding *exemplum* (example) of chivalric virtues, and a man who used arms and letters in executing his offices. And he was without peer in his age.

Interpreting the major themes of the biographies is simple compared to discovering the character portrayed by the palace. Seeing it as something other than an example of Renaissance style requires a secure building history and abundant descriptions. Although such evidence is relatively incomplete or unstudied, there is enough to draw some conclusions.

The palace was built in three campaigns (Figs. 1 and 2).[36] The first was begun in about 1450, probably under the supervision of Maso di Bartolommeo (d.1456), a mediocre Florentine from Michelozzo's shop. It consisted of renovations and additions to older buildings. The result was a two-story wing along what is now the southeast part of the palace, with another wing projecting to the west from near the center. This wing may have turned north when it reached the declivity on the western side of the site, although that entire west wing may belong to the second campaign. The Iole suite, in the east range of the piano nobile, was the most important part of the original palace. Most of the palace's windows and much of its decoration, both inside and out, postdate the first campaign.

The larger part of the palace dates from two later campaigns. The second, begun about 1465, followed a model made by Luciano Laurana that established the palace's character. The third continued the work and added decorative and other elements, apparently within Laurana's fabric.[37] Begun in 1472 when Laurana transferred to Naples, construction was directed by Francesco di Giorgio Martini.

Largely complete in 1482, it was enlarged later, and the additions must be stripped away to recover Federigo's palace.[38] Guest rooms in a superelevation reduced the palace's apparent horizontality, cut off light from the cortile and the Sala del Trono, and erased the crenellations that ran around the entire silhouette and gave the building "the guise of a castello."[39]

Contemporary sources show how to divide the palace into parts for purposes of analysis. They indicate that quattrocento palaces contained three parts: utilitarian, public, and private. The utilitarian parts, while giving the palace dignity and serving necessary functions, were unimportant in defining its character. When possible, they were arranged so as not to detract from the more important public and private parts. In 1455 Giannozzo Manetti said that at the Vatican they were scattered about the base of the Vatican hill behind the palace.[40] At the Palazzo Piccolomini in Pienza (1458–62) they were inserted in the slope of the hill and used to support the garden. In Urbino, they were also inconspicuous. The stables were in an independent structure below the palace,[41] while shops, storerooms, a cone for collecting snow and ice, and other facilities were arranged at the bottom of the steep hillside beneath the palace. Fully half the palace's volume was devoted to various utilitarian functions.

The public and private parts are the significant ones that constitute the palace proper. In Urbino they face the countryside and the town. Within the town, the most conspicuous part is the facade of the L-shaped block from the second campaign that unites the Iole suite with the cathedral, closing the two sides of a piazza that flanks the cathedral.[42]

The facade facing the piazza has obvious representational significance (Fig. 3). It is incomplete and problematic, but when considered as a surface only, it can provide the key to understanding the design procedure and thence the final intentions of its designers.

Rotondi's analysis revealed four stages in the facade's evolution, but he found it difficult to relate these phases directly to either the second or third campaigns.[43] All phases, with the possible exception of the fourth, predate Federigo's death. In the first phase, a brick fabric was raised with apparent disregard for the placement of openings, except along the ground floor where windows fitted with the present modest surrounds were rather regularly placed. In the second phase eight piano nobile windows were given their present handsome frames. These frames are revisions of the ones that were already in place on the west facade overlooking the countryside. In the third phase new elements were added in order to tie together those already integrated. Handsomely carved string courses, corner pilasters, five portal frames, and a bench along the base formed parts of a coordinated design that included the piano nobile windows.[44] These elements were inserted into the facade by cutting into the brick wall, a procedure already followed for the piano nobile windows and one that would have to be followed in all later work. Finally, in the fourth phase, thin slabs representing drafted ashlar were added on the ground floor within the fields already defined by the benches, pilasters, portals, windows, and string courses.

All this was added to a fabric with a highly irregular face. The three windows in the Sala del Trono (Fig. 2, no. 112) were nearly evenly spaced and in sequence with the door from the Sala del Trono into the Sala delle Veglie (no. 113) and the Sala del Trono's ceiling vaults, but they are relatively unevenly spaced in relationship to the ground floor windows and the single portal.[45] The other (west) facade reveals the same characteristics. One portal was placed toward the end of the room it serves. On the piano nobile level, a window was placed above the portal and centered in the chamber it lights, and another was placed above the ground floor window and like it centered in the wall of its room. The window at the opposite end of the facade was placed

relative to the vaults in the Sala delle Veglie, while the other window in that room represents an exceptional case. It was more or less centered between the windows that flank it rather than placed precisely between the vault corbels in the Sala delle Veglie.

In each phase the designer of the facade elements attempted to diminish the apparent irregularity of the original construction.[46] Three of the five portals were blind, and therefore functionally unnecessary.[47] Only one of the two windows lighting the stairhall could be integrated into a regular sequence on the piano nobile; the other was simply ignored, as was the lack of a window under two of the piano nobile windows and a lack of a piano nobile window above one of the ground floor windows. The additions reveal an attempt to give a more sound articulation to the facade and to tie together openings that otherwise would have been floating unanchored on a vast surface of undisguised bricks, to obscure the irregular sequence of openings, and to emphasize the distinction between the ground floor and the piano nobile. How the crenellations would have been handled remains a mystery. The facade might have been given a stucco coat, as was common in Rome; instead, a stone revetment was begun but remains incomplete.

At each stage the piazza facade was handled exclusively as a facade. Other facades on the palace, which need not be discussed, reveal the same general principle: the design and disposition of rooms preceded the design of facades, and openings were placed in response to interior, not exterior, facade demands.[48] The facades, however, do not suffer unduly because their designs managed to obscure disharmonies.

There was nothing strange about this. The palace in Urbino was built in several campaigns from parts assembled on an irregular site, a common procedure except in dense urban areas with high land values and with a tradition of building palaces in single blocks that covered the entire available site. It was easier to achieve a sense of clear articulation on the facade of a blocky palace, but an entirely coherent articulation was not guaranteed (as Michelozzo's Palazzo Medici shows). The windows on the piano nobile and piano superiore are regularly spaced, but the sequence ignores the locations of openings on the ground floor. The facade Alberti added to the Palazzo Rucellai was the first to maintain coherence among all three floor levels, but at the cost of openings related to the arrangement of rooms on the interior.

These observations correspond to contemporary theory. In *De re aedificatoria*, Alberti explained that beauty resides in the congruence of design and construction and in the resolution of problems related to usefulness, firmness, and delight brought together with proper *concinnitas*. He added that ornament is

1
Ducal Palace, Urbino, ground floor.
(From Rotondi, *The Ducal Palace of Urbino*)
2
Ducal Palace, Urbino, piano nobile.
(From Rotondi, *The Ducal Palace of Urbino*)

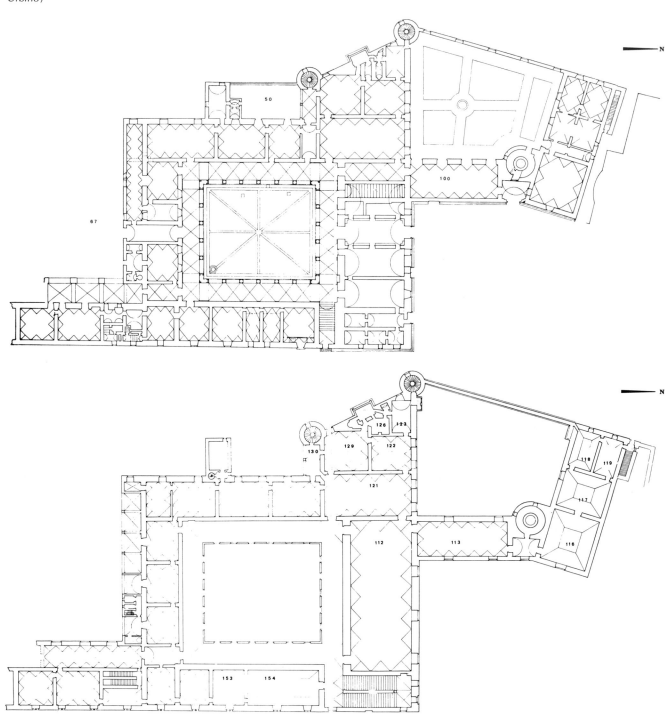

3
Ducal Palace, Urbino, piazza facade.
(Photo: Anderson, Rome)

an additional luster added to, indeed, worked into the design of a beautiful building, and that ornament includes such elements as window and portal forms, pilasters, string courses, entablatures, and others that might be derived from the classical vocabulary of forms.[49] Beauty and ornament are intimately related, as are the thing and attributes of the thing. The fabric and its interiors constitute the thing, and the facade conveys its attributes.

The facade is an ornament that conveys attributes of Federigo's character. Although incomplete, its elements convey a consistent representational program that may be recovered by discovering the elements' prototypes.

The piazza facade does not draw on either of the important available models, the Palazzo Medici and the Palazzo Rucellai, although it is unthinkable without Alberti's Florentine works. Instead, its source is Rome. The drafted ashlar revetment resembles the representation of ancient Roman buildings as they appear, for example, on Filarete's doors at St. Peter's, completed in 1445. The pattern had already appeared on the facade of Nicholas V's new wing at the Vatican palace. Similarly, the corner pilasters, the string courses, and the portal and window frames bear the rich decorations of ancient Rome. The Palazzo Rucellai facade, with its emblematic blowing sails, rings, and feathers, could have suggested the way Federigo's heraldic and chivalric emblems and decorations were woven into the architectural articulation, but Federigo's emblems came from his chivalric superiors, not from his family heraldry. Federigo's palace shares with Rucellai's the impression of being a studied presentation in two dimensions of a three-dimensional system of structural forms derived from ancient Roman practice and theory, but the Urbino palace is luxuriant rather than sober, as is appropriate to a prince.[50] Lacking in Florence are the bench reliefs showing engines of war and the martial crenellations.

The ornamentation conveys quite specific attributes of both the palace and its builder. It shows that its design descends from ancient Rome, because ancient Rome provided the formal prototypes for the ornamental elements. It reveals that the inhabitant occupies a clearly defined place within a chivalric hierarchy, because the emblematic devices reveal the sources of the inhabitant's honors and imply the obligations he accepted in receiving them. And because the architectural elements are clearly articulated and are based on the manipulation of elements representative of structural solidity, the palace shows that it was intelligently designed. The attributes of Roman precedent, chivalric virtue, and intelligence have already been observed in biographies of Federigo, and will be encountered repeatedly throughout the palace.

The facade presents attributes of Federigo's character, but the palace contained him. Only in three dimensions are design and construction conjoined to produce beauty; only inside does one penetrate to the qualities of the thing. The palace was a setting for Federigo's virtuous actions. To discover what the palace revealed about his character, one must examine its programmatic, functional qualities.

These qualities were given the palace by providing certain places for specific activities, and these places were based upon certain design motifs drawn from traditional and other sources. An analysis of the meaning of these motifs in their original settings conveys important information about the qualities of the actions undertaken in them and about the person undertaking the actions. But first the motifs must be identified.

Particularly important in identifying them is a description from after 1480 written by Francesco di Giorgio, who was intimately familiar with the palace. The description's organization and emphasis are closely related to the descriptions and prescriptions in Alberti's and Filarete's earlier treatises; it may, therefore, be used to represent a professional quattrocento opinion.

"Finally," he begins, "there remains to be treated the *case di particulari signori o vero principi*. First it seems to me that in front there should be an ample piazza with free and unencumbered surroundings; one should be able to make in front of the entrance a portico as long as the facade with loggias above it. Then there should be an ornate portal and entrance into the middle of the *casa* (house), with an *andito* (entranceway) or with an *atrio* (atrium) or with a cortile of porticos and loggias running round it from which one could enter all the rooms on that floor, where there would be salons, dining rooms, rooms, anterooms, chancellery rooms, baths, bathing rooms both hot and cold." He describes utilitarian rooms below this level, and continues, "Above the first floor one arrives by means of a side stairway at a loggia above that cortile; and next to this loggia would be a grand and principal hall that would be above the piazza. At each end of the hall should be a salon the length or breadth of which should be the same as that of the principal hall," and other rooms including a chapel and studies. "These rooms and salons should be for visitors, with all proper conveniences." On the other side of the palace should be a duplication and augmentation of these facilities for the private uses of the household, which he describes in some detail. Finally, above this level should be the kitchens and other service facilities, lodgings for staff, and facilities for the household's functionaries.[51]

The descriptions of several quattrocento laymen parallel Francesco di Giorgio's in emphasis and organization, as does Bernardino Baldi's from 1587.

29
Chivalric
Declaration: The
Palazzo Ducale
in Urbino as a
Political
Statement

His table of contents reveals what he believed were the principal topics: "Who was the architect of the palace; on the palace's site; on the palace in general." Next he lists motifs: "On the vestibule and cortile; on the stairs; on the upper loggia and the hall; on the apartments; on the library, studiolo, ball court, bath, and *capellette* (small chapels); on the towers; on the garden." Finally, general topics reappear: "On parts not finished and not begun; on the architecture of the fabric; on the ornaments of the palace; on the material of the palace; the artifice (that is, ingeniousness) of the palace; responses to some objections made about the fabric of the palace."[52]

These descriptions have two things in common: none discusses facades as parts of the palace's substance,[53] and each stresses functional blocks of space. Each moves successively from one to another while giving only the most meager sense of the relationship of one block to another, relating them instead to a functional program for the palace as a whole. A similar procedure will be followed here.

One motif is the entrance and a related public area. There are two entrances from the piazza to the palace, one to the enclosed garden, the other to the cortile. A sentence by Vespasiano da Bisticci gives the clue to the character of this first motif. He wrote that after his early morning inspections of the countryside, Federigo would hear mass, and "afterwards go into a garden (*orto*) with all the doors open and give audience to all who wished, till the hour of repast."[54] Francesco di Giorgio's description makes the same point but in a different way. Only the ducal palace in Venice precisely fits this part of his formal description; the palaces in Mantua, Pesaro, and other north Italian states come close, but they lack the upper loggia. But to look for a formal analogy is to miss the point, which demands a functional analogy. He called for a loggia, and a loggia was used for governing. Francesco is saying that the governor should be in a proper setting. The garden loggia (Fig. 1, no. 100) immediately beyond the piazza could easily be the functional analogy in Urbino to the loggia above the entrance portal in Francesco's description. Francesco and Vespasiano, then, are describing a similar functional motif. The source for Federigo's design for this motif will be discussed later.

Francesco's specifications lead to another motif, the other portal and its cortile (Fig. 4). He describes it both as a part of the sequence of spaces leading into the palace and as an area ringed by utilitarian facilities that are not related in any significant way to the cortile. The important rooms are on the piano nobile, and these facilities are useful in raising them to that level.

The cortile in Urbino obviously receives the visitor. The entrance portal that is asymmetrically placed on the piazza facade opens into a barrel vaulted androne leading to the middle of the five bays of the cortile's shorter side. The other side has six bays, denying a central position for an entrance and making the principal entrance more conspicuous.

The design of the cortile's facade shows that the portal, androne, and cortile form an autonomous motif inserted within the blocks that constitute the palace. Each cortile facade is simply a face placed on the side of a hollow area; the four faces do not form a three-dimensional architectonic fabric that encloses a space.[55] On the ground floor each face is a simple columnar arcade terminated by a half-column abutting a pier. Each corner pier is faced with a pilaster. The design simply extends the front of the Rucellai loggia in length, adds occuli in the spandrels, and uses stone and brick rather than stone alone.

Alberti's example did not assist the cortile's designer in turning the corner, however. It is one thing to turn forward, another to turn backward. The stage-flat faces in Urbino touch one another only at the uppermost moulding of the cornice, that is, at the point of each face's farthest projection. At the corner the entablature breaks forward, continuing the vertical line of the corner pilaster and suggesting structural mass at the corners, but this only produces ambiguity, as do the pilasters' truncations of the occuli.

There is additional ambiguity on the back corner of each pier where a quarter column has been carved out of the mass of the pier, joining the two faces of the pier with a structural member but depriving the pier of mass. This runs counter to the idea that columns are added onto piers, not carved out of them.

Although laden with problems first resolved by High Renaissance architects, the cortile evokes Roman sources. Formally, it suggests ancient Roman architecture by going beyond the simple and prevalent Florentine cortile design that turns a corner with a column. It also recalls the very Roman Loggia Rucellai and the newer garden loggia at the Palazzo Venezia. Functionally, it is related to a Roman example that was completed only in a description of its use. Giannozzo Manetti stated that at the Vatican Palace, Nicholas V had intended to provide a new entrance and to renovate the areas known as the *curia prima* and the *curia secunda* with porticoes in order to form a properly noble entrance.[56] Like the facade, the portal with its frame, the androne with its vault, and the cortile reveal an attempt at the intelligent manipulation of structural elements and an allegiance to Roman precedent. The pompous inscription in the cortile friezes tells of Federigo's

4
Ducal Palace, Urbino, cortile.
(Gabinetto Fotografico Nazionale,
Rome)

5
Ducal Palace, Urbino, stairway,
stemma of Federigo da Montefeltro,
Gonfaloniere della Chiesa, after 1474.
(Gabinetto Fotografico Nazionale,
Rome)

virtù, but it postdates Federigo's death even if it is in character with the original theme.[57]

The next important motif, the stairhall, is part of the sequence of spaces leading to the piano nobile. Inserted as a block at the end of the Iole wing, it opens from a corner of the cortile. Throughout, it is a carefully articulated spatial construction with highly decorated arched openings and corner pilasters and a robust three-quarter column sustaining a richly treated composite capital and the ribs of the vaults of the two stair tunnels that meet at the return landing. On the lower landing the coat of arms of Duke Federigo, Gonfaloniere della Chiesa, faces up the stairs (Fig. 5). Count Federigo is represented in the vault bosses by the initials FC. A statue of Federigo posed in a mannerist sway, now in a niche in the return landing, is a posthumous production.

Once again, intelligent design and chivalric virtues surround a person in what Baldi called "one of the most principal parts of the palace in the judgment of all . . . which, to be sure, serves not only commodity, but adds ornament here as well."[58] And Rome is both source and place of later development. The stairs Pius II had recently completed at his palace in Pienza may have been the direct prototype, although the relationship between the stairs and the great hall is different, and Pius's are crammed within the block of the palace.[59] The prototype for Pius's stairs may have been the ones Nicholas V had built at the Palazzo dei Conservatori in Rome.[60] The later stairs in the Cancelleria would resemble those in Urbino, while Bramante's simple stair at the cloister of Santa Maria della Pace was a preliminary sketch based on Urbino for the new stairhall he was to design for the south end of Julius II's Vatican palace.

At the top of the stairs Francesco di Giorgio said there would be a corridor (loggia) and that next to this "would be a grand and principal hall that would be above the piazza." The hall belonged to what Francesco called a group of public rooms, and the massing of the palace in Urbino suggests that the public rooms were conceived of as a single block forming a distinct motif.

This block satisfied functions transferred from the earlier construction. There, the original stairway opened into a foyer that was followed by three square rooms and by the Sala degli Affreschi (no. 153), which was apparently the original throne room. Federigo was stationed against the wall opposite the window and was flanked by two frescoed men-at-arms holding pikes.[61] Around the room was a now-defaced cycle of worthy warriors. Surviving are coats of arms of the Montefeltro family, fragments of a fictive backdrop of a pomegranate-patterned damask, flower vases, putti, and life-sized warriors, of whom only Mucius Scarevola and

Horatius Coclus are identifiable.[62] Last was the largest room in the older wing, the Sala della Iole (no. 154), a council room. It was decorated predominately with generalizing elements defining virtue rather than with Federigo's particular attributes.

In the new construction the spaces leading to the new public rooms were more august, the rooms themselves were more directly accessible and larger, and the decorative elements in them were less generalizing. The motif of the public block comprised the Sala del Trono, placed between the piazza and the cortile, the Sala degli Angeli, placed to the west of the Sala del Trono, and, apparently, the wing along the west side of the cortile. The Sala del Trono dominated this block and was the largest interior space in the palace. A vast vaulted hall, it was originally lit by the three great windows opening onto the piazza and clerestory windows on the opposite side. Their simple surrounds were reflected on the piazza side by blind windows.[63]

The ornament here is heraldic. The lintels of the doors and fireplaces, the vault corbels, and the vault bosses constantly remind the visitor that the man in the hall, Federigo, is Duke of Urbino and Knight of St. Peter, Knight of the Frmine, and servant of the pope and of the king of Naples. Tapestries, now lost, showed the famous battles and warriors from earlier history that provided him with a stirring incentive for his own actions in preserving order by engaging in battles. Here was Federigo the chivalric warrior, the counterpart to Federigo the governor who held counsel in the garden.

Appended to the public block are two other motifs that together constitute the major private area in the palace. One is the duke's suite (nos. 121–130) which projects from the Sala degli Angeli; the other is the duchess's suite (nos. 116–119) which was fitted out next to the cathedral.[64] The duchess's suite was joined to the public block by the Sala delle Veglie, which stood above the garden loggia and was apparently used for entertainments and receptions. The portal that led from the piazza through an antechamber to the enclosed garden's loggia also led to an entrance to the duchess's suite. Francesco di Giorgio had recommended, perhaps on the basis of this design, that while women should be separated from the men, they should also be able to pass back and forth secretly.[65] This is accomplished by means of a walkway across the wall enclosing the western side of the garden.[66] Enclosed balconies on the intimate western part of each suite and next to the walkway allowed the duke and duchess to salute one another across the intervening garden and then to reach one another privately by means of the walkway.

31
Chivalric
Declaration: The
Palazzo Ducale
in Urbino as a
Political
Statement

The duke's suite is by far the most complex motif in the palace. It was in the center of the realm over which Federigo presided, poised between the public rooms of the palace that were accessible from the town, and the countryside beyond the Mercatale, a great piazza that he had thrown across the ravine below the stables.[67] On the piano nobile are two small rooms, another smaller room, and the tiny studiolo (no. 126). Below it are three more rooms and two tiny chapels, and below that are small rooms, one of which was used for playing ball,[68] and baths. The floors are connected by circular stairs within the towers on the western facade.

It is very important to clarify the sources for this complex area. Professor Heydenreich has pointed out that neither Alberti nor Filarete, the only two Renaissance theorists who wrote before this part of the palace was built, discussed private baths. He added that because Pliny did discuss baths when describing his villa, and because other elements in the duke's suite bear close relations to Pliny's hideaway, he is "inclined to assume a direct connection" between Pliny's description and Federigo's construction.[69] What Heydenreich has called a "charming concetto" may earlier have inspired the designer of Nicholas V's Vatican palace, who fitted out several rooms, including a bedroom, the renowned but now lost studiolo, and the chapel that Fra Angelico frescoed. These rooms, spread over two floors, were accessible from the public counsel rooms facing across gardens to Rome and from the new wing Nicholas had extended across the future Cortile del Belvedere.

The arrangement of the private apartment was perhaps traditional in case regie, and at the Vatican a designer familiar with Pliny's description may have given it a new coherence. More certain is a connection between the arrangement at the Vatican and the duke's suite in Urbino. In each, the more public facilities overlook gardens, and the smaller rooms that constituted the private recesses are in the inner, more intimate areas. The arrangement of the duke's suite, having been sketched out at the Vatican, was transported to Urbino and skillfully modified and integrated into the construction, achieving about the same relationship to the garden and the public rooms as occurred at the Vatican. In Urbino, this motif assumed an independence that had been prevented by its insertion into extant construction at the Vatican, and it exploited a seemingly disadvantageous, clifflike site.

Towers and balconies are appended to the western facade of the duke's suite (Fig. 6). The conical turrets atop the towers are probably not later additions.[70] Originally the towers were crenellated, and they and the great eagle emblematic of the Montefeltro family, which would have appeared above the palace's crenellated silhouette, forcefully dominated the western facade.[71]

The towers and balconies are often treated as a unit, and that unit is usually said to have come from the triumphal arch and towers at the Castel Nuovo in Naples. They should, however, be considered two separate elements with two separate sources and meanings.[72]

Towers convey a martial theme commonly found in fortified residences of princes. Because examples are legion, they contain no particular reference. The Urbino towers simply represent Federigo's military prowess and his ability to defend the palace and the city. The designer turned the theme to domestic advantage by inserting the spiral stairs within each tower, just as he carefully balanced their mass and placement among the other elements to the benefit of the overall design.

The balconies do contain a particular reference. They are like the loggias that overlook a realm whose order is protected by the virtù of the man in the rooms opening onto them, and they have huge Fs and Cs to identify him. In a sense, the towers protect the balconies as much as they do the palace, but otherwise the towers and balconies are unrelated. Directly off the lower balcony (the lowest two are buttresses, not balconies) are the Cappella del Perdono and the Tempietto delle Muse, and directly behind the upper balcony is the studiolo. These are the three places within the palace most intimately related to the sources of Federigo's virtù, communion with God, communion with personifications of excellence in fields of human endeavor, and a more complex program that will be discussed later, as will the theme of having balconies or loggias overlook protected realms.

The duke's suite contains one more element, the two bay, two-story Loggia del Gallo (no. 130) attached to its south flank. The loggia is accessible from small audience rooms within the palace, and it overlooks the Terrazza del Gallo (no. 50) on the ground floor level. The terrace is defined by the loggia and by a tier of rectangular rooms attached to the south reach of the western facade. The loggia provides projections from council rooms similar to the balconies attached to the duke's suite.

The final motif, the Cortile del Pasquino (no. 67), was conceived at about the time of the second campaign and was added to the south of the palace (Fig.7). Fabric with a ground floor arcade, arcuated windows on the piano nobile, and crenellations extended the palace to the south; the oldest palace wing received an addition on its west side containing an arched doorway opening on the ground floor, an arcuated loggia along the piano nobile, and crenellations.[73] To the south some sort of enclosure was to be built, and a simple balustrade defining the west side would open this enclosed, private courtyard to the countryside.[74] A barrel vaulted androne in line with the entrance from the piazza and a ground floor loggia begun along its eastern side would be its only entrances. In its center was to be a circular mausoleum for the duke and duchess.[75] The duchess's death in 1472 apparently terminated construction here.

This motif was without precedent but not without sources. It is an amalgamation of two different types of mausoleum that were being explored at mid-century. One type was located in a centralized area of a functioning ecclesiastical space. Cosimo de' Medici interred his parents in the sacristy that Brunelleschi had built at San Lorenzo. Alberti and Michelozzo in about 1449 had begun to add a centralized east end to SS. Annunziata in Florence, in which Lodovico Gonzaga could bury his father, Gian Francesco. There are suggestions that the domed crossing of Alberti's Sant' Andrea in Mantua from 1470 and of Bramante's Santa Maria della Grazie in Milan from the 1490s were also meant to receive the bodies of their ducal builders.[76] The tomb Michelangelo planned to place under Bramante's great dome in the centralized scheme for St. Peter's so that Julius II could be placed above Peter was the most daring example of this type, and it is little wonder that it was abandoned.

The other type illustrated Alberti's proposal that the dead be interred elsewhere than in functioning churches, but it met with little success except at mid-century. In about 1450, Sigismondo Malatesta had Alberti rebuild and enlarge the church of San Francesco in Rimini with a row of massive arches along the external flanks to receive the sarcophagi of court humanists and other favorites. He also added a facade that combined a temple front and a triumphal arch, creating two large spaces for the sarcophagi of Sigismondo and Isotta. Matteo de'Pasti's medal shows that the east end of the Tempio Malatestiano was to have received a drumless Pantheon-like dome. In about the same years Nicholas V also pursued Alberti's proposal. He began to rebuild Santa Maria delle Febbre, a domed, circular structure at the south transept of St. Peter's that was believed to be ancient. According to Manetti, it was to provide a proper burial place for the mortal remains of the popes.[77]

Federigo rejected an alternative that he could have known, the San Sepolcro Rucellai that Alberti had designed. The Rucellai tomb was a conscious, careful imitation of the Holy Sepulchre in Jerusalem; undomed, it stands in a chapel at the Rucellai parish church of San Pancrazio in Florence. Its dedication and its function, however, relate it typologically to the other current Florentine example of the Holy Sepulchre, the church of SS. Annunziata. Federigo instead began a burial precinct that bears the character of the Vatican example in that it is independent of an ecclesiastical space and contains a domed mausoleum.

Francesco di Giorgio was its most likely designer, and he turned to obvious sources for the mausoleum. Even though nothing is known about the details of its form, it is typologically related to the Christian church of S. Stefano Rotondo that Nicholas V restored, to Santa Costanza that was originally an imperial mausoleum and that Francesco drew and labeled "tempio di Baccho,"[78] to some pagan temples destroyed during the pontificate of Sixtus IV,[79] and to circular tempietti within imperial villas and palaces that Francesco restored in a fanciful way.[80] These circular tempietti were the most likely sources for Francesco's design, because they were parts of the residences of ancient Romans and enabled the palace in Urbino to relate its builder to Roman precedents. The original suggestion for the precinct may have been made by the Vatican project of Nicholas V, and referring to that source would have allowed another important point about the palace's builder to be made.

Having reviewed the motifs that provide the substance of the palace's program and reveal the qualities of Federigo's character, and having earlier examined the formal elements and ornaments that convey attributes of his character, certain conclusions may now be drawn. One is that the palace's program conveys the same broad points as the biographies do. Another is that the palace provided Federigo with a setting for his exertions in arms, letters, and governing.

The palace was arranged in five broad divisions, two public and three more private. One public area began in the piazza and included the portal near the cathedral. This conducted the visitor to a loggia overlooking an enclosed garden, the setting in which Federigo governed his realm with intellect and reason. Another began at the portal leading to the cortile and continued up the stairs to the Sala del Trono, the public room where Federigo was surrounded with emblematic representations of the place he as a man of arms had assumed in the chivalric hierarchy. These two public areas were set apart from the three private ones, the apartments of the duke, those of the duchess, and the secluded Cortile del Pasquino.

The ornament of the palace commented on these places. The facade ornamentation and the decoration in the public areas stressed Federigo's intelligence, Roman precedent, and chivalric virtue. These same themes are found in the private areas, and they

6
Ducal Palace, Urbino, west facade.
(Photo: Anderson, Rome). The Loggia
del Gallo is shown bricked up. The
large structure below the palace is the
teatro del Raffaelo, its apse standing
on the so-called *Data* of Federigo's
stables, whose foundations are seen
running off to the right from the *Data*.
The Mercatale is visible below the
stable foundations.

7
Ducal Palace, Urbino, Cortile del
Pasquino, reconstruction. (From
Rotondi, *The Ducal Palace of Urbino*)

are brilliantly summarized in the most beautiful room, the studiolo located in the heart of the duke's suite (Figs. 8 and 9).

The studiolo surrounded Federigo with three topics—letters, arms, and concern for the perpetuation of virtue in his ducal realm. The topic of letters was represented in the attic by painted portraits of twenty-eight ancient, modern, pagan, Jewish, and Christian authors classified, according to Santi, as theologians, philosophers, poets, and jurists,[81] and according to Vespasiano as philosophers, poets, and doctors of the Church.[82] The portraits included Pius II and Sixtus IV. The lower level has intarsia panels representing cabinets that seem to be open to display a collection of musical, mathematical, geometric, and chronological instruments mingled with books whose authors include Cicero, Seneca, and Virgil. The topic of letters is completed by a panel on the back wall of the south alcove. Here the duke's lectern appears with a full load of closed books standing in what is clearly a fictive extension of the reading alcove, which the viewer himself can physically inhabit.

The topic of arms is less fully developed here. While letters, which guided arms, could be pursued in the studiolo, arms were carried in the field, and the studiolo became a place to display the result of the duke's virtù at arms. The intarsia contain shelves that appear to form benches and ledges above supports rising from the floor. The duke's chivalric emblems are scattered about on the shelves among the books and other intellectual instruments as well as elsewhere in the scheme and in the coffers of the rich ceiling. In the depths of the north alcove, balancing the lectern in the south alcove, the duke's armor is seen carefully put away in the cupboard. A gauntlet leaning against the ledge in front indicates that the real space of the viewer and the fictive space of the cupboard are continuous, thus establishing an increased immediacy between the viewer and that which he sees fictively presented in the intarsia.

The topic of virtue's perpetuation in the ducal realm is developed in three ways. One shows that Federigo's legitimate successor is Guidobaldo, his son, who was tutored by his father. This is presented in the large portrait by Pedro Berruguete (or Justus van Ghent) in the attic, among the exemplary men of letters. It shows Federigo reading while dressed in armor covered by his robe of state and conspicuously displaying the Order of the Garter and the Order of the Ermine. Below the lectern that holds Federigo's book and the hat given him by ambassadors of the Shah of Persia stands Guidobaldo dressed in princely robes and holding a mace while gazing thoughtfully into the studiolo.

The second theme in this topic is in the form of an admonition concerning virtuous conduct. The sequence of cabinets in the intarsia is interrupted by several niches. In three that are seemingly half round in plan with shell half-domes stand the three Christian virtues. two other niches are seemingly rectangular in plan and elevation and could be covered with curtains that have been drawn aside. These are located within the actual alcoves on the east side. The one next to the duke's lectern contains a pipe organ, an apparent complement to the order discovered through pursuit of letters. The one next to the duke's armor holds Federigo himself (Fig. 8). He is dressed in long robes and ducal cap rather than in armor. Like Queen Tomyris in Castagno's frescoes in the Villa Carducci at Legnaia, and like the Trojans, Etruscans, and Arcadians in the funeral procession of the hero Pallas in the *Aeneid*, Federigo holds a spear with the tip down. He appears here as an exemplum for his son similar in character to the three Christian virtues.

The third theme concerns death. It is quite apparent that the studiolo, which was completed before Federigo's death, is a posthumous memorial and a display of Federigo's virtue, not a presentation of the duke in everyday life when alive. The books on the lectern are closed; the armor is put away; the duke takes his place as an exemplum for his son who will succeed him. The studiolo is a metaphor, if not a symbolic representation, for the reward Federigo will receive, and explains why he merits that reward (Fig. 9). On the east wall, between the alcoves with the lectern and the armor and below the portrait of Federigo and Guidobaldo, is a panel that gains great impact because it is flanked by actual recesses and because of the large scale of its elements. On its foremost ledge, between the fictive pilasters that belong to the space of the viewer, is a wicker basket filled with leaved apples and pomegranates whose ripeness bursts their skins, and an industrious squirrel wearing a collar, busily gnawing at a nut. Beyond, beginning at a point made indeterminate by the ledge across the front, stretches an empty piazza with a pavement that recedes in carefully marked squares. At its base is a robust arcade with piers that are faced with heavy pilasters, a mature evocation of ancient Roman architecture. Beyond the arcade can be seen a lower, distant landscape with hills, trees, a lake, and, on a distant plain, a city walled and towered and dominated by a dome.

The content of this panel and of the studiolo that surrounds it is simple: Federigo merits the paradise beyond the piazza and the arcade because by exerting himself in arms and letters he has, like the collared squirrel, shackled the abundant gifts of Venus represented by the basket of fruits, and he has become an exemplum of virtue like the three Christian

37
Chivalric
Declaration: The
Palazzo Ducale
in Urbino as a
Political
Statement

virtues. A paradisaical realm may be established by exercising a just government based on intellect.

This concept permeates the palace and other products of Federigo's patronage. The garden in which Federigo would "give audience to all who wished," as Vespasiano reported, or where "Commanding a thing, *el Padrone* is obeyed," as another biographer put it,[83] was a paradise that included all the appropriate elements—a loggia, an enclosure, planting beds, and a fountain that was supplied from a cistern atop the structure containing a ramp between the Sala delle Veglie and the duchess's suite.

The relationship of the duke's and duchess's suites to one another and to the garden is also paradisaical. Each suite had a private balcony overlooking the garden, and the two suites were connected by the passage that ran across the garden wall. It probably allowed the duchess to arrive at the Alcova del Duca, a bed chamber decorated with the arms of the Montefeltro, with Federigo's personal emblems, and with *armorini,* rich stuffs, evergreens, and ripe fruits hanging from citrus trees.[84] This is a mature representation of the theme Patroni had used when discussing the soldier's lustful youth in Urbino. Here it is clear that in Federigo's household, which he regulated as if it were a religious institution,[85] love was pure, sanctified by the sacrament of marriage, free of lust, and intended to provide an example and an heir for his subjects.[86]

Another example of this theme again reveals that chaste love within the ducal household helped maintain an orderly realm. In the double portrait of the duke and duchess by Piero della Francesca now in the Uffizi, Federigo is a knight seated on a campaign chair and dressed in armor. He holds a scepter as he is crowned with the wreath of victory by a winged figure standing on a ball. The four cardinal virtues also ride on the car as it is drawn across the landscape by large horses driven by a putto. The inscription, which explicitly refers to the image, states that Federigo is equal to the greatest martial leaders and that the virtues who guide his government celebrate his perpetual fame. His orderly government is shown by the ships riding peacefully across the luminous lake in the distant landscape. The pendant to this portrait shows Battista. Her inscription calls her an example of chastity, and this is emblematically repeated by the castles in the distant landscape. Her chaste life and the virtues that accompany her on the car drawn by white unicorns are attributes complementary to Federigo's.

The Cortile del Pasquino was also intended as a paradise. In its mausoleum the bodies of the duke and duchess would have received a final resting place resembling the one in the distant landscape in the central studiolo panel.

The paradise program that permeates the palace had a long tradition and a variety of interpretations. Locating the source for the Urbino program and discovering the origin for the numerous important motifs that compose the palace will add an additional level of meaning to Federigo's character.

Federigo himself said that when he undertook the second campaign he had sought his architects in Tuscany.[87] He eventually hired Laurana in Mantua, not in Tuscany, and although Tuscan practice stands behind some ornamental and architectural elements, it contributed none of the important motifs.[88]

Some of the motifs are commonly found in other palaces of the same type, and their appearance in Urbino would be generic rather than specific. The piazza, the west facade towers, and perhaps the studiolo (but not its decoration) are of this nature.[89] The piazza and cortile facades are based on Roman precedents or concepts even if their articulation reveals a clarity found at this time only in Tuscany. The stairs point to Nicholas V's work on the Capitol, and the balconies attached to the duke's suite point to the Vatican palace of Nicholas V, as do other elements. But here difficulties arise; the relationship between the public rooms and the duke's suite could derive from the Vatican only vaguely because the pope had renovated older fabric and therefore could not control that relationship as Federigo could, and the duchess's suite would hardly have a parallel at the Vatican. Still, the Vatican is the source for several important motifs, and these motifs form the most fundamental part of the program of the Urbino palace.

According to Manetti, Nicholas had designed the Vatican palace to serve him in much the same role that Federigo was playing in Urbino. The close analogy is most clearly revealed by a surviving fragment of the pope's decorative scheme.[90] Its emphasis was closely parallel, mutatis mutandis, to the emphasis of the decoration of the studiolo in Urbino. Nicholas had a room decorated with the four virtues and with sportive, clear-eyed putti playing with objects indicating that his love was directed at governing actively in the world. The room was used for counsel and was placed between the pope's private apartment and the *mons saccorum,* an area Manetti called a paradise. The point of Nicholas's program was that exercising virtue and controlling lust leads to loving concord and an orderly, paradisaical realm.

The Vatican palace allowed the pope to use charity in governing superbia. It included interior public and private areas and an enclosed garden with halls, a chapel, and a loggia (theater) where the pope could perform ceremonial duties and hold counsel with others such as counts and dukes involved in maintaining order.

Federigo's palace allowed the duke to emulate the pope in striving for virtue by governing justly. The paradise theme in the studiolo parallels the pope's. The formal and spatial character of the garden and theater loggia between the duke's and duchess's suites resembles the layout of the Vatican palace as it faced the paradise on the *mons saccorum,* which had loggias overlooking it that were functionally analogous to the Urbino balconies. Similarly, the balconies between the west towers in Urbino overlook an orderly, protected realm, a theme suggested by the Vatican loggias. The Cortile del Pasquino also derives most directly from Nicholas's ideas and once again repeats the theme of loggias, balconies, and enclosed gardens as a setting for paradise. These elements, when added to the clearly Roman character of the facades and cortile d'onore, reveal a more fundamental debt to the Vatican palace than to any other palace, and one that is specific, not generic.

Nicholas's palace at the Vatican was a paradise. As Manetti put it, it was a paradise beyond the abilities of poets to describe. Although the paradise theme had a long tradition in decorative and literary programs, Nicholas's project was the first to translate it into an architectural program and render it in actual architectural construction. After Nicholas had sketched out his plans, and after they had been made accessible through construction, decoration, Manetti's description, and other, less important sources, others saw that a major clarification of long-standing ideas had been laid down. Themes lacking clear representation suddenly gained force, and Nicholas's Vatican palace became a model no one subordinate to the pope could ignore. They could now copy the program of the pope's palace, adapting its motifs as required by particular sites and circumstances, to reveal their relationship to their superior.[91]

To copy the palace of one's superior was to show that one was guided by the same virtues that guided his superior. As Aristotle had said, "The ruler ought to have moral virtue in perfection, for his function, taken absolutely, demands a master artificer, and rational principle is such an artificer; the subjects, on the other hand, require only that measure of virtue which is proper to each of them" (*Politics,* 1260a, 17–20). The various virtues Aristotle cited had become the chivalric virtues, and they, along with clearly articulated hierarchical distinctions, were basic to an orderly princely realm in the quattrocento. Filarete expressed this with great clarity throughout the architectural treatise he addressed to Francesco Sforza. At one point he had the duke lecture his son and heir: "I leave you a beautiful domain, as you can see. I leave you the love of our people. If you wish to maintain it, you need first to use justice, which is a laudable virtù and which encompasses all the others." He continues, "A domain

is like a wall made of many and various *ragioni* (orders) of stones. . . . As it is necessary for you to maintain all the qualities of stone in this wall, so it is necessary for you to maintain and to preserve all your people according to their quality. . . . See to it that you are the master and the architect of this wall."[92]

Two of the principal chivalric virtues were magnificence and intellect, and according to Federigo's biographers, his palace revealed these qualities. Paltroni cited "the splendid court and . . . the magnificent and splendid buildings" as evidence of Federigo's chivalric character,[93] and Vespasiano stressed the "grand order and the measure of every element as he had supervised it."[94] Santi began his description of the palace immediately after he had dealt with Battista's death. The beautiful building, he said, and the active life he led in it deserve the admiration of all men.[95] Its architect was Laurana, who "with highest intellect and ability directed the work with the intentions of the Count, whose directions were higher and more lucid than [those of] any other Signor."[96] He continued with a description of Federigo's library, introduced the palace again, and concluded with a recitation of Federigo's "demonstrations of a faithful heart/ More than sufficient to show the Count/ beyond all others in his high splendor."[97] Baldi introduced the palace immediately after he described how Federigo had routed Sigismondo Malatesta and had earned the pleasure of Pius II, and again turned to Federigo's patronage of building and devoted a long section to his support and pursuit of learning, immediately after recounting Federigo's investiture with the ducal title by Sixtus IV.[98]

These apostrophes resemble the one that connected Nicholas V to the design of the Vatican palace, except that Nicholas's intellect tended to be extolled while Federigo's intellect and magnificence receive about equal emphasis, in part because of the later date of Federigo's biographies, and in part because of the differences in their respective offices.[99] The quattrocento reasons for connecting the pope with the design of the Vatican palace are similar to those that would lead observers to attribute the Urbino palace to Federigo. But from a twentieth-century point of view, the problem in Urbino is more complex. More information is available about Urbino than about Rome, more of the palace survives, and what was built is of much higher architectural quality. Nevertheless, from both quattrocento and twentieth-century points of view, it seems reasonable to take Federigo's patent to Luciano Laurana at face value: ". . . having decided to make in our city of Urbino a beautiful residence worthy of the rank and fame of our ancestors and our own standing, we have chosen and deputed . . . Laurana to be

39
Chivalric
Declaration: The
Palazzo Ducale
in Urbino as a
Political
Statement

engineer and overseer of all the master workmen employed on the said work . . . who [are] to obey the said Master Luciano in all things and perform whatever they are ordered to do by him, as though by our own person."[100] His rank was that of count, later duke, of a papal vicarate, and his fame was that of being skilled in arms and learned in letters. The former he could reveal by copying the pope's palace, and the latter he could reveal by imitating the pope's intelligence in design and adding magnificence.

That is what a quattrocento observer might have noted. Federigo did have help in designing, perhaps from even more individuals than are named in quattrocento sources. Mario Salmi believed that he detected the aesthetic of Piero della Francesca,[101] while Baldi attempted to imply that Alberti had a role in the palace's design. He pointed out, while naming a number of architects who were involved in the design and a number, such as Brunelleschi, who were not, that Federigo "also had great familiarity with and the service of Leon Battista Alberti, a singular man, and one of the luminaries of Florence, his country. We also have it on good authority" that Alberti had intended to dedicate *De re aedificatoria* to Federigo.[102] Alberti had begun the treatise for the Gonzaga in Mantua, close friends of Federigo; it was eventually presented to Nicholas V, and finally dedicated, after Alberti's death, to Lorenzo de' Medici. But the point that Federigo and Alberti shared a close relationship is well authenticated, and it seems improbable that Federigo would have been immune to Alberti's advice.[103]

According to quattrocento descriptions the palace is magnificent and splendid, it shows intelligence in its grand order and measure, and it is beautiful. But these quattrocento terms, in which beauty means the congruence of design and construction and the clear exposition of a functional program based on a man's office, have little to do with the terms that refer to the source of the aesthetic experience one has when contemplating an object with pure visual forms and no references to goodness and truth. Still, even in present terms, the palace is beautiful. Is that beauty attributable to any conscious quattrocento concerns?

It is, as is indicated by the place of the Urbino palace relative to other projects built for Federigo. The cortile in Urbino, for example, is superior to the one in the ducal palace in Gubbio which is largely a copy of the one in Urbino.[104] Constructed for the same patron and by the same crew of designers and builders, it is much less pleasing. Its proportions are less satisfactory, symmetry is lacking (its opposite sides are discordant with one another), and the colors of the materials do not blend with the same subtlety. But this is proper because Gubbio was only the secondary seat of the Montefeltro family. It was a cheaper job, and the materials available in Gubbio were less satisfactory. A prudent patron would hardly be profligate at a secondary seat of the family.

Gubbio lacks an independent aesthetic value because it was the product of a half-hearted quattrocento effort. Urbino has abundant independent aesthetic value as well as quattrocento value because the architects had managed to reveal the character of the duke while also producing excellent proportions and symmetry and using materials harmoniously. It is now difficult to accept the notion that the design can be attributed to a building committee that included Federigo, architects, painters, and consultants. We require that some one person be held responsible, and art historians are probably correct in identifying Laurana and Francesco di Giorgio as the prime designers. Indeed, they were excellent architects, but they were not working in a vacuum. They lived in an exciting moment when Rome, both ancient and modern, and Florence were providing new sources for formal elements. There was a freshness then that mitigated the grossness found in earlier productions—for example, the Palazzo Vitelleschi in Tarquinia—and the excessive finesse found in later works—for example, the Cancellaria. The quality of the moment contributed to the architects' skill in finishing the design.

But responsibility for the substance of the palace, the part in which its beauty resides, for its programmatic motifs, their arrangement, and their selection from proper sources, must be given to Federigo. Vespasiano and others indicated that his ability to direct architectural affairs was quite good. He could dictate how best to render the "rank and fame of our ancestors and our own standing" in motifs drawn from proper sources and assembled with intelligence.[105] Without his talented supervision of the architects and workmen, the palace would have lacked proportion, symmetry, and beauty in its ornamental finishing. But more importantly, without his own clear understanding of his political position and of the ability of architecture to represent it, the program itself and the assemblage of motifs within a program—that is, the thing that was beautiful—would have been substantially deficient.[106] The palace would have lacked the coherence required for beauty both then and now.

Like Nicholas V, Federigo built a palace with a coherent program that revealed his intentions as a signore, and as Alberti, on the basis of Bartolus and Salutati, required of a benevolent prince, his intentions were virtuous. The palace decorated the prince's realm, and this revealed the prince's magnificence. Its superiority over the realm reveals his legitimate position over his subjects. His accessibility within it shows his concern for their affairs. And furthermore, the arrangement of its major motifs and the content of its ornamentation reveals the place he occupied within the political system and his attitude toward the values of that system.

Federigo was part of a political system that operated because charity conquered superbia and because those above were conspicuous examples of virtue for those below. In copying the pope's palace, Federigo showed that he maintained the trust of his superiors, that he preserved his reputation and honor, and that he was therefore more than a mere condottiere. He was a legitimate vicar, de facto and de jure. In governing in a setting that established a paradise like the popes', he revealed that their ideals and values in governing were his own. He shared love with his subjects, and was therefore their legitimate signore. Urbino was not a republic, Florentine, Jeffersonian, or otherwise. Vespasiano reported that he treated his subjects "not as subjects, but as his children, and . . . they loved him as children love their own fathers."[107] The children respected order and did not attempt to usurp the father's position. To settle a dispute, Federigo once said to a young man of low estate, "If I desired you to become a relative of mine, would you not consent, having regard for my station? Would it not seem to you a desirable relationship?" Vespasiano reported that the youth, no opportunist as Burckhardt might have predicted, replied "that in this case it would not be fitting, between so great a man as the Duke and one like himself."[108]

Federigo governed during a period that was propitious for formulating an articulate and coherent statecraft and building program, although he could not have known that in 1444. When he succeeded his half brother, he had to gain the trust of his subjects and the authority vested by his superiors. He gained the former through benevolent government, and the latter through faithful service. He began the first phase of his palace only after his rule had become secure, and he launched the second building campaign about fifteen years later. There was a significant difference between the political climate in 1450, when conditions were only beginning to stabilize, and 1465, when conditions had been stable for a decade or so. When he said that the palace was to be "worthy of the rank and fame of our ancestors and our own standing," it was clear to him and to others what his rank was, how his fame had been earned and would continue to be deserved, how his own virtues were part of a dynastic heritage that he had protected and promoted, and what architectural program could be pressed into his service. The tentative beginnings of the first campaign could be extended to the larger program of the second to celebrate past successes and to promise future glory for himself, for his family, and for the subjects within the Montefeltro's jurisdiction. His statecraft and his building program satisfied the criteria of the dynastic mythology of a Renaissance prince. Both noted Federigo's and his family's origins, proclaimed their virtues, and revealed his own particular qualities and abilities while demonstrating that the state was the family writ large and the state was Federigo in person.[109]

Federigo's abilities as a statesman may be appreciated in his statecraft, and his abilities as a patron of the visual arts are evident in the products of his artists and architects. His own abilities in both of these fields may also be seen in the palace, which is good not only because it has the proportion, symmetry, and beauty that could be given it by its architects, but also because its program has these qualities and because it clearly reveals and portrays its inhabitant's beliefs about what makes a political system function well.

To say this is to claim that a coherent conjunction of form and content has more value than an incoherent one. Had it been a coherent statement of a malevolent tyrant rather than of a benevolent prince, it would still be better than an incoherent statement by a benevolent prince. To claim that the palace is good because Federigo was benevolent, and that had he been malevolent the same palace could be judged bad, would be to lapse into what Scott called the "ethical fallacy." To claim that a good man will inevitably produce works of high visual quality is belied by experience. The point of assessing Federigo's moral value need have nothing to do with assessing the visual quality of the objects that represent him. But the claims made by the good are always to be respected above those made by the evil, and one cannot help but respond to those claims when they are illustrated by beautiful visual forms.

Notes

1
Geoffrey Scott, The Architecture of Humanism, 2d ed. (Garden City, N.Y., 1956), p. 29. Original emphasis.

2
Jacob Burckhardt, The Civilization of the Renaissance in Italy, trans. S. G. C. Middlemore (Harper Torchbook edition, New York, 1958), p. 107.

3
Ernst Gombrich, In Search of Cultural History (Oxford, 1969), passim.

4
Werner L. Gundersheimer, Ferrara: The Style of a Renaissance Despotism (Princeton, 1973), p. 9.

5
Rudolph Wittkower, Architectural Principles in the Age of Humanism, 3d ed. (London, 1962), p. 1. Emphasis added.

6
Erwin Panofsky, "Iconography and Iconology: An Introduction to the Study of Renaissance Art," in Meaning in the

Visual Arts (Garden City, N.Y., 1957), pp. 26–54, especially in the chart, pp. 40–41. The essay is reprinted from *Studies in Iconology* (Oxford, 1939). See also Ernst Cassirer, *An Essay on Man: An Introduction to a Philosophy of Human Culture* (New Haven, 1944).

7

Wittkower, *Architectural Principles,* p. 1.

8

De re aedificatoria, edited with Italian translation by Giovanni Orlandi, 2 vols. (Milan, 1966), V, i, 1: 333; and *Ten Books on Architecture,* trans. James Leoni from the Italian translation of Cosimo Bartoli (London, 1755), reprinted and edited by Joseph Rykwert (London, 1955), p. 82. Compare the opinions of Bartolus of Sassoferrato, *De tyrannia,* trans. E. Emerton, in *Humanism and Tyranny* (Cambridge, Mass., 1925), pp. 126–154; and Coluccio Salutati, *De tyranno,* in ibid., pp. 70–116.

9

For a brief review that suggests the background of these *topoi,* see Ernst Robert Curtius, *European Literature and the Latin Middle Ages,* trans. Willard R. Trask (Harper Torchbook edition, New York and Evanston, 1963). Chap. 9, especially sections 4–9.

10

Pierantonio Paltroni, *Commentari della vita et gesti dell'illustrissimo Federico Duca d'Urbino,* ed. Walter Tommasoli (Urbino, 1966), hereafter cited as Paltroni.

11

Vespasiano da Bisticci, *Le Vite,* ed. Aulo Greco, vol. 1 [Florence (Istituto Nazionale di Studi sul Rinascimento) 1970]; hereafter cited as Vespasiano. See also *Renaissance Princes, Popes, and Prelates: The Vespasiano Memoirs,* trans. William George and Emily Waters, ed. Myron P. Gilmore (Harper Torchbook edition, New York, Evanston, and London, 1963), hereafter cited as Vespasiano, translation.

12

G. Zannoni, "Commentarii della Vita e delle imprese di Federico da Montefeltro di Francesco Filelfo," *Atti e memorie della R. Deputazione di Storia Patria per le provincie delle Marche,* 5 (1901). I have been unable to consult this publication.

13

Giovanni Santi, *Federigo di Montefeltro, Duca di Urbino, Cronaca,* ed. H. Holtzinger (Stuttgart, 1893), hereafter cited as Santi.

14

Unpublished; fragments appear in August Schmarsow, *Melozzo da Forlì* (Berlin and Stuttgart, 1886).

15

Unpublished; fragments appear in Schmarsow, *Melozzo da Forlì.*

16

Girolamo Muzio (Mutio), *Historia de' Fatti di Federico di Montefeltro, Duca d'Urbino* (Venice, 1605), hereafter cited as Muzio.

17

Bernardino Baldi, *Vita e fatti di Federigo di Montefeltro,* ed. Francesco Zuccardi, 3 vols. (Rome, 1824), hereafter cited as Baldi.

18

Paltroni, p. 42. Guidantonio had Martin V register a formal legitimation on December 22, 1424, declaring Federigo to be his son by an unnamed Urbino girl; James Dennistoun, *Memoirs of the Dukes of Urbino,* ed. Edward Hutton, 3 vols. (London and New York, 1909), 1: 62; and Tommasoli's note in Paltroni, p. 43, n. 2.

19

For this period, see Gino Franceschini, *Figure del Rinascimento urbinate* (Urbino, 1959), p. 14.

20

Paltroni, pp. 44–46.

21

Paltroni, p. 68; compare Baldi, 1: 67–72.

22

The accord is transcribed in Dennistoun, *Memoirs,* 1: app. IV, 438–442.

23

Eugenius excommunicated Federigo, thus depriving him of his titles, but Nicholas V lifted the censure and confirmed them on September 26, 1447, soon after his ascension to the pontifical throne; see Baldi, 1: 95–114.

24

Quoted in Dennistoun, *Memoirs,* 1: app. VII, 457.

25

Paltroni, p. 40.

26

Baldi, 1: 95; see also Bernardino Baldi, *Encomio della Patria* (Urbino, 1706), pp. 69–72 (hereafter cited as Baldi, *Encomio*).

27

Santi, I, iv, 20. See also idem, Preambolo, v.

28

Paltroni, p. 54. See also Santi, 1, viii: 68–70.

29

Muzio, p. 6; see also pp. 391–393. See also Santi, 1, ii: 47–49. Federigo had been betrothed at age three to Gentile Brancaleoni, whom he married in 1437; she died in 1457. The marriage was barren. In 1460 he married Battista Sforza (1446–1472). This marriage produced seven daughters and one son, Guidobaldo. There were also four illegitimate offspring, two of whom were males, both of whom Federigo had legitimated, one of whom predeceased his father. See Dennistoun, *Memoirs,* 1: 289–291.

30

See especially André Chastel, *Art et Humanisme à Florence,* 2d ed. (Paris, 1961), pp. 261–264, and pp. 359–372; Ruggero Ruggieri, *L'umanesimo cavalleresco italiano* (Rome, 1962), especially pp. 180ff; and Marilyn Aronberg Lavin, "Piero della Francesca's Montefeltro Altarpiece: A Pledge of Fidelity," *The Art Bulletin,* 51 (1969): 367–371, passim. See Gustave Reese, "Musical Compositions in Renaissance Intarsia," in *Medieval and Renaissance Studies* (Proceedings of the Southeastern Institute of Medieval and Renaissance Studies, Summer, 1966), ed. John L. Lievsay (Durham, S.C., 1968), 74–97, for romance *chansons* represented in the *studiolo* intarsia. For the subject in general, see most recently Gundersheimer, *Ferrara,* pp. 133–135, 266–267, and references given later.

31

Vespasiano, p. 353. This preamble does not appear in Vespasiano, translation.

32

Vespasiano, p. 380; Vespasiano, translation, p. 99.

33

Vespasiano, pp. 382–383; compare Vespasiano, translation, pp. 100–101.

43
Chivalric
Declaration: The
Palazzo Ducale
in Urbino as a
Political
Statement

34
Vespasiano, p. 390; Vespasiano, translation, p. 103.

35
Vespasiano, p. 399; Vespasiano, translation, p. 105.

36
The literature is reviewed in Howard Saalman, review of Pasquale Rotondi, *The Ducal Palace of Urbino*, in *Burlington Magazine*, 113 (1971): 46–51 (hereafter cited as Rotondi, review). I have been unable to consult P. Rotondi, *Francesco di Giorgio nel Palazzo Ducale di Urbino* (Milan, 1970).

37
Giuseppe Marchini, "Il Palazzo Ducale di Urbino," *Rinascimento* 9 (1958): 43–78 (hereafter cited as "Palazzo Ducale"), wishes to attribute more work to Francesco di Giorgio in the third campaign than Rotondi does.

38
G. Marchini, "Aggiunte al Palazzo Ducale di Urbino," *Bollettino d'Arte,* series 4, 45 (1960): 73–80 (hereafter cited as "Aggiunte"); on p. 80, he points out that some of the guest apartments were begun by Federigo, but that they would not have risen above the crenellations. He also suggests that, contrary to Rotondi's opinion, the roof covering the Sala del Trono's roof would not have projected above the crenellations.

39
Bernardino Baldi, *Descrittione del Palazzo Ducale d'Urbino,* in Baldi, *Verse e Prose* (Venice, 1590), pp. 503–573, 557 (hereafter cited as Baldi, *Descrittione*).

40
The relevant section from book II of the *Vita Nicolai V* is given in Torgil Magnuson, Studies in Roman Quattrocento Architecture, *Figura,* 9 (Stockholm, 1958): app. 351–362, especially ss. 54–82. *Figura* is an irregularly issued series of studies subtitled "Studies Edited by the Institute of Art History, University of Uppsala." No. 9, published by Almgvist & Wiksell in Stockholm, is devoted to a single title, *Studies in Roman Quattrocento Architecture*.

41
See Francesco di Giorgio Martini, *Trattati di architettura ingegneria e arte militare,* ed. Corrado Maltese, 2 vols. (Milan, 1967) 2: 339–340.

42
The present loggia along the flank of the cathedral possibly replaces a quattrocento structure. Baldi, *Descrittione,* pp. 569–570, states that the largo along the old wing was opened by Guidobaldo II, Federigo's son. See also the captions to the first three photographs in Marchini, "Palazzo Ducale." Federigo continued the work of his father on the cathedral, apparently with a new plan by Francesco di Giorgio, but an earthquake cleared the site for the present late eighteenth-century structure.

43
A résumé of the longer argument in Pasquale Rotondi, *Il Palazzo Ducale di Urbino,* 2 vols. (Urbino, 1950–1951), is given in idem, *The Ducal Palace of Urbino* (London, 1969), pp. 68–72. The latter work hereafter cited as Rotondi, 1969.

44
The panels from the bench show engines of war and other mechanical devices. They are now on exhibit within the palace. Recently it has been suggested that Francesco di Giorgio was not their designer and that they postdate Francesco's activity in Urbino; Frank G. Prager and Gustina Scaglia, *Brunelleschi: Studies of his Technology and Inventions* (Cambridge, Mass., and London, 1970), especially p. 105.

45
The other windows, lighting the top flight of stairs, leading to the guest rooms above the east wing, are later additions to the fabric; the vault bosses in these stairs have the initials FD.

46
See also Marchini, "Palazzo Ducale," pp. 71–72.

47
Two of these three are still blind; the one opening into the chancellery was originally blind according to Baldi, *Descrittione,* p. 554.

48
See also Rotondi, 1969, pp. 68–69, for similar conclusions about the two facades facing the piazza.

49
For this interpretation see my "Society, Beauty, and the Humanist Architect in Alberti's *De re aedificatoria*," *Studies in the Renaissance,* 16 (1969): 61–79, and my *In This Most Perfect Paradise: Alberti, Nicholas V, and the Invention of Conscious Urban Planning in Rome, 1447–55* (University Park and London, 1974), chap. 3. The latter work hereafter cited as *Paradise*.

50
For an analysis of this aspect of quattrocento palace architecture see my "Alberti and the Vatican Palace Type," *Journal of the Society of Architectural Historians,* 33 (1974): 101–121.

51
Francesco di Giorgio, *Trattati,* 2: 351–352.

52
Baldi, *Descrittione,* p. 573 for the table of contents.

53
Baldi, ibid., includes the facade as something unfinished, p. 546, and as part of the ornament, pp. 550 ff.

54
Vespasiano, p. 404; Vespasiano, translation, p. 108.

55
Compare similar, brief remarks in Ludwig H. Heydenreich, "Federigo da Montefeltro as a Building Patron," in *Studies in Renaissance and Baroque Art Presented to Anthony Blunt on his Sixtieth Birthday* (London, 1967), pp. 1–6, p. 4 (hereafter cited as *Studies*), and Marchini, "Palazzo Ducale," p. 49. Marchini, idem, 44ff., and idem, "Aggiunte," passim, suggests that the present cortile replaced an earlier one, or an earlier, partially completed project for one, a view questioned by Saalman, Rotondi review, pp. 46–51.

56
Manetti, *Vita Nicolai V,* in Magnuson, *Studies,* 9: app. 351–362, ss. 54–55.

57
Muzio, p. 390, states that the inscription was installed by Guidobaldo II. The same inscription appears in the church of San Bernardino which serves as Federigo's mausoleum.

58
Baldi, *Descrittione,* p. 527.

59
This was suggested by Heydenreich, *Studies,* p. 3. Pius's own description of his stairs is particularly dry; see *Memoirs of a Renaissance Pope: The Commentaries of Pius II,* trans. Florence Gragg, ed. Leona Gabel (New York, 1962), pp. 283–284.

60

See *Paradise,* chapter 5.

61

This wall is incorrectly represented in the reconstruction in Rotondi, 1969, Fig. 13.

62

Identifications in ibid., p. 21.

63

The external masonry indicates that these windows were never open. The clerestory windows on the cortile side were blocked by the later superelevation.

64

Federigo, of course, never had a duchess; Battista died two years before he became duke.

65

Francesco di Giorgio, *Trattati,* 2: 352.

66

Baldi, *Descrittione,* pp. 544–545, apparently incorrectly, attributes the walkway to Bartolomeo Genga working for Duke Francesco Maria I della Rovere.

67

Baldi, ibid., pp. 522–523, claimed that the Mercatale stabilized the palace's foundations, which seems unlikely.

68

Mentioned ibid., p. 537. Baldi states that ball playing is an "essercitio lodatissimo fra tutti gli altri."

69

Heydenreich, *Studies,* pp. 4, n. 19, and p. 5. He cites II, xvii, lines 8–9 and 20–24. See also line 12 for a ball court (*sphaeristerium*) and a tower (*turris*), both located away from the hideaway. The description is available in Pliny, *Letters and Panegyricus,* ed. and trans. Betty Radice, Loeb Classical Library, 2 vols. (Cambridge, Mass., and London, 1969), letter addressed to Clusinius (?) Gallus.

70

Contrast Marchini, "Palazzo Ducale," p. 69.

71

Baldi, *Descrittione,* p. 540, mentions the crenellations. Crenellations are conspicuous in the view in the frontispiece in Baldi, *Encomio,* and in the view in the background of the portrait of Federigo in Muzio, frontispiece. One merlin is still visible, and appears in the far right side of Fig. 60 in Rotondi, 1969. Restoration underway in 1974 revealed the original tile roofs above the vaults of room 123 and above the access area leading from that room to the studiolo (room 126), as mentioned earlier by Marchini, "Aggiunte," 80. It also revealed an intact corner merlin above the northwest corner of the studiolo projecting above the level of those roofs, and the fragment of another at the same level above the wall between rooms 122 and 123. The indentation of the crenellation line at that corner indicated that these merlins would have made the northern tower extremely prominent.

72

Compare Baldi, *Descrittione,* pp. 539–542, and p. 557, who discusses them separately. Marchini, "Palazzo Ducale," pp. 48ff., 67ff., proposes that the bases of the towers are perhaps originally part of the city walls built beyond the limits of the first campaign or even in the trecento by Albernoz, and later reached by the second campaign's enlargement of the palace when they were incorporated into its fabric.

73

See Rotondi, *Palazzo Ducale,* 1: 296 ff.

74

Baldi, *Descrittione,* pp. 546–547, lists the southern and western elements as parts of the intended but uncompleted project, but states clearly that he saw no model for the courtyard.

75

Santi, 12, lix: 14–20, 46–49, for its function; Baldi, *Descrittione,* pp. 546–547, for the form of a model he reports having seen in a "guardaroba." Foundations for the mausoleum exist.

76

Carlo Pedretti, "The Original Project for S. Maria della Grazie," *Journal of the Society of Architectural Historians,* 32 (1973): 30–42, passim.

77

Manetti, *Vita Nicolai V,* in Magnuson, *Studies,* 9: s. 119. This element has been analyzed in *Paradise,* chapter 6.

78

Francesco di Giorgio, *Trattati,* 1, plate 163, from Codice Torinese Saluzziano 148, fol. 88^r.

79

Earl Rosenthal, "The Antecedents of Bramante's Tempietto," *Journal of the Society of Architectural Historians,* 23 (1964): 55–74, 65, n. 45.

80

Francesco di Giorgio, *Trattati,* 1, plates 151 ff., from Codice Torinese Saluzziano 148, fols. 82^r ff.

81

See Chastel, *Art et Humanisme,* p. 367.

82

Vespasiano, 384; Vespasiano, translation, 101.

83

Antonio di Francesco (Feltresco) Merchatello, quoted in Schmarsow, *Melozzo de Forlì,* p. 355.

84

The *alcova* was reassembled from pieces found in the cellars in 1912; hence, its quattrocento location is unknown. F. Mazzini, *Guida di Urbino* (Vicenza, 1962), p. 124.

85

Vespasiano, p. 401; Vespasiano, translation, p. 106. Muzio, pp. 356–357, attributes this form of administration to Battista's influence, but he does not suggest that Federigo objected. Muzio's attribution is unique and seems fanciful, however; it appears in the glowing but brief tribute he devotes to her.

86

An amusing analogue occurred in Ferrara in 1444. When Leonello d'Este and Maria of Aragon were married, there were elaborate festivities. At one point, a "collection of wild animals was released in the garden at Belfiore, and as the newlyweds watched from a balcony, hunters killed them all." Gundersheimer, *Ferrara,* p. 121.

87

In the patent dated 1468 to Laurana, given most recently in a transcription in Heydenreich, *Studies,* p. 3, n. 8, and in English in D. S. Chambers, *Patrons and Artists in the Italian Renaissance* (Columbia, S.C., 1971), pp. 165–166.

88

Saalman, Rotondi review, p. 51, promises a study of the Badia in Fiesole, which may suggest a revision of this judgment.

89

For the studiolo, see for example the small study at the papal palace in Avignon, decorated with birds and hunting scenes. A studiolo decorated with mythological scenes was

45
Chivalric
Declaration: The
Palazzo Ducale
in Urbino as a
Political
Statement

in place at Belfiore at Ferrara by 1449; Rotondi, *Palazzo Ducale*, I: 335; Kenneth Clark, *Piero della Francesca* (London, 1951), p. 15.

90
Discussed in *Paradise*, chap. 7, which also discusses points raised below.

91
The role of the Vatican palace in the use and development of the paradise program must remain speculative until more is known about secular construction by princes, although on the basis of present evidence, it seems to have been decisive because of the clarity with which the motifs of paradise were rendered in architectural form, and because of the position occupied by the popes in the hierarchy. The wholesale destruction and alteration of many palaces, *castelli,* and *luoghi di delizie* may render it impossible to recover an exact understanding of the role of the Vatican palace. For examples from after Nicholas's death (1455), when the incomplete palace was forced to exert its influence primarily through descriptions of its builder's intentions, see the many such places described in Filarete's treatise, and the descriptions of the products of d'Este patronage in Gundersheimer, *Ferrara,* pp. 249–265. I have not been able to consult the descriptions in *Art and Life at the Court of Ercole I d'Este: The 'De triumphis religionis' of Giovanni Sabadino degli Arienti,* ed. W. L. Gundersheimer (Geneva, 1972).

92
Antonio Averlino, called Filarete, *Trattato di Architettura,* ed. Anna Maria Finoli and Liliana Grassi, 2 vols. (Milan, 1972), book 20 (Bib. Naz., Florence, Codex Magliabechianus II, IV, 140, fols. 168^{r-v}): 622–623; compare Filarete, *Treatise on Architecture,* trans. John Spencer, with facsimile of codex *idem,* 2 vols. (New Haven and London, 1965), 1: 288. See also Baldi, *Descrittione,* pp. 510–512.

93
Paltroni, p. 40.

94
Vespasiano, 382–383; compare Vespasiano, translation, 100–101.

95
Santi, 12, lix: 4–5.

96
Ibid., pp. 29–30; see also pp. 39–44.

97
Ibid., lx: 32.

98
Baldi, 3: 55ff., and 3: 239 ff., respectively. See also Baldi, *Encomio,* pp. 75 ff.

99
For the first reason, see A. D. Fraser Jenkins, "Cosimo de'Medici's Patronage of Architecture and the Theory of Magnificence," *Journal of the Warburg and Courtauld Institutes,* 33 (1970): 162–170, passim; for the second reason see *Paradise,* Epilogue.

100
Quoted in Heydenreich, *Studies,* and Chambers, *Patrons and Artists.*

101
See Mario Salmi, *Piero della Francesca ed il Palazzo Ducale di Urbino* (Florence, 1945).

102
Baldi, 3: 55–56. See also Baldi, *Descrittione,* pp. 517, 548–550, and Girolamo Mancini, *Vita di Leon Battista Alberti* 2d ed. (Florence, 1911), pp. 479 ff.

103
See for example the paraphrase of Alberti's discussion (*De re aedificatoria,* preface) of the relative merits of the architect and the captain that Santi gives with attribution to "the moderns" in his report on the discussion of art held between Ercole d'Este and Federigo, Santi, 23, xcvi: 101–103. Many other points in Santi's long discussion of this topic depend upon Alberti. Saalman, Rotondi review, is the latest to suggest links between Federigo and Alberti in the palace's design.

104
For details, see Marchini, "Aggiunte," pp. 63 ff.

105
Rotondi, *Palazzo Ducale,* 1: 54ff., discusses Federigo's role, claiming that he must be dismissed from consideration as its designer because the palace was built in two phases, and he could only have tolerated one design, the single one he could have conceived. This overlooks the distinction between substance and attributes in designs, and ignores the possibility that as his "rank and fame" changed, so too would his palace design, no matter who its architect was. Rotondi's analysis is flawed throughout by his tendency to believe that an independent and Scottian aesthetic impuse moved the designers in Urbino.

106
See the important connection drawn between Alberti's distinction of what here has been called the substance and the attributes (or *pulchritudo* and *ornamentum*) and distinctions in Cicero's *De officiis,* in John Onians, "Alberti and Filarete," *Journal of the Warburg and Courtauld Institutes,* 34 (1971): 96–114, especially 96–104.

107
Vespasiano, pp. 403–404; Vespasiano, translation, pp. 107–108.

108
Vespasiano, p. 409; Veaspasiano, translation, p. 111.

109
These criteria for a dynastic mythology are taken, along with the term, from Gundersheimer, *Ferrara,* pp. 279–280, where they are contrasted with the republican mythology, discussed ibid., pp. 278–279.

3
The Palace as a Fortress: Rome and Bologna under Pope Julius II

Stanislaus von Moos

This paper is on political symbolism in Renaissance architecture—or more precisely, it discusses some ways political ideas and political interests may have influenced or even determined the choice of architectural forms at a certain moment in time. This is not, of course, a problem that is of interest from the point of view of a history of style, nor even, from the point of view of iconography in the traditional sense. A quote from Heinrich Wölfflin's *Renaissance and Baroque* that deals precisely with the period under question may illustrate the dilemma. In fact Wölfflin's description of the Roman cinquecento palace-type is, for good reasons, still widely accepted as the trademark of High Renaissance architecture in Rome:

The width of the facade is, in relation to its height, in most cases very considerable. One wants the splendid, comfortable extension. Even where the palace extends to unusual width . . . , the volume forms a unified mass; neither projecting lateral wings, as in the Cancelleria, nor central portions articulate the surface.[1]

However, [Wölfflin then adds,], there is a significant number of palaces that have these vertical articulations. There are projections at the corners of the Palazzo Sora-Fieschi, slightly reminiscent of Bramante's project for St. Peter's with its towers. Bramante himself wanted to equip the Palazzo S. Biagio with projecting corner portions and a central tower. The baroque seems to have tolerated this motif for rhythmical reasons, although it quite naturally reduces the sense of unity of the block.[2]

And he gives two examples: Michelangelo's Palazzo del Senatore on the Capitol and Martino Lunghi's Palazzo Borghese.

How can the seemingly eccentric formal particularities of this "significant number of palaces" be explained? Wölfflin doesn't suggest an explanation; he just notes the fact. The problem cannot be resolved in terms of stylistic interpretation and on the grounds of any supposedly intrinsic "Wesen" of the period's style. But a quite straightforward explanation applies as soon as the function and meaning of the buildings in question are considered in their political and institutional context.

At least two of the previously mentioned palaces are of the highest public prestige. The patron as well as the purpose of the Palazzo S. Biagio are extraordinary: Bramante's Palazzo S. Biagio is, in fact, Julius II's most important building project outside the Vatican. It is the new Palace of Justice, symbol of the pope's authority over law and order in the public sphere (Figs. 2–5). As to the Capitol in general and the Senator's Palace in particular, it was, since the Middle Ages, the most important architectural visualization of both the Commune's and the papacy's political power. Its amplification in the sixteenth century represents the only secular counterpart to the new Borgo and St. Peter's (Figs. 1; 15–19; 33–35).[3]

Both these buildings have strongly projecting corner portions (*torri*) as well as *campanili* (central towers). Furthermore, they have both been focal points of important urban renewal campaigns, a fact that underlines their public function as highly visible images of power. So their stylistic eccentricities seem to be charged with a message, though not primarily an aesthetic one.

Julius II, Bramante, and the Building of a Palace of Justice in Rome: Context and Background

When, in 1503, Giuliano della Rovere was elected to the papacy as Julius II, he faced a difficult moment in the history of Rome. The sources speak of foreign troops and frequent riots that endangered the security of the streets; the papal finances, the public administration and jurisdiction seem to have been in a dramatic state of corruption and inefficiency; the supply of water and grain was precarious.[4] There was no autonomous communal administration able to provide order and reasonable living conditions for all. Noble families lived secluded in their fortified palaces and towers; the Vatican itself was an efficiently isolated fortress, sitting firmly on the city's strategic northern flank.

The economic crisis, the decadence of the nobility, and, at the same time, the increasing economic and political power of the papacy provided the circumstances for a papal dictatorship—a dictatorship that aimed far beyond the ideals and dreams of imperial glory of Pope Nicolaus V or, in Milan, Duke Francesco Sforza a half a century earlier. The political goal was the creation of a national Italian empire, equal in political and military power to the great kingdoms of France and Spain. The Roman Empire served as a model. Around 1506 the Pope circulated a medal with the inscription: "IVLIV(S) CAESAR PONT II" (Julius Caesar Pope II).[5]

The building program that was intended to visualize this new papal policy had two focal points in Rome (Fig. 2): first, the rebuilding of St. Peter's and a gigantic amplification of the papal residence, the Cortile del Belvedere; and second, urban renewal of the city itself. Unlike the ambitious program of the rebuilding of the Vatican, which aimed at a "renovatio" of the splendors of antiquity, the urbanistic plans of Julius II served more practical goals. A few decades earlier Sixtus IV had started to redevelop the area immediately across the river from the Castel S. Angelo as a new business district, cutting the Via dei Coronari and the "trident" of streets radiating from the Ponte S. Angelo into the popular and mostly poor and socially unstable neighborhood.[6] But the traffic situation, among other things, had remained precarious; a system of streets that would create easy access to the Vatican for large

numbers of pilgrims as well as for the merchandise unloaded at the Porto della Ripa was urgently needed.

As soon as the economic situation was stable enough, probably in 1507,[7] the plan was put to work to establish direct connections between the densely populated parts of the town—Trastevere, Porto di Ripa, Ghetto, Campo di Fiori—and the Borgo Vaticano. Two long streets were laid out: the Via della Lungara on the right, the Via Giulia—one kilometer long, cut into the compact cluster of the medieval center—on the left bank of the Tiber. This whole urbanistic reorganization was to be accentuated by a number of new buildings and dramatized by large squares. The most spectacular among these piazzas was to be opened on the Via Giulia. Vasari recalls around 1550 the pope's plan to establish a large administrative center at the Via Giulia: "The Pope decided to locate at the Via Giulia, which had been laid out by Bramante, all buildings and offices of Rome in one place, for this would have been convenient for the merchants in their business transactions, which up to then had been extremely inconvenient."[8] Not too far from the point where, according to a rather utopian idea by Bramante, the Via Giulia was to be connected with the Borgo by a bridge (which was never actually built)[9], a palace was to be erected for the most important secular institution of the papacy: courts of law. This palace—the Palazzo S. Biagio—was to be equipped with four massive corner towers and a central tower in the middle of its main facade overlooking the Via Giulia. Moreover, a large piazza, measuring about fifty by one hundred meters, was to be opened between this main facade and the older Palazzo Sforza Cesarini.[10] The idea was, in fact, to create a monumental civic center, a "Forum Julium" in the midst of the city's commercial district. This urban renewal campaign foreshadowed not only enterprises like the Piazza Farnese but—and this fact is of particular importance—the creation of the Piazza del Campidoglio on the Capitol some decades later.

Although neither palace nor piazza were completed, the Palazzo dei Tribunali was praised by the chroniclers of the early cinquecento as the largest and most significant papal building campaign outside the walls of the Vatican. Egidio da Viterbo, a contemporary of Bramante and Julius II, mentions two buildings of the pope that "cum Romanorum splendore contendant": the Belvedere and the Palace of Justice.[11] Another contemporary author, Francesco Albertini, not only gives a precise idea of the outstanding features of the project but also anticipates its completion when he writes in 1510: "The new Palace of Julius with its church of S. Blasius . . . has towers and extremely safe quarters

1
Rome, Senator's Palace on the Capitol
on an Italian postal stamp, 1935.
(From Saxl, ''The Capitol during the
Renaissance,'' in *Lectures,* vol. 1)

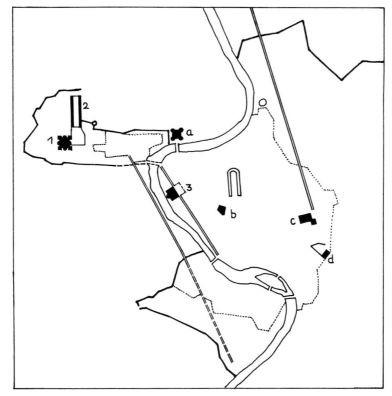

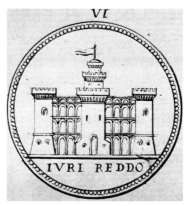

2
Rome, building campaigns under
Julius II (1–3) and older monuments of
state authority (a–d). 1: Bramante's
project for the rebuilding of St. Pe-
ter's; 2: Belvedere; 3: Palazzo dei
Tribunali with Piazza (unexecuted); a:
Castel Sant'Angelo; b: Cancelleria; c.
Palazzo Venezia; d. Senator's Palace
on the Capitol. (Drawing by Martin
Steinmann)
3
Medal, commemorating the founda-
tion of the Palazzo dei Tribunali in
Rome. (From Bonanni, *Numismata*)

4
Rome, Via Guilia, detail of the
Palazzo dei Tribunali and its rusti-
cated base. (Photo: author)

5
Antonio di Pellegrino, plan of the
Palazzo dei Tribunali in Rome, after
Bramante's project, Piano Nobile.
(UA 136)

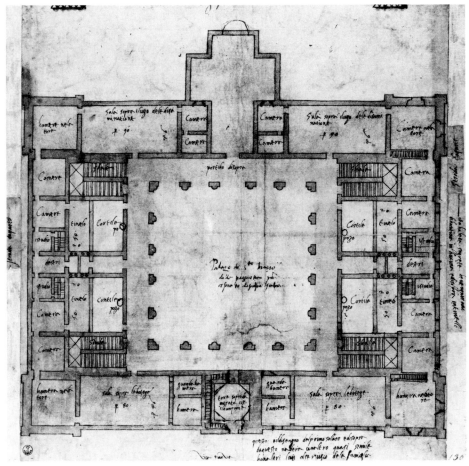

for public commodity and utility; such is the famous work built on new foundations by your Holyness, together with the wide and straight Via Nova."[12] Today, however, only a few remains of the building's base with its projecting corner portions and its massive rustication are to be seen in the Via Giulia, between the Carceri Nuovi and the Palazzo Sacchetti (Fig. 4). The size of the planned building can at least be identified: the main facade, seventy-eight meters long, exceeds the main facade of the Cancelleria by six meters.[13] In fact, the area of the palace was large enough to allow a great number of smaller palazzi and no less than three churches to be installed on its foundations (Fig. 6).

The Struggle for a New Legal Order

The reform of jurisdiction was one of the most urgent political goals of Julius II. At the time of his ascendancy to the throne roughly six different jurisdictions were operating in Rome,[14] partly controlled by the commune, partly by the church. The attempt of Sixtus IV to reorganize jurisdiction (1473) had been a failure. Julius made a new and even more vigorous attempt to centralize the powers. In 1505 he established the *baroncello*, a sort of commander-in-chief of the police corps who was, wherever he appeared, accompanied by a mounted escort.

At about the same time the pope must have felt the need to relocate the judiciary administration of the church. Its offices and halls were then partly accommodated in several buildings of the Vatican Palace, between the Atrium of old St. Peter's and the Sala Regia (especially the fifteenth century "Palatium Innocentianum"), and partly dispersed among the residences of the prelates in Rome, including the Palazzo Sforza Cesarini.[15] Around 1506, when the rebuilding of St. Peter's started, these Vatican accommodations were about to be demolished: the building of a new seat of law outside the Vatican was an immediate practical necessity. In August 1508, a building on the site of the future Palace of Justice was demolished; soon thereafter the foundations were built according to Bramante's project.

As Frommel has shown in his monumental work on Roman palace architecture, the new Palazzo dei Tribunali was to become the seat of the following organs of the papal curia: the "Penitenziaria," the "Dateria," the "Sacra Romana Rota," the "Segnatura di Grazia e Giustizia" and the "Camera Apostolica."[16] Besides the "Camera Apostolica," none of these institutions were tribunals in the narrow sense of the term; but the Camera alone controlled three tribunals, among which the tribunal of the Governatore di Roma was politically the most important. The intention was to increase the control of this tribunal over public life in the urbs, and this meant of

course a serious threat to the competences of the older tribunal of the Roman commune, which was controlled by the Senator. The seat of communal justice had been the Senator's Palace; but given the bad state of the building on the Capitol, law was spoken in the cloisters of Aracoeli or even in the church S. Maria in Aracoeli itself, despite repeated prohibitions by the popes.

In recent decades, the authority of the Capitoline Curia had been restricted by the papacy: in 1473 Sixtus IV had declared that only those Romans who had no connection whatsoever with the Vatican could be judged by the Capitoline court. The building of a new Palazzo dei Tribunali can thus be understood as a further step in the process of centralization of jurisdiction undertaken by Julius II. The idea seems to have been not only to accommodate the papal institutions and to increase the competences of the Governatore di Roma but to bring the Curia Capitolina as well under the roof of the new palace and thus under the papacy's direct control.[17]

This attempt to establish a new and centralized judiciary authority in Rome is the premise and the background for the building of the Palazzo dei Tribunali, and the difficulties in realizing this attempt are drastically mirrored in the collapse of the building campaign on the Via Giulia. By 1511, the Pope's financial and political position had been weakened by unfortunate military campaigns and, among other things, the loss of Bologna as the church's northern outpost. He was now inclined to grant concessions to the commune and its claims of judiciary sovereignty. Thus, in a bill of April 15, 1512, he once again denounces the pitiful state of law and order in Rome: "It seems as if there is not one jurisdiction, but a multitude of laws and courts, a fact which results in numerous murders and crimes."[18] In the same bill, however, he reinstates the Capitoline Curia as the supreme court for all matters concerning citizens of Rome born in the urbs, with the sole exception of wholesale merchants, diplomats, members of the papal curia and cardinals. At this moment, the building of the Palazzo dei Tribunali had already come to a stop, and the Romans may have interpreted this as a confirmation of their privileges.

A few decades later, around 1588, Sixtus V toyed with the idea of completing Julius's project, but nothing happened and so the site was gradually occupied by the patchwork of buildings which we see today (Figs. 4, 6).[19]

The "Military Look" of the Palazzo dei Tribunali

The only detailed information about Bramante's project is given by a carefully drawn plan of the piano nobile by Antonio di Pellegrino (Fig. 5).[20] It shows a slightly elongated, rectangular building with a large central courtyard, four corner towers and, in the middle of the main facade, a "torre sopra la entrata col champanile." On the back side of the complex, toward the Tiber, the choir and the transept of the S. Biagio church project from the rectangular mass.[21]

The plan suggests an articulation of the corner towers through pilasters, a solution reminiscent of the somewhat later Palazzo Sora Fieschi. A papal medal, however, whose inscription (IVRI REDD)[22] establishes its connection with the Palace of Justice, shows a more severe elevation: massive towers on strongly scarped bases, with heavy battlements on the top; and on the ground floor botteghe (Fig. 3). Abstract and schematic as this representation is, it seems to relate to an early project for the Palazzo dei Tribunali by Bramante. This early project has later been modified, as Pellegrino's drawing shows. The massive towers were to receive a colossal order of pilasters, the strength of the base was to be accentuated by a massive rustication rather than by a strongly scarped outline, and the wide, arcaded windows in the upper floors, suggested by the medal, were to become smaller and more numerous. But despite these (and other) modifications, the essential character of the early project remained the basis of the design: the regularity of its plan and the castle-like articulation of its elevation and silhouette.

The program has obvious antecedents: the idea of a complex amalgamation of offices, dwellings, ceremonial courtyard, and church is prefigured in the large cardinal's residences of the quattrocento, such as the Palazzo Venezia (Fig. 17) and, especially, the Cancelleria. But here, the functional complexity of a cardinal's residence has received a rigidly regular shape, recalling Bramante's original plan for St. Peter's if not the plans of imperial baths.[23] The corner towers too have Roman antecedents: they were outstanding features of Roman Quattrocento palaces such as the Palazzo Venezia or—to remain in the immediate neighborhood of the Palazzo dei Tribunali—the Palazzo Sforza Cesarini.[24] While the torri of these quattrocento palaces usually emerge from the top of the facades, without influencing the articulation of the building's faces, Bramante has emphasized them through strong, projecting vertical articulations. In doing this, he varied an idea that had been introduced in Rome in the Cancelleria.

But on the whole, the project for the Palazzo dei Tribunali has an archaizing, heraldic quality that, curiously, seems more reminiscent of Lombard architecture than of anything Roman.[25] This is perhaps no mere coincidence, given the fact that Bramante had spent some twenty years of his career as an architect in Lombardy. In fact, the planning of the palace occurred at a moment when, especially through the increasing contacts with France, images

of fortified castles began to exert a certain influence on Italian palace architecture, especially in the North. Leonardo was fascinated with the idea of towered palaces. His frequent use of octagonal or cylindrical corner towers in a number of palace-projects between 1506 and 1516 suggests that he was familiar with French castles such as Le Verger and Gaillon (Fig. 10).[26] Furthermore, his sympathy with the imagery of French châteaux seems to indicate a political as well as an esthetic preference—an homage, as it were, to French rule in Lombardy. However, I don't think that the Tribunali concept has much to do with Leonardo and with France. Its roots go deeper. The articulation of the towers seems to owe something to Filarete's idealized rendering of Milan's Ospedale Maggiore in his Trattato, if not to the towers of Jersalem on Giovanni da Montorfano's crucifixion fresco in the refectory of S. Maria delle Grazie in Milan (Figs. 7, 9).[27]

The most obviously Lombard feature of Bramante's Tribunali project is the central tower dominating the main facade of the palazzo. Milan seems, once again, to be a likely point of reference. It is in the famous Castello Sforzesco that the idea of a central tower, protecting and dramatizing the main entrance of a large, symmetrical building, had received its most impressive architectural image (Figs. 11, 12). It had been an idea of Francesco Sforza and his architects. The older Castello Visconteo, carefully reconstructed by Francesco Sforza after its practically total demolition during the short intermezzo of the Ambrosian Republic, had no such tower.[28] But once realized in Milan around 1460, this monumental torre dell'orologio (clock tower) rapidly became a symbol of ducal rule throughout Northern Italy. The towers of the Sforza residence in Cusago and of the Castello Sforzesco in Vigevano are direct copies of their Milanese antecedent; the entrance tower in front of Alberto Pio's palace at Carpi demonstrates that this feature was rapidly accepted as a symbol and a tool of ducal sovereignty, even outside the domain of the Sforza.[29] But the idea of the Milanese entrance tower reaches further back: since the beginning of the fifteenth century, Venice used to build clock towers on the strategic points of the cities of the terraferma which had fallen under its domination. One may think of Padua—whose orologio of 1428 was restored in the sixteenth century and incorporated in the western front of the Piazza de Signori (Fig. 14)—, of Udine or of Brescia. The torre dell'orologio in Venice itself, built in 1496–99 as an entrance gate from the Piazza S. Marco to the city's commercial district and particularly the Merceria dell'orologio, illustrates again the principle and the ceremonial function of this important instrument of rule (Fig. 13).[30] So there are numerous North Italian buildings from which Bramante could take off. But there were Roman examples as

6
Rome, buildings between the Vicolo
del Gonfalone, Via Giulia and Vicolo
del Cefalo (partly built on the foundations of the Palazzo dei Tribunali).
Plan from the nineteenth century.
(Pius VII's land-registry office)
7
Antonio Averlino Filarete, view of
the Hospital at Sforzinda. (*Trattato,*
Book XI)

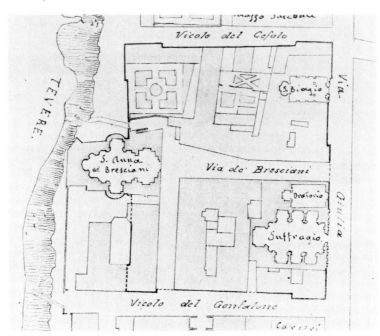

8
Caradosso, medal, with view of
Bramante's first project for the rebuild-
ing of St. Peter's (1506).

9
Giovanni da Montorfano, crucifixion,
fresco in the refectory of S. Maria
delle Grazie, ca. 1495. (Photo:
Alinari)

10
Leonardo da Vinci, sketches for a
palace for Lorenzo di Piero de'
Medici, to be built opposite the existing Palazzo Medici in Florence. Plan,
top, and view of the main facade,
center. (Codex Atlanticus)

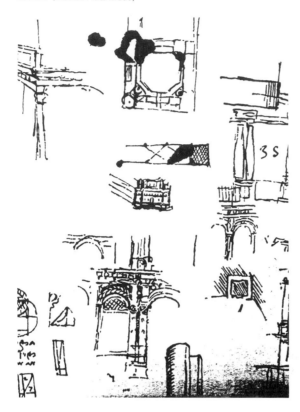

11
Milan, plan of Castello Sforzesco after
its rebuilding under Francesco Sforza.
(From Beltrami, *Il castello di Milano*)

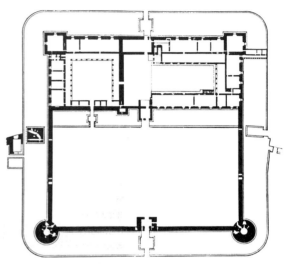

12
Milan, Castello Sforzesco, facade toward the city with the so-called *torre
del Filarete.* (From Beltrami, *Il castello
di Milano*)

13
Venice, view of Piazza S. Marco and
the *torre dell' orologio,* separating the
Piazza from the *mercerie nuove.* Detail of Jacopo de Barbari's plan (1500)

14
Padua, *torre dell'orologio.* (Photo:
Alinari)

well for the combination of a ceremonial gate with clock and bell tower crowning the facade of a palace. The gateway to the Vatican Palaces, realized under Innocent VIII, illustrates the principle, though still—like the earlier cardinal's residences, but unlike the Lombard examples—with no concern for symmetrical integration of the tower into the palace facade.[31]

A simple enumeration of formal and stylistic precedents does not explain the choice of the architectural type. The question is not only What are the formal antecedents? but Why were they chosen as points of reference for this important project? The purpose of the building, as outlined, proves to be extremely helpful in the determination of the meaning of its formal typology. It allows us to go further than Bruschi, who laconically states that the secluded character of this towered complex is due to the ideology of a socially and culturally isolated elite,[32] and even further than Tafuri, who emphasizes the political overtones of the project's allusions to the older towered palace complexes of the Roman nobility and the cardinals.[33]

The Capitol in Rome and the Architectural Imagery of Papal Law

One of the most controversial aspects of the new Palace of Justice must have been its pretension to replace the traditional seat of the Curia Capitolina, the Senator's Palace on the Capitol. For it is probable, as we have seen, that the pope intended not only to relocate the judiciary institutions of the papacy in the new palace but to bring the judiciary organs of the Commune under the same roof and thus under the papacy's control. Nothing was more obvious than to illustrate and comment on this procedure through the choice of architectural forms.

For decades, if not centuries, the Palazzo del Senatore had been closely linked with the idea and the propaganda of the papacy's secular power. In the first decade of the sixteenth century, when the building of the Palazzo dei Tribunali was begun, the Senator's palace on the Capitoline Hill appeared more or less in the shape that Marten van Heemskerck has documented in a famous drawing executed somewhat later, in 1536.[34] Two strong towers flanked the facade, while a crenellated campanile dominated the whole complex. With the exception of the loggia, which is a copy of the benediction loggia in the Vatican and which was built later, under Leo X, we have here the shape Pope Nicholas V had given to the palace in the 1450s (Fig. 19). Given the historical significance of this building, it is not unlikely that its architectural form should have played some role in the conception of the Tribunali.

The complex building history of the Palazzo del Senatore does not need to be exposed here.[35] But it is interesting to note that already the first palace, built on top of the Tabularium around the middle of the twelfth century, after the *renovatio Senatus* (1144), had two towers, flanking a central hall. This was not changed by Pope Boniface VIII, who remodeled and fortified the palace around 1300. The golden seal of Ludwig of Bavaria, who was crowned as emperor on the Capitol in 1328, shows this facade in heraldic reduction (Fig. 15). And so does the map of Rome by Taddeo di Bartolo in the Palazzo Pubblico in Siena (Fig. 16) (1414) and the similar map in the *Très Riches Heures du Duc de Berry.*

In the first half of the fifteenth century the Capitol, "tantis olim aedificiis exornatus" (at one time so richly decorated with buildings, Flavio Biondo), was a deserted area, if not a rubbish heap,[36] with the exception of the church of S. Maria in Aracoeli and the architectural collage of the Senator's palace itself. It was Eugene IV, and especially Nicholas V, who reestablished its ancient splendor and dignity. Nicholas V built the first Palazzo dei Conservatori and gave the Senator's palace its modern shape: four wings, a courtyard in the middle, and four towers at the corners (Fig. 19).

This amplification of the Senator's palace was one of the most important among Nicholas's campaigns toward the architectural renewal of Rome. Here the pope was able to realize the kind of fortified palace he seems to have had in mind when he was starting to modernize the Vatican Palace itself—a project that was only partly executed and whose intention appears today only in the north wing of the Palazzo Vaticano, which overlooks the Cortile del Belvedere (Fig. 20).[37] The analogy between the Vatican and the Senator's Palace underlines the significance of the latter: it had to visualize the papal authority over the civic and legal institutions of the urbs. There was no place in Rome more appropriate for such a demonstration. The Capitol was the physical as well as the symbolic center of the city, as it appears in Taddeo di Bartolo's plan;[38] its buildings reflect, throughout the Middle Ages, the complex interdependence of communal autonomy and papal authority, each relying on the other's complicity in their struggle against the overpowering presence of the local nobility.[39] Thus arose the complex political meaning of the Capitol as the traditional seat of the civic institutions of the *populus romanus* and, at the same time, the theater for a splendid demonstration of the secular authority of the church. The complex architectural typology of the Senator's palace owes in fact as much to the tradition of medieval communal palaces as it does to the fortified castles of the North Italian dukes, the Neapolitan kings and the pope himself.

Among the institutions traditionally housed in the Senator's palace, jurisdiction was one of the most important. "From the tenth century onwards, state criminals had been executed by throwing them down from the tarpeian rock."[40] Early in the fourteenth century the palace was equipped with an open staircase, seventeen meters long, from which sentences were pronounced and executions performed; the antique spolia lions, adjacent to the staircase, symbolized strength and tradition of the law. A drawing by Heemskerck shows that as late as 1536, a column of justice was standing not far from the stairs.[41] Another, anonymous drawing in Brunswick from around 1553 conveys the character and function of this place even more directly: A gallows projects from the tower to the left, with a victim of justice hanging in the air as a grim memento of the severity of papal law.[42]

Papal Colonialism and Its Architecture under Julius II and Before: Bologna

A brief examination of the situation in Bologna in the first decade of the cinquecento may throw some additional light on the function and meaning of the fortified palace-type under Julius II. For the Tribunali palace was not Julius's first architectural campaign toward the reinforcement of law and order in the papal empire. In the early sixteenth century Bologna was the largest and most important city of the papal state, second only to Rome. The city stood in the foreground of Julius's political and military attempts to strengthen the authority of the papacy in the territories of the church. Julius had been Bishop of Bologna from 1483 to 1502, which must have contributed to his interest in the city. Thus the newly elected pope was eager to break the Bolognese tyranny of Giovanni Bentivoglio and to reestablish church control over this most important northern outpost of the papal state.

He succeeded in the fall of 1506. After a cumbersome campaign the pope entered the city, triumphantly received by its inhabitants (as the official chroniclers report), Giovanni Bentivoglio having fled shortly before.[43] Now the reform of the political and legal institutions was tackled: The previous Council of the Sixteen was replaced by the Council of the Forty and given equal rank with the Papal Legate. Reestablishment of the privileges that had been granted to the Bolognese by Nicholas V was the declared intention of the new papal jurisdiction and tax policy.[44]

A series of medals commemorate the papal takeover. One of these medals shows the elevation of a fortress with corner towers and a campanile or *mastio* in the middle, with strong, rusticated scarps; in the foreground, justitia stands next to a seated blacksmith (Fig. 21).[45] What does the building stand

for? Is it an abstract architectural symbol of the *justitia papalis*? Or does it represent the fortress Julius II built next to the Porta Galliera on the city's northern flank (Fig. 22), and at whose foundation on February 20, 1507, he personally assisted?[46]

One doesn't know precisely what this fortress looked like; soon after the departure of the pope from Bologna it was taken over by the populace, and as soon as Giovanni Bentivoglio's heirs returned to the city in 1511 they wisely ordered its demolition.[47] Today, only a few fragments of a tower and a part of the adjacent wall of the city are to be seen. As a result of this state of affairs, scholarly interest in this building has been less than scarce. However, the importance of the Fortezza di Porta Galliera in the history of the papal empire under Julius II is indicated by its early date and its extraordinary size. In its bulk the fortress is one of the largest enterprises of this sort undertaken by Julius, comparable only with the building of the Rocca at Civitavecchia (Fig. 23), whose foundation stone was laid by the pope almost two years after the foundation of the Bolognese *arx*, on December 14, 1508.[48]

Four fortresses had been built before on the same location, next to the Porta di Galliera. The first around 1330 (destroyed after 1334); the second in 1404 (destroyed 1411); the third in 1414 (destroyed 1416) and the fourth in 1435 (destroyed 1441). The foundations of Julius's arx coincide to a large degree with those of the first Rocca built by Cardinal Bertrando del Poggetto around 1330,[49] with the exception of the so-called Cittadella built—after 1508—to the left of the Rocca, along the city's wall (Figs. 12a, 12b). Guidicini recalls that the new fortress was "the largest and the strongest among all the preceding ones," having walls measuring twelve *braccia* (yards) in thickness and eight strong towers. Furthermore, he emphasizes the fact that the southern flank of the arx, its facade (which must have measured around 200 meters) toward the city had received a special treatment: The walls were scarped and the ditch was filled with water.[50] Novacula, a contemporary chronicler, gives more details. In the center of the facade toward the city there was, he says, a tower with the pope's arms; a similar entrance tower was located on the northern flank, toward the countryside, again with the arms of the pope and those of the cardinal of Pavia.[51] One may assume that the new Rocca was equipped with cylindrical corner towers and, on both its southern and northern flanks, with entrance towers, whose form was perhaps not unlike that of the so-called Torre del Filarete in Milan's Castello Sforzesco.[52] If that assumption is correct, the foundation medal of the Bolognese fortress does indeed correspond with the actual situation, and the central tower of the Palazzo dei Tribunali has found its most plausible model.

15
Golden seal of Ludwig of Bavaria,
with symbolic representation of
Rome. First half of the fourteenth
century.

16
Taddeo di Bartolo, plan of Rome,
fresco in the Palazzo Pubblico, Siena.
(Photo: Gabinetto Fotografico
Nazionale)

17
Etienne Dupérac, plan of Rome. De-
tail: the Capitol with the Senator's
Palace, *left,* and Palazzo Venezia,
right. (Photo: Biblioteca Hertziana,
Rome)

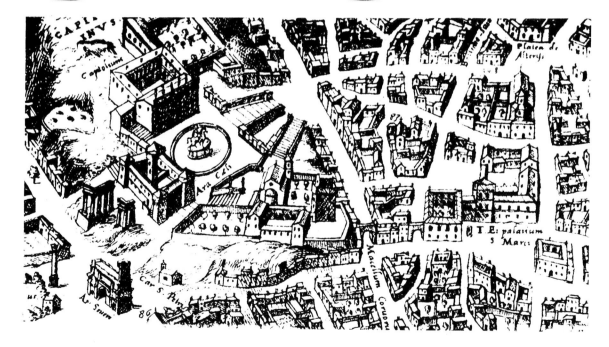

18
Anonymous artist of the sixteenth century, view of the Senator's Palace on the Capitol, ca. 1554–1560. (Louvre)

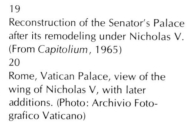

19
Reconstruction of the Senator's Palace
after its remodeling under Nicholas V.
(From *Capitolium*, 1965)
20
Rome, Vatican Palace, view of the
wing of Nicholas V, with later
additions. (Photo: Archivio Fotografico Vaticano)

21
Medal, commemorating the rebuild-
ing of the Fortezza di Porta Galliera in
Bologna[?], 1507. (From Bonanni,
Numismata)

22

(a) Bologna. plan of Fortezza di Porta Galliera, as built around 1330. (After Marinelli, "La fortezza alla Porta di Galliera," in *Il Comune di Bologna;* drawing by Martin Steinmann); (b) Bologna, plan of Fortezza di Galliera, as rebuilt under Julius II, 1507. *Left,* the new "Cittadella" (built after 1508). The arrow indicates the location of remaining portions of the fortress. (After Marinelli, "La fortezza," in *Il Comune di Bologna;* drawing by Martin Steinmann)

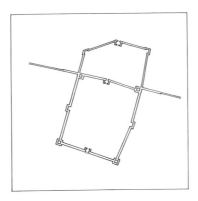

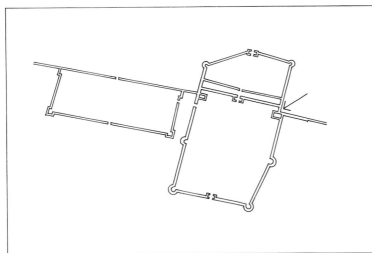

23
Ignazio Danti[?], aerial view of Civitavecchia and its fortifications. *Bottom right,* Julius II's maritime fortress. Detail of a fresco in the Galleria delle Carte Geografiche, Vatican. (Photo: Gabinetto Fotografico Nazionale)

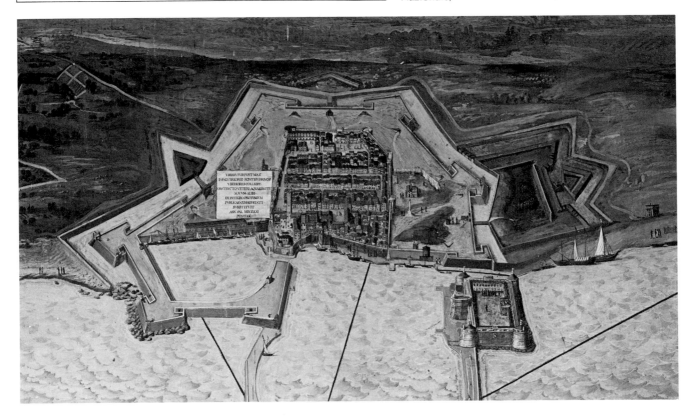

Be that as it may, the kind of entrance tower suggested by the medal was certainly not unknown in Bologna in the early sixteenth century. As a collection of architectural *vedute* from the second half of the cinquecento can show, the Villa Hercolani, just outside Bologna, built around 1490 by Giovanni II Bentivoglio, was originally equipped with a similar tower, overlooking the surrounding gardens and *fattorie* (Fig. 24).[53] Here too, as in the sphere of the *Sforza* dynasty, these towers, usually equipped with *orologi* seem to have been accepted icons of feudal sovereignty.

Bramante must have been aware of all this. He had accompanied Julius II on his trip to Bologna and was busy there with the design of "molte cose ingegnose e di grandissima importanza" (many ingenious and extremely important things), as Vasari recalls.[54] One would expect him to be involved in the building of the new Fortezza di Porta Galliera, but no evidence of such an involvement seems to have survived.[55] However, with or without Bramante's direct assistance, Julius has used Bologna as the theater for a first, grand display of buildings guaranteeing and symbolizing the strength of the new papal empire. As can be seen from Guidicini's description, the rebuilding of the arx was more than just a matter of military security; it served to visualize, through its imposing southern flank, a political claim which was to be reaffirmed almost two years later in the new Rocca at Civitavecchia and the Palazzo dei Tribunali in Rome.

Thus, once again Bologna had become, if only for a short period, the main outpost of the papal empire. It had played this role before. And it preserved—and still preserves—in its center the monuments of earlier attempts of the church to establish a permanent rule in this part of Italy. In fact, Julius's rebuilding of the arx is nothing but the continuation of a military and political strategy of the church that reaches back at least into the fourteenth century. It is interesting to note that around 1327, when Cardinal Bertrando del Poggetto decided to build the first fortress at the Porta di Galliera, he spread rumors that the pope had chosen Bologna instead of Rome as his permanent residence after his eventual return from Avignon.[56] However, a few decades later the Holy See was still in Avignon, and new attempts were made to reestablish the political and military sovereignty of the church in Italy. The man who realized the program was Cardinal d'Albornoz. He, too, attributed a crucial role to Bologna in his campaign, which finally managed to subject Italy to the pope's military, political, and judiciary control.[57] However, unlike Julius II, he felt safe enough in Bologna to renounce, after his takeover in 1360, the building of

a fortified palace or a fortress guaranteeing the security of the newly established rule. This was done only a few years later.

A military treatise by Giovanni da Legnano, *De bello,* sent by its author to the cardinal while he was still residing in Bologna, indicates the ideological climate that colored the cardinal's campaign. This treatise not only glorifies the church as the reincarnation of the Roman imperial idea, it also justifies the building of fortresses in the name of the *virtus romana:* for it is more courageous, the author insists, to wait for an assault than to assault. Furthermore, Giovanni da Legnano praises Bologna as the political and religious center of Christianity, as it had been renewed by the Cardinal.[58] It is no coincidence that Cardinal d'Albornoz was rediscovered in the sixteenth century as a champion of the church's claims to be the trustee of the imperial idea, a claim that had more recently played such a crucial role in Julius II's political ideology. In fact, Genesio di Sepulveda, Albornoz's sixteenth-century biographer, doesn't hesitate to compare his hero with Trajan, Hadrian, and Theodosius.[59]

Albornoz, who built many fortresses throughout Italy (Spoleto, Narni, Assisi, and others)[60] seems not to have felt the need to fortify the seat of the papal administration in Bologna. But this situation changed under Androino di Grimoard, the brother of Pope Urban V, who became cardinal legate in 1364 after Albornoz had left the city for other diplomatic and military campaigns. Under the new legate, the palaces on the west side of the Piazza Maggiore, where the papal administration was accommodated,—the Palazzo d'Accursio and the houses of the Tebaldi, the Uberti, and the Caccianemici—were united in a large, fortified palace complex, later called Palazzo Pubblico or Palazzo Apostolico, today known as Palazzo Communale (Fig. 25).[61] It was the paradigm of a *palazzo fortificato* until late in the nineteenth century, when a part of the scarped base of the Palazzo's main facade was removed in order to expose the original Dugento arcade in the ground floor of the Palazzo d'Accursio (Fig. 26). When, in 1506, Julius arrived in Bologna, it was in this papal stronghold that he took residence. One of his first measures seems to have been the isolation of the palace from its immediate surroundings through the demolition of a number of adjacent houses and especially of thirty–three botteghe that had been leaning against the palace's flanks; furthermore, he modernized its defenses through the placement of twenty–four *bombardiere*.[62] It is for this palace that Bramante designed a new *scalone cordonato* and various decorative improvements.[63]

At the time of Julius, the Palazzo Apostolico must have had almost the status of a second Vatican, and in the following decades it received all possible insignia necessary to qualify it as the main branch of

24
Ignazio Danti[?], view of Villa Hercolani in Bologna. (From Fanti, *Ville,
castelli e chiese bolognesi*)

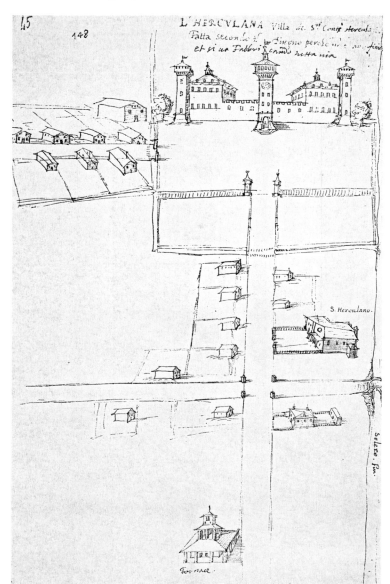

25
Bologna, the center with S. Petronio
and the Palazzo Comunale. Detail
from Filippo de Gnudi's plan (1702).
(Fotofast, Bologna)

26
Bologna, Palazzo Comunale. *Left,*
Palazzo d'Accursio, as reconstructed
with its original arcade (nineteenth
century). *Right,* Palazzo del Podestà.
(Photo: Alinari)

the Holy See, including a Swiss guard. All improvements and modifications of the Palace's exterior undertaken by Julius's legate, the cardinal of Pavia, and his successor, Francesco Alidosi, maintained the fortresslike severity of its appearance. Among other measures, the northeastern and the northwestern corner towers were modernized around 1509, and so was the western flank, today overlooking the Piazza Roosevelt.[64] But it was only in 1565 that the facade in front of the Palazzo di Re Enzo received its present form (Fig. 28), at the same time as the *fontana vecchia* was added in the center of the palace's northern flank. And finally, in 1580, the main facade toward the Piazza Maggiore was amplified by the grandiose entrance dominated by the statue of Gregory XIII.[65] Such was the facade of the Palazzo Apostolico, which served as a background for the city's ceremonial events and popular entertainments until the eighteenth century, as numerous representations among the *Insignia* show (Figs. 27, 28). All this is not of direct relevance here. What counts is the fact that the papal takeover of Bologna in 1506–1507 brought a spectacular renewal of older architectural instruments and images of military rule; these images, blended into the perhaps abstract and ideal representation of the *arx* on the Bolognese medal, remained a point of reference for a significant number of papal campaigns tackled in the following years. The Forum Iulium to be built together with the new Palace of Justice was in many ways an attempt at creating in Rome a civic center à la Bologna's Piazza Maggiore.

A Note on Serlio

The Bolognese Piazza Maggiore and its buildings may in short be regarded as not the least important among the antecedents of Bramante's project. The new Palazzo dei Tribunali seems to combine the features of the Palazzo Pubblico opposite S. Petronio with those of the adjacent Palazzo Apostolico. And throughout the sixteenth century, the typology underlying the Palazzo dei Tribunali seems to have been considered an appropriate way to visualize the state's institutions guaranteeing law and order. Serlio is aware of it. In his Book VI he gives two versions of an ideal Palace of Justice. The first version, a "Palazzo del pretore, cioè del podestà," has arcades on its main facade, a ceremonial staircase in the courtyard and a high torre, "sopra la quale vi sarà la campana della giustizia" (on top of which there will be the bell of justice), (Fig. 29).[66] The second version gives, in addition to these typical features of medieval *palazzi pubblici,* four corner towers. These are motivated by the specific character of the political authority to be represented in this palace: It is not the local podestà but the governor of an alien power

who lives here. In Serlio's words: "After the Palace of the Podestà I still have to mention the Palace of the governor, or lieutenant, called captain in some places, president in others. These apply justice more rigorously than the Podestà, especially so in those parts where I have been born. . . ." The severity of this justice is visualized through the towers, which are supposed to protect the governor from the *strani scherzi* of the people.[67]

In fact, Serlio could hardly have been more explicit about the background of these architectural concepts. He was born in Bologna; his Palazzo del Podestà is a modernized and regularized version of the homonymous building opposite S. Petronio (Figs. 26, 27). That, in turn, the governor of an alien power needs a strongly fortified residence was documented, more than anywhere else, in the adjacent Palazzo Apostolico; and Serlio's long list of dignitaries who are likely to require such a palace (governatore, luogotenente, capitano, presidente) is a polite and diplomatic way of circumscribing the oppressive presence of the Cardinal Legato in his own home town.

The Renovation of the Senator's Palace in Rome, Sixteenth Century

If we summarize the outstanding features of Serlio's two schemes—campanile, arcades, corner towers, and open staircase, descending in two symmetrically arranged and broken wings from the piano nobile—we are reminded once more of the Senator's Palace in Rome, where Michelangelo was about to complete a similar staircase while Serlio was compiling his sixth book. In fact, after the breakdown of Julius's project of a civic center on the Via Giulia nothing had happened for a few years, until the Farnese begun building their nearby Palace and Piazza—in many ways a private nouveau riche version of the much larger but never built Palazzo S. Biagio. Finally Pope Paul III had decided to concentrate his efforts on the Capitol again, the traditional theater of papal authority, that Julius had boldly intended to substitute by his new and controversial "Forum" downtown. The different stages of the renewal, which ultimately led to the present shape of the Senator's Palace, need not be repeated here.[68] It is enough to remember that the facade was completed only between 1593 and 1612 (by Giacomo della Porta and, after his death in 1602, Girolamo Rainaldi), while Michelangelo's staircase, begun in the forties and then interrupted for many years, was finished in the early fifties. Neither Michelangelo nor any other architect working on the Senator's palace seems ever to have thought of a removal of the corner towers, despite their antiquarian character with respect to the High Renaissance typology of Roman palace facades of the Farnese type.

27
Bologna, Piazza Maggiore with the facades of S. Petronio, *left,* the Palazzo Comunale, *center,* and the Palazzo del Podestà, *right,* in the seventeenth century. (*Insignia,* vol. IX, c.7)

Bologna, view of Palazzo Comunale,
with its facade in front of the Palazzo
di Re Enzo (built ca. 1565). (*Insignia*,
vol. XIII, c.9)

LEGATIONE FELICISSIME' FUNCTA
EMINENTISS. ET REVERENDISS.
D. GEORGIJS CARD. SPINOLA.
È BONONIA DISCEDIT.

29
Sebastiano Serlio, elevations of the
Palazzo del Podestà (Book VI).
(Staatsbibliothek, Munich)

36
Rome, Collegio della Sapienza; street
facade. (From Letarouilly)

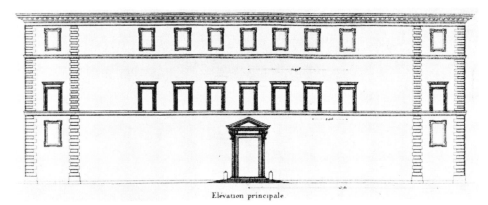

Élévation principale

37
Granada, Spain, main facade of the
Chancillieria (completed 1587). (From
Kubler, *Art and Architecture in Spain*)

Postscript

Perhaps the present discussion allows some cautious generalizations concerning the intercourse between politics and architecture in the Renaissance. Or rather, between politics and architectural form, for it should be clear that architectural forms play only a secondary part within the complex economic, social, and political role of building in society. (A straight social and political history of architecture will therefore have to look at the building processes themselves, the information they provide on the organization of labor in a society, and the ways by which the ruling powers manipulated the given system of production in order to secure economic and political stability; but that is not at stake here.) [74]

It has been argued that the presence of towers and towerlike articulations in a series of Italian Renaissance palaces has—quite apart from their possible military motivation—something to do with the institutional function of these buildings. As architectural images the *torri* of the Palazzo dei Tribunali represent the idea of papal sovreignty over public life in a similar way as, for example, the three terraces of the Belvedere court represent the idea of an imperial Roman villa like the Domus Aurea. [75] In both the Belvedere court on one side and the Palazzo dei Tribunali on the other, architectural forms provide a cultural reference for the purposes the two buildings are designed to serve, and the difference of the program calls for different cultural references and thus for different forms. In the idealistic terms of an architectural iconology, the difference between the meaning of the two buildings is mainly that one celebrates a humanist, antiquarian ideal, while the other varies a traditional imagery of state representation.

But that is not all; there is a more categorical difference between the two projects, and that difference may have to do with what art in the service of politics is all about. It is also a difference that the established techniques of formal analysis, iconography, or the aseptic dissection of "architectural principles" tend to overlook. For what separates the two campaigns is not only their style and their meaning as such, but the social range of the forms and meanings they incorporate. The Belvedere is humanist, antiquarian, hermetic in its symbolic references—and literally hermetic in its enclosed form and perspective drama that can only be visually experienced appropriately from one point: the pope's Camera della Segnatura. The Palazzo dei Tribunali (and for that matter the Palazzo dei Senatori) in turn is public, simple, and unequivocal in its symbolism. It is not contained in a papal garden, secluded from the city; quite the contrary, it addresses its message to the city, amplified by an urbanistic setting that allows it to dominate large public spaces. And its imagery is conservative and popular—popular in that it displays no (or few) signs of elitist humanist creativity that might blur the political message. In short, what motivates the formal choice in both cases is not only the (supposedly intrinsic) content of the program but pragmatic considerations, such as the wish to address certain target groups within society to whom the idea of the papacy's grandeur and deep-rooted legitimacy has to be marketed.

It should not be overlooked that even the pattern of form-idea relations in architecture is subject to change according to pragmatic considerations that have to do with the choice of a public towards which a demonstration of authority is directed. For example, most discussions of iconology in medieval architecture presuppose a safely established continuity between symbolic contents and building types. [76] Now, whether or not such a continuity ever existed, it is interesting to note that in the period under examination here there are certain architectural tasks that tend to be realized in terms of long-established iconographic rules and others that don't. The Tribunali project and some buildings directly related to it can be understood as examples of a traditional iconography of papal rule; but in the Belvedere the symbolism that charges the building with meaning had to be invented together with the forms—it did not really exist before. Insofar this complex is more typical for the circumstances under which architectural meaning is produced in the Renaissance and ever since: [77] It realizes an open pattern of idea-form relations, flexible and subject to creative improvisation.

Not that, on the other side, towers and other archaizing military paraphernalia in Renaissance palaces always stand for law and order (as they actually do in the Tribunali project). Here too it is just not possible to use architectural forms and types, whenever and wherever they appear, as a sort of a litmus paper for the identification of certain political ideas or ideological conditions. [78] If a synthetic interpretation of the meaning of towers in sixteenth century palaces is possible at all, I suspect that this meaning does not coincide with clearcut political programs and ideas. It has more to do with political pragmatism in view of a stabilization of certain political institutions and with the wish to visualize political ideas and claims—not primarily with these institutions and ideas themselves. Traditional images of military architecture may occur in the sixteenth century whenever there is the need of actual fortification and wherever there is the wish to dramatize the age and tradition of an institution whose origins lie in the Middle Ages. Among these pragmatic aspects there is also the question of the public toward which a demonstration of political power and legitimation is directed.

So it is rhetoric more than iconography that tends to charge art in the service of politics with meaning, especially when the political interests involved are those of a head of state trying to build up an empire. It is interesting, in this context, that the first pope who envisaged an urban renewal of Rome was also singularly aware of the possibilities of architecture as a mass medium in the service of the church and its ideology. Nicholas V, whose renewal of the Capitol (see Figs. 18 and 19) was the point of reference for Julius's project of a civic center, summarized his intentions when he declared on his deathbed that the beliefs of the illiterate, of "people ignorant of letters and wholly untouched by them" would "gradually collapse in the course of time . . . unless they are moved by certain extraordinary sights. But when that vulgar belief founded on doctrines of learned men is continually confirmed and daily corroborated by great buildings . . . it is forever conveyed to those both present and future, who behold these admirable constructions."[79] In his buildings (see Figs. 19, 20) the pope made it clear that what strengthens the belief of the illiterate is an architecture that operates with traditional, familiar, well-known concepts—such as the fortified palace of the ruler.

Notes

This article is a revised and substantially enlarged version of a chapter in my book *Turm und Bollwerk. Beiträge zu einer politischen Ikonographie der italienischen Renaissancearchitektur* (Zurich, 1974). I would like to thank Prof. Henry A. Millon for having given me an opportunity to rediscuss and clarify some problems I have dealt with in a more summary fashion in the book.

I owe special gratitude to James S. Ackerman and Naomi Miller, whose criticism of the first draft of this paper was invaluable. Furthermore, I have had the advice of many friends in my attempts to elucidate the situation in Bologna under Julius II and before: Richard J. Tuttle, Franco Bergonzoni, Lorenzo Bianconi, Oscar Mischiati, and Giancarlo Roversi have been most helpful. Gail Geiger has generously shared my pains in translating this piece into English.

1
Heinrich Wölfflin, *Renaissance und Barock. Eine Untersuchung über Wesen und Entstehung des Barockstils in Italien,* ed. Hans Rose (Munich, 1926), p. 128; the translation is mine.

2
Ibid., pp. 128 ff.

3
See Fritz Saxl, "The Capitol during the Renaissance. A Symbol of the Imperial Idea," in *Lectures,* vol. I, (London, 1971), pp. 200–214; especially p. 208.

4
See Ludwig von Pastor, *Geschichte der Päpste,* 25 vols., Freiburg i. Br., 1891–1933, vol. 3, pp. 4–8.

5
G. F. Hill, *A Corpus of Italian Renaissance Medals* (London, 1931), Nr. 874, pl. 139.

6
On Sixtus IV and his campaigns see G. Simoncini, *Città e società nel rinascimento* (Turin, 1974), vol. II, pp. 228–233. On the premises for Julius's endeavors, such as the catastrophe of 1450 when hundreds of pilgraims were squashed on the Ponte Sant'Angelo by the masses arriving from the city, see E. Rodocanachi, *Histoire de Rome de 1354 à 1471* (Paris, 1922), pp. 465 ff.

7
Arnaldo Bruschi, *Bramante architetto* (Bari, 1969), pp. 625–647. On urban planning in Rome under Julius II and his successors see Christoph Luitpold Frommel, *Der römische Palastbau der Hochrenaissance,* Tübingen, 1973, vol. I, pp. 11–24, and Arnaldo Bruschi, *Bramante* (Bari, 1973), pp. 197–217, especially pp. 210 ff.

8
"Si risolvé il Papa di mettere in strada Giulia, da Bramante indirizzata, tutti gli edifici e le ragioni di Roma in un luogo, per la comodità ch'ai negoziatori avria recato nelle faccende, essendo continuamente fino allora stato molto scomode." Vasari, *Le vite de' più excellenti pittori, scultori ed architetti,* ed. Milanesi (Florence, 1878–1885), vol. IV, p. 159. The sources and the recent literature concerning the Palazzo dei Tribunali are listed in Luigi Salerno, Luigi Spezzaferro and Manfredo Tafuri, *Via Giulia. Una utopia urbanistica del '500* (Rome, 1973), pp. 314–322, and in Frommel, *Der römische Palastbau,* vol. I, p. 96; vol. II, pp. 327–335.

9
See Frommel, *Der römische Palastbau,* vol. I, p. 16.

10
The main source for the projected piazza is a sketch—possibly by Bramante himself—on the back of the well-known plan of the Palazzo dei Tribunali, UA, 136. See Frommel, (who has discovered and identified this sketch), *Der römische Palastbau,* vol. II, p. 330; vol. III, pl. 146b.

11
Quoted in Bruschi, *Bramante architetto,* p. 946.

12
"Palatium novum Julianum, cum ecclesia S. Blasii de panetta ibidem inclusa, habet turres et loca fortissima pro comodite et utilitate publica quod quidem praeclarum opus a fundamentis ipsis tua Sanctitas extruvit cum ampla et recta, via nova." *Francisci Albertini Opusculum de Mirabilibus Novae Urbis Romae,* (1510), ed. August Schmarsow (Heilbronn, 1886), p. 22; see also p. 11.

13
See Frommel, *Der römische Palastbau,* vol. I, p. 96.

14
E. Rodocanachi, *Rome au temps de Jules II* (Paris, 1912), pp. 269 ff.

15
See Frommel, *Der römische Palastbau,* vol. II, p. 331.

16
Ibid.; See, for a more detailed discussion of papal jurisdiction under Julius II, N. Del Re, *La curia romana* (Rome, 1952), pp. 205–275.

17
Frommel, *Der römische Palastbau,* vol. II, p. 332.

18
Bullarium, vol. V, p. 533; see Pastor, *Geschichte der Päpste,* vol. III, 2, pp. 697.

19
I owe this information on Sixtus V to René Schiffmann. He also was kind enough to indicate the respective sources:

Cod. Urb. Lat. 1055, fol. 260 r; id., 1056, fol. 278 r, where the "Tribunali" project is referred to as "Zecca" (mint); id., 1057, fol. 412 r (all in the Vatican library).

20
The plan is in the Uffizi collection, UA, 136. The attribution to Antonio di Pellegrino is Frommel's; see Der römische Palastbau, vol. II, pp. 329ff. For Bramante's sketch on the back of this plan see note 10. Cf. also Peruzzi's plan of a part of the building, UA, 109v.

21
The church was built, but not entirely according to Bramante's ideas.

22
IVRI REDD = juri reddendo; See Domenico Gnoli, "Il Palazzo di Giustizia di Bramante," in Nuova Antologia, (April 16, 1914), pp. 3–15; especially p. 7, n. 2.

23
I would like to mention at least randomly another possible source for Bramante's design of the Palazzo dei Tribunali: Giulio da Sangallo's project of a palace for Ferdinand of Aragon in Naples (1488; the plan is in the Vatican, Cod. Barb. Lat. 4424, fol. 41v.). G. L. Hersey has recently interpreted the plan—which was never executed—as a project for a palace of justice; see Alfonso II and the Artistic Renewal of Naples, 1485–1495 (New Haven and London, 1969), pp. 79ff. If this interpretation is correct, then this plan throws additional light onto the prehistory of Bramante's project.

Bramante's combination of a complex amalgam of residential and ceremonial functions and a rigidly geometric shape had a rapid success throughout Italy. It reappears in Antonio da Sangallo's partly executed project for the apostolic palace in Loreto (Bruschi interprets Sangallo's drawing as the copy of a drawing by Bramante himself; see Bramante architetto, pp. 652–667; here p. 652). Here the towers actually receive military significance under the impact of the threatening Turkish invasions, while the modest church of S. Biagio has been replaced here by the large "Santuario" of Loreto. Palladio brought the scheme to Northern Italy; cf. his Palazzo Thiene in Vicenza (Renato Cevese, I palazzi dei Thiene [Vicenza, 1952], pp. 47, 77). And Serlio introduced it to France, with his château in Ancy-le-Franc. (See Marco Rosci, Il trattato di architettura di Sebastiano Serlio [Milan, 1966], vol. II, p. 68). But further aspects of the Tribunali type's influence abroad will have to be discussed later.

24
In my book Turm und Bollwerk, pp. 74–78, I give a brief survey of the Roman quattrocento palaces of the cardinals and the nobility, especially from the point of view of their frequent use of towers—an aspect that connects them with the Vatican Palace itself, whose main facade was, at the time of Nicholas V, and even earlier, dominated by towers. For more details see the fundamental studies by Piero Tomei, L'architettura a Roma nel quattrocento (Rome, 1942) and Torgil Magnuson, Studies in Roman Quattrocento Architecture (Stockholm, 1958). While Magnuson emphasizes the political significance of these towers, for example, the towers of the Palazzo Venezia—I am trying to show that they often had a military function as well. Much of what I try to summarize in my book has now been studied in great detail by Carroll William Westfall, "Alberti and the Vatican Palace Type," in Journal of the Society of Architectural Historians (May, 1974), pp. 101–121.

25
As has already been noted by D. Gnoli, "Il Palazzo di Giustizia."

26
See in particular the sketches on Ms.K., vol. III, fol. 116v, and Windsor, 12591r (around 1506), and the project for a new Medici palace in Florence, opposite the old one by Michelozzo, on Cod. Atl., fol. 315r–b and fol. 315r–a (around 1515–1516). In my book, I give more details concerning these sketches, on the basis of Carlo Pedretti, A Chronology of Leonardo da Vinci's Architectural Studies after 1500 (Geneva, 1962) and id., Leonardo da Vinci. The Royal Palace at Romorantin (Cambridge, Mass, 1972).

27
Geymüller had suggested that this architectural fantasy has something to do with Bramante's original project for St. Peter's; See S. von Moos, Die Kastelltyp-Variationen des Filarete (Zurich, 1971), pp. 35 ff.

28
The reconstruction of the Castello di Porta Giovia was started in 1450; the present entrance tower is a partly conjectural reconstruction by Luca Beltrami (1893). See Luca Beltrami, Il castello di Milano sotto il dominio dei Visconti e dei Sforza, 1368–1535 (Milan, 1894).

29
On the torre of the Sforza castle at Vigevano cf. F. Malaguzzi Valeri, La corte di Ludovico il Moro (Milan, 1913–1923), vol. I, pp. 659 ff., and Vittorio Ramella, "Il Castello Sforzesco di Vigevano," in Castellum, 7 (1968): 69–74. On Carpi see H. Semper, F. O. Schulze, W. Barth, Carpi, ein Fürstensitz der Renaissance, Dresden, 1882 (where, however, the torre is wrongly interpreted as a baroque addition to the palace).

30
See Turm und Bollwerk, pp. 61–63.

31
Bramante's solution of the entrance tower as a part of a palace complex had again far-reaching consequences in Italian architecture of the cinquecento; see for example Vignola's project for the Farnese palace at Piacenza, in Maria Walcher Casotti, Il Vignola (Trieste, 1960), vol. II, fig. 156.

32
Bruschi, Bramante architetto, p. 645; see also id., Bramante, pp. 215 ff., for a more subtle interpretation of the project's "immagine turriforme."

33
See Manfredo Tafuri in Via Giulia, p. 319. Frommel, in turn, seems to have emphasized (in his contribution to the Bramante congress of 1970) the project's dependence upon the typology of medieval palazzi comunali and brolleti; but in his more recent book he doesn't follow up this line of thought and discusses the project more in the stylistic context of its closely Roman antecedents such as the Cancelleria. See Der römische Palastbau, vol. I, pp. 93, 96; vol. II, pp. 327–335. The "Atti" of the Bramante congress of 1970 were not available at the time this paper was written; see Werner Oechslin, "Congresso Internazionale di Studi Bramanteschi. Zum Bramantekongress in Mailand, Urbino und Rom," in Bibliothèque d'Humanisme et de Renaissance, 33 (1971): 191.

34
See C. Hülsen and H. Egger, Die römischen Skizzenbücher von Marten Heemskerck, 1913, fol. 32r; 92r.

35
Jürgen Paul gives a detailed account of the dates in Die mittelalterlichen Kommunalpaläste in Italien (Freiburg i.

Br., 1963), pp. 253–260, with rich bibliography. There are however some more recent contributions, especially by Carlo Pietrangeli: "I palazzi capitolini nel medioevo" and "I palazzi capitolini nel rinascimento," in the special issue of the review *Capitolium: Il Campidoglio* (Rome, 1965), pp. 21–28; see also id., "I palazzi capitolini prima di Michelangelo," in *Il Campidoglio di Michelangelo* (various authors) (Milan, 1965), pp. 1–20. Herbert Siebenhüner's monograph, although superceded in some minor details, is still fundamental: *Das Kapitol in Rom. Idee und Gestalt*, Munich, 1959, especially pp. 24–36. See also Fritz Saxl, "The Capitol during the Renaissance."

36
Flavio Biondo, *Roma Instaurata* (1443), chap. 2, ed. Valentini-Zucchetti, IV, p. 275. See Poggio Bracciolini: "Stercorum ac purgamentorum receptacutrium," in *De Varietate Fortunae*, quoted in E. Rodocanachi, *Le Capitole Romain antique et moderne* (Paris, 1904), p. 30.

37
The regular "castle type" that played such an important role in Nicholas's architectural ideas owes something to the traditional typology of the Roman cardinals' residences, but it may have been inspired by the ducal palaces of Northern Italy as well (Pavia, Milan, Mantua, Ferrara, and others); palaces that are the background for Alberti's definition of the tyrant's castle in his treatise *De re aedificatoria*, a copy of which was dedicated to Nicholas V. Concerning the significance of Nicholas's project for the renewal of the Vatican see C. W. Westfall, "Alberti and the Vatican Palace Type," and especially Westfall's recent monograph, *In This Most Perfect Paradise. Alberti, Nicholas V, and the Invention of Conscious Urban Planning in Rome, 1447–55* (University Park and London, 1974).

38
Quite naturally, Alberti used the Capitol as the center of his topographical survey of ancient Rome, which he compiled around 1450 in his *Descriptio urbis Romae*; see Luigi Vagnetti, "La 'Descriptio urbis Romae'," in *Quaderno dell' Università degli Studi di Genova*, 1, (1968): 25–80.

39
See Gaetanina Scano, "Storia e istituzioni capitoline dal medioevo all'età moderna," in *Il Campidoglio*, pp. 13–20.

40
Siebenhüner, *Das Kapitol*, pp. 22 ff.

41
Hülsen/Egger, *Die römischen Skizzenbücher*, fol. 16r.

42
All that does not prove however that the Senator's Palace was Bramante's actual model for the Tribunali: it seems doubtful for example whether it is necessary to trace back the botteghe of the Tribunali project to the arcades of the Roman Tabularium (underneath the Senator's Palace, overlooking the Forum); a much more likely antecedent is the Palazzo del Podestà in Bologna (as I try to show below), but there were arcades in many buildings in the commercial district of Rome. Concerning the role of the staircase in medieval Palazzi Comunali see J. Paul, *Die mittelalterlichen Kommunalpaläste*, passim. It is interesting to note that Filarete has chosen for the *prigione* a building with four corner towers; see Antonio Averlino Filarete, *Treatise on Architecture. Being the Treatise by Antonio di Piero Averlino, Known as Filarete*, ed. Spencer (New Haven and London, 1965), vol. II, fol. 70v ff.

43
Von Pastor, *Geschichte der Päpste*, vol. III, 2, pp. 734 ff. He died 1508 in Milan.

44
Paris De Grassis, *Le due spedizioni militari di Giulio II*, (ed. Luigi Frati) (Bologna, 1886), pp. 140 ff.

45
See Filippo Bonanni, *Numismata pontificum romanorum*, Rome, 1706, pl. next to p. 138; comments p. 159; G. F. Hill, *A Corpus of Italian Renaissance Medals*, nr. 227; Roberto Weiss, "The Medals of Pope Julius II (1503–1513)," in *Journal of the Warburg and Courtauld Institutes* (1965), pp. 163–182; pl. 32.

46
Both G. F. Hill and R. Weiss connect the medal with the Roman Palazzo dei Tribunali. Weiss adds that the inscription "ARCIS FVNDATOR" on the back of the medal is taken over from another medal commemorating the foundation of the Rocca at Civitavecchia (1508). See R. Weiss, "The Medals," pp. 177 ff. Frommel reiterates this information; *Der römische Palastbau*, vol. II, p. 329. All these scholars seem to have overlooked Bonanni's information, according to which this medal was coined in the context of the Bolognese arx; See *Numismata*, p. 159.

47
See Niccolò Macchiavelli, *Discorsi sopra la prima deca di Tito Livio* (Milan, 1960), vol. II, 24; Domenico Zanelli, *I papi a Bologna* (Rome, 1857), p. 32; von Pastor, *Geschichte der Päpste*, vol. III, 2, p. 743.

48
On Civitavecchia see Bruschi, *Bramante*, pp. 204ff. See also, in this context, Bramante's plans for the remodeling of the papal Rocca at Viterbo, around 1506; A. Bruschi, "Un intervento di Bramante nella rocca di Viterbo," in *L'Arte* (1971), pp. 75–109.

49
See Lodovico Marinelli, "La fortezza alla Porta di Galliera," in *Il Comune di Bologna* (January 1926). I am told by Mr. Franco Bergonzoni, the chief architect of the Comune di Bologna, that new attempts to reconstruct the size and form of Julius's arx are underway. This is all the more welcome since Marinelli's reconstruction is to a large degree purely conjectural.

50
Giuseppe Guidicini, *Cose notabili della città di Bologna*, 3 vols., (Bologna, 1869/1870); vol. III, p. 274. See also ibid., vol. II, p. 159, and Ghirardacci, *Historia di Bologna* (*Rer. ital. script.*, vol. 33), who claims that the fortress was "meravigliosa e tale, da essere reputata una delle prime d'Italia" (p. 363).

51
Andrea Bernardi (Novacula), *Cronache dei monumenti istorici pertinenti alle provincie della Romagna*, 3 vols., Bologna, 1895 ff., vol. II, pp. 206 ff.

52
Marinelli however suggests only small half-cylindrical "rivellini" in front of both the southern and the northern entrances; cf. "La fortezza,", pp. 15 ff. But his plan clearly suggests the presence of a tower similar to that of the Castello Sforzesco in Milan.

53
Mario Fanti, *Ville, castelli e chiese bolognesi da un libro di disegni del cinquecento* (Bologna, 1967), plate 148. As I hear in Bologna, this collection of drawings has recently been attributed to Ignazio Danti. According to Fanti, the villa Hercolani was begun in 1530 (p. 56). However, typology and style of the villa suggest a much earlier date; see Giampiero Cuppini and Anna Maria Matteucci, *Ville del bolognese* (Bologna, 1967), p. 345. Equally strange is the usual dating of the villa Palata Pepoli, which has a

similar entrance tower (1541); cf. Cuppini/Matteucci, ibid., pp. 18 ff. and Fanti, *Ville, castelli e chiese,* plate 39.

54
Vasari, *Le vite,* ed. Milanesi, vol. IV, p. 159. On Bramante's activities in Bologna cf. the few indications in Francesco Malaguzzi Valeri, *L'architettura a Bologna nel rinascimento,* Rocca S. Casciano, 1899. Bramante played an important role in the siege of a fortress called Mirandola and designed the *scalone cordonato* and a few decorative details in the Palazzo Comunale; see pp. 100 ff., 111, 125, 168. Bruschi is even more scarce of information; see *Bramante architetto,* p. XXXVIII.

55
Novacula tells us that Julius has visited the site of the arx "come le multi inzigneri et architaturi," in *Cronache,* vol. II, p. 206. I was unable to find, with the help of Dr. Oscar Mischiati, even a mention of Bramante's name in the documents concerning the Fortezza di Porta Galliera in the Bolognese Archivio di Stato.

56
Guidicini, *Cose notabili,* vol. III, p. 273.

57
On Cardinal d'Albornoz and his role in Bologna—especially as the founder of the Spanish College there—see Francesco Filippini, *Il Cardinale Egidio Albornoz* (Bologna, 1933), especially pp. 244 ff.; Juan Beneyto Perez, *El Cardenal Albornoz, Canciller de Castilla y Caudillo de Italia* (Madrid, 1950); Berthe M. Marti, *The Spanish College at Bologna in the Fourteenth Century* (Philadelphia, 1966); Cecil H. Clough, "Cardinal Gil Albornoz, the Spanish College in Bologna, and the Italian Renaissance," in *Studia Albornotiana,* vol. XII, n.d., pp. 225–238.

58
See Filippini, *Il Cardinale,* pp. 249 ff.

59
Genesio di Sepulveda, *Vita del cardinale d'Albornoz* (Bologna, 1521); see Berthe M. Marti, *The Spanish College,* p. 16.

60
See John White, *Art and Architecture in Italy, 1250–1400,* Harmondsworth, 1966, p. 330; but Albornoz's activity as a building patron would deserve a special study.

61
See Giuseppe Guidicini, *Cose notabili,* vol. III, pp. 345–359; especially p. 350; Hieronymus De Bursellis, *Cronica gestorum ac factorum memorabilium civitatis Bononiae* (*Rer Ital. Script.*), vol. 33, part II, p. 51; F. Malaguzzi Valeri, *L'architettura a Bologna,* passim; Guido Zucchini, *Edifici di Bologna* (Rome, 1931), pp. 112–115; Umberto Beseghi, *Palazzi di Bologna* (Bologna, 1956), pp. 53–70; Jürgen Paul, *Die mittelalterlichen Kommunalpaläste,* p. 130; Giuseppe Rivani, *Le torri di Bologna* (Bologna, 1966), pp. 187–192; Franco Bergonzoni, "Note sul restauro dei prospetti del Palazzo Comunale di Bologna," in *Strenna storica bolognese,* 19, 1969, pp. 9–34.

62
Guidicini, *Cose notabili,* vol. III, pp. 351ff.

63
Especially, next to the scalone, a third loggia towards the courtyard; cf. Guidicini, *Cose notabili,* vol. III, p. 352. Cf. also Malaguzzi Valeri, *L'architettura a Bologna,* p. 100 and passim.

64
For a rather detailed description of the palace's modernization under the Cardinal of Pavia and his successors cf.

Novacula, *Cronache dei monumenti,* pp. 225 ff. See also Bergonzoni, "Note sul restauro." However, these were improvements of an already fortified palace; Malaguzzi Valeri is misleading in stating that it was only in 1509 that the palace was fortified; *L'architettura a Bologna,* p. 100.

65
See Richard J. Tuttle, "Le opere di Galeazzo Alessi nel Palazzo Comunale di Bologna," in *Galeazzo Alessi e l'architettura del cinquecento (Atti del convegno)* (Genova, 1975), pp. 229–237.

66
The sixth book of Serlio's compendium, written between 1540 and 1553 in France, has never been printed. It survives in two manuscripts: one is in the Staatsbibliothek in Munich, the other in the Avery Library of Columbia University in New York. A facsimile edition of the Munich version exists, probably prepared for printing by Serlio: Marco Rosci, *Il trattat o di achitettura di Sebastiano Serlio* (Milan, 1966), vol. I. The text on the Palace of Justice is on fol. 59v. Concerning the importance of the sixth book see also William B. Dinsmoor, "The Literary Remains of Sebastiano Serlio," in *Art Bulletin,* 24 (1942): 130–141 and, more recently, Myra N. Rosenfeld, "Sebastiano Serlio's Late Style in the Avery Library Version of his Sixth Book on Domestic Architecture," in *Journal of the Society of Architectural Historians,* 28 (Oct. 1969): 155–172. Myra N. Rosenfeld is at present preparing a critical edition of the Avery Library manuscript.

As far as Serlio's functional explanation of the campanile is concerned, it is interesting to note that the earlier, Avery version of the sixth book is more precise than the later: "questa torre sarà per la campana della giustizia ed anche per dare allarmi secondo gli bisogni e per gli incendi ancora," see Ms. of the Avery Library, fol. 63 (the transcription into modern Italian is mine). This detail is an interesting anticipation of later developments such as the typology of New England fire houses from the eighteenth century onwards. I would like to take this opportunity to thank Mr. Adolf K. Placek for his kind permission to consult the Avery manuscript.

67
"Dipoi lo palazzo del podestà, è necessario ancora quello del governatore, o luogotenente, altri lo dicono capitano, altri presidente, secondo li luoghi. Questi tali amministrano la giustizia più rigorosamente del podestà, e massimamente nelle contrade, dove io sono nato. . . ." S. Serlio, *Il sesto libro,* (ed. Rosci), fol. 61v.

68
Cf. Siebenhüner, *Das Kapitol,* pp. 107–114 and James S. Ackerman, *The Architecture of Michelangelo* (London, 1961), vol. I, pp. 54–74 and vol. II, pp. 49–66, and Tilmann Buddensieg, "Zum Statuenprogramm im Kapitolsplan Pauls III.," in *Zeitschrift für Kunstgeschichte* (1969), pp. 177–228.

69
Siebenhüner, *Das Kapitol,* pp. 99, 109ff., for the foundation medal of the campanile cf. Bonanni, *Numismata,* plate next to p. 322; comments p. 348.

70
An important basis for the distinction of two different stages in the building of the Villa d'Este is a fresco in the pianterreno of the villa, which shows the facade without the lateral torri. (The fresco is dated around 1568). See David R. Coffin, *The Villa d'Este at Tivoli* (Princeton, N.J., 1960), pp. 11ff.

71
Michelangelo's project is documented in a series of engravings by Dupérac (1568 and 1569); cf. Siebenhüner, *Das Kapitol,* Figs. 47, 48, 70.

72
See Ackerman, *The Architecture of Michelangelo,* pp. 59 ff. Concerning the problems of funding, especially the conflict between Senator and "Conservatori," see also Guglielmo de Angelis d'Ossat, "L'opera michelangiolesca," in *Il Campidoglio di Michelangelo* (Rome, 1965), p. 47.

73
De Angelis d'Ossat, "L'opera michelangiolesca," p. 47.

74
For additional references see *Turm und Bollwerk,* pp. 216–221.

75
See James S. Ackerman, "The Belvedere as a Classical Villa," in *Journal of the Warburg and Courtauld Institutes,* 14 (1951): 70–91.

76
There can be no doubt that the work done in the field of medieval architecture is fundamental for any discussion of architectural symbolism. Some among the classics are Richard Krautheimer, "Introduction to an 'Iconography of Early Medieval Architecture'," in *Journal of the Warburg and Courtauld Institutes* (1942), pp. 1–33; Hans Sedlmayr, *Die Entstehung der Kathedrale* (Zürich, 1950); Günter Bandmann, *Mittelalterliche Architektur als Bedeutungsträger* (Berlin, 1951); Louis Hautecoeur, *Mystique et architecture. Symbolisme du cercle et de la coupole* (Paris, 1954), and E. Baldwin Smith, *Architectural Symbolism of Imperial Rome and the Middle Ages* (Princeton, N.J., 1956).

77
See for example Martin Gosebruch, '"Varietas' bei Leon Battista Alberti und der wissenschaftliche Renaissancebegriff," in *Zeitschrift für Kunstgeschichte* (1957), pp. 229–238. The autonomy of art with respect to its underlying social and cultural forces and their established imageries has been recently discussed by Michael Müller, Horst Bredekamp, Berthold Hinz, Franz-Joachim Verspohl, Jürgen Fredel and Ursula Apitzsch: *Autonomie der Kunst. Zur Genese und Kritik einer bürgerlichen Kategorie* (Frankfurt a. M., 1972). For earlier, still useful discussions of these problems see Arnold Hauser, *The Social History of Art* (New York, n.d.), vol. 2, pp. 52–84; Paolo Rossi, "Arte e scienza," in *Enciclopedia universale dell'arte,* vol. XII, col. 300–309, or Erwin Panofsky, *Idea* (Berlin, 1924), where the autonomy of art is discussed in the context of the philosophical rationalizations of the Renaissance itself.

78
This is where I disagree with Reinhart Bentmann and Michael Müller, who still must be credited for having proposed, at least in Germany, a way of looking politically at Renaissance architecture. In their interesting study *Die Villa als Herrschaftsarchitektur. Versuch einer kunst- und sozial-geschichtlichen Untersuchung* (Frankfurt a. M., 1968), they use an extremely generic concept of "Herrschaftsideologie" that allows them not only to offer an overall explanation for the whole complex phenomenology of Italian villa architecture of the century but also to bring a large number of architectural ideas and realizations from the fifteenth to the twentieth century under a common ideological denominator. In such a philosophical rather than historical perspective, different forms and different historical contexts out of which buildings are generated and the different meanings they have had within this context become practically irrelevant.

79
Giannozzo Manetti, "Vita Nicolai V. Summi pontificis ex manuscripto codice Florentino," in Muratori, *Rer. Ital. Script.,* III, 2 (Milan, 1734), col. 932ff; quoted after William C. Westfall's translation in his monograph, *In This Most Perfect Paradise. Alberti, Nicholas V, and the Invention of Conscious Urban Planning in Rome, 1447–55* (University Park and London, 1974), pp. 33 ff. Unfortunately, Westfall's important monograph became available to me only after the completion of this manuscript.

4
Ingres's *Vow of Louis XIII* and the Politics of the Restoration

Carol Duncan

In November, 1826, Ingres's *Vow of Louis XIII* was installed in the Cathedral of Montauban with great pomp.[1] The event, more a political than a religious affair, was in keeping with the spirit and meaning of the new altarpiece. The elaborate installation ceremonies not only recalled but in many ways recreated the coronation of Charles X at Rheims Cathedral in 1824. The crowning of Charles, the last Bourbon king, was controversial. In the judgment of many of his contemporaries and of most modern historians, this coronation was a farcical attempt to revive the trappings of a pre-Revolutionary France, a France irretrievably lost to the vicissitudes of history. Then, two years later, the king's men staged a reenactment of that event. The *Mass* that Cherubini composed for the ceremony at Rheims was once again performed and Ingres's image of Louis XIII was substituted for the anachronistic figure of his descendant.

The modern literature on the *Vow of Louis XIII* has focused almost exclusively on whether Ingres solved the artistic problems the work posed—how he treated the double subject of the King and the Virgin, how he utilized the art of Raphael, and so forth.[2] And, although modern scholars are aware that the painting pleased official government circles and gave ideological support to the Bourbon dynasty, the painting has nevertheless been discussed as if it were purely a product of Ingres's artistic judgment. The modern reader is left to conclude that men and women of the 1820s experienced it with only such artistic and stylistic questions in mind.

The *Vow of Louis XIII*, however, attests to far more than Ingres's imaginative activity. Indeed, to understand fully even the artistic problems Ingres resolved, it is necessary to consider the work within the broader political and ideological context of the times. In imagery flattering to the Bourbon house, the *Vow of Louis XIII* affirmed a definite ideology and reinforced one of the most contested doctrines of the Right: the alliance between the throne and the altar. Generated in a particularly reactionary moment of a generally reactionary period, the *Vow of Louis XIII* was both a specific response to events of 1820 and a reflection of an outlook that thrived during the Restoration as a whole.

In 1814, after the fall of Napoleon, the Bourbon house returned to a France exhausted by war.[3] Long years of absence combined with the presence of a new generation had both mellowed and dimmed the memory of the Bourbons in the minds of the French. Their return was the work of Tallyrand and the Allies, who were anxious for a peaceful and unified France. To them, the Bourbons were the only house with luster enough to fill the vacuum left by

1

Ingres, *The Vow of Louis XIII,* Cathedral of Montauban, 1824, (Photo: Service de Documentation Photographique de la Réunion des Musées Nationaux)

Napoleon, the only name with sufficient past glory to rally French national pride and identity. The Bourbons were recalled not because the French people wanted to reject the past twenty-five years and return to pre-Revolutionary days, but because no one could think of anyone better to unify the nation.

Of the returning emigrés, few besides Louis XVIII seemed to understand the conditions of their return. Even before he reached Paris, he issued a charter calculated to appease the fears and to win the cooperation of those who had served France during the past quarter century. After a conciliatory preamble, it granted basic civil liberties, established a representative government with two houses, promised taxation with consent and guaranteed existing property rights and new titles. Louis XVIII understood the necessity of compromise.

Surrounding Louis, however, was a crowd of emigrés who regarded constitutional government with horror and fear. Led by the King's younger brother, the arrogant Comte d'Artois—the future Charles X—they were known as the Ultra-Royalist or Clerical Party. These old aristocrats and high church officials had never wavered in their loyalty to the Bourbons, and now they were rewarded with key government posts. The Charter—a document venerated by Liberals—infuriated them, and throughout the Restoration, they dedicated themselves to preventing the fulfillment of its promises. More Royalist than the king, they were aptly described by their contemporaries as having forgotten nothing and learnt nothing during their years of exile. In their eyes, the Restoration was a mandate to return France to the way it had been in 1789. They were especially determined to see all confiscated properties returned to the church and the aristocracy, the revival of all privileges abolished since 1789, and the return of education to the hands of the church. Although denied their full will by Louis XVIII's more realistic policies (between 1816 and 1820, the Ultras were the opposition party), they were an active and influential force, enjoying special relationships to the king. At bottom, Louis XVIII and his supporters shared many of their views, and their Ultra prejudices often set the tone of the official Restoration.

To the Ultras, the past twenty-five years were a scorge, a punishment sent by God to an aristocracy that had allowed itself to be led astray by the teachings of Voltaire, Rousseau, Diderot, and the like. In the view of Ultras, the poisonous ideals of the Enlightenment philosophers had eroded and undermined the institutions and beliefs without which no ordered society could exist: the authority of the church and the doctrine of the divine right of kings. To them, the Revolution was the design of Providence—like the Biblical flood, it swept away the evil excesses of the eighteenth century so that France might begin anew. They even believed that they had been called back by a repentant people to reestablish absolute monarchy. The task now was to put France back on her pre-Revolutionary course, avenge the crimes of the past and purge the nation of all Revolutionary elements.

The Right—the King's Party—while not sharing the wilder fantasies of its Ultra faction, was nevertheless bent on significantly undoing many of the changes brought about in the previous twenty-five years. Above all, it was determined to secure the sovereignty of the throne, and, like its Ultra faction, it was convinced that religion was monarchy's best ally. The Revolution had proven that when the authority of the church crumbled, all other institutions would topple with it. Therefore, as Bonald, De Maistre, and other theorists of the Right argued, the authority of the church must be strengthened. The Right urged the restoration of the church to its ancient position and power not because Catholicism was the true faith, but because Catholicism provided the most effective ideological sanction for monarchy. Religion, as Georges Brandes wrote, "was employed as the police, the army, the prisons were employed, to keep everything quiet and support the principle of authority."[4] Or, to quote Chateaubriand, "To *the most Christian King* religion was no more than a medicinal liquor, well adapted to form one of the ingredients of the brew called monarchy."[5]

The alliance between the throne and the altar, then, was a cornerstone of Bourbon policy. Insensitive to the widespread anticlericalism of the populace, especially where it concerned the education of their children, a zealous church, under the protection of the government, set out to reeducate Frenchmen in matters of religion. None of the hundreds of outrages perpetrated by the Revolution—the desecration and confiscation of church property, the destruction of relics, the suppression of orders, the massacres of priests who refused to accept the authority of the state over that of Rome, the blasphemous attempts to replace Christianity with the worship of secular ideals—none of these crimes had been forgotten, and the church was determined to impress the people with the sinfulness of their recent ways.

Missions—bands of fanatical priests—swept into every district, holding revival meetings and preaching loyalty to the throne. Their visit to a town usually culminated in a large, outdoor assembly, attended by the mayor and other officials. There, around a great bonfire, public penance would be made for the crimes of the Revolution, and copies of Voltaire and the *Encyclopedia* were thrown into the flames. The church also turned to more conventional methods to reeducate the people. State-supported convents and government-financed seminaries were established.

Officially, the latter were meant for prospective priests only, but they also served—illegally—as an alternative to the secular educational system established after the Revolution; parents wishing to stay on the good side of local officials and hoping for the future advancement of their sons' careers found it expedient to send them there. The Jesuits, although still outlawed in France (they had been expelled in 1757), were secretly encouraged to teach in schools and even opened schools of their own—without, however, acknowledging their identity. The government also commissioned scores of religious monuments and church decorations. In return for all of this, the clergy were relentless and fervent campaigners for the Right, preaching its doctrines from every pulpit in the land. These activities, often exaggerated by rumor and the Liberal press, aroused real anxiety in the middle classes, which feared a return to the *Ancien Régime* and the loss of their newly acquired property and privileges.

A rigid and reactionary Catholicism became the official ideology of the Restoration. An ambiguity in the Charter justified this, for while guaranteeing religious freedom, it also declared Catholicism the religion of the state. Throughout the Restoration, loyalty to the government was expressed as support for the church, and at all levels of society, individuals found it useful to visibly support the church. Indeed, such activities were secretly noted and often recorded by members of the clergy, lay religious societies, government men and the police—Stendhal's *The Red and the Black* hardly exaggerates the conspiratorial climate of the times. Prefects and the police kept copious files on individuals (among other things, they were useful in rigging the lists of voters at election time), noting what cafés they frequented, who their friends were, and what newspapers they read.[6] In the drawing rooms of the illustrious, those unofficial centers of power where men advanced their political and artistic careers, one took care to hold the "Right opinions." Here it was mandatory to express horror at the Revolution, Napoleon and all Liberal ideas and to show ardent support for religious education, the king's legislation, Sunday laws, the poetry of Lamartine and De Maistre's *Du Pape*, an ultramontane tract beloved by the Right. Above all, one's relationship to the church was regarded as the key to one's political sympathies. As Stendhal wrote, religion was "a powerful corporation with which it is most advantageous to be affiliated."[7]

What one said about the past was as politically charged as one's attitude toward religion. As the historian Stanley Mellon has shown, political controversy in the Restoration frequently raged around conflicting claims regarding the history of France—both ancient and recent.[8] The Right wanted the past

twenty-five years stricken from the official record of French history, seeing in them only a period of regicide and national crime. They adamantly refused to acknowledge in the acts of the Revolution or the Empire any precedents for the present. Conservative historians contrasted those years to idealized accounts of Old France, and with many artists and writers, portrayed bygone monarchies as golden ages, the old aristocracy as inherently noble, and past kings as wise and good. For Liberals, on the other hand, as for most middle-class Frenchmen whose lives, feelings, and fortunes had been shaped by them, the past twenty-five years were a source of deep pride, a dazzling era of military glory and enlightened social progress. Unable to attack the monarchy directly—such attacks would constitute treason—Liberal historians such as Thierry and Guizot exposed the corruptions of past monarchies and the class conflicts of pre-Revolutionary France, representing the Revolution as an inevitable outcome of earlier French history. During the Restoration, history was the most popular, the most controversial, and the most ideologically charged literary pursuit. In this context, every image and utterance of and about the national past could be ammunition in an ideological battle.

The literary men of the Restoration gave poetic substance to Rightist views of the past. Chateaubriand, De Maistre, Lamartine, and Hugo expounded the beauty and wisdom of societies founded on the authority of the church and governed by divinely appointed monarchs. In their poems and novels, the past is envisioned as a socially harmonious world in which rulers and the ruled accept without question the given political and religious order. Their writings, along with the "troubadour" subjects fashionable in Romantic art, evoke shimmering images of medieval life in which Christianity invests even simple relationships and everyday experience with grandeur and significance. Yet these post-Enlightenment intellectuals, while disaffected with the Enlightenment ideals of their fathers, were nevertheless heirs of the Age of Reason. The innocent, unquestioned faith for which they envied the past—that faith that assured men of the purposefulness of existence—eluded them. Their writings express more the desire to believe in some absolute authority than authentic faith in Christianity.[9] Chateaubriand, whose *Génie du Christianisme* was the inspiration of this generation and whose rhapsodic eulogies of the church and the king made him the most effective propagandist for the Restoration, made no pretense to faith in his memoirs: "A Republican, I serve the Monarchy; a philosopher, I honour religion. These are not contradictions: they are forced consequences of the uncertainty of theory and the certainty of practice among men."[10]

In the place of faith, Restoration literature substituted self-conscious sentimentality and a reverence for the symbols and trappings of tradition. The dogmas, rituals, and artifacts of the church and the throne were researched, revived, and made the objects of enthusiastic aesthetic transport. "The kind of piety was coming into vogue which consisted in looking at religion pathetically, gazing at it from the outside, as one looks at an object in a museum, and saying: How poetic! how touching! how beautiful!"[11]

Ingres' *Vow of Louis XIII* faithfully reflects the religious sentimentality of the Restoration and the counterfeit piety of official state religion. The insistent presence of past art,[12] the airlessness of the spaces, the sharp-edged and atrophied Raphaelesque forms—these and the strict hierarchical relationship between King and Virgin suggest the rigid dogmas and calculated faith of official Catholicism. At the same time, the lurid colors, the rouged mouths and the too-explicit textures make exaggerated appeal to the emotions and the senses.[13] Ingres speaks of the beyond, but unconvincingly, and only on the authority of past art. He is distanced from the transcendental reality he portrays: between it and himself he has placed both older art and a mass of concrete, meticulously observed objects. The king's act of faith goes almost unnoticed in the assemblage of researched visual facts. Yet the visual facts suggest contradictory realities. The illusionism is unstable: the king's vision, rendered in a broader style than the foreground, flattens out into a pastiche of Raphael, an art object before which Louis XIII absurdly kneels; or, more disturbingly, it threatens to materialize as a concrete, voluptuous woman, who, with her cupidlike son, is displayed before him. The flaming torches and the sultry climate suggested by the blushing light emanating from the holy realm contradict the spiritual effect they were meant to enhance.

Beyond its affirmation of the general tone and spirit of the official Restoration, Ingres's *Vow of Louis XIII* fulfilled more specific political and ideological functions. As a state-financed commission destined for the Cathedral of Montauban, it benefited a particular group of politicians. The officials who commissioned it were the Mayor of Montauban, the local prefect, deputies from Tarne-et-Garonne (one of whom was a former mayor of Montauban), and the Baron Portal, one of Louis XVIII's ministers. During the Restoration, politicians frequently commissioned religious art for local churches as a means of influencing their conservative constituencies or reassuring church and higher state officials of their ideological colors.[14] The combination of officials involved in the commission of Ingres's *Vow of Louis XIII* can leave little doubt that the work was meant to serve such purposes. They not only represent the alliance between the church and the government, they also exemplify the chains of authority that linked local town halls to the king's cabinet.

The commission stipulated that the subject had to be approved by the prefect, but was to be chosen by the mayor in consultation with the Bishop of Montauban.[15] The subject they agreed upon clearly reveals their political intent, and although altered by Ingres, the finished work was well suited to affirm their allegiance to the Bourbon house and its policies. The subject—the vow of Louis XIII—is not a traditional Christian subject, nor is it even a very religious one.[16] Designed to glorify the Bourbons and to sanctify the present throne and altar alliance, it honors an earlier Bourbon king as he prayed for divine aid in the midst of political and religious strife. Louis XIII's vow was taken in 1636,[17] at a moment when his throne was threatened and heresy divided the land. As Ingres's painting illustrates, the king, who offers his crown and scepter to the Virgin, placed France under her protection in return for her help. Two years later, the king, now victorious, published and made good his promises to her. He decreed that every year, on the Day of the Assumption, in every church of the realm, a procession to the Virgin was to take place along with the celebration of High Mass. The Revolution put an end to this tradition, but Louis XVIII, on his return to France, immediately revived it.[18] The seventeenth-century Louis had also donated a painting to the main altar of Notre-Dame of Paris representing himself kneeling before the Virgin and the dead Christ. Several of these were executed in the seventeenth century,[19] and it was this subject that the mayor, the prefect and the Bishop of Montauban had in mind when they commissioned Ingres to execute a painting for the altar of the cathedral.

Besides glorifying the Bourbon line in general, the choice of subject alludes more specifically to Louis XVIII. Historians of the Right had already pointed out analogies between the reigns of Louis XIII and Louis XVIII, both of which followed a period of religious and civil conflict. As one Restoration historian, Anaïs de Raucou Bazin, wrote in the preface to his *Histoire de France sous Louis XIII,* "The reign of Louis XIII emerged, after the great commotion of the religious wars, almost into the same conditions where we ourselves are, in the wake of the double upheaval caused by the Revolution and the Empire.[20] Ingres's altarpiece not only evokes the same comparison, it suggests that the Virgin takes a special interest in the Bourbons and that as long as they occupy the throne, France will enjoy her personal protection.

85
Ingres's *Vow of
Louis XIII* and the
Politics of the
Restoration

Such flattery was not unusual in the Restoration, but in 1820, when the work was commissioned, government officials had a particularly strong motive to laud the Bourbon line and the alliance between the throne and the altar. Between 1816 and 1820, Louis XVIII had opposed the more reactionary ideas of the Comte d'Artois and his friends. Events of 1820, however, initiated a dramatic shift to the Right. In February, the young Duc de Berry, the only male member of the Bourbon family capable of producing an heir to the throne, was fatally stabbed by an obscure stablehand named Louvel, a fanatical Republican. The assassination produced a great wave of fear and reaction throughout France, and the Comte d'Artois and his clique were quick to exploit it to their advantage. With no supporting evidence, they insisted that the assassination was the result of a conspiracy and that the really guilty parties were the moderate Royalists, for under their Liberal-leaning policies, subversive and revolutionary elements of society had been able to grow and organize. The assassination of the Duc, they pointed out, proved the wisdom of the hard line that they had been advocating all along. In the climate of shock and fear generated by the Duc's death, they successfully pressed their demand that the king dissolve his moderate Royalist cabinet. After this, the Comte d'Artois and his party took increasing control of the government, and the sick old king increasingly became their willing tool.

As the Comtesse de Boigne remarked, "The death of the Duc de Berry was more useful to his family than his life."[21] People in all levels of public life hastened to affirm their faith in Christianity and to assure the Bourbons of their loyalty. Funeral orations by clerics, memorial speeches by politicians, and poems and odes by Chateaubriand and his followers lamented the murdered Duc, emphasized the national tragedy of his death and recounted the nobility of his line.[22] It was a time to remember all of the Louis' and the Bourbons of the past, and to glorify one was to glorify all. When it was learned that the Duchesse de Berry was pregnant, there was more public proclaiming.

The *Vow of Louis XIII* was conceived, then, at a moment when everyone connected with the government was making a point of displaying their allegiance to the Bourbon house and to the policies of the Right. It is conceivable that the subject of the painting was even meant to allude to the pregnancy of the Duchesse de Berry. Louis XIII, at the time he made the vow, had prayed for an heir, and in January 1638, it became known that the queen was pregnant.[23] Since the family history of the Bourbons was being told and retold with such frequency and ardor in 1820, it is not unlikely that the Montauban group thought to draw this analogy, too, and thus

underline the idea that the Virgin habitually intervenes in the affairs of the Bourbons. Lamartine's *Ode* on the birth of the new heir, the Duc de Bordeau, developed this idea at length, calling the new heir "the miracle child," his birth a "divine marvel," and his cradle "sacred."[24]

When Ingres received news of the commission in Florence, he immediately pronounced the subject ill-conceived. There followed a complex correspondence between Florence and Montauban, with letters to and from the town officials and the lawyer Gilibert, Ingres's boyhood friend who had been instrumental in securing him the commission and who now acted as his intermediary.[25] From his side, Ingres objected to the double subject of the king's vow and the Pietà. First of all, it broke the classical law of unity; its two subjects would divide the viewers's attention and produce a disturbing effect. Second, lacking the necessary documents in Florence, he would be unable to portray Louis XIII with satisfactory accuracy. The Virgin alone would be a better subject. From Montauban came the reply that the painting not only must commemorate the Assumption of the Virgin, but must also allude to the special celebrations and meanings that the Day of the Assumption held for the Bourbons. Then, in 1821, both sides changed their minds. Evidently, Ingres's arguments had gotten to the mayor and the prefect. Not wishing to violate this law of unity about which the artist spoke, they approved the Virgin of the Assumption as the subject of their painting. In response, however, Ingres abruptly withdrew his aesthetic objections and proposed an altered version of the double subject: the vow of Louis XIII before the Virgin and Child.

Ingres scholars—that is, Ingres scholars who admire the finished work—have attributed the artist's change of mind to purely artistic motives.[26] According to this explanation, Ingres accepted the double subject in place of the Virgin alone only when—and because—he resolved the compositional problems it posed. The imagination and originality of the work are taken to be sufficient proof of the artist's motives. To argue the purely artistic merits or faults of the work, however, demonstrates nothing about Ingres's motives—assuming that one can isolate and weigh such ingredients. Anyone familiar with Ingres and his obsessive ideal of beauty must grant that he would not have undertaken a task that seriously violated his artistic credo. However, it is more difficult to agree that Ingres accepted a commission that so obviously praised the Bourbons only as an opportunity to meet its pictorial challenges. To assume such an idealistic, politically disinterested motive is to accept an ideological rationalization of the political content of the work. That Ingres—doctrinaire idealist that he was—eventually took this very position is understandable; but, Ingres's letters and the contingencies of his career suggest a more complex explanation.

In 1820, when Ingres received the commission for the *Vow of Louis XIII,* he was forty-three years old, had lived outside of France for years, and, except for a few artist-friends and patrons, was little known or appreciated. His exhibits to the Paris Salons were never well received, and disheartened, he had been sending fewer paintings there as the years went by. As he himself so often lamented, his career seemed to be under the influence of an unlucky star. Ingres's career options had always been more limited than those of Delacroix, Eugène Devéria, and other luminaries of the art world. Without inherited means, he also lacked the charm and easy manners necessary for acceptance into the drawing rooms of the fashionable. Then as now, wealthy patrons of art decorated their social gatherings with artists as well as art. Always a stiff and sober petit bourgeois, awkward in his speech and ill at ease in educated society, Ingres was never able to advance his career by this route—as he himself knew.[27] Moreover, he simply did not *look* like an artist—or what people expected artists to look like.

If he passed you in the street, you would take him for a Spanish priest dressed up as a bourgeois: a swarthy, bilious complexion; a dark, alert, suspicious, ill-humoured eye; a brow narrow and receding; short, thick hair, jet-black once and always greasy, divided by a parting down the centre of a pointed skull; large ears; veins beating vigorously at the temples; a prominent nose, incined to be hooked and made to appear short on account of the vast space separating it from the mouth; cheeks coarse and baggy; chin and cheekbones very pronounced; jaw like a rock, and lips thin and sullen.[28]
Genius was expected to have more fiery, nervous looks—the unruly hair, sensitive brow and smoldering gaze of a Delacroix, for example.

By 1821, after much correspondence with Montauban, Ingres hardly could have remained innocent of the propagandistic nature of the commission—if, in fact, he ever was innocent of it. Indeed, his letters after 1821 reveal a very shrewd understanding of the opportunity the commission provided for a virtually assured success in Paris.[29] He frequently refers to the painting as a decisive change in his fortunes, "the most important moment in my life." From the moment he dedicated himself to the double subject, he resolved to accompany the finished work to the Salon, and he wrote Gilibert that he intended "to strike while the iron is hot." As he repeatedly told his friend, he was putting into it three times the work he normally would, but as he was doing it for "ma gloire," it was worth it.

Thus, if the government would use his artistic skills to further its ends, Ingres would use the government to further his own. In any case, glorifying the Bourbons probably did not violate any of his personal convictions. Politically, he appears to have resembled many of his compatriots in the nineteenth century: of Royalist sentiments and, in principle, inclined toward constitutional monarchy, he was fearful of revolution; and, needing to earn a living, he was adaptable to and willing to serve a succession of authoritarian régimes.[30] Like many petits bourgeoises, he was in awe of established authority, impressed with the official honors it bestowed, and flattered to be recognized and patronized by men of rank and title.

Moreover, this was neither the first nor the last time that Ingres lent his talents to political interests. Among the few patrons he had attracted since the fall of the Empire were several Ultra-Royalists who had already given him commissions of this kind.[31] The Duc de Blacas, a violent reactionary, a crony of the Comte d'Artois and one of the most notorious and unpopular Ultras of the Restoration, had commissioned from him *Henry IV Playing with his Children,* 1817–one of those themes illustrating the charm and humaneness of pre-Revolutionary monarchs that pleased the Right. In 1819, Blacas also bought Ingres's *Roger and Angelica* for the king's collection. Between 1815 and 1819, Ingres undertook two commissions glorifying the Berwick-Alba family, and although he found one of them too repugnant to complete (*The Duc of Alba at Saint-Gudule, Brussels*—an event commemorating the Duc's bloody massacres of the Dutch in the sixteenth century), he did finish the second, *Philip V Investing the Marechal of Berwick with the Golden Fleece.* Finally, in 1821, the Comte Amidée de Pastoret, a fervent convert to the Bourbon cause, commissioned *The Dauphin Entering Paris,* showing a supposed fourteenth century ancestor of the Pastoret family demonstrating his loyalty to the future Charles V, who had recently vanquished a challenger to the throne.

Having divined the kind of opportunity that the Montauban commission presented, it is little wonder that Ingres's artistic imagination came up with a pictorial solution that fulfilled its original purpose. By accepting the Bourbon subject matter, he preserved the overt ideological intent of his patrons, thus increasing by several times the probability of a favorable reception for the work in Paris. And by substituting the Madonna for the Pietà (and also by facing Louis XIII away from the viewer and showing only a small part of his face), he mitigated the causes of his original "aesthetic" objections. Those aesthetic objections, however, especially his complaint that the subject as first proposed was not a unified one, hardly make sense without considering the ideological import of the work. The image of a king before the Pietà is no more disunified than the one Ingres finally chose. As realized by Philippe de Champaigne and other seventeenth-century artists, it emphasizes the idea of the king's Christian piety by showing him before the dead Christ—that is, as a penitent. It is understandable that now, in 1820, the subject should strike Ingres as lacking in a compelling central idea. Its strong appeal to traditional religious feeling and its prominent display of royal religious affect must have seemed not to the point—judging from the finished work. His resolution of the problem was not a matter of bringing unity out of something disunified, but of changing the emphasis of the iconography in order to render it more relevant to the ideological needs of his patrons and to the sensibilities of his nineteenth-century audience.

Ingres's substitution of the Adoration theme for the Pietà enabled him to focus upon and stress the Bourbon claim to legitimacy. The central issue of the King-Virgin relationship as it is presented here is not the king's piety as a good Christian ruler but the king's right to rule. The figure of Louis is conceived largely as a reigning Bourbon monarch. Ingres dwells upon his Bourbon costume and the symbols of his power but skirts the matter of his subjective religious experience. The transaction in which the king is engaged is to the point: he offers to the Virgin the symbols of his power, and, in return, will receive from her (in the form of a military victory) the confirmation that they are his to hold. Truer to his times than he might have been able to admit consciously, Ingres created an altarpiece in which the alliance between throne and altar is starkly portrayed as political in nature. Of course, seventeenth-century images of the *Vow of Louis XIII* also promulgate the legitimacy of the Bourbon house; but in Ingres's altarpiece, the emphasis of the doctrine of divine right so overwhelms the issue of the king's Christian virtue that the latter is supressed as a distracting countertheme. The very insistency with which the doctrine is argued testifies to its shakiness in the minds of Ingres' countrymen. Following his artistic intuition, he shrewdly took their measure when he decided to base his appeal not on their religious faith but on their respect for authority, divinely or otherwise sanctioned.

The opening of the Salon on September 24, 1824, came two weeks after the death of Louis XVIII. On September 27, the Comte d'Artois entered Paris as King Charles X. Two weeks later, the *Vow of Louis XIII* was put on display at the Salon. Ingres, after eighteen years of absence, now enjoyed the triumph he had anticipated for the last three years. To his friend Gilibert, he stressed the purely artistic nature

of his triumph, repeating the flattering comments made to him—how the painting came just in time to stop bad taste and how it was inspired by Raphael without being a copy of him—and assuring his friend that the most respected artists—Gérard, Girodet, Gros and Dupaty—had personally lauded his work to him.[32] Most twentieth-century scholars have followed Ingres in choosing to believe that the *Vow of Louis XIII* was judged strictly on the basis of its artistic qualities and that Ingres's triumph was purely a matter of aesthetics. In fact, published opinion of the time was divided about the artistic merits of the work;[33] Stendhal, for example, while admiring Ingres's drawing, found the work lacking expression.[34] Yet, many voices did declare the painting an artistic triumph and Ingres the champion of tradition. These accolades, however, must be taken at least in part as a way of flattering the new Bourbon king. In any case, the critical response cannot be understood only in the light of academic disputes over style and certainly not as a reflection of disinterested aesthetic taste. Critics commonly registered their support of a work's ideological content by praising its artistic qualities. Of course, Ingres's painting had to fulfill some notion of artistic quality. To function ideologically, the work had to be measurable and justifiable on separate, aesthetic grounds—good drawing, a proper understanding of tradition, and so forth. But without its ideological import, it is unlikely that it would have been thus extolled.

That the Liberal press remained silent about the political meanings of the altarpiece is not surprising. The conventions of art criticism did not lend themselves to such analysis easily. Moreover, angering the king by attacking the ideology of a monumental artistic effort undertaken on his behalf would have been unwise. The Bourbons were extremely sensitive to the least criticism and did not hesitate to prosecute even inuendos they thought mocking or disrespectful to the king, the church, and their symbols of authority. As Stanley Mellon has shown, it was official dogma that the king was loved by the people, and anyone contesting this in print was liable to legal prosecution.[35] The elaborate censorship and press laws habitually legislated by the Bourbon government could bring severe damages to periodicals or to individual journalists.[36] The art press was as closely scrutinized as the political press, and publications could be suspended for what they published about paintings.[37] Stendhal probably went as far as one dared when he wryly commented that Ingres's figures lacked a feeling for the divine, that they were without celestial "onction," and that, despite the attention the work was receiving in the press, it was not popular among visitors to the Salon.[38] Finally, at that moment, there was a temporary truce between the king and the press—Louis XVIII had just been interred and Charles X had just arrived on the throne. The storm would break over issues much bigger than a painting that glorified the Bourbon monarchy.

Much has been written about the role of Ingres and the *Vow of Louis XIII* in the art politics of 1824. Ingres is often represented as the upholder of classical tradition in the face of a Romantic opposition led by Delacroix, whose *Massacre of Chios* was also exhibited in the Salon. The implication is that classicism was becoming identified with reaction while the Romantic school, with its love of color and open brushwork and its disdain for rules, was the artistic corollary of forces demanding social and political change. It is true that after 1824 leading Romantic writers like Chateaubriand and Hugo became disenchanted with the Bourbon monarchy and that the growing Liberal opposition was attracting talented young painters like Géricault and Delacroix. However, at this time, there were no ideological claims being made about styles themselves, and in painting especially neither Romanticism nor Neoclassicism can be firmly identified with the Right or the Left, either in the Restoration or in the decades following. Open techniques, vibrant colors, and emotionally appealing subjects appeared in works both pleasing and displeasing to the Right. Moreover, paintings were not judged merely on their formal and stylistic characteristics.

Delacroix's *Massacre of Chios* was no more unconventional in its form than paintings exhibited by Eugène Devéria and other young colorists who were doted on by the Right. It was its subject that was more controversial. The Greeks' struggle to liberate themselves from the Turks was a great Liberal rallying cause in the '20s, and the spectacle of Greek victims could easily be taken as an indirect criticism of French foreign policy, which—while it did not hesitate to crush constitutional government in Spain—had so far refused to extend aid to the Greeks. To espouse liberty for the Greeks was also a way to espouse liberty at home without directly attacking the monarchy. "At a time when it was impossible to cry 'Long Live Liberty,' those who were disaffected were quick to see the advantage of shouting 'Long Live the Greeks.'"[39] In 1826, from the floor of the Chamber of Deputies, Benjamin Constant invoked the Greek cause in an indictment of Charles X's ministry. His words seem to articulate the political message of Delacroix's painting: ". . . The inhumanity of your diplomacy is witnessed in the ruins of Greece, the corpses of martyrs, old men, women, and children."[40]

Ingres's *Vow of Louis XIII,* on the other hand, affirmed all the ideals Ultras invoked to justify their policies—the alliance of the throne and the altar and the doctrine of the divine right of kings. Charles X was notoriously indifferent to art, good or bad, and it was surely for political and not aesthetic reasons that his first minister, Villèle, offered to buy the painting so that it might be kept permanently in Paris. His bid of 80,000 francs—Montauban was getting it for 5,000—was turned down, but the work was detained in Paris for two years (even while Montauban clamored for it), and a large, official engraving of it was made widely available.[41] Nor is it surprising that Ingres's name was advanced for the Legion of Honor by two of Charles X's most fervent and important supporters—the Vicomte de La Rochefoucauld, a fanatical Ultra, and the Minister of the Interior Corbière.[42]

To the extent that it please the Right, the *Vow of Louis XIII* must have annoyed Liberals. For during the two years that the work remained in Paris as an officially revered object, the concepts it glorified were increasingly attacked by a growing opposition and defended by an ever more vociferous Right. Popular prints of the time attest to the anger and distrust with which the urban crowd regarded the king, the church, and the aristocracy.[43] Even as Ingres was receiving his Cross at the closing ceremonies of the Salon, the king's new legislative program was beginning to stir hot debate.[44] It included two bills that especially signaled his intentions to annul everything accomplished by the Revolution. The first, the Law of Sacrilege, would make it a crime to profane the sacred vessels and wafers used in the mass. The prescribed punishment was as bizarre as it was drastic: the criminal, in black hood and barefooted, was to be decapitated— after having had his hand cut off. The bill, which made Catholic religious dogma civil law, was passed, but at a price to the king. It stirred deep-seated anticlerical feelings among the people, and seemed to confirm the popular fear that the Jesuits and the Clerical party were dictating state policy. Indeed, the bill inspired a wave of clerical fanaticism, with priests refusing burial and marriage to suspected Liberals.[45] The second bill, which would have reinstituted the ancient laws of primogeniture, was defeated, but not before it, too, convinced the people of the king's intention to turn back the clock and revive the privileges and inequalities of feudalism. Its defeat was celebrated in Paris for days, and the city rang with the cry, "Down with the Jesuits."[46]

Other events of 1825 and 1826 exacerbated these fears. But nothing raised anticlerical feeling more than the king's coronation in Rheims Cathedral, in May 1825. This controversial event also seems a kind of dramatization of Ingres' altarpiece, and it was fitting that Ingres was chosen as its official artist. The coronation manifested in reality the same desire to reconstruct a dead past through archaeological detail. "The present coronation," wrote Chateaubriand, "will be not a coronation, but the representation of a coronation."[47] All of the ancient coronation rituals and dressings were adhered to as if there had never been a Revolution. The king was even annointed with what was purported to be some of the original holy oil miraculously given to Clovis by a heaven-sent dove in the fifth century. Pieces of the ancient vial, smashed during the Revolution, were conveniently produced and authenticated by a clerical commission, and traces of the original oil were used as a base for a new supply. Besides striking people as absurd—Béranger's poem mocking the pompous ceremonies was immensely popular[48]—the business of the holy oil raised important issues. The revival of this and the other rituals was interpreted as a reassertion of ancient absolutism. To Liberals, the Charter was the ultimate authority upon which the monarchy rested, and through it, the king was responsible to the people. The Bourbons, however, had always insisted that ultimate authority resided in the King by divine right and that the Charter was a grant from the king to the people.[49] The coronation rituals seems to sanctify a return to absolute monarchy, to the days when the king's will was law.

Worst of all, the ceremony of annointment required the king to lie on the floor while a high church official applied the oil. That is, the ceremony would have the king do precisely what Napoleon had refused to do in his coronation of 1804—grovel before priests. The image of the pious king prostrating himself before the powers of the church—Louis XIII comes close to this in Ingres's painting—was extremely disturbing to this generation of French, who nurtured strong Gallican sentiments and vivid memories of 1804, when Napoleon had seized the crown from the hands of the pope and placed it on his head himself. People were now convinced that Charles X was the tool of the Jesuits. So went Béranger's poem, *The Coronation of Charles the Simple:*

Charles in the dust now prostrate lies;
"Rise up, Sir King," a soldier cries.
"No," quoth the Bishop, "and by Saint Peter,
The Church crowns you; with bounty treat her!
Heaven *sends* but 'tis priests who *give;*
Long may legitimacy live!"[50]

Two years later, when the *Vow of Louis XIII* was installed in the Cathedral of Montauban and the *Coronation Mass* by Ingres's friend Cherubini was heard again, both Liberals and Ultras must have remembered afresh the ritual enacted at Rheims. That same year, in the church Jubilee celebrations, Charles X could be seen again submitting to priests, meekly trailing them in the public processions. Rumor had it that he had been secretly ordained as a priest and was now the complete captive of the Jesuits.

Ingres's *Vow of Louis XIII* was unveiled at a moment when the church, the king, and the symbols of their allied authority were targets of mounting popular hatred and ridicule. By creating a lucid symbol of that alliance—a reminder of everything that was to bring down Charles X—Ingres might well have claimed a modest contribution to the deepening tensions of the time: he helped furnish the trappings of the dispised monarchy whose pompous rituals increasingly aroused the conscious hostility of the people. That hostility would continue to grow as Charles X blindly pursued his Ultra policies and as the nation, increasingly polarized by the politico-theological issue, moved closer to revolution.

Notes

1
Ingres d'après une correspondance inédite, ed. Boyer d'Agen (Paris, 1909), p. 175; and Paris: Petit Palais, *Ingres* (exhibition catalog), October 27, 1967, to January 29, 1968, p. 190.

2
For examples, see P.-M. Auzas, "Observations iconographiques sur le'Voeu de Louis XIII,'" in *Colloques Ingres,* a special number of the *Bulletin du Musée Ingres* (Montauban, October 15, 1969), pp. 1–11; J. Alazard, *Ingres et l'ingrisme* (Paris, 1950), pp. 68–70; F. Elgar, *Ingres* (Paris, 1951), p. 7; Petit Palais, *Ingres,* p. 190 (catalog entry by Daniel Ternois); and N. Schlenoff, *Ingres, ses sources littéraires* (Paris, 1956), pp. 140–147.

Not all Ingres scholars see the painting as an artistic success. See R. Rosenblum, *Ingres* (New York, 1967), p. 126, for a most perceptive visual analysis of the work; and W. Friedlaender, *David to Delacroix* (New York, 1968), pp. 80–81. Friedlaender found the work so derivative that he could "not quite understand why just this particular picture should have had such a tremendous success." The explanation he offered is the one accepted by most scholars: established academic taste needed a champion of classical traditions to oppose Delacroix and the young Romantic painters who were out in force at the Salon of 1824.

3
For the political history of the Restoration, I have relied mainly on the following: F. B. Artz, *France Under the Bourbon Restoration, 1814–1830* (New York, 1963) and *Reaction and Revolution, 1814–1832* (New York, 1963); V. N. Beach, *Charles X of France, His Life and Times* (Boulder, Colorado, 1971); G. de Bertier de Sauvigny, *The Bourbon Restoration,* trans. L. M. Case (Philadelphia, 1966); G. Brandes, *Main Currents in Nineteenth Century Literature* (New York, 1901–1906), Vols. I and III; J.-P. Garnier, *Charles X, le roi, le proscrit* (Paris, 1967); M. D. R. Leys, *Between Two Empires* (London/New York/Toronto, 1955); S. Mellon, *"The Politics of History: A Study of the Historical Writing of the French Restoration"* (Doctoral dissertation, Princeton University, 1954, also available as a book); R. Rémond, *The Right Wing in France, From 1815 to de Gaulle,* trans. J. M. Laux (Philadelphia, 1969); J. H. Stewart, *The Restoration in France, 1814–1830* (a collection of documentary texts) (Princeton, New Jersey, 1968).

4
Main Currents, III: 197.

5
In ibid., III: 164. Napoleon had similarly used religion as a prop to his authority. Following the Terror and its devastating attacks on the church, France experienced a wave of proclerical sentiment. Rather than risk opposing it, Napoleon sought to use it as a support to his throne. The Concordat of 1802 and the Coronation of 1804 were in part designed to disassociate Catholicism from the Bourbon house and to identify it with his own (ibid., III; 35–37 and 52–56).

6
Artz, *France* pp. 49, 75–79.

7
Stendhal, *The Life of Henri Brulard,* trans. C. A. Phillips (New York, 1955), p. 292.

8
Mellon's *The Politics of History* is devoted entirely to this subject.

9
Artz, *Reaction,* Chap. 3; and Brandes, *Main Currents,* Vol. III.

10
The Memoirs of Francois René Vicomte de Chateaubriand, trans. A. Teixeira de Mattos (New York, 1902), III: 37.

11
Brandes, *Main Currents,* III: 85.

12
For the artistic sources of the *Vow of Louis XIII,* see Auzas, "Observations," pp. 3 ff.

13
See also the visual analysis by Robert Rosenblum in *Ingres,* p. 126; and W. Hofmann, *Art in the Nineteenth Century,* trans. B. Battershaw (London, 1961), p. 152.

14
S. Kent, *Electoral Procedure Under Louis Philippe* (Yale Historical Publications, No. 10) (New Haven, 1937), pp. 125–127.

15
Petit Palais, *Ingres,* p. 190; and Schlenoff, *Ingres,* pp. 141–142.

16
P. Angrand, *Monsieur Ingres et son époque* (Paris, 1968), pp. 34–36. Angrand is an exception among Ingres scholars for the attention he gives to the relationship between politics and the artist's work.

17
For the text of the vow, see Auzas, "Observations," p. 1.

18
Ibid., p. 7.

19
Ibid., pp. 3 ff. The best known is the one by Philippe de Champaigne, formerly in Notre-Dame, Paris, now in the Musée de Caen.

20
Paris, 1840, I: iii–vi. Although published in 1840, Baxin's sentiments belong to the Restoration.

21
In Stewart, *Restoration,* p. 139.

22
Mellon, *Politics,* p. 100.

23
Bazin, *Histoire,* pp. 13 ff.

24
Lamartine, *Oeuvres* (Paris, 1826), I: 96–97

25
Ingres . . .correspondance, pp. 55–82; and Schlenoff, *Ingres,* pp. 142–146.

26
Alazard, *Ingres,* pp. 68–70; Petit Palais, *Ingres,* p. 190; J. Pope-Hennessy, *Raphael* (New York, 1970), pp. 254–255; and Schlenoff, *Ingres,* pp. 145–147.

27
Amaury-Duval, *L'Atelier d'Ingres* (1878) (Paris, 1924), pp. 215, 219. Ingres was fully aware that the social skills he lacked could make a difference in his career (*Ingres. . .correspondance,* p. 85).

28
Th. Silvestre, quoted in M. Easton, *Artists and Writers in Paris* (London, 1964), p. 168.

29
Ingres. . .correspondance, pp. 60–71; 114–116; 119; and Angrand, *Ingres,* pp. 44–45.

30
Angrand, *Ingres,* passim. Ingres glorified every French régime from the Consulate to the Second Empire—with the exception of the Second Republic.

31
Ibid., pp. 36–43; Petit Palais, *Ingres,* pp. 112, 142, 174.

32
Ingres. . .correspondance, pp. 120–125.

33
Dorathea K. Beard, "Ingres and Quatremère de Quincy: Some Insignts into Academic Maneuvers" (Paper delivered at the Annual Meeting of the College Art Association of America, January 23–26, 1974). According to Beard, many newspapers simply ignored the work.

34
Stendhal, "Salon de 1824," in *Mélanges d'art* (Paris, 1932), pp. 116–119.

35
Mellon, *Politics,* pp. 101–102.

36
Artz, *France,* pp. 82–83 and *Reaction,* pp. 224–25; Beach, *Charles X,,* pp. 236–238; I. Collins, *The Government and the Newspaper Press in France, 1814–1881,* (London, 1959); C. Ledré, *La Presse à l'assaut de la monarchie, 1815–1848* (Paris, 1960); and Stewart, *Restoration,* pp. 131–137.

37
Collins, *The Government,* p. 17; and Ledré, *La Presse,* p. 18.

38
Stendhal, "Salon de 1824," pp. 116–119.

39
Beach, *Charles X,* pp. 231–235; and Artz, *Reaction,* p. 207.

40
Beach, *Charles X,* p. 231.

41
Petit Palais, *Ingres,* p. 190.

42
Angrand, *Ingres,* p. 48.

43
Artz, in *France,* reproduces a lithograph of 1824, "The Past and the Present," which is especially interesting for the way it reverses the throne-altar relationship as depicted by

91
Ingres's *Vow of
Louis XIII* and the
Politics of the
Restoration

Ingres. While the left side of the print remembers the Empire as a time of enlightenment and justice, the right side depicts the Restoration as a modern dark age: figures representing the monarch and his aristocratic supporters are shown to be *above* and resting upon a fanatical, fire-and brimstone-preaching clergyman.

44
Beach, *Charles X,* pp. 182–197, 224–225; and Stewart, *Restoration,* pp. 154–155.

45
Artz, *France,* p. 159.

46
Beach, *Charles X,* pp. 224–226.

47
Memoirs, IV: 109.

48
The Coronation of Charles the Simple, in Stewart, *Restoration,* pp. 150–152. The poem earned him nine months in jail.

49
Artz, *France,* pp. 37–38; Beach, *Charles X,* pp. 198–199; and Mellon, *Politics,* p. 82.

50
Stewart, *Restoration,* p. 151.

5
Long Live the Revolution, the Republic, and Especially the Emperor!: The Political Sculpture of Rude

Ruth Butler

Four works by Francois Rude signify for us the most outstanding group of political sculptures done in France during the nineteenth century: the *Departure of the Volunteers of 1792* (Fig. 1, popularly referred to as *La Marseillaise*), *The Awakening of Napoleon to Immortality* (Fig. 2), the tomb of Godefroi Cavaignac (Fig. 3), and the *Marshal Ney* (Fig. 4). They are Rude's best-known sculptures, and they are the ones most responsible for our view of him as an important Romantic sculptor. If we were to remove them from his oeuvre, we would have quite a different idea of Rude as an artist. Without them it would be less easy to overlook the first twenty-five years of his creative life when he was making only Neoclassical works, or to skim over the fact that in 1834 he was engaged on an important relief in addition to the *Departure of the Volunteers:* the extremely classical *Prometheus Giving Life to the Arts* for the facade of the Palais Bourbon. We would also have to pay more attention to the works that absorbed him during the last years of his life: the marble, mythological works of *Hebe and the Eagle of Jupiter* and the *Rule of Love.* And we would have to consider his preferred reading about his profession: Emeric David's *Recherches sur l'histoire de la sculpture,* the same book that meant so much to Canova and, in fact, to every Neoclassicist in the first part of the nineteenth century. In many ways Rude was one of them. Then how to account for the fact that his most interesting work was not in a classical mode? The answer lies in understanding the nature of the particular subjects and the degree to which Rude was involved in them. According to these factors he would change his style. And he altered it especially when the content was political.

Two of Rude's political sculptures, the *Departure of the Volunteers of 1792* and the *Marshal Ney,* were commissioned by the government, and though one is a colossal allegorical relief and the other a free-standing, life-size statue, they are similar in spirit. We even find that when Rude went to create his *Marshal Ney,* he fused the screaming, sword-bearing "Genius of Liberty" with the central striding warrior of his relief in order to create the figure of the hero of Moscow. He worked on his other political pieces—both life-size bronze recumbent figures eulogizing dead leaders—simultaneously. Neither was a regular commission; he received no pay, but created them because of his commitment to the men and to what they stood for. These two works were perhaps the best things he ever did.

By all contemporary accounts Rude was not the kind of person to become automatically *engagé.* He was fond of a quiet life at home; he disliked leaving the quartier for fashionable Parisian events, preferring to play at boules near the house, to walk in the countryside on Sundays, or to read his numerous books, particularly those dealing with great deeds and the heroism of the ancients. He was honest and direct in his politics; Theophile Silvestre, who knew Rude toward the end of his life, found them "démocratique-napoléoniens [qui] manquaient de lucidité et de direction."[1] But Rude was a man of temperament, and the experience of living through the first half of the nineteenth century in France had drawn from him a special response to the political events of his time. He translated that response into works that still project something about the contemporary meaning of those events, and about the lives and deaths of three individuals—Cavaignac, Ney, and especially Napoleon.

Before examining Rude's approach to political ideas in sculpture, there are a few facts to keep in mind. Two things about his childhood stand out: he was the son of a worker-artisan (a stove-maker), and he was the child of a family committed to the Revolution. And when both of Rude's parents died shortly after the turn of the century, he allied himself with the family of an ardent Bonapartist, Louis Frémiet.

After preliminary training in Dijon, Rude went to Paris, an imperial Paris in the process of being redone by Napoleon's impresario, Vivant Denon. It was Denon who best understood that the grandeur of contemporary events could only be commemorated by colossal monuments. And it was Denon who saw to it that Rude was able to work on the reliefs of one of the most important of those colossal monuments—the Vendôme column. Rude learned at first hand just how the deeds of the emperor, the glory of the regime, and the high principles of national life could be splendidly evoked in the squares and streets of the capital. And Paris offered him schooling and competitions; by 1812 he had won a Prix de Rome. But because he did not have enough money to leave for Italy, he worked for two more years in Paris. The years 1812–1814 were difficult for France, but as far as we know, Rude thought more about Rome than about Russia and more about gaining the experience of Italian art than about the loss of Italy from the Empire. Finally, in early 1815, he was on his way; he stopped in Dijon for a brief visit before leaving France. March 1 changed everything: Napoleon landed at Fréjus. Rude's passionate feelings for his country and his emperor flamed to life. He took to the streets to rally those loyal to the imperial cause; he even faced Royalist troops with tricolor in hand shouting "Vive l'Empereur!" Thoughts of Italy became remote. We have only one sculpture from that period—a terracotta bust of the emperor. And Waterloo? Surely that was the moment to leave for Italy. But Rude had entered the fate of those around him and he would share it; Frémiet was in danger and had fled to Brussels. Rude assumed responsibility for his old friend's family and brought them north that they might be reunited.

Brussels was a city of exiles, where the greatest artist of the Empire, Jacques-Louis David, worked on a second version of the *Sacre of Napoleon*. His studio provided a place where Republicans and Bonapartists could freely mingle. David introduced Rude to persons who could give him work; he was also part of the young sculptor's life, for he was Sophie Frémiet's teacher. In 1821—the year Napoleon died—Rude and Sophie Frémiet were married. From what Sophie reveals in her letters of that year, the two had little time to think of the possible consequences of the emperor's death. They had put their concern for politics aside; now they sought commissions and expanded their atelier. Sophie entered the salons of Ghent and Antwerp and in 1823 gave birth to Louis-Amédée.

Rude's reasons for returning to Paris in 1827–1828 were professional; Sophie explained to a friend: "Rude wants to make a figure for the Paris exhibition. . . ."[2] The Salon of 1828 was a great success for him and commissions followed. The largest was from the state for the arch at the Etoile, where the government of the Restoration had rededicated Napoleon's great heap of stone to the recent Bourbon triumphs in Spain. Rude was one of fourteen sculptors assigned to carry out the frieze that would show the deeds of Charles X and his army. By March of 1829 the sculptors had gone over the terms of their agreement with the state and decided that there were both economic and aesthetic disadvantages in the proposal as it stood. So they sent a letter to Huyot, the architect in charge of work. This letter ended with a phrase to indicate that, in spite of the difficulties, the artists were most anxious to "attacher nos noms à un monument glorieux pour la France, le roi, les princes et l'armée. . . ." Louis de Fourcaud, who published the letter in 1904, admitted he could not suppress a little "surprise and also some displeasure to see this fierce republican as much as a fiery admirer of Bonaparte vowing his zeal for the royal government and to work on a piece that is evidently contrary to his faith. . . ."[3] Rude delivered his plaster for the frieze early in 1830, a few months before the July Revolution. How far Rude had strayed from his political beliefs of fifteen years earlier is evident from his feelings during the summer and fall of 1830. As far as we know, his greatest worries were about the future of his reliefs for the arch.

Louis-Philippe was extremely interested in the Arc de Triomphe. He committed himself early in his reign to complete it and to restore its original Napoleonic meaning—but with a subtle shift: it would no longer specifically pay tribute to the Grande Armée but to all brave men who had fought to defend France since the Revolution. Rude was still a sculptor of the Arc de Triomphe, but there was

1
Departure of the Volunteers of 1792,
Arc de Triomphe, L'Etoile, Paris,
1833–1836.

2
The Awakening of Napoleon to Immortality, Fixin, 1845–1847.
(Photo: Kirk T. Varnedoe)
3
Tomb of Godefroi Cavaignac, Cemetery of Montmartre, Paris, 1846–1847.
(Photo: Photographie Giraudon, Paris)

4
Marshal Ney, Paris, 1852–1853.
(Photo: Bulloz)

no work going on. Early in 1832 Sophie wrote: "The future is not reassuring; we are moving to an inevitable crisis. Our government, in spite of its liberal thinking, follows a direction that will ruin it, and perhaps ruin us as well."[4] By midsummer a change in personnel took place at the Arc de Triomphe, and things got going again. Huyot was replaced by Guillaume-Abel Blouet, who totally reorganized the work on the arch, now dedicated to "la gloire de toutes les Armées françaises depuis 1792." By the end of the year he was ready to think about the sculpture, particularly the four "trophées" for the immense front and back wall-surfaces. Blouet considered four colossal victories surrounded by the arms and flags of the defeated European powers, and he thought about having four soldiers, each standing for a principal corps of the army, with the figures placed amid the attributes of their corps. But his favorite program was one in which the prosperity of France was glorified through symbols of War, Science and Art, Commerce, and Agriculture. Each was to be personified by the appropriate Roman god or goddess. Such were the kinds of proposals in the air early in 1833. How is it then that such a different program was completely established by the following summer when the commissions were handed out? The answer must lie in the office of the powerful Minister of the Interior, Adolph Thiers. Thiers, a writer, considered to be a liberal in 1830, had been instrumental in bringing Louis-Philippe to power. Now he reaped the benefits. He personally had done much to give vigor to the cult of Napoleon, and he was learning ever more ably how to exploit it. Once he became such a significant figure in the new regime, he set out to put to use the monuments of the Empire as supports for a government that took its shaky existence from neither the people nor from God. Napoleon was necessary; his shadow buttressed the foundation of the July Monarchy. As another of Louis-Philippe's ministers, Guizot, said about Napoleon: "C'est beaucoup d'être à la fois une gloire nationale, une garantie révolutionnaire et un principe d'autorité." The July Monarchy needed all those things. But how to show that it was in a direct line of descent from Napoleon, just as he had descended from the Revolution? Theirs knew that no monument gave a better opportunity for revealing such an interpretation of history than the Arc de Triomphe at Etoile. So he began to work on a more specific program than the nebulous ones under consideration by Blouet. There is a note of February 1833 from Thiers asking about the proposals for subjects and the sketches in connection with the arch.[5] Thiers must have assumed the major portion of responsibility for recasting the program between February and July 23rd, when the commissions were handed out. How did he come to his solution? It appears that historic dates were of major importance

to him. The young sculptor Antoine Etex, who was to receive the commissions for both of the large reliefs on the Neuilly side of the arch, said that not long after his return to Paris in the fall of 1832 after two years at the Academy in Rome, Thiers contacted him about the possibility of doing a relief for the Arc de Triomphe. In his memoirs Etex recounted that the minister mentioned only two facts at their first meeting: it was to represent "1814," and it would be forty-five feet high. Etex did not like the idea very much: ". . . it seemed to me extraordinary that this date of 1814, date of our great misfortune, should appear as a 'trophée' on our Arc de Triomphe." When he said this, Thiers responded: "I don't care; I'm keeping it; I need 1814 as a date."[6] Etex finally had the idea of focusing on the "Defense of 1814." He submitted this to Thiers as a sketch; Thiers liked it and asked him to think about "1815." He then prepared a terracotta maquette for each "trophée."

Rude was another person to whom Thiers turned for suggestions about how to work out the subjects. We know this from two sets of sketches Rude made for the four reliefs, plus several single sketches, all anticipating the final choices. The least developed set (hence, we assume, the earlier) in the Musée de Dijon shows the Departure of the Volunteers of 1792, the Egyptian Campaign, the Retreat from Russia, and the Peace of 1815. Each is a static composition with a central male figure in front of a tree or a standard hung with the emblems of war. The drawings of the second group in the Cabinet des Dessins at the Louvre are more vigorous and more interesting. The composition of the Departure of the Volunteers is now dominated by the great winged figure. She blows a trumpet and has been referred to as symbolizing the "Call to War." He dropped the Egyptian Campaign (Rude ended up doing this subject for the frieze on the Neuilly side of the arch) and changed the Retreat from Russia (Fig. 5). He now showed the cruel fate of the men of 1792: the old, mutilated, blinded warriors returning home; their horses are dying while wolves howl under the aegis of a great bearded allegorical figure of Winter secured above on a craggy rock. The one hopeful sight in the relief is the young soldier in the rear. He turns to protect the retreat; and in so doing seems to symbolize the role that was played by Ney during the retreat. Rude then added the Resistance of 1814, in which he showed a female allegory of "Imperial France" looking upon the exhausted defenders of France who have come before the altar of "la Patrie." His Peace of 1815 was dominated by a beautiful allegory wearing a Phrygian bonnet and carrying an olive branch in one hand while indicating with the other that the warrior should put away his sword. The existence of these sketches prompted

5
Retreat from Russia, Cabinet des Dessins, Musée du Louvre, ca. 1833.
(Photo: Réunion des musées nationaux)

nineteenth-century writers to believe that at some point Rude was being considered for all four reliefs, and that because of jealousies and political double-dealing he was edged out of the enormous commission. There is no evidence to support this. It is far more likely that Rude was simply one of the people whose ideas Thiers solicited during the crucial months of 1833. Thiers may even have asked Rude's help in a manner that implied more than it involved. The shrewd politician and the hard-working sculptor never seemed to understand each other fully; Thiers' offers were surrounded by implications of further possibilities never fully described; Rude's replies were frank and direct and he appears to have been genuinely indifferent to "favors."

The commissions were handed out on July 23, 1833.[7] Rude would do the *Departure of the Volunteers of 1792* on the Paris side of the monument, Jean-Pierre Cortot would do its pendant showing the *Triumph of 1810* with the winged "Genius of Fame" proclaiming the glories of the Empire and a Victory crowning Napoleon as the Vanquished Cities of Europe offer submission at his feet. The *Resistance of 1814* and the *Peace of 1815* for the Neuilly side of the arch were both assigned to Etex. The only major difference between Rude's second set of sketches and the final reliefs was his choice of the year 1812 and the *Retreat from Russia* to represent the imperial period rather than the year 1810 and the *Triumph of the Empire*. The dramatic contrast of the *Departure of the Volunteers of 1792* and the *Retreat from Russia* was a characteristic choice for Rude; it indicated interest in something of the complex reality of the revolutionary and imperial periods—that it was not all triumph. It also brought to mind the heroic fight of Ney which fascinated Rude. But Thiers wanted the "Triumph" as one of the four events in the recent past that could be seen as the significant steps leading to the present: 1792 and the accomplished Revolution, 1810 and the triumph of France in Europe, 1814 and the French people unifying to defend themselves against the foreigner, 1815 and a France at peace. Building on this foundation, the government of 1830 would complete the work for reconciliation and peace.

Rude probably did not start working on the big relief immediately. We know he was busy through the summer on his portion of the frieze showing the *Egyptian Campaign*.[8] In 1834 he divided his time between the *Volunteers of 1792* and *Prometheus Giving Life to the Arts* for the Palais Bourbon, but by 1835 he must have been devoting himself principally to the colossal work. Beginning with small sketches and maquettes, then augmenting the size, the complexity, and the number of figures, he finally came to a solution that pleased him; he wrote to a friend, "I believe that this time I have succeeded, because there is something there that makes my

blood run hot and cold. My warriors hasten to defend their country and not in search of *la gloire*."[9] As Rude's designs took on solidity, we feel his mounting enthusiasm. The subject is about the response of thousands of men to the threat the Allies—the Prussians and the Austrians—posed to France in 1792. The men came from all over France—clerks, shopkeepers, and workers; together they formed the first volunteer army in modern Europe. The men from Marseilles made their marching song the hymn of the Revolution.

Rude's town of Dijon was a part of the provinces where anti-royalist feelings were strong, and in 1792 he had had his first real taste of the Revolution. His father had inscribed the eight-year-old boy in the "jeunes volontaires de Dijon." Surely the nude youth looking trustingly into the face of the ruddy old Gaul in Rude's relief has something to do with his remembrance of 1792, of his father, and of his initial contact with the revolutionary struggle. In working out the composition Rude juxtaposed the complex masculine response to the call of war and the "Genius of Liberty," in which he embodied the spirit of the nation. Her face has fantastic force as it emits a cry: a cry of anguish, of war, but also a call to liberty and to unity. Rude wanted to project that cry across great distances. Sophie was his model; evidently when her pose would slacken he would call out: "Cry louder!" Beneath this ferocious symbol of the "Marseillaise" he put men of different ages, each with a particular ability to respond and to comprehend. The dynamism, the number of figures, the depth of relief distinguish this sharply from the other three. But Rude did not know if it would carry as he hoped it would. Late in her life Mme. Rude remembered those days when the reliefs were in place but not yet unveiled:

I never saw him so tormented. He could not keep still. The Arc de Triomphe attracted him invincibly, and he kept repeating to me in such a sad voice while walking on the Champs-Elysées: "It would be too beautiful to really be able to show what one feels! That's the only thing to be desired. Nothing else counts . . ."[10]

Perhaps it is not easy for the twentieth-century viewer to read the reality that Rude wanted to fashion in his relief, even while he used allegory and Roman armor. His contemporaries saw it better, though often critically: Gustave Planche disliked its lack of idealism, particularly in the "Genius"—"Si c'est là le Génie de la guerre, les rues de Paris sont peuplées de pareils génies."[11] And David d'Angers saw only an "expression d'une fausse chaleur . . . ."[12]

The inauguration of the Arc de Triomphe took place on July 29, 1836, the sixth anniversary of the revolution that put Louis-Philippe on the throne. A medallion was struck for the occasion showing the king's profile superimposed on that of Napoleon.

People bought them as though they were holy medals. But the king was not present—it was too dangerous, there had been another attack on his life three weeks earlier. So Thiers, now head of the government, reviewed the troops alone. He overlooked mentioning the names of the sculptors in his address. Nor were they invited to the royal banquet at the Tuileries that evening where a crowd toasted Louis-Philippe for having brought Napoleon's monument to such noble completion.

By 1836 Thiers was no longer considered a friend to artists. For several years dissatisfaction had been mounting. They were angry because they knew he was committed to the arts and they had hoped he would introduce liberalizing measures into the national policy for the arts. But by 1834 it was clear that he would uphold past traditions. The artists remembered how when he took his place in the administration he had announced his "intention to stop refusing work and recompense for artists who were outside of academic circles. . . ." But now when an artist went to the ministry to put his name on the list of potential recipients of State commissions, the first question he was asked was, "Monsieur, êtes-vous allé à Rome?"[13] Further, the artists found Thiers presumptuous for announcing that he would complete the Napoleonic program of public monuments. And they found evidence at the Arc de Triomphe that he could not, in fact, carry out his grand plan, for he failed to commission anyone to execute a work to crown the entire arch. He had begun to ask for designs in 1834; many were submitted, but he never made a decision. This, too, was part of the dissatisfaction of July 29, 1836.

Rude made as many as twenty sketches for the top of the Arc de Triomphe. Only one is known. At the Louvre we can look at a pale drawing for the *Triumph of Bonaparte*—a beautiful young, nude, sword-bearing Caesar, astride his horse rearing up on the orb of Earth and accompanied by a wild and menacing eagle. The government of the Orleans monarch was continually seeking the right balance between its own identity and that of its identification with Napoleon. It is probable that in the mid-1830s a "Triumph of Bonaparte" would have tipped the scales too far in the direction of Bonapartism.

Rude must have felt considerably let down in the late 1830s. He suffered, as did many artists, from the growing conservatism of the July Monarchy. For Rude, the Arc de Triomphe, rather than beginning a brilliant public career, was the threshold of official neglect. 1838 was the last time he entered a Salon during the July Monarchy; it was the same year in which he tried to obtain a seat in the Academy, but he was strongly opposed and was never elected. He received almost no state commissions; what he did get failed to excite his imagination. Thiers asked him to do a *Marechal de Saxe* for Versailles in 1836 and

the following year requested him to make a copy of his own *Mercury* for the statesman's personal collection. The Ministry of the Interior came to him for a *Baptism of Christ* for the Madeleine in 1838; this was not Rude's kind of work and it shows.

But one great event in 1840 did brighten his days, as it did for many French people; it was the "Retour des Cendres."

Thiers took charge of the government for a second time on March 1, 1840. In doing so he took over a country assailed by dissensions and bitterness. As he moved to restore equilibrium, he hoped a public manifestation might aid in securing greater stability for the State. As so often in the past, he relied upon the magic of the emperor. The project he proposed was not new, but it was the ultimate move: to bring Napoleon's body back to France. Louis-Philippe announced on his own birthday, May 1, that his gift to the nation would be "les restes de Napoleon." He would send his son to Saint Helena to bring back the precious remains. Not everyone was pleased; Lamartine wrote: "Thiers himself is in the hands of the passions he has kindled. . . . The ashes of Napoleon are not extinguished and he blows on them. God save us."

Over the next six months the people of France, roused by the press and the government, sang songs and told stories about the expedition to Saint Helena and its meaning for the country. Finally on December 15 the "mountain of gold" bearing the body appeared beneath the Arc de Triomphe. Women knelt and crossed themselves as it passed; cries of "Vive Napoleon," "Vive l'Empereur" mingled with "A bas les traîtres!"—the latter referring to Louis-Philippe and his ministers. The veterans of Napoleon's old guard were there; they had gotten out their uniforms and stood close to his remains. At one point when municipal councilors asked them to move aside so that they might take the guards' places beside the casket, a captain from Côte d'or—Noisot—informed the officials that: "Those who have organized the festival have forgotten that the emperor always marches with his own guard."[14]

Rude met Captain Noisot that week. They were compatriots and almost the same age. Noisot, wounded at Esslingen, veteran of Wagram, Spain, and Moscow, present at Elba and at Waterloo, imprisoned by the Restoration government, after which, except for a brief tour in his old uniform during 1830, had retired to live with his memories in Fixin. The focus of his life was, and remained, Napoleon. As Rude's friend Maximin Legrand described it: "The passionate cult that he devoted to the emperor expressed itself in such a sympathetic fashion that it appealed even to people of the opposite religion."[15] Rude was hardly of another religion. He loved talking with Noisot, whom he would visit

99
Long Live the
Revolution, the
Republic, and
Especially the
Emperor!: The
Political Sculpture
of Rude

while on summer holidays in Burgundy. During one of these visits—probably 1844—Noisot spoke of his sadness because nowhere could he find a monument that really "recalled the man for whom he had so much love and for whom he had sacrificed everything."[16] So Rude promised him one, and the two agreed to place it on Noisot's land in Fixin.

Rude went back to Paris and to work. The idea of doing a Napoleon monument was not new to him. He had thought a great deal about it during the 1830s. But his initial *maquette* (Fig. 6) for Fixin was far from the triumphant spirit he projected in his drawing for the crown of the Arc de Triomphe. For here he modeled Napoleon as a partially nude cadaver covered by a cape, lying starkly on rocks, washed by waves, and bound by chains. He wanted a sculpture that would be realistic as well as monumental; the aura is solemn and the design conceived so that the rhythmic movements of crape, waves, and rocks come to rest in the imperial body. The conception is allied to a view of the burial on Saint Helena that was very much alive during the 1830s: that lonely tomb in the woods covered by a simple stone as a modern day Holy Sepulchre. This was depicted often in prints of the day. Another well-known image in popular prints was the body of Napoleon covered with the cape he had worn during the Battle of Marengo, just as it had been for two days after his death in May 1821.

Rude's "Dead Napoleon" is an example of the kind of transposition of Christian martyr iconography for the depiction of the deaths of contemporary heroes that David had used when he isolated the image of the bodies of Marat and of Le Pelletier de Saint Fargeau. In his *Marat* David had included the attributes of the passion and death much as earlier painters had depicted Christ. Like a religious image-maker, Rude wanted authentic reminders. He talked with Napoleon's valet, Marchand, who had been with the emperor when he died and was willing to lend Rude a "Death Mask" and a mantle of Marengo. The things of Napoleon's person, the things he had touched at crucial moments in his life, had now become relics.[17]

In his sketch for the Fixin monument Rude placed the eagle beside the body of the martyred Napoleon. It is an alert and watchful presence that still draws inspiration from the body. The concept echoed the thinking of many people during the July Monarchy who knew that, though Napoleon was in his tomb, Bonapartism was not dead. It also relates to the spirit of an 1830s popular print like "Ils n'ont plus peur" (Fig. 7) that bore the cautionary message: "Approchez doucement vous tous . . . car s'il se reveillait vous ne dormiriez plus. . . . ," telling the countries of Europe that the spirit of Napoleon's Empire could still become a force to reckon with in their midst.

By tradition it is believed that Noisot was the one to change Rude's mind about the kind of monument proper for Fixin. However the change came about, by the time Rude showed the large plaster in his studio in the spring of 1846, he had completely reversed the scenario. Now we have *The Awakening of Napoleon to Immortality* (Fig. 2) and the young Bonaparte is crowned with victor's laurels. The mantle of Marengo, no longer covering death, gives way to life; Napoleon's body begins to move, to push away the shroud, and to break the chains that fall upon the rocks over the "petit chapeau" of Eylau, the sword of Iena, and the oak leaves clustered on the rocks, each bearing the name of a victorious battle. Napoleon's body takes on life, while the eagle lies dead with his great broken wing over his body and his sharp long tongue limp upon the rock— "figure l'extinction de la splendeur matérielle de l'Empire, comme son maître en travail de résurrection en présage le retour spirituel."[18] The spirit of the "Awakened" Napoleon fills the remote Burgundian hillside with generative life. It was created as the idol of a powerful cult that had been developing in France since the early days of the Restoration, and on September 19, 1847, thousands of veterans came to Fixin to be with Noisot and Rude for the inauguration. Noisot gave an impassioned dedicatory speech, speaking of the "Christ moderne" whom he had followed to the ends of the earth. He was no longer thinking of the old emperor but of the young Bonaparte. The concept that lived in Fixin that day was much akin to that shown in a print of the 1830s (Fig. 8),[19] with the young general joined to but rising from the defeated emperor. Here is Bonaparte, the poetic figure of liberty, "représantant de la Révolution, absous par le malheur et purifié par la mort."[20] He was also the Man who broke his chains on the rocks of Saint Helena in 1840, calling out to his people: "J'attendais! . . . ." (Fig. 9), and the veterans had come. Among those present at Fixin in the fall of 1847 were surely some who had shouted "A bas les traîtres" in 1840. As the decade progressed, that spirit had become stronger. This Bonaparte of Burgundy was awakening to liberty; he was not the Napoleon of the Invalides imprisoned under the red porphyry of Emperors (the tomb of the Invalides was planned though not yet finished) by the regime. It is no wonder that there was no official representation that September in Fixin.

The only major sculpture Rude had in his studio in 1845 was his *Napoleon*. But in 1846 he was working on another important project that he approached in the same spirit in which he had come to *Napoleon*. Etienne Arago, one of France's leading republicans, asked Rude to make the tomb for Godefroi Cavaignac. His reply, as reported by Arago, was given with characteristic directness: Why speak about money? You want me to make a mausoleum for Godefroi Cavaignac—I will do it for nothing. Long ago I knew his father in Belgium; I even had the occasion to see Godefroi himself and I know what he was worth. I don't need anything else. I am happy to have been chosen to be the sculptor of his tomb.[21]

Godefroi Cavaignac had been the kind of radical most feared by Thiers and his government. He was the son of a regicide of the Convention who died in exile in Belgium. After the July Revolution, during which he was prominent on the barricades, Godefroi began systematically comparing the faint-heartedness of the present government to the greatness of the Republic. That was in the early 1830s, the same years during which Thiers would publicly repeat that contemporary Frenchmen felt horror when they heard the word "republic," for everyone knew that this "form of government turns to blood or imbecility." Godefroi was arrested in 1834, escaped to England in 1835, and returned in 1841. He helped found La Réforme and through it conspired against the government with words. He died on May 5, 1845, after a long illness. The following day his coworkers at La Réforme, under the leadership of Louis Blanc, wrote their editorial speaking of Godefroi's "haute mélancolie qui est la gloire et le tourment des natures d'élite." They told their readers that the best way to honor him was by carrying on the work of the Revolution that had consumed his life. They buried him in the Cemetery of Montmartre; the government was unable to stop the well attended funeral. He was laid beneath a simple stone. On May 25 La Réforme announced the opening of a public subscription for a sepulcher monument. Though donations came in steadily, even from republicans beyond French borders—from England and Mexico—there was not enough money to cover more than expenses. And so Arago made his hesitant approach to Rude. For Rude it was totally appropriate in 1846; here was another hero whose name was identified with the cause of liberty and who lay beneath a stone that did not indicate his greatness, just as Napoleon had lain for nineteen years following his death. Maximin Legrand understood perfectly:

He accepted happily. If this eagerness appears strange on the part of an artist who, concurrently and using the same motifs, was fashioning a bronze with which to sing the praises of the Empire, then one should note that the two expressions, which seem irreconcilable to us, were barely separated under Louis-Philippe. And under the Restoration they were absolutely identified. One thought about the Emperor as le petit caporal of the Revolution. He personified it and in his own life had realized equality![22]

The link between the two monuments is evident; for his Cavaignac (Fig. 3) Rude returned to his first sketch for the Napoleon monument. He laid out a cadaver—a body, stiff in death, skin taut, head thrown back, with craggy features and sunken cheeks—on a simple slab of marble. It is the starkest, most realistic work Rude ever made. He placed all focus on the body, the body as bearer of the evidence of this man's suffering for liberty. A piece of cloth laid upon the body both covers and reveals its form. The sole emblems to remind us of Cavaignac's struggle are the pen and the sword close to his right hand.

Rude had help in arriving at his conception. One of Godefroi's friends who was with the republican hero when he died was Philippe-Auguste Jeanron, the painter who would soon play such an important role in protecting the arts during the Revolution of 1848. Together with Arago, Jeanron made the death mask that aided Rude in his work. Evidently he also made some sort of visual record, for it was described by Théophile Thoré in La Réforme five days after Cavaignac's death:

The head of Cavaignac explains marvelously this character of a moral man, one who was just and courageous. After the last breath his face kept the sign of a superb serenity which is even more accentuated with the repose of death. The harsh veil of death like the draperies of a fine Greek monument firmly reveals the principal planes of the structure and then illuminates them. . . . Thus, the features of the character of Cavaignac are resplendent on his death bed attended by his overwhelmed friends. What a beautiful image to keep in a faithfully executed painting![23]

Jeanron was on the committee to oversee the tomb; his visual and verbal descriptions of the great civic martyr's death must have inspired Rude.

Eck and Durand cast both the Napoleon and the Cavaignac in 1847, and Rude put them on view in his studio during the summer—first the Cavaignac and a few weeks later the Napoleon. The press described them together, and the subversive nature of their combined force could not have been overlooked. Just as there were no officials present at Fixin for the inauguration of the Napoleon, there was no inauguration of the Cavaignac (it finally took place in 1856, the year after Rude's death). But Rude must have felt proud that summer; people poured into his studio and wept over the figures they found there. He had never done more beautiful work, and it had sprung from his deepest personal convictions.

Rude lived through the turmoil of the 1848 spring, once again as a man involved in the present and the future of his country. He showed at the Salon for the first time in a decade. In March the people of Dijon considered asking him to be their representative in the Provisional Government of the Second Republic (just as the people of Maine et Loire had asked David d'Angers to serve). Rude felt about this in much the same way he felt about his two great monuments: he would give himself without reserve. "I will tell you simply that I am a radical democrat," he wrote to his countrymen.[24] In the end he did not serve as a legislator (the prefect of Dijon had the wisdom to think twice about the candidacy), but he

6
The Imperial Eagle Watching Over the Dead Napoleon, Musée de Dijon, 1844–1845. (Photo: Musée de Dijon)

7
''Ils n'ont plus peur,'' Collection de Vinck, Cabinet des Estampes, Bibliothèque Nationale, Paris), ca. 1832. (Photo: Bibliotèque Nationale, Paris)

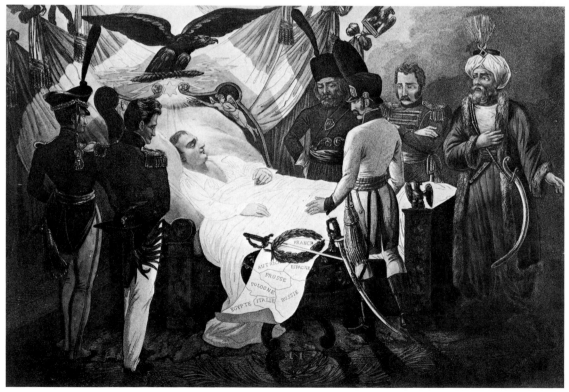

8
Le Songe, lithograph by Delpech,
Cabinet des Estampes, Bibliothèque
Nationale, Paris, early 1830s. (Photo:
Bibliothèque Nationale, Paris)

9
"J'attendais! . . . .," October 15, 1840,
Cabinet des Estampes, Bibliothèque
Nationale, Paris. (Photo: Bibliothèque
Nationale, Paris)

10
Marshal Ney, terracotta sketch, Musèe
de Dijon, ca. 1848–1850. (Photo:
Musée de Dijon)

served his country by setting up a colossal allegory in plaster of the *Republic* in front of the Panthéon for the Fête des Ecoles in May. Nothing permanent came of it; in June cannon shot of another revolutionary action pulverized the fragile piece.

The Second Republic, as a patron of the arts, has been judged a failure; its programs for a state art came to very little.[25] Though this is true, a number of ideas did take root during the days that followed the February Revolution. One of them was important for Rude. The government decided that Marshal Ney, executed by decree of Louis XVIII in 1815, was due national honor. Even during the Restoration many recognized that the execution of Marshal Ney had been a blunder. For all his mistakes, this particular marshal was a hero of extraordinary popularity. He alone had saved the honor of the French army in Russia. There had been petitions before the government of the July Monarchy for his remains to be moved to the Panthéon and for a monument to be erected in his memory. People visited the wall where he was shot as if it were a national shirine.

When Louis-Napoleon Bonaparte became the first president of the new Republic, the French people found that they had actually elected a Bonaparte and they hoped he would, indeed, be a savior of their society. Throughout 1849 he presented himself as the defender of the rights of the people while, in fact, he was the chief of a government becoming ever more restrictive. It was during the spring of 1850, at a time when he was quite involved in new repressive measures (that is, a law denying the vote to anyone ever found guilty of an offense in the courts) that he first received reports of the project, which had been dormant for almost two years. Ferdinand Barrot told the Prince-président in his report of March 5 that the moment had come to execute this monument, which would translate so well "un des plus vifs et des profonds sentiments du pays." Barrot stated that by the nature of the memories it awakened, it should be "austere and of great simplicity." It was to stand on the place near the Observatory where Ney had died "without a single witness save that of his executioners." Barrot said that he felt sure the Prince-président did not want a monument to the man the emperor had called the "brave des braves" to be "a public testimony to a bad memory, but rather a sign of the rehabilitation already proclaimed by the cry of public consciousness." Then he went on to describe the proposed monument: "it will represent Marshal Ney pointing to his chest and opening his heart to death," and he assured the president that he had chosen "one of our greatest sculptors" to carry out the work.[26] He did not mention Rude by name, but other communications make it clear that Rude had already been the choice in 1848.[27]

De Fourcaud has suggested that Rude must have been thinking about such a statue since 1838 when he made André Dupin's bust. Dupin had been Ney's lawyer, and during the hours he sat for the sculptor evidently he recounted the details of the trial and execution.

There is still another personal note in the background of Rude's monument to Ney: Rude believed that his own life had been tied to Ney's confused political journey. Ney had played a significant role in securing Napoleon's abdication in 1814: he then vowed allegiance to Louis XVIII and went at his bidding to capture Napoleon in the spring of 1815. But rather than arrest the emperor, he joined him. At some point in his life Rude recollected that Ney's change of loyalties took place in Dijon, that as he and his friends ran through the streets shouting "Vive l'Empereur" they were joined by Ney's troops. This story was never questioned until the twentieth century, when De Fourcaud took note of the fact that Ney did not pass through Dijon before he met with Napoleon at Auxerre. De Fourcaud did not doubt that the elderly Rude remembered such an incident, as it was recorded by Rude's contemporary biographers, but he believed that Rude had compounded two incidents: that of taking to the streets and encountering troops after receiving the news of Napoleon's presence in France, and one involving the presence of Ney in Dijon after his reconciliation with Bonaparte.[28]

Barrot must have seen Rude's first sketch (Fig. 10) before he wrote his letter to Louis-Napoleon. Rude represented Ney in civilian clothes looking at his executioners, his body still, his head bare, chin high—an elegant, severe, proud man. Only the thick coat, which Ney pulls back with his left hand as he indicates "right to the heart," moves. It is in the spirit of the first sketch for the Napoleon monument and of the Cavaignac tomb. As he had for the two earlier works, Rude thought intensely about the death of the great man and gathered every detail he could about the moment it occurred. In addition to what he learned from Dupin, he spoke with the concierge at the Observatory, who had helped carry the body back to the Hospice de la Maternité, and who loved to evoke "l'ombre ensanglantée du vaillant homme."[29] He must have looked at the prints that were made at the time of Ney's death, some published in England, others in France during the 1830s (Fig. 11). And Rude was able to visualize how his monument would look each day as he passed the wall where it would stand, but a short distance from his home and studio.

The president approved the project, but it never went any further in 1850 because of insufficient funds. Barrot's successor, F. de Persigny, also wrote to the Prince-président about the Ney project. This was in the spring of 1852; Louis-Napoleon had just

11
*Mort du Mar*échal Ney, Cabinet des
Estampes, Bibliothèque Nationale,
Paris. (Photo: Bibliothèque Nationale,
Paris)

12
Poster for "Les Négriers," Paris, 1973.
(Photo: Author)

accomplished his coup d'état and was about to give France another empire. The spirit of the monument had changed:

It appears to me, in effect, that this monument should not be considered just a tardy rehabilitation, but it should be an homage to the memory of one of our greatest military figures, the hero of Moscow.

It is necessary then, while conserving the simple and austere character given to it initially, to give more importance to it by realizing a greater connection with the personage to whom it is consecrated . . . by [creating] a statue representing him in military dress.[30]

This is no longer the work of a republican government that would expose a monarch's injustice against a hero of the people; it is the work of an empire directing attention to one of its own past heroes.

Rude went to work again, now with explicit orders for a military figure. He left aside his first, and probably preferred, sketch of the stoic hero at the moment of death to create the figure of a leader in action. He first developed the powerful body in the nude, one that turns in space with strong contrapposto, then a *maquette* in which he developed the uniform, the boots, the sword, and sheath to elaborate further the dominant diagonals of the design. In the final work (Fig. 4) he gave Ney's face that shout and noisy aura of a military leader which echoes the cry and the pose of *La Marseillaise* done twenty years earlier. The finished monument is rich in detail. Rude wanted to fuse the energy and action expressed in the gesture and the face with a careful description of reality in the uniform and the objects around the base. His aim was to give both the intensity of a moment—we learn from the scroll at Ney's feet that it is "le 7 Septembre 1812," and to show that this is the "Ordre du jour. . . ." from Napoleon on the day of the day of the Battle of Borodino—and the type of action that could stand as a symbol for the entire meaning of a person's life. Rude finished it in less than a year and had it back from Eck and Durant ready for mounting by spring. The inauguration took place on December 7, 1853, the thirty-eighth anniversary of Ney's death, on the spot where he was killed.

Of the four sculptures examined, *Marshal Ney* is the one whose import and substance probably carries the least meaning for us today. Rude responded to a hero's martyrdom, while the regime wanted a fighting general; so the man of action was placed a bit incongrously beside the wall of death. And the new Empire was honoring the military success of the old Empire at the very moment when Louis-Napoleon was proclaiming "l'Empire, c'est la Paix." If its meaning was fuzzy in 1853, it was not helped at the end of the century when work on a railway forced the city to move *Marshal Ney* to a spot at a nearby confluence of two busy streets in front of the charming old restaurant of the Symbolists, the Closerie des Lilas. There it remains, a bit out of place, but, nevertheless, a brilliantly executed figure suggesting something of the glory and swagger of Napoleon's wars.

Each of the other three monuments, however, can still tell us something about certain political feelings in France: *La Marseillaise* has come to stand for the entire Arc de Triomphe and stands so firmly in the imagination of people that it is an immediately recognizable image with enormous power when turned into a symbol of oppression (Fig. 12). The *Cavaignac* remains one of the most austere Republican monuments in its place among the people of Paris in the cemetery of Montmartre. As for *The Napoleon Awakening to Immortality* amidst the forest of pines from Corsica planted by Noisot in Fixin, with its "hundred steps" in the woods to symbolize the "Hundred Days," and Noisot's fortress grave on the edge of the hill, it is a total ambient dominated by the spirit of Bonapartism where twentieth-century people can learn well how nineteenth-century Frenchmen felt about Napoleon.

In order to make such images, it was necessary for Rude to feel the force of the ideas behind them. As his commitment mounted, his style took on the new strains of romanticism and of realism. Both contributed to his ability to project his ideas. When Rude relinquished the neoclassicism that he knew best, it was neither due to a lack of stylistic identity nor to a simple evolution from the style of youth to a personal one of maturity. Rather it was part of the acquisition by a nineteenth-century artist of his full power as a sculptor—to be able to have at his command more than one style in order to respond adequately to the multiple demands of a complicated and changing culture. It was parallel to his ability as a citizen to embrace divergent political ideas, not through a well-worked out intellectual analysis but through a full emotional response to the moment. To study a career like Rude's is to be continually aware of both stylistic and ideological flexibility. It is also to recognize artistic achievement in the face of repression. If, after the Arc de Triomphe sculpture was completed, the government had continued to engage Rude in work worthy of his talents, and if he had been active during the 1840s, it is unlikely that he would have created either the *Napoleon* or the *Cavaignac*.

If there is anything unifying Rude's political sculptures—a people's army, a conqueror of Europe and his general, a fighter for working-class justice—it is his sense of the hero. These men were all heroes to Rude; Napoleon was the greatest of them all. Rude was able to realize his most concentrated effort in sculptural form in the 1840s, during the final period of a repressive monarchy but when the

107
Long Live the
Revolution, the
Republic, and
Especially the
Emperor!: The
Political Sculpture
of Rude

memory of the "Retour des Cendres" was still alive. The decade has been beautifully described by Henrich Heine, who wrote after the "Retour des Cendres":

The Emperor is dead. With him was extinguished the last hero fashioned according to the ancient taste, and now we have the new world of the grocery people who breathe with greater ease as if extricated from a brilliant nightmare. Upon the imperial tomb awoke a bourgeois and industrial era which admires other heroes, like the virtuous Lafayette or the cotton mill maker James Watt.[32]

Rude was of that "ancient taste." If he had lived through the Second Empire, he surely would have found it difficult to have made the same kinds of statements in sculpture, taking inspiration from his very personal political feelings, for it was a make-believe Empire led by a new Napoleon who was anything but a hero.

Notes

The research for this paper, aided by a grant from the American Philosophical Society, was carried out in Paris and Dijon during the summer of 1973. I took pleasure and benefited greatly from conversations with Nicole Villa at the Cabinet des Estampes of the Bibliothèque Nationale, Gérard Hubert, Conservateur at the Museum of Malmaison, and Pierre Quarré, Conservateur at the Museum of Fine Arts in Dijon. I also wish to give substantial thanks to H. W. Janson for his ever insightful comments on my manuscript.

1
Théophile Silvestre, Les Artistes français, (Paris: G. Charpentier, 1878), p. 191.

2
Letter of April 16, 1827. Louis De Fourcaud, François Rude, sculpteur, ses oeuvres et son temps (Paris: 1904), pp. 124–125.

3
Ibid., p. 178.

4
Letter of January 19, 1832. Ibid., pp. 157–158.

5
Archives nationales F¹³1030. See De Fourcaud, p. 195.

6
Antoine Etex, Les Souvenirs d'un Artiste (Paris: E. Dentu, 1877), p. 192.

7
Archives nationales F²¹579.

8
Rude wrote to Blouet on October 14, 1833 to tell him that he could come by his atelier to take the measurements of the piece. Letter in the Bibliothèque Doucet, Paris.

9
Stanislas Lami, Dictionnaire des sculpteurs de l'école française au dix-neuvième siècle (Paris: 1914–21), IV: 204.

10
De Fourcaud, p. 220.

11
Gustave Planche, Portraits d'artistes (Paris: 1853), II: 199–200.

12
David d'Angers, Les Carnets (Paris: André Bruel, 1958), II: 89.

13
L'Artiste, Ser. I, VIII (August 1834): 28.

14
J. Lucas-Dubreton, Le Culte de Napoléon (Paris: Editions Albin Michel, 1960), p. 377.

15
[Dr. Maximin Legrand], Rude, sa vie, ses oeuvre, son enseignement (Paris: Dentu, 1856), p. 59.

16
Notice sur le monument élevé à Napoléon à Fixin (Côte d'Or) le 19 septembre 1847 (Dijon: Imprimerie Loireau-Feuchot, 1847), p. 10.

17
The statue of Napoleon by Seurre which was raised to the top of the Vendôme Column on July 28, 1833 can probably be seen as the first sculptural "Apotheosis of Napoleon." And Seurre, too, had borrowed "authentic" models to use when modeling his statue—a sword and a uniform used by Napoleon.

18
Lucas-Dubreton, p. 407.

19
Mlle. Nicole Villa has suggested that this is a work of the 1830s because of the references to Egypt which were then so in vogue. Also it relates to other works by Delpech in the 1830s.

20
Heinrich Heine, De la France, p. 120. Quoted by Lucas-Dubreton, p. 311.

21
De Fourcaud, p. 310.

22
Legrand, p. 87.

23
Théophile Thoré, "Portrait de Cavaignac," La Réforme (May 10, 1845).

24
This letter of March 30, 1848, was published in the Dijon journal, La République (I, April 12, 1848). See De Fourcaud, p. 347.

25
See T. J. Clark, The Absolute Bourgeois (Greenwich, Connecticut: New York Graphic Society, 1973), pp. 70–71.

26
Archives nationales F²¹583. The letter has been published by Gabriel Vauthier, "La statue du maréchal Ney," La Révolution de 1848, 27 (December 1930–February 1931), pp. 249–50.

27
De Fourcaud, p. 373. Gérard Hubert, "Nouvelles Esquisses de Rude," La Revue des Arts (September 1952), p. 174.

28
De Fourcaud, p. 368.

29
Ibid., pp. 87–88.

30
Ibid., p. 374.

31
Heinrich Heine, Lutèce [letters on the political, artistic, and social life in France written for the Gazette of Augsburg, 1840–1843 (Paris: Calmann Levy Editeur, 1892)], letter of January 11, 1841, p. 161.

6
The Revolutionary Theme in Russian Realism

Alison Hilton

"Truth to Life" was the fundamental idea of the Russian realist movement of the 1860s to 1880s. It meant more to the artists concerned than refusal to idealize the depictions of rural villages, woodland meadows, and peasants that dominated most of their exhibitions. For them, as for many contemporary writers, the very choice of a subject was necessarily a realistic choice and represented the concerns and values of their own times.

The realist philosophy was stated by Nikolai G. Chernyshevskii (1828–1889) in his master's essay, "The Aesthetic Relations of Art to Reality" (1853, published 1855). Chernyshevskii wrote that art was man's means of contact with life, the vehicle for understanding and responding to the experiences life presented. He insisted that art, like any creative work, was a moral activity that must not only reflect but also probe into phenomena in the physical, social, and moral spheres.[1]

Chernyshevskii was a major contributor to the radical journal *Contemporary (Sovremennik)* until 1862, when he was arrested for disseminating anti-government ideas and sentenced to hard labor in Siberia. He suffered the chilling ritual of a civil execution, which deprived him officially of citizenship and identity; his name was not permitted in print, but he became a hero to a generation of students and other so-called "new people." Sporadic rescue attempts during the politically tense late 1870s only caused his sentence to be extended and he was not released until 1883, so exhausted that he died six years later. In 1862, while still in prison, Chernyshevskii completed the novel *What Is To Be Done?*, which, thanks to fortuitous oversights by the police and censors, was published in *Contemporary* in 1863.[2] Subtitled "Tales about New People," it was intended to encourage those people who were trying to break down some of the most restrictive traditions of Russian society. Chernyshevskii urged young people to make themselves independent of their parents and conventional society and to lead useful lives; he suggested the formation of communal workshops in which property, profits, and responsibility for mutual well-being would be shared. This hopeful solution to the practical problems of life was widely adopted in the 1870s. "*What Is To Be Done?* fired the minds of a whole generation; it was read with passion, in tattered, printed, or hand-written copies, and preserved, together with other prohibited literature and pictures of the politicals," the artist Ilia Repin later wrote.[3]

Influenced by Chernyshevskii's essay on aesthetics and *What Is To Be Done?*, the painter Ivan Kramskoi (1837–1887) led the secession of a group of young art students from the Petersburg Academy of Arts in 1863, in protest over the authoritarian conditions of the diploma competition of that year.[4] For their economic survival, the group founded a cooperative art workshop, replaced in 1870 by the Association of Traveling Art Exhibitions, called the *Peredvizhniki*, or Wanderers, for short. The Wanderers' major activity was the organization of traveling exhibitions, which brought art, chiefly realist painting that dealt with subjects meaningful to ordinary people, not only to the two capital cities, Petersburg and Moscow, but also to provincial towns. This program was comparable to that of the populists, who took medicine, education, and other aid to the people of the provinces during the same period.[5]

The government fought the populist movement by closing universities, censoring publications, and, beginning in 1874, arresting the populists on a wholesale scale. Many of the leading activists went abroad or underground; during the next decade some began to engage in terrorism against the tsar and high officials.[6] After many attempts, the hardcore group The People's Will assassinated the tsar with a bomb on March 1, 1881, but this was a suicidal victory. Within three years, nearly all the terrorists were captured and most of the leaders were executed. During this ten-year revolutionary period, about 1874 to 1884, the probing, moral aspect of realist art was put to the test. Artists who sympathized with populist ideals had to decide how far they could go in accepting terrorism and how clearly they could reveal their political views. To paint a political subject was in itself a moral decision. Perhaps more difficult for some artists than judging the revolutionaries' goals was analyzing honestly the real situation and questioning the validity of terrorism as a means of bringing better political and social conditions.

Explicit statements made by some of the artists and their associates reveal their concern over the moral issues raised by political events and their determination to search out the truth of these issues. Years before his break away from the Academy, Kramskoi wrote: "The true artist has an enormous task: to hold up a mirror before the face of the people . . . that will make their hearts beat in alarm."[7] Ilia Repin (1844–1930) who, while still a student at the Academy had become a follower of Kramskoi, wrote in his letters and memoirs about his concern for current events and he painted an important group of works dealing with incidents and issues of the revolutionary period. In 1883, when he was planning his major work on a revolutionary subject, *They Did Not Expect Him* (Fig. 1), he wrote to a friend: "With all my meager strength I strive to embody my ideas in truth. The life around me upsets me too much; it gives me no rest, but demands the canvas. Reality is too shocking to allow one to embroider its patterns peacefully, like a well-bred young lady."[8] A short time after the assassination, he

stated his intention to put his art at the service of the "best" element in Russia, those people, who through their "disinterested and heroic actions" sought to bring good to their country, "having faith in her future and fighting for this idea."[9]

Repin, not an exceptionally politically minded person, was very much a product of both the political and the artistic situation of his time. The intense moral basis of some of his work of the 1870s and 1880s conformed to the chief point of the realist philosophy. This moral involvement focused on the major political conflict of the time, the struggle between the revolutionaries and the government.[10]

How did the realists' commitment work out in terms of actual paintings? How did the artists' sense of their moral obligation affect the styles of their art, and, conversely, how did their efforts to visually represent political ideas contribute to the development of these ideas? Some artists evidently toned down their political message in order to get their works exhibited. Some works with very explicit political content, such as Repin's *Arrest of a Propagandist* (Fig. 8) and *Revolutionary Woman Awaiting Execution* (Fig. 4), were not exhibited until the mid-1890s, when the events that inspired them were long past. Nevertheless, equally overt political works like *They Did Not Expect Him* were exhibited and discussed at great length in the press, in articles representing all shades of critical opinion. To some extent the critical dividing line between political ephemera and high art dealing with major human issues lay in the sphere of style rather than content.

In order to examine in concrete terms the relationship between the political intentions of the Russian realists and their handling of their subjects, I have focused on the work of Repin. Repin is the best known and most thoroughly documented Russian nineteenth-century artist[11] and his works on revolutionary subjects cover a wide range of themes treated by the realists as a group. Further, *They Did Not Expect Him* has been considered from the time of its first exhibition to be a masterpiece of politically motivated painting. The first part of this paper will discuss some aspects of revolutionary iconography, themes, and symbols developed by Repin and other artists during the 1870s and early 1880s. The second part concerns a group of Repin's political paintings, culminating in *They Did Not Expect Him*. In discussing the styles of these works, I will suggest ways in which Repin sought to rise above the charge of producing merely topical work[12] and asserted the importance of both his theme and his style, his moral and artistic integrity.

The Concept of the Revolutionary

Two basic elements, the representational and the symbolic, can be recognized in most paintings on revolutionary subjects. An individual political figure might be portrayed as an agitator, a prisoner, or an exile (represented in a specific action or situation), but he might also be universalized in some way, identified symbolically as a prophet or messiah, a redeemer of mankind. This kind of symbolic expansion of the particular and concrete is a key concept in Russian realism. Chernyshevskii had written that the function of art was not only to represent life but also to interpret it and to serve as a guide or handbook for those unable to read life directly from its sources.[13] The Russian artist, seeking to make his ideas about political issues as clear as possible to his audience, would try to make use of familiar images or, as Kramskoi wrote, "natural language . . . accessible to all."[14]

Kramskoi's *Christ in the Desert* (Fig. 2) symbolizes, through a familiar, iconlike image of Christ, the choice between good and evil that every man must make.[15] Although it does not portray a revolutionary, it represents the moral struggle that an artist, revolutionary, or any thinking person, must go through at some crucial moment. According to Repin, Kramskoi interpreted Christ's struggle in the desert against the temptation of Satan as a symbol of the universal struggle against "the dark side of human nature."[16]

Illuminating a complex idea by means of a well-known religious image was a common technique of radical writers, whose works were always subject to censorship. The related technique of embodying a universal in a particular object, the concept of the "type" embodied in an individual entity or personality introduced by the critic Vissarion Belinskii in the mid-1830s, was also stressed by Chernyshevskii: "A work of art must contain as little of the abstract as possible; everything in it must be . . . expressed concretely in living scenes and individual images."[17] This concept of types was extremely important for the representation of revolutionary subjects. Many figures appearing in such paintings were not actual portraits but were composites of the traits of several individuals, based partly on photographs of the "politicals," which were widely distributed at one time.[18] These generalized revolutionary types came to be as easily recognized as any religious image of previous centuries. One of these types, the young woman student or *kursistka,* was painted a number of times by Repin, Nikolai Iaroshenko (1846–1898), and Vladimir Makovskii (1846–1920). The kursistka came into being with the opening of higher education to women in the 1860s; because of the unrest among students during these years many conservatives associated the kursistka and the "advanced" woman generally with disruptive, anti-government tendencies.[19] A drawing by Iaroshenko, entitled *Progressivist* (Fig. 3) illustrates this type. The best known portrayal of this figure, Iaroshenko's *Kursistka* (1883,

Kiev, Museum of Russian Art), aroused a storm of controversy when it was first exhibited. Conservative critics complained of the "unsound tendentiousness" in the painting, while more liberal writers declared that the artist had depicted "a new type in our society" with great sympathy and intelligence.[20]

The populist critic Gleb Uspenskii, a close friend of the artist, published an article analyzing the painting and the repository of conflicting attitudes toward the "woman question" which it aroused. He interpreted this positive image of the woman student as the embodiment of a new ideal. Her self-sufficiency, so disturbing to some, was a quality to be cherished because it gave to the face "an extraordinary light of thought and spirit." Uspenskii concluded that the artist had created, in one figure, not only the prototype of the new woman but the representative of the "new people," who would bring about the most far-reaching social changes.[21]

Images of this sort had multiple connotations, just as symbols from older art and religious tradition had. Of course the women students and women revolutionaries painted by Iaroshenko and others, though typified, were based primarily on real people of whom the artists and the public knew a considerable amount through rumors or the press. One of Repin's most unflinching and convincing portrayals of such a figure is *Revolutionary Woman Awaiting Execution* (Fig. 4). It was probably painted at the time of the arrests of the terrorists after the assassination of the tsar. "What a time of nightmare that was," Repin later wrote, "pure horror . . . and I remember the placards bearing the inscription 'regicide' that hung on their chests."[22] The large painting was exhibited in St. Petersburg only in 1896, and even then it bore the ambiguous title *Anguish.* It is possible, as some who saw the painting in 1896 thought, that Repin based the figure of the solitary prisoner on Vera Figner, one of the leaders of the terrorists' Executive Committee, who was captured some time after the execution of the regicides and sentenced to life imprisonment instead of hanging because of the public outcry at the execution of Sophia Perovskaya.[23] The identification is plausible in that Figner had been in contact with Iaroshenko, Uspenskii, and other friends of Repin, though it is uncertain whether Repin ever met her; in any event, Repin did follow the trials and he must have known about Figner's defense speech, in which she declared that the absolute power of the autocracy could only be broken by terrorism.[24] The woman in Repin's painting bears no close likeness to photographs of Vera Figner or the other well-known woman revolutionaries; it is not a portrait but rather a generalized image that combines the forward-looking intelligence of Iaroshenko's woman student and the fatalistic courage of one who, like Kramskoi's Christ, understands and accepts her fate.

1
I. E. Repin, *They Did Not Expect Him*
(Ne zhadli), 1883–1888, Moscow,
Tretiakov Gallery. (Photo: Tretiakov
Gallery)

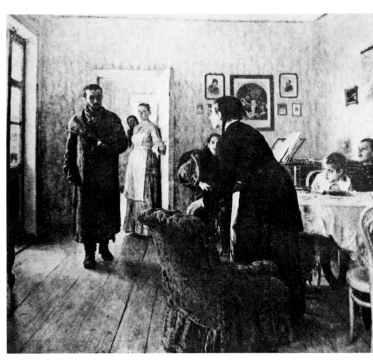

2
I. N. Kramskoi, *Christ in the Desert,*
1872, Moscow, Tretiakov Gallery.
(Photo: Tretiakov Gallery)

3
N. Iaroshenko, *Progressivist,* 1878,
Moscow, Tretiakov Gallery. (Photo:
Academy of Arts Research Photo-
Archive, Leningrad)

4
Repin, *Revolutionary Woman Await-
ing Execution,* n.d., ca. 1884, Prague,
National Gallery. (Photo: *Repin:
Khudozhestvennoe Nasledstvo,*
Moscow, 1948, 1, 176)

Aside from the real-life revolutionaries, there were some important models or companions for these universalized portraits in the works of writers associated with Repin and the Wanderers. Indeed, the relationship between the works of writers and artists is an important aspect of the development of the revolutionary theme.

Nikolai Nekrasov, an editor of the *Contemporary* and the foremost populist poet of Russia, was admired by all the realist artists. One of his most famous poems, "Russian Women" (1872–1873), was based on the accounts of two noblewomen, wives of the Decembrists who followed their exiled husbands to Siberia in 1825. Nekrasov treated these women, who gave up homes, families, and hereditary privileges to become "one with the common people," as personifications of the courage, self-sacrifice, and endurance of Russian women.[25]

Chernyshevskii's more prosaic and contemporary heroine of *What Is To Be Done?* escaped from her vulgar and mercenary parents by means of a "legal marriage" to a medical student and resolved to make herself useful to society by establishing a cooperative workshop for seamstresses and by studying medicine. The lives of Vera Pavlovna and her friends illustrate the ramifications of certain ethical issues, including the right, or duty, of the "new people" to live according to their own convictions, even at the risk of hurting others. The immediate problem in the novel is whether Vera and the two men who love her can live together or must make some compromise in order to continue as accepted and productive members of a society less advanced than they. Although they compromise, Chernyshevskii's epilogue offers the hope of a future society in which individuals' needs and obligations will be more rationally balanced.

Many young radicals of the 1860s and '70s were actually faced with similar personal conflicts. Willing to risk their own lives, they had to fear the penalties that might ruin their friends and families. Vera Figner's memoirs, for example, are full of concern for her mother and sisters, especially when, as a leader of The People's Will, she must break all ties with them.

In painting, the importance of family ties is shown in a simple and direct way in Vladimir Makovskii's (1846–1920) *The Acquitted Woman* (Fig. 5), in which a woman, obviously not an important terrorist, joyously greets her child, her sister and old parents in a police station. Repin's painting of a political exile's unexpected return deals with the relationship of the revolutionary to his family and the conflict of political and personal obligations in a much less simple and conclusive way. In *They Did Not Expect Him*, this relationship stands for issues beyond the plight of the individual. It is worth noting, however, that the original version of the work,

The Unexpected Return (Fig. 6), shows, instead of a man, a young woman who is clearly a sister of Iaroshenko's *Kursistka*.[26] Even without a textual explanation, it is evident that this woman is not returning to her sisters but is stopping only to say goodbye for the last time. She holds a satchel and wears a clumsy overcoat and cap and stands sturdily apart from the others. She has already gone, politically, far beyond them, having accepted the "Revolutionary Catechism" of Bakunin's followers: "Hard with himself, he must be hard toward others. All the tender feelings of family life, of friendship, love and gratitude, and even honor must be stifled in him by a single cold passion for the revolutionary cause."[27] This oath is one item from a long pamphlet smuggled into Russia by Bakunin's associate Nechaev; it was discovered by the police, decoded, and made public at the Nechaev conspiracy trial of 1871, which Dostoevskii used as background for his novel *The Possessed*.

Vera Zasulich, a member of the Nechaev circle, whose trial in 1878 aroused more attention than almost any other event that year, may have provided a model for Repin's young revolutionary. Zasulich had shot the Governor of St. Petersburg, the notorious General Trepov, in full view of a group of petitioners; though she did not kill him, there was no doubt of her intention. However, the jury acquitted her, and thanks to the confusion caused by a violent demonstration, she managed to escape police detention and get out of the country. The trial was considered a victory for the populists. The liberal press praised the jury and made hopeful references to the French Revolution and Charlotte Corday.[28] The authorities reacted by curtailing the jury system and suppressing newspaper reports on Zasulich. For both sides, the trial was a catalyst. At this point, too, the public was courted by both radical and conservative press. Repin and Iaroshenko, who had some contact with liberal circles, were apparently more concerned with current events and more sympathetic to the radicals than most of their artist colleagues were.[29] The young writer Vsevolod Garshin, who became a friend of Repin at about this time, created a third type of revolutionary heroine in his short novel *Nadezhda Nikolaevna* (1885).[30] This heroine was not a populist or a "progressive" woman, but a true terrorist, almost certainly inspired by Vera Zasulich and her trial.

The story is especially relevant because it deals with an artist's effort to express his political sympathies in a work of art. The narrator, the painter Lopatin, envisions a portrait of Charlotte Corday that would embody all the strength, fanaticism, and tragedy of this legendary champion of the people. He cannot find the right model until he meets a prostitute, Nadezhda Nikolaevna, whose air of hopelessness and dignity overwhelms him. For him, she becomes Charlotte Corday. Lopatin almost completes his painting when an enraged colleague, a former client of the prostitute, suddenly attacks the artist and his model and kills Nadezhda. The artist goes mad and can think of nothing but his portrait of the French terrorist, a solemn, powerful, full-length figure striding forward. Garshin's description of the portrait is so close to Iaroshenko's *Kursistka* that it might have been deliberately intended to remind readers of the painting. The portrait of Charlotte Corday contained the essential qualities of the woman student, the intelligence and determination, raised to a higher pitch. At the same time, the truly religious fanaticism that Garshin attributes to Corday unites this figure with a more generalized image of a Christlike sacrificial victim.[31]

Identification of the revolutionary with Christ depends on a traditional Russian interest in sacrificial victims, rooted in the Orthodox martyrology. In the nineteenth century, the meaning of the incarnation of Christ and the humanity of Jesus was examined by such artists as Alexander Ivanov and Nikolai Ge and Ivan Kramskoi. Ivanov's monumental painting, *The Appearance of the Messiah to the People* (1837–1858, Moscow, Tretiakov Gallery), and Ge's *Last Supper* (1863, Leningrad, Russian Museum) were both thematic and philosophical sources for Kramskoi's interpretation of Christ's role and for various representations of the revolutionaries who tried to save the Russian people.[32] By the end of the 1870s, it seemed to some that the revolutionaries, along with the Russian people, were doomed to crucifixion: a belief that Dostoevskii developed in his "Legend of the Grand Inquisitor." This changing interpretation of the symbolic identification of the revolutionary hero with Christ can be seen in the political paintings of Repin.

Repin and the Revolutionary Theme

As a student at the Petersburg Academy in 1866, Repin witnessed the execution of Dmitrii Karakozov, the first of many terrorists who failed to kill the tsar.[33] He may also have come into contact with revolutionaries during his three-year term (1873–1876) as an Academy pensioner in Paris; he lived in Montmartre, collected local stories of the Paris Commune, and asked his correspondents for reading matter on French history, particularly the 1848 revolution and the Commune.[34] Repin began to paint revolutionary subjects upon his return from France, just after the mass arrests of the populists, and he continued to record political events and express his own attitudes toward them in a series of works throughout the following decade.

Among Repin's first paintings of revolutionaries, *Guarded Convoy on a Muddy Road* (Fig. 7), shows an open wagon in which a prisoner, presumably one of the populists arrested in 1874, is being conveyed toward Siberia. The painting is very small, done in a sketchlike manner that vividly conveys the physical sensation of a cold, gloomy drizzle. It is a generalized, rather romantic image, which communicates sympathy for the exile without analyzing the situation or raising political questions.

In *Arrest of a Propagandist,* begun in 1878 (Fig. 8), Repin explores the motivations of the activists and the reactions of the people they tried to change. A revolutionary has just been apprehended. Incriminating pamphlets are scattered about. The peasant woman who has boarded him looks out fearfully from behind a doorway, while a group of villagers watch unemotionally from the far end of the room.

All the types in a peasant village are represented, and the picture is thus a microcosm of Russian rural life.[35] Focusing on one dramatic moment, the painting is also a compendium of the activity and goals of the populists. In one sense it is a documentary work, illustrating the dangers caused by the peasants' distrust of the intelligensia, as described in the memoirs of Vera Figner and other activists. Yet the main point of the work lies in the composition itself. Some of Repin's preparatory drawings, particularly one of 1879 (Fig. 9), resemble Rembrandt's *Hundred Guilder Print* and *Christ Preaching* to the extent that Repin may indeed have used these readily available models, directly or indirectly, as sources for his composition.[36] A study of this relationship may elucidate Repin's interpretation of his subject. The village elders near the far window, those responsible for informing the police about the propagandist,[37] correspond to Rembrandt's pharisees, and the peasant woman on the right to Rembrandt's poor; the large figure in the left foreground and the small child (omitted in the painting) also echo Rembrandt's figures. As in the *Hundred Guilder Print,* the people represent a cross section of humanity and they show various responses to the central figure. The unmistakable Christlike physiognomy of the propagandist follows the tradition of Ivanov's, Ge's, and Kramskoi's humanized Christs. Repin, however, gave new dimensions to the context of revolutionary activity by showing an active relationship between Christ and the people, comparable to that in Rembrandt's etching. The *Arrest of a Propagandist* reveals not only Repin's apprehension of the central issues of the populist movement but also his appreciation of the visual requirements and possibilities of the theme.

Three other paintings illustrate the expressive means by which Repin gave his revolutionary subjects a heightened emotional and moral impact. *Refusal of the Last Confession* (Fig. 10) shows the confrontation of a condemned prisoner and a priest who offers the last rites. The subject was taken from a poem printed in an illegal journal of the terrorist group, N. M. Minskii's "The Last Confession."[38] Early drawings (Fig. 11) are rather descriptive and seem to depend on both the poem and a recently ended trial of the terrorists, which attracted a great deal of attention because of its length and secrecy and because some of the defense statements were published illegally.[39] In the final painting, however, Repin eliminated details and adjusted the balance of the two figures in a composition that recalls Rembrandt's *David and Saul* in the Hague and *The Prodigal Son* in the Hermitage.[40] The prisoner's rejection of the last confession and the psychological abyss between the revolutionary and the representative of conventional religion are conveyed by the thick darkness separating the figures. The contrasting spotlighting of the face of the condemned man and the crucifix held by the priest reinforces a comparison with Rembrandt's works. Ironically, the theme of spiritual reaching out and acceptance of contact expressed in Rembrandt's works is totally absent in Repin's.

Revolutionary Meeting (Fig. 12) may be compared with Vladimir Makovsky's earlier painting of the same subject, *Evening Meeting* (Fig. 13). Makovsky's style is descriptive and narrative, giving due attention to each one of the radical types who take part in the scene: a student in a peasant's blouse, an officer, a white-bearded veteran revolutionary, and a young woman speaking at the center of the group. Repin's handling is unspecific and expressive. Repin stresses the coherence of the group; instead of delineating types he blurs the individualities by the intensity of the highlights, the dark, hot colors and extremely close focus. There is an effect of urgency, even melodrama, recalling the mood of Rembrandt's *Julius Civilis*. Repin left the painting unfinished, but even so it seems clear that he deliberately avoided Makovsky's prosaic approach in order to heighten emotional involvement in the drama.

The undated *Woman Revolutionary Awaiting Execution* (Fig. 4) belongs with this thematic group. It is more laconic and pathetic than *Refusal of the Last Confession* or *Revolutionary Meeting;* it portrays no action or confrontation but only the fate of the revolutionary.

Repin was in Petersburg on March 1, 1881, when Tsar Alexander II was killed by a terrorist bomb. His letters of the following months contain only brief, oblique comments on the assassination. The most direct was in a letter to his patron Pavel Tretiakov, an attack on a prominent reactionary publisher: "The ideals of such people contain all the slavery, the merciless punishment, the arbitrariness of power [that] call forth such horrible opposition and such horrifying events as that of March 1."[41] He said that

Tretiakov should display in his gallery the portraits of such people as Tolstoi, Nekrasov, and others "dear to the nation, her best sons, who bring positive good through their selfless actions for the good of their native land, believing in a better future and fighting for this idea."[42] No one expressed the agony of the times or the hope for some redemption more forcefully than Tolstoi. Within days after Tsar Alexander III's succession, Tolstoi wrote to him pleading forgiveness for the regicides, urging the divine gesture of pardon, which alone could bring true victory over terrorism. "The death penalty is useless against revolutionaries. Their numbers are not what counts, it is their ideas. . . . Their ideal is universal well-being, equality, liberty. To combat them some other ideal must be advanced, superior to theirs, larger than theirs. There is only one ideal that can be opposed to them . . . the ideal of love and forgiveness. . . . Then, as wax melts in the fire, the revolutionaries' opposition will melt in the deed of their emperor, the man who fulfills the law of Christ."[43] It is unlikely that Repin knew about this letter, though he saw Tolstoi almost daily during this period and he must have been equally appalled by both the assassination and the executions.[44] The events of March, 1881, marked a philosophical turning point for Tolstoi, who became increasingly occupied with the idea of nonresistance to evil. Repin's reactions were more ambiguous, both passionate and in a strange way self-conscious. His two most important works inspired by these events, *Ivan the Terrible and his Son Ivan, November 16, 1581* (1885, Moscow, Tretiakov Gallery) and *They Did Not Expect Him* (Fig. 1) represent opposite poles of Repin's style. Repin wrote later that he had conceived the image of Ivan the Terrible murdering his heir in a fit of madness under the impact of "the bloody events of March 1, 1881," and that he worked in a fever, unable to tear himself from the canvas: "My feelings were overwhelmed by the horrors of the present. This was the mood of life then. Such pictures stood before our eyes, but no one dared to paint them. It was natural to seek an escape into the painful tragedy of history. . . ."[45]

In contrast to the dramatic historical painting and the emotionally engaging, close-up images of revolutionaries, *They Did Not Expect Him* appears decidedly contemporary, documentary, almost prosaic. In visual and narrative terms it represents a change of focus. Attention is centered on the man just entering the room, but this attention is different from the unflinching concentration of the solitary prisoner. The concrete details and the daylight diffuse the dramatic focus and establish a convincing, everyday reality. The sunny garden visible through the windows, the shadow of the footstool on the polished

5
V. Makovsky, *The Acquitted Woman,*
1882, Moscow, Tretiakov Gallery.
(Photo: Tretiakov Gallery)

6
Repin, *The Unexpected Return*
1883–1898, Moscow, Tretiakov Gallery. (Photo: Academy of Arts)

7
Repin, *Guarded Convoy on a Muddy Road*, 1876–77, Moscow, Tretiakov Gallery. (Photo: Academy of Arts)
8
Repin, *Arrest of a Propagandist*, 1878–1892, Moscow, Tretiakov Gallery. (Photo: Tretiakov Gallery)

9
Repin, drawing for *Arrest of a Propagandist*, 1879, Moscow, Tretiakov
Gallery. (Photo: Tretiakov Gallery)
10
Repin, *Refusal of the Last Confession*,
1879–1885, Moscow, Tretiakov Gallery. (Photo: I. Grabar, *I. E. Repin,*
Moscow, 1963–1964, I, 254)

11
Repin, drawing for *Refusal of the Last
Confession*, 1879, Leningrad, Russian
Museum. (Photo: Grabar, *I. E. Repin,* I,
254)

12
Repin, *Revolutionary Meeting,* 1882,
Moscow, Tretiakov Gallery. (Photo:
Tretiakov Gallery)

13
Makovsky, *Evening Meeting,* 1875–
1897, Moscow, Tretiakov Gallery.
(Photo: Tretiakov Gallery)

floor boards, the old armchair, the table covered with schoolbooks, piano, map, and pictures all belong to the familiar environment of a family, suddenly disrupted by the coming of an alien figure, a political exile. Repin presented the situation through the responses, and as if through the eyes, of the family members.

The central figure caused the artist a great deal of difficulty from the very beginning.[46] The exile was intended to represent all the revolutionaries and yet had to be depicted as a concrete personality. Two drawings, 1883 and 1884, (Figs. 14a,b) show the alternative characterizations: a middle-aged man and a young woman carrying a satchel. For the small first version of the painting (Fig. 6), Repin decided on the woman, keeping to a type of revolutionary already established, and perhaps intended, like Iaroshenko's *Kursistka,* to represent both the men and the women of the new, revolutionary generation.

The impact of the painting depends on the tension between the normally close family members and the estrangement forced on them by their opposing paths in life, a contrast more shocking and more touching than the barrier between the returning male exile and the women and children at home. Repin emphasized this contrast by using an impressionistic technique like that of his small painting of a guarded convoy of 1876 (Fig. 7) to produce an atmosphere of peaceful intimacy in the room; he also resorted to a conventional symbol of the forces of catastrophe behind the scene by including a framed print of Mount Vesuvius erupting on the far wall.

However, Repin's understanding of the revolutionary theme was at a point where the intimacy of the smaller painting was inadequate.[47] In turning to a larger canvas, Repin also changed the proportions and gave the scene more breadth, both physical spaciousness and a wider framework of associations. He replaced the girl with an older man, possibly because he already identified the positive image of the revolutionary heroine with a previous stage of the revolutionary movement. As Repin's conception of the situation changed after 1883, he perhaps came to identify the returning exile with other aspects of the era of terrorism and repression that went beyond the immediate events.

In his representation of the revolutionary and his situation, Repin faced a task similar to that of Kramskoi in *Christ in the Desert* to a recognizable image by means of a "natural language, accessible to all," and to express his own judgment about the subject. Repin handled these problems in a way that still owed much to Kramskoi, but which placed a new emphasis on style as a decisive aspect of the painting's content. This can be seen by examining the iconography and style of *They Did Not Expect Him.*

Details of the setting are directly related to the ideological content of the painting; they are connected with Repin's own attitude toward the subject and with literature and other art which he felt was related to the theme, and they are critical to its interpretation. Aside from the furnishings, appropriate to the modest, middle-class status of the family, the decor consists of a map on the right-hand wall and a group of framed photographs and engravings. A photograph of Tsar Alexander II lying in state on the right indicates the time at which the scene occurs and suggests that the family remain sympathetic or at least loyal to the monarchy. The exile must have been freed in the amnesty arranged for the coronation of Alexander III, so the presence of the photograph,[48] and its position nearly opposite the exile's head, underline the irony of the revolutionary's return to this home.

On the back wall, at either side of the large engraving, are reproductions of portraits of Nikolai Nekrasov and Taras Shevchenko. Nekrasov, Chernyshevskii's friend and collaborator, was the best known of the populist writers; his poems, memorized by both the illiterate and by intellectuals, dealt with poverty and exploitation and with personal sacrifice for ideals. Shevchenko was a Ukrainian serf, a self-taught artist and poet who had obtained his freedom through the efforts of leading cultural figures, but was arrested in the 1840's for involvement in political activity. During his exile, Shevchenko produced a series of engravings, *The Parable of the Prodigal Son* (1856–1857, Kiev, Shevchenko Museum), which gave the biblical story a modern interpretation. The portraits in Repin's painting appear to be based on two by Kramskoi: a copy of Shevchenko's 1860 self-portrait, done in 1871, and a lithograph portrait of Nekrasov done in 1878 shortly before the poet's death.

Repin borrowed the combined portrait motif from Kramskoi and made his debt obvious not only out of respect for the older artist but also because this citation let him introduce still other allusions to revolutionary figures. Kramskoi's *Portrait of Nekrasov at the Time of his "Last Poems"* (Fig. 15) shows the poet on his deathbed, surrounded by journals and notes for his poems, working as if under the auspices of a marble bust of Belinskii and portraits of Chernyshevskii's follower Dobroliubov and the Polish patriotic poet Mickewics.[49] Like Kramskoi, Repin clearly spelled out the influence of the subject of the paired portraits on the fate of his revolutionary.

There is yet another, more symbolic level of interpretation for *They Did Not Expect Him.* The revolutionary artists are purposely given more prominence than the dead tsar: their portraits seem to belong on the wall as if they have been there for some time, whereas the recent photograph belongs to the immediate present, and is connected with return of the exile. In the place of honor between the two portraits hangs a large engraving, identified as one which Repin himself owned, after a Golgotha painted about 1833 for St. Isaac's Cathedral.[50] This conventional, academic religious work ties together all the victims represented—the revolutionary writers, the dead tsar, and the exhausted exile—under the universal theme of Christ's sacrifice. The composition reinforces this iconography. The limited space of the room is opened out in three directions, through the still open doorway, the window on the garden, and the political map of Russia on the wall. But within the space of the picture, the exile is physically isolated, both from his family and from his symbolic counterparts in the framed pictures, by the firm dividing line of the door. He is pinioned in a cell-like space by the converging lines of the floorboards and the frame of the door behind his head, which echoes the shape of the cross of Golgotha. In the 1880's, "golgotha" was a popular expression for the prisoner's dock.[51]

The face of the returning exile underwent many revisions, even after the painting had been shown in the Traveling Exhibition of 1884. When Repin mentioned his dissatisfaction with the face, both Tretiakov and Stasov hastened to agree, adding that the expression was excessively tragic and that it destroyed the verisimilitude of the painting.[52] The original appearance can be seen in a photograph that Repin sent to Stasov in 1884,[53] in which the exile appears haggard and exhausted, quite different from Repin's previous revolutionaries. It is possible that this revision of the face shows Repin's reaction to the release of Chernyshevskii from exile in August, 1883. This gesture of clemency was obviously intended by the authorities to show that Chernyshevskii and the other defeated revolutionaries no longer threatened the *status quo*. Chernyshevskii's life and philosophy epitomized the ideals of the sixties, in which Repin sincerely believed, but after twenty years of exile Chernyshevskii would be completely out of touch with events, just as Repin portrayed the exile in the painting. The juxtaposition of this figure with the portraits of Nekrasov and Shevchenko reinforce the identification of the returning exile with the spirit of the sixties and the social and moral problems discussed in *What Is To Be Done?*. The irony of the true situation and the realization that the hopes for reform and reconciliation could no longer be salvaged becomes all the harsher. Finally, just as the exile is cut off from his family and the past, the artist of the 1880s realizes that his own decision to portray contemporary life requires him to abandon the ideals of the previous generation.

Tretiakov and Stasov, somewhat insensitive to the problems that lay behind Repin's difficulty with the exile, made suggestions for improving the figure;

Tretiakov finally urged Repin to find a "younger, more sympathetic" model, like the writer Vsevolod Garshin.[54] It is not known whether Garshin actually posed for *They Did Not Expect Him,* but he had recently been Repin's model for the murdered tsarevich in *Ivan the Terrible,* and in 1884 Repin did a large three-quarter length portrait of the writer.[55] The sad, vulnerable expression in Garshin's eyes seems to have been carried over from the portrait to the face of the exile, but in other features the exile more closely resembles studies of another model, the young artist Menk. Repin may have tried to combine the features of various models, on the plan of the familiar composite portraits of revolutionaries, but the results remained sketchy, and, in Stasov's words, "unconvincing and untypical."[56] Repin's wavering may also be related to a new image he attached to Garshin when he was working on illustrations for the latter's partly allegorical, partly confessional short story, "The Artists."[57] The story contrasts a successful landscape painter and a tormented realist who paints the sufferings of real people but is unable to reach an unconcerned, exhibition-going public. In his illustrations (Fig. 16), Repin gave Garshin's features to the despairing realist and, after the writer's suicide in 1888, Repin and other contemporaries remembered him as a Don Quixote in spirit.[58]

When Repin repainted the face of the exile for the last time he reduced the ambiguous suggestions of physical likenesses and made the hero seem stronger and less hopeless than the exile of 1884, a more generalized and apparently a more satisfying image. Stasov wrote that the painting was "definitely the *chef d'oeuvre* of the entire Russian school . . . no other painting . . . can compete with this one, as far as *characteristic type* and *expression of profound ideas* are concerned."[59]

In contrast to the *Refusal of the Last Confession* (shown at the same Traveling Exhibition) and to *Ivan the Terrible, They Did Not Expect Him* was both contemporary and specific in setting and very restrained in its drama. One element of this difference can be seen in Repin's use of thematic and stylistic references to older art. Whereas the dynamic engaged style associated with Rembrandt corresponded perfectly with Repin's emotional reaction to events, the cooler, more composed style of *They Did Not Expect Him* suggests a conscious effort to achieve a kind of stability or balance between emotion and analysis.

Repin may have been guided toward this goal by his study of Velasquez, one of the artists he most admired. Compositional similarities to *Las Meninas*—the structure of the deep, interior space and the arrangement of figures, the tricky interplay

14a
Repin, Study for *They Did Not Expect Him,* 1883, Moscow, Tretiakov Gallery. (Photo: O. Liaskovskaia, *Repin,* 1962)

14b
Repin, study for *They Did Not Expect Him,* 1884, Helsinki, Museum of the Atheneum. (Photo: Atheneum)
15
Kramskoi, *Portrait of Nekrasov at the Time of his "Last Poems".* Moscow, Tretiakov Gallery. (Photo: Tretiakov Gallery)

16
Repin, illustration for V. Garshin's
story "The Artists," 1888, Leningrad,
Russian Museum. (Photo:
Khudozhestvennoe Nasledstvo II, 243)

17
Repin, *Annual Meeting at the Wall of
the Communards at the Père Lachaise
Cemetery*, 1883, Moscow, Tretiakov
Gallery. (Photo: Tretiakov Gallery)

of real people and pictures, and the emphatic lateral lighting—are no accident. Shortly before beginning work on *They Did Not Expect Him,* Repin made a trip to Europe with Stasov, during which he made a special point of studying and copying works of Velasquez in the Prado.[60] Other features of *They Did Not Expect Him,* particularly the way the details of the setting are used almost like theatrical properties to support the action and point to its meaning, suggest the influence of Dutch or English narrative painting, although it would be difficult to point to specific sources. During his stay in Paris in 1883, Repin also took the time to experiment with the impressionist style in a small painting of a political rally on the anniversary of the Paris Commune, *Annual Meeting at the Wall of the Communards, Père Lachaise Cemetery in Paris* (Fig. 17),[61] Moscow, which seems to be an especially appropriate application of a modern style to a timely subject.

These various artistic experiences gave Repin the means of making *They Did Not Expect Him* a visual vehicle for expressing his ideas and feelings about a very complex subject, and, at the same time asserting the importance of the subject. The combination of apparently contradictory effects—the apparently objective description of the room and its inhabitants, the realistic lighting and cool coloration along with a very carefully worked-out composition and deliberate echoes of older art—answered to Repin's desire to create a work that was immediately relevant to real concerns and also of lasting, universal value.

The tragedy of the revolutionary era, as Repin and some of his contemporaries were beginning to see it, was not only in the brutal killing of the tsar and the execution of scores of terrorists, but in an ironic failure of historical continuity. The original populists had hoped to be unifying agents between the classes, but their successors were forced to destroy all ties with family life, ordinary friendship, and humanity. The revolutionary became a "lost man." In his study of terrorism and anarchism, *The Rebel,* Camus expressed the terrible transformation of a virtually religious faith that the future would justify extreme actions into a sad confrontation with reality. The honesty with which the terrorists tried, "with bombs and revolvers, and also with the courage with which they walk to the gallows, to escape from contradiction and create the values they lack" did not lead to a good end but, inevitably, to devaluation of human life.[62] The fact that Repin connected the assassination of Tsar Alexander II with the crime of Ivan IV, who murdered his heir and broke the line of succession, and the way in which Repin united the images of all the martyrs of the revolutionary struggle, the older populists, the dead tsar, and the exile, with the image of Christ on Golgotha, shows that he perceived the current conflict as part of a recurrent failing in Russian history.

They Did Not Expect Him is not only the final and culminating statement in painting of the revolutionary theme of the 1870s and 1880s. It is also a summing up of a much broader historical theme of conflict, a universal tragedy seen through the perspective of the most idealistic and most destructive struggle of the artist's own time.

Notes

1
N. G. Chernyshevskii, "The Aesthetic Relations of Art to Reality," in *Selected Philosophical Essays* (Moscow, 1953), pp. 373–375.

2
Evgenii Lampert, *Sons against Fathers: Studies in Russian Radicalism and Revolution* (Oxford, 1965) p. 364, n. 51. The police confiscated all writing found in Chernyshevskii's cell, but they passed the manuscript because the novel seemed to have no bearing on his case, and the censor approved it for publication. The authorities soon recognized the danger the book represented and banned it. The English translation is *What Is To Be Done?,* trans. B. Tucker, (New York, 1961).

3
I. E. Repin, *Dalekoe blizkoe* (Moscow, 1953) pp. 189, 350–351.

4
As part of a broader program of reform, the Academy administration liberalized the rules for the concourse of diploma students in 1863, setting general themes instead of specific subjects. Encouraged by this gesture, Kramskoi and his friends unsuccessfully petitioned for complete freedom of choice of subject. Kramskoi's decision to leave the Academy is explained in an unpublished article, "Sud'by russkogo iskusstva" (1877), in which the oppressive authorianism of the Academy is stressed. Cf. S. N. Gol'dshtein, *I. N. Kramskoi. Zhizn' i tvorchestvo* (Moscow, 1965), pp. 46ff. The fourteen secessionists were under police surveillance and were in a very serious economic position, since without Academy affiliation they were denied many commissions. Under Kramskoi's leadership they formed an artists' cooperative (artel' khudozhnikov). Meanwhile, a group of Moscow artists approached them with the idea of organizing traveling art exhibitions. The Association of Traveling Art Exhibitions was formed in 1870; its charter stated the goals as the creation of a wider audience of lovers of art in Russia and improving the market for artists' works. See E. P. Gomberg-Verzhbinskaia, *Peredvizhniki* (Leningrad, 1970), pp. 36–43. The most recent and thorough discussion of the origins and social context of the Wanderers is Elizabeth Valkenier, *Russian Realist Art* (Ann Arbor, 1977), pp. 17–73.

5
Populism in Russia was based on the belief in the revolutionary potential of the peasantry, which must be aroused by propaganda and social work by the radical intelligentsia. The failure of reforms from above (emancipation and land reforms of the 1860s) and the inciting of Herzen, Ogarev, and other publicists led to the massive movement of university students out into the provinces, "to the People" in 1874.

6
See Franco Venturi, *Roots of Revolution,* trans. F. Haskell (New York, 1960), p. 595 on the 1874 arrests. Well over a

thousand were arrested but less than half of them were brought to trial; nearly all were under thirty.

7
I. N. Kramskoi, "Vzgliad na istoricheskuiu zhivopis'," in Kramskoi, Pis'ma, stat'i, 2 vols. (Moscow, 1965), II, p. 272.

8
I. E. Repin, letter to N. Murashko, November 30, 1883, in I. A. Brodskii, ed., Repin, Pis'ma, 2 vols. (Moscow, 1969), I, pp. 292–293.

9
Repin, letter to P. Tret'iakov, April 8, 1881, Repin, Pis'ma, I, p. 250. The artist explained his refusal to paint a portrait of the publisher Katkov for Tret'iakov's gallery.

10
This paper does not attempt to encompass either the real range of the realists' interests or the complexities of the political situation.

11
Besides Repin, several of the Wanderers, including Nikolai Ge, Ivan Kramskoi, Konstantin Savitskii, Vladimir Makovskii, and Nikolai Iaroshenko dealt with political subjects in their works; many others focused on the conditions of life among peasants and the urban poor, potentially political subjects in themselves.

The major sources of biographical and documentary material on Repin are the monographs I. E. Grabar', Ilia Efimovich Repin, 2 vols. (Moscow, 1963–1964) and O. A. Liaskovskaia, I. E. Repin: zhivopis', skul'putra, grafika (Moscow, 1962); the collections of documents and articles by I. E. Grabar' and I. S. Zil'bershtein, eds. Repin. Khudozhestvennoe Nasledstvo, 2 vols. (Moscow, Leningrad, 1948) and I. A. Brodskii and V. N. Moskvinov, eds. Novoe o Repine (Moscow, 1969); Repin's memoirs Dalekoe blizkoe, and his published letters, Repin, Pis'ma.

12
Vladimir Stasov, the critic who championed Repin and the realists, wrote that "tendentiousness" was a positive quality in Repin's They Did Not Expect Him ("Nashi Khudozhestvennie dela," [1884] in V. Stasov, Izbrannoe: Russkoe iskusstvo [Moscow, Leningrad, 1950], p. 194), whereas most critics held that tendentiousness or topicality confined a work to the level of genre.

13
Chernyshevskii, "The Aesthetic Relations of Art to Reality," p. 375.

14
I. N. Kramskoi, letter to V. M. Garshin, February 16, 1878, in Kramskoi, Pis'ma, 2 vols. (Moscow, 1937), II, p. 140.

15
Ibid. Kramskoi wrote a detailed reply to Garshin's questions about the meaning of Christ in the Desert.

16
Repin, Dalekoe blizkoe, pp. 146–148.

17
Chernyshevskii, "The Aesthetic Relations of Art to Reality," p. 371. See R. Welleck, Concepts of Criticism (New Haven and London, 1963), pp. 244–245 on Belinskii's concept of types.

18
On Repin's and Iaroshenko's interest in these photographs see Repin, Dalekoe Blizkoe, p. 189, and Mikhail Nesterov, Davnie dni. Vstrechi i vospominaniia (Moscow, 1959), p. 67.

19
An outbreak of student strikes in the early 1860s caused many conservatives to blame the disruptions on the presence of women students. The advanced woman student was caricatured by Dostoevskii in The Possessed and treated more sympathetically by Turgenev in his Poems in Prose. A good discussion of the feminist movement and higher education in Russia is in Daniel Brower, Training the Nihilists: Education and Radicalism in Tsarist Russie (Ithaca, New York, 1975), pp. 83 ff; I am grateful to Dr. S. Frederick Starr for bringing this book to my attention.

20
I. S. Zil'bershtein, "Obraz peredovoi russkoi zhenshchiny v maloizvestnykh proizvedeniiakh Repina (1880-e gody)," in Repin. Khudozhestvennoe nasledstvo, I, p. 170, quotes hostile criticism in S.-Peterburgskie vedomosti (1883, Nos. 121, 235) and favorable comment by V. Stasov in Vestnik Evropy (1883, No. 12).

21
G. Uspenskii, "Po povodu odnoi malen'koi kartinki," in Otechestvennye zapiski (1883, No. 2), pp. 557–558.

22
M. Troitskii, "Repin i 'Narodnaia Volia'" (Iskusstvo, 1971, No. 9) p. 57, citing an interview with Repin in V. Kamenskii, "'Sredy v Penatakh," Repin—k 10 letiu so dnia smerti (Leningrad, 1940), p. 14.

23
P. I. Neradovskii, Iz zhizni khudozhnika (Leningrad, 1965) identifies the figure as Vera Figner, recalling his impressions at the 1896 exhibition.

24
Repin's possible contacts with members of revolutionary groups are discussed in Troitskii, "Repin i 'Narodnaia Volia,'" pp. 56–57, Z. I. Krapivin, "Revoliutsionnaia tema v tvorchestve I. E. Repina" (unpublished dissertation, Moscow Pedagogical Institute, Moscow, 1961), Krapivin, "Iz zhizni i tvorchestva I. E. Repina v Parizhe," in Novoe o Repine, p. 381. In the most recent study of Repin intellectual contacts, G. I. Pribul'skaia, "Peterburgskii period v zhizni i tvorchestve I. E. Repina" (unpublished dissertation, Academy of Arts, Leningrad, 1975), p. 175, states that Repin was not personally close to any of the terrorists, but he followed the trials attentively. Cf. Repin, letter to Stasov, February 16, 1881, Repin-Stasov. Perepiska (Moscow, Leningrad, 1948–1950), II, pp. 59–60.

On the trial of Figner and her codefendants, see V. Figner, Memoirs of a Revolutionist (New York, 1927), pp. 142–143.

25
N. Nekrasov, Poems, trans. J. Soskice (London, 1929).

26
I. S. Zil'bershtein, "Obraz peredovoi russkoi zhenshiny," and O. A. Liaskovskaia, "Proizvedenie I. E. Repina 'Ne zhdali' i problema kartiny v russkoi zhivopisi vtoroi poloviny XIX veka," Gos. Tret'iakovskaia Gallereia. Materialy i issledovaniia (Moscow, 1958) II. pp. 102–103 discuss the relationships between the two paintings but come to no satisfactory conclusions.

27
See Venturi, Roots of Revolution, pp. 364–369, on this document and its impact.

28
See Venturi, Roots of Revolution, pp. 604–606, on Zasulich's trial and reactions in the press.

29
Repin, letter to L. Tolstoi, November 18, 1880, Repin. Pis'ma, I, p. 241, writes of his desire to be near the center of events in Petersburg and his disgust with a kind of stagnation of ideas in Moscow. His close friends, the artists

Polenov and Surikov were unsympathetic to political activism. Repin and Iaroshenko became acquainted with the prominant liberal Mikhailovskii at this time. See James Billington, *Mikhailovsky and Russian Populism* (Oxford, 1958), p. 82.

30
V. M. Garshin, *Nadezhda Nikolaevna*, originally serialized in *Russkaia mysl'*, February, March, 1885; English version in V. Garshin, *The Scarlet Flower and Other Stories*, trans. B. Isaacs (Moscow, 1955).

31
Another story by Garshin, "The Artists" (1879) made use of a still more monumental image, Iaroshenko's *Stoker* (1878, Moscow, Tret'iakov Gallery). While Iaroshenko's paintings were, on the surface, quite objective, they clearly invited symbolic interpretations.

32
Kramskoi's essay, "Vzgliad na istoricheskuiu zhivopis'" was dedicated to Ivanov. Repin once stated that *They Did Not Expect Him* followed the tradition of Ivanov's painting as a moral and historical work; cf. A. Fedorov-Davydov, "Chemu uchit'cia u peredvizhnikov," *Tvorchestvo* (1971, No. 11) and I. Il'in, "O Repine," *Khudozhnik* (1972, No. 3). Ge's *Last Supper* represents the moment after Christ's announcement that one of the disciples would betray him and it also symbolically represents the falling apart of the liberal circle of Alexander Herzen (Christ's face was based on a photograph of Herzen); see V. I. Porudominskii, *Nikolai Ge* (Moscow, 1970), pp. 28–29. Both paintings stress the spiritual isolation of Christ.

33
Repin describes his reaction to the execution in "Kazn' Karakozova," *Dalekoe blizkoe*, pp. 198–209. A sketch he made of Karakozov's head (1866) is published in *Repin. Khudozhestvennoe nasledstvo*, I, p. 99.

34
Repin, letter to Stasov, October 15, 1873, *Repin, Pis'ma*, I, p. 86.

35
The Russian word *mir* for "village commune" also means "world". Some populist thinkers idealized the peasant commune and saw in it the embryonic form of a future Russian society. Repin, however, is concerned with the typicality of this scene.

36
I. S. Zil'bershtein, *Arest Propagandista* (Moscow, 1951) describes the progress of the work, illustrating preparatory studies. I have not found any suggestion in Soviet literature of Repin's use of Rembrandt's etchings. Repin had admired Rembrandt from his student days, when he frequently studied the Rembrandts in the Hermitage. V. Stasov introduced Repin to collectors, including Dmitrii Rovinskii, who showed Repin his collection of Rembrandt etchings; cf. *Dalekoe blizkoe*, p. 291; Pribul'skaia, "Peterburgskii period," p. 184; D. Rovinskii, *L'Oeuvre Gravé de Rembrandt: Catalogue raisoné* (St. Petersburg, 1890). During his trip to Paris in 1883, Repin visited the collection of Rembrandt engravings at the Bibliotheque nationale; *Dalekoe blizkoe*, p. 290.

37
Repin touched up the faces in 1892 to emphasize the informers' characters.

38
The poem was printed in the illegal journal of "The People's Will," *Narodnaia Volia* (October, 1879); Repin and Stasov read it together. Cf. S. Ivanov, *Moskva v zhizni i tvorchestve Repina* (Moscow, 1960), p. 94.

39
See Venturi, *Roots of Revolution,* pp. 587–590.

40
One of Repin's chief purposes in traveling abroad in 1883 was to study the works of Rembrandt, Hals, and Velasquez; after visiting Holland, he affirmed that Rembrandt's best works were at the Hermitage. Letter to P. Tret'iakov, July 10, 1883, *Repin, Pis'ma*, I, pp. 282–283. Repin's letters mention few individual paintings; it is not known whether he knew *David and Saul* (then in a private collection) or *Julius Civilis* in the original.

41
Repin, letter to P. Tret'iakov, April 8, 1881, *Repin, Pis'ma*, I, p. 250.

42
Ibid.

43
Quoted in Henri Troyat, *Tolstoy,* trans. Nancy Amphoux (New York, 1967), pp. 405–407.

44
Repin and Tolstoi became friends at this time and may have discussed the events; there is no correspondence from these months. See Repin, letter to Stasov, January 20, 1882, *Repin, Pis'ma*, I, p. 265.

45
Repin, "Zametki I. E. Repina o sozdanii im kartiny (*Ivan Groznyi i syn ego Ivan*)" (undated, Archive, Academy of Arts, Leningrad) fond A-3, K4, op. 54, p. 4. Repin's feelings had been brought to an emotional pitch when he heard Rimskii-Korsakov's new work, a trilogy called "Love. Power. Vengeance." performed in Moscow in 1882, which Repin understood to be on the same theme.

46
See Liaskovskaia, "Proizvedenie I. E. Repina 'Ne zhdali'," pp. 102–105 and Grabar', *Repin,* I, p. 256, on the early stages of the work. Details of studies and revisions of this figure are given in: N. Iu. Zograf, "Novye podgotovitel'nye raboty k kartine I. E. Repina 'Ne zhdali'," *Gos. Tret'iakovskaia Galereia. Ocherki po russkomu i sovetskomu iskusstvu* (Leningrad, 1974), pp. 155–168, and S. V. Korolkevich, "Rabota I. E. Repina nad kartinoi 'Ne zhdali'," (unpublished article, Archive, Academy of Arts, Leningrad, 1951) fond 11, op. 1, ed. khr. 409.

47
I. S. Ostroukhov, letter to S. Flerov, undated 1899[?]. Quoted in Liaskovskaia, "Proizvedenie I. E. Repina 'Ne zhdali'," pp. 102–103.

48
Liaskovskaia, "Proizvedennie I. E. Repina 'Ne zhdali'," p. 109, suggests that the photograph was included to assure censors that the painting was not seditious.

49
See S. N. Gol'dshtein, "Iz istorii sozdanii proizvedenii I. N. Kramskogo 'Nekrasov v periode poslednykh pesen'," *Gos. Tret'iakovskaia Galereia. Materialy i issledovaniia* (Moscow, 1958), II, pp. 155–159. Dobroliubov's book, *Good Intentions and Actions,* dealt with the barrier between the merely well-meaning liberals and those who sacrificed everything in order to act according to their convictions.

50
K. K. Shteiben's *Golgotha,* still in St. Isaac's Cathedral, was very popular in its time and several copies were made in provincial churches. Repin, *Dalekoe blizkoe,* p. 85, mentions a large engraved version in a church near his childhood home and he later copied the work for himself.

51
James Billington, *The Icon and the Axe*, (London, 1966), p. 435.

52
Stasov, letter to Tret'iakov, April 8, 1884, *Perepiska P. M. Tret'iakova i V. V. Stasova* (Moscow, 1949), pp. 91–92.

53
Published in Grabar', *Repin*.

54
Repin, letter to Tret'iakov, April 6, 1884, Repin, Pis'ma, I, p. 295; Stasov, letter to Tret'iakov, April 8, 1884, *Perepiska*, p. 91; Tret'iakov, letter to Repin, March 10, 1885, *P. M. Tret'iakov, Perepiska* (Moscow, 1940), pp. 93–94.

55
Zograf, "Novye podgotovitel'nye raboty," p. 159, discusses recent research on models for the exile. Cf. D. V. Sarab'ianov, "Repin," in I. E. Grabar' *et al.* eds., *Istoriia russkogo ishusstva* (Moscow, 1968) IX, Part 1, p. 518.

56
Stasov, letter to Tret'iakov, April 8, 1884, *Perepiska*, p. 91.

57
V. M. Garshin, "Khudozhniki" (1879) in *Polnoe sobranye sochinenii*, (St. Petersburg, 1910) pp. 154–170. Repin's illustrations were for a memorial edition and he did a portrait of Garshin for a frontispiece. Illustrations are published in I. Lazarevskii, "Repin—Illiustrator," *Repin, Khudozhestvennoe nasledstvo,* II, p. 243.

58
Repin, "V. M. Garshin," in *Dalekoe blizkoe*, p. 371.

59
Stasov, letter to Tret'iakov, April 8, 1884, *Perepiska,* pp. 92–93 (the italics are Stasov's). See Stasov, "Nashi khudozhestvennye dela" (1884), *Izbrannoe,* I, p. 194.

60
Repin, letter to Stasov, October 20, 1881, *Repin, Pis'ma,* I, p. 262; on his experience of Velasquez in the Louvre and the Prado, letters to Tret'iakov, May 29, July 10, 1883, and to V. Polenov, July 17, 1883, *Repin, Pis'ma,* I, pp. 280–285, pp. 285–290. Repin idolized Velasquez and Spanish and Dutch seventeenth-century painting in general.

61
Repin describes the ceremony and its participants (who included Lavrov and other exiled Russian revolutionaries) in a letter to Polenov, July 17, 1883, *Repin, Pis'ma,* I, p. 289, and in his memoirs of Stasov, *Dalekoe blizkoe,* p. 297. He made a pencil sketch on the spot and painted the scene immediately afterwards, using a bright, impressionist palette. Material on this event and the trip to Europe from Stasov's diaries is published in I. S. Zil'bershtein, "Puteshestvie I. E. Repina i V. V. Stasova po zapadnoi Evrope v 1883 godu," *Repin. Khudozhestvennoe nasledstvo,* I, pp. 429–524.

62
Albert Camus, *The Rebel,* trans. Anthony Bower (New York, 1961), pp. 164–173.

7
Rome's First National State Architecture: The *Palazzo delle Finanze*

Eberhard Schroeter

For Katrin

The question of art as political propaganda is mainly concerned with obvious artistic manifestations favoring a political group or movement. This purely propagandist art produces works with a direct political meaning and a "readable" political text.

In the case of state architecture it is nearly self-evident that there is an intent to represent state or nation; this might be done in different ways but is usually conveyed through the choice of the architect or the choice of stylistic forms. Such political intent is too general, insofar as any person who commissions any kind of art or architecture will aim at the representation of himself through the artifact. The only difference in state-commissioned architecture is that the state is already a political institution—the political manifestation is far more obvious and immediate than in the case of private commissions.

To equate the term *politics* with propaganda is to use it far too narrowly to describe the intent and character of political and especially of ideological factors in state-commissioned art. On the one hand there is a quite simple, clear notion of politics as party politics, using the arts as pure propaganda. On the other hand we have to deal with a wider notion of politics, describing the current politics of a state and its rulers. The art production does not need to be related directly to the politics in this case. The political content of art can be implicit. Finally we have to work with politics defined by the ideological description of the social and economic situation. It refers to the entire social and political system in its actual practice. Art and architecture reflect the basis and superstructure of the political system.

For my example of state architecture I shall deal with the latter two notions of politics. The pure propagandistic aspect does not clarify the political meaning of such a building, but mainly ideological concepts define its character.

I will demonstrate the political quality of the Italian Ministry of Finance in Rome through the historical and ideological situation of the time as it is related to the client and the construction itself. The architects will be mostly neglected for reasons inherent in the special case of this building, while the main point of observation will be the intent of the client, the Minister Quintino Sella, who will prove to be the decisive figure for the building and an advanced proponent of capitalist ideology.

I shall study the Ministry of Finance in terms of the historical factors that determined its construction, an examination of the building itself, and finally, an analysis of its political meaning. Within these three categories I shall treat the general historical and ideological circumstances of the time, particularly the figure of Quintino Sella, the Minister of Finance, and his role as client of the *Palazzo delle Finanze*. In studying the building itself, I shall deal with its external architecture and its internal organization resulting from a series of modifications during its construction. Finally I shall consider the meaning of the *Palazzo delle Finanze* in terms of the pragmatic intent of the client, the relation between the actual political situation and the building's site and architectural decoration, and the utilitarian objectives as an expression of a new ideology.

Historical and Ideological Summary

The historical situation around 1870 in Rome, important with respect to this building and the man who commissioned it, should be mentioned briefly.

Rome, that is, the choice of Rome as the capital of the young Italian national state, was one of the great aims and one of the main points of controversy of the Risorgimento. It was, however, not only an internal political question, it was also an international problem. The entire Catholic world as well as the governments of Europe felt, and took the right to interfere, against or in favor of international Rome, as cosmopolitan Rome, capital of Catholicism. The decision of Napoleon III to withdraw the French troops stationed in Rome in support of the pope and transfer them instead to the Prussian front gave the Italians the military and the political opportunity they needed to take the city.

Based on feudal concepts, the argument of Pius IX was that the territorial power of the Vatican was essential for the survival of the spiritual power of the church. Pius IX maintained this view in spite of the extremely profitable offers proposed by the Savoy kingdom. A similar offer was accepted only later in 1929, when the Vatican had changed the basis of its power from feudal land holdings to capital. The change had begun as early as 1870 by a special kind of capitalization—the transforming of clerical property into corporate entities—before the national secularization laws had been extended to Rome.[1]

The social situation of the papal city was disastrously underdeveloped. The absence of any industrial activity (the only exception was the tobacco factory in Trastevere) and the low standard of the infrastructure (the first dispositions had been made only with the railways to Frascati and Civitavecchia) conditioned the economic existence of the population. This consisted of the Roman nobility, their administrators, some corn merchants and the artisans, and the large group of inhabitants living on occasional services or benefits from the Vatican and ecclesiastical orders. The surrounding country, owned mainly by the nobility, was exploited and cultivated according to old feudal principles.

In sharp contrast to this basic weakness, we can observe intentions and associations of grandeur that

had no correspondence to any form of real power based on economic strength. The idea of Rome consisted chiefly of power images borrowed from history. Conquering merely these associations and the ideological and emotional content in 1870 provided the basis for national policies that had little effect on the social and economic structure of Rome for generations. Rome as the capital of the new national state had been one of the central terms of the spirit of the Risorgimento. It had been the unifying idea as against many regional and political interests. Although there had been proposals for founding a completely new capital, the ideological significance of Rome was far too strong to be swayed by technical, functional, or even economic arguments:

On 20 September 1870 it seemed that through the breach of Porta Pia there entered only great ideals, sublime political and moral aspirations. It wasn't easy to perceive the considerably more prosaic, complex, underlying reality: that of a nation and a ruling class weak and constrained by compromises with the past, which had just established the center of their power in a city that was equally weak and retarded in its basic structure, thus also displaying one of the typical characteristics of the general development of united Italy.[2]

The decisive group in Italian politics from the foundation of the Italian state in Turin in 1861 was the north Italian ruling class, representing that part of the country which was most developed economically. The shift of the capital from Florence to Rome was accomplished by the government of Giovanni Lanza, also called the Gabinetto Lanza-Sella. The proclamation of the new capital on 1 February 1871 was accompanied by the institution of the Commissione Governativa pel Trasferimento della Sede del Governo a Roma (Government-Commission for the Transfer of the Seat of the Administration to Rome) on 3 February 1871.[3] The Lanza-Sella administration remained in power from 12 December 1869 until 23 June 1873. Minister of Finance Quintino Sella became especially involved in the formation of national Rome, theoretically as well as practically, by proposing and promoting his ministry building in Via XX Settembre.

Quintino Sella, the Client of the Palazzo delle Finanze

Before examining the history of the construction and the factors that conditioned the building, two interrelated aspects of Sella's ideas for the new capital and their presumed positivist origin should be cited. His ideas seem to have been dominated by social considerations on the one hand and pure ideological principles on the other.

According to him, the cosmopolitan references of papal Rome, once the city had become the national capital, should neither be eliminated nor focused on the Vatican but should be profoundly altered. The cosmopolitan Christian values should be changed

129
Rome's First
National State
Architecture: The
Palazzo delle
Finanze

into values of science, introducing science as the new universalism instead of Catholicism. In a parliamentary speech in 1881 he affirmed this idea, recalling a meeting with Mommsen in 1871.

Mommsen asked him:

But what do you mean to do in Rome? This is worrying everybody; you cannot be in Rome without having cosmopolitan references. What do you mean to do?—[Sella:] Yes, we cannot avoid having a cosmopolitan reference in Rome; that of science. We must be aware of the position we hold vis-a-vis the civilized world, since we are in Rome.[4]

Although this might have been a marginal remark, its significance is underlined because Sella mentions this interview in front of parliament when discussing the development of Rome. But, together with another parliamentary declaration that refers to more practical aspects of the future of Rome, we are able to connect these science-ideas with economic and social arguments. In 1876, three years after his tenure as Minister, he alluded to these social terms of Roman development:

For my part I admit I believe that Rome must be the seat of the supreme direction of the general interest of the country. I believe, as I said the other day, that a country, so to speak, in the same way as a human body must have its brain in the capital; but that the other members must be perfectly healthy and such that the whole can function in harmony.

And further on he continues:

But if you should think, as it is said, that I am an adherent of the concept of concentrating so many factories, so many work shops in a capital city, you believe precisely the opposite of what I think. As far as we are concerned, I have always wanted Rome to be the administrative center, the intellectual center, but I have never desired that it should contain great agglomerations of workers. In an overwhelming agglomeration of workers in Rome I foresee a real inconvenience, because I believe that this should be the place where many questions, which need to be discussed intellectually, which require the effort of all the intellectual forces of the country, should be dealt with: But the proletarian impetuosity of great masses of workers would not be appropriate. I believe that a structure of this type would be dangerous or at least inconvenient. Nevertheless I think that production and labor of all types should be stimulated in the other parts of the kingdom.[5]

These proposals for Rome express Sella's vision of a rigid division between the basis and superstructure and, in local terms, show his interest in industrializing the country but excluding Rome from such development. According to him, the intellect—the sciences—must be separated from production and should rule society, untouched by social struggles. This concept seems very close to certain aspects of the positivism of Auguste Comte, who had been a much discussed philosopher in Paris during the years when Sella studied in the French capital.

Comte developed a social theory that provided the sciences as a substitute for the church as moral ruler of the world—as a power standing above social struggle and group interests, ruling in "objectivity"

the morals of the world. In his *Cours de philosophie positive*[6] Auguste Comte gives a very clear, purely instrumental interpretation of the social function of the Christian church in the Middle Ages. He describes the role of the church as reconciling the different class interests for the benefit of all and as the essential stabilizing factor of medieval society. In other words, he exposes a perfect system of social control, working for the interest of the ruling class and keeping down the lower classes through the Catholic moral laws.[7] Comte also sees that the church cannot reestablish this role after the Enlightenment and the French Revolution. But the system itself seems very convincing to him, even for postrevolutionary times. He concludes—and this in a totally ahistorical manner—that this concept has to be applied to modern society, giving the control function to the sciences instead of the church. According to him, the sciences build the modern equivalent of the church—being empiric, objective, independent, and without any class interest—and he admits the practical advantage that the public reputation of the sciences is already very good.

This aspect of Comte's ideas that attracts our interest with respect to Sella's politics is mainly set forth in the last volume of the *Cours,* published in 1842. He also sees intellectuals as the promoters and carriers of his social system. Their task, according to him, would be to create a postrevolutionary, "positive," not critical but progressive moral system, which means in practice the installation of a highly paternalistic intellectual elite society.

These theories probably influenced Quintino Sella. Sella, who was born in 1827 in Biella in Piedmont, finished his studies in Turin with a degree in engineering in 1847. Immediately thereafter he went to Paris to continue his studies at the Ecole des Mines.[8] He stayed in Paris over two full years between 1847 and 1851,[9] where he also became interested in social sciences and economics.[10] This interest may account for his presumed contact with Comte. Comte had been examiner at the Ecole Polytechnique up to 1844 and was still in contact with this famous school for his *cours populaires,* which had been instituted by the Ecole. The Ecole Polytechnique and the Ecole des Mines were closely allied at this time. Students of each of the schools would attend lectures in both institutions. Also, the Société Positiviste was founded in 1848 while Sella was in Paris. Even though there is no direct evidence of contact between Sella and Comte, it seems likely that Sella must have heard of Comte and may have read his works.

Sella, however, was no philosopher. He published valuable articles in different areas of the natural sciences. He sojourned in Paris, made extended trips through Germany, visited the Great World Exhibition in London in 1851, which gave him wider knowledge than most of his colleagues. These experiences in countries far more developed than his native land gave him an advanced view of the value and demands of a growing industrial capitalist system. He started his political career in 1860 and was extremely successful because of the support of Cavour. His own political ideas were, however, only put in practice when he received his first important portfolio, the Ministry of Finance, in 1869.

His idea of Rome as an unindustrialized capital, without a proletariat, for the benefit of the intelligentsia that would discuss and solve the problems of the nation in untroubled freedom, unconditioned by and free from any group interest, seems to refer to the elite system of Comte. It appears to approximate in practice some aspects of Comte's theory.

Sella introduces no industry in the area of the capital, but reserves this basic activity for the northern regions. Rome should fulfill only the ideological aims of the national state. It should continue its old ruling function, not change its social and economic structure. Only the contents of its ideology should be altered by modernizing the surface, substituting the "objective" bourgeois sciences for the superannuated church. Sella's political position toward the church has to be seen in the light of Cavour's formula: A free church in a free state. It sees the church as one of many elements in the society, not as a dominant one. Sella expressed this viewpoint, according to his biography, during a meeting with workers in Biella in 1883: "We are studying science for its own sake, Monsignore . . ., without preconceived ideas. If you find that this science confirms your faith, so much the better; but permit us to remain unconcerned with that."[11]

The modern, "scientific," and instrumental position of Sella affects his view of the city of Rome and its urban development. Although the technically advanced viewpoint of this politician has already been noted by some authors, such as Gramsci,[12] Caracciolo, and Insolera, his relation to the ideas of Comte should be emphasized again. Caracciolo observed a very strong contradiction in Sella's ideas and politics and showed him to be technologically advanced but also deeply reactionary.[13] His interpretation is right but incomplete. He does not see the contradiction as part of a single view, that is, the application of Comte's ideas in an attempt to resolve the antinomies of capitalism. Caracciolo takes the antiproletarian statement of Sella to be his reactionary side. But this statement has to be related to the elite system of Comte. Sella tried to introduce Comte's system, providing the productive sector for the more developed northern regions and leaving Rome totally unproductive industrially. Rome was to be, instead, the center of decision and was to balance the different interest groups in the country. The con-

tradiction seen in Sella is not a personal one; it is a contradiction of the capitalist system and the antihistorical positivist theory, which tried to create an instrumental division between the basis and superstructure. Sella, the industrialist from the North,[14] is not split into progressive and reactionary parts but, rather, he appears as a representative of an advanced capitalism. His technical and instrumental progressiveness, working for practical and functional progress, is not an absolute progressiveness but a position that integrates, as Comte's theory does, "progress" in a paternalistic elite system of order.

The Role of Quintino Sella

Sella's views about capitalist society, demonstrated in his ideas for Rome as the national capital, seem to find their correspondence and expression in the history of the formation of the Palazzo delle Finanze, which was mainly carried through by Sella as head of the Ministero delle Finanze.

There is not much literature about the building on Via XX Settembre, a fact with significance for our argument. Contemporaries apparently did not accord artistic value to the construction.[15] Only some modifications and details of the internal decoration, added some time after Sella left office in 1873, found a strong echo in the public. The most informative article, which appeared in the Illustrazione Italiana in 1879,[16] will be referred to later.

More recent publications concerned with the "Third Rome" mention the building but do not discuss it because of its low artistic value. However, a few remark its functionality and unpretentious architectural decoration.[17] Recent publications, however, agree on one point: the urban intent and effect of Sella's initiative for the ministry building. Insolera and Caracciolo, together with many others, affirm the importance of Sella for the growth of the city toward the hills of Rome and the decisive role Sella played in starting an administrative center along the axis of Via XX Settembre.[18] Credit for the site chosen for the first construction of the national government in Rome, in fact, should be given to Sella.

He was the one who persuaded the government to start this construction. He opposed the general tendency of locating the entire governmental administration in exmonastic buildings. He finally got his plans through the National Council (Consiglio di Stato) in the meeting of 9 September 1871, when an approval was voted for construction along the Via XX Settembre (Fig. 1). Later, in 1881, Sella confirmed his responsibility for the building itself but not for its location.[19]

The following documents, however, leave no doubt about his influence on all the preliminary matters of the ministry building and its location:

131
Rome's First
National State
Architecture: The
Palazzo delle
Finanze

1. At a meeting on 9 September 1871 Sella presented not only a plan for its location but also a general construction cost estimate of six million lire (Doc. 1). The estimate allows us to assume that an architect's preliminary project already existed.

2. Raffaele Canevari, the architect, was mentioned as charged with the realization of the project and as author of the project from October 1871 (Doc. 2).

3. Minister Sella proposed Canevari as architect to Commissioner Gadda, chief of the Commissione pel Trasferimento, and Canevari received the commission for a general master plan for the building. The context proves that the proposal was practically an order and confirms, thereby, that the choice of the architect was made by Sella (Docs. 3 and 4).

4. Canevari was chosen by Sella for his knowledge of the city and the municipal plans (Docs. 3 and 4). Canevari himself was at the same time a civil officer of the civil engineering corps and also involved in the development of a future master plan of Rome.

5. As far as the choice of the site is concerned, it must be assumed that the contact between Sella and the city was mainly through Canevari. It should be emphasized, however, that the later negotiations between the central government and the municipal administration about the disposition of the area along Via XX Settembre show no initial coordination between the Finance Ministry plans and the housing district plans (*Quartiere Castro Pretorio*) of the city (Doc. 5). There are two facts that confirm the predominance of the governmental plans: expropriation of land for governmental usage in this part of the city dates much earlier (6 August 1871)[20] than the final agreement between nation and city (25 March 1872);[21] and the city had to concede in certain aspects during the negotiations.

Under such conditions the coordination between city and national government must have been a very general one as the government's plans were elaborated. Sella seems to have seen an advantage in having his ministry lie close to a private housing district, which would provide housing for the transferred ministry employees. Beyond this, the choice had other practical advantages, such as the proximity to the new main railway station *Termini,* the modern gate of the city, and the better hygienic conditions on the hills.

Undoubtedly, however, there was another, less practical reason for the location of the building in this area. It was certain that the new parts of the city would be easier to equip with a modern technical infrastructure, which was one way to start a serious competition against the papal center. National Rome would be a modern alternative with modern issues; it would not touch the historical center. It was to convince by means of better organization and more efficiency.

Description of the Building

The Palazzo del Ministero delle Finanze occupies an area 300 by 118 meters, bounded on the long sides by Via XX Settembre and Via della Cernaia (toward the Baths of Diocletian and the railway station), and on the short sides by Via Goito (toward Porta Pia) and Via Pastrengo, formerly Via della Corte dei Conti (toward the Quirinal Palace) (Fig. 2). In addition to the Segretariato Generale delle Finanze, the building contained six financial departments.[22]

The construction consists first of a rectangular projecting central block that surrounds the central courtyard, and two long symmetrical setback sections of three wings, one to either side of the central block. Each setback section forms on the interior a rectangular secondary courtyard (Fig. 3). The side toward the Quirinal Palace is called Lato della Corte dei Conti, the opposite one toward Porta Pia, Lato del Debito Pubblico. The four farthest corners of the enormous construction are accentuated by salient pavilions in the same plane as the central block.

The complex should not be characterized as a unified compositional whole but as a system of joined pavilions (Fig. 4).[23] Only the smaller transversal fronts can be seen as facades of a unified composition with flat corner projections, formed by the corner pavilions (Fig. 5), while the longitudinal main fronts are architecturally split and only accentuated in the facades of the projecting central block (Fig. 4).

The distinction between a main facade on Via XX Settembre and a rear facade toward Via della Cernaia is merely a practical one. There is no architectural or decorative difference between the two, except for the sculptural program of the pediments (Figs. 6 and 7). The distinction is due only to the greater urban importance of the Via XX Settembre, leading from Porta Pia to the Quirinal Palace.

The building, which reaches an average height of thirty-one meters from the street level, contains six floors—two of them as basements below the street level—and the roof. The remaining four floors are readable from the external elevation of the whole construction (Fig. 4). The ground floor is contained within the pedestal zone of drafted blocks, which starts above a very low travertine socle with openings to the first basement and ends in a continuous stringcourse. The main and second floor form the next zone of the elevation, crowned by the main cornice. The main floor dominates with its aedicula windows, while the second floor shows simply framed windows. Above the main cornice is the third floor, treated as an attic zone with mezzanine windows.

The elaboration of the general system of the elevation differs according to the architectural and functional importance of the various parts of the

1
The area of the future *Palazzo delle Finanze* along Via XX Settembre. Drawing (58.9 × 44.8 cm), 16 January 1872, presented to the *Consiglio Superiore dei Lavori Pubblici* the 17 January 1872. (ACS, RC, b. 71, s. M IV, *fasc.* 1, f. 19)

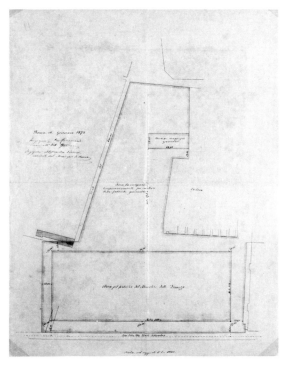

2
Air View of Via XX Settembre. (Fotocielo No. 12/4—Rome)

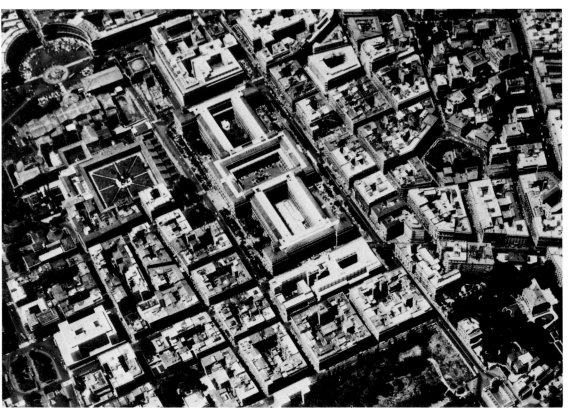

3

Palazzo delle Finanze. Ground floor
Left: Debito Publico; *right: Corte dei Conti; above:* Via della Cernaia; *below:* Via XX Settembre. Plan of the 20 April 1881, date of official consignment of building (79.8 × 47.1 cm). (ACS, RC, b. 81, s. M IV, *fasc.* 45, f. 216)

4

View of the rear elevation (Via della Cernaia). Drawing by Canedi, published by Pesci in the *Illustrazione Italiana*, IV, 50, 14 December 1879, p. 376.

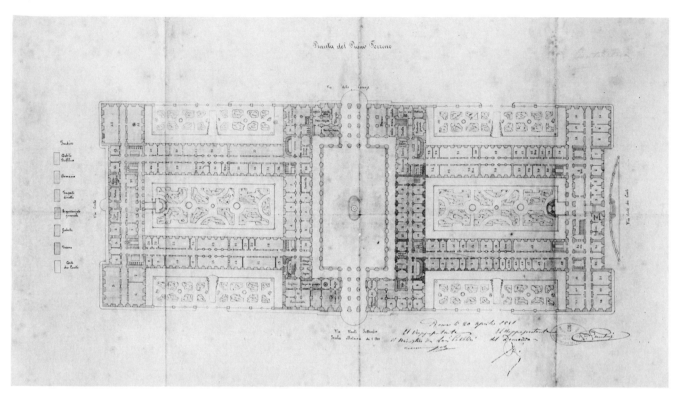

5
Facade of the *Corte dei Conti.* Drawing by Canedi, published by Pesci in
the *Illustrazione Italiana,* IV, 50, 14
December 1879, p. 376.

6
Elevation of the central block, the entrance arches facing Via XX Settembre. (Photo: Schroeter, 1973)

7
Central projecting block facing Via
della Cernaia. (Photo: Schroeter,
1973)

building. The most accentuated fronts are the two identical ones of the central block on the longitudinal sides of the complex (Figs. 3 and 7). Their fifteen frontal bays and four bays on each flank of the projection are emphasized by an ionic colossal order unifying the main and second floor, rusticated pilasters in the ground floor, and pilaster strips in the attic floor, and also by more elaborate window forms in ground, main, and third floor. A centralization is effected by proceeding from ionic pilasters to ionic columns in the central seven bays, while the four columns above the three entrance arches are engaged in the main entablature, ending on the top of the attic in large segmental pediments (Fig. 6). The pedestals of the seven middle bays are linked with balusters forming balconies (Fig. 7).

The least important longitudinal wings follow the general elevation, are not decorated by a colossal order, and their twenty-one bays are defined in the main floor by narrow standing simple windows with tympana (Fig. 4).

The side elevations are both centralized in the three middle bays through different window forms in ground and main floor and balconies above the arched door. The Corte dei Conti, considered as the second most important department of the whole ministry, has a more representational aspect because of the balustered ramps leading to the entrance[24] and the lower number of bays (Fig. 5). The facade of the Corte dei Conti contains thirteen bays without the corner projections, the facade of the Debito Pubblico fifteen smaller bays. Therefore we see on the latter facade two pilasters, which try to provide rhythm for the crowded wall.

The three visible facades of each corner pavilion, each consisting of five bays, achieve their special character through pilasters at the corners and one accentuated central window in the main floor. The small square *belvederi* on the top of the pavilions emphasize the extreme corners of the complex and contain water tanks (Fig. 4).

The two flanking secondary courtyards, the Cortile della Corte dei Conti and the Cortile del Debito Pubblico, are identical in their measurements (81 by 35 meters) and in the elevation of the longitudinal sides, repeating very simple arched windows, articulated by stringcourses, frames, and flat pilasters or pilaster strips (Figs. 8 and 9).[25] The floor level of both courtyards is shifted because of the lower ground level, so that the first basement appears here as the ground floor with drafted blocks and the external attic zone corresponds in the courtyard to an integrated fourth floor. The attic floor of the courtyards visible today (Fig. 8) is a modern extension of the roof level, as can be seen when compared with the drawings of 1879 (Fig. 9). Only the elaboration of the elevation of the transversal sides of both secondary courtyards varies. Their extreme ends follow in

their decoration the example of the central courtyard, the Corte dei Conti, with a gallery on ground and main floors, the Debito Pubblico only on the ground floor, as we see on the drawing of 1879 (Fig. 9) and the plans of the main (Fig. 10) and second floors (Fig. 11). On the opposite sides toward the central block the Cortile del Debito Pubblico follows the decoration of the central courtyard as well, while in the Cortile della Corte dei Conti the system of the longitudinal wings is continued (Fig. 8). The last two floors of these tracts were added after the completion of the building, following the drawing of 1879 (Fig. 9) and the plan of the second floor (Fig. 11).

The central courtyard (69 by 36 meters) is, compositionally, the most elaborate part of the building, with a double arcade that was once planned opened but was later closed for climatic reasons (Figs. 12 and 13). The upper two floors are set back by the depth of the arcade and are articulated by pilaster strips, the second floor with arched windows under tympana, the third floor treated as a mezzanine. The tuscan-doric and ionic orders of the double arcade follow obviously Roman traditions, with their open arcades and wall piers with pilasters and projecting attached columns. We will discuss the importance of this courtyard later.

The architectonic decoration was neither a primary nor even an important detail in the intent of the client, although it should be considered as one possible contribution to the political ideological content of the construction. The primary elements in the formation of the Palazzo delle Finanze were technical, tectonic, and functional.

The Construction of the Palazzo delle Finanze

The original project of the engineer Raffaele Canevari was primarily a building with an iron structure. The vertical structure was planned to be cast-iron columns and the horizontal to be iron beams, producing the possibility of easily alterable spaces (Doc. 7). This advantage must have interested Minister Sella, who may have been calculatedly thinking about potential later necessities of his administration. Notice of the early iron concept is contained in a memorandum of Canevari prepared for the Ministro dei Lavori Pubblici in connection with a court case between the construction firm and the government that ended only in 1885:

The original concept of the Palazzo delle Finanze was that of a structure for the greater part in iron and for a lesser part in masonry. The company has gradually provoked a total change of structure, in which the iron has now been reduced to a minimal quantity and has been substituted by masonry.[26] (Doc.6)

Canevari's memorandum brings us to the discussions that affected decisively the formation of

8
Secondary courtyard (*Corte dei Conti*).
View from the transverse wing of the
Corte dei Conti to the transverse wing
of the central block. (Photo: Schroeter,
1973)

9
The three courtyards. View from the
roof of the Debito Pubblico. Drawing
by Paolocci, published by Pesci in the
Illustrazione Italiana, IV, 50, 14 December 1879, p. 373.

10
Palazzo delle Finanze. Main floor.
Plan of the 20 April 1881, date of official consignment of building (82.5 ×
46.7 cm). (ACS, RC, b. 81, s. M IV,
fasc. 45, f. 217)

11
Palazzo delle Finanze. Second floor.
Plan of the 20 April 1881, date of official consignment of building (83.2 ×
47.1 cm). (ACS, RC, b. 81, IV, *fasc*.
45, f. 218)

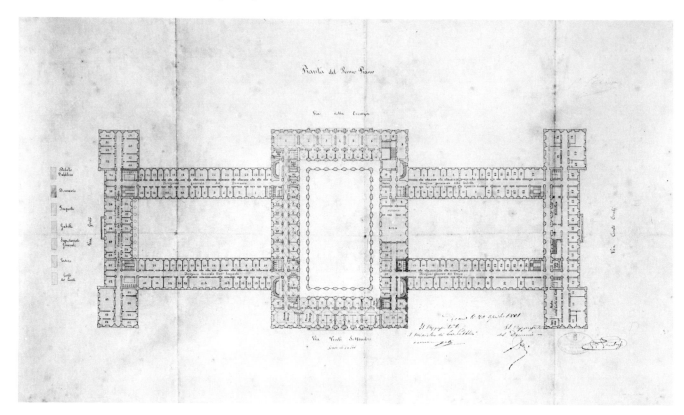

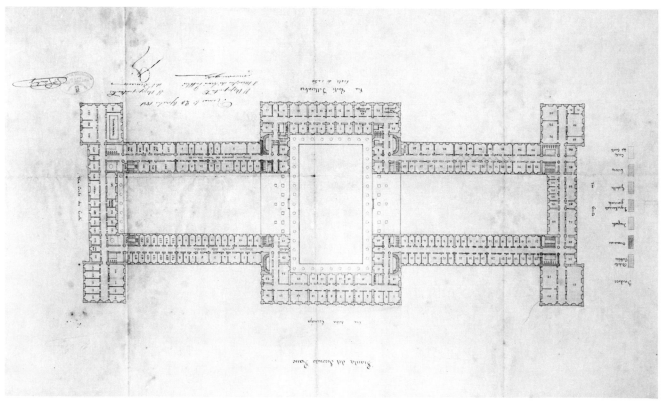

12
Central courtyard. Drawing by
Paolocci, published by Pesci in the *Illustrazione Italiana,* IV, 50, 14 December 1879, p. 372.

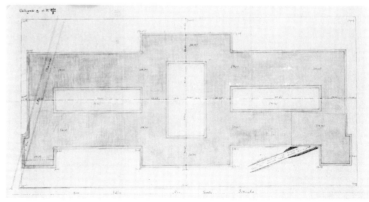

13
Central courtyard. (Photo: Schroeter,
1973)
14
Excavation plan without the rear
corner pavilions. Drawing (70.4 ×
36.0 cm) of the construction firm, 9
May 1872. (ACS, RC, b. 72, s. M IV,
fasc. 9, f. 51)

the finance ministry. These concerned the modifications introduced before and during the execution of the construction, which will de described chronologically.

It is necessary to distinguish two different periods in the history of the construction and the respective decisions: The first period includes the contract with the construction firm Società Veneta per Imprese e Costruzioni Pubbliche of 6 March 1872 and the final, definitive contract with the same firm, the contract (convenzione) of 30 June 1872, ending with the resignation of the Lanza-Sella government on 23 June 1873; the second period extends up to the completion of construction in 1879 and the official delivery of the building on 20 April 1881.

From the decision of the government to build a finance ministry building in the area of Via XX Settembre on 9 September 1871, the construction history was primarily determined by financial considerations. Canevari's first project was criticized in the meeting of the Commissione pel Trasferimento on 26 October 1871 mainly on three points: the waste of space in the central block (too pretentious), the excessive number of windows in the longitudinal wings, and the small amount of usable space in the four corner pavilions (Doc. 7). All these points had been extensively discussed up to the final contract with the Società Veneta on 30 June 1872 and were followed by variations. Agreeing with the argument that there was little usable space, the Commissione pel Trasferimento decided on 8 February 1872, in conformity with Minister Sella, to cancel the two corner pavilions of the rear facade facing Via della Cernaia (Doc. 8). A design of the construction firm, indicating the area that had to be excavated for the foundations, shows the formal effect of this decision (Fig. 14). The excavations were started on 1 April 1872.[27]

Already on 17 January 1872 the Consiglio Superiore dei Lavori Pubblici, responsible for the technical execution of the building, had decided to reduce the width of the corridors from 4 meters to 3.5 meters, the depth of the offices from 6.5 meters to 6.0 meters, and the air space within the exterior walls from 0.6 meters to only 0.1 meters. Following Canevari's calculations, this decision produced a diminution of the total area from 67,924.0 to 60,540.4 square meters, while preserving the same effect and not losing any usable space. The financial advantage is evident—the costs were lowered from 7.0 to 6.2 million lire. The cancellation of the two rear corner pavilions, once again, pushed the costs down to 5.8 million lire (Doc. 9), in this way meeting and even underbidding the first approximate estimate of expenses of 9 September 1871 (6.0 million lire). The first contract between the government and the Società Veneta of 6 March 1872 was signed on the basis of 5.8 million lire. The definitive designs for the execution of the building were to be delivered to the firm by 30 June 1872.

Although the official builder of the new construction was the Ministro dei Lavori Pubblici, Finance Minister Sella had to approve, had to communicate his placet as head of the Ministry of Finance and future resident of the new building. His intention was to "limit the size to the indispensable minimum," agreeing even to the decision to cancel the two rear pavilions (Doc. 10).[28] This would have made the building assymetrical in plan and created the practical disadvantage of omitting space for two sections of the Ministry of Finance.[29] Sella's interest was obviously to provide the best functional and spatial results at the lowest possible cost.

As we have seen, the first contract (6 March 1872) specified delivery of the working drawings by 30 June of the same year. During their preparation it became more and more evident that the designs of Canevari had been far too general and, consequently, that the calculation of costs and material was wrong. Therefore the whole project had to be revised, and new modifications, also structural ones, were introduced.

With the new calculations of 14/15 June 1872 and the approval of the plans by the Consiglio Superiore dei Lavori Pubblici (Council of Public Works) on 21 June 1872, the problem of increased costs was solved: The definitive contract (convenzione) with the construction firm (30 June 1872) limited the execution of the building to the central block and the part of the Corte dei Conti for the previously contracted sum of 5.8 million lire. For the construction of the remaining part (Debito Pubblico) a new contract was drawn up with the same firm on 18 December 1875.

During the review of the project the former solution, which included the two rear corner pavilions, was confirmed. Their reintroduction was related to administrative planning, which anticipated an increase up to 2,500 of the number of employees (Doc. 11). The reduced plan did not provide for the relocation of the two sections that had been omitted.

The definitive contract, however, did not stop the effort for modifications, although it prescribed that the essential character of the building not be changed, in case of necessary variations of the project. But, in fact, the most drastic modifications were introduced after 30 June 1872.

Immediately after the contract had been signed, the Commissione pel Trasferimento agreed to Canevari's proposal, as architect and supervisor of construction, to reintroduce the windows that had been removed previously for aesthetic reasons (Doc. 12).[30] Each floor in the longitudinal wings received two more windows, increasing their number from nineteen to twenty-one. This modification created the possibility of seventy-two more offices, with each window corresponding to one office for three employees.

Other variations after 30 June 1872 started to change the entire original structure of the project. Offering high cost reductions,[31] the Società Veneta first proposed the substitution of masonry and stone piers for the entire vertical cast-iron structure and obtained approval on 12 October 1872. Although this replacement reduced slightly the inner space and limited the mutability of the spaces, because of the lower cost Sella had no objection (Doc. 13).[32] The long-span, horizontal iron structure, which afforded a potential variability of the inner-room distribution was retained. But this structure was the next item challenged by the construction firm.

A new proposal in September 1872 provided for the substitution of barrel vaults for the iron beams throughout the ground floor and in a considerable part of the main floor (Doc. 12).[33] Sella was asked for his opinion. He replied negatively (Doc. 13),[34] and the variations were only accepted in March 1874, that is, eight months after the Lanza-Sella government lost its majority in parliament.

We cannot be certain that these plans would not have been approved with Sella as head of the Ministry of Finance, but he had strong reservations, relating also to the delivery date of the building, against the new proposal in spite of the one million lire potential reduction in construction cost (Doc. 14). The exterior walls were to be increased by 0.2 meters, and the completion of construction was in this way retarded. The second and third floors kept their iron beams, permitting an easier functional distribution of the office space.

In any case, from the beginning the modifications made during Sella's term of office show a general tendency for economic solutions that insofar as possible do not destroy the functional character and use-space requirements. He did not aim for a building that would be technically innovative but rather for a functional one. Cost was carefully weighted against the modifications, without disregarding either.

After the tenure of Sella this concept of utility was not applied anymore to the building. There were two important variations under the government of Depretis, who served as both Prime Minister and Minister of Finance:

1. On 11 April 1874 the Consiglio Superiore dei Lavori Pubblici decided to leave out the upper two floors of the transverse wings between the central and the secondary courtyards, which emphasized the already impressive double arcade of the central courtyard and combined, formally, the three divisions of the construction (Fig. 9) but reduced the usable space.

2. The plan of the main floor of the transverse wing of the central block toward the Corte dei Conti was changed. Parts of the small-sized rooms of the apartments of the minister and surrounding offices were demolished, in order to install a large aulic meeting room for the Consiglio di Stato, the so-called Aula del Consiglio (today the Sala della Maggioranza) with one antechamber, the Anti-Sala (Fig. 15). Together with this alteration, ordered by Depretis, on 2 November 1876, it was decided to change the space distribution of the front section of the central block facing Via della Cernaia. Instead of office rooms with one window, corresponding to the solution on the opposite side, Depretis introduced a long sequence of large decorated *saloni* along the rear facade (Doc. 15) (Fig. 15).

The Aula del Consiglio became the most appreciated part of the building artistically in the view of contemporaries. The decoration and the painted ceiling of Cesare Mariani, who received the commission for the painting after a competition held by the Direzione delle Belle Arti del Ministero della Pubblica Istruzione—one of the very few competitions in the history of this building—has an allegorical political program with historical references to Italian unification. The present context does not allow an explanation of the iconographical program.[35] It is of interest, however, that the later modifications of the building tended to give more pomp, more artistic and spatial effects to the first national building in Rome, while under the Lanza-Sella administration the modifications showed the opposite tendency.

The essential terms of the construction were already fixed by the government of Lanza-Sella. The primarily technical and functional character of the building is reflected in the general distribution of the spaces. One need only calculate and compare the representational spaces with the purely functional office space. The comparison holds good even on the traditionally most decorated main floor of the building.

Considering the fact that the construction extends over a tract 300 by 118 meters and houses seven different departments with facilities for libraries, archives,[36] and meeting rooms, the areas devoted to ceremonial purposes, as luxury space, are considerably limited.[37]

There are mainly two areas where this representational demand is evident. Both are located around a functionally superfluous *scala nobile,* a staircase used only on special occasions. The first area, in the central block, starts with the staircase on the left of the entrance arches of the rear facade and extends in the main floor over the rear section and

141
Rome's First
National State
Architecture: The
Palazzo delle
Finanze

15
Palazzo delle Finanze. Main floor.
Detail of Fig. 10: Central block.
16
Palazzo delle Finanze. Main floor.
Detail of Fig. 10: Corte dei Conti.

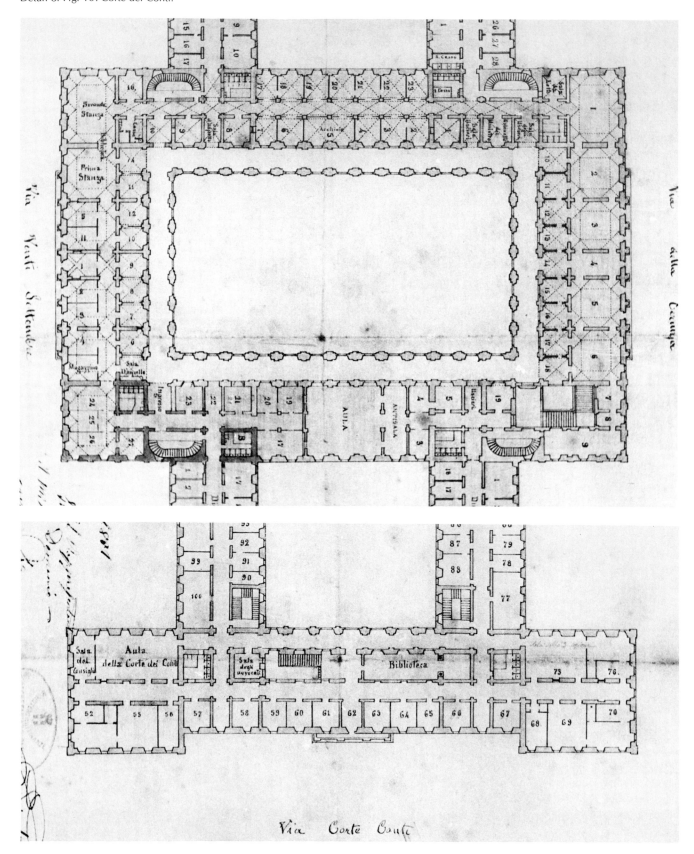

the transverse wing toward the Corte dei Conti (Figs. 3 and 15). The atrium of the entrance arches with three aisles opens to the left to a wide pronaos which leads to the scala nobile.[38] The staircase ends at the main floor. The decoration with materials such as marble and *pietra serena* produces a relatively respectable appearance. On the main floor the staircase opens onto a narrow corridor, crosses the entering corridor of the longitudinal wings, and ends finally at the antechamber and the Aula del Consiglio. This inconvenient conjunction of the staircase and the Aula is due to the alteration that had been introduced by Depretis in 1876. The old system provided in this area apartments of much narrower size for the Minister. Also following Sella's concept, the frontal section consisted of smaller rooms, used as offices. Following his intent, the representational zone would have been limited to the rooms annexed to the staircase.

The second area, similarly disposed, is located in the transverse wing of the Corte dei Conti, with its facade facing Via Pastrengo. It runs along the whole extension of the interior side of the wing and includes the two corner pavilions. It consists of the staircase, the library, and the two meeting rooms of the Corte dei Conti (Fig. 16). The central part with the library is on one side, accompanied by an arcade toward the courtyard, while on the other side there is a corridor with offices toward the facade.

Apart from these two areas, the two vestibules of the entrances of the transverse facades are emphasized through decoration and choice of materials, and the main floor arcade of the central courtyard produces a more ceremonial accentuation, especially through its measurements (Fig. 15).[39] The remaining space was used primarily for offices, interrupted from time to time by larger rooms for administrative needs. The eight secondary stairways, four in the corners of the central block and four at the junctions of the longitudinal and the extreme transverse wings (Figs. 3 and 10), served purely practical purposes.

Practicality as Intent

As we have seen, Minister of Finance Sella, as the commissioner of the building, is the central figure for the interpretation of our political questioning. The decisions made during the government of the Lanza-Sella Cabinet show a precise tendency characterized by financial and technical functional criteria. Sella himself affirmed his unartistic intent quite often. In a letter written during the preparation of the definitive contract with the Società Veneta of 30 June 1872, he gave, among others, a very indicative order: "All types of decoration should be eliminated, except in the two central projections, where

also it must be restricted to an absolute *minimum* [Sella's italics]."[40] (Doc. 16).

He adds neither detail nor motive, and he even rejects any involvement in choosing the scheme for architectural decoration: "Let me say it once and for all, that I take neither credit nor discredit for the architecture of this building, therefore you should neither praise me nor blame me for the external structure of the edifice."[41]

Although these two quotations might seem contradictory, the implications are quite clear. He did not care about the external architectural character of the construction; he merely wanted to reduce costs. By reducing both the costs and the decoration, he consequently influenced the artistic formation of the building.

Sella chose Raffaele Canevari as architect on the basis of Canevari's knowledge of the city and his technical expertise (Doc. 3).[42] This choice fell not on one of the important architects of the time but on a man who had little experience in archiecture and was a specialist in hydraulic engineering. There was no competition held for the first national government building in Rome. Canevari's collaborator Francesco Pieroni (1829–1883),[43] who designed the central courtyard, was probably working with Canevari from the very beginning (Docs. 3 and 4). It is also certain that there was no competition to select the collaborators who appear in the documents as designers under the leadership of Canevari (Pieroni, Martinori, Garofoli). Canevari was responsible for the development and the execution of the project.

Being a second-rate architect, however, Canevari did not play the role of an architect who produces a self-representative piece of architecture. He had to accept, instead, as the history of the building confirms, practically any variation wanted by the administration. Already in October 1871, in the preparative phase for an abortive contract with the construction firm Tatti, the *Capitolato speciale* (appendix to the contract) of the contract provides explicitly the right of the administration to introduce modifications (Doc. 7).[44]

Actual Politics and the Building

Counting the various decisions and determining factors that formed the Palazzo delle Finanze, we now have to answer the question of the political artistic intent and the potential political meaning of the building.

In spite of Sella's antiartistic tendencies in this enterprise, Portoghesi cites *"intenzioni celebrative"*[45] in the building. This celebrative element must be excluded as an explicit intent; it may, however, be included as an implicit effect. We can, in fact, summarize some arguments that confirm a political rep-

143
Rome's First
National State
Architecture: The
Palazzo delle
Finanze

resentative value of the building and are concerned with the site and the architectural decoration.

The enormous extent of the new construction itself certainly represents an aspect of grandeur, apart from its artistic quality. To place such a huge block in an area that lies outside the actual city is an important urbanistic and political statement. The foundation of "New Rome," removed from the papal city, gave concrete form to actual politics through the creation of the governmental "Avenue" of Via XX Settembre. It connects two important antipapal sites of the recent history of the Risorgimento. At the one end the Quirinal Palace was sequestered as the new residence of the royal home of Italy, and at the other was the Porta Pia, where on 20 September 1870 Italian troups victoriously concluded Italian unification.

There was also a political reason for doing it: It was necessary to demonstrate to the Romans and to Europe that henceforth for Italy the possession of Rome was a question of *to be or not to be* and that the Italians like the Centurion of Titus Livius—whose statue, according to the idea of *onorevole* Sella, should have been erected in this building—had said unanimously HIC MANEBIMUS OPTIME.[46]

Besides this evident manifestation of the new nation, of the Italian Rome, which, in spite of its administrational character, introduced the quality of national monument into the building, there was the choice of the architectural style, which could also play a political/ideological role. The architectural details are generalized adaptations of Roman baroque. There is no single Roman palace that served as the source for the articulation of the Palazzo delle Finanze.[47] The elevation is certainly a traditional Roman baroque one in the way it distinguishes the different floors, but this is in contrast to the ground plan, which is not Roman, with the volumes distributed in wings and pavilions.[48] And even the main facades, the two of the central block, are Roman only in their morphology not in their composition with the crowning pediments.

The most expressive part, in Roman terms, is the central courtyard of Pieroni. The double arcade with the tuscan-doric and ionic order embracing the free space is the strongest element of Roman tradition in this building. It evokes the monumental effects of Roman architecture since the Palazzo Venezia. The double arcade of the central courtyard not only refers to Roman traditions in its details but it is an integrally quoted Roman architectural form. General stylistic associations were considered because the Commissione pel Trasferimento in choosing between two alternative designs for the courtyard, voted for a solution with a double arcade of two orders and rejected one with a unique colossal order (Doc. 12).[49] This chosen solution, however, coincides only with the formal tradition of the Roman renaissance baroque type of courtyard. The fact that

in the Palazzo delle Finanze the central courtyard is opened to the public means that very different functions were envisaged for it.

The stylistic issue was noted by contemporaries. The journal *Roma Artistica,* when publishing the Mariani painting in the ceiling of the Aula del Consiglio, mentioned the architecture of the building in one sentence: ". . . as the architectural character of the building required, it was the Italian style of the seventeenth century that provided the concept for the entire decoration."[50] The Roman Journal, as we see, does not use the term *Roman,* but rather *Italian,* style of the seventeenth century. This choice might refer to the already initiated general Italian dispute about a national style, which began influencing architectural practice in the 1880s and ended under fascism. The dispute arose from efforts to find a unifying style for the nation and aimed preferably at revivals of the morphology of quattrocento, cinquecento, and imperial Roman architectural periods. One important monumental contribution to this discussion was the Monument to Victor Emanuel (1885–1911), but the main tendency was the revival of quattrocento and cinquecento architecture, the latter in Rome especially. Roman baroque adaptations were rare, except for the minor architecture of *ambientamento* (conforming in character) in the historic center.

In Rome, the neoclassic tradition of Valadier and Camporesi had begun to recede during the 1850s. The following disparate tendencies of eclecticism led only in the 1880s, to a unified stylistic revival, the cinquecentesque *stile umbertino* (umbertine style). In this context it is quite uncertain whether the Roman baroque detailing of the external decoration of the Ministry of Finance can be seen as an artistic political decision or just as the revivalist continuation of the quantitatively most important stylistic expression of the papal city.

While no documentation has yet come to light to confirm or deny that the baroque references were a deliberate expression of political historical intent, Sella, the architect, and the government cannot have been insensitive to the stylistic associations. The stylistic choice may, therefore, express an implicit political character. This character discloses the contradiction of the political situation of that time. The use of historical power connotations identified with papal Rome, visible in the style, indicates a continuity with papal Roman social and power structures. This continuity is emphasized in spite of the actual antipapal national politics of unification, which were evident in the siting of the building on the Avenue du Risorgimento.

Utility as a Political Quality

The discussion of questions of style and national imagery should not deflect our attention from the predominant functional technical aspects of the formation of the Palazzo delle Finanze in Via XX Settembre. Architectural decoration is a minor aspect of this building. The political ideological content in terms of the decoration turns out to be quite limited and refers mainly to the momentary political situation.

The celebrative expression of the Palazzo delle Finanze should not be investigated only in terms of style but, more important, in the ideological value of the functional, and not artistic, intent of Sella, the building's commissioner, and the functional end product, which according to all critics is of low aesthetic value.[51]

As we have seen, the building does not contribute any sort of architectural innovation to the history of architecture, and in the same way we cannot attribute to it an innovative technical scope. The development shows that Sella did not intend a revolutionary new construction but merely the best possible lodging for his administration; he did not want a Crystal Palace, which he must have seen when he visited the Great World Exhibition of 1851 in London, but a construction which had to be, above all, practical.[52] The initial plan of an iron-structured building was abandoned partially because of financial disadvantages. At the base of all the decisions stood the interest in efficient office space. This issue becomes especially evident if we look at the four facades. Following Sella's concept, the space behind the four fronts is not distributed in representational saloni, as we would expect it in conformity with the external pretension, but consists, instead, of small entities for office use (Figs. 10, 15, 16).[53] Also, the relatively wide secondary courtyards have the functional scope of lighting the offices and the corridors of the longitudinal wings. In addition, the large number of windows in these wings provides for more office space and light.

The practicality of the construction satisfied the first technical needs of the installation and settlement of the national government in Rome. The size of the building was conditioned by the need for a centralized administration of finance, the largest ministry in the nation.[54] But in spite of its merely meeting these necessities, the Palazzo delle Finanze still must be considered a monument of the new nation in the eternal city. It is the first visible step of the nation in Rome. And this step is not just a ceremonial but an administrative one, not a Monument to Victor Emanuel but a building, whose main scope consists of the installation of a modern bureaucracy, underlined by the fact that the first building is for the Ministry of Finance, one of the basic institutions of the new capitalist nation.

The construction is an integral, but also dominant, part of the new housing district Castro Pretorio. Apart from the width of Via XX Settembre and Via

della Cernaia, it is not emphasized urbanistically (Fig. 2). The concept of a free-standing block with a wide, impressive, and authority-evoking free space surrounding it had not yet been established as in later equivalent national buildings, such as the Palazzo di Giustizia by Calderini (begun 1885). The latter is part of a new district too, but its longitudinal facades are both free-standing; on the one side it faces the Tiber, and on the other side it establishes an honorable distance from the district through the huge Piazza Cavour, which occupies more than half of the area covered by the building. In this way the Palazzo di Giustizia (155 by 170 meters), only half the size of the Palazzo delle Finanze (300 by 118 meters), becomes extraordinarily more impressive and monumental. The Sella-Canevari construction shows quite the opposite urban concept. Here the public square is shifted to the interior and becomes a public central courtyard on an axis with the two centrally joining streets (Via Q. Sella and Via Volturno), again an element introduced by Sella (Doc. 7).[55] It functions as a passage for the whole Quartiere Castro Pretorio, with the public offices on the ground floor, and avoids the monumental urban distance (Fig. 2).

This urban concept seems consistent with the technical functional practicality of the building itself. The architectural decoration, which did not interest Quintino Sella, cannot be interpreted as the substantial representative element of this building. The new government under the leadership of Lanza-Sella did not try to take over the traditional terms of representation in Rome as later governments did. Sella seems to compete with papal Rome through other methods. Supported by connotations of Roman history, he founded a "Third Rome" by infusing the new ministry building and the new role of the city with a new concept.

Carroll Meeks observes simplicity as the main characteristic of the building and attributes to it a political expression that stands for the dignity and confidence of the new government.[56] But this cannot be interpreted as the new concept of Rome. The wider urban, social, and political context, which forms the background of the building and determines its realization, cannot be omitted. The interpretation of a political intent and a political expression of the architecture in itself is difficult to accept. The predominant value of utility, which overrides any kind of intent of beauty, is not utility per se.

The substitution of the one for the other can be seen as the new concept. The unpretentious character of the building—the practicality, the utility—becomes the central political ideological element. And this utility, which Sella (trained in the northern

145
Rome's First
National State
Architecture: The
Palazzo delle
Finanze

part of Europe) intended, is the expression of his positivist viewpoint of Rome. For Sella the city in its new role was to be only the producer of ideology, as the city had been before. Instead of the church, the sciences and the intellect were to form the universal reference of the city, the new ruling "objectivity."

The positivist objectivity of the sciences as an important contribution to the ideology of the advancing capitalist system corresponds exactly to the technical objectivity of pure utility, of the practicality of the Palazzo delle Finanze. The objectivity of the sciences and pure utility shield the interest of the nonobjective ruling class, which provided neither for social nor economic independent development of the city of Rome.

Progress in aesthetic and technological development may be absent, but the architecture of the Palazzo delle Finanze marks, in fact, progress toward the organization of an expanding capitalist system.

Notes

I want to thank first Henry A. Millon for the invitation to participate in this symposium and for his technical and linguistic assistance. I would like to recognize publicly the assistance given me in the preparation of this study by the Archivio Centrale dello Stato, Rome; Manlio Spanò, and Franco Pepe of the Ministero del Tesoro, Rome. I would also like to thank Elisabeth Schröter, Bibliotheca Hertziana, Rome, for reading the manuscript and offering helpful suggestions, Gail Geiger and Mary Conlon for their advice in matters of language, and Wolfgang Lotz, the director of the Bibliotheca Hertziana, for his special interest in this study and his technical assistance. Finally I would like to thank my professor, Heinrich Thelen, Berlin, and Ernst Coenen of the Fritz Thyssen Stiftung, Cologne, for the generous support that allowed me to extend the first meeting of the symposium to a study tour of the most important centers of architecture in the United States. I would like to point out that this article was written in 1973. Therefore it has not been possible to consider more recent publications in the study.

1
Italo Insolera, *Roma Moderna* (Turin, 1962), pp. 19, 43.

2
Alberto Caracciolo, *Roma Capitale dal Risorgimento alla crisi dello Stato liberale* (Rome, 1956), p. 35 (my translation). Original text: "Il Venti Settembre del 1870 sembrò che entrassero dalla breccia di Porta Pia soltanto grandi ideali, sublimi aspirazioni politiche e morali. Non era facile intravedere quale fosse nel fondo la realtà ben più prosaica, e più complessa. Le realtà di uno Stato e di una classe dirigente deboli a avvinti da compromessi con l'antico, che venivano a stabilire il centro del loro potere in una città altrettanto debole e arretrata nelle sue strutture profonde, manifestando anche in ciò uno dei caratteri tipici dello sviluppo generale dell'Italia unita."

3
The title Commissione Governativa pel Trasferimento della Sede del Governo a Roma will be cited in subsequent references as Commissione pel Trasferimento.

4
Quintino Sella, *Discorsi parlamentari* (Rome, 1887–1890),

5 vols. 1, (*Discorso* 14 March 1881): p. 292 (my translation). Original text: "Ma che cosa intendete fare a Roma? Questo ci inquieta tutti; a Roma non si sta senza avere dei propositi cosmopolitici. Che cosa intendete a fare? Si, un proposito cosmopolita non possiamo non averlo a Roma; quello della scienza. Noi dobbiamo renderci conto della posizione che occupiamo davanti al mondo civile, dacchè siamo a Roma."

5
Sella, *Discorsi*, 2, (*Discorso* 27 June 1876); pp. 278–279 (my translation). Original text: "Per parte mia confesso che credo doversi avere in Roma la direzione suprema degli interessi generali del paese; credo, come diceva l'altro giorno, che un paese, per dir cosi, alla stessa guisa del corpo umano, debba avere nella capitale il cervello; ma che le altre membra debbono essere perfettamente robuste e tali che il tutto possa funzionare armonicamente." And further on he continues: "Ma se voi credeste, come si diceva, che io sia un'ammiratore della concentrazione di tante officine, di tanti laboratori in una capitale, credeste precisamente il contrario di ciò che io penso. In quanto a noi, io ho sempre desiderato che sia in Roma la parte direttiva, la parte intellettuale, ma non ho mai desiderato che vi sieno grandi agglomerazioni di operai. In una soverchia agglomerazione di operai in Roma io vedrei un vero inconveniente, perchè credo che qui sia il luogo dove si debbono trattare molte questioni che vogliono essere discusse intellettualmente, che richiedono l'opera di tutte le forze intellettuali del paese: ma non sarebbero opportuni gli impeti popolari di grandi masse di operai. Crederei pericolosa o almeno non conveniente un'organizzazione di questa natura. Bene io penso che debbasi spingere la produzione e il lavoro, sotto tutte le forme, nelle altre parti del regno."

6
Auguste Comte, *Cours de philosophie positive,* 6 vols. (Paris, 1830–1842).

7
Ulrike Prokop, *Soziologie der Olympischen Spiele: Sport und Kapitalismus* (Munich, 1971), pp. 9–22. Prokop's interpretation suggests that Comte's positivism was a fundamental ideological contribution to the stabilizing of capitalist society in the second half of the nineteenth century.

8
The registration list of the Ecole des Mines (bound volume in the administrative office of the *Ecole des Mines*) contains *Sella's entrance under the date 27 August 1847 and entitles him ingenieur hydraulique.*

9
Sella, *Discorsi*, 2, (*Discorso,* 27 June 1876): 278. In this speech Sella himself indicates his sojourn in Paris between 1848 and 1851.

10
Pierre Larousse, ed., *Grand Dictionnaire du 19ᵉᵐᵉ siècle,* vol. 14 (Paris, *s.d.* [1876?]), Entry: Sella, Quentin.

11
Alessandro Guiccioli, *Quintino Sella* (Rovigo, 1887), vol. II: 413–414 (my translation). Original text: "Noi studiamo la scienza per la scienza, Monsignore, . . ., senza idee preconcette. Se Lei trova che questa scienza conferma la Sua fede, tanto meglio; ma permetta a noi di non occuparci di ciò."

12
Antonio Gramsci, *Il Risorgimento* (Turin, 1949), p. 159.

13
Caracciolo, *Roma,* pp. 60–67.

14

Larousse, *Grand Dictionnaire*. "Issu d'une riche famille de manufacturiers, il accrut lui-même considérablement sa fortune par la fabrication des gros draps de Piedmont." Translation: "Descendent of a rich family of manufacturers, he increased his fortune considerably through the manufacture of cloth in Piedmont." (my translation)

15

Among others: Luigi Broggi, *Prima Esposizione Italiana di Architettura in Torino, Conferenze* (Turin, 1891); Ugo Pesci, "Il Palazzo del Ministero della Finanze," *L'Illustrazione Italiana*, IV, No. 50 (14 December 1879): pp. 373–375. Anonymous, without title, *L'Illustrazione Italiana*, IV, No. 9 (4 March 1877), p. 130. The only exception with an artistically positive statement is: Pietro Bonelli, "Il Palazzo del Ministero delle Finanze," *Il Buonarotti,* serie II, No. 11 (1876), pp. 298–305.

16

Pesci, "Il Palazzo," pp. 374–375.

17

Among others: Castagnoli-Cecchelli, *Topografia di Roma* (Bologna, 1969), pp. 567–569. Emilio Lavagnino, *Arte Moderna*, I (Turin, 1956), p. 534. Carroll Meeks, *Italian Architecture 1750–1914* (New Haven, 1960), pp. 331–332.

18

Three ministry buildings followed the example of the Palazzo delle Finanze: Ministero di Guerra (1882–1885); Ministero dell'Agricultura (1908–1914); Ministero dei Lavori Pubblici (1911–1925) at Piazzale Porta Pia.

19

Sella, *Discorsi*, 1 (*Discorso* 15, March 1881), pp. 313–314.

20

The expropriation for public utility in that area concerned the Vigna ed Orti dei Certosini, land of the Collegio Romano, and of the Noviziato dei Gesuiti.

21

The contract also fixed an agreement about the execution of the deviation of the Acquedotto Felice, what had been necessary for the construction of the Palazzo delle Finanze. The costs fell to the city. For this deviation see: Arturo Bianchi, "Le vicende e le realizzazioni del piano regolatore di Roma Capitale," *Capitolium,* 9 (1933), pp. 61–66.

22

The ministry contained the Corte dei Conti (General Accounting Department), the Debito Pubblico (National Debt), the Demanio (Government Real Estate), the Tesoro (Treasury), and the Gabelle and Imposte (two specialized tax divisions). Today the situation is changed; a new Ministry of Finance has been built in EUR (1957–1962).

23

The drawings of Paolocci (Figs. 9, 12) and Canedi (Figs. 4, 5) have been used because of the difficulty in photographing the huge complex and in order to compare them to the actual situation of the building. They are illustrations from the article by Pesci, "Il Palazzo."

24

The technical reasons for the ramps is the falling level toward the side of the Corte dei Conti.

25

The courtyard of the Debito Pubblico is occupied by a cinema today and cannot be photographed.

26

See Document 6 (my translation). Original text: "Il concetto originario pel Palazzo delle Finanze fu quello di una costruzione per la massima parte in ferro, e per una minore in muramento. L'Impresa provocò successivamente un assoluto cangiamento di struttura, mentre il ferro è ora ridotto a minima quantità, essendo sostituito dal muro."

27

The contract of 6 March 1872 prescribed 9 meters depth for the foundations, while the later works required a depth of 12–18 meters due to the ancient Roman structures that appeared during the works. This slowed completion of the foundations, in parts as late as June 1874. For the foundation work see also: Raffaele Canevari, *Sulle fondazioni dell'edificio del Ministero delle Finanze, Atti dell'Accademia dei Lincei, serie* II, vol. 2 (Rome, 1875): pp. 35–37.

28

See Document 10. ". . . restringere l'ampiezza al *minimum* indispensabile." The italics are original.

29

The Direzione Generale del Lotto and the Intendenza di Finanza.

30

See Document 12. "Questa modificazione era suggerita di estetica e di simmetria nella pianta . . ." Translation: "This modification was suggested for purposes of aesthetics and symmetry of the plan . . ." (my translation). The fewer windows would have enlarged the width of the bays from 3.875 to 4.3 meters and in this way they would have been closer to the normal width of the bays, which lies between 4.5 and 5.4 meters, the latter regarding the central block. The same reintroduction of two more windows was applied to the transverse facade of the Debito Pubblico, while the facade of the Corte dei Conti kept the wider bays.

31

Iron had to be imported and was expensive at that time.

32

See Document 13. ". . . io non ebbi difficoltà nel suffragare la sostituzione dei muri di facile prosciugamento alle colonette di ghisa, sia perchè si diceva risultarne un risparmio di spesa . . ., sia perchè danno sostanziale non mi pareva venire all'edificio." Translation: ". . . I had no difficulty in accepting the substitution of easy drainage walls for the cast iron columns, both because it was said to result in a saving of money . . . and because it did not seem to me that it would do substantial damage to the building." (my translation)

33

Most of the consequences of this variation are registered in the document.

34

See Document 13. "Ma se si tratta ora di sostituire volte a botte alle volticelle fra travi in ferro temo che ne avvengano parecchi inconvenienti: cioè che si perda spazio in altezza, si perda tempo nella costruzione e nell'asciugamento, si rendano più gravi le conseguenze di qualche movimento nei muri. Quindi non nascondo che la impressione prodotta in me dalla proposta variazione è del tutto sfavorevole." Translation: "But if we are now concerned with substituting barrel vaults for the flat vaults between iron beams, I am afraid that several inconveniences will result: that vertical space will be lost, that time will be lost in the construction and the drying process, and that the consequences of any movements of the walls will become more serious. Therefore I cannot deny that the proposed variation has produced in me an overall unfavorable impression." (my translation) In fact, later, when the substitution had been put in practice, Canevari tried to recover space in the second and third floors.

35
For an approximate iconographical description and a reproduction, see Cesare Mariani, (without title), *Roma Artistica*, 5, (18 August 1879): pp. 209–210, hereafter cited as Mariani untitled article.

36
The great archives with storage rooms and printing office were installed in the first basement, while the second basement contained equipment of mechanical services.

37
In the context of this study the problem of the very interesting typological history of ministries of finance since the eighteenth century must be passed over, although it could be very enlightening.

38
Unfortunately the disposition is hardly visible in the present reproduction.

39
In contrast to all other corridors, the full width of the arcade of the central courtyard is 5.0 meters.

40
See Document 16 (my translation). Original text: "Si opprima ogni specie di decorazione, salvo nei due avancorpi centrali, ove pure sarà da ridursi al *minimum* possibile." Italics from the original.

41
Sella, *Discorsi*, 1, (*Discorso* 15, March 1881): p. 314 (my translation). Original text: "Non ho alcun merito e nessun demerito per l'architettura di quello stabilimento, e lo devo dire una volta per tutte, acciò non mi dia lode o biasimo per l'architettura esterna di quell'edificio."

42
Paolo Portoghesi, ed., *Dizionario enciclopedico di Architettura e Urbanistica* (Roma, 1968), Entry: Canevari, Raffaele: Canevari, in addition to this building, worked also on the bridge of S. Giovanni dei Fiorentini, and later designed the Museo Geologico.

43
Luigi Callari, *Storia d'arte contemporanea italiana* (Rome, 1909), pp. 129–130. According to him, Pieroni was a collaborator of Letarouilly in his work *Edifices de Rome moderne* (Paris, 1840–1857). He also worked on the models of the Colosseum and the Pantheon for the Crystal Palace, designed a project for the planned national Archives and the "ampio cortile del Palazzo delle Finanze, che fabbricò per desiderio del Canevari." Translation: ". . . wide courtyard of the Palazzo dell Finanze which he built for the will of Canevari." (my translation)

44
See Document 7. "Durante la esecuzione dei lavori è però riservata facoltà alla Amministrazione d'introdurre nel progetto tutte quelle parziali modificazioni che non alterino la natura ed entità complessiva delle opere." Translation: "During the execution of the construction the administration reserves the privilege to introduce into the project all those partial modifications that do not alter the nature and the complexity of the project." (my translation) The essentials are not specified.

45
Portoghesi, *L'ecletticismo a Roma 1870–1922* (Rome, 1968), p. 17.

46
Pesci, "Il Palazzo," p. 374 (my translation). Original text: "Vi era anche una ragione politica per farlo: bisognava dimostrare ai Romani ed all'Europa che ormai per l'Italia il possesso di Roma era questione di essere o di non essere e che gli italiani, come il Centurione di Tito Livio—la cui

statua, secondo l'idea dell'on. Sella doveva sorgere in questo palazzo—avenavo detto tutti d'accordo HIC MANEBIMUS OPTIME!" The statue with the inscription has not been executed, and the reference appears only in this article. I have not been able to confirm the plan by documents. It would, however, coincide with the national politics.

47
Meeks, *Italian Architecture*, pp. 331–332. Meeks saw as the main recourse of inspiration for the building the Senatorial Palace of Michelangelo, without proving this association by a stylistic, comparative description. I cannot agree with him in this matter. I see nothing in the elevation or in the details that would support such a conclusion.

48
I deliberately exclude any discussion of a potential French or other source for the ground plan. In our context we are only interested in potential Roman traditions of the architecture.

49
The decision fell during the preparation of the definitive contract (convenzione) of 30 June 1872.

50
Mariani, untitled article, p. 209 (my translation). Original text: " . . . come richiedevasi dal carattere architettonico dell'Edifizio, fu lo stile italiano del secolo XVII il concetto, a cui si informò tutta la decorazione."

51
Among others: Umberto Botazzi, "L'architettura a Roma nella seconda metà del XIX secolo," *Capitolium* VII (1931): pp. 288–289. Guglielmo De Angelis d'Ossat, "L'architettura in Roma negli ultimi decenni del secolo XIX," *Annuario dell'Accademia di S. Luca*, No. 6 (1942): p. 17. Callari, *Storia d'arte*, pp. 129–130: "R. Canevari, romano, . . ., autore del colossale Palazzo delle Finanze in Roma, che da molti è stato chiamato il monumento della terza Italia, ma che nella sua troppo nuda semplicità nulla ha di artistico e degno di Roma. . . ." Translation: "R. Canevari, Roman, . . ., architect of the colossal *Palazzo delle Finanze* in Rome which has been called by many the monument of the third Italy, but which in its excessively bare simplicity has nothing of the artistic style and dignity of Rome. . . ." (my translation)

52
The Palazzo delle Finanze did not win any prize at the International Exhibition of 1878 in Paris, as reported by Pesci "Il Palazzo." The *Rapport du Jury international* does not mention the building in the prize list of the respective group (groupe I, classe 4, section d'architecture). See *Minstre de l'agriculture et du commerce, Exposition universelle internationale de 1878 à Paris, Rapport du Jury international* (Paris, 1880).

53
As we remember, the saloni of this wing are due to the modification of 1876.

54
Pesci, "Il Palazzo." According to him, the Ministry of Finance had nearly as many employees as all the other ministries together.

55
Already during the meeting of 26 October 1871, Canevari affirmed that Sella preferred not to install the wrought-iron gates at the entrance arches of the central block, as Canevari had planned, but that he insisted on leaving the entrances open.

56
Meeks, *Italian Architecture*, pp. 331–332.

153
Votes for Women?
A Graphic
Episode in the
Battle of the Sexes

charms. The rebuttal to this argument was proposed by Jane Addams in an article, "Why Women Should Vote," which first appeared in the *Ladies Home Journal* in 1909[3] She urged women to use the ballot to *preserve* the home, by electing governments that would provide clean milk, sanitary surroundings, and good education for their families in the new urban environments. She pointed out that the farm woman could assume personal responsibility for the safety and cleanliness of the milk from her own cow, but that in the cities, mothers were dependent on the community for such services. Women's traditional responsibilities were education and protection of children; they must bring their superior spiritual forces to bear on a materialistic world. A woman must, wrote Jane Addams, even though it was an extra burden, "bring herself to the use of the ballot." Many posters emphasize this motivation. Images of motherly suffragists who gently asked for the vote in order to provide better homes for their families offered an analgesia to the antisuffrage forces and soothed masculine misgivings.

An antisuffrage article by George Holland in the *Sewanee Review* of 1909[4] predicted that if the suffragists were successful in gaining the ballot, all women would in time become "large-handed, big-footed, flat-chested, and thin-lipped." These unfeminine characteristics were often used by caricaturists to satirize feminists. A long tradition of popular prints from the fifteenth century through Grandville and Daumier in the nineteenth century to the cartoonists for *Punch* and *Life Magazine* in the early twentieth century mocked the "over-emancipated" woman by picturing her as stringy, angular, and sexless or as self-satisfied and matronly with an overwhelming bosom and bottom. Role reversal is a common caricatural device in this tradition; men are shown caring for the squalling baby, cleaning and washing up while the women laze about, congregate in saloons, smoke cigars, or write novels. (See Fig. 4, "The Age of Iron." Men seem always to have recognized that housework was a very undesirable thing to do when *they* were pictured doing it.) The prosuffrage poster artists countered with images of the "womanly" woman, whose sources in the history of art were traditional madonna or classical goddess types. (See Fig. 5, "Votes for Women" and Fig. 6, "Give Her of the Fruit.") These images, in general, suppressed the sexual characteristics of the woman and presented her as a creature somewhere between a nun and a nineteenth-century nature goddess.

The Style of the Posters as Suffragist Strategy

The relationship between artist and work, when the work is intended to serve the ends of a political faction, is quite different from the twentieth-century ideal of the artistic process. According to this ideal, the artist acts as a free individual to translate his or her own emotions, ideas, and experiences into an individual language of visual form. If he or she succeeds in creating a genuinely personal amalgam of life experience and artistic forms, the result will be an original "style."

But originality of style is not so desirable a quality in art with a political (or commercial) message, except insofar as some superficial novelty will attract attention. In 1933, Cassandre (Jean-Marie Moreau), the French advertising designer famous for his "Dubonnet" and "Etoile du Nord" posters, spoke about his own experience as a maker of commercial posters, in which the personal convictions of the artist about the product are relatively unimportant.

> It is difficult to determine the status of the poster among the pictorial arts. Some reckon it as a department of painting, which is mistaken, others place it among the decorative arts and I believe they are no less mistaken. . . . The poster demands utter resignation on the part of the artist. He must not assert his personality. If he does so it would be contrary to his rights.
>
> Painting is an end in itself. The poster is only a means to an end, a means of communication between the dealer and the public, something like a telegraph. The poster designer plays the part of the telegraph operator; he does not initiate news, he merely dispenses it. No one asks him for his opinion; he is only required to bring about a clear, good, and exact transmission.[5]

If Cassandre were exactly right, the style of posters would never change, as the style of transmitting a message in Morse code varies only minimally with minor idiosyncrasies of the operator. But poster styles do change because their style, as well as their content, carries the message. The "how" is part of the "what," and poster makers knowingly choose the forms that they judge will transmit the content most appropriately. When the designer of a German World War I poster consciously chooses to imitate the style of a late Gothic woodcut, or the maker of a modern advertising poster for canned strawberries chooses the forms of children's book illustration, both artists clearly intend the selected style to project a set of connotations that will form an aura around the content and communicate to the id as well as to the ego. The propaganda artist finds the styles of the past particularly useful for the resonances they contain and because we are emotionally conditioned to respond to them in a more or less predictable fashion. Whether or not the content of the poster springs from the personal convictions of the artist, as it does with "amateur" political posters, the choice of a style that communicates to the right public with the right voice is crucial.

The poster artists for women's suffrage seem to have, to some extent, chosen styles appropriate to their intentions. In general they followed the stylistic tradition of persuasive art by using modes of either illusionism or stylized realism to represent figures,

4
"The Age of Iron. Man as He Expects
to Be." Currier and Ives, 1869. Lithograph, 18 × 24 in. (Library of
Congress)

5
"Votes for Women." B. M. Boye, ca.
1913. Lithograph, 26 × 18 in. Sierra
Art Engraving Co., San Francisco.
(Schlesinger Library, Radcliffe
College)

6
"Give Her of the Fruit." Evelyn Rum-
sey Cary, ca. 1915. Lithograph, 48 ×
30 in. (Library of Congress)

attributes, and emblems. But unlike most political poster makers, they drew inspiration from the romantic pre-Raphaelite and decorative art nouveau styles. The forms of art nouveau influenced commercial art and the design of home furnishings and arts and crafts even into the 1920s. It was a style generally considered unsuitable for political posters and rarely used in the World War I posters. But the pre-Raphaelite and art nouveau styles have this advantage: they romanticize women. They are "feminine" styles not created by women but carrying connotations of what constitutes femininity from a masculine point of view. (See Fig. 5, "Votes for Women," and Fig. 6, "Give Her of the Fruit.")

The suffrage posters are also influenced by magazine and book illustration and in some cases by children's book illustration, an intentionally "innocent" and even "cute" style. (See Fig. 2.) The colors of all the posters tend to be pastel, the lines pliant; the emphatic color contrasts and aggressive forms of most twentieth-century political posters are avoided. The choice of the styles of the suffrage posters seems to be politic; their forms soften and neutralize the content. The women's suffrage posters do not shout, they speak in a voice ever soft and low.

Great Britain and the United States: A Contrast

The differences between the posters produced in Great Britain and the United States seem to reflect the differences in the political realities and the ideology of suffragists in the two countries. On the whole, the British posters tend to be more aggressive than the American, occasionally on the attack rather than on the defense. (See "Handicapped!," Fig. 7.) In England, militancy was greater and reaction stronger. The first militant action of the suffragists took place in 1905, when an election meeting in Manchester on behalf of Winston Churchill was disrupted by Emmeline Pankhurst's daughter, Christabel, and Annie Kenney, her working-class associate in the WSPU. They chanted "votes for women!" from the back of the hall, were arrested for disturbing the peace and manhandled. Christabel Pankhurst went to jail for a week rather than pay the ten shilling fine. The incident was reported in the Manchester and London press and set a pattern for increasingly well-publicized confrontations between militant suffragists and government and parliamentary officials. Attracting attention to their cause and enlisting public opinion, which was significantly influenced by the press, was one of the most effective methods, for the British suffragists, of putting pressure on the party in power.

American suffragists were not limited to appealing to public opinion; by 1914 they controlled ninety-one electoral votes from the nine states that had granted suffrage to women. Alice Paul, leader of the National Women's Party, insisted that these votes should be used as a partisan political weapon against the Democrats in the 1916 presidential election, a position that split the National Women's Party from the nonpartisan NAWSA. NAWSA favored "indirect influence" and eschewed political coercion, relying instead on the desire for reform and justice on the part of men, a position that the more militant suffragists identified with helplessness and ineffectiveness. But even though the National Women's Party was considered militant by NAWSA, they never used tactics as aggressive as those of the British suffragists. And it is the more indirect approach favored by NAWSA that most of the American posters take.

The British poster makers, like the Americans, mainly addressed themselves to a well-educated, middle-class audience. However, there are some English posters that plead the special cause of working-class women, a group almost totally ignored in the American suffrage movement. (See Fig. 8, "They Have a Cheek. I've Never been Asked.")

The British posters also seem to place far more stress on the intellectual achievements and professional accomplishments of women and less on the importance of motherhood and the "womanly nature." The anonymous poster, "Polling Station." (Fig. 9) refers to a parade held in London on June 13, 1908, in which 13,000 women marched in groups; professional women, university graduates, artists, writers, and actresses among them. Homemakers brought up the rear of this parade, and motherhood has been treated with some ambivalence by the poster designer. The mother is shown front and center—the most important figure in placement—but her position of bending down to the child lowers her in relation to the erect figures of the professional women flanking her on both sides.

Aileen Kraditor in her book, *Ideas of the Women's Suffrage Movement, 1890–1920,*[6] notes that up into the 1890s the suffrage movement in the United States was educational, basing its appeal on the equality of men and women and on the justice of suffrage for both. But as the movement took on a more activist stance, new and more politically sophisticated arguments were introduced, based not on justice but on expediency. Suffragists campaigning in northern cities, for example, pointed out that the male, lower-class immigrant vote could be outbalanced by the female, middle-class, 100% American vote. These tactics of practical persuasion depended less on the idea of the simple fairness of suffrage for women, a concept expressed in the British poster of 1908, "Justice Demands the Vote." (See Fig. 10.) But British poster makers were also willing to use arguments based on political "expediency."

157
Votes for Women?
A Graphic
Episode in the
Battle of the Sexes

"Polling Station" (Fig. 9) shows distinguished professional women barred from a voting place which is being entered freely by a motley crew of men, some obviously of inferior status. The appeal of this poster and also of "Convicts, Lunatics, and Women Have No Vote," of 1909 (Fig. 11) is based on the idea of the superiority of the educated woman to some male citizens, and the loss to society of her contribution to government. The concept for "Convicts, Lunatics and Women Have No Vote" was borrowed from an American postcard-size photomontage which was widely circulated in the 1890's. (See Fig. 12, "American Woman and Her Political Peers.") In the center of this curious image the refined and respectable face of Frances Willard, president of the International Women's Christian Temperance Union, appears. In the four corners are representatives of the other groups in American society who, like women, cannot vote: clockwise from upper left, the congenital idiot, the convict, the lunatic, and the Indian. The message, however, is not that all men and women are equal and that Indians and idiots should be allowed to vote.

The Case of the Missing Theme; or L'homme Manqué

The posters most often present women themselves. In British posters they often appear in academic robes or other professional costume, in American posters more often as mothers or symbols of nurturing. The image of woman as nurturer is so strong and frequent in the history of visual art that one British prosuffrage poster was misinterpreted as a result. The poster shows "Mrs. John Bull" refusing to dish out any more from a large bowl labeled "political help" to a group of little boys marked with the names of various political organizations. The legend reads, "Now you greedy boys. I shall not give you any more until I have helped myself." (See Fig. 13.) The woman in the poster, since she is refusing food to children, was interpreted as a "bad mother," and therefore the poster was antisuffrage propaganda; this was the impression of several art historians at the first MIT conference in December 1972. This momentary misunderstanding illuminates one of the weaknesses of the women's posters; their reluctance to attack and caricature the opposition. If the little boys in the poster had been shown as grossly fat and ugly as well as aggressively greedy (the way Gillray might have pictured them, for instance) and the mother obviously undernourished and needy, the poster would carry its message with force and clarity. This lack of audacity may account for the missing theme in the posters of the women's suffrage movement. There are no attacks on men.

In other visual propaganda campaigns of politically weak groups against groups in power—the Protestants versus the Catholics in the sixteenth century, the republicans against the monarchists in nineteenth-century France, and the socialists versus capitalists in the later nineteenth and twentieth centuries—the enemy was always specifically defined and clearly attacked through mockery, exaggeration of his animal or subhuman nature (as demonstrated by external appearance), or by association with the devil or satanic powers. But where, for example, is the suffragist poster depicting a monstrous male with his cruelly booted heel grinding down on the neck of the voteless, helpless female? Not to be found. The poster makers for women's suffrage avoid attacking men in favor of presenting a positive image of women. Perhaps it was distasteful to women to lose dignity by admitting their oppression. Perhaps they feared losing advantages they already had. Perhaps there was a natural reluctance on the part of the weaker half of the human race to define the stronger half as the enemy. It was only men, after all, who could give women the vote; antagonizing them was not good political strategy.

Some Conclusions

The posters, by their peculiar lack of forcefulness and their gentility and timidity, visually illustrate the dilemma of the suffragists, who wanted political power and freedom from an oppressive social status but hesitated to part with their traditional sexual identity (even though it was one that had been defined by men), perhaps for fear of being left sexless.

The women artists who made the posters faced this problem in concrete terms: they had no tradition of imagemaking to draw upon except the masculine one in which they were embedded as second-class citizens. This tradition did not serve them: it provided few images of women except male-created ones. The poster artists could only make a selection from this available tradition and fit the suffragist image, more or less uneasily, into it. The Pre-Raphaelite woman often chosen was graceful, elegant, idolized, and above all, ladylike. Her clothing flowed in liquid but modest folds, her hair was her crown and train. It was an image that connoted sexual and social privilege and one with which, most probably, many of the suffragists found it pleasant to identify. But was it a self-image that, once adopted, impeded the suffragists from clearly challenging a political system that denied women equality in exchange for giving them privilege and a social system that emphasized the superiority of an educated, cultivated minority? In other words, can the status quo truly be opposed by an art that uses the artistic conventions acceptable to that status quo? A conviction that it cannot is behind the present-day search of many women artists for new forms and content that are based on their own experience and not selected or modified from available, primarily masculine,

7
"Handicapped!" Anonymous, ca.
1910. Lithograph, 30 × 20 in. (Library
of Congress)

8
'They Have a Cheek.'' Emily Ford,
1908. Lithograph, 40 × 29 in. Published by Artists' Suffrage League,
London. (Library of Congress)
9
''Polling Station.'' Anonymous, ca.
1908. Hand colored linoleum block
print, 25½ × 23½ in. Designed and
printed at Atelier, 6 Stanlake Villas,
Shepherd's Bush, London.

10
"Justice Demands the Vote."
Anonymous, ca. 1908. Lithograph,
39× 24 in. Published by Women's
Franchise Society, London.
(Schlesinger Library, Radcliffe
College)

11
"Convicts, Lunatics, and Women
Have No Vote." Emily J. Harding An-
drews, ca. 1909. Lithograph, 40 × 30
in. Published by Artists' Suffrage
League, London. (Library of Congress)
12
"American Woman and her Political
Peers." Henrietta Briggs Wall, 1893.
Composite Photograph, 6½ × 4¼ in.
(The Sophia Smith Collection, Wom-
en's History Archive, Smith College,
Northampton, Mass.)

13
"Now You Greedy Boys. I Shall Not
Give You Any More Until I Have
Helped Myself." D. Meeson Coates.
Lithograph 30 × 40 in. Published by
National Union of Women's Suffrage
Societies, Great Britain. (Library of
Congress)
14
"Won't You Let Me Help You, John."
Anonymous, ca. 1915. Hand-colored
lithograph, 40 × 30 in. (Schlesinger
Library, Radcliffe College)

15
"National League for Women's Service." Anonymous, ca. 1918. Photo-
lithograph, 40 × 30 in. (Library of
Congress)

tradition. But the suffragists looked into the mirror of art and believed they saw themselves. This belief may have conditioned not only the style of their posters but their style of political action.

The suffrage posters seem ineffective when compared with present-day posters, but they also seem weak when compared with posters made during World War I. In these posters, made by men at almost the same time, women are cast in another role. They are shown as strong, capable, engaged in manual labor, in heroic "masculine" poses or as powerful allegorical figures. The contrast between the timid, self-deprecating woman in "Won't You Let Me Help You, John?" (Fig. 14) and the glamorous operetta heroine in the poster for the National League for Women's Service of World War I (Fig. 15) is startling. Which image won the vote for women? The result (if not the aim) of both kinds of propaganda was the same; to convince men that women were harmless, that they would not threaten the social status quo, and that they believed in and would work for the same ends as men. Women's efforts in World War I substantiated this. Patriotism and the "Americanization" of aliens were specific war aims of NAWSA. Without the proof women gave in World War I that they could make a contribution to the national war effort, it is doubtful they would have received the vote, either in the United States or in Great Britain. The campaign of the British suffragists resulted in partial victory in 1918, when university graduates over thirty, women householders, and householders' wives over thirty were granted the vote. Full suffrage on an equal basis with men did not come until 1928. In the United States, the Nineteenth Amendment to the Federal Constitution, passed by Congress in May, 1919, was ratified by the necessary three-fourths of the states and proclaimed August 26, 1920, so that all women citizens over twenty-one could vote at the presidential elections in November of that year, when Woodrow Wilson was returned to office.

As it turned out, the women were harmless. The vote was conceived of as an end, not as a means to an end, by most. After winning it, American women did not begin to wield it for their own advantage until the era of the new feminism which began in the late 1960s, forty years after the moving victory of our grandmothers, the suffragists.

Notes

1
Preserved in the collections of the Department of Prints and Photographs and the National Women's Party Papers at the Library of Congress, the Department of Political History at the Smithsonian, the Schlesinger Library of Radcliffe College, the Sophia Smith Collection of Smith College, the Laidlaw Collection at the New York Historical Society, the Rare Books Division of the New York Public Library.

2
See James M. Buckley, *The Wrong and Peril of Woman Suffrage* (New York, 1909).

3
Reprinted in *Woman Suffrage, History, Arguments, Results,* ed. Mrs. Frances Bjorkman (New York, 1915).

4
"The Suffragette," *Sewanee Review 17* (July, 1909): 270.

5
Quoted by John Barnicoat, *A Concise History of Posters* (Thames and Hudson, London, 1972), p. 80.

6
Columbia University Press (New York, 1965). Kraditor's book contains an excellent bibliography of the history of the suffrage movement.

161
Votes for Women?
A Graphic
Episode in the
Battle of the Sexes

9
Five Artists in the Service of Politics in the Pages of *L'Assiette au Beurre*

Ralph E. Shikes

Behind the facade of the Paris Exposition of 1900, France was a nation in the turmoil of transition to an industrial society. The gap between the affluent and the impoverished was brutally wide. As France had lagged behind England and Germany in industrial development, so had it failed to provide any but a few of the services essential to protect the weak, the unemployed, the sick, and the elderly. Paris was filled with the inevitable byproducts of this society—the prostitutes and other "street people," the castoffs and homeless—sketched in life by Steinlen, Van Dongen, and other artists.

Daumier's dream of a democratic France, responsive to the will and the needs of the people, was still far from fulfillment. The Dreyfus affair seemed to end the threat to the Republic by the right wing military-church-aristocracy coalition, but the issues of clericalism and militarism remained. And the state, instead of being an instrument of the people, was a huge, bureaucratic machine dominated by "l'assiette au beurre"—the butter dish—the nice, fat job with the prerogative of dispensing favors for a price.

Into this scene of contrasting human conditions, artists from all over the world poured into Paris in the first decade, by the hundreds, then by the thousands. In 1900, 164 artists exhibited at the Salon des Indépendants; in 1901, the entrants had risen to 1012; by 1903, this figure had doubled; in 1905, as many as 4209 exhibited, and by 1909, the incredible total reached 6701.[1]

This tremendous influx of artists, or would-be artists, obviously meant hunger and poverty for most and intense competition for the few sources of income—fashion drawing, book illustration, and so forth. Many contributed satirical sketches or caricatures, occasionally even strongly political drawings, to the "journeaux amusants," especially *Le Rire* or *Le Courrier Français,* for which they were paid sometimes generously, other times not at all.[2]

Many managed to scrape by, but protest was in the air. The more social-minded of the artists often turned toward anarchism as the political expression of their reaction against the injustices they observed and the frustrations of their own condition. As a philosophy, it was amorphous enough to appeal to their humanitarian instincts without requiring much discipline or participation. With its stress on the individual, its appeal to artists in an era of experimentation was especially strong. The authoritarianism of Marxian communism was alien to their philosophical bent. "It was the anarchist cultivation of independence of mind and of freedom of action and of experience for its own sake that appealed to the artists and intellectuals," writes George Woodcock, historian of anarchism.[3]

The anarchist tradition among artists was a strong one when the new century began. Among the neo-impressionists, Pissarro, Signac, Luce, Cross, and Van Rysselberghe were still close to Jean Grave, editor of *Les Temps Nouveaux*, official anarchist organ, to which they occasionally contributed, as did one of the Nabis, Félix Vallotton. Among the Fauves, Van Dongen and Vlaminck were to embrace anarchism, at least for a while; later in the decade, most of the cubists were anarchists, with the notable exception of Braque; and the futurists had an anarcho-syndicalist philosophy.

With the tradition of dissent so firmly established among artists, it was a masterstroke of timing when Samuel Schwarz launched *L'Assiette au Beurre* on April 4, 1901. It offered a unique opportunity to the social-minded artist. For most of its twelve years, it was almost entirely visual, its sixteen pages nearly all full-page drawings, at least half in color. Since it was issued weekly, almost 10,000 drawings appeared in *L'Assiette au Beurre,* usually with brief captions. Shrewdly, as protective coloration, Schwarz and his successors balanced the strident issues attacking society with *Punch*-like, gentle, often genial comment on innocuous subjects—Paris in the summer, mothers-in-law, dentists, omnibuses, and so forth. Violent as its attacks were, *L'Assiette au Beurre* was banned for only one issue. Published every Friday, it circulated throughout France and had some distribution in many countries of western Europe.

The size of the page gave the artist full scope for his drawings. Many were one-man issues on a single subject. The wide distribution gave him an audience and a certain fame or notoriety, and the income was welcome; however, the artists were frequently offered a good sum for their drawings but often actually paid very little, and sometimes they went unpaid.[4]

Favorite targets were capitalism, colonialism, the courts, the Catholic church, bureaucracy, the crowned heads of Europe, England, the czar, prostitution, monopolies. As the years went by, the magazine frequently attacked the ex-Socialists—especially Briande and Clemenceau—who they felt had betrayed their political origin when they attained power. Some of the stereotypes of anti-Semitism occasionally appeared, even in work by the most radical of artists, like Franz Kupka, Jules Grandjouan, and Aristide Delannoy, yet the same artists attacked pogroms and anti-Semitism.

As Jean Cassou has pointed out in reviewing the work of one of the artists, Grandjouan, "It is an epoch that lives again, and an epic. The epoch of syndicalism, of socialism . . . the élan of the anarchist revolt. Among all publications that expressed the revolt, the most significant was *L'Assiette au Beurre*. When leafing through it, one rediscovers in its ex-

treme virulence, the spirit that inspired '48 and the Commune, and that continues in the new struggles . . . In *L'Assiette au Beurre* art blended with action in a most natural way."[5]

Among those who contributed were artists who had become or were to become famous: Jacques Villon, Alexandre Steinlen, Franz Kupka, Kees Van Dongen, Jean Louis Forain, Félix Vallotton, Juan Gris, Louis Marcoussis, Alfred Kubin, even poster-artist Jules Chéret, who illustrated an entire frothy issue with his Chérettes. "We were all anarchists without throwing bombs, we had those kinds of ideas," Van Dongen reminisced years later.[6]

Many others who contributed regularly for the twelve years are lesser known today but were familiar to the readers of the ubiquitous satirical magazines of the day, several of them highly respected artists then: Grandjouan, Delannoy, Demetrios Galanis (who was to become one of France's leading book illustrators), D'Ostoya, Roubille, Hermann-Paul, A. Willette, Jossot, Radiguet, and others.

Altogether, *L'Assiette au Beurre* had on its roster about fifty artists who sought to bare what lay behind the facade of the Belle Epoque. Some had only a brief flirtation with radicalism, especially anarchism; others never wavered in their devotion to it.

Let us examine the work of five of these artists in the service of politics at that time as reflected in their drawings of protest in *L'Assiette au Beurre*. Three eventually devoted themselves more to painting, gained reputations, and gradually lost interest in art as a political weapon and probably in social protest. The other two adhered to their convictions. The motives and the degree of intensity were as mixed, in these five, as were their styles and techniques.

The variety of approaches—and the dynamic impact—are reflected in these covers: Jacques Villon's loose, flowing *The Easy Life* (Fig. 1);[7] Aristide Delannoy's tight, pinched magpies symbolizing *The Small Town* (Fig. 2);[8] Franz Kupka's *Money* (Fig. 3)[9]—Art Nouveau in the service of politics, at least in the lettering; Jules Grandjouan's *The Strike* (Fig. 4),[10] dominated by the ominous shadow of unseen soldiers; and Juan Gris's ironic, understated tableau, *The Suicides* (Fig. 5)[11].

Jacques Villon (1875–1963) was probably the least committed of the five, his span of appearance in *L'Assiette au Beurre* the briefest. Perhaps like Gris his political stance was equally compounded of radicalism and bohemianism. But among the twenty-five drawings he contributed between 1901 and 1902 were some of the most elegant and graceful in the magazine's history. At times his delicate line was almost insipid when applied to political protest; but when the two were successfully fused, he was extremely effective.

1
Jacques Villon, *The Easy Life.* From
L'Assiette au Beurre, no. 46, February
15, 1902.

2
Aristide Delannoy, *The Small Town.*
From *L'Assiette au Beurre,* no. 134,
October 24, 1903.
3
Franz Kupka, *Money.* From *L'Assiette
au Beurre,* no. 162, May 7, 1904.

4
Jules Grandjouan, *The Strike.* From
L'Assiette au Beurre, no. 214, May 6,
1905.

5
Juan Gris, *The Suicides.* From *L'Assiette au Beurre,* no. 438, August 21,
1909.

Although Villon sketched mostly for *Le Courrier Français* from 1897 to 1910—work he later regretted for diverting him from painting—his remarks about this newspaper work apply equally to his drawings for *L'Assiette au Beurre:* "At that time the influence of the press on art was incontestable. It helped to speed up the liberation of painting from academicians.... And let's make it clear that the press of those days just doesn't compare with today's papers. The press had a most advanced spirit and cartoons were done with love, and not just dished out as today. This love for drawing owes a lot to the influence of Toulouse-Lautrec...."[12]

This "love for drawing" was reflected not only in the lithographs and etchings he executed in this period, but in some of the polemical work he did for *L'Assiette au Beurre.* Stylistically, the two were related. As Jean Cassou has pointed out, "the line appears less like the stroke of a draughtsman than the stroke of an engraver."[13] Often the masses of his figures, printed in delicate reds, seemed to step out of aquatints. And the line was never harsh or abrasive. Villon reacted against the issues of the day, but he was much too gentle to project the ferocity of some of his contemporaries in *L'Assiette au Beurre.*

Several of his drawings were sardonic comments on the demimondaines, with the bite in the caption rather than in the drawing, or satirical views of art patrons; but many grapple strongly with more political content. In *Associations!!!* (Fig. 6),[14] his worried priest almost spits out the caption referring to the Associations Law, which effectively dissolved many of the religious orders engaged in teaching. His military allies, their power fading, desert him.

With *The Monopolists* (Fig. 7),[15] he attacks the clergy again, as the elderly rich move over to make room for the fat priest in the carriage of the privileged. Here Villon shows that elegant representational drawing can sharpen rather than diminish pointed political comment.

In 1902, Villon used pen, brush, and watercolor to draw an entire issue depicting "the easy life" of the idle rich—especially their mistresses—and the bureaucracy (minister snores at desk, caption says: "The administration that Europe envies us for."). His most scathing drawing, based on a quotation from Zola, epitomized the anarchist concept of the social structure, with one of Villon's parasitical ladies driving the workers "like domestic animals," the peasants curtsying, and in the distance, smoke pouring from the factories that enriched her (Fig. 8).[16] The mass of the woman's costume dominating the lighter brushstrokes of the exploited provides effective contrast, though the concept is marred by her facing the reader as if she were posing.

The last drawing of the issue, *"Conclusion!"* (Fig. 9),[17] appropriately depicts a pimp—or possibly a detective—collecting his share from the prostitute,

epitomizing "l'assiette au beurre." To many of the contributors to *L'Assiette au Beurre,* prostitution symbolized the degradation of capitalist society, and they returned to the theme again and again.

Villon did not appear in *L'Assiette au Beurre* after 1902. Perhaps he felt the need to be loyal to *Le Courrier Français;* perhaps he was more at home in its less ideological pages, often satirizing bourgeois women, in the spirit of Gavarni. In 1906 he moved to Puteaux, partly to escape the camaraderie that made serious work difficult, and soon thereafter devoted himself almost wholly to painting.

Villon's connection with anarchism was peripheral, but his closest friends in the last part of the decade were Kupka and Gris, at that time still anarchist in philosophy. A lingering residue of Villon's antimilitarist attitude may be found in his "Soldats en Marche" of 1913. It may be wholly a study in dynamic diagonals, with no political connotation, but in 1913 war was threatening, and one is reminded of a sardonic antiwar drawing he did for *L'Assiette au Beurre* a dozen years before, showing an old man reminiscing—"Yes, young people, war is very beautiful, very noble. And I speak of it without having taken part, because I was more than forty-five years old."[18]

If Villon's connection with *L'Assiette au Beurre* was brief, that of the lesser-known Aristide Delannoy (1874–1911) was almost lifelong. From 1901 until shortly before his death he made more than 300 sketches, drawings, and paintings for *L'Assiette au Beurre.*

Delannoy was one of the hundreds of artists who poured into Paris in 1900 eager to gain a career as a painter. He exhibited in the Salon des Indépendants in 1903 and 1904 but received little recognition as a painter during his lifetime, although he became well known for other reasons. To earn minimum expenses, he made drawings and sketches for *Le Bon Vivant, Le Rire, L'Indiscrèt,* and other weeklies. He contributed free drawings to Jean Grave's anarchist weekly *Les Temps Nouveaux,* to *Almanach de la Révolution,* and to Gustave Hervé's *Almanach de la Guerre Sociale.* "There are not enough of us anarchist draughtsmen," he wrote Grave in 1905.[19]

His major graphic effort, however, was in *L'Assiette au Beurre,* where there was hardly a target in the lexicon of the anarchist that he didn't attack: the clergy, the police, factory owners, colonialism, abuse of children and unwed mothers, exploitation of workers, and a dozen others including, for personal reasons, Clemenceau and Briande. Many were cartoonlike sketches, hastily done; others were carefully wrought, well-composed watercolors. His more serious work was usually much more successful than his lighter attempts.

In an issue on the church in the service of the factory owner, a weary worker collects what few coins are left in his pay after deductions for factory-enforced novenas, candles, attendance at sermons, and so forth. Delannoy's Steinlen-like figure has dignity without bathos, weariness carved in his face, the shapeless mass of his clothes lending stress to his anonymity (Fig. 10).[20]

In *The Small Town* (Fig. 2), Delannoy explored life in a clerical-dominated small town with vignettes of pettiness and hypocrisy and a series of wash drawings or paintings of the laborers' lot.

Three men haul a river boat, like beasts of burden, the massive, straining figures predecessors of Kollwitz's Peasant's War series (Fig. 11).[21] His mining scenes are ironical and compassionate. Some were far more ambitious than most drawings in *L'Assiette au Buerre*, as his *The Miner's Bath* (Fig. 12)[22] indicates—a nineteenth-century genre scene with muted protest, again his handling of the body mass impressive, the dark tones, the fading light imparting an overall tone of melancholy, infinitely more effective than the strident tone often used by his colleagues—and frequently by Delannoy himself.

L'Assiette au Beurre often devoted the Christmas issue to savage portraits of a debauched upper class carousing through the holiday. Delannoy's dynamic cover for "Les Petits Noëls" (Fig. 13)[23] was a much more original concept, with dozens of outstretched "gimme, gimme" hands reaching for a bloated, grimacing Marianne's gifts of medals and other handouts.

Delannoy did many covers and eight complete issues, most notably one on the barbarism of insane asylums, and dozens of ephemeral, hasty sketches. His undoing was a drawing he made for a four-page weekly, *Les Hommes du jour*. On October 3, 1908, he portrayed General d'Amade, occupier of Morocco, as a butcher, with bloody hands and apron in a corpse-strewn scene. He was convicted and sentenced to a year in jail, but a presidential pardon cut short the term. Delannoy lashed out with two complete issues of *L'Assiette au Beurre*, eloquently and bitterly attacking Briande and Clemenceau for betraying their previous stands in defense of free expression. He continued to draw for *L'Assiette au Beurre* through 1910, but the hereditary lung condition he suffered from worsened considerably while he was in jail, and he died early in 1911 The editors of *L'Assiette au Beurre* urged its readers to contribute to the support of his widow and daughter and helped form a committee for the sale of his paintings and drawings. Anatole France, Octave Mirbeau, Signac, Luce, Forain, Elie Faure, Jean Grave, and others served on the committee.

In 1926, a retrospective of his paintings, some city scenes but mostly views of the countryside, was held at the Grand Palais.

Delannoy's anarchism was leavened by a humanistic regard for people; Franz Kupka's (1871–1957) was intensified by a virulent anticlerical, anticapitalist, antimilitarist hatred. He hated with such intensity that his gusto carried over into his drawing with a vitality and vigor of movement that enlivened and enriched the pages of the weekly.

Kupka reached Paris in 1894 after a restless, wandering youth and art study in Prague and Vienna. He scraped by with some fashion illustration and commercial posters, spent a decade from 1900 on concentrating on the satirical weeklies. He painted occasionally—he won a Gold Medal at St. Louis in 1902—but in 1900 he wrote his Prague journalist friend, Josef Machar, that he wanted to devote himself to graphic work as it seemed to him to be more "democratic."[24] Seven years later he wrote Machar that he would gladly give his paintings to the Czech miners and not to the Prague establishment.[25]

Throughout the decade Kupka was consistently anarchist. As his biographer, Ludmila Vachtová, put it, "Kupka's criticism of class structure was philosophically reasoned: it was not the protest of a mere humanitarian moralist."[26] His three-part cycle in *L'Assiette au Beurre*, on "Money," "Religion," and "Peace," won him international fame in left-wing circles. He corresponded warmly with Jean Grave from 1905 to 1908[27] and gave him several drawings for *Les Temps Nouveaux*. In 1908 he thanked Grave for sending him a copy of "Terre Libre," a view of an anarchist commune. "You demonstrate that it is feasible," he wrote. He devoted a great deal of time and effort to illustrate a book by the anarchist geographer Elisée Reclus, and he made sketches in 1909 for Kropotkin's book on the French Revolution. In that period he was active, with his friends Juan Gris and Grandjouan, in protest against the execution of the Catalan anarchist Ferrer, whom he knew personally.[28]

Stylistically, Kupka ranged from art nouveau to representation to distortion for dramatic effect. In *The Guillotine* (Fig. 14)[29] Robespierre and Danton, with guillotine looming behind them, look down on what their revolution had wrought: Kupka's symbolic capitalist, hook-nosed Mr. Rich, with mistress and cornucopia being hauled by exhausted workers, while a child starves, a mother cries, and Mr. Rich's factories belch smoke in the distance. It is encased in an art nouveau frame, and the swirling smoke from the factories hints of Kupka's abstract whorls of color a dozen years later.

"L'Argent," Kupka's first single-topic issue, is an encyclopedia of the abuses of money, page after page of inspired polemic. His Mr. Rich, as Jean Adhémar has pointed out,[30] reminds one of M. Prudhomme—albeit an infinitely more corrupt and malevolent one—and he reappears for years. The

6
Jacques Villon, *Associations!!!* From
L'Assiette au Beurre, no. 9, May 30,
1901.

8
Jacques Villon, *The Domestic Animals.* From *L'Assiette au Beurre,* no.
46, February 15, 1942.

7
Jacques Villon, *The Monopolists.*
From *L'Assiette au Beurre,* no. 13,
June 27, 1901.

L'ASSIETTE AU BEURRE

9
Jacques Villon, *Conclusion!* From
L'Assiette au Beurre, no. 46, February
15, 1942.

10
Aristide Delannoy, *Paycheck.* From
L'Assiette au Beurre, no. 66, July 5,
1902.

Conclusion!

— Qu'est-ce que vous réclamez encore?... Un sou pour les chandelles, deux sous pour le syndicat mixte, trois sous pour la " Croix ", une heure à décompter pour le sermon de vendredi, six heures en moins pour la neuvaine... ça fait bien 5 fr. 35 de semaine!

11
Aristide Delannoy, *The Long Haul.*
From *L'Assiette au Beurre,* no. 134,
October 24, 1903.

12
Aristide Delannoy, *The Miner's Bath,*
From *L'Assiette au Beurre,* no. 134,
October 24, 1903.
13
Aristide Delannoy, *Les Petites Noëls.*
From *L'Assiette au Beurre,* no. 195,
December 24, 1904.

14
Franz Kupka, *The Guillotine.* From
L'Assiette au Beurre, no. 1, April 4,
1901.

gold-filled pot belly theme was picked up from his oil painting of 1899, *Women and Money*. In scene after scene, Mr. Rich acts the role of the all-powerful. In the opening scene he is a marionetteer, manipulating the heads of states while the goddess of war beats her drums. In Kupka's triad of *Liberty* (Fig. 15),[31]*Equality,*and *Fraternity,* he looms like a Colossus over his helpless workers. He backs both sides of the Boer War—for profit. A priest appeals for alms while he conceals a hoard of gold. People fight, whore, gamble for money. Surprisingly, in the final scene, the goddess of reason triumphs over money, and wreath-carrying men, women, children, and scientists enter a portal marked "Humanitas." Like many anarchists, Kupka was convinced that science held the key to man's liberation.

The cover of "Religions" (Fig. 16)[32] is an extraordinary use of art nouveau in the service of brutality, with the priest's hands squeezing the coins out of the mouth of his victims. The issue is a satire on all religion, with Kupka drawing each scene in the appropriate art style— Chinese, Japanese, Turkish, Egyptian, and so forth, with strong attack reserved only for the Catholic Church. His original version was rejected by the cautious editors of *L'Assiette au Beurre* as too inflammatory.

Kupka was particularly adept at crowd scenes, several alive with movement. In *The Push* (Fig. 17),[33] on the Alsace-Lorraine question, hundreds of flag-waving, shrieking Germans—Uhlans, bishops, bourgeoisie, soldiers, and cripples shove a priest across the frontier. His satire on bureaucracy, *The Administrative Hierarchy* (Fig. 18),[34] uses the throne theme, as ancient as art, to present his captive administrator, while his supplicants, like Daumier's deputies, are his humble—and voracious—subjects.

Just a few months after his "Religions" issue, Kupka struck again with the third of his triad, "La Paix." Children are taught military history, they play war games, bishops bless armies. Many of Daumier's themes are modernized. In the final scene, Kupka strikes a revolutionary note. His Mr. Rich tosses a few coins to sycophantic employees: "One pacifies sometimes . . ." reads the caption; but on the facing page, the workers have revolted, "private property's" head is impaled, and ". . . but not always!" is the defiant retort.

Kupka contributed occasionally to *L'Assiette au Beurre* in 1905, 1906, and 1907, but after his move to Puteaux in 1906 his search for a rational approach to painting gradually absorbed him. He studied physiology, biology, mechanics, even prepared himself physically by cold showers and sunbathing. "Artistically, he still could not find his way. He accused the moderns of decadence and found the academicians repulsive. The Old Masters in the Louvre seemed to him full of religious and social

hypocrisy. He was not satisfied with being a first-class draftsman. He wanted to be a great painter. . .," Vachtová comments.[35]

Did Kupka's decade of anarchist activity affect his development as a painter? Possibly it slowed his emergence as a pioneer abstractionist, but it is equally possible that it made a contribution to the paths his painting finally entered. Aside from the obvious fact that at Puteaux experimentation was in the air, his disgust with what he saw in the world possibly contributed to his seeking a nonrepresentational course. The anarchist artist's concern with the application of science to art was almost a generation old. Two decades had passed since the neo-Impressionists—almost all of whom were anarchists— had applied their theories to pointillism.

Kupka, like almost all of the artists with whom we are concerned, was primarily a painter. Jules Grandjouan (1875–1968) remained a draftsman all his life. Pen and ink, watercolor, and crayon rather than oil were his natural and principal tools. And he maintained a radical stance throughout most of his long life.

Jean Cassou has remarked, "Bohemianism and rebellion, at certain moments of turmoil, meet each other in the same confines. But within these confines there are also some artists with whom the revolt took precedence over all other aspirations and remained the essence of their life as artists. Grandjouan is one of those."[36]

Of all the artists who contributed to *L'Assiette au Beurre*, Grandjouan was the one most closely identified with it. From 1902 to 1912 almost 800 of his drawings appeared in its pages—almost 10 percent of its total. He drew thirty-five complete, one-subject issues and collaborated with another artist in a dozen more. To the French public at that time he was the personification of the artist in revolt.

Grandjouan grew up in the seacoast city of Nantes, prowled the city wharves, markets, and streets, sold sketches to a Nantes newspaper, turned to engraving in wood and on stone, and in 1899 fifty of his lithographs were published under the collective title, "Nantes la Grise." In 1900 he settled in Paris, illustrated books, drew for *Le Rire* for a few years, but most of his work was for weeklies and monthlies of the left—socialist, anarchist, or whatever. Throughout the decade he was a star contributor to the protest journals, occasionally drawing lucrative commissions from the more "respectable" journals after his fame had spread.

In 1902 Grandjouan burst upon the readers of *L'Assiette au Beurre* with "L'assiette au beurre municipale," a satire on the self-serving bureaucracy of the municipal government. Particularly noteworthy were his caricatures in woodcut style of the Paris city councillors, executed in color with a striking accent and movement that revealed a strong new

15
Franz Kupka, *Liberty*. From *L'Assiette
au Beurre,* no. 41, January 11, 1902.

16
Franz Kupka, *Religions.* From *L'Assiette au Beurre,* no. 162, May 7, 1904.

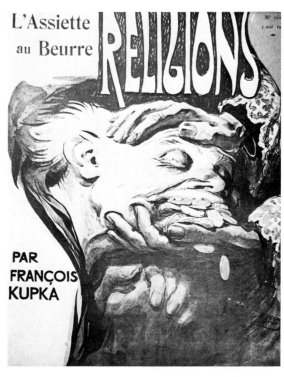

17
Franz Kupka, *The Push.* From *L'Assiette au Beurre,* no. 148, January 30, 1904.

18
Franz Kupka, *The Administrative
Hierarchy*. From *L'Assiette au Beurre*,
no. 164, May 21, 1904.

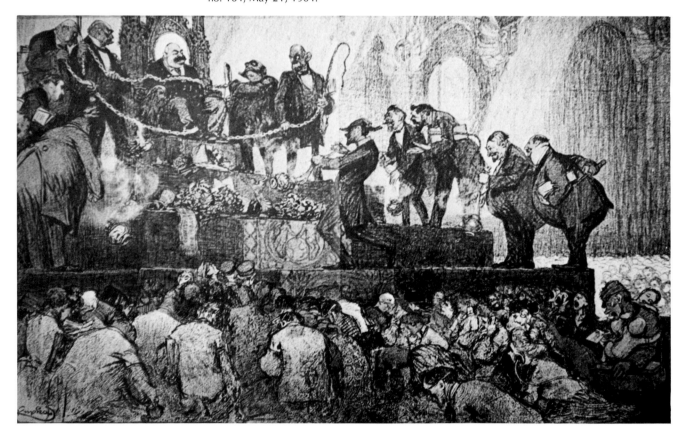

talent. His *A Patriot* (Fig. 19),[37] like several other caricatures in the issue, had an exciting vigor of draftsmanship not wholly reflected here in a black-and-white reproduction.

Grandjouan struck again two months later with an issue devoted to his and the other artists' obsessive hate—czarist Russia. They were outraged when republican France allied with the repressive, church-dominated, pogrom-ridden imperialist Russia. Most of the drawings were bitter caricatures, but two spreads were full of swirling movement and action that leaped off the page, such as *Vive l'Alliance* (Fig. 20),[38] an ironic tableau of the orgy of false patriotism on the facade of the unholy alliance.

In an issue on the gas monopoly, Grandjouan switches to watercolor and relies wholly on his contrapuntal composition to make his political point. While the chief engineer extols the benefits of the huge gas tanks (Fig. 21),[39] the viewer's eye is drawn to the worker shoveling coal in the lower foreground by the device of projecting the shovel handle beyond the frame of the picture, and the eye is led by the curve of the coal pile to the other worker wheeling a barrow and upward to the huge factories that, with the tanks, dwarf the workers.

Grandjouan was even more comprehensive than Kupka in his attacks on the social order. Issue after issue flowed from his drawing board: free Algeria, the crimes of the czar, an end to all monopolies, freedom of education from church control, prostitution (where Grandjouan, in contrast to Van Dongen, used a harsher, more realistic, though sympathetic approach).

When he returned to the city government again, "reporting" a ball at the city hall, in contrast with his "patriot-butcher" treatment, his hatred has softened to contempt and the versatile Grandjouan falls back on Lautrec's milder irony and massive-figure composition, in *After the Ball* (Fig. 22).[40]

His style ranged from directly representational to a romantic, curvilinear art nouveau, from hasty sketch to detailed, careful, and occasionally inspired composition; his mood and subject varied from harsh and bitter and despairing to light, funny, almost frivolous. With Juan Gris he did an issue on airplanes in gay pastels to set the tone for their jaunty approach.

Grandjouan occasionally made editorial comment. In one of his most interesting issues, he collaborated with Delannoy to report "with a cold and righteous anger," he said, a disaster in which 1500 miners were killed. Grandjouan's striking cover, *Courrières* (Fig. 23),[41] aroused France; his on-the-spot reportage of the victims' families and the ruthlessness of the owners moved his readers. In one inspired conception he drew the pit as a huge sphinx, towering over and dominating, as it did, the gesticulating, helpless widows.

As *L'Assiette au Beurre* began to fade and its tone of protest softened, Grandjouan turned to a Chéret-like fin-de-siècle style, bubbly and light as champagne, but his political and philosophical position had not changed. While contributing in his spare time to all the journals of the left, including Emma Goldman's American anarchist magazine, *Mother Earth*,[42] he also made flaming posters—for Francisco Ferrer, for "the imprisoned art" of Delannoy, for a variety of causes. After *L'Assiette au Beurre* closed in 1912, he drew for *La Bataille Syndicaliste* and remained an anarchist until 1914, but spent most of that time in exile. Grandjouan was summoned to court for his drawings (not those in *L'Assiette au Beurre*) a half dozen times between 1907 and 1911, when he received an eighteen-month sentence. He fled France, returning when Poincaré pardoned him a year later. Typically, when the French Lithographic Federation raised a collection for him while he was in exile, he proposed to use the money to buy 2000 copies of *La Voix du peuple* to give to conscripts.

After the war,[43] he became enthusiastic for Russian Communism, did posters paying homage to Liebknecht and other Communists, though at times he quarreled with *l'Humanité*, the Communist organ. He visited Russia twice, but a declaration he signed was considered anti-Soviet, and for years he had little contact. (However, in 1967, a Warsaw exhibition of fifty revolutionary posters included fourteen by Grandjouan.) In 1932, he ran for the Chamber against his pet hate, Briande, and was thoroughly defeated.

From 1940 on, he spent most of his remaining years in Nantes. After his death, a retrospective exhibition of 400 of his works was held at the Musée des Beaux Arts in Nantes—scenes of Nantes, portraits, book illustrations, travel sketchbooks, his polemic art, song books—as well as a group of sketches of Isadora Duncan. In 1901 Grandjouan had seen Duncan dance, tried to sketch her. Three years later he sketched her from backstage; she liked the drawings and agreed to pose. "The meeting changed my life and art," Grandjouan said.[44] For years he sketched her, in pastel, charcoal, watercolor.[45] At one point he became her lover; when she died, he drew and wrote a lamentation of despair. In 1856, the California Palace of the Legion of Honor held a memorial exhibition of Grandjouan's drawings of Isadora Duncan, invited him to the occasion, and the eighty-one-year-old ex-revolutionary was feted by San Francisco society.

When the nineteen-year-old Juan Gris went to Paris in 1906, he moved into the ramshackle tenement, the Bateau-Lavoir, where Picasso had his studio and was still living in penury. Gris was even poorer, his studio even more sparse. It was inevitable that the struggling and impoverished artist

19
Jules Grandjouan, *A Patriot*. From
L'Assiette au Beurre, no. 55, April 19,
1902.

20
Jules Grandjouan, *Vive l'Alliance!*
From *L'Assiette au Beurre,* no. 63,
June 14, 1902.

GODAILLE, RIPAILLE, PATRIOTISME, SOULOGRAPHIE, APOTHÉOSE

21
Jules Grandjouan, *Profits.* From *L'Assiette au Beurre,* no. 87, November 28, 1902.
22
Jules Grandjouan, *After the Ball.* From *L'Assiette au Beurre,* no. 203, February 18, 1905.

23
Jules Grandjouan, *Courrières.* From *L'Assiette au Beurre,* no. 260, March 24, 1906.

should absorb some of the anarchist philosophy from Picasso and his friends and this should be reflected in his drawings for L'Assiette au Beurre. Between 1908 and 1911 he made approximately 125 drawings, including four complete issues. A devotion to liberty and justice, a contempt for fraud and profiteering and the vast gaps between the rich and poor, and a preoccupation with the hypocrisies of bourgeois women were reflected in Gris's work. His satire was rarely bitter, usually gentler and much less ferocious than that of either Kupka or Grandjouan. Only occasionally, as with the execution of Ferrer—an event that outraged the Parisian artists and much of the Western world—did passion break through. His conception, however, was a static takeoff on Manet's painting "The Execution of Maximilian."

The young Gris was amusing, occasionally moving, often ironic in his comments on society in L'Assiette au Beurre, but never as profound or as committed as some of his colleagues. Stylistically, however, Gris was especially interesting. At times he ranged from the black, mass figures of Vallotton, as in The Suicides (Fig. 5), to the softer tones of Seurat, Forain, Toulouse-Lautrec, and Beardsley. But more significant were those that reflected his growing preoccupation with the pre-cubist aesthetic.

In many of his drawings, Gris was much more concerned with the careful construction of a scene, and the linear and geometric patterns, than he was with the people, as in two drawings on the Turkish revolution. In Liberty (Fig. 24),[46] he is more absorbed with the effect of the verticals than with the figure inside. In the other ironic drawing (Fig. 25, ". . . two classes: those who work, and those who watch them work."),[47] again it is the pattern of cross beams, the angles of the ladders, the rectangles of the bricks that obviously interest Gris equally with the problem of integrating the silhouette of his figures into the composition.

Gris's figures were often static, stiff, devoid of movement. His faces were often expressionless, cartoonlike. In his children, especially, the eyes were but circles, like Little Orphan Annie, as in Truth (Fig. 26),[48] but again the construction was solid, tightly woven, architectural. In an issue on frauds, however, Gris's pre-cubist evolution is most apparent (Fig. 27)[49] in the faces of his con men. The Cézanne-like face of the standing man is constructed of shadow (there are no shadows in the picture except in the two faces), planes, line and angulation. It is a structured face, so unlike any that had appeared before in L'Assiette au Beurre. There is a discipline, a tight control to Gris's drawings.

By 1911 Gris was wholly immersed in his painting. A lingering trace of his antiwar attitude was indicated in an anguished letter he wrote Maurice Raynal in 1916: "I can't understand as you do this urge to massacre, to exterminate, unless there is an absolute guarantee that it will end satisfactorily . . . I am amazed by my own stupidity and inability to swim with the tide."[50]

As there were hints of cubism in some of Gris's drawings for L'Assiette au Beurre, so, one can ask, were there elements in anarchism that contributed to the evolution of Gris's cubism? One cannot answer that without considering the circles in which he moved and which had so much influence on his early development, even though he was to find his own individual vision.

The center of that circle was Picasso, of course, Picasso from strongly anarchist Barcelona, where in 1901 he had briefly published a "bourgeois-hating, essentially anarchist paper."[51] Picasso had recently stopped painting the poor and destitute, but all of the cubists were still surrounded by poverty and destitution, and reacted accordingly. With the probable exception of Braque, nearly all of the cubists had manifested hatred of the bourgeois world, nearly all had embraced anarchism at some time—Picasso, Gris, Léger, Marcoussis, Gleizes, Metzinger. Apollinaire was an anarchist; his first writing on Picasso's work appeared in the Socialist magazine La Plume.

It may have been coincidence, but the subject of Les Demoiselles d'Avignon was a Barcelona whorehouse. As we have seen, to many of the anarchist artists prostitution symbolized the degradation of a bourgeois society, and the Demoiselles was painted at a time when Picasso was "still steeped in compassion for humanity and concern with reality and emotion."[52] The Demoiselles may also be interpreted as a violent defiance of the bourgeois concept of painting and a symbolic attack on what seemed to Picasso—and to many other artists—an ugly society.

Possibly, too, cubism was a linear reaction against the curve, symbol of bourgeois decoration at the time. Paul W. Schwartz has pointed out, "This was the epoch of the art nouveau. Restaurant mirrors coiled themselves into elliptically ovoid postures, and even the ironwork entrances to utilitarian Metro stations were graced with flowing patterns. The succinct linear principles of the currently admired Japanese art were adapted to the most decorative of purposes. Picasso remarked that he and his allies were part of all that as well, precisely because they reacted directly against the tide."[53] If the curve represented bourgeois society in all its materialism, of which the cubists shared very little, it is possible that they would instinctively seek the opposite.

Finally, by painting the most utilitarian and ordinary of subjects, as if to emphasize the ascetic scale of their own living, and by adding bits of newspaper, cloth, tin, glass, to their pictures, as John Berger has pointed out, "They challenged the whole bourgeois

24
Juan Gris, *Liberty*. From *L'Assiette au Beurre*, no. 387, August 29, 1908.
25
Juan Gris, *The Two Classes*. From *L'Assiette au Beurre*, no. 387, August 29, 1908.

26
Juan Gris, Truth. From *L'Assiette au Beurre*, no. 475, May 14, 1910.
27
Juan Gris, *The Con Men*. From *L'Assiette au Beurre*, no. 447, October 23, 1909.

concept of art as something precious, valuable, and to be prized like jewelry."[54]

Juan Gris was obviously influenced by the trends developed by Cezanne, Braque, and Picasso, and their tradition was undoubtedly the principal factor in the evolution of his cubism. But his anarchist, idealist, antibourgeois stance cannot be wholly ignored as a factor. As with Villon and especially Kupka, Gris's alienation from the social order may have played a role in the development of his painting style.

Notes

1
Cited in Louis Chaumeil, *Van Dongen—L'homme et l'artiste—La Vie et l'oeuvre* (Geneva, 1967), p. 65.

2
See Francis Steegmuller, *Introduction to Jacques Villon Master Printmaker*, exhibition at R. M. Light and Co., Seiferheld Gallery, New York, 1964; and A. Warnod, *Ceux de la Butte* (Paris, 1947), p. 255. cited in Jacques Lethève, *La Caricature et la Presse sous la IIIe République* (Paris, 1961), p. 50.

3
George Woodcock, *Anarchism* (New York, 1962), p. 306.

4
Mme. Giselle Lambert, unpublished thesis, *Les Illustrations de L'Assiette au Beurre, Une thèse de l'Ecole du Louvre*, and statements to the author by Lucien Grandjouan, grandnephew of Jules-Félix Grandjouan.

5
Jean Cassou, *Introduction to catalogue, Jules Grandjouan (1875–1968)* (Musée des Beaux Arts, Nantes, 1969).

6
"Bums, Madmen, Masters," *Life*, February 8, 1960, p. 92.

7
L'Assiette au Beurre, no. 46, February 15, 1902.

8
Ibid., no. 134, October 24, 1903.

9
Ibid. no. 162, May 7, 1904.

10
Ibid., no. 214, May 6, 1905.

11
Ibid., no. 438, August 21, 1909.

12
Dora Vallier, *Jacques Villon, Oeuvres de 1897 á 1956* (Paris, n.d.), p. 116.

13
Jean Cassou, Preface to *Jacques Villon: master of graphic art* (Museum of Fine Arts, Boston, 1964), p. 1.

14
L'Assiette au Beurre, no. 9, May 30, 1901, p. 156.

15
Ibid., no. 13, June 27, 1901, p. 229.

16
Ibid., no. 46, February 15, 1902, p. 731.

17
Ibid., p. 740.

18
Ibid., no. 8, May 23, 1901, p. 135.

19
File of "Letters to Jean Grave," at Institut Français d'Histoire Sociale, Archives Nationales, Paris IIIe Delannoy's drawings for *Les Temps Nouveaux, Almanach la Révolution, Almanach de la Guerre Sociale* will also be found there, as well as a file of the weekly, *Les Hommes du Jour*, of which Delannoy was cofounder.

20
L'Assiette au Beurre, no. 66, July 5, 1902, p. 1098.

21
Ibid., no. 134, October 24, 1903, pp. 2256–2257.

22
Ibid., p. 2261.

23
Ibid., no. 195, December 24, 1904.

24
Ludmila Vachtová, *Frank Kupka, Pioneer of Abstract Art* (New York, 1968), p. 41.

25
Ibid.

26
Ibid.

27
See n. 19 of this chapter.

28
Vachtová, *Kupka* p. 23.

29
L'Assiette au Beurre, no. 1, April 4, 1901, pp. 16–17.

30
Jean Adhémar, "Les journeaux amusants et les premiers peintres cubistes," *L'Oeil*, IV, April 15, 1955, p. 40.

31
L'Assiette au Beurre, no. 41, January 11, 1902, p. 647.

32
Ibid., no. 162, May 7, 1904.

33
Ibid., no. 148, January 30, 1904, pp. 2476–2477.

34
Ibid., no. 164, May 21, 1904, pp. 2735–2737.

35
Vachtová, *Kupka*, p. 24.

36
Jean Cassou, *Introduction to catalogues, Exhibition of Jules Grandjouan (1875–1968)*, (Musée des Beaux Arts, Nantes, 1969), p. 9.

37
L'Assiette au Beurre, no. 55, April 19, 1902, p. 898.

38
Ibid., no. 63, June 14, 1902, pp. 1052–1053.

39
Ibid., no. 87, November 29, 1902, p. 1456.

40
Ibid., no. 203, February 18, 1905, p. 3366.

41
Ibid., no. 260, March 24, 1906.

42
Emma Goldman, *Living My Life* (2 vols., N.Y., 1931), 1:407. Mrs. Goldman quoted Grandjouan: "He expressed his belief that the mission of art is to inspire the vision of a new dawn."

181
Five Artists in the
Service of Politics
in the Pages of
*L'Assiette au
Beurre*

43
For these and many of the facts of Grandjouan's life that
follow, the source is the Catalog Notes; See footnote no.
36, By Mme. Vige Longevin, Grandjouan's daughter.

44
*Isadora Duncan: A Memorial Exhibition of Drawings by
Jules Grandjouan* (Artist's Guild of America, California
Palace of the Legion of Honor, San Francisco, December 1,
1956). Introduction by Harold Smithson.

45
*Vingt-cinq planches desinées, gravées, et imprimées par
Grandjouan,* 1912, New York Public Library.

46
L'Assiette au Beurre, no. 387, August 29, 1908, p. 358.

47
Ibid., p. 363.

48
Ibid., no. 476, May 14, 1910, p. 125.

49
Ibid., no. 447, October 23, 1909, p. 1328.

50
Daniel-Henry Kahnweiler, *Letters of Juan Gris, 1913–1927,*
tr. by Douglas Cooper (London, 1956), p. 42.

51
Donald Drew Egbert, *Social Radicalism and the Arts* (New
York, 1970), p. 324.

52
Robert Rosenblum, *Cubism and Twentieth Century Art*
(New York, 1966), p. 10.

53
Paul W. Schwartz, *Cubism* (London, 1971), p. 12.

54
John Berger, *Success and Failure of Picasso* (Baltimore,
1965), p. 57.

10
Russian Sculpture and Lenin's Plan of Monumental Propaganda

John E. Bowlt

The formation and development of the so-called monumental style in Soviet sculpture, architecture, and painting arose very much as a direct result of governmental attitudes and policies immediately after the Russian Revolution of October 1917 and, in the case of sculpture, virtually owed their existence to Lenin's resonant call in April 1918 for a program of monumental propaganda. Historically, the chronological framework we discuss here, ca. 1917–1922, was one of the utmost importance for Russian/Soviet sculpture, even though both aesthetically and in terms of propaganda sculptural achievements of these years left a great deal to be desired. But the actual interaction between politics and art, or perhaps one should say between politicians and artists, was a very curious and distinctive one.

The sudden, unprecedented attention the discipline of sculpture received just after 1917 is all the more striking when we consider it against the background of the eighteenth and nineteenth centuries. If we stop to ask ourselves where the focus of artistic energies had been during the pre-Revolutionary period, then we find that painting, literature, and music, from a professional or idealist viewpoint, had achieved much of permanent value and had, as the nineteenth century advanced, become increasingly Russian. For better or worse, the process of "russification" of the arts culminated in the tendentious and explicitly Russian depictions of the famous realists such as Repin, Surikov, Tolstoi, and Dostoevsky; later, of course, a second culmination of Russian art was reached with the avant-garde in the figures of Kandinsky, Larionov, and Malevich, all of whom, unquestioningly, were profoundly Russian. But the radical fervor, the constant wish for political and ethical change that the realists supported, found no acceptable equivalent in the realm of sculpture. Indeed, when we pause to examine Russian sculptural accomplishments of the nineteenth century, we are forced to repeat the question once raised by the eminent artist and critic Alexandre Benois— "Was there really a Russian sculpture?"[1] Certainly, there were no Repins or Tolstois in sculpture and, in the main, the kind of works produced by sculptors in Russia up until the end of the nineteenth century were academic in the extreme and based on classical concepts of formal precision and nudist perfection, elements that had been much more at home in the heyday of Russian neoclassicism during the eighteenth and early nineteenth centuries, especially since the architectural boom in St. Petersburg had provided unprecedented opportunities for the decorative sculptor. Even then, of course, there had been nothing specifically Russian about such works and, on the whole, they had owed nothing to the indigenous, tentative traditions of Russian folk sculpture, that is, the so-called *lubochnaya skulptura* of carved wooden toys, church figurines, and so forth. Indeed, as one observer indicated later, it was both absurd and fruitless to attempt to transplant monumental concepts from the blue skies and elevated topography of Athens and Rome, where everyone lived practically out of doors (and therefore decorated their outdoor residence with statues), to the misty "pit" of St. Petersburg where, by the end of the nineteenth century, St. Isaac's Cathedral— one of the most striking examples of Russian neoclassicism— was sinking into the morass beneath it.

If we glance at general catalogs of Russian art exhibitions from the nineteenth century, we see that sculpture, if included at all, was always relegated to the last section. We note, too, that while there were several eminent schools of painting in both the capitals and the provinces, there were no schools of sculpture as such. Moreover, the few great names of Russian sculpture in the late nineteenth century— such as Mark Antokolsky (1843–1902) and Paolo Trubetskoi (1867–1938)—were transients who spent most of their creative lives abroad; in addition, the remarkable and innovative artist Mikhail Vrubel (1856–1910), now celebrated for his majolica sculptures, turned to this medium only late in his career and hence produced comparatively few finished works. We should remember, too, that the arbiters of public taste and supporters of the status quo, in particular the royal family, purchased pictures and prints, but very few sculptures: that is one reason why we find an endless number of Russian paintings in the Tretyakov Gallery in Moscow, but scarcely any sculptures. The lack of governmental and private patronage for young sculptors, peculiar to Russia during the nineteenth century, was extremely pernicious, since of all the conventional arts, excluding architecture, sculpture involves the most expense in material, equipment, and production. Ultimately, this state of affairs meant that sculpture commissions were placed either with members of an official, academic institution with its own workshops, or with the financially independent—and we note that both Antokolsky and Trubetskoi were both men of more than adequate means.

It was only in the early 1900s that the situation regarding sculpture in Russia changed, that is, with the rise of a young generation which included such names as Anna Golubkina (1864–1927), Sergei Konenkov (1874–1972), and Aleksandr Matveev (1878–1960) who, variously, earned the title of "impressionist" and "stylist." But although both Golubkina and Konenkov were involved directly in the civil disturbances of 1905, and although in retrospect they magnified their involvement, their sculptural products remained aesthetic, ornamental,

or in the folk tradition—in other words, political awareness did not affect the development of their art in any substantial way; true, Konenkov did carve a remarkable head of a Moscow worker in 1906, but essentially he remained content, at least until 1917, with his series of mythological and legendary figures. Similarly, Golubkina's and Matveev's portraits of friends, vestal maidens, and idealized peasants were scarcely contributions to a radical or, for that matter, even a realist movement in sculpture. However, the redeeming feature of this new generation of sculptors was that they did begin to concentrate more on the expressive qualities of the material itself and to react against the academic strictures that had held sway throughout the nineteenth century, even though their subjects remained representational and often sentimental: and, certainly, when we look for a Russian avant-garde sculpture to place beside the canvases of Kandinsky, Larionov, and Malevich we find none. Of course, Alexander Archipenko (1887–1964), Jacques Lipchitz (1891–1973) and Ossip Zadkine (1890–1967) are names that come to mind in any discussion of modern sculpture, but they had very little relevance to the mainstream of Russian, or rather East European, art and relied on Paris for the main stimulus to their artistic development.

By 1912 the problems concerning the lack of a real sculptural tradition in Russia were being aired in public, as, for example, at the large All-Russian Convention of Artists organized in St. Petersburg under the auspices of the czar and czarina. Ilya Gintsburg (1859–1939), later to become famous as a realist sculptor under the Soviets, called for immediate action in order to give sculpture its rightful place within the general cultural spectrum: he suggested that the public at large should be made aware of sculpture as an art form, that schools should contain sculpture classes, and even that a special government commission should be set up to investigate the whole situation.[3] But, inevitably, with the widening rift between the governmental hierarchy and artists and with the Great War only a short time away, Gintsburg's proposals remained on paper.

Curiously, however, early in 1917, particularly after the February Revolution, there was a sudden upsurge of interest in the formal organization of art affairs on the part of artists themselves, especially since government attention was directed elsewhere at the time, the official and august Imperial Academy was hopelessly out of date in both aesthetic evaluation and artistic output, and many radical artists,—Altman, Rodchenko, and Tatlin among them,—already felt a lack of cohesion and overall direction and were beginning to question validity and relevance of their abstract or semiabstract work. On an organizational level matters came to fruition in the serious, collective proposal for the establishment of a Ministry of Fine Arts,[4] and although this was not realized, several large, umbrella societies or artists' trade unions did emerge in the spring of 1917. With a number of sculptors in their ranks these grand, eclectic organizations in which Malevich and Meierkhold, Rodchenko and Tatlin rubbed shoulders, strove to narrow the gap between the artist and society, specifically between the leftist painter and the ordinary worker on the one hand (some of whom were invited to enter artists' studios to receive free tuition) and the leftist painter and the radical politician on the other. This new state of affairs gave many artists organizational experience that was to stand them in good stead during the leftist dictatorship just after October 1917. On a more immediate level, since these organizations provided a very democratic forum and one in which artists could speak for themselves, more attention was given to the problems of sculpture and sculptors. Indicative of this revival of interest was the idea of creating a monument to the victims of the February Revolution in March 1917, although, ironically, the winning entry of the competition was designed by an architect with the help of a painter-graphist.[5] A stimulus to sculptural activity was provided also by the widespread concern at this time for the preservation of Russian artistic monuments such as palaces, statues, villas threatened already by neglect and vandalism—sculptors were summoned for the repair and maintenance of statues, bas-reliefs, and so forth. It is worth remembering in this context that the accusation cast at the Soviet régime of neglect and wanton destruction of czarist art treasures should be qualified at least by a reference to the situation before October 1917—the slogan ''Rasstrelivai Rasstrelli'' (''Shoot up Rastrelli'') was heard surely both before and after the proletarian revolution.

Even so, despite this new, but tentative call for sculpture early in 1917, it was restorational rather than originally creative, applied rather than self-sufficient. And ironically, the most dynamic pieces of sculpture or three-dimensional work were being created not by professional sculptors but by painters or former painters—Tatlin and his reliefs, Pougny (Puni) and his relief paintings and constructions, Baranoff-Rossiné with his wooden, polychrome constructions. Consequently, sculpture within the arena of the Russian avant-garde became more and more painterly, for its gravitational center shifted from volume to mass, from visual/tactile qualities to visual qualities alone. Perhaps, to use Lissitzky's terms, we might submit that the move was from ''composition'' to ''construction,''[6] because the idea of applying certain elements to a basic surface, as in Tatlin's reliefs or Gabo's constructions, is fundamentally a pictorial conception and not a sculptural one. The autonomy

of sculpture as such was undermined still further when we recall that between 1914 and ca. 1922 there was little significant architectural activity, so that decorative sculpture, except in restoration work, had no real outlet.

By the autumn of 1917 sculpture was the most backward and most adulterated of all the arts in Russia. There were few sculptors in existence. Radical forces in this area had long emigrated and there was little public interest in statues, bas-reliefs, busts, stone ornaments—as Antokolsky had said thirty years before, ''sculpture is outside the pale, it's not in fashion, there's no demand for it''.[7] Indeed, when we remember the severity of line, the restraint and innate discipline of traditional Western sculpture, we realize that it was an art form totally alien to the expansive and tortuous paths of the Russian soul. It was amazing, therefore, that in April 1918 Lenin should have called for a plan of monumental propaganda that was to have created numerous statues and bas-reliefs in the main metropolitan areas of Soviet Russia: this was his decree, signed and published on April 14th, entitled ''On the Dismantling of Monuments Erected in Honor of the Czars and Their Servants and on the Formulation of Projects of Monuments to the Russian Socialist Revolution.''

It would seem that Lenin had formed the idea of decorating metropolitan streets with statues of revolutionary and popular heroes as early as the winter of 1917–1918, when Anatolii Lunacharsky, Head of Narkompros (People's Commissariat for Enlightenment), after a meeting with Lenin, pronounced breathlessly to an audience of painters and sculptors: ''I've just come from Vladimir Ilich. Once again he has had one of those fortunate and profoundly exciting ideas that have shocked and delighted all of us so many times. He intends to have the squares of Moscow decorated with statues and monuments in honor of revolutionaries, great fighters of socialism. This denotes both agitation for socialism and a wide field for our sculptural talents to manifest themselves''.[8] It is difficult to understand Lunacharsky's enthusiasm, since as Commissar he knew very well the real situation regarding the lack of sculptural talent in Russia. A more realistic view was supported by Lunacharsky's seconds-in-command, the artists Shterenberg and Tatlin, Heads of the Visual Arts Sections (IZO Narkompros) in Petrograd and Moscow respectively. Shterenberg said outright that Lenin's plan to put up monuments was impossible because of the sheer lack of artistic ability in this area;[9] Tatlin maintained that the plan had to be thought over very carefully, since to hurry would mean to detract from any possible artistic value of the proposed monuments.[10]

Such were the initial reactions to Lenin's plan—one that has received such wide publicity in the annals of Soviet criticism—because, ostensibly, it demonstrated Lenin's awareness of art as a vital propagational medium and his wish to make art a mass experience. At this juncture it would be well to examine in detail the main stipulations of the decree:

1. Monuments erected in honor of the tsars and of their servants and that do not present interest either from a historical or from an artistic viewpoint are to be dismantled and taken off the squares and streets; in part they are to be transferred to depositories, in part they are to be used for utilitarian ends. . . .
2. The same committee (the Soviet of People's Commissars) is entrusted with mobilizing artistic forces and organizing an extensive competition for producing projects of monuments intended to commemorate the great days of the Russian Socialist revolution.
3. The Soviet of People's Commissars expresses the desire that certain of the more hideous idols be dismantled and the first models of the new monuments be put up for verdict by the masses by May 1.
4. The same committee is entrusted with urgently preparing the decoration of the city by May 1 and with the replacement of inscriptions, emblems, street names, coats of arms and so forth by new ones reflecting the ideas and feelings of the working class of revolutionary Russia.[11]

The first proposal of the decree was to be expected from a new and radical régime. Moreover, the destruction of artifacts belonging to the feudal and capitalist past was very much in keeping with the general doctrine of futurism that pervaded IZO Narkompros. Nikolai Punin, one of the most active and influential art critics within Narkompros, summed up their attitude: "Futurism is the strongest of all existing artistic trends, and we certainly lay claim to this; and we wouldn't be loath to employ government power for putting our artistic ideas into practice."[12] Undoubtedly, Lunacharsky strove to counteract the extremism of the futurists in Narkompros and Proletkult (the Proletarian Culture organization) who tended to believe that a communist culture could begin only by rejecting the cultural heritage by maintaining that no single art group had the right to consider itself the spokesman for the proletarian mass.[13] And, certainly, when we remember Lunacharsky's own rather retrospective and nostalgic tastes in art, we can understand why Lunacharsky was so slow to put demolition plans into effect, especially when such imposing statues as those of Alexander II and Catherine the Great were at stake. On the other hand, we can sense the delight with which the very young, leftist sculptors such as Aleksei Babichev (1887–1963) and Boris

Korolev (1883–1963) dismantled Alexander III and General Skobelev. Indeed, although the deadline for demolition was set at May 1, only one statue had been dismantled by then and not even a draft list of new names had been compiled by the Commissariat. This procrastination annoyed Lenin intensely, as he indicated in a telegram he sent to Lunacharsky on May 13, 1918: "I'm surprised and indignant at your . . . inactivity in preparing good quotations and inscriptions for the public buildings of Petrograd and Moscow."[14]

The other sections of the decree were of much direct significance to the development of Russian sculpture, even though Lenin was attempting to draw on an artistic tradition that scarcely existed in Russia. In a letter to Lunacharsky, Lenin explained what his motives for the project were: "You remember that Campanella in his *City of the Sun* speaks of frescos on the walls of his fantastic socialist city, frescos that were to serve as graphic lessons in natural science, history. . . . I think that this is by no means naive and with certain modifications could be assimilated by us and realized right now. . . . I would name what I have in mind monumental propaganda . . . in furtherance of this, concise but expressive inscriptions containing the most permanent radical principles and slogans of Marxism could be disseminated. . . . Let this be just cement blocks with inscriptions on them as legible as possible. For the moment I'm not even thinking in terms of eternity or permanence. . . . Even more important than the inscriptions I consider monuments: busts or full-length figures, perhaps bas-reliefs, groups. . . . We should compile a list of the predecessors of socialism or its theoreticians and fighters, as well as those luminaries of philosophical thought, science, art, and so forth, who, while not having direct relevance to socialism, were genuine heroes of culture. . . ."[15] We know from many contexts that Lenin's taste in art was "average," even conservative, that is, he preferred Nekrasov to Mayakovsky, Levitan to Malevich—as he said himself: "I just cannot consider the works of expressionism, futurism, cubism, and other "isms" as the highest manifestation of artistic genius. I do not understand them. I do not experience any pleasure from them."[16] From the communication of Lenin to Lunacharsky cited earlier, it is clear that Lenin was more interested in the didactic, simplistic value of the proposed statues than in any intrinsic, aesthetic qualities. This wish for a laconic and obvious art form in "telegraph style" Lenin advanced in one of his articles on the press in 1918: "A little less political chatter. A little less intellectual reflection. A little closer to life. . . ."[17] What, therefore, Lenin envisaged in his statues and bas-reliefs was a series of, as it were, three-dimensional posters recognizable immediately as historical personages to the mass spectator. Unfortunately, Lenin's high aspirations were not fulfilled.

By the end of May 1918, Lunacharsky, as head of Narkompros and directly responsible for the implementation of Lenin's plan, had begun to consider details, although a definitive list of names for "monumentalization" was still not ready. In an article entitled "Monumental Agitation," dated July 14,[18] Lunacharsky wrote that in addition to statues in Moscow and Petrograd, there would be bas-reliefs and blocks of stone or marble that would bear wise popular sayings or utterances of great historical figures. Like Lenin, Lunacharsky, however, was still thinking in temporary terms for the statues and suggested plaster of Paris or terracotta as media, then, if desired, to be cast in bronze or carved in marble. Although in his statement Lunacharsky did propose certain names for perpetuation, including Ryleev, Belinsky, Dobrolyubov, Chernyshevsky and Nekrasov—writers and thinkers of socialist sympathy—the definitive list appeared only in August. Moreover, in this statement Lunacharsky suggested that the moderate sculptor Leonid Shervud (1871–1954) be general supervisor and that a jury for judging proposals be set up to include Shterenberg and himself—although both these measures were changed shortly thereafter.

At this time the head of the professional union of Moscow sculptors and the sculptors' representative within the Art Collegium of IZO Narkompros was Konenkov, an artist who, while extremely competent, had had little experience in actual monumental design. He was consulted by Lenin and Lunacharsky on contiguous problems and in his recommendations made some guarded comments about the whole plan: "The great difficulty in implementing this idea is that the speed of completion might override the artistic considerations, for the government, as it is now, cannot and must not be the initiator of bad taste. . . . In rejecting any sorts of prizes, the Art Collegium finds it expedient to allow the sculptor/artist to express himself freely by simply supplying his material needs during his work [on the sculpture]. The Collegium considers it also essential . . . to destroy the conventional jury and to settle for public review and judgment of the model projects. . . . From the day of the competition-commission to completion no more than three months must elapse, during which time sculptors must make draft-projects . . . out of light material . . . after which public verdict will decide which of the draft projects are to be finished in hard materials, bronze, marble, and granite. . . . The work must be completed approximately by the end of September this year."[19] It is interesting to note from the above text read by Konenkov in the presence of Lenin at a

session of the Soviet of People's Commissars on July 17, 1918, that it already contradicted certain parts of Lunacharsky's text published three days earlier and cited above. At this session Konenkov read out a list of names of those to whom statues were to be erected, which was, in turn, debated and supplemented; Lenin discussed generalities with Konenkov, and the latter commented that pedestals and figures should be in position before the frosts came, that figures should be presented in plaster of Paris, life-size, and that the cost per monument would be about 8,000 rubles—a sum that was made available to every participating sculptor. In the August issue of the journal *Art (Iskusstvo)* final details were published concerning both the mechanics and the name-list itself: we find that the concept of "heroes of culture" has come to embrace many artists and musicians and that a specific invitation was included for designs for a bas-relief on the Kremlin wall in memory of the fallen heroes of the October Revolution.[20] Simultaneously, Lenin signed a statement ratifying the proposal, but emphasizing certain priorities: to erect monuments first and foremost to Marx and Engels, to include in the list great foreign writers such as Heine, to exclude Vladimir Solovev, and so on.[21] With these modifications the definitive list, divided into six categories, encompassed sixty-seven names and, apart from the expected choices of Marx, Chernyshevsky, Herzen, Robespierre (Fig. 1), included such unexpected personages as Spartacus, Chopin, Garibaldi, Gogol, Kiprensky, Rublev, Skryabin, Tyutchev, Vrubel, and Lermontov; yet, for unaccountable reasons, it did not include John Stuart Mill, Dickens, or Joan of Arc. A more haphazard list of historical luminaries could scarcely be imagined, especially when the list was lengthened shortly thereafter to include Cézanne, Lord Byron, Voltaire, and Rimsky-Korsakov.

Symptomatic of the very tolerant attitude toward art affairs from the governmental apparatus at this time was the fact that a minimum of conditions was laid down for work on these monuments. The sculptor was to have complete freedom, there was to be no jury except that of the general public, the artist could present a bust, a bas-relief, or a full-length figure, although in the latter case the minimum height was five arshins (11' 8"), which allowed the statue to Dostoevsky, for example, to be over ten meters high.[22] Because of such license, sculptors and would-be sculptors of all directions participated, although contrary to some sources, it would seem that leftism or cubo-futurism was not the dominant tendency. Of course, very few statues were ready by the November 7 deadline, although, among others, the bust of La Salle by Viktor Sinaisky (1893–1968) was opened in October (Fig. 2), and Matveev's plaster statue of Marx opened on November 7. Thereafter openings were frequent, although sporadic. Essentially, of course, the deadline was too soon, because Lenin's request in his resolution of August 2 that the monuments be ready by the first anniversary of the October Revolution (November 7, new style) left only two and a half months for drafting projects and casting plaster prototypes. In addition, there were, frankly, very few sculptors who had had any monumental experience and whose studios were equipped for such work, and, moreover, materials were in very short supply. One journal summed up the situation: ". . . almost all the sculptors of Moscow responded to their Union's call to work, to a mobilization of sculptural forces, despite the fact that the time limit (three months), the rather low compensation (the principle of labor payment was applied for an estimate), the shortage of material and the technical difficulties . . . should have scared off a lot of people."[23] En passant, we can note that during the period 1918–1921 twenty-five of the monuments were opened in Moscow, fifteen in Petrograd, and forty-seven remained at the model stage; 280,000 rubles were expended, about half of the sum originally allocated, and sixty-one sculptors took part.

After the first few statues and busts had been unveiled together with appropriate music and speeches declaiming the virtues of the historical figure in question, a general feeling developed that something somewhere had gone wrong. Lenin was dismayed at the poor results; Shterenberg declared that this was exactly what he had foreseen and he fully expected the failure; Lunacharsky remained silent. First, many of the monuments were created by incompetent sculptors and hence were just technically weak and often unrecognizable because of this, so that in some cases a supplementary description had to be provided. Second, winter came early that year and the frosts cracked the clay and plaster figures; alternatively, heavy rain washed away the plaster of Paris figures, so proving Michelangelo's assertion that a work of sculpture "lives in clay, dies in plaster (and is resurrected in marble)."[24] Third, most of the monuments, despite the 12-foot minimal limit, were not big enough, a fault that derived directly from the pre-Revolutionary tradition of intimate studio sculpture not destined for large, public places—as Punin observed, "Every day I walked past the Radishchev monument, but only on the eighth day did I notice that it had fallen over."[25] The general response, then, was one of dissatisfaction either because the aesthetic quality of the monuments was so low or because they appeared to many to be mere caricatures of beloved historical figures (Fig. 3).

Not all the lack of semblance was, however, the result of amateur or poorly organized work, since a few statues were constructed deliberately in a highly schematic and cubo-futuristic way. Even Matveev's plaster statue of Marx, unveiled in front of Smolnyi

in Petrograd, was very stylized and gave the impression of a thick-set dwarf, rather than of an overbearing, revolutionary thinker, an impression voiced by Lenin that contributed to the statue's ultimate dismantling—even though Lunacharsky did talk about its "originality in plastic rendition."[26] The center of criticism became, however, a single statue put up in Moscow in the winter of 1919, but never opened officially: Korolev's statue to Bakunin (Fig. 4). Korolev, a colleague of Altman, Mayakovsky, and Punin, was at that time an ardent follower of futurism and shared Punin's view that "the artist must forget sculpture in the narrow sense of the word; the form of the human body can henceforth no longer serve as an artistic form; form must be invented anew."[27] Korolev's severe distortion of Bakunin's figure, his evident interest in the spatial juxtaposition of blocks of varying dimensions, dispensed with any claim to mimetic representation— as the man in the street was quick to acknowledge: ". . . The statue is not exactly just a narrow slab of stone, and it's not exactly the remains of some kind of ugly tree, but one thing's certain—it's a scarecrow very much resembling a man. . . . Workers and Red Army men are surprised and outraged when they find out that the monument is about to be unveiled."[28] In fact, the wooden scaffolding around the statue was not removed, at least not until it was taken down for firewood, and then the statue was removed and broken up. Similar criticisms were leveled at the statue to Perovskaya by Grizelli in Petrograd, at the Saltykov-Shchedrin statue by Aleksandr Zlatovratsky (1878–1960) in Moscow, and at the morbid, twisted monument to Heine by Georgii Motovilov (1894–1963) also in Moscow (all of 1918). Behind the public outcry at the unrecognizable features of certain figures, one does detect a general resentment at the vast amounts of money being spent on the whole agitational program. The poet Blok, in his famous poem *The Twelve*, pinpointed this issue in the form of an old lady's reaction to a poster declaring "All Power to the Constituent Assembly": "she is in tears, she just can't make out what this poster and its huge piece of material are all about. How many pairs of pants it would make for our children—and none of them has any clothes or shoes."[29] Indeed, on a practical level the whole plan lacked discipline, coordination, or even a unanimity of vision. Many sculptors were oblivious of questions of local environment and created their monuments with no reference to their ultimate positions in the streets or squares, and, in many cases, especially, in Petrograd, sculptors were left to choose their own locations. In addition, since the sculptors concerned had no definite guidelines as to the desired treatment of the historical figures, the most absurd positions, expressions, and gestures were to be met with: Heine was depicted in a severe

1
Sarra Lebedeva, *Robespierre* (bas-relief). Plaster of Paris, 1920. Photo: *Iskusstvo* [Art], Moscow, 1970, no. 9, p. 21)

2
Viktor Sinaisky, *La Salle* (bust), 1918. Silhouette by Elizaveta Kruglikova. (Photo: *Pechat i revoliutsiia* [The Press and the Revolution], Moscow, 1927, no. 8, p. 211)

3
S. Smirnov, *Beethoven* (bust). Plaster of Paris, ca. 1920. (Photo: *Pechat i revoliutsiia* [The Press and the Revolution], Moscow, 1927, no. 7, p. 191)

4
Boris Korolev, *Bakunin*, 1919. (Photo: *Pechat i revoliutsiia* [The Press and the Revolution], Moscow, 1927, no. 8, p. 109)

state of malnutrition and physical enervation; Bakunin had no face; the scientist Timiryazev was depicted as a graduate of Cambridge University with appropriate gown (Fig. 5).

Less acerbic criticisms were passed on the several bas-reliefs that appeared on the walls of important institutions in Moscow, Petrograd, and other cities. To a considerable extent, of course, the whole artistic approach in this area was wrong, that is, in its original, pristine condition, the bas-relief had never been "applied" to the wall, but had been carved from it and had thus acted as an organic part of the whole structure. Most of the Soviet bas-reliefs were, however, carved and cast in studios and then attached to the appropriate surface. This lack of immediate contact between the sculptor and his ultimate working locale became evident in the frequent disproportion and disharmony between the bas-relief and the expanse of the wall. Some reliefs were too small for their positions high up on a standing surface and could not, therefore, be recognized; others lacked the formal clarity and precision essential to the relief and relied more on surface narrative scene than on three-dimensional volume. Again we can see the elements of painting rather than of sculpture at work, and indeed, some reliefs looked more like canvases than exercises in stone. Such a criticism could be leveled at Konenkov's relief "To Those Fallen in the Struggle for Peace and Fraternity of Peoples," unveiled on the Kremlin wall on 7 November 1918, where it remained until 1948, when it was removed because of its disrepair (Fig. 6). This relief was, in any case, too allegorical to be widely understood, and the winged celestial figure playing the main role made Lenin rather suspicious. Similarly, not all quotations written on these reliefs were to the point—one artist put plaques with inscribed texts from Marx, Bakunin, and the Apostle Paul; another carved the slogan "He who doesn't work, doesn't eat" beneath a genre scene of a worker and his wife having their dinner; yet another mounted the very wise maxim "All our hope rests on those people who feed themselves." All in all, as one correspondent wrote in a German magazine: "The young sculptors have proved that they were not yet capable of creating a distinctive monumental style."[30]

One result of the monumental failure of the monumental plan was that both critical and public interest in sculpture diminished considerably and was revived only during the mid–1920s and thereafter when the proclivity toward strictly representational forms became very pronounced. Of course, parallel to the decline in the popularity of sculpture emerged the industrial constructivist movement, with its proclamation that easel art (and

hence the statue) was dead and that industrial design was the only viable outlet for creative energy. And, therefore, as architecture became increasingly linear and severe, so the demand for external stone ornamentation dwindled accordingly (at least until ca. 1930 when the Palladian style reasserted itself). It is significant that after the first stages of the monumental plan, many statues were produced through a combination of sculptural and architectural forces. Hence, for example, we find that in one of the Karl Marx projects of 1920 the pedestal was designed by the Vesnins (Fig. 7) and that the monument to Lenin speaking from an armored car was designed by two architects (Shchuko and Geilfreikh) and one sculptor (Sergei Evseev, 1882–1959).

Even if some artists, such as Gabo, believed that easel art was still very much alive, any concept of progressive sculpture was, in fact, replaced by construction, by "engineerism." Some critics, especially Punin, believed that realism/naturalism, whether in sculpture or in painting, was outmoded and that, unfortunately, the monumental plan had shown that the average sculptor had not managed to conceive of a new artistic form worthy of the new age. This was one reason why Punin welcomed Tatlin's scheme for a monument to the Revolution (the prototype of the model to the Third International), for he saw its synthesis of art and technology as a logical extension of the Revolution and a true reflection of the age.[31] But Tatlin's model was an isolated case and orthodox forms continued to dominate the sculptural arena: after the mid-1920s imposing, professional statues to Lenin and other leaders were commissioned very widely, and the miniature bust or figurine also enjoyed a vogue as the new middle class, the product of the new economic policy, began to furnish its salons with appropriate knickknacks and to dictate artistic taste. At the other extreme there was a brief endeavor to make art truly monumental by carving the faces of Lenin and other leaders in rock cliffs, rather in the tradition of the Mount Rushmore presidential complex.

Although born premature, thanks to Lenin's ill-timed plan of monumental propaganda, Soviet monumental sculpture did achieve its most impressive and emphatic results after the rise of Stalin. The age of monolithic decrees, of political autocracy, of extravagant rhetoric could thus stimulate such colossal phenomena as the 500-foot statue to have been placed on the projected Palace of Soviets (Iofan et al., early and mid-1930s, (Fig. 8), already to have been much higher than the Empire State, the Worker and Collective Farm-Worker in Moscow (designed in 1937 by Vera Mukhina, 1889–1953), or the towering statue of Stalin overlooking the Dnepropetrovsk Hydroelectric dam (1930s). Such sculpture became identifiable with the Soviet Union until

5
Sergei Merkurov (with the architect D.
P. Osipov): *Timiryazev*. Granite,
1923. (Photo: *Iskusstvo* [Art],
Moscow, 1969, no. 12, p. 3)

6
Sergei Konenkov. *Relief: ''To Those
Fallen in the Struggle for Peace and
Fraternity of Peoples''*. Cement, 1918.
(Photo: *Iskusstro* [Art], Moscow,
1972, no. 6, p. 3)

7
Sergei Aleshin (with the architects
Aleksandr, Leonid, and Viktor Ves-
nin), Project of a monument to Karl
Marx, 1919–1920. Not realized.
(Photo: A. Chiniakhov, *Bratia Vesniny*,
Moscow, 1970, p. 53)
8
Boris Iofan, Vladimir Gelfreikh, Vla-
dimir Shchuko (architects): Project for
a Palace of Soviets, Early and mid–
1930s. Not realized. (Photo: I. Grabar
et al., eds., *Istoriia russkogo iskusstva*,
Moscow, 1961, vol. 12, p. 93)

9
Vasilii Borodai, *Monument to
Chekisty* [Security Police]. Detail.
Granite, 1967. (Photo: *Iskusstvo* [Art],
Moscow, 1971, no. 11, p. 27)

about 1960, especially during the 1950s when many monumental complexes of statues and murals to the Second World War were put up in the iron curtain countries. Unfortunately, the way the trend developed was toward grandeur at all costs, devoid both of mimetic and of intrinsic aesthetic value.

The lesson we learn from the implementation of the monumental program of 1918–1922 is twofold. On the one hand, it becomes very clear that art and politics do have strict demarcation lines and that art in the service only of politics degenerates accordingly; this is not to say that art cannot be political, of course, but it would seem to be more at home in disharmony than in harmony with a given régime (Fig. 9). On the other hand, an issue almost as broad emerges from this general context, that artists are incapable of organizing their own affairs: the failure of Lenin's plan rested not merely on his own unawareness of certain problems but also on the distinct lack of organization and communication among the artists themselves. This becomes especially apparent when we remember that IZO Narkompros was manned, for the most part, by practicing artists who were far more interested in their practical and pedagogical work than in administrative and bureaucratic duties. But however negative the immediate results of Lenin's plan, we must not forget that it formed only part of a much greater vision: the tentative endeavor to populate the streets and squares with statues and reliefs was but the first stage in the transformation of the industrial city into a garden city, "of the grey squares into a living museum."[32] In this respect, Lenin's conception was a progressive, albeit utopian one and in its proposals anticipated ideas fundamental to the development of Soviet architecture and society in the late 1920s and early 1930s.

Notes

1
I. Gintsburg: "Po voprosu o razvitii skulptury v Rossii," *Trudy Vserossiiskogo sezda khudozhnikov v Peterburge dek. 1911—yanv. 1912* (Petrograd, 1914), v. 3, p. 47 (hereafter cited as Gintsburg).

2
A. Vasyutinsky in reply to Gintsburg, p. 51.

3
See Gintsburg, pp. 47–50.

4
See S. Makovsky: "Ministerstvo iskusstv," *Apollon* (Pentrograd, 1917), no. 2/3, pp. I–XVI.

5
The basic design belonged to the architect Lev Rudnev and the monument was later landscaped by the architect Ivan Fomin; the artist Vladimir Kozlinsky contributed to the minor decorative designs.

6
El Lissitzky: "New Russian Art. A Lecture" (1922), in S. Lissitzky-Küppers: *El Lissitzky* (N.Y., 1968), p. 336.

7
Gintsburg, p. 47.

8
I. Grabar: "Aktualnye zadachi sovetskoi skulptury," *Iskusstvo* (Moscow-Leningrad, 1933), no. 1/2, p. 155.

9
For details see A. Mikhailov: "Programma monumentalnoi propagandy," *Iskusstvo* (Moscow, 1968), no. 4, pp. 31–34. See also D. Shterenberg: "Agitatsionnye pamyatniki i otnoshenie k nim Soyuza skulptorov," *Izobrazitelnoe iskusstvo* (Petrograd, 1919), no. 1, pp. 71–72.

10
For details see *Iskusstvo* (Moscow, 1918), no. 2 (6), p. 15 et seq.

11
Izvestiya VTsIK, Moscow, April 14, 1918. Reprinted in I. Grabar et al. (ed.): *Istoriya russkogo iskusstva* (Moscow, 1957), v. 11, p. 25 (hereafter cited as Grabar et al.). In his formulation of the decree Lenin seems to have drawn substantially upon the very similar proposals supported by the Revolutionary government in France in the early 1790s. Diane Kelder brought my attention to this in December 1972, during the first meeting of the symposium from which this volume developed.

12
A. Galushkina et al., eds.: *Agitatsionno-massovoe iskusstvo pervykh let Oktyabrya* (Moscow, 1971), p. 34.

13
Ibid., p. 34.

14
Grabar et al., eds., p. 26.

15
S. Konenkov: *Moi vek* (Moscow, 1972), p. 214.

16
Lenin o kulture i iskusstve. Sbornik (Moscow, 1956), p. 250.

17
I. Matsa et al., eds.: *Sovetskoe iskusstvo za 15 let* (Moscow-Leningrad, 1933), p. 27 (hereafter cited as Matsa).

18
Ibid., pp. 27–29.

19
S. Konenkov, *Moi vek,* pp. 216–217.

20
Iskusstvo (Moscow, 1918), no. 2 (6). Quoted from Matsa, p. 21.

21
Izvestiya VTsIK (Moscow, 1918), no. 163 (427). Ibid., p. 20.

22
This according to K. Umanski: "Die neue Monumental skulptur in Russland," *Der Ararat* (Munich, 1920), no. 5/6, p. 31 (hereafter cited as Umanski).

23
Grabar et al., eds., p. 32.

24
M. Dillon: "O skulpture," in *Trudy Vserossiiskogo,* v. 3, p. 54.

25
N. Punin: "O pamyatnikakh," *Iskusstvo kommuny* (Petersburg, 1919), no. 14, March 9, p. 2 (hereafter cited as Punin).

26
Quoted from "Vsesoyuznaya vystavka monumentalnogo iskusstva," *Iskusstvo* (Moscow, 1969), no. 6, p. 4.

27
Punin, p. 3.

28
"Uberite chuchelo!," *Vechernie izvestiya Moskovskogo Soveta rabochikh i krasnoarmeiskikh deputatov* (Moscow, 1920), February 10.

29
A. Blok: *Dvenadtsat* (Petrograd, 1918), p. 10.

30
Umanski, p. 33.

31
Punin, pp. 2–3.

32
Iskusstvo (Moscow, 1918), no. 6 (10), pp. 7–9. Quoted from I. Nikonova, ed.: *Stanovlenie sotsialisticheskogo realizma v sovetskom izobraziteĺnom iskusstve* (Moscow, 1960), p. 90.

11
Political Iconography in the Diego Rivera Frescoes at Cuernavaca, Mexico

Stanton L. Catlin

When his scientific researches and sociological projects from the Valley of Teotihuacan had piled ponderous data on his desk for a resumé of his findings, [Manuel] Gamio pushed them aside and called in an artist to crown the pyramid. "It was necessary," he wrote," that a painter, a true painter . . . be sent to live in the valley; to identify himself . . . with the brilliant blue heaven, the hostile arid mountains, the eternally verdant plains; with the aged colonial temples of stately legend . . . and with the stark huts grasped in the claws of the magueys and the cacti. . . . He must live with and become the brother of the native of the valley, accept for himself so long as he remained, the customs, the ideals, the pain, the pleasure, the beliefs and amusements of that man."
Anita Brenner in *Idols behind Altars* (New York, 1931), p. 231, on the Zacatecan artist, Francisco Goitia.

The Diego Rivera murals at Cuernavaca are in the out-of-door, second-floor gallery or loggia of the Cortés Palace, an early sixteenth-century building which in recent years has served as government headquarters of the State of Morelos. They were painted in 1930 when Rivera was forty-four years old and were his fifth mural undertaking in Mexico.[1] They vary in height from about 13 to 15 feet, are just under 120 feet in overall length, and are painted entirely in fresco (Fig. 1). They look eastward through the loggia's stately sixteenth-century arcade across the valley of Cuernavaca toward the snow-covered peaks of Popocatépetl and Ixtaccihuatl. They were commissioned in October 1929 by the late Dwight W. Morrow, United States Ambassador to Mexico from 1927 to 1930.

The subject matter of the main panels traces the history of Cuernavaca and the surrounding regions from the battles of the Spanish Conquest in 1521, to the Agrarian Revolt under Emiliano Zapata in 1911 in two main divisions: first, the military conquest by Spain, followed by Spanish settlement and its nineteenth-century aftermath. The historical theme is divided into eight sub-parts arranged chronologically in continuous design (except for a dividing central pier) along the three faces of the main and end walls. Arched window and door openings, with windows well below the loggia ceiling, make boundaries and transitional areas at irregular intervals for the selected historical themes. Following the order in the diagram (Fig. 2), these are:

I. The battle for Cuernavaca between Aztecs and Spaniards and Indian allies in April 1521.

Revised and extended form of the article, "Some Sources and Uses of Pre-Columbian Art in the Cuernavaca Frescoes of Diego Rivera," first presented at the 35th Congreso Internacional de Americanistas, in Mexico, 1962, and thereafter published in English by the Instituto Nacional de Antropologia e Historia in the *Actas y Memorias* of the Congress, pp. 439 ff. The study was continued for a Master's thesis with the same title at the Institute of Fine Arts, New York University, 1967.

1
General view of Rivera frescoes in
loggia, looking south. 1930. State
Palace, Cuernavaca.

2
Diagram of loggia walls showing sequence of mural themes (see text).
State Palace, Cuernavaca. (Isometric
drawing: James Garrison)

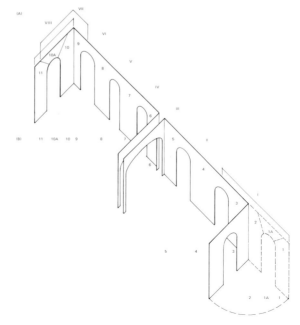

II. Spaniards crossing the *barranca* (ravine) into Cuernavaca.

III. Spaniards seizing Cuernavaca from its Tlahuican inhabitants.

IV. Cortés taking title to the lands awarded him by Imperial decree in the name of The Spanish Crown and Church.

V. The building of Cortés's palace by Indian labor and Cortés receiving Indian tribute.

VI. Colonial sugar farming and processing at the Cortés's family plant at Atlacomulco, near Cuernavaca.

VII. The role of the Spanish Church after the Conquest.

VIII. Oppression of the peasants, their revolt and assumption of power in Morelos under Emiliano Zapata in the spring of 1911.

Underneath the main panels, other events of the Conquest are interpreted in eleven grisaille panels, also in fresco. In addition, the central piers are painted with full-length portraits of Morelos (for which Rivera used himself as model) and Zapata (a composite based on verbal descriptions of associates and acquaintances); the faces of the depressed arch above are decorated with reclining female figures, emblems, and slogans, on one side symbolizing the Mexican Independence movement, on the other the Zapatista guerrilla war against the landowners of the State of Morelos a century later. Six heraldic designs based on Aztec place glyphs of native villages of the region are painted on the inner spandrels of the gallery archway facing the main walls.

Historical Background

Landing at what is now the port of Veracruz on the Gulf of Mexico on April 21, 1519, Cortés explored the neighboring coastal regions and subdued various Indian communities that were tributaries of the Aztecs and their priest-king, Moctezuma II. His curiosity and ambition heightened by reports of the wealth and power of a great inland empire, he decided to march to its capital in the highlands to the west. Burning his ships, he set forth into the interior in August of the same year with 15 Spanish horsemen, 415 foot soldiers, and some 2,300 Indian auxiliaries. After marching across the tropical coastlands and up the high, eastern cordillera, he encountered the Tlaxcalans, an Indian nation that had stood off Aztec rule. Cortés hoped to make an alliance with this powerful tribe and, if necessary, use their warriors against the Aztecs. But their leaders mistrusted him because of his dealings with the emissaries of Moctezuma, who had been using every diplomatic strategem and divinatory rite he could think of to keep the Spaniards away. After three hard-fought battles the Tlaxacalans decided to throw in their lot

with Cortés. Moctezuma, seeing that his policy to divert the strange newcomers was failing, reversed himself and offered the invaders his hospitality. Accordingly, in December 1519, the band of Spanish soldier-adventurers was received in Tenochtitlán, the Aztecs' island metropolis, and put up in one of the Emperor's palaces in the main temple enclosure in the center of the city.

Once established in the capital, Cortés hoped to rule the empire from behind Moctezuma's throne. But after six uneasy months in Tenochtitlán there was a general uprising of the Aztecs when the Spaniards killed a group of Indians taking part in a religious festival in the central square. At the time, Cortés was in Veracruz fighting a counter expedition sent against him by his superior, the Governor of Cuba, Diego Velázquez. His lieutenant in charge, the impulsive Pedro de Alvarado, suspecting the ceremony to be a ruse (it was a feast of the Sun- and War-God, Huitzilopochtli), ordered his men to attack the gathering. Confounded and enraged, the population as a whole rose against the visitors and drove them back into their quarters. Hearing of these developments Cortés marched to Tenochtitlán in haste and managed to reenter the capital and rejoin his beseiged troops. But he was unable to control the situation. Obliged to abandon the city at night, the members of the Spanish company, laden with gold, were attacked and nearly overwhelmed by masses of Indian warriors as they crossed from the island to the mainland over the city's western causeway. His forces were decimated during what, with the human sense of a Renaissance man, he called the "noche triste."

Cortés determined to remain in the Valley of Mexico. He established headquarters in the friendly village of Texcoco on the east shore of the great lake surrounding Tenochtitlán and went about the task of preparing a full-scale amphibious siege the following summer.

It was during the course of these preparations that Cortés undertook the Cuernavaca expedition. Its purpose was to reconnoiter the region beyond the lakes surrounding Tenochtitlán and to gain allies or break the resistance of potentially hostile tribes before his assault on the capital. The Spanish, supported by thousands of Tlaxcalan and Texcocan allies, completed their circling of the lakes after three weeks of trail blazing, mountain climbing, scaling of Indian-held cliffs, and rugged marching in all kinds of terrain and weather, most of the time under attack. Five fierce battles were fought, including the one for Cuernavaca, which took place on April 21, 1521.

Ideology

The whole first phase of Rivera's mural painting, particularly that part following his Preparatory School mural (finished March 1923) and continuing through all but the left wall of the National Palace stairway (that is, until late in 1930), is conceived as an instrument of political indoctrination and action within the context of Mexican life and history. Cuernavaca is no exception. It fits into, rounds out, and epitomizes major phases of a revolutionary ideological system that had become increasingly clear in his previous comprehensive public documentation of the life and twentieth-century history of the Mexican people at the Ministry of Education building and at Chapingo. In keeping with this purpose it applies dialectical principles derived from a developed social revolutionary philosophy to achieve what the artist deems the proper goals of the Mexican Revolution: a native Mexican dictatorship in which sovereign power is vested not only in the peasant and worker class but explicitly and fundamentally in that element of the working population identified with the Indian ethnic matrix of the nation before Western colonization. As such he deliberately gives to his art theoretical and tutorial roles as primary missions, integral with its aesthetic function and thus essential to its artistic genesis and existence. In these terms art becomes not only a humanistic activity of intellect and sensibility, traditionally independent and autonomous, without regard for social implications or lack of them, but an activity with broad ideological aims to define and impart for the benefit of a national society and those elements of the Mexican population he considers most needful of and politically essential to their realization. This is no different in principle from any art that has been part of or has served to further belief in sociopolitical or socioreligious doctrine. One must, however, eliminate from Rivera's system any element of belief in metaphysical absolutes and substitute Hegelian teleology as the mainspring of its determinism.

In the broad outlines and substance of its social revolutionary philosophy, Rivera's mural art realized in Mexico during the 1920s shows that the selection, organization, and treatment of its artistic materials as well as its ideological content is based on political ends, means, and dialectical principles that are clearly Marxist in origin. At the same time, however, quite independently of Marxist tradition, it gives precedence in attention to Mexican national over international revolutionary objectives and tacitly equates the importance of native cultural values with what he considers the political imperatives in the general revolutionary process. Within this dual system three principles may be seen to affect the formal character of Rivera's murals at this time: (1) the use of Marxist-Leninist social revolutionary philosophy and dialectical method as the philosophical base of his new politically directed career; (2) the greater attention given Mexican national as distinct

from (but not in opposition to) world revolutionary objectives; and (3) the parity given cultural vis-a-vis political-economic facts, both as means and end, in the Revolutionary struggle. These three principles not only govern the formal character but also the social revolutionary content of the Cuernavaca murals, with the social revolutionary content, put forward and argued for dialectical and immediately political reasons, as the most important aspect of the work, no matter how this content is dependent upon and involved in other aspects of its artistic form.

Giving precedence to the social revolutionary content and purpose of the murals is entirely in keeping with Marxist theory and practice. The intended Proletarian-dictated Socialist state is the end that subsumes all means, including art. However, points 2 and 3 of the previously stated tenets, which Rivera followed in formulating his personal style and version of social revolutionary content, stand outside of and, in effect, are antithetical to orthodox Marxist revolutionary thought and practice. The particular elements associated with these interests, comprehensively developed throughout his Mexican work of the 1920s—Mexican nationalism and its indigenous Mexican-American cultural characteristics—proclaimed the artist's independence of attitude and action as well as the uncontainable artistic imagination that contributed to his break with the Mexican Communist party in 1929. The humanistic and political legacy of this independence was that Rivera not only devised new and generally viable thematic and compositional forms for didactic mural painting but helped create a new and durable independent image for the Mexican nation, establishing major conceptual and symbolic features of this image. The thematic and compositional forms that gave rise to this new, visually formed self-conception have one of their clearest articulations in the individual themes at Cuernavaca. The resulting mural as a whole is an essential part of the now established and generally accepted image of post-revolutionary Mexico, embodied as well in the historical series he painted simultaneously in the stairway of the National Palace in Mexico City.

Definition and Perspective

Ideology: 4. The intellectual pattern of any widespread culture or movement; as, exposure to Anglo-Saxon ideology; specif., the integrated assertions, theories, and aims that constitute a politico-social program. . . .[2]
—*Webster's New Collegiate Dictionary*, 1949 edition

The word *ideology* in this study has been used in the sense quoted in the dictionary entry.[3] The meaning will be obvious if *Hispanic* or, as one may now say, *Mexican* (albeit within the purely national

197
Political
Iconography in
the Diego Rivera
Frescoes at
Cuernavaca,
Mexico

scope) is substituted for *Anglo-Saxon*. Applied specifically to Diego Rivera's work as an art in the service of politics, its use is based on the broad purpose of his artistic activity, which is to carry out a politico-social program that will result in a new comprehension of Mexico as a nation, replacing the previous colonialist ideology and subservience of its people.

Since both means and ends are involved in achieving the new ideology, and since the total work of art is involved in the dynamic process of engaging the observer in beliefs and activity that will favor the realization of the politico-social program, political content, that is, the service of political ends, is concomitant with all aspects of its formal existence as art. In thus bringing the actual world of political means and ends into art, Rivera brings art into the actual world of politics.

Considering the scope of Rivera's detailed inventory of Mexican life and potentialities in this and the aggregate of his other mural works of the 1920s, the artist may be said to have also assumed a universal role not unlike that of the early Renaissance muralists in Italy, as in the civic fresco programs of the Palazzo Publico in Siena. However, he takes this role not as interpreter and reformer within an established religious system following classical precepts but as lawgiver and theologian, undertaking the elaboration of a new faith and social order for his reemergent nation on his own.

Iconographical Sources: Battle of Aztecs and Spaniards

Sometime within six months before receiving the Morrow commission and less than a year following his return to Mexico from his first trip to Moscow, Rivera had started the planning and, to some extent not yet precisely determined, the work of painting his general mural history of Mexico on the walls of the National Palace stairway. Not only the subject of the first section of this history, the legend of Quetzalcoatl and the spectacle of Indian civilization and ceremonial life before the Conquest, but the whole subsequent history of Mexico confronted him with the need for literary and visual source materials. With his interest thus focused upon problems of historical representation, the more limited but analogous historical theme of the Cuernavaca commission underscored the importance of documents from the past. Whenever he may have first taken hold of this problem, it is in connection with the Cuernavaca project that he said, "I took care to authenticate every detail by exact research because I wanted to leave no opening for anyone to try to discredit the murals as a whole by the charge that any detail was a fabrication."[4] This requirement was meant to

apply not only to pre-Spanish aspects of his theme but to all phases of his historical survey. The resulting number of visual references, even of identifiable specific pictorial sources in both murals, is exceptionally large.

To determine the sources of these references—here limited to principal motifs in a selection of the historical themes of the mural series and concentrating first on those found in the three battle scenes of the Cuernavaca frescos (see Fig. 2, Theme I, Parts 1, 1A, 2, and 3)—the present inquiry has sought pictorial, literary, and journalistic material from the late pre-Conquest and early colonial periods (approx. 1490–1560) to the Zapatista revolt (early twentieth century) insofar as this material was published or otherwise available to the artist (and found by the writer) before completion of the main panels of the mural series in September 1930. Most important, it includes examples or representations of popular painting, sculpture, and graphic art as well as artifacts of ritual or practical daily use either continuing pre-Conquest traditions or assimilating colonial and nineteenth-century strains down to the time of the murals' execution.[5]

Within this broad research area, the following are some of the specific sources in Mexico Rivera must have consulted for the Battle Theme at Cuernavaca and others that he is likely to have found readily available for consulation:

1. Among the pictorial codices, the *Lienzo de Tlaxcala* and the *Matrícula de Tributos,* both in the National Museum.
2. Among monuments of pre-Columbian art and architecture and their traditions, the remains of Aztec and pre-Aztec architecture, particularly the Aztec temple of Teopanzoloco at Cuernavaca; Aztec sculpture in the National Museum and elsewhere; Indian popular art and artifacts of use.
3. Among publications—Sahagún's *Codex Florentino* in the Paso y Troncoso edition of 1905–1907; Sahagún's *Codice Matritense, Primeros Memoriales,* in the same edition; the *Codex Mendoza* in the Galindo y Villa edition, with the Paso y Troncoso facsimile in black and white; the first three volumes of Kingsborough's *Antiquities of Mexico* (1831), which included color reproductions of the *Codex Mendoza, Codex Vaticanus* (No. 3738), *Codex Telleriano-Remensis,* and other pictorial manuscripts in Oxford, Berlin, Vienna, Dresden, Liverpool, Rome, and Paris; the *Lienzo de Tlaxcala,* Junta de Colombino edition, in *Antigüedades Mexicanas* (1892); and Eduard Seler's massive *Gesammelte Abhandlungen* (1904).

The three-part battle theme at the north end of the portico area, *Battle of Aztecs and Spaniards,* is the locus of Rivera's greatest concentration of subject matter deriving from the pre-Columbian phase of

Mexican history (Figs. 3a and 3b). The manner of the artist's use of these sources is considered here not only with respect to the artist's fidelity to the source but to possible new meanings given these sources as elements forming part of the style and educative purpose of the Cuernavaca mural program. The plan is to consider several of the chief motifs as these would be seen by following the normal chronological sequence beginning with the lower right section of the first panel on the north-end wall.

The action in the progression of historical events begins without preliminaries in the first event of the three-part battle scene on the lower right: two Tlaxcalan allies of the Spaniards direct a cannon against a Mexican flanking attack under the command of an armored Spanish officer (Fig. 3a, lower right). The realistically painted Tlaxcalans are naked except for a loin cloth (*temillotl*), their ears are pierced, their columnar headdresses are bound with rings, and the foremost wears a necklace of green stone. The cannon is placed between the Tlaxcalans and the Spanish officer, who wears a half-suit of burnished armor.

Using subjects and pose as well as style as the basis of comparison in order to locate possible sources of these motifs, the Tlaxcalan warriors seem to correspond most closely to the central figure of the Spaniards' messenger who first approached the Tlaxcalans (on the march from Veracruz to Tenochititlán) in panel No. 1 of the *Lienzo de Tlaxcala* (Fig. 4). Details such as the headdress, pierced ears, and necklace, which appear in the Rivera figure but not in this particular *Lienzo* panel, and conversely, the lack of sandals in the Rivera rendering, are attributes found in other parts of the *Lienzo* drawings of Tlaxcalan warriors and officials that could have been introduced in the fresco figures in keeping with the artist's wide-ranging eclecticism. In terms of style one finds that, although Rivera's modeling and details are more realistic and the contours more angular than round, the artist's emphasis on the nakedness and profile of these figures as well as their role as Spanish auxiliaries further point to the *Lienzo*, particularly No. 24 (Fig. 5), as the chief pictorial source of his representation.

The Spanish officer, on the other hand, indicates a freer but less convincing interpretation of its sources. As suggested in the same *Lienzo* drawing, Rivera's officer owes a great deal to the *Lienzo* renderings of armored Spanish soldiers, again in its sharp outlines, suggestion of the texture of shiny armor plate, and adoption of certain details of helmet and armor. However, the tassets of Rivera's soldier seem improvised and, compared with prototypes of Maximilian armor of the early sixteenth century, incorrect, and there is ambiguity in the handling of shoulder plates and coudes. This is due in part, to the artist's effort

to give the flat, relatively unmodeled *Lienzo* drawings a three-dimensional quality and material substance by combining them with a second source, namely, the drawings of armored Spanish soldiers in Book XII of the *Codex Florentino,* which are less formal and often more realistic in conveying body, texture, and spacial depth as well as action (*Codex Florentino,* XII, 18, Fig. 6). One finds evidence of this fusion of two or more sources again and again at Cuernavaca, even to the extent where it seems deliberately adopted dichotomy in the artist's method, with emphasis shifting from one to the other.

The third motif in this first group is the cannon. Here the examples of Spanish artillery found in the *Lienzo de Tlaxcala* and *Codex Florentino,* although welcome as thematic sources, probably fell far short of Rivera's demands for realistic representation; he could have met these by corrective reference to another source, in this case an illustration in Vol. VI of the 1905 edition of the *Enciclopedia Universal Ilustrada,* showing an early sixteenth-century *basilisco* (wheeled cannon) (Fig. 7). In Rivera's rendering the splayed mount with crosspiece at the base and coincidence of breech with the angle of the mount, the wheel rim, and other details suggest a turn to this more explicit source to obtain authenticity and three-dimensional realism.

Next in this consideration are the three groups of warriors on the left of the doorway, starting at the top (Fig. 3a, top left). There the Mexican knight is dressed as an eagle, hurling a stone with a sling, and holding a blue and white shield with insignia of dotted black circles. There is no problem in identifying this military dress as that of an Eagle Knight (*quauhtín*) one of the three warrior orders named in the *Codex Mendoza* (Clark I, 62n). The nearest pictorial source of the pose as well as the eagle dress may be found in a *Codex Florentino* illustration (*Codex Florentino,* II, 54, Fig. 8) of a gladitorial sacrifice (*Tlauauanalitzli*). As previously noted, Rivera gives his knight the shield of the sun and warrior god Huitzilopochtli, to whom the Mexicans owed the rite of human sacrifice. The more plastic treatment of Rivera's helmet, however, suggests classic Aztec sculpture, recalling the Scopas-like Grecian head of an Eagle Knight in the National Museum (Fig. 9).[6] Consideration of sources may here be widened, however, because the figure of an eagle knight placed at the top of the left wall composition and shown opposing Spanish firearms with a stone and sling would indicate that Rivera wanted this motif to strike the observer not only as an example of intrepid battle action but as a general symbol of Mexican resistance to the conquerors. Considering the motif in these terms, the artist could well have noticed a pertinent historical and compositional

199
Political
Iconography in
the Diego Rivera
Frescoes at
Cuernavaca,
Mexico

3a
Rivera: *Battle of Aztecs and Spaniards*
(First Section), Theme 1, Parts 1, 1A,
and 2. State Palace, Cuernavaca.
(Photo: Álvarez-Bravo, Mexico City)

3b
Rivera: *Battle of Aztecs and Spaniards*
(Second Section), Theme 1, Part 3.
State Palace, Cuernavaca. (Photo:
Álvarez-Bravo, Mexico City)

4
Messenger before Tlaxcalan tribal
council. *Lienzo de Tlaxcala,* No. 1.
(From Chavero)

5
Armored Spanish soldiers. *Lienzo de Tlaxcala,* No. 24 (detail). (After Chavero)

6
Armored Spanish soldiers in Mexico. Sahagún: *Codex Florentino,* XII, ill. 18.

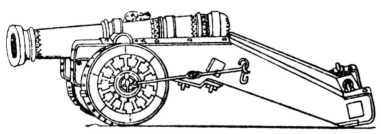

7
Sixteenth-Century Spanish basilisco. (From *Enciclopedia Universal Ilustrada,* VI, 507)

8
Ritual combat of Eagle Knight and prisoner. Sahagún: *Codex Florentino,* II, ill. 54. (From Paso y Troncoso)

9
Head of Eagle Knight. Aztec, ca.
1500. Mexico City, National Museum.
(Reproduced with permission from
*Thirteen Masterpieces of Mexican Ar-
chaeology.* Detroit: Blaine-Ethridge
Books. 1938.)

10
Aztec defending Tenochtitlán.
Sahagún: *Codex Florentino,* XII, ill.
152. (From Paso y Troncoso)

11
Aztec Ocelot Knight and Spaniard.
Detail of Fig. 3a (Photo: Álvarez-
Bravo, Mexico City)

precedent for it in a drawing (No. 152) in Book XII of the *Codex Florentino,* illustrating an episode just before the fall of Tenochtitlán (Fig. 10).

To the observer the nearest part of the first wall of the battle theme, left of the doorway (Part 2), is the much reproduced triumph of an Indian warrior over an armored Spaniard. An Aztec brave in the full war dress of an ocelot pins his adversary to the ground and drives a stone dagger into his throat (Fig. 11). The prototype of this warrior is the Ocelot Knight; another of Rivera's versions of this Knight, without helmet, was seen in the figure of the Tlaxcalan with spiral headband. Its pictorial source was found in the *Lienzo de Tlaxcala.* Here, however, one is struck by the heightened graphic effect. Whereas up to this point Rivera's treatment has fluctuated between the simplified linear stylization of the *Lienzo de Tlaxcala* and the freer drawing of Book XII of the *Codex Florentino;* in this representation he seems to aim for the first time at detailed realism through close imitation of the more objective style of *Mendoza Codex* or the *Matrćula de Tributos* (Fig. 12). The vengeful intensity of the effigy of the Ocelot Knight as well as the action might be explained by illustration No. 72 in Book XII of the *Codex Florentino* (Fig. 13). In this almost expressionistic drawing an armored Spaniard in a barred helmet is about to give an unconscious Indian warrior a death blow. It is hard not to think that the sight of this so disturbed Rivera that he could not resist the personal retaliation of reversing the protagonists and giving the conquistador an even more decisive death blow.[7]

The third part of the Cuernavaca battle theme occupies a full panel that joins the north-end wall around a ninety-degree corner angle without interruption of the painting. Dominating the foreground of this panel is the encounter between an armored Spanish knight on horseback and a Mexican Eagle Knight on foot. (Fig. 3b) We have considered the prototype of the Eagle Knight in connection with the previous panel on the left side of the north-end wall. In this case drawing No. 79 in Book VIII of the *Florentine Codex* can be suggested as a likely specific source (Fig. 14). Corresponding similarities are the near completeness of the eagle war dress including the tail feathers, obsidian-bladed club, the inside of the shield and its pendant, chest support of the overhead standard, and, the overhead standard itself. The mounted Spanish knight, on the other hand, seems to derive partly from several drawings of the Spanish horsemen in the *Lienzo de Tlaxcala,* of which No. 73 is a close example for the position of the sword (Fig. 15). This figure also seems to be a good illustration of the range of Rivera's eclectic method of combining motifs and treatments from diverse sources. The details of armor, the horse's long tail, rump strap, stirrup, the generally archaic

character of the armor, despite the effort toward greater naturalism on Rivera's part, again seem to be from the *Lienzo* (*Lienzo de Tlaxcala,* 39, Fig. 16).

Another source, if not, indeed, the chief origin of the white horse, however, is to be found in the Italian quattrocento painting, the *Battle of San Romano* (by Paolo Uccello, in the Uffizi Gallery), specifically in the foreshortened white horse, facing the rear, on the far right (Fig. 17). Rivera made posture studies as well as details of weapons and armor from this painting in 1921.[8] In adapting a Florentine Renaissance horse to his Cuernavaca composition, Rivera has modified its form to the point where it would be stylistically consistent with the realism of other elements adapted from the *Lienzo de Tlaxcala.* Further, going beyond the naturalistically conceived profile, modeling, and details of the Tlaxcalans and Spaniard in the previous cannon group, the artist exaggerates realistic appearance in a manner bordering on caricature to portray the actions and features of one of the conquerors. This contrasts with the quite different approach in his treatment of the Eagle Knight, here not only symbolizing Indian opposition to the conquerors but also representing Mexican indigenous civilization. Instead of a naturalistic norm we find the profile as well as individual shapes of limbs, beak, and feathers almost schematically stylized. On the basis of this and the cannon group, together with recurrences of similar treatment in later parts of the mural, one may believe that Rivera associated naturalistic realism with the Spanish and all those whom, in Rivera's personal view and application of Marxist theory, the Spaniards' actions of conquest, pillage, enslavement, and exploitation symbolize. He associated stylized realism, on the other hand, with the Mexican nation and its opposition to all he considered committed to such aims and actions.[9] Thus we have an artistic distinction applied generally as a device for differentiating between two of the chief realities he proposes as confronting the contemporary Mexican—foreign versus native proletarian interest.

Next for consideration among motifs from the battle theme are the Aztec standards, specifically overhead standards constructed on a frame and supported by poles attached to the backs of Indian warriors of higher rank (Figs. 18 and 19). These standards were made of light wood and were most often effigies or symbols of gods with whom the warrior was associated and whose power he may have wished to invoke in battle. Such effigies were often of frightening aspect so as to overawe their Indian adversaries. There are thirty-three such overhead standards in the battle scenes of Rivera's mural: fourteen so-called effigy devices and nineteen other devices, including eleven flag, five sheaf, and three

203
Political
Iconography in
the Diego Rivera
Frescoes at
Cuernavaca,
Mexico

12
Battle dress of Ocelot Knight with
Nose-Moon shield. *Codex Mendoza.*
f. 21 vo. (detail).
13
Aztec warrior in battle for
Tenochtitlán. In background, Spanish
knight and fallen Aztec. Sahagún:
Codex Florentino, XII, ill. 72. (From
Paso y Troncoso)

14
Military gladitorial combat with Aztec
Eagle Knight and overhead standard.
Sahagún: Codex Florentino, VIII, ill.
79. (From Paso y Troncoso)

15

Mounted Spanish knight with sword.
Lienzo de Tlaxcala, No. 73. (detail).
(After Chavero)

16

Mounted Spanish knight with lance.
Lienzo de Tlaxcala, No. 39 (detail).
(After Chavero)

17

Paolo Uccello (Florentine, 1397–
1475): *The Battle of San Romano* (detail). Florence, Uffizi.

18
Line reconstruction of overhead standard worn by Eagle Knight in Fig. 3b (Theme I, 3).

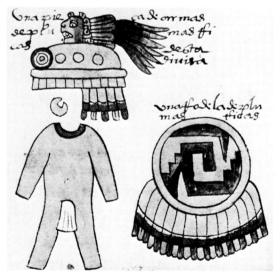

19
Overhead battle standard with dog effigy and shield with fret motif. *Codex Mendoza,* f. 27 vo. (detail).
20
Overhead battle standard with dog effigy. *Lienzo de Tlaxcala,* No. 62 (detail). (After Chavero)

spiral standards. Consideration here is limited to the exemplar of the effigy devices carried by the Aztec warrior fighting the Spanish horseman in the foreground of part 3 of the battle theme.

In the Rivera painting there is only one type of effigy device: the head of a dog or coyote (Fig. 3b, center left, and Fig. 18).

Overhead standards surmounted by a dog's head and supported by an apparatus strapped to the warrior's back were identified by Sahagún as the *Quaxolotl*, "those with the Xolotl head" (Sahagún, Academia de la Historia ms., in Seler, *Gesammelte Abhandlungen*, p. 581). Xolotl was the Aztec god of twins and monstrosities and was a twin brother of Quetzalcoatl. The quaxolotl device representing him was also, according to Seler, a name of Chantico, the fire goddess of Xochimilco, symbolizing the forked flame—a further manifestation of the twins idea. Representations of this device appear in the *Codex Mendoza, Matrícula de Tributos, Lienzo de Tlaxcala,* and Book XII of the *Codex Florentino*. A reliable prototype is on f. 21 vo. of the *Mendoza Codex,* in which the greater part of the device is an arched frame, covered with yellow feathers and with a feather pendant at the back (Fig. 19). The small coyote head appears at the top. A similar device appears in the *Lienzo de Tlaxcala* (No. 62) except that the feather pendant extends all the way around (Fig. 20). However, I have found no representations in the sources Rivera was most likely to have consulted directly, or anywhere else, of a canine effigy as large as any of his versions, nor any without the arched frame. An example similar to the Mendoza illustration, but with a somewhat larger head, appears in No. 110 from the battle scenes of Book XII of the *Codex Florentino* (Fig. 21), and a second of the same type is shown in illustration No. 139 (Fig. 22). It is in the first of these illustrations in Book XII that one may find a clue to Rivera's improvisation. He was just beginning organized research for his historical projects, both at Cuernevaca and the National Palace, and probably had not covered much ground before starting work. By visual coincidence of sword, arched frame, and its supporting pole in the drawing of the warrior in the upper-left-hand corner, the whole frame of this quaxolotl device is given the aspect of a fierce animal's head. This example may have been the starting point for the iconic image that takes on, in its conspicuous and repeated use in Rivera's National Palace series as well as at Cuernabaca, the value of a major symbol of defiant resistance to conquest—one with the contemporary political function of evoking latent feelings of ancestral pride and reviving sympathies and sense of common cause among the Indian and mestizo population to whom it was chiefly addressed.

General Aspects of Style and Ideological Function

Organization of Eclectic Elements Rivera's study of European art of the more distant past during his many years abroad—before and throughout the revolutionary period at home—contributed to the formation of his three-dimensional representation method, his preference for mural painting, and his use of thematic elements from specific European works of art. If, subsequently, the Mexican indigenous heritage and contemporary scene, became the primary determinants of his style, it does not follow that previously assimilated elements were left behind. The continuing influence of large-scale Italian quattrocento painting can be seen at Cuernavaca in much more than the Ucello horse; this influence can be noted in, for example, his concern for solid, overlapping figures, and for the representation of two or more related events in a compositional frame or stage unified in extended space and time, similar to that of Masaccio in the *Tribute Money*. Such elements, along with much of the color taste and objectivity of quattrocento painting, remained basic to his organizational structure and an integral part of his sensibility; in their fusion with indigenous elements, they became effective aids in the formation of his conception and his transmission of Mexican values.

We have noted Rivera's skillful combination of naturalistic and stylized representation of his subject matter and suggested that he applied these norms in two ways: a more naturalistic treatment, on the one hand, for themes identified with foreign and private interests, and, on the other, more stylized treatment for themes associated with indigenous values and potentialities. Coupled with mean faces, scowling expressions, and shiny metal armor, this more specific treatment of individual features appears consistently in the figures of Spanish soldiers, the conquerors themselves, and almost as frequently in the faces of the priests; whereas the more generalized and stylized handling is found most consistently of all in the figures, faces, dress, comportment, and action of Indian subjects. Reinforcing the latter method and, in consequence, giving a pervading symbolic as well as stylistic reference of indigenous and thus ideological character to the mural as a whole, is the similar conception and rendering of native vegetation, agricultural husbandry, and craftsmanship.

Interesting variations within both systems occur, such as the flatter, more geometrical design of the Aztec pyramid and battle flags, the flags approaching pure abstraction yet still showing their derivation from Indian heraldic symbols and architecture. The curious angularities in the drawing of the figures of the *peones* in the sugar cane theme in the second section of the mural (Fig. 2, VI), contrast with the

207
Political
Iconography in
the Diego Rivera
Frescoes at
Cuernavaca,
Mexico

21
Battle scene at Tenochtitlán. Sahagún:
Codex Florentino, XII, ill. 110. (From
Paso y Troncoso)

22
Battle scene at Tenochtitlán. Sahagún:
Codex Florentino, XII, ill. 139. (From
Paso y Troncoso)

23
Rivera: *Crossing the Barranca of Amanalco*. 1930. Fresco. State Palace, Cuernavaca. (Photo: Álvarez-Bravo, Mexico City)

undulant drawing of the rest of the composition and thus echo the artist's cubist period; and, on the side of the more realistic treatment of subjects, carry the delineation of objectionable acts and traits of Spanish soldiers and priests into personifications of evil through satirical portraiture. These suggest derivation from one or more of the illustrated French political journals of the early 1900s, during Rivera's own years in Paris, such as the graphic weekly, *L'Assiette au Beurre,* to which Kupka, van Dongen, Villon, Gris, and other artists contributed "satirical and often violent attacks on a society they considered corrupt and decadent."[10]

As previously suggested, the realistic representation of Tlaxcalan subjects, such as the Indian positioning the Spanish cannon in Part 1 of the battle theme, is logically extended to native motifs in other parts of the mural where these were shown in alliance with the invader.

Taking the mural from end to end, however, it is quite evident that the ideological dichotomy is not everywhere reflected by consistent application of the two manners of stylistic treatment. There are both overlappings and inversions of the double approach—for example, the more particularized features in the head of Zapata's closest Indian follower in the revolt scene (Fig. 2; VIII) suggesting a portrait, and the circular semistylized forms of the Spaniards in *Crossing the Barranca* (Figs. 23; 2, II) probably to convey a whirling effect and thus the dizziness that (according to Bernal Díaz) almost overcame the clambering soldiers. Nevertheless, it is consistent enough in its application to passages of key meaning to cite as an important tie to, and artistic means of realizing the ideological program of the work as a whole.

The key to separation of his method is to be found in the range of styles he discovered in the pre-Columbian sources he studied. Among the pictorial codices, he seems consistently to have preferred those from after the Conquest and under European influence, rather than the complex hieratic images of pre-Conquest documents. In the variations afforded by the flat linear style of the *Lienzo* (for example, Fig. 5), in the intuitive expressionism of the Sahagún Book XII illustrations of the Conquest (Fig. 13), and in the more objective observation and reporting of the Matrícula, the Mendoza codices, and books other than XII of the Sahagún manuscripts (Figs. 8–14), he found ample range for the development of his contrapuntal figurative method as well as the basic ingredients of an independent, personal, and humanistically viable Mexican mural style.

Together with everyday artifacts of Indian popular art continuing pre-Columbian formal traditions—practical vessels of clay, wood, and vegetable fiber, not excluding toy and decorative figures in terra cotta and other materials—fifteenth and early sixteenth-century Mexican sculpture was a fundamental source in the evolution of Rivera's stylized norm applied to indigenous subjects. In its particular qualities of closed form, evenness of surface, and fidelity to character, combining formality with objectivity, it seems so close to Rivera's norm of stylization for all indigenous subject matter that it can be thought of as the prototype of his plastic figuation in general. This model is used within a Renaissance spatial and perspective system and is varied for ideological reasons, but it sets the figural norm and the general tone and is the central focus of the basic unities of his generic style.

Relation of Mural to Audience   In shaping his many influences into a consistent art form, Rivera's purpose is not to provide his Indian and mestizo observers with a work of art in the traditional sense, which the individual can take or leave according to personal predilections. His mural art is first and foremost a method and a program of inculcation aimed at appealing to the contemporary Mexican peasant and worker and intended to contribute to the development of a Mexican, self-conscious, working-class political and cultural ethic.

In assuming this pedagogical task, the problem of creating a style that would effectively communicate his message to his audience was complicated by the fact that his revolutionary doctrine was a product of Western civilization and involved rational analysis of social issues and the adoption of practical forms of organization and thinking in terms of Marxist, but now Trotzkyist rather then Stalinist, proletarian class intent. On the other hand, the audience to whom he addressed himself was an Indian one, whose habits were based on an aesthetic, sensory, and religious orientation to experience, and to whom the rational, practical, dialectical approach, in spite of four centuries of life under European precepts and a decade of revolution, remained essentially foreign.

In order to bridge this gap, Rivera had to invent an art form that contained the tenets and program of his social philosophy but also presented this content in terms that would accord with the habits, sensibilities, and beliefs of his Indian and mestizo audience and would sway them to other beliefs and action.

As pointed out, one of his approaches to this problem can be seen in his method of stylizing Indian subject matter by adapting forms endemic to the Indians' visual environment, this stylization being paralleled by a realistic treatment of subject matter derived from the European world. It would logically follow that to achieve an integrated presentation he would have to envelop this dichotomy in a larger formal element that would make both strains intelligible and sympathetic to his Indian audience.

To achieve this, he daringly crosses the boundary lines of visual art into a musical form, the Mexican *corrido*. He adopts the outward form of this popular ballad as a denominator of thinking and feeling that, by visual translation of its rhythmical flow and its political and cultural associations, can create the disposition to combine Western rational philosophy with familiar native tradition in the Mexican popular mind.

A statement Rivera made when he began his commission at the Ministry of Education in Mexico City in 1923 provides a key to this source. At that time he said he would "choose as subject matter a revolutionary program based on the popular aspirations expressed in the *corridos*."[11] The most obvious use of this popular musical form is to be found on the third floor of the second patio of the Ministry of Education building, where he reproduced in literal fashion the context of two ballads, the so-called Agrarian (sometimes called Bourgeois) and Proletarian Revolutions, illustrating the themes, stanza by stanza, in a sequence of descriptive panels carefully designed to capture both the form and spirit of the musical narrative. The words of the songs themselves are reproduced on festooned streamers running from the beginning to the end of both series (Fig. 24).

At Cuernavaca there are no such obvious references to another art. But in the continuous design scheme, the progression of themes, and the sensuous quality of the color one feels a conscious attempt to continue and further develop the form and sharpen the political effect of his earlier metaphor. In the broadened color program, the multiplied action, the increased articulation of individual figures, and especially the parallel flow of realistic and schematized treatment, it may be said that he has simply developed a more subtle and orchestrated version of the revolutionary ballad series of the Ministry of Education.

Conclusion

Within ten years of Manuel Gamio's invitation to the painter Francisco Goitia, other Mexican artists had painted other mural versions of their indigenous heritage. The aggregate of their work comprises the first formulation of the Indian past as a symbol of national patrimony and modern nationhood on a popularly achieved and constitutionally confirmed national plane. In consequence, for the first time in over 400 years the descendants of that patrimony could identify themselves and dwell in their ancient past with open pride. This is a unique and monumental achievement, for which mural painting is as,

if not more, responsible than any other field of influence in modern Mexico's postrevolutionary history. In the process of its realization the Mexican spirit and heritage was reborn, introduced into the public life, and rooted in the public mind.

Many artists, contemporaries of Gamio and Goitia, were part of the movement that soon came to be known as the Mexican Mural Renaissance. Nearly all of them created individual styles or works of individuality, some of towering stature. All reflect controversy over artistic, intellectual, and public issues and highly personal interpretations of those issues, making the field of the movement as a whole one of unusual diversity of viewpoint and character. Diego Rivera's particular contribution was his comprehensive formulation and documentation of Mexico's life and history in terms of a consistent and systematically applied ideology based on socialist principles adapted to the total Mexican national experience. As such, it stands as a kind of Summa Theologica of the modern Mexican Revolution. It is also an exemplar of the political role of art in that it succeeded in formulating and to a degree making known an unprecedented sense of nationality, with its own demos and ethos, for a major part of the Indian and mestizo community in Latin America.

Afterword

If one were to look for an epitome of Rivera's early Mexican mural work directed to this end, it might well be found in *The Ancient and Indigenous World* of his "History and Perspective of Mexico," the right section of his stairway mural in the National Palace of Mexico (Fig. 25). In it the creator-god Quetzalcoatl, surrounded by his votaries, presides over the ancient Mexican civilization that had its center in the ceremonial complex of Teotihuacán (ca. 100 to 700 A.D.)[12] His beard and white skin contrast with the bronze of the priestly attendants who do him homage. Below and to the right, Indian craftsmen and musicians symbolize the arts of peace he encouraged. Directly below and to the left, an Indian of lower rank, awakening to the realities of ancient society, points to the spectacle of subject tribes bearing tribute to their overlords. To the left, a battle is fought under the system of ceremonial warfare by which the later Aztecs extended their power, captured prisoners, and exacted tribute from their neighbors. In the background rise the pyramids and volcanoes of the Valley of Mexico during the classic age of ancient Indian society there. At the upper right of the same panel appears Rivera's interpretation of the popular legend about Quetzalcoatl. Outraged by indifference to his teachings, the great god departs to the east on a plumed serpent, vowing his eventual return. The artist's vision of this greatest metropolitan center of the ancient American world is idyllic, proud, and probably the purest synthesis of

211
Political
Iconography in
the Diego Rivera
Frescoes at
Cuernavaca,
Mexico

24
Rivera: First theme from the series,
''Ballad of the Agrarian Revolution.''
ca. 1925. Fresco. 3d floor, 2d patio,
Department of Education, Mexico
City. (From Rodríguez, *History of
Mexican Mural Painting*)

25

Rivera: *The Ancient Indigenous World*
from the scene, "History and Perspective of Mexico." 1929–1930. Fresco.
Main Stairway, National Palace,
Mexico City. (From Rodríguez, *History of Mexican Mural Painting*)

native ideology among his various interpretations of the indigenous patrimony of Mexico.

Painted in 1929–1930 while Rivera was working at Cuernavaca, "History and Perspective of Mexico" has become a visual cornerstone of the modern Mexican's patriotic consciousness. It represents both the grandeur of ancient Indian civilization and the social-revolutionary origin of the modern nation.[13]

Notes

1
Each of the five mural groups painted by Rivera in Mexico before his Cuernavaca work involved programs of multiple subjects, often of very large scale in connecting or related wall and room complexes in which existing architectural character was respected through extensive supplementary decoration in fresco. The total area of wall surface painted by Rivera during this eight-year period has been measured at 2,663.43 square meters. The five-part grouping of works here referred to are in: (1) the National Preparatory School (*Creation*, 1921–1922); (2) Department of Education Building (*Courts of Labor and Festivals* on three levels and lateral stairway, 1923–1928); (3) National Palace (*History of Mexico* in the principal stairway, 1929 continued through 1934); (4) the National Agricultural School, Chapingo (*Social Evolution and the Land*, 1926–1927); and (5) the Department of Health Building (*Social Hygiene*, 1929–1930). All are in Mexico City or the Federal District. (Dates and measurements from Suzanna Gamboa in *Diego Rivera, 50 Años de su labor artistica*. Mexico D. F., 1949, pp. 297–309.)

2
The definition continues: "... often with an implication of factitious propagandizing; as, Fascism was altered in Germany to fit the Nazi *ideology*."

3
An intensive study of Rivera's Cuernavaca work, begun in 1950, established the basic frame of reference, terminology, and sources quoted in the present essay.

4
Diego Rivera with Gladys March: *Diego Rivera—My Art, My Life* (New York, 1960), p. 168.

5
This field may be divided into seven types of material:

1. Early codices, those in European collections in cities Rivera visited before his return to Mexico in 1921 as well as those in the National Museum and other collections in Mexico.
2. Pre-Columbian architecture, sculpture, mural painting, and artifacts.
3. Manuscripts and literary records with or without illustrations, of personalities, events, customs, dress of the colonial and postcolonial periods in Cuernavaca and the State of Morelos.
4. Facsimile publications, and/or reeditions of these records.
5. Post-Columbian architecture, sculpture, mural painting, and objects of ritual or practical use associated with the post-conquest history of Cuernavaca and the State of Morelos.
6. Word-of-mouth accounts and descriptions of the personalities and events of the Zapatista Revolt.
7. Reproductions of this material in books, journals, and newspapers published before the completion of the murals.

6
Compare also Greek warrior headdress from pediment of Temple of Aphaia, Munich, Glyptothek. Reproduced in *Horizon*, Vol. II, No. 1, September, 1959, p. 43.

7
See also Rivera's drawing of a fallen armored knight, similarly foreshortened, taken from the extreme right foreground of Paolo Uccello's *The Battle of San Romano*, Florence, Uffizi. Original in the Diego Rivera Museum, formerly the house of Frida Kahlo de Rivera, Londres 127, Coyoacán, D. F.

8
Diego Rivera, *50 Años de su labor artistica*, pp. 104–05. See other drawings from this source in the Diego Rivera Museum, Coyoacán, D. F.

9
Confirmed personally by Rivera to the writer in August 1949, at San Angel, after having reviewed the draft of the first text stating this principle.

10
I am grateful to Ralph E. Shike's paper, *L'Assiette au Beurre*, given at the first meeting of the Symposium on Art and Politics, for bringing out this very likely model for Rivera's treatment of the faces of Spanish soldiers and priests at Cuernavaca. Although Mexican political caricature reached one of its highest points of development in Rivera's early years, and found its way into the work of many Mexican artists of the 1910–1920 Revolutionary period, this Parisian journal is undoubtedly also a main source for his formal treatment in representing villainy throughout his mural *oeuvre*, especially his composite caricatures for the Reforma Hotel in Mexico (1938), and for many personalities in the "Portrait of America" series painted in New York (1934).

11
Paine, Frances Flynn. In a biographical introduction to *Diego Rivera*, Museum of Modern Art exhibition catalogue (New York, 1931).

12
Based on Kubler in *The Art and Architecture of Ancient America*, 2nd ed. (Baltimore, 1975).

13
Revised from the writer's "Mural Painting, Notes on the Art Renaissance," in *Mexico, Its Cultural Life in Music and Art*, Columbia Records, Legacy Collection, 1964.

Bibliography

Clark, James Cooper, ed. and trans. *Codex Mendoza*. London, 1938.

Curtis, F. S., Jr "Spanish Arms and Armor in the Southwest." In *New Mexico Historical Review* 2 (1927): 2.

Danbila y Collado, Francisco. *Trajes y armas de los españoles desde los tiempos prehistoricos hasta los primeros años del siglo XIX*. Madrid, 1877.

Díaz del Castillo, Bernal. *The True History of the Conquest of New Spain*. Translated by A. P. Maudslay. London, 1908–1916.

Hewitt, John. *Ancient Armor and Weapons in Europe*. Oxford and London, 1960.

King, E., Viscount Kingsborough, ed. *Antiquities of Mexico*. London, 1830–1848.

Mann, J. G. "Notes on the Armour worn in Spain from the tenth to the fifteenth century." In *Archaeologia* 83: 285–305. Oxford, 1933.

del Paso y Troncoso, Francisco. *Códice Mendocino.* Phototype facsimile. Introduction and commentaries by Jesús Galindo y Villa. Mexico, 1925.

Peñafiel, Antonio. *Indumentaria Antigua—Vestidos guerreros y civiles de los antiguos Mexicanos.* Mexico, 1903.

_____.*Monumentos del Arte Mexicano Antiguo.* Berlin, 1890.

Prescott, W. H. *History of the Conquest of Mexico.* New York, 1844.

Radin, Paul. "The sources and authenticity of the history of the Ancient Mexicans." In *Univ. of California Publications in American Archaeology and Ethnology* 17: 1. Berkeley. 1920–1926.

Rivera, Diego. *50 Años de su Labor Artística.* Mexico, 1951.

_____. with Gladys March. *Diego Rivera, My Art, My Life.* New York, 1960.

Von Sachen, Freiherrn. *Rüstungen und Waffen der K.K. Amraser-Sammlung.* Vienna, 1862.

de Sahagún, Fray Bernardino. *Historia de las Cosas de Nueva España.* Francisco del Paso y Troncoso, ed. and pub. Madrid, 1905–1907.

Seler, Eduard. *Gesammelte Abhandlungen zur Amerikanischen Sprach- und Alterthumskunde.* Berlin, 1902–1903.

Du Solier, W. *Ancient Mexican Costume.* Mexico, 1950.

Vaillant, G. C. *Aztecs of Mexico.* Garden City, 1948.

de Villar Villamil, Ignacio. *Cedulario Heráldico de Conquistadores de Nueva España.* Mexico, 1933.

215
Political
Iconography in
the Diego Rivera
Frescoes at
Cuernavaca,
Mexico

12
The Rivera Frescoes of Modern Industry at the Detroit Institute of Arts: Proletarian Art under Capitalist Patronage

Max Kozloff

They look as complex and involuted as machines themselves. But if the ensemble is hard to remember, the large masses of these paintings are immediately felt. The eye notes a thousand independent stages entered into a pattern that has yielded to them without interrupting its flow. The more simplified "technological" styles of Western Europe—in Holland, France, Germany, and Russia—are *not* more monumental. Rivera's pictorial economy takes into itself the insatiable need to show how things work, and his frescoes, loaded with an almost bewildering amount of information, are more descriptive than any other works with a comparable subject. Instead of a utopian mystique of machines' effects, incarnated by a supreme abstract order, he is interested in how machinery came to be. The origins of modern industry are summoned up before us as part of current experience. Though expressively as powerful as the ultramodern Italian futurists, he parts ways with them because his technology has an ancient pre-Columbian history, though now transfused by a collaboration of all cultures and lives. What we achieve today, no matter how advanced, does not represent a cut with the past, but its fruition in the millennial efforts of man, the artificer. Rivera's determinism will truck neither with evanescent phenomena—though his every image is activated—nor with a rigid, impersonal geometry—though his will is incredibly authoritative.

The main inset of the north wall in the Detroit Institute of Art's garden court represents the manufacture of the internal combustion engine at the Ford River Rouge plant in 1932 (Fig. 1). In the upper left, molds are made, and the conveyor belts feed parts and move the motors past furnaces, drills, and presses to a final polishing on the left. Above this panel, from top down, one sees giant reclining figures, archetypes of the Asiatic and black races, flanking a volcano whose slopes sprout enormous clenched metal-holding fists. Beneath this, a subterranean world of mineral crystals and organic materials wells open at center with a kind of great gush. Directly below the latter the artist locates a blast furnace. But now the work loses its central axis as well as its fabled space. The scheme recalls a traditional Italian Renaissance device, which separated the symbolic from the earthly actors, the divine from the material worlds. Rivera has even followed through with "predella" panels, inserted at bottom level, and a donor portrait of Edsel Ford on the south wall (Fig. 2).

At its most synthetic, the large panel displays an asymetric three-part partitioning, established by the

Reprinted with permission from Kozloff, Max. "Rivera Frescoes of Modern Industry at the Detroit Institute of Arts: Proletarian Art under Capitalist Patronage." In *Artforum* 12 (1974): 49.

main verticals of the off-center, portal-like presses. These are reinforced by right-angle girder patterns throughout (as if, somehow, the environment is being constructed before our eyes). Of course, these girders buttress and compartmentalize the action at the same time they compose it with an informal grid (which no Renaissance master could have quite envisaged because it is cubist in origin). The artist challenges himself with a great design problem: how would the eye navigate this composite, multi-episodic space, which oscillates so drastically between near and far, with its miles of depth, disparate eye levels, scales, and vantages, closed and open environments, and casts of thousands—how could the viewer accept this as one totality rather than as an arbitrary patchwork of separate narratives?

Rivera, remembering that the snake was a symbol of life to the ancient Mexicans, finds the answer in his concept of wavelike or serpentine form. He gives us vast conveyor belts circuiting through the archaic, static masses. They comprise a slow lateral entanglement, sensuous in its curves, convincing as realistically observed detail from the assembly line, and, above all, as an infusion of continuous energy that rhymes with the allegorical "chapter-headings" above. Further, he populates this environment with the angular figures of workers who invariably counterpoint each other—bent elbows thrust up or forearms bearing down—the push of any work in the foreground answered by comparable pulls (Fig. 3). Rivera shows those close up to us as dense, rounded, solid forms, intent and concerted in their postures. Surely this is how Piero's figures would move if they had jobs. One can no longer tell if the exact placement of the workers' volumes results from their assigned stations or the almost mathematical acuteness of the artist. The "farther" the eye penetrates, the more contraction is signified by background clustering of these men, while the widening of graded intervals in the foreground frieze, with the strongest decorative contrasts, individuates the play of human forces. Though his hard edges and firm lines are everywhere appropriate to this metallic forest (and viewing from a distance), Rivera varies, not the focus, but the transparence of his subjects, keeping them always under optical control. (Another reason he can compress so much incident on the wall emerges from the almost telephoto packing of left and right areas.)

But what really dramatizes and orchestrates these tableaux is color. From on high, where the deep azures, siennas, and umbers sink in with a saturation uncommon in fresco, the eye descends to airier terrains, signaled by the whites of the massive machines upon which play delicate blue and orange reflections (Fig. 4). Skylights and blast furnaces both diffuse the light of day and tear open the shadows of night. The healthy freshness of Rivera's paint, every gentle stroke guiding a form, is not even compromised by the nacreous greens of the foundry sequences, as if the artist were in realistic accord, here at least, with old Henry Ford's mania for cleanliness in the factory. But one is impressed by the high-powered metaphors of this palette, as well. For, in producing the internal combustion motor, man is shown harvesting and releasing, by his ingenuity, the raw energies of underground minerals, and Rivera's color symbolism, by its echoes, works to clarify his argument about the union of man, earth, and machine. His program is condensed overall by covert montage, although particulars are distributed as if in one long tracking shot, left to right. If not in technique, in concept this work presents affinities with nineteenth-century historical or allegorical panoramas, like Ford Madox Brown's "Work." Still, in neither our century nor the last had an artist introduced into such a mode references to "the Nahautl cosmogony of earliest prehistoric America, that historical substratum in which plunge the roots of our continental culture."[1]

On the south wall of the garden court (body presses and assembly of chassis), no less than in the many subsidiary panels, this genetic, cross-racial and temporal program is inescapable (Figs. 5, 6). At Detroit, Rivera produced one of his few major works not reminiscent of popular Mexican painting or engaged with the revolutions of his homeland. Rather than simply articulating a native consciousness, he brought it to the picturing of what was, for him, an entirely new society. This citizen of an underdeveloped, agrarian economy, obsessed by the working of all phenomena, had one of the most sophisticated pictorial intelligences of his time. In the United States he encountered a spectacle of collective effort within an overwhelmingly mechanized world whose example might harmonize all national energies. The art that resulted was as rich and unique as the circumstances that brought it about. As an insight into the conditions of the modern working class, as an analysis of mass product assembly with its support systems, planning, and processing, as a public and political document of the possibilities of technology, the epic Detroit frescoes have no peer in Western art. Yet, when they were unveiled in 1933, public outcry against them was so great that for a time there was serious danger they would be destroyed by the community to which they had been bequeathed.

There were reasons—steeped in irony. If Rivera's art in this country once had to make its way uphill against popular opinion, the critical establishment, represented by persons as diverse as Thomas Craven and Lewis Mumford, rushed to its defense. Today, long after the Detroit frescoes have become the

1
Rivera, *Detroit Industry*. North wall.
Parts production and assembly of
motor. Courtesy of The Detroit Institute of Arts, Gift of Edsel B. Ford.

4
Rivera, *Detroit Industry*. South wall.
Machinery detail. Courtesy of the Detroit Institute of Arts, gift of Edsel B. Ford.

2
Rivera, *Detroit Industry*. South wall. Portrait of Edsel B. Ford and Dr. Valentiner. Courtesy of The Detroit Institute of Arts.
3
Rivera, *Detroit Industry*. North wall. Body presses and assembly. Courtesy of the Detroit Institute of Arts.

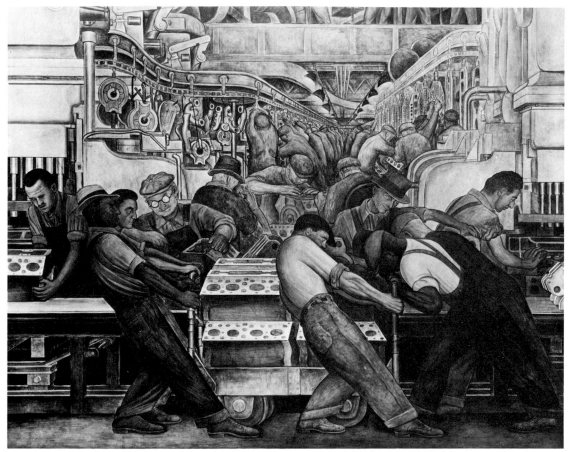

5
Rivera, *Detroit Industry*. South wall.
Detail. Courtesy of the Detroit Insti-
tute of Arts, gift of Edsel B. Ford.

7
Rivera, *Detroit Industry*. North wall.
The vaccination panel. Courtesy of
the Detroit Institute of Arts.

8
Rivera, *Detroit Industry*. North wall.
The making of poison gas. Courtesy of
the Detroit Institute of Arts, gift of The
Edsel B. Ford Fund.

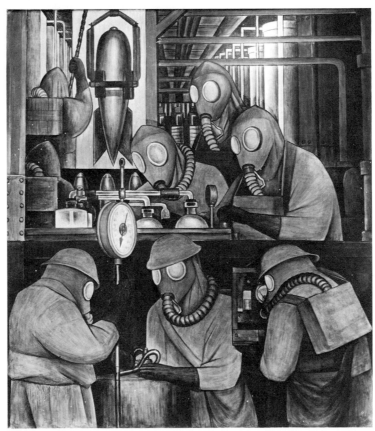

9
Rivera, *Detroit Industry*. West wall.
Courtesy of the Detroit Institute of
Arts, gift of the Edsel B. Ford Fund.

10
Rivera, *Detroit Industry*. South wall.
The pharmaceutical industry. Courtesy of the Detroit Institute of Arts, gift
of The Edsel B. Ford Fund.

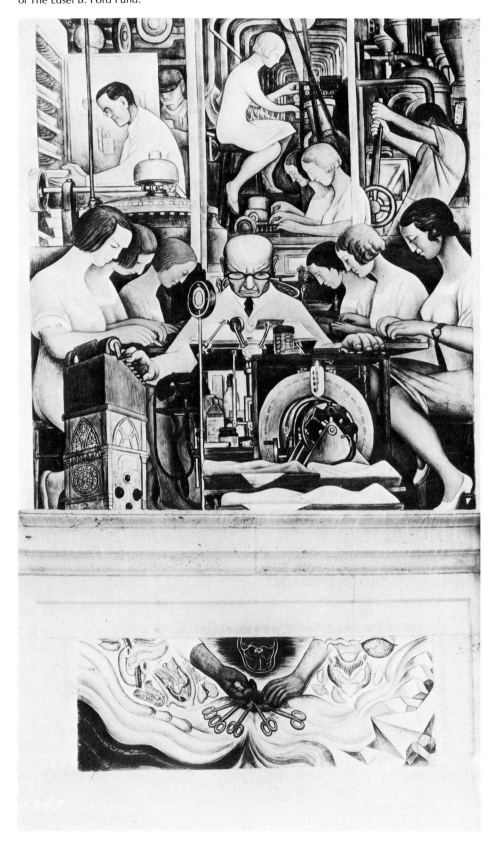

resented by shocked corporation wives who did not find in their temple of art a reflection of the Grosse Point leisure that was, in fact, built upon the clangorous input of the Dearborn factories Rivera so vividly showed them. In the *New York Times,* he said, "Some society ladies have told me that they found the murals cold and hard. I answer that their subject is steel, and steel is cold and hard."[9] But there turned out to be greater inducements to uproar when all the Catholic and many of the Protestant groups in the city saw in the thematically peripheral vaccination panel (Fig. 7) a quote from traditional Nativity scenes. In a country where the Scopes monkey trial was a recent charade, where Father Coughlin was listened to on the radio by untold millions, this rather benign parody was judged an utmost affront to religious faith. Ignoring the more amusing Temptation of St. Anthony theme in the pharmaceutical panel, gathering outrage that moved even into the city council called for the destruction of the paintings. The *Detroit News* called them un-American, incongruous, unsympathetic. Yet, at approximately the same time that Dr. George Derry, president of Marygrove College, conceived that Rivera had "perpetrated a heartless hoax on his capitalist employer . . . a communist manifesto," the artist's Stalinist compatriot and fellow artist, David Alfaro Siquieros, railed against him as a "mental tourist," "trade union opportunist" (it's difficult to know what that meant), and "Esthete of Imperialism." Rivera himself was quick to sally against the parochialism of his Detroit critics:

And now we have the curious spectacle of the local prelates of two religious organizations of European origin—one of which openly avows allegiance to a foreign potentate, while the other has its roots deep in alien soil—stirring up the people in patriotic defence of an exotic Renaissance patio against what they decry as an "unAmerican" invasion, namely, the pictorial representation of the basis of their city's existence and the source of its wealth, painted by a direct descendant of aboriginal American stock![10]

Large bodies of vigilantes, no doubt of left-wing sympathies, thought it necessary to guard the frescoes after they had been opened to the public. In the end, the works were probably saved only by the bewildered Edsel Ford, who said: "I admire Mr. Rivera's spirit: I really believe he was trying to express his idea of the spirit of Detroit."

What can be said about that "spirit" in 1932, one of the worst moments in the city's and nation's history? Ridden by Mafia gangsterism, racial hatreds, and virulent anticommunism, Detroit was also the setting of the first serious sit-down strikes in labor tradition. Employment reached its lowest ebb. Ford was doing only one-fifth its production of 1929. And the municipal government came so close to bankruptcy that Edsel Ford had to pay for the running of the Institute of Arts for a whole month out of his own pocket. Without social security or unemployment insurance, out-of-work masses lived on dwindling savings quickly exhausted in this, the nadir of the Depression. President Hoover's Secretary of the Treasury, Andrew Mellon, a great art benefactor, thought the solution was to "liquidate labor, liquidate stock, liquidate the farmer, liquidate real estate."[11] Bread lines and soup kitchens dotted the city, as elsewhere. As for the "genetics" of speed, huge Pullman trains would make cross-country trips practically devoid of passengers. In factories, there was a terrible management fear of outside agitation. Detroit was the most refractory city for union organizers. All the large companies opposed any steps for collective bargaining. Old Henry Ford despised unions because he saw in them the seeds of class warfare. He thought the United States was fortunate in having no fixed classes, except that major division between the men who will work and those who will not. "People are never so likely to be wrong as when they are organized."[12]

Obviously this stricture did not include the "organization" the bosses imposed upon the workers. "As soon as you went through the door and punched your card, you was nothing more or less than a robot. Do this, go there, do that. You'd do it."[13] Rotating two-week shifts that constantly disoriented workers, factory rules that prohibited talking or sitting, that allowed only fifteen minutes for lunch, that fired workers if they were late, and that set spies and spotters among them everywhere: these were normal conditions at River Rouge during Rivera's stint in the city.[14]

Rivera limned a world in which such practices were entirely imaginable, though he himself discreetly overlooked them. More important, at what seemed a crisis point for laissez-faire capitalism, the moment when its earlier confidence and inevitable workings became fatally open to question, he rendered it prophetically as a fount of terrifying and beautiful creativity. In this respect, he does not depict the historical moment of 1932 at all, but one conceivably five years before or ten years after it. And this was necessary, not only to avoid offending Ford, but because he wanted to portray the might of those worker masses who had not yet rebelled. In Mexico, that rebellion had already been traduced, a fact that makes his works there more brilliantly strident in their disillusion and even more remotely Marxist in their temporal specifics. While behind the scenes he financed the trip back home of a number of Mexicans unemployed and stranded in the City, he gave his parting shot to his fractious audience:

If my Detroit frescoes are destroyed, I shall be profoundly distressed, as I put into them a year of my life and the best of my talent; but tomorrow I shall be busy making others, for I am not merely an "artist," but a man performing his biological function of producing paintings, just as a tree produces flowers and fruit, nor mourns their loss each year, knowing that the next season it shall blossom and bear fruit again.[15]

Vita Brevis Longa Ars.

229
The Rivera
Frescoes of
Modern Industry
at the Detroit
Institute of Arts:
Proletarian Art
under Capitalist
Patronage

Notes

1
Diego Rivera, "Dynamic Detroit—An Interpretation," *Creative Arts* (April, 1933), p. 293.

2
Diego Rivera, Museum of Modern Art (New York, 1931), p. 35.

3
Quoted by Margaret Sterne, "The Museum Director and the Artist: Dr. William R. Valentiner and Diego Rivera in Detroit," *Detroit in Perspective,* Vol. 1, No. 2, Winter, 1973, p. 102.

4
Ibid., p. 98.

5
Bertram Wolfe, *The Fabulous Life of Diego Rivera,* (1963), p. 216.

6
Rivera, "Dynamic Detroit," p. 289.

7
Fortune Magazine, February, 1933.

8
Octavio Paz, *The Labyrinth of Solitude,* (1961), p. 70.

9
New York Times, March 22, 1933.

10
Rivera, "Dynamic Detroit," p. 295.

11
Samuel Eliot Morison: *The Oxford History of the American People,* (1966), p. 945.

12
Alan Nevins and Frank Ernest Hill: *Ford: Expansion and Challenge, 1915–1933,* (1957), p. 540.

13
Bob Stinson, a Ford worker, in Studs Terkel, *Hard Times,* (1972), p. 156.

14
Nevins and Hill, *Ford,* p. 514.

15
Rivera, "Dynamic Detroit," p. 295.

13
With Red Flags Flying: Housing in Amsterdam, 1915–1923

Helen Searing

In 1912, at a meeting of Architectura et Amicitia, Ary Keppler (1876–1941), an important and controversial housing reformer,[1] challenged the architects of Amsterdam to new political and architectural directions. After berating them for neglecting workers' housing in favor of more lucrative but socially irrelevant private commissions, he exhorted them to become involved in "the struggle of the working class" and to create "beautiful workers' dwellings, the monuments to that struggle."[2]

The response to Keppler's challenge was a series of remarkable housing complexes that arose in Amsterdam between 1915 and 1923, the result of a happy weaving together of various strands of political and architectural activity. This activity was generated not only by a group of young architects who saw in housing a new and exciting field for their own creativity but also by a vigorous faction in the city council that made workers' housing its chief issue, by the elected and appointed officials (of whom Keppler was one) who brought imagination and daring to their involvement with housing, and by the housing societies that participated in the planning and execution of better dwellings for the workers and their families. Those individuals and organizations affiliated with the social democratic party or with socialist leanings made the major contribution in this area. Keppler's statement, so tinged with "red" rhetoric, will form the leitmotif of this investigation of housing and politics in Amsterdam.

Behind Keppler's words lie several interesting assumptions. The call for "beautiful workers' dwellings" implies that housing should not merely satisfy the physical need for hygienic shelter but that it should provide aesthetic pleasure as well, that is, that it should be *architecture*. At a time when most dwellings were produced by speculators and private contractors without the service of architects, Keppler's demand was startling and had political overtones, since it indicated that the proletariat no less than the propertied classes had a right to carefully designed surroundings. That the working man richly deserved the beauty of which he had been so long deprived was one of Keppler's insistent themes.[3]

Another fundamental assumption is revealed by the phrase "monuments to the class struggle." Monument suggests commemorative sculpture, but now the monument is to provide shelter as well as to function symbolically. Keppler seems to be urging architects to design housing so that its forms express the history and aspirations of the working class and commemorate socialist ideals.

The spirit behind Keppler's words is specifically red. The Marxist doctrine of class struggle, of the need to raise class consciousness so that the worker would be willing to fight to emancipate himself from capitalist exploitation, was accepted, in theory at least, by most Dutch social democrats of Keppler's generation. Housing that commemorated the class struggle at the same time that it met physical needs would aid in developing the workingman's sense of solidarity. It would also advertise social democratic success in obtaining such housing for its constituents. To understand fully the purpose of Keppler's challenge, it is necessary to have some understanding of the Social Democratic Workers' Party—SDAP (Sociaal Democratische Arbeiderspartij).[4]

The SDAP was born relatively late in socialist history. The industrial and political revolutions of the late eighteenth century, which brought modern capitalism and socialism in their wake, were slow to reach the Netherlands, as were the consequences of those revolutions—urbanization and the concentration of industry, the rise of trade unionism and class consciousness, the struggle for universal suffrage and social welfare, and the creation of activist left-wing political groups. It was not until the 1870s that the Netherlands experienced the evolution of large-scale capitalism and with it those evils chronicled so vividly for England by Friedrich Engels.[5] In Britain, workers realized that they had to organize to protect their interests; in the Netherlands, they were inhibited by a tradition of apathy[6] and by the fact that many of them were deeply religious and had been taught to accept their condition as ordained by God. The first unions were organized mainly to raise funds for the sick and elderly and to provide social and cultural activities rather than to create economic pressure for better pay and working conditions. Most of these unions shunned the International[7] in favor of the Dutch Workers' Association (ANW), founded in 1871, which renounced social revolution and violence, holding that tangible improvements like higher wages and shorter hours could be achieved only through cooperation with employers. Strikes were virtually unknown.

The workers, of course, lacked political representation. The franchise was based on the amount of taxes paid and the electorate consisted entirely of well-to-do citizens. The Liberals dominated parliament in the second half of the nineteenth century, and while they were ordinarily men of sound humanitarian sentiments, they were reluctant to interfere with the free functioning of the economy. Faced with the social problems created by modern capitalism, most Liberals believed in reform through private action and philanthropy rather than through government action. In the area of housing, for instance, Liberal members of the bourgeoisie founded societies to provide decent dwellings for the working class. But since a major objective was to demonstrate that this could be done within the existing economic system, those who participated in these

early housing associations expected, and received, a modest profit (usually about 3 percent) on their investment.[8]

Opposition to the Liberals formed along religious lines. The strongest denominational groupings were the Roman Catholics, who exercised power by voting as a bloc, and the Calvinists, whose main political organ was the Anti-Revolutionary party.[9] Despite the fact that workers and small tradesmen made up the bulk of the churchgoing populace, the denominational parties tended to support the interests of the propertied classes. The working class still lacked a champion in government.

By the mid 1880s there were signs that the workers were ready to struggle against a system in which they had no representation. Suffrage demonstrations took place in 1885, and the leaders hinted at the possibility of violence if popular sovereignty was not granted—this was something new for the Netherlands, which even the revolutions of 1848 had left unscathed.[10] In July 1886, one of the first proletarian riots occurred. This was the so-called *paling oproer* (Fig. 1), which took place in the Amsterdam slum known as the Jordaan. The city government, perhaps fearing that the workers would openly reveal their deep discontent when assembled for the annual festival occasioned by the eel (*paling*) migration, forbade the celebration. But the people refused to obey this arbitrary dictate; they drew up the bridges and barricaded the streets so that they could proceed with their festival. The police were sent in, and in the melée that ensued, twenty-seven died and thirty-four were injured. This event constituted a rare nineteenth-century example of class conflict in the Netherlands.[11]

One of the leaders of the new revolutionary spirit was the fiery former minister, F. N. Domela Nieuwenhuis (1846–1919), whose wealthy background did not prevent him from taking up the cudgels on behalf of the proletariat. He guided the Sociaal Democratische Bond (SDB, founded 1881) to electoral victory in 1888, when he became the first socialist member of the Dutch parliament.[12] With this event the red flag was raised aloft in the Netherlands for the first time. Its subsequent vicissitudes are germane to this study of social democratic housing policy in Amsterdam.

In the course of the nineteenth century the international socialist movement had split into two hostile camps. One believed that parliamentary means could eventually bring about the socialist state; the other, generally against all forms of centralized power, believed that socialism could be attained only by revolution and the breakdown of the capitalist system. Marx, although he "provided rationales for both the revolutionary and peaceful transitions to socialism,"[13] came to find the anarchist direction increasingly distasteful, and in 1872 he had the Bakhuninists, who represented this tendency, expelled from the International. But anarchism remained a powerful force and disrupted the Second International as well. It continued to create a breach among various factions of the left and led them to expend their energies fighting each other. Its attraction was strong in the Netherlands, and under its sway Domela Nieuwenhuis resigned his seat in the Second Chamber shortly after his election to launch an antiparliamentary campaign.

The SDB adopted the beliefs and methods of anarchism, rejecting the idea of working through elected government and concentrating instead on disruptive tactics to thwart and wound the capitalist giant. Amsterdam especially, with its huge working-class population, was susceptible to anarchism, and trade unions were established in the related syndicalist mold. But so many socialists found this turn toward anarchism unacceptable that in 1894 the rival SDAP was founded, with the goal of working within the democratic system. The SDAP soon became the major socialist party in the Netherlands; in 1896 it was recognized by the Second International as the legitimate Dutch section in place of the SDB.[14]

The original manifesto of the SDAP, signed by the ''Twelve Apostles,''[15] who would lead the party in the years to come, sets forth the reasons for the birth of the new party:

For years the Sociaal Democratische Bond was considered the organ of the working class . . . but it never succeeded in uniting under its banner any considerable part of that class. . . . Instead of concerning itself with the needs of the moment and struggling for actual improvement of the workers' condition, the so-called ultrarevolutionary position held by the Bond has led to nothing but talk about violent revolution, which like a Messiah will bring salvation for everyone and everything. . . . This utopian attitude estranged the Bond from the people . . . it lived above, not in and with the people.[16]

This makes an important point about the SDAP—its pragmatism (or as its leftist opponents would say, its opportunism). Its members in Amsterdam concentrated on attaining solid results in the housing field, even when this meant seeking the support of other parties and of the private sector. This was in contrast to the SDB, which was

determinedly inimical to social democracy; indeed it considers this as great an enemy to the workers as the bourgeoisie itself . . . [But] we want our men to form into a new corps in which we will struggle with new courage and passion and power for the realization of our dearest principles. Maintaining the social-democratic standpoint that has been abandoned by the SDB, picking up the democratic red flag cast down by the Bond, placing ourselves by the side of international social democracy . . . we stand firmly united under the red flag.[17]

The SDAP's faith in parliamentary democracy seemed justified, for it grew steadily in electoral strength, from three seats (out of one-hundred in the Second Chamber) in 1897 to seven in 1901, eighteen in 1913 and twenty-two in 1918. It could accomplish its legislative goals, however, only in concert with another party. Its natural allies were the Liberals,[18] who stood clearly to the left of the denominational parties and who had proved their devotion to social reform by passing at the turn of the century such important legislation as the National Housing Act, the Compulsory Education Act, and measures for workmen's compensation and child protection. But the Liberals lost their dominance in 1901 and thereafter, until 1936, a coalition of right-wing religious parties ruled the government, except for a progressive interlude between 1913 and 1918.[19] It was during this five-year period that the SDAP and the Liberal parties had a majority of seats in parliament, and together they achieved in 1917 the socialist goal of universal manhood suffrage (women were enfranchised in 1919).

No single Dutch party could ever have a clear majority because of the factional nature of Dutch society.[20] For example, workers in any given trade had at least four local unions to choose from: socialist, syndicalist, catholic, and protestant. Each had different aims and tactics, and therefore labor could never confront management as a united bloc. Solidarity was difficult to achieve. Nonetheless the SDAP became the most popular party with the workers.[21] This enabled it to be effective at least on a local level, in those cities with a large working-class population.

Since voting requirements for municipal elections were less stringent than for national, socialists began to win seats on city councils even before the advent of universal suffrage.[22] Henri Polak, one of the ''Twelve Apostles'', became in 1902 the first SDAP delegate to sit in the Amsterdam gemeenteraad; in 1904 he was joined by P. L. Tak. By 1907 there were six social democrats, and in 1913 fully fifteen of the council's thirty-nine members represented the SDAP. On the eve of the First World War, red Amsterdam experienced a further triumph, when F. M. Wibaut (1859–1935)[23] became the first socialist alderman. In 1913 it was decided to create a sixth wethouder who would be chiefly concerned with housing, and in 1914 Wibaut accepted the position of wethouder voor de volkshuisvesting. With the support of his brother-in-law Keppler, fellow social democrats on the council, and housing societies and architects, Wibaut was able to make Amsterdam the ''mecca of housing'' in the 1920s.[24]

Yet mecca had other prophets than the faithful of the SDAP. One of these was J. W. C. Tellegen (1859–1921), who first as director of the Amsterdam Bouw-en Woningtoezicht (Department of Building and Housing Inspection) and then as mayor from

1915 until his death, devoted his considerable energies and expertise[25] to finding viable solutions to the housing problem. The others were N. G. Pierson (1839–1909), H. Goeman Borgesius (1847–1917), and P. W. A. Cort van der Linden (1840–1935), members of the Liberal Ministry of 1897–1901 that had been responsible for the passage of the Dutch National Housing Act (Woningwet), on which the SDAP based its housing policy.[26]

The Woningwet was the Liberal government's response to a number of investigations into housing conditions made during the second half of the nineteenth century,[27] which indicated that the Netherlands was experiencing the same cycle of overcrowding, deterioration, and jerrybuilding other countries had undergone after industrialization and unplanned urbanization. The act's purpose was to undo the blight and prevent future problems by improving the quality and increasing the quantity of dwellings. Its character was typical of Liberal legislation in that it was permissive rather than coercive.[28] Only two measures were mandatory: cities with more than 10,000 inhabitants were required to make extension plans, and all municipalities, rural or urban, had to establish building codes. However, the content was not prescribed, and therefore the effectiveness and severity of the codes varied greatly from place to place.

The remaining measures were permissive; for example, the demolition of slums was facilitated through granting the municipalities explicit authority for condemnation and expropriation in order to improve housing, but the municipality itself decided whether to utilize this authority or not. One of the most significant sections, whose vast consequences were not then foreseen, was that which dealt with finances. The Woningwet made funds available for the construction of dwellings at the same interest rate (originally 3 percent, later it rose to more than 4½ percent) the government itself had to pay on the national debt. Since it was first and foremost the scarcity and expense of capital that had made the erection of workers' housing such a difficult and discouraging business in the nineteenth century, the financial provisions of the act would prove to have a dramatic effect.[29]

The loans were granted either directly, to the municipality itself (which could borrow from the state to purchase land and existing dwellings in need of rehabilitation and to construct housing for families displaced by slum clearance), or indirectly, to the woningbouwvereenigingen (housing associations). These were legal entities composed of private individuals, but they worked with money borrowed from the state and in some cases received state and municipal subsidies; they developed in a typically Dutch way.[30]

The framers of the National Housing Act no doubt thought of the woningbouwvereenigingen as successors to the philanthropic housing societies of the nineteenth century, but in fact most Woningwet housing societies were founded by the workers themselves and were thus composed of interested parties (that is, the tenants). They were considered non-profit organizations whose members might not make financial gain (any profits were put toward new construction); the advantage in belonging lay in the attainment of a good dwelling. They had to maintain certain fiscal standards and to conform to specific rules of incorporation (although they had a choice among the legal forms of corporation, cooperative, or foundation). After sending in their statutes for approval, they could be named by royal decree as a "society active exclusively in the interests of housing," and then they were eligible to receive long-term (fifty-year) loans if the municipality recommended their projects. By advancing the loans indirectly, through the municipality, the government guaranteed that the interest and amortization would be paid, since the municipality was responsible for the debt. This method was also advantageous to the municipality, for it allowed the local authorities to exercise control over the planning, execution, and operation of housing erected by the woningbouwvereenigingen. The societies first presented detailed plans to the Bouw- en Woningtoezicht and the Public Health Commission for advice and approval, then to the mayor and aldermen, and finally to the council, in which was vested the final decision-making power to request funds from the national government. In this way, a number of experienced and concerned municipal officials, who were aware of the entire housing picture in a given city, aided the members of the housing society and their architect in finding a just solution.

The woningbouwvereenigingen have indeed lived up to the fine ideals of the framers of the Housing Act, and although quantitatively they have been surpassed by private builders, the dwelling standards they established have been strikingly higher than those achieved by private enterprise or by most local authorities. With the introduction of the woningbouwvereenigingen, Keppler's statement may now be fully translated, for he declared that it was *their* dwellings (*vereenigingsgebouwen*) which must become the "monuments to the class struggle."

Some of the first woningbouwvereenigingen to be incorporated were offshoots of the nineteenth-century philanthropic associations; a group of well-to-do housing reformers might set up a society, apply for a government loan, and do with public funds what had previously been achieved with private. Such was the Amsterdamsche Bouwfonds, established as a Woningwet organization in 1906. But while such societies of "disinterested parties" did

1
The paling oproer, 1886. (Historische topografische atlas, Gemeentelijke archiefdienst, Amsterdam)

2
Zeeburgerdijk, dwellings of Eigen Haard. J. H. L. Leliman, 1915–1917. (Photo: Gemeentelijke dienst volkshuisvesting, Amsterdam)

excellent work, the future belonged to the associations founded by the workers themselves. Amsterdam had a number of these, and, not surprisingly, they were formed along sectarian lines. For example, the large central organization of Protestant trade unions, Patrimonium, established housing foundations in various cities and did excellent work in providing spacious, airy dwellings for its members. There were also Roman Catholic housing societies such as Het Oosten in Amsterdam, incorporated in 1912 and today one of the largest owner-operators of housing in the Netherlands. Then there were the social democratic housing associations, some of which were organized via trade affiliations. The cooperative housing society Rochdale (named after the English weaving town that in 1844 became the birthplace of the cooperative movement) was formed by municipal employees (such as tram conductors, gas and electricity workers) and in 1909 had the distinction of completing the first dwellings built with Woningwet funds in Amsterdam. Other large societies whose founding membership chiefly comprised social democrats were Eigen Haard, founded in 1909, whose first dwellings were located in eastern Amsterdam (Figs. 2–7), Algemeene Woningbouw Vereeniging, established 1910, and De Dageraad, approved by the authorities in 1916. Eigen Haard and De Dageraad are of particular importance to this study. Also socialist was the separate housing foundation set up by the predominantly Jewish organization Handwerkers Vriendenkring, which concerned itself particularly with rehousing families who had lived in the inner city slums of Amsterdam and wanted to remain together as a community when they were moved to new lodgings.[31]

Many of these societies received assistance from city officials concerned with the housing problem in the often bewildering task of drawing up statutes and making concrete plans. Wibaut, for example, gave useful criticism to Het Oosten, and Keppler took an active part in the founding of Rochdale and the Algemene Woningbouw Vereeniging. He therefore was well acquainted with the potentialities of the housing associations when he issued his challenge of 1912.

It must be recognized that the woningbouwvereenigingen were created by a proletarian elite (the equivalent of those usually referred to as artisans in histories of Victorian England). In order to qualify as a member-tenant, the worker had to earn enough to be able to save weekly dues out of his salary; most of the societies required the purchase of an initial share at about one guilder and weekly contributions of ten to twenty-five cents.[32] Further, because the aim was to provide sound and comfortable housing, rents were not minimal but often were

in the same range as those charged for flats in privately owned tenements, but the housing society member received much more for his money, and there were long waiting lists for membership. Workers who were at the poverty level could not afford to live in dwellings operated by most of the housing societies;[33] ultimately, in Amsterdam at any rate, the city would have to provide them with heavily subsidized dwellings. The Woningwet housing erected by the municipality constituted an important share of new construction in Amsterdam in the years from 1915 to 1923, but it forms a subject in its own right and cannot be examined in this paper.[34]

As mentioned, housing societies had to have their plans approved by the Bouw-en Woningtoezicht. This municipal agency was of extreme importance to the goal of improving housing because it administered the building code. Amsterdam had already established a code in 1896, before it was required by national legislation, but in 1905 the city council passed a new and much stricter one. Tellegen was the key figure in the framing of this code. He had come to Amsterdam in 1900 to organize a department to supervise all the construction and renovation in the city, and he worked hard to develop an effective code that would promote wholesome and safe housing. His success may be measured by the fact that Amsterdam's code became a model for the rest of the country.

Tellegen was assisted in his task by members of the Public Health Commission and by some of the city councilors. Two of the social democrats in particular were helpful: P. L. Tak and Henri Polak, who were responsible for an amendment that decisively improved the code in that it forbade the heretofore ubiquitous alcove. This was an interior space used for sleeping; it was created by walling off an area between rooms and had no direct access to light and air. Health commissioners believed that the alcove was a major factor in the incidence of tuberculosis, but it was in widespread use in the Netherlands. The builders liked alcoves because they were a cheap means of providing a separate sleeping space, and the population liked them because they were warm and cozy during cold winter months. There was resistance to the Tak-Polak proposal from those councilors who represented landlords, because it was feared that such an improvement would increase building costs. However, the amendment was passed, twenty-eight to six, making Amsterdam the first Dutch city to do away with this unhealthy practice.[35]

When the Gemeentelijke Woningdienst was established with Keppler as its director in 1915, it took over some of the advisory duties of the Bouw-en Woningtoezicht in the area of housing. Keppler's agency also was charged with laying out the new working-class districts around the rim of the old city

3
View of Zeeburgerdijk, dwellings of
Eigen Haard. (Photo: Author)

4
Detail of Fig. 3. (Photo: Author)
5
Detail of Fig. 3. (Photo: Author)

6
Rear view of Fig. 2. (Photo: Author)
7
Plan of Fig. 3. (Photocopy: Bouw-en
Woningtoezicht, Amsterdam)

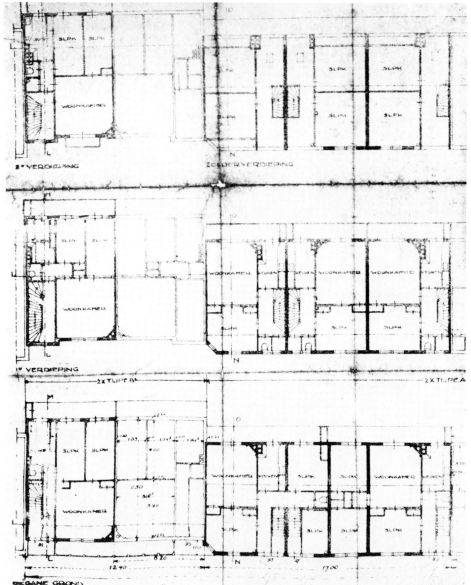

and assigning sites in them to the housing societies. In the second decade of this century Amsterdam, guided by Keppler's suggestions, pursued a vigorous policy of land purchase; it did not sell the property it acquired but preferred to lease the sites to prospective builders. This gave the city a great degree of control over the purposes for which the land would be used and over the types of buildings to be erected. The leases were for periods of fifty to seventy-five years and originally provided that at expiration the buildings would revert to the municipality. Later the leases were made renewable. The system of leasehold (erfpacht) was advantageous to the housing societies as well as to the community, because it meant that they did not have to raise large sums for land purchase. The land was leased at a yearly rate (canon), which in the years under discussion varied from about .80 to 1.40 guilders per square meter, compared with average land prices of 20 to 35 guilders per square meter. The rate was based on the cost of acquiring and preparing the land for building. The preparation of the land, which was done by the municipal Department of Public Works, could be very expensive in Amsterdam, because usually the level had to be raised considerably from its marshy base before it became suitable for construction.

While the Woningdienst and the Bouw-en Woningtoezicht were municipal agencies with paid employees, there were also commissions, made up of private citizens and members of the city council, which were involved in housing policy in Amsterdam. One has already been cited—the Public Health Commission, which included physicians and housing reformers and on which Wibaut served from 1907 to 1914. It investigated complaints and made recommendations for improvement and for condemnation to the Bouw-en Woningtoezicht. Soon after the passage of the Woningwet the commission and the agency set to work energetically on the task of slum clearance; however, experience showed that such action on any scale had to be preceded by a dramatic increase in housing production, because old dwellings could not be torn down until their occupants had new ones to move into. In 1909 some of the inner-city slums were cleared, but from 1914 to 1925 condemnation proceedings were virtually at a standstill. Only in the second half of the 1920s was there a sufficient housing supply to allow an effective slum clearance program.

Another city commission that came to exercise a powerful influence on housing in Amsterdam was the Schoonheidscommissie (Commission on Aesthetic Advice). Again Amsterdam was in the vanguard, for it was the first municipality—in 1898—to set up such a body. Representatives of the major architectural organizations (including Architectura et Amicitia) had delegates on the commission, whose task was to review the exteriors of all buildings to be erected on municipally owned land. If the commission decided that the facade designs were not satisfactory from an artistic point of view, they returned them to the builder or the woningbouwvereniging for revision: this process was repeated until a satisfactory solution was found. There was a right of appeal to the mayor and aldermen who had the final say; but they tended to support the commission. Obviously it was in the interest of all parties wishing to build on municipal land to employ an architect; without one, designs had little chance of being approved. The demand for "beautiful workers' dwellings" voiced by Keppler found support through this commission, since almost all of the housing erected in Amsterdam was on land leased from the city and therefore in addition to sound planning and construction had to offer aesthetic qualities to the community.

The architects in turn made their contribution in 1916 by setting up a special honorarium table for woningbouwvereenigingen. The professional organizations had established different levels of fees according to the amount of work required, and although the design of housing could be a time-consuming and painstaking task, it was put in the lowest category, the first class (buildings for which few drawings were needed). Thus on a commission of 50,000 guilders, the fee was reckoned at 4.10 percent of the building costs, compared with 5.10 percent for a second-class building and 6.54 percent for third class (buildings, whose execution required long hours of study, calculation and drafting). With building costs of 100,000, the honorarium was 3.7 percent, 4.71 percent, and 6.11 percent respectively.[36] Architects thus did respond to Keppler's challenge and made a small financial sacrifice so that the woningbouwvereenigingen could afford their fees.

With the various agents now assembled to implement Keppler's appeal, one final ingredient was necessary: capital. At first the financial provisions of the Woningwet were utilized only modestly: Amsterdam received its first funds in 1908, for twenty-eight dwellings erected by Rochdale,[37] and gradually other woningbouwvereenigingen set to work with government loans. But World War I brought a tremendous blow to the slowly improving housing situation, even though Holland remained neutral. Shortages of building materials and labor brought a fantastic rise in prices; it is estimated that building costs rose to 225 percent of prewar prices in 1917 and reached a peak of 350 percent in 1920.[38] It was impossible to erect housing whose operating costs could be covered by the rent, much less housing which would yield a profit. Private building came to a standstill, but at this period the woningbouwvereenigingen, which were not motivated by a desire for financial gain, could come into their own. However, they needed to be heavily subsidized; that is, not only did the government grant repayable loans, but it offered to pay, for a period of five years, the extra costs resulting from wartime inflation, so that rents could be held at a level the population could afford.

The decision to offer subsidies to the housing societies was made during the Liberal Ministry of Cort van der Linden, one of the framers of the Woningwet. It should be pointed out that the vagueness of the Woningwet allowed it to be interpreted in various ways depending on one's political position. The left believed in generous financial support for housing[39] and accordingly, during the period when it was in control (see note 19), a new system of loans plus subsidies was introduced. When the woningbouwvereenigingen sent in their budgets, they were to include, in addition to an estimate of actual costs, a calculation of what the costs would have been in 1914. The government then pledged to pay 50 percent, subsequently 75 percent, of the difference, with the municipalities picking up the remaining tab to make a subsidy of 100 percent of excess costs caused by inflation.

Although the 1918 elections brought a turn to the right (ironically, universal suffrage brought into power the very parties that had opposed it most vigorously), the state did not immediately withdraw these subsidies. Indeed, at first the denominational parties demonstrated their good faith by creating a new cabinet position—Minister of Labor—for the purpose of administering the Woningwet. This post was held by the Roman Catholic, P. J. M. Aalberse, who had a reputation for sensitivity to the housing needs of the workers. In 1919 he simplified the method whereby the government covered the war-related excess costs; it was found more workable for the authorities to pay the difference between operating costs and rental income (75 percent charged to the state and 25 percent to local authorities). But the following year he decreed that, depending on the size of the dwelling, 50 to 70 percent of the expenses had to be covered by the rents. This proportion was increased to 90 percent and finally to 100 percent, thus effectively cutting off all subsidies for new housing. The woningbouwvereenigingen were forced to raise rents and/or build much more cheaply (it was estimated that before the war they built 33 percent more expensively than private builders, and immediately after the figure was 53 percent).[40]

Injury to the housing societies was compounded when in June 1921, Aalberse froze all grants for housing, because he believed that enough schemes

had been approved to use up available resources of labor and materials for at least two years, and because private builders were again contributing to the dwelling supply. In fact, it soon became clear that conservative housing policy was designed to favor the private sector. The government instituted a system of premiums (premies), outright grants to private builders, who would receive a fixed sum for every dwelling constructed. This action did accomplish its intended purpose of stimulating the private building industry, so much so that the premies ceased in 1923. But the government then supported the builders by lending them second-mortgage money. The woningbouwvereenigingen, by contrast, had to turn to other sources for capital, to mortgage banks and semipublic institutions like the National Insurance Bank; they were able to do this only if the municipalities would guarantee these mortgages. Their share in dwelling production steadily declined, from 64 percent in 1921 to 35 percent in 1923, 27 percent in 1924 and 1925, and 15 percent in 1926.[41] It was not until after the Second World War that housing societies would again dominate the housing market.

It is true that because private industry built faster and cheaper than the woningbouwvereenigingen, it made an enormous quantitative contribution to housing; even Amsterdam's social democrats recognized this and from 1921 on approved plans for various combinations of private builders to develop housing sites in the new districts of Amsterdam. But there is no question that qualitative improvement—the main purpose of the Woningwet and a cornerstone of SDAP policy—was due to the activities of the housing societies. Their dwellings were the true "monuments to the class struggle."

The major examples of those monuments were erected by two of the social democratic societies, Eigen Haard (Our Own Hearth) and De Dageraad (Dawn), and were the most eagerly visited shrines in the "mecca of housing." Stylistically they are representative of the Amsterdam School,[42] a local architectural movement that flourished between 1915 and 1926. Its members were characterized by a tendency toward expressionism and a delight in fantasy, and this led to strikingly conceived housing complexes that had the visual impact of a May Day demonstration (Fig. 8) and that seemed to embody the triumph of the working class.

The first housing to arise under the banner of the Amsterdam School was designed by Michel de Klerk (1884–1923). It was located in the Spaarndammerbuurt, a triangular area northwest of the center between the railroad and the harbor, which the municipality was shaping into a workers' district (Figs. 9, 10). Pushed by the SDAP members of the city council, Amsterdam began after 1910 to

8
May Day, 1917, Amsterdam. (Historische topografische atlas, Gemeentelijke archiefdienst Amsterdam)

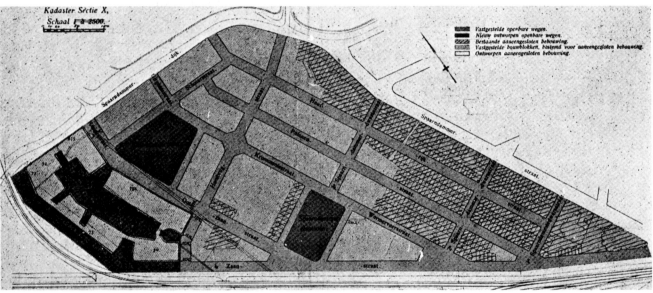

9
Proposed plan of the Spaarndammerbuurt, 1915. Hatched areas are existing buildings, dark areas are proposed new streets and parks. (*Gemeenteblad, Afd. I*, 1915)

10
Spaarndammerbuurt, aerial view from
the southwest, after its development
as a workers' quarter. (Photo: Afdeling
stadsontwikkeling, Dienst publieke
werken, Amsterdam)

purchase land there on a large scale for the purpose of leasing it to housing societies and in some cases to private builders who wished to construct workers' dwellings. One such builder was Klaas Hille, who, knowing that on such leased land his project would have to pass review by the Schoonheidscommissie, hired the young de Klerk in 1914 to design several housing blocks.[43] These bordered on a park proposed by the city for that neighborhood, the Spaarndammerplantsoen. In 1915 the first block was completed, and de Klerk made a drawing for the second (Fig. 11). However, because of financial difficulties associated with the war, Hille was unable to proceed further with his scheme, and Keppler encouraged a housing society to take over the relinquished terrain. Presumably the society employed the fledgling architect, de Klerk, because he had already prepared a design for the site, and indeed there were but minor changes between the drawing and the executed building (Figs. 12–16).

The housing society was Eigen Haard, founded in 1909 by a group of workers who had already tasted the fruits of collective endeavor through their membership in a consumers' cooperative. Tellegen and Keppler helped them with legal and technical advice, and by 1912 their first 155 dwellings, in two-story blocks of great simplicity, were executed.[44] In 1915, work was begun on a group of ninety-three dwellings on the Zeeburgerdijk (Figs. 2–7), designed by the established architect, J. H. W. Leliman (1878–1921).[45] These were completed in 1917. Both complexes were in the Indischebuurt, a neighborhood in the eastern part of the city which, like the Spaarndammerbuurt, was being developed by the municipality during the second decade as a working-class quarter.

While its building on the Zeeburgerdijk was under construction, Eigen Haard decided to build in the Spaarndammerbuurt as well, in order to give those members who worked in the western part of Amsterdam access to good housing also. The society commissioned the experienced Leliman to create a housing block there (which resembles his first one, being conservative in style and rationalist in concept), and in addition, it took over, along with Hille's site, the project prepared for him by de Klerk. In October 1916, the municipality approved Eigen Haard's request for a Woningwet loan for the purpose of erecting the fifty-nine dwellings and one shop that comprised de Klerk's scheme. The following year the society asked de Klerk to design a second block (Figs. 17–25). This faces the earlier one but is larger and takes up all sides of the triangular site, with the exception of the area occupied by an existing school. It consists of 102 dwellings, plus a post office and, in the courtyard, a small assembly building for members of the society.

Since Leliman and de Klerk represent antithetical responses to Keppler's call for "beautiful workers' dwellings," it may be instructive to compare their work for the same client. One will find certain similarities imposed by building codes and building practices as well as by the needs and desires of the housing society. But the differences reveal a significant split between the rationalists (both those of the older generation who fought the historicizing excesses of the nineteenth century, and their younger followers) and the members of the Amsterdam School. The former believed that the logical and economic fulfillment of programmatic requirements was the main, if not exclusive, task of the architect; the latter group sought to create a unique and expressive solution to the particular problem of workers' housing. While the rationalists believed that a building attained sufficient beauty when functional and structural demands were met in a consistent and truthful manner, the Amsterdam School architects believed that aesthetic effects were distinct from such demands and must be deliberately sought.

In terms of organization of space, the buildings share some characteristics peculiar to almost all workers' housing in Amsterdam. The flats are arranged as distinct stacks, each grouped around an entry and stairhall, rather than in a continuous series connected by interior corridors and served by one main entrance and a limited number of stairs. During the period of speculative building, when ownership of dwellings on any one street was fragmented, it was necessary that each parcel (*perceel* or *opstal,* that is, one vertical stack of dwellings) have its own means of access. This system of separate parcels was continued even when the housing societies were able to command the entire block. Indeed the system was prescribed in the building code. There are advantages—one section of the building can be easily quarantined in case of an epidemic, and also, once back-to-back dwellings were prohibited (as they were in 1905), cross ventilation is possible. In addition, the system seemed to afford more privacy to tenants, because only a portion of the occupants of a block would use each entry.

The arrangement of the dwellings themselves in Leliman's and de Klerk's plans of 1915 (Figs. 7 and 14) is also similar and was no doubt worked out in consultation with the Municipal Housing Service. Each flat has a large room for general purposes and a varying number of small bedrooms (it was considered a moral danger for a child to share a bedroom with a sibling of the opposite sex, and thus families with girls and boys were supposed to have three-bedroom dwellings). Kitchens have been placed in the rear of the building, in the space left over behind the stairs, and waterclosets in the entry, an unattractive but standard practice, preferable at least to no sanitary facilities whatever, which had been the case with many nineteenth-century tenements.

There are differences in planning and composition, to be sure. In the two-story portion of his block, Leliman has somewhat eccentrically reversed the position of living room and bedrooms. Although this may have resulted in noisier sleeping quarters, the charm of a living room that overlooked the Lozingskanaal probably compensated for that disadvantage. The siting of the Zeeburgerijk building is indeed unusual in that a canal rather than a garden defines the rear facade. Moreover, Leliman has given some tenants an additional balcony on the front, perhaps to add three-dimensional interest to his facade (although by means of a functional element). He has increased plastic interest also by combining two-, three- and four-story elevations. This device does visually mitigate the relentless length of the building, but as used here it results in a somewhat disunified facade. De Klerk too, in his second block for Eigen Haard, joined two- and four-story portions (Figs. 19–20), but he succeeded in avoiding a discordant effect. The combination of high and low sections may have been done at the request of the society or it may have been suggested by Keppler, for he liked that method of achieving a lively silhouette.

With twenty-nine three-room, forty-eight four-room and sixteen five-room dwellings, the Zeeburgerdijk block has proportionately more large flats than either of de Klerk's buildings. His block of 1915–1918 has nine two-room, twenty-seven three-room and only twenty-three four-room flats, and this may be a reflection of the fact that it was originally intended for a private builder. In de Klerk's second complex, of 1917–1920, where he worked to Eigen Haard's specifications, there is only one two-room dwelling, plus eleven five-room and thirty-five four-room flats. There are fifty-five three-room units, so the smaller dwellings do predominate,[46] but this is the result of increased building costs, which necessitated more modest responses on the part of the housing societies to the spatial needs of their members.

While all Woningwet housing includes differently-sized dwellings, de Klerk in his second block has made a noticeable departure from typical planning procedure by varying the shape and arrangement as well as the number of rooms. The stairways are not all located on one facade but sometimes appear on the front and sometimes on the rear (in which case the kitchen is placed in the front, next to the living room). Not all of the rooms are rectangular, but oblique walls often make curious spaces. In part, de Klerk was trying to accommodate an awkward site, where absolute standardization would have been difficult to attain without sacrificing square footage. He has been criticized on economic grounds for the lavish variety of dwellings, but one must acknowledge that he was willing to spend extra time without compensation (except insofar as higher building costs increased his commission) to work out a number of different plan types. In this he certainly contributed to assuaging the workers' fears that mass housing meant tenements made up of identical units which had the barracks-like monotony of prison cells.[47]

It is in external appearance that de Klerk's dwellings differ most markedly from Leliman's and from other Woningwet buildings of the time. While each man has used the interior spatial divisions as the starting point for facade articulation (so that, for example, windows of living spaces differ in size and shape from those of circulation areas), Leliman has taken the rationalist position that any ornamental elements must be integral with construction and not superfluous to function. He has provided some decorative interest by his handling of the brickwork in the corbels that support the balconies (Fig. 4) and the projections of the upper stairs (Fig. 5). The chimneys, which extend down the facade in a thin plane (Fig. 4), also provide a visual flourish that is not at odds with the nature of the brick wall. The windows of the transoms and the doors (Fig. 5) are perfectly simple, yet their shape has been carefully considered and a disciplined play of rectangles provided. These modest touches have something in common with the more grandiose treatment of geometric forms by members of de Stijl and suggest, perhaps, the relationship of that avant-garde group to the Dutch rationalist tradition.

Although Leliman has given some consideration to detail, his chief concern is to solve the purely physical needs of the program. Large windows, sturdy walls, and roomy balconies are his contributions to the occupants. He believed in simplicity and solidity and abhorred unnecessary flourishes, particularly for workers' housing. In *De Bouwwereld,* he often printed articles ridiculing the architecture of the Amsterdam School. His attitude toward the movement is clear in his review of de Klerk's competition design of 1918 for an Academy of Fine Arts, which won second prize. After indicating the weakness of the plan, "which determines the usefulness of a building," he continued: "This project, with its complicated and affected games—the product of a decadent conception of art—manifestly is to be appreciated primarily, if not exclusively, for its exterior." In the same review he scornfully noted that Henri Polak announced that de Klerk should have won first prize because his was the most artistic entry, although the social democrat admitted that "technically his design did not fulfill all the requirements."[48]

11
M. de Klerk, project for workers housing, Spaarndammerplantsoen. (Historische topografische atlas, Gemeentelijke archiefdienst Amsterdam)
12
Spaarndammerplantsoen, dwellings of
Eigen Haard. M. de Klerk, 1915–
1918. (Photo: Gemeentelijke dienst
volkshuisvesting, Amsterdam)

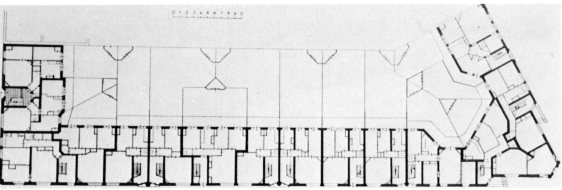

13
View of Fig. 12, from the Zaanstraat.
(Photo: Author)
14
Plan of Fig. 12. (*Wendingen,* Vol VI
(1924), No. 9–10, p. 7)

15
Detail of Fig. 13. (Photo: Author)

16
Detail of Fig. 13. (Photo: Author)
17
Site plan, Spaarndammerplantsoen,
housing blocks by de Klerk, 1914–
1920. (*Wendingen*, Vol. VI (1924),
No. 9–10, p. 9.)

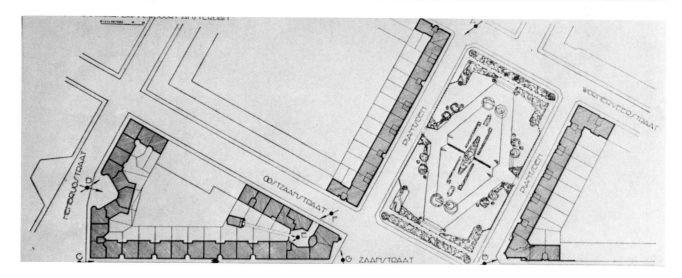

18
Zaanstraat and Oostzaanstraat,
dwellings of Eigen Haard, view from
the Spaarndammerplantsoen. De
Klerk, 1917–1920. (Photo: Author)

19
Zaanstraat, dwellings of Eigen Haard.
Drawing, de Klerk, 1917. (Historisch
topografische atlas, Gemeentelijke-
archiefdienst, Amsterdam)

20
Hembrugstraat, dwellings of Eigen
Haard. De Klerk, 1917–1920. (Photo:
Gemeentelijke dienst volkshuisvest-
ing, Amsterdam)

21
Courtyard and assembly hall, Eigen
Haard. (Photo: Gemeentelijke dienst
volkshuisvesting, Amsterdam)

22
Detail of Zaanstraat and Oostzaanstraat, post office. (Photo: Author)

23
Detail of Zaanstraat. (Photo: Author)

24
Dwelling types, Spaarndammerplantsoen. *A,* Living room, *B,* bedroom,
C, kitchen, *D,* entry. (*Arbeiderswoningen in Nederland,* Rotterdam, 1921,
p. 80

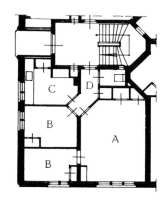

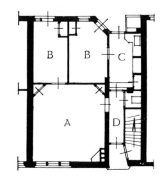

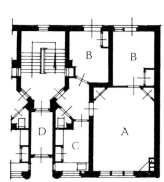

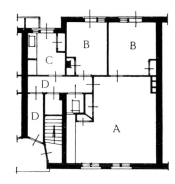

25
Plan of Fig. 18. (*Wendingen,* Vol VI
(1924), No. 9–10, p. 8)

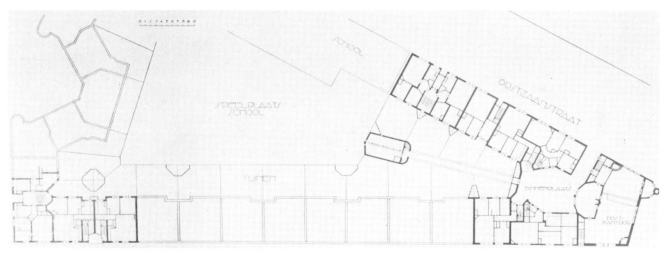

De Klerk had no intention of being inhibited by rationalist strictures. In his first work for Eigen Haard he did not have the program of varying heights to fall back on in order to avoid monotony, so he relied on his sense of fantasy. Although he has created an intriguing complex full of visual incident, he has also achieved the unity that eluded Leliman. For all its modulation, his building is perceived first as an organic whole rather than as a collection of adjacent parts. A comparison of the plan with the elevation reveals his method of emphasizing the basic continuity of the block. The walls perpendicular to the facade, which provide the main vertical support for the floors and which separate the "parcels," have not been expressed, except perhaps very subtly in the cylindrical bulges along the main facade. On the contrary, the interior divisions are bridged by the tiled extrusions of the stairhalls and by the masonry projections over the doors (Fig. 15). The fact that the party walls are the major structural element has been suggested in another way, and becomes the point of departure for de Klerk's treatment of the exterior wall, which serves chiefly to cover interior space. His treatment is the opposite of the rationalist one that emphasizes the bearing quality of the masonry. De Klerk, in contrast, makes the facade wall analogous to a fabric suspended from above, by his handling of the fourth story and attic windows and by the creation of atectonic patterns at the lowest story, where one would expect a firm base. De Klerk has not so much denied the structural and spatial facts as he has played with them to introduce elements of paradox.

As in Leliman's block, the alternation of semipublic and private spaces has provided a rationale for the articulation of the long slab. Yet the same interior arrangement that sanctifies this articulation seems to have been manipulated in the interest of the visual rhythms of the elevation. There is surely no logical reason why some stairhalls should serve two sets of dwellings on each floor and others (the tile-covered double stairhalls) only one. But that arrangement has allowed de Klerk to introduce an almost mannerist complexity into his composition.

If the single stairhall (defined by the triangular windows) is *a*, the double stairhall (signaled by the tiled portions) is *b*, and the concluding cylindrical stairhall is *c*, the rhythm of the main facade is read as *abababc*. (The original version, Fig. 11, would have had an *abbbac* rhythm.) A similarly alternating rather than symmetrical rhythm animates the paraboloid windows of the fourth story. Taking the single window as *a*, the paired paraboloids as *b*, one discerns an *ababba* progression, then a pause for *c* in the form of some square windows and, finally, in the prow-shaped corner, *a* again (thus *ababbaca*). It may seem perverse to apply such traditional methods of visual analysis to de Klerk's stridently novel work, but surely he was deliberately introducing such complex rhythms into his design.

De Klerk has been criticized for sacrificing function to artistic effect. The repetitious windows of Leliman's stairhalls, it is true, admit lots of healthful light and fresh air, while de Klerk's stairs are but dimly lit and ventilated by tiny triangular and cylindrical windows. Further, the occupants of the corner dwellings must accept some awkwardly shaped rooms. Given the site, however, an irregular corner was unavoidable, and de Klerk has turned the disadvantage into a positive element, creating a prow form which introduces a dynamic feature. De Klerk's main concern, after fulfilling basic requirements, was to confront the observer with a powerful monument, one that sheltered a class whose expectations and strength were on the rise.

For the building is not a neutral backdrop to the park but commands the attention in a somewhat disquieting manner. Viewed from across the Spaarndammerplantsoen (Fig. 12), it suggests a vaguely menacing being, capable of motion. The section at the left, on the Wormerveerstraat, seems about to advance toward the park; the sense of potential or arrested movement is maintained in the tile-covered stairtowers that have struggled outward from the main wall plane. At the prow-shaped corner on the Zaanstraat (Fig. 13) the movement gains a new direction, one oriented toward the railroad track. The reference to mobility is given a piquant touch by the wheels of brick that conclude the balusters of the corner stairs (Fig. 16).

Yet the menace is mitigated, and relegated to the world of the fairy tale, by the humorously irreverent handling of architectural details, some of which may perhaps be linked with working-class history. Waves created by dark, vertically laid bricks lap the base of the building; above the entrance, the wavy rhythm quickens and the curving brick patterns suggest a school of eels (Fig. 15). Another sea creature may be visualized in the sinuous yet simultaneously spiky band of iron slithering up the baluster (Fig. 16). The prow at the corner is reminiscent of the eel boat. Although it may be frivolous, it is perhaps not entirely uninstructive to suggest that such details refer to that singular event, the *paling oproer*. De Klerk's origins were proletarian,[49] and although he was only two years old when the riot occurred, it is not impossible that he knew about this stirring affair. Perhaps the mocking tongue protruding from beneath the "school of eels" (the "mouth and tongue corbel," as Suzanne Frank so ingeniously describes it)[50] implies that the working-class occupants of the building have had the last laugh.

The mood evoked in de Klerk's second block for Eigen Haard seems gayer. Further, the details are more integrated with the whole. Despite the diversity of shapes found in the block of 1917–1920, the separate functions have been quite skillfully united within one billowing envelope. On the other hand, some may find the scale insufficiently urban; the earlier block does seem more successful in relating to the generous new scale of the Spaarndammerbuurt.

Vincent Scully has seen in the section containing the post office, which forms the apex of the triangular plan (Figs. 19, 22, 23), the image of a train, and he is no doubt correct, although the "train" has been taken apart and reassembled for architectural and functional demands. The windows along the flank of the low portion, for example, resemble the pistons that drive the wheels. This reading is corroborated by the fact of location along a railroad track; the building merges with its actual environment in a strikingly literal way.[51] There are other dynamic touches in the long flank of dwellings extending along the track, where the wall bulges out over the entrance and, doubled in rhythm, at the attic story, as if in response to the shock waves created by the speed of the train. Yet surely such glorifications of the locomotive coexist with references of a less futuristic nature. An interpretation of the building as a medieval town in miniature, with its religious spires and secular turrets, is also defensible,[52] and suggests the ties that link the modern unions and housing societies with the guilds, a reading reinforced by the provision of the Lilliputian "guildhall." To be sure, the building can be enjoyed simply as a knowing and masterful play of volumes in light, without reference to symbolic allusions. The most crucial point is that the housing block has become an arresting artifact that conveys by its uniqueness that it is a special place. De Klerk wanted to achieve "the sparklingly new, the sensationally shocking . . . that which characterizes the properly modern,"[53] and such sentiments proved compatible with the call for visible monuments to the class which represented the new age. The worker who lived here came home to an identifiable environment; its exuberance and novelty were intended to refresh his spirit at the end of a hard day.[54]

At this point the question of building costs should be introduced. The loans required by the society amounted to 246,000 guilders for the ninety-three dwellings and one office of Leliman's block of 1915–1917, 330,200 builders for the fifty-nine dwellings and one store of de Klerk's building of 1916–1918, and almost one million guilders for his one-hundred-three dwellings and post office of 1918–1920.[55] These sums include items such as architects' and supervisors' fees, interest on the loan and the leasehold payments during the construction period when no rents were coming in, and other minor entries in addition to the actual costs of materials and labor. But the latter were the major item, and in comparing the figures one must recall that by 1920 building costs had risen to 300 percent of 1914 prices. In the case of the third building under discussion, contractors' costs were first estimated at 638,951 guilders when the budget was drawn up in January 1918. By August 1920, these had increased to 928,122 guilders. The cubic meter costs of this block were more than 33 guilders, compared to an average cost at that time of 30 guilders per cubic meter for the other woningbouwvereenigingen buildings.[56]

Eigen Haard's request for a larger Woningwet loan to cover the increase of almost 300,000 guilders came before the Gemeenteraad on October 8, 1920. A number of the councilors took the occasion to accuse the society of irresponsiblity and to claim that the dwellings were ridiculously and unnecessarily luxurious for workingmen. The social democrats, on the other hand, defended Eigen Haard and charged that the opposition was trying to lower housing standards. The architect, Z. Gulden (1875–1960),[57] who was an SDAP representative on the council, praised de Klerk's blocks in the Spaarndammerbuurt as demonstrating a new sensitivity and concern in the design of a workers' district. He went on to explain that

this commission was given to one of our young and most gifted architects . . . in the time when, under the leadership of Minister Cort van der Linden it was decided that workers' dwellings must also fulfill aesthetic demands. Now Minister Aaalberse [who in a government circular had criticized the "capricious forms" found in some of the work for the housing societies] claims to love the workers but at the same time he takes all possible measures to depress the level of housing.[58]

The contributions to the debate by the wethouder voor de volkshuisvesting are of particular interest, because they constitute a dispassionate defense of the social democratic position on housing and complement Keppler's more emotional rhetoric. In Wibaut's words:

It is true that these dwellings are somewhat more expensive than the average. But the mayor and aldermen have taken the standpoint that the new workers' districts are intended for future generations and therefore are cultural objects on which other demands than those of cheapness should be placed: we take this standpoint as well with regard to schools and even bridges. In our municipality inexpensiveness is not the only consideration, but aesthetic criteria must be fulfilled. . . . Already we had asked ourselves, shouldn't we give major architects the opportunity to design housing? Naturally all architects are not equally important, and certainly not all are so significant as the artist de Klerk. There is always a sort of aversion to the new, and therefore de Klerk was not used for the first housing complexes, but he must be used now. If you give a commission to such a significant architect then you

must expect high building costs, but one must accept the aesthetic conception of the artist. . . .
We are convinced that it was worth a bit more to let that architect create something in that part of the city. Who is we? In the first place Eigen Haard, which sent in the plan. Then the Woningdienst, the inspector of Public Health, . . . and finally the government approved the plans. It is only now that the bills have been received that difficulties are being made. In that district there is need of architectural distinction. And when one is going to *timmeren met metselsteen* [be a carpenter in brick], of course it is expensive. And the tower [Fig. 20], yes, that cost a few thousand guilders, but in that large urban area there was need of such a small monument.[59]

In the end, the aesthetic qualities of de Klerk's designs were paid for not only by the local and national authorities but also by the housing society and its tenants. While a portion of the excessive building costs were absorbed by the government as war-related expenses, the original decision to use fine and varied materials[60] and the subsequent difficulty of maintaining complicated details has involved a continuing drain on the resources of Eigen Haard. Nevertheless, the society has asserted that "Although the operation of this block is a burden . . . we consider ourselves very fortunate to be able to have it in our possession. It is truly a monument to people's housing."[61]

But is is another "monument to people's housing" that probably constitutes the most successful of the productions created jointly by the members of the SDAP and of the Amsterdam School. This is the housing complex erected by De Dageraad, (Figs. 26–39), and its history is deeply intertwined with the social democratic dream.

De Dageraad's success as a housing society was assured because it was founded by an existing organization, a consumer's cooperative of the same name,[62] with a pool of members at hand. A large proportion of these were Jewish working-class intellectuals; all the members "came from the circles of the social democratic workers' movement. From the first it was clear that the activities of De Dageraad would not be restricted to the improvement of housing in the narrow sense, but that the society would also try to give expression to that pressure for cultural renewal which was so strongly marked in this movement."[63]

In 1919 the society's first request for Woningwet funds was approved. These were to be used to build some 300 dwellings, plus a few shops, in the new quarter of Amsterdam that had been planned by H. P. Berlage (1856–1934).[64] The scheme for Amsterdam Zuid (South), as this section is called, was approved by the city in 1917,[65] but subsequently, many of the areas that had been reserved for public buildings and parks had to be utilized for housing. A site north of the newly dug Amstel Canal, which had

been designated by Berlage for a hospital, was annexed by the Municipal Housing Service for a workers' district. The land was leased to six housing societies, which eventually built 1,686 dwellings (including a few with retail shops attached); the city added two schools and a library.

The site plan (Fig. 26) was prepared by Keppler's department in consultation with the various architects who received commissions from the housing societies. The area is bounded by two north-south circulation spines (Tweede van der Helststraat and van Woustraat), which cross the canal and link the quarter with the rest of Amsterdam South, and by two east-west streets (Lutmastraat and Amstelkade), which are relatively narrow and do not encourage fast traffic. Within the housing area itself, traffic is discouraged because of the labyrinthine street layout. At the center of the complex is the P. L. Takstraat, which connects with a pedestrian bridge over the canal; De Dageraad's dwellings (Fig. 27), which for the most part are only three stories high, lie along this street and also on the two squares of the quarter and thus form the climax of the entire district.

All the dwellings are laid out in the now standard Amsterdam way, extending around the periphery of the block and enclosing gardens. Although the layout is symmetrical when viewed on the plan in two dimensions, the buildings to either side of De Dageraad are not mirror images of one another, so there is a three-dimensional differentiation. The housing blocks vary in height from two to four stories and range in style from traditional to modern (that is, Amsterdam School). The dwellings of each of the societies (which included the Protestant Patrimonium, the Catholic Dr. Schaepman, and the social-democratic Rochdale and Amsterdam Zuid) are readily identifiable. All have a system of vertical entries and all are of brick, but there is a range of color (from deep red to brownish mauve to bright red-orange, to the yellow and rose of De Dageraad). A balance has been achieved between the community need for a coordinated ensemble and the desires of each society for its own distinctive image.

De Dageraad was ready with its plans in this quarter in 1920 (most of the drawings are dated July of that year).[66] The designs had been prepared by de Klerk in association with Pieter Kramer (1881–1961),[67] another of the Amsterdam School's very gifted practitioners. In any meaningful account of the execution of these designs, two more institutions linked with the social democratic movement must be considered—the Centrale Bouwvoorziening (CBV; Center for Building Materials), and the Federatie van Zelfstandige Werkende Groepen in het Bouwbedrijf (henceforth Federation or Federatie van groepen; Federation of independent groups in the construction industry).[68]

26
Site plan, housing societies' quarter,
Amsterdam South, c. 1920. (*Amsterdam: Stadsontwikkeling, Volkshuisvesting*, Amsterdam, 1924, p. 4a)
27
Site plan, dwellings of De Dageraad,
ca. 1920. (Photocopy: Bouw-en
Woningtoezicht, Amsterdam)

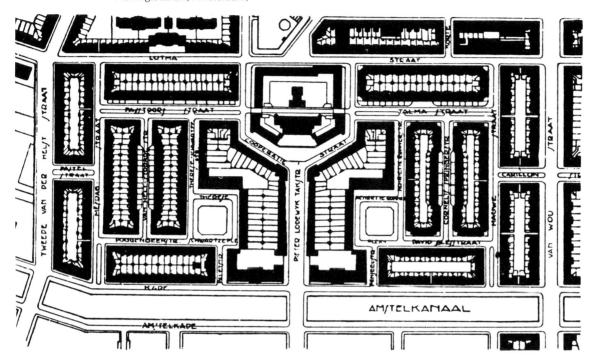

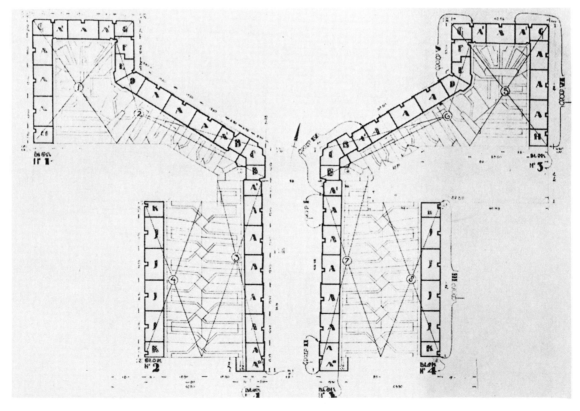

28
Henriette Ronnerplein and Therese
Schwartzeplein, dwellings of De
Dageraad. De Klerk, 1920–1923.
(Photo: Gemeentelijke dienst volks-
huisvesting, Amsterdam)

29
Rear view of Fig. 28. (Photo: Gemeen-
telijke dienst volkshuisvesting,
Amsterdam)

Detail of Fig. 28. (Photo: Author)

31
Plan of ground and second floors, section (see Fig. 28). Types J and K, Fig. 27. Photocopy: Bouw-en woningtoezicht, Amsterdam)

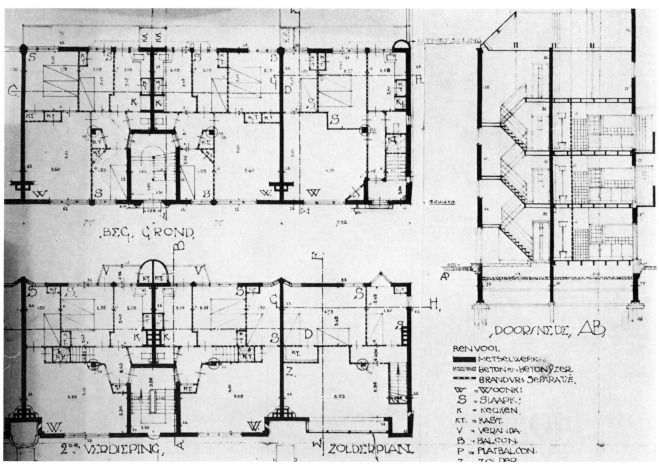

32
P. L. Takstraat, dwellings of De
Dageraad. M. de Klerk and P. Kramer,
1920–1923. (Photo: Gemeentelijke
dienst volkshuisvesting, Amsterdam)
33
View of Fig. 32. (Photo: Gemeentelijke dienst volkshuisvesting,
Amsterdam)

34
Corners at P. L. Takstraat and Bur-
gomeester Tellegenstraat, dwellings of
De Dageraad. (Photo: Author)

35
Burgomeester Tellegenstraat,
dwellings of De Dageraad. De Klerk
and Kramer, 1920–1923. (Photo:
Author)

36
Plan of ground and first floors, Fig. 32.
Type *A,* dwellings of De Dageraad.
(Wendingen, Vol VI (1924), No. 9–10,
p. 22)

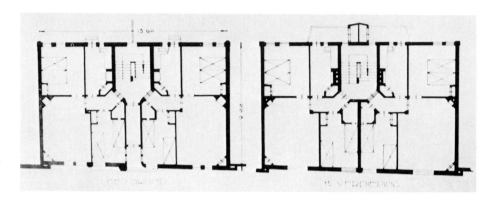

37
Rear view of Fig. 32. (Photo: Gemeen-
telijke dienst volkshuisvesting,
Amsterdam)

38
Detail of Fig. 35. (Photo: Author)

39
Corners at P. L. Takstraat and Burgomeester Tellegenstraat. Drawing, Kramer, 1920. (*Arbeiderswoningen in Nederland,* Rotterdam, 1921, p. 88)

The first of these institutions was very short-lived. The CBV was set up in April 1918, during the last days of the Liberal ministry. It was established by the state, the cities of Amsterdam, Utrecht, and The Hague, and the central organization of Dutch municipalities, for the purpose of buying and selling building materials. The justification for such government intervention was that it was the only way to assure an equitable distribution at reasonable prices of the scarce supplies of construction goods. The manufacturers and importers of brick, tile, mill products, cements, and so forth, were asked—the CBV's enemies said coerced[69]—to sell their products to the CBV in preference to private suppliers, at a price considered fair by the authorities. Unfortunately, the CBV was not a success. Its detractors claimed that it was not only inefficient, failing to fill orders on time, but that despite government support it charged more for its materials than private firms. It was liquidated a few years after its founding, another socialist ideal killed, admittedly, as much by its own bureaucratic muddle as by the hostility of the conservative government and private interests.

The CBV was intended to act as the main supplier to the Federatie van groepen. This was an organization of productive associations, which were cooperatives oriented toward production rather than consumption. The Federatie van groepen, in fact, accomplished on a small scale the socialist dream of ownership of the means of production by the workers, for its members, although they were paid wages, were in effect working for an organization they themselves owned and operated.[70] Most of the individual productive associations were formed by workers skilled in one trade—masons, carpenters, painters, and others, although several related trades might also be grouped in one association. The Federation employed the members of the associations to execute works it had contracted to build and thus eliminated the middleman—the contractor and subcontractors. Since the Federation was not motivated by desire for financial profit, it was able simultaneously to raise wages and decrease building costs. Lower costs enabled it not only to compete with private builders but also to fulfill its pledge to aid the woningbouwvereenigingen, which were the Federation's chief clients.

A major goal of the Federatie van groepen was to equalize wages in the building trades. Masons and stuccoworkers were relatively highly paid, but other workers, such as piledrivers and carpenters, were not. The Federation paid all its workers at the same rate—1.35 guilders per hour. This was more than most of them would have earned from private contractors, although the masons and plasterers had to take a slight hourly decrease in pay in order to work for the Federation. But this was compensated by such provisions as paid vacations and sick leaves, and pay on the job even when the weather made it impossible to work. There was also the psychic income derived from greater independence and a sense of purpose. By most accounts the quality of the construction was very high, because so many of the workers were experienced and highly skilled.

De Dageraad was one of the housing societies that chose the Federatie van groepen as its contractor when the work was put out to bid at the end of May 1921,[71] and the Federation was responsible for the execution of this amazing housing complex. The CBV presumably supplied the materials, but its role was overshadowed by a bitter union struggle that delayed the completion of De Dageraad until late in 1923.

Although the sixteen productive associations in the building trades in Amsterdam counted about 1,250 members, these were not sufficient to fulfill all the Federation's contracts, and nonmembers formed about one-third of the work force.[72] Many of these belonged to syndicalist unions, which in turn were grouped in the Landelijke Federatie van Bouwvakarbeiders (National Federation of Construction Workers). This organization, with its partially anarchist, partially communist affinities, viewed the proponents of the productive associations as dupes of the capitalists and took a negative attitude toward them, although it did not refuse outright to cooperate with the Federatie van groepen. The syndicalist unions were the most aggressive in the building industry and prided themselves on driving harder bargains than the Catholic, Protestant and socialist unions. In 1922, they demanded that the hourly wage paid by the Federation be increased to 1.50 guilders. The Federation was financially unable to meet this demand and those construction workers affiliated with the Landelijke Federatie struck.

Ironically, one of the reasons for the initial success of the Federatie van groepen was that it had seemed immune to the series of strikes and lockouts that had afflicted the building industry in 1921. But for various reasons, including the long-standing enmity between the SDB, whose policies survived in the syndicalist unions, and the SDAP, which supported the productive associations, the Federatie van groepen found itself the victim of a destructive power struggle. In this dispute can be discerned basic theoretical differences. The social democrats, with their background of Fabianism and their reluctance to disrupt society, revealed an idealistic commitment to equality and cooperation, while the anarchosyndicalists, with their sustained heritage of bitterness and distrust, concentrated on obtaining immediate tangible gains for their own comrades, whatever the social costs.

Eventually the strike was resolved, for the most part in the Federation's favor, and work was resumed on De Dageraad. The strife that marred its birth has been forgotten in the glory of its being. Almost 300 families inhabit these superb structures, roughly half in three-room and half in four-room dwellings (there are a few five-room flats as well, plus *winkelwoningen*—dwellings with shops attached). The cost slightly exceeded one million guilders, not very much more than that of de Klerk's second block for Eigen Haard, which contained only about one-third as many units. Yet there has been no sacrifice in quality or visual excitement; indeed De Dageraad is a more mature and successful performance. The symmetrical organization of the complex helps to unify the parts and adds a formality more suitable for a large urban quarter. Furthermore, the formality has been attained without any loss of intimacy or charm.

There are certain similarities between the two projects that generally identify any product of the Amsterdam School. Native brick and tile have been retained as the primary materials, but they are employed with such inventiveness that they seem to be new substances. (Reinforced concrete has been used at certain points for heavily-loaded or projecting floors, but it is not visible; structural expressionism was not a concern of the Amsterdam School.) Color contrasts—orange-red tiles, purplish-red brick at the base, wheat-yellow brick for the walls—have been used to unify large areas, not to articulate structure or to subdivide the wall-surface (as in the nineteenth century). The exterior of the building has been designed with an awareness of its role in the cityscape; the street wall has been treated not as a mere mirror of the interior space but as something with its own raison d'être. Kramer explained that not only should the tenant be given a well-arranged dwelling but that the passerby, who views the building from the exterior, should be presented with attractive facades.[73] A final Amsterdam School characteristic is that the composition of the street walls has been inspired by the nature of the location. In the facades of the dwellings on the two squares (Figs. 28–31), vertical caesurae have been accentuated to give a sense of rest and stability, while in those that run down the street (Figs. 32, 33), dynamic rhythms that sweep the eye along have been emphasized.

The dwellings on Henriette Ronnerplein and Therese Schwartzeplein (Types J and K in Fig. 27), are generally credited to de Klerk. Type J is a four-room unit with the living room fronting the square. The kitchen, as customary, is fitted into the space left over behind the entry and the stairs, and faces the garden; two bedrooms are placed beside it. The units on the first and second stories have a third bedroom on the front; those on the third floor have a larger living room instead, with the third bedroom located in the attic story. This difference in dwelling type is indicated on the facade by the fenestration; the broader windows of the first two floors admit light to two adjacent rooms, the narrower ones at the third story only to a living room. The diminution in window width also accommodates the illusionistically sloping walls.

Framing the Type J series are the units in the two-story blocks (Type K). On the ground floor is a small three-room dwelling, and above is a five-room unit. This is comprised on the second floor of a spacious living room and two bedrooms, and on the third story of two more bedrooms, plus generous storage space. The bedrooms are in the rear and are lit by a variety of windows—a prow-shaped one for the small bedroom, rectangular and semitriangular ones for the larger room (Fig. 29). All of the upper level dwellings have access from the kitchen to a balcony; those of Type J are provided with additional storage space in the hollow semicircular walls between those balconies.

The dwellings are separated from one another and from the hall by sturdy bearing walls and are subdivided within by fireproof partitions, the standard Amsterdam system used, for example, in de Klerk's first block for Eigen Haard. Here, as there, the stairs are at the front of the building, but de Klerk has articulated the stairs and the party walls differently, although he has continued to insist on vertical accents. In the block for Eigen Haard the stairhalls provided the dramatic focus of the facade, but in the De Dageraad complex, the division between the dwellings has been stressed. By pulling the wall back at the second-story level (and thereby cutting a piece out of the living rooms of the upper stories), de Klerk has given to what is actually a simple slab the appearance of a row of houses. They are not ordinary houses, to be sure, for the fairy-tale quality he achieved in the Spaarndammerbuurt informs this design as well. They are Brobdingnagian habitations, such as might be drawn by a schoolchild asked to depict the homes of giants, and they express the same attitude about the nature of the inhabitants as was discerned in the work for Eigen Haard, a mixture of admiration and affection. Thus the almost threatening scale of these houses suggests the titanic character of the occupants, yet humorous touches, such as the baskets (Fig. 30) that link the houses and the treatment of the chimneys as enormous faucets, dispel any doubts about the friendliness of the inhabitants. The portions to either end of the row are more modestly scaled, and the red tile roof that is pulled down over the facade to mask the attic storage area confers another domestic touch.

One might say that in this project de Klerk has constructed an architectural model of the ideal socialist society. By the vertical divisions and by the differentiation of each story through color, fenestration, and other details, he has shown that the collective unit shelters individual families. By repetition of forms and by the horizontal linkages created also through color and through details such as the baskets, he has expressed the fact that the families are members of a larger unit, the housing society. He thus has succeeded in striking a balance between the claims of the individual and of the community.

The facades on the aptly-named P. L. Takstraat and Burgomeester Tellegenstraat (marked Cooperatiestraat in Fig. 26) present a more dynamic appearance in keeping with their location on a street rather than a square, yet the same method of indicating each group of dwellings (or parcel) by a sloping and projecting wall prevails. Here, the stairs are located on the rear, but the parcel or stack of dwellings remains the basis of the visual organization. From the Amstel Canal (Fig. 32), the party wall between each group reads as the controlling structure. It begins at right angles to the street, then curves to make the facade, then ceases at the next group, except at the base where it continues into the entryway of the neighboring unit. The effect is rather like waves upon a shore, or perhaps like bolts of cloth unfolding. From the corners (Fig. 34) on the Burgomeester Tellegenstraat (Fig. 35), the rolling rhythms at the roofline carry the eye in the opposite direction. The composition has been designed for the moving observer and, like the traffic, moves up and down the street.

Most of the dwellings here are the three-room type (Fig. 36) marked A on the site plan. On the first two stories are dwellings with a living room and two bedrooms; the top dwellings get an additional bedroom at the rear of the attic story, reached by a private stair. Also on the attic story is the usual storage space, plus an open terrace, sheltered behind the street wall. Balconies are provided on the rear at the second and third story, while the ground floor has direct entry into the garden (Fig. 37).

Wherever the street and the building change direction, the architects have marked it as an event. At D (on the site plan), the stairhall juts out like a prow, and the windows also partake of the third dimension (Figs. 35, 38). The most spectacular of these junctures is at point C (Fig. 34), the climax of the composition. Visually, these famous corners (which contain stairs) collect the counter movements of the long facades and create an episode of epic proportions at their point of meeting. It is here that the shops are located and that the name of the housing society is emblazoned (the corners were altered slightly in execution; compare Figs. 34, 39).

Similarly, where the buildings terminate on the P. L. Takstraat, there is a bold acknowledgment. Volumes interpenetrate, edges are softened, and color

and texture participate to emphasize the plastic wholeness of the building. The viewer is never confronted with lifeless surfaces but is constantly forced to respond to the power of the building as a rich variety of impressions unfolds.

The celebrated corners are the work of Piet Kramer, whose personal style was broader than de Klerk's, being marked by greater emphasis on general forms and less on details. The authorship of the adjoining parts of the building, however, is more problematic. The drawings on file with the Bouw-en Woningtoezicht were signed by both architects, but these include portions known to be by one alone. Then there exists a perspective rendering of the buildings on the P. L. Takstraat that bears only the signature of de Klerk,[74] and the shapes of the windows and patterns of color are certainly met with in other works designed by him. On the other hand, the way the buildings terminate resembles Kramer's handling of 90° angles. It is true that Kramer, when discussing the project with a member of the city council,[75] spoke as if de Klerk had been its guiding genius, but that may have been due to his natural modesty and his desire to pay homage to his late friend. Perhaps the soundest conclusion is that these portions were designed jointly. The exact attributions, in any case, are less important than the fact that two architects could together produce a work marked simultaneously by such unity and such individuality. That is one of the striking achievements of the Amsterdam School—each building was unique yet exhibited a recognizably collective style.

The complexes of Eigen Haard and De Dageraad that have been described constitute only a small part of the fine housing erected by the woningbouwvereenigingen of red Amsterdam.[76] They are probably the most striking examples, but there are other extremely satisfying groups that make the Spaarndammerbuurt and Amsterdam South a necessary pilgrimage for the person interested in architecture and politics. This housing could not have been erected without the support of the national government, but the municipality played the major role in fostering it and keeping the housing societies solvent during difficult times. It was the municipal officials who demanded that the working-class districts be a worthy and dignified addition to the beautiful, existing cityscape of Amsterdam.

Political ends were an inherent ingredient of the housing schemes, because the projects had to be approved by the elected representatives on the city council. All of the dwellings constructed by the housing societies with the assistance of the city contributed to raising the physical level of housing, and most of them attained an unusual degree of attractiveness as well. But the housing designed by members of the Amsterdam School and erected by the social democratic woningbouwvereenigingen achieved more than that. It seems to be a genuine embodiment of Keppler's challenge. It was new, it was monumental, and it commemorated in permanent materials the courage of the men and women who inhabit it. Might not the observer familiar with the history of the SDAP see in many of the forms of De Dageraad an evocation of the massed standards of a May Day parade? To either side of the corners, the flags stream forth, slightly overlapping as they are borne aloft. At some points, red pennants seem to flutter from the roofline. Finally, at the corners, the banner of De Dageraad itself looms on high. Its windwhipped folds have been permanently cast in masonry and form an enduring monument to the struggle, and brief triumph, of Amsterdam's working class.

Notes

1
Keppler received a degree in civil engineering from the Technical High School at Delft. In 1905 he went to Amsterdam to work in the Department of Building and Housing Inspection; in 1908 he was named Inspector in that department, with the special task of running the section in charge of housing. This section was made into a separate agency in 1915—the Gemeentelijke Woningdienst (Municipal Housing Service)—with Keppler as its director. He held this position as a very active and outspoken official until his retirement in 1937. He made no secret of his social democratic sympathies, to the chagrin of some of the right-wing members of the city council, particularly as he believed in sparing no expense to provide workers of all ranks with sound and attractive dwellings. When the Woningdienst needed new quarters, one of Keppler's critics suggested that his office be moved to the Mint!

2
Keppler's speech was reported in *De Bouwwereld*, 11 (1912): 24. "Ten slotte spoorde de spreker de architecten aan belang te stellen in den strijd der arbeidersklasse. Eerst als gij iets voor den strijd voelt, zult gij hunne [woningbouw]vereenigingensgebouwen, de monumenten van hun strijd, schoon kunnen bouwen." Architectura et Amicitia was a club for architects and those interested in architecture as an art. For a discussion of its importance in the development of an Amsterdam housing style, see the author's *Housing in Holland and the Amsterdam School* (Diss., Yale University, 1971), pp. 206–215.

3
See, for example, his statement that "nothing can be too beautiful for the workers who have done without so much for so long," made in answer to a question about the luxury of some of Amsterdam's working-class housing. Quoted in *Le Soir* of Brussels, October, 1920.

4
For the general political history of the Netherlands, see especially P. E. Kramer, *The Societal State* (Meppel, 1966); and Dr. Willem Verkade, *Democratic Parties in the Low Countries and Germany* (Leiden, 1965). For working-class movements and the development of socialism, see Dr. I. J. Brugmans, *De Arbeidende Klasse in Nederland in de 19e eeuw* (The Hague, 1929); Henriette Roland Holst, *Kapitaal en Arbeid in Nederland* (Rotterdam, 1932); J. J. 't Hoen,

Op naar het licht: De Zaanstreek in de periode van de opkomst der arbeidersbeweging, 1882–1909 (Wormerveer, 1968); and especially H. van Hulst, A. Pleysier, and A. Scheffer, *Het Roode Vaandel volgen wij* (The Hague, 1969). I would also like to cite here the superb resources in the Instituut voor Sociale Geschiedenis in Amsterdam.

5
Friedrich Engels, *The Condition of the Working-class in England in 1844* (London, 1892).

6
Every commentator on the nineteenth-century working class in Holland has made this point. Thus Brugmans, *De Arbeidende Klasse*, pp. 178–181: "If we consider the personality of the worker as a whole, we see before us someone who remains at an extremely low level of existence, who lacks the spiritual and physical strength to raise himself up, whose development is too slight to even think of the possibility of an improvement in his lot." And H. Roland-Holst could still write in the twentieth century: "With capitalism in the Netherlands comes the modern workers' movement. But that movement is weak, uncertain and unusually subject to disintegration. It shows a notable lack of solidarity, regulated growth and stability," *Kapitaal*, 1: 5–6.

7
The first International was the IWMA—the International Working Man's Association, which grew out of the trade union movement. As a result of theoretical and personal rivalries, such as those between orthodox Marxists and anarchists, the First International effectively ceased in 1871. The Second International, founded in 1889, was not free from conflict, but in 1896 the anarchists were expelled and the International, while remaining Marxist, granted the possibility of parliamentary action. The nationalist passions stirred by World War I wrought havoc on the Second International, though some socialist parties continued to support it. With the founding of the Third or Communist International (Comintern) in 1919, the schism between the essentially democratic socialist parties and the extreme left-wing factions that supported bolshevism, was confirmed. See David Caute, *The Left in Europe Since 1789* (New York-Toronto, 1966); and Leslie Derfler, *Socialism Since Marx* (New York, 1973).

8
In this they were similar to the model dwelling agencies in England, which J. N. Tarn, *Working-class Housing in 19th century Britain* (London, 1971), describes as "philanthropic in name but effectively commercial organizations dependent on profit of some kind." The first Dutch society was founded in Amsterdam in 1852, the Vereeniging ten behoeve van de arbeidersklasse. See Helen Mercier, *Over Arbeiderswoningen* (1887); and Frank Smit, "Geboorte van de volkshuisvesting," *Wonen TA/BK*, No. 13, 1973.

9
The Anti-Revolutionary party, founded in 1879, was mainly the party of the *kleine luyden*, the petit bourgeoisie. Most of its members belonged to the very orthodox Gereformeerde Kerk. Another Calvinist political party was made up of the less puritanical and more anti-Catholic members of the Hervormde Kerk—this was the Christian Historical Union. See Stanley Henig, ed., *European Political Parties* (New York), pp. 259–260; and Kraemer, *Societal State*, p. 95.

10
There was a minor disturbance in Amsterdam, but this was evidently fostered mainly by German immigrant laborers. See Brugmans, *De Arbeidende Klasse*, pp. 188–190.

11

Hoen, *Opnaar het licht,* p. 124.

12

The first formal socialist organization in the Netherlands was the Sociaal Democratische Vereeniging, founded in 1879. There had been individuals who had allied themselves with socialism by joining the First International, but most of these had been members of the Liberal intelligentsia rather than working men. Many belonged to an organization of freethinkers called De Dageraad (Dawn), established in 1856. With its wholeheartedly democratic and anticlerical orientation, De Dageraad became a breeding ground for many who would lead the socialist movement.

13

Derfler, *Socialism Since Marx,* p. 10.

14

The SDB continued to have strength, particularly in certain quarters in Amsterdam, and within the SDAP itself extremist tendencies similar to those held by anarchists manifested themselves. in 1909 a dissident group split off to form the Sociaal Democratische Partij, SDP, which revealed its true sympathies when it changed its name in 1917 to the Dutch Communist Party (*Roode Vaandel,* p. 25). The Communists in Amsterdam held a few seats on the city council and were violent enemies of the SDAP, accusing them of opportunism and capitulation to the capitalist parties. The insults they hurled at social democrats, recorded in the *Amsterdam Gemeenteblad* (the published minutes of all the meetings of the Amsterdam City Council) make lively reading.

15

These included Henri Polak (1868–1943), chief of the powerful Diamond Workers' Union, and P. J. Troelstra (1860–1930), the head of the party.

16

Na Tien Jaar: Gedenkschrift bij het Tienjarig bestaan der Soc. Demo. Arb. Partij (Amsterdam, 1904), p. 4.

17

Ibid., pp. 6–7.

18

The Liberals, predictably, were split up into factions. The Free Liberals were comparatively conservative, the Liberal Union members were moderate, and the Radical Liberals were relatively left-wing. See Verkade, *Democratic Parties,* passim.

19

The 1913 elections brought the left fifty-five seats. The Liberals wanted to form a government that would include the SDAP and offered that party three portfolios. The party refused to accept ministerial responsibility however, because of its belief in the Marxist doctrine of class struggle; that is, the party could not condone bourgeois action, however enlightened, to the extent of participating in the government. This event is lengthily reported in *Roode Vaandel,* pp. 36–47.

20

The results of the 1918 election, in which for the first time all adult male citizens could vote, might be inserted here to underscore the extremely sectarian character of Dutch society. No fewer than thirty-two parties competed in that election, and eight obtained one seat each. The remaining ninety-two seats were split among nine parties. Since each party or religious group tends to have its own press and radio, its own schools. unions, social organizations, and housing societies, the divisive nature of life is further increased.

21

This can be measured by the membership in the union organizations affiliated with major political parties. By 1914 the membership of the NVV (Nederlandsche Verbond van Vakvereenigingen), associated with the SDAP, comprised 31% of all workers, compared with 3.6% for the anarchosyndicalist, 9.7% for the Catholic, and 4.6% for the Protestant organizations. See Verkade, *Democratic Parties,* p. 50.

22

The municipal council (Gemeenteraad) is the legislative branch, while executive power is vested in the College of Mayor and Aldermen—B en W (Burgomeester en Wethouders). The council is elected directly, the mayor is appointed by the crown, and until recently the aldermen were elected by the council from among its own members.

23

Wibaut was a major figure in the SDAP. He had been born a Roman Catholic but renounced his religion while still in his teens and subsequently, driven by compassion for the working class, he became a socialist. He began as a Fabian but after 1906 embraced Marxism, and for a time he belonged to the extreme left section of the SDAP. However, after accepting a seat on the council, he became more willing to work through elective office, although "he never let his position in the municipal administration come into conflict with the class interests of the workers." See *Roode Vaandel,* p. 81. A man of great intelligence and high ideals, he continued his service to housing when he moved from the position of wethouder for housing to wethouder for finances in 1921. See F. M. Wibaut, *Levensbouw* (Amsterdam, 1936).

24

I am not certain where this term originated, but the social democrats continually used it in the meetings of the city council to justify municipal expenditures on housing. It appears, for example, in *The Builder,* April 21, 1922, p. 594.

25

Tellegen had been trained as an engineer. His experience as director of the Department of Municipal Works in Arnheim stood him in good stead when he moved to Amsterdam in 1900 to set up its Bouw-en Woningtoezicht, the first such installation in the Netherlands to be organized along the lines of a modern agency. See E. F. Samson "40 jaar Woningtoezicht," *Tijdschrift voor Volkshuisvesting* (February, 1943).

26

Some commentators believed that it was the pressure of the workers' movement and the presence of three socialists in the Second Chamber that forced the inclusion of the financial paragraphs in the bill. See, for example, Jacques Nycolaas and Rein Geurtsen, "70 jaar Woningwet," *Plan,* vol. 9, 1972. For the history and provisions of the housing act, see *De Woningwet 1902–1929,* ed. H. P. J. Bloemers (Amsterdam, 1930), and *50 Jaar Woningwet,* ed. G. van der Flier et al. (Alphen a.d. Rijn, 1952). For an English summary, see Catherine Bauer, *Modern Housing* (Boston, 1934).

27

Among them, *Kort Verslag aan den Koning . . .* (Short Report to the King about the needs and arrangement of workers' housing), 1853; the report of the Staatscommissie voor de Arbeidersenquete, 1892; and the report of the Maatschappij tot Nut van 't Algemeen (Society for the General Good) 1896.

28
Probably British laws in the public health and housing domain had the most influence on the shape and extent of the Dutch Housing Act. (French laws were not as extensive as British, and German housing reform had not yet attained state levels but mainly occurred through the action of the municipality.) In the third quarter of the nineteenth century, England established precedents for the dual requirements of destroying insalubrious housing and encouraging the creation of healthy new dwellings. A number of public health acts passed after 1851 granted local authorities (the English equivalent of the Dutch municipality) statutory powers to improve housing and eventually to demolish slums. Lord Shaftesbury's Act of 1851, allowing the authorities to establish lodging houses, though it was not utilized very often, was the beginning of a series of Housing Acts that encouraged local authorities to build working-class housing. Nevertheless, at the time the Dutch Act was passed, Britain had no *national* system of subsidies as envisaged by the Dutch law.

29
A very helpful discussion of the financial problems encountered by the private builder is to be found in the master's thesis of F. C. D. van Wijk, *De volkshuisvesting te Amsterdam 1850–1914*, Economische Instituut voor de Bouwnijverheid (1973). Mr. van Wijk gave invaluable advice to the author.

30
Most European countries had some type of housing association by the beginning of the twentieth century. Such semiprivate agencies were sometimes called public utility societies, when they received support from the municipalities or from the state, directly or through such institutions as national pension banks. Thus the woningbouwvereenigingen were not unique; they probably resembled most closely those German housing associations with trade union affiliations. But they did have the Dutch stigmata of being narrowly defined not merely along trade or class lines but according to religious or political affiliation. For a summary of types of housing societies existing at this time in Europe, see the article on "Housing" in the 11th edition of the *Encyclopaedia Brittannica*, and Catherine Bauer, *Modern Housing*.

31
Most of the societies have published memorial booklets, and the information about their history, membership, and goals is culled from such sources. The author is grateful for the resources of the Gemeentelijke Archiefdienst, the Nationale Woningraad, and the Instituut for Sociale Geschiedenis.

32
The average workingman's salary during the war years ranged from 11 to 25 guilders a week (this figure is from M. J. van der Flier, *War Finances in the Netherlands up to 1918* [Oxford, 1923], p. 107); after the war, wages, like prices, rose considerably. The Dutch consider that no more than one-sixth of one's income should be allotted to rent. The rents of the housing societies varied, according to the size of the dwelling, from about 3.25 to 4.75 guilders weekly during the period under review. To allow them to maintain such rents after 1918, when building costs became astronomical, national and local authorities subsidized the societies.

33
There was one housing society, De Arbeiderswoning, established under the provisions of the Woningwet with the goal of providing dwellings for large families at low rents; it was philanthropic in that it was composed not of the tenants but of housing reformers. Government subsidies were necessary to enable the society to fulfill its aim, but the difficulties, not only financial but also managerial (for example, teaching slum families how to be good tenants) proved so insurmountable that the municipality had to take over the society in 1918.

34
In 1925, 4,836 Amsterdam families lived in dwellings operated by the municipality, all of which were subsidized, and 8,331 lived in housing owned by the housing societies, of which 5,229 were subsidized. Information from a report made by the *Gemeentelijke Woningdienst*, published in the *Gemeenteblad* (1925), Afd. 1, Bijlage E.

35
Gemeenteblad (1905), Afd. 2, 953.

36
Maatschappij tot het Bevordering der Bouwkunst (MBVA) and Bond van Nederlandse Architekten (BNA), *Regelen en tabel voor de berekening en uitbetaling van het honorarium van architecten,* 1915; and MBVA, BNA, and Nationale Woningraad, *Regelen en tabel voor de berekening en uitbetaling van het honorarium van architecten, voor bouwwerken voor woningbouwvereenigingen . . .* (1916).

37
For a discussion of these dwellings, see the author's "Eigen Haard: Workers' Housing and the Amsterdam School," *Architectura*, 2 (1971): 150–152.

38
Gemeente Amsterdam, *Amsterdam: Stadsontwikkeling, Volkshuisvesting,* Amsterdam, 2d ed. (1925), p. 27.

39
That is, the social democratic left. Following Engels (*Zur Wohnungsfrage;* published in Dutch as *Over het Woningvraagstuk* in 1872–1873), the far left (those who were anarchists and those who would become communists in 1917) believed that palliative measures were counterproductive in that they postponed the revolution and ultimately aided the capitalists. Engels' solution, echoed by the communist members of the Amsterdam gemeenteraad, was the redistribution of the dwelling supply according to need (that is, size of family), with rents based on ability to pay. While social democrats like Wibaut and Keppler believed in municipally subsidized housing for the poorest families, they did not favor the idea of redistribution.

40
Figures from "De Goedkoope bouw der bouwondernemers," *Tijdschrift voor Volkshuisvesting,* 1 (1920): 127.

41
H. G. van Beusekom, *Getijden der volkshuisvesting* (Alphen a.d. Rijn, 1955), p. 108.

42
For the Amsterdam School see Wolfgang Pehnt, *Expressionist Architecture* (New York, 1973); G. Fanelli, *Architettura moderna in Olanda* (Firenze, 1968); and Reyner Banham, *Theory and Design in the First Machine Age* (London, 1960). The excellent catalogue *Amsterdamse School,* published in August, 1975, in connection with the Stedelijk Museum's exhibition of the same title, is accessible only to those who read Dutch. The most complete discussion in English remains the author's *Housing in Holland and the Amsterdam School* (Diss., Yale University, 1971).

43
Hille gave de Klerk his first significant commission. This was for a block of luxury flats (*Hillehuis*) on the Johannes Vermeerplein, which was completed in 1912. As with the Amsterdam School, so with de Klerk: the most complete up-to-date considerations thus far are in English, and unpublished. See Suzanne Shuloff Frank, *Michel de Klerk (1884–1923): An Architect of the Amsterdam School* (Diss., Columbia University, 1970), as well as the author's doctoral thesis. For recent discussions of de Klerk's entire complex around the Spaarndammerplantsoen, see Suzanne S. Frank, "Michel de Klerk's Designs for Amsterdam's Spaarndammerbuurt," *Nederlands Kunsthistorische Jaarboek* (1971), and the author's article cited in note 37.

44
Eigen Haard, *40 jarig bestaan* (1949), and *De Gouden Mijlpaal* (1959).

45
Leliman was a fairly traditional architect whose basic sympathies lay with the strong current of rationalism propounded by the Netherlands' most respected and internationally known architect, H. P. Berlage. Leliman introduced no new motifs in his work, but in accord with rationalist practice, simplified and economized, emphasizing the structural elements of the building. He was an author (*Het Stadswoonhuis in Nederland, Het Moderne Landhuis in Nederland*), and he founded in 1901 and published until his death the periodical *De Bouwwereld*. This could be counted on for a jaundiced view of the Amsterdam School, but it gave useful information to architects about the Woningwet and their obligations toward the housing societies.

46
Figures from *De Gouden Mijlpaal* and from the *Gemeenteblad*.

47
This attitude came through very clearly at the housing congress held in Amsterdam in February 1918. There was a discussion of the proposal of the engineer, J. van der Waerden, to create a few standard dwelling types which could be built throughout the country and which, by being standardized, could be constructed quickly and cheaply. It was the representatives of the unions and the housing societies who spoke out most strongly against this proposal. Berlage, on the other hand, defended it in a special lecture. The proposal and the lectures are printed in *Normalisatie in Woningbouw* (Rotterdam, 1918). I have summarized the issues on pp. 155–163 of my article "Berlage and Housing, 'the most significant modern dwelling type'" (*Nederlands Kunsthistorische Jaarboek 1974*, 25: 133–179).

48
De Bouwwereld, 17 (1918), 152. "Dit ontwerp met zijne ingewikkelde en gezochte *Spielereiën*—product van een dekadente kunstopvatting—is blijkbaar voornamelijk, zoo al niet uitsluitend naar het uiterlijk gewaardeerd." It is significant that Leliman uses the *German* word for games, or childish pastimes; he considered that the Amsterdam School was heavily dependent on German sources. In another article he called its members mere "phrasemakers" and applied to them Rodin's judgment: "They called it originality but it was nothing" (*De Bouwwereld*, 1919 [18], p. 4). Leliman further believed that economic conditions forbade *luxe-bouw*, especially in housing, and recommended that it be prevented in Holland by legislation as it had been in England and Germany (*De Bouwwereld*, 1920 [19], p. 1).

49
De Klerk's father was a diamond worker. The family was Jewish and resided in the Joodenbuurt, the Jewish quarter, one of the inner-city slums of Amsterdam. See Suzanne Frank's dissertation, and the doctoral exam of A. W. F. M. Meij for the Kunsthistorische Instituut, Utrecht, 1968.

50
Frank, "Michel de Klerk's Designs," p. 202.

51
The train imagery would be even more apt if Eigen Haard had been "formed by rail workers," as Frank states in her article, p. 180, but I have been unable to corroborate this point. It is true that a number of the first members of Eigen Haard were employed by Werkspoor, a company that manufactured products used by the railroad industry. The report cited in n. 34 of this chapter surveyed the occupations of Eigen Haard's tenants in 1925 and found that 158 of them were metalworkers, 133 worked in the service of the municipality, 76 worked in stores and offices, 48 were dockworkers, 22 carpenters, and 18 railroad workers, to name a few of the more popular occupations. I regret to say that Eigen Haard itself was very uncooperative and refused to answer any of my questions.

52
See the author's "Eigen Haard," pp. 161–164.

53
De Klerk's own words, from a statement submitted to *Bouwkundig Weekblad*, 36 (1916): 331–332.

54
See the two letters cited in the author's "Eigen Haard," p. 175, where two workers' wives express their pleasure in de Klerk's architectural creations.

55
Figures from *De Gouden Mijlpaal* and from the *Gemeenteblad*.

56
Gemeenteblad (1920), Afd. 2, pp. 1387 ff.

57
Gulden founded the firm of Gulden en Geldmaker, which was responsible for the designs of many Woningwet dwellings. Stylistically Gulden may be considered a member of the Amsterdam School.

58
Gemeenteblad (1920), Afd. 2, pp. 1389–1390.

59
Ibid., pp. 1392–1396.

60
According to councilman Peters, one of the Roman Catholic faction, fine Groningen brick was used in this block, which was most unusual for workers' housing; its beautiful warm red color does enhance the wall surfaces. Also many of the bricks had to be hand formed into the innumerably varied shapes de Klerk had specified.

61
De Gouden Mijlpaal, p. 21.

62
There was no connection with the freethinkers' organization of the same name, mentioned in note 7. At first the housing society was called the *Amsterdamse Woningstichting De Dageraad*, then in 1921 the *woningbouwvereeniging De Dageraad* was established and the two were merged.

63
50-Jaar Arbeiderswoningbouwvereeniging De Dageraad
(Amsterdam, 1966), p. 3.

64
For an account of the life and thought of this great Dutch
architect, see P. Singelenberg, *H. P. Berlage: Idea and Style*
(Utrecht, 1972). Regrettably, Berlage's activities as a city
planner are not discussed in this otherwise excellent
monograph.

65
Berlage's first scheme was created in 1904, but it was too
picturesque and rural for Amsterdam's needs, and he made
a new plan in 1915. Portions of it were executed as designed; for example, the area south of the Amstel Canal
along the Vrijheidslaan and the western section around the
Marathonweg.

66
These are on file at the Bouw-en Woningtoezicht. I am indebted to the secretary of the archive, Mr. H. de Koning,
for his kind cooperation and assistance.

67
There is no recent monograph on Kramer. A small booklet
by W. Retera Wzn. exists in the series *Nederlandsche
Bouwmeesters,* published in 1927.

68
The information about these institutions has been culled by
the author from polemical pamphlets and articles that
hardly offer objective historical data but are the only
sources. For the CBV I referred to an undated pamphlet
issued by lobbyists for the private building industry, called
simply De CBV, and to the *Gemeenteblad.* For the
Federatie van Zelfstandige Groepen, I read *Het Bouwvak,
1919–1923,* the organ of the Landelijke Federatie van
Bouwvakarbeiders; *Het Bouwbedrijf, 1922–1923,* the
organ of the Federatie van groepen, and a pamphlet by L.
B. Spanjer, *De Broederstrijd in het bouwbedrijf te Amsterdam: Tragedie der Wankelmoedigen,* no date. These scarce
pamphlets and trade papers are available at the Instituut
voor Sociale Geschiedenis, Amsterdam.

69
In *De CBV,* it is said that the government threatened to stop
all deliveries of coal to brick manufacturers who would not
sell to the CBV at low prices.

70
Keppler's hand may be seen behind the Federatie van
groepen, and in 1922 he addressed their congress. In 1918
he had tried to form a bouwgilde, based on the English
building guilds and the German bauhütte, but this organization never took hold. The Federatie van groepen, however, followed some of the principles of the bouwgilde, but
it too disappeared from the scene in the later 1920s.

71
The printed specifications are on file at the Gemeentelijke
Archiefdienst.

72
Amsterdam was the leader in this movement; there were
thirteen productive associations elsewhere in the Netherlands with 300 members. Information from *Het Bouwvak*
(1922).

73
From an interview by Edmond Visser in *De Vrijheid,*
August 13, 1924.

74
The drawing is in the possession of the *Documentatiecen-
trum voor de bouwkunst,* Amsterdam.

75
Gemeenteblad (1926), Afd. 2, p. 1107.

76
In a future publication I hope to examine all of the
Woningwet housing erected in Amsterdam in the first quar-
ter of the century.

14
The Emperor and the Duce: The Planning of Piazzale Augusto Imperatore in Rome

Spiro Kostof

In memory of Ernest Nash

On 22 October 1934, a few days before the twelfth anniversary of the Fascist march on Rome, Benito Mussolini stood on the roof of a building on Vicolo Soderini and delivered a brief address to a crowd of workers and dignitaries (Fig. 1). They had gathered for the start of demolitions that would liberate the mausoleum of the emperor Augustus from the untidy accretion of centuries. The Duce said that this ambitious project, which must be completed within three years in time for the bimillennial of the emperor's birth, had a triple utility: that of history and beauty, that of traffic, and that of hygiene.[1] Many streets would have to disappear, as had many for the opening of Via dell'Impero several years before. One had to make an effort now to recall those streets as one went by. He enumerated them for his audience: Via Alessandrina, Via S. Lorenzo, Via del Lauro, Via Salara Vecchia, Via della Croce Bianca, Via Bonella, Via del Priorato, Via delle Marmorelle, Via Cremona, Via dei Carbonari, Via S. Lorenzo ai Monti, over an area of forty thousand square meters. And for the liberation of the mausoleum the following streets would have to go: Via dei Pontefici, Via delle Colonnette in part, Vicolo Soderini where this ceremony was taking place, Via degli Schiavoni, Vicolo degli Schiavoni, Vicolo del Grottino—one hundred and twenty houses in all, covering an area of twenty-seven thousand square meters. This project too, with the creation of a large piazza and a wide passage toward the Corso, would be of the greatest benefit to urban traffic, as Via dell'Impero had been. It was not then a matter of archaeology alone but of the imposing and continual life of the city.

As for the houses to be demolished, they represented a grave backwardness with respect to health. The Duce assured his audience that he had ordered that a thorough photographic record be made of the exterior and interior of the condemned buildings, to satisfy "some rare survival of nostalgia for so-called local color."[2]

Finally, there was a fourth benefit to be derived from the work he was about to initiate. "With this project of demolition and the construction of new buildings, we provide jobs for three years to numerous workers in every category."

And then he raised his pick with the exhortation, "la parola al piccone!"

By mid-1937, the pick had done its work. A vast area of some one hundred thousand square meters, circumscribed by the Tiber and the Corso to the west and east, Via della Frezza to the north, and Via Tomacelli to the south, had been cleared of its buildings (Fig. 2). The mausoleum of the first emperor of Rome, freestanding again after at least one thousand years, looked for a time desolate and unfamiliar in the giant hollow, at the edges of which browsed the churches of S. Carlo al Corso, S. Rocco, and S. Girolamo degli Schiavoni. The scene—"grandeur and abandon"—reminded one observer of a print by Piranesi.[3] In physical size, Romans had been repeatedly and pridefully told, the new piazza would surpass Piazza del Popolo to its north. But to get his splendid oval, Giuseppe Valadier had merely enlarged an existing square of considerable size. The new Piazzale Augusto Imperatore had been carved out of dense urban tissue, where the only public space had been the tiny Piazza degli Otto Cantoni, almost a perfect square in shape, in the solid construction between the mausoleum and the Corso.

Although the liberation of the mausoleum was of the first priority and the Duce's inaugural picking took place in its immediate vicinity, the actual demolition proceeded from the periphery inward. The mausoleum could thus continue to serve for a while longer as Rome's symphony hall, the Augusteo, a function it had fulfilled since 1907. The last concert was held there on 13 May 1936. By this time the area bounded by Via della Frezza, Via di Ripetta, Via degli Schiavoni, and the Corso had been bared. Soon afterward the foundations were laid for the new buildings that were to define the piazzale on its north and east sides (Fig. 3). In January 1937 the Palazzo Valdambrini (Soderini) to the north of S. Rocco, built by cardinal Riminaldi in 1774, was brought down. The Palazzo Correa, abutting on the mausoleum and fronting on Via dei Pontefici, came down in March. The last to be cleared were the buildings between Via di Ripetta and the river; and the buildings along the south side of the new piazzale with only three exceptions—the palazzetto of the Torlonia at the corner of Via Tomacelli and Largo degli Schiavoni, built ca. 1910 from the designs of Gustavo Giovannoni; a late nineteenth-century palazzo a little to the west; and the Unione Militare building at the corner of Via Tomacelli and the Corso.

The restoration of the mausoleum was speedily concluded, under the direction of Antonio Muñoz in time for the bimillennial of Augustus's birth, celebrated spectacularly, with many ceremonies and a vast exhibition, from September 1937 to September 1938. But the peripheral buildings of the piazzale were not completed until 1941, the last major structure to rise being the Collegio degli Illirici on the Via Tomacelli side, adjacent to S. Girolamo. Still, the achievement was remarkable. It had taken about six years to create in the thick of Rome one of the largest of its squares—and also one of the least known and least attractive (Fig. 4). To the Duce and his regime it was one more essential Fascist monument in the name of archaeology, better circulation,

slum clearance, and the curbing of unemployment. That is, a work of political propaganda—illustrating not only the general worthiness of the regime that these stated objectives stood for but in this instance a historical congruity as well between Augustus, the founder of the Roman empire, and Benito Mussolini, who had brought it back to life.

Most urban surgery in Rome during the Fascist decades had been anticipated in earlier proposals, but the Duce's untrammeled power could actually dispose of these now, often in grander and costlier form. The liberation of the Mausoleum of Augustus is no exception. It was first seriously advanced in the Piano Regolatore of 1909, the second official master plan for the city since its designation in 1870 as the national capital of a united Italy. We may discount a project by Giuseppe Valadier about one hundred years earlier, because it involved only partial clearing of the building's circumference, and also because it was unconcerned with any larger scheme of urban circulation.

The mausoleum in the early nineteenth century served as an amphitheater. It had been converted to this use in 1789 by its new owner, the Marchese Francesco Saverio Vivaldi-Armentieri, who had acquired the property from the Correa family.[4] In the mid-sixteenth century the interior of the mausoleum had been laid out as a hanging garden for the Soderini family, and it still maintained this form when Vivaldi-Armentieri, (or more probably a Correa tenant, the Spaniard Bernardo Mates) decided to overlay this with a bull ring of wood. In 1796 Vincenzo Correa improved the structure and extended the program to include, besides bullfights, musical events, sack races, and fireworks. Valadier's scheme, dated in 1814, aimed at improving upon the design of the amphitheater and its setting (Fig. 5).[5] A new piazza was to be opened to the east, by destroying the block of houses defined by Vicolo degli Otto Cantoni, Vicolo Soderini, and Via delle Colonnette. The small Piazza degli Otto Cantoni would be retained but would now become the southeastern protrusion of the new trapezoidal piazza. A monumental entrance to the amphitheater from the Ripetta was to be cut between the Palazzo Valdambrini/Soderini and the block of S. Rocco. Finally, the interior of the amphitheater would be crowned by a continuous row of columns in the original manner of the Colosseum.

Nothing came of this project, and Valadier had to content himself with covering the amphitheater by a *velario* (awning). Bullfights were prohibited in 1829 and fireworks a few years later. The Anfiteatro Corea [*sic*] led a desultory existence as an equine circus until the late nineteenth century, when it was acquired by the state. For some years it housed the

1
Mussolini inaugurates the clearance
project of the Mausoleum of Augustus, 22 October 1934. (From
Capitolium, 13, 1938, p. 491)

2
Mausoleum of Augustus exposed,
1937. The dome in the background
belongs to S. Rocco; to its left, the
north side of Via Tomacelli in the
process of demolition. (Museo di
Roma, C/3558)

3
Aerial view of Piazzale Augusto Imperatore under construction, early 1938. Fabbricato *B* is to the right, and along the river in the background the Busiri Vici block is being demolished. (Aerofototeca, Rome)

4
Aerial view of Piazzale Augusto Imperatore today; the Ara Pacis is in the bottom left-hand corner. (Fototeca Unione, 4371)

5
Map of the area around the
Mausoleum of Augustus as of 1870.
(From *Studi per una operante storia
urbana di Roma* [Rome, 1963])

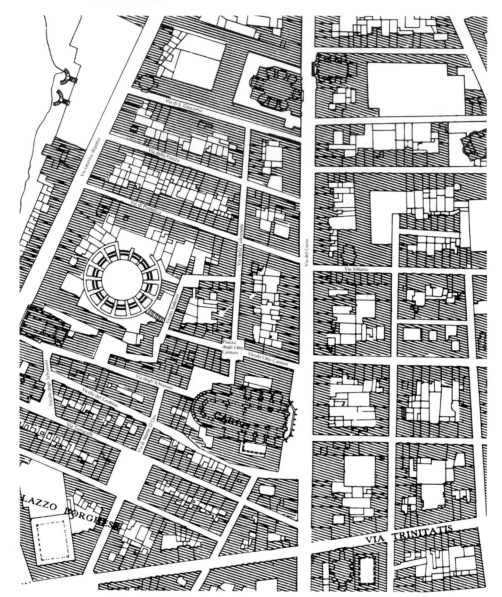

studio of the sculptor Enrico Chiaradia, in which he fashioned the giant equestrian statue of Victor Emanuel II for the monument on Piazza Venezia to this first king of Italy. Later the building was ceded to the commune of Rome and converted into a concert hall called Augusteo at the initiative of Conte Enrico di San Martino, then president of the Reggia Accademia di Santa Cecilia, and according to the designs of one Rebacchi (Fig. 6).

The Piano Regolatore of 1909 was not interested in altering this aspect of the Augusteo but rather in revealing its original form externally by freeing the circumference wall of the ancient mausoleum. On the north side only, the Palazzo Correa would continue to abut upon the building. Around the historic monument a modest and odd-shaped heptagonal piazza was to be created (Fig. 7). Actually, this latter arrangement was almost an afterthought. The mausoleum was simply benefiting from the fact that it sat between the busy new quarters of modern Rome to the east, such as Monti and Esquilino, and the developing quarters north of the Borgo. The need for a major artery to connect these two became imperative when the population of Prati di Castello on the right bank, beyond the Vatican and Castel Sant'Angelo, rose to about thirty thousand by the end of the first decade of this century.

The development of Prati was very much a matter of dispute in 1873, when the first Piano Regolatore for modern Rome was being drawn up. Even in 1883 when the plan was made legal, less than three thousand people had moved into new housing there. The city was committed during those years to the completion of Via Nazionale and Corso Vittorio Emanuele. These formed the main east-west artery of modern Rome, starting at the train station and cutting through the papal city by way of Piazza Venezia, to end up at the Borgo by means of the new Ponte Vittorio Emanuele. Consequently, the first Piano Regolatore left the urban fabric north of Corso Vittorio intact, with the exception of some minor revision in the area around Piazza dell'Oca. The growth of the city since then, however, had brought about new traffic needs, of which east-west passage north of Via Nazionale/Corso Vittorio was of considerable urgency.[6]

The Piano Regolatore of 1909 proposed to open a wide avenue at precisely a ninety-degree angle to Via del Corso, which still remained the main north-south axis of the city.[7] The new avenue was to commence east of the Corso with a widened Via della Croce and then be carried west of the Corso in a straight line until it linked up with Via di Ripetta just north of S. Girolamo degli Schiavoni. Beyond the Ripetta, the ragged outline of the Lungotevere that had resulted from the recent construction of massive embankments for the Tiber was to be filled

up with new buildings, so as to present, from Ponte Cavour to Via della Frezza, a smooth concave frontage paralleling the curve of the embankment.

The proposed avenue was designed to assist with the traffic between Piazza di Spagna and Piazza Cavour north of Castel Sant'Angelo. The burden of linking these two foci was carried only by a tramline, established a few years earlier by the liberal city administration of Ernesto Nathan. It ran along Via Condotti and the recently widened Via Tomacelli. Nathan had given assurances that this would be a temporary solution. With the prevalence of other means of transportation in the near future, the tram would be put underground to spare the characteristic Via Condotti the curse of fixed tracks. In the meantime, the Piano Regolatore of 1909 proposed to move the tracks from Via Condotti/Tomacelli to Via della Croce and its new direct extension along the Augusteo.

These provisions were not executed. Expropriation laws, overwhelmingly in favor of property owners, made progress difficult and the cost prohibitive. In addition, the new artery along the Augusteo was considered complementary to the more important improvements in the area of Via Due Macelli-Via Tritone that had precedence. The war interrupted the realization of the Piano Regolatore altogether. Only with the advent of Fascist government in 1922 could attention be focused again on planning.

By this time both altered conditions in the physical makeup of the city and the realities of expropriation, as well as ideological demands made upon the historic city by the new regime, required substantial revision in the master plan. A municipal commission was appointed by the Reggio Commissario pel Comune di Roma to study the plan. Their work was incorporated in a Variante Generale, prepared in 1924 and published in two installments in 1925/1926. Marcello Piacentini and Gustavo Giovannoni, two of the most influential personalities in the Fascist remaking of Rome, were members of this commission; and their current view—that the older city be tampered with as little as possible while the major thrust of modern development be confined to the historically less burdened periphery—seems to have prevailed.

For the area around the Augusteo, this view showed itself in the abandonment of the straight avenue that would continue the line of Via della Croce all the way to the Ripetta (Fig. 8). Rather than the dictates of traffic, which favor abstraction, the commission chose to be guided by the integrity of the chief historic buildings in the area, so that not only was the Augusteo to be disengaged completely from surrounding construction, including the Palazzo Correa spared by the Piano Regolatore of 1909, but

6
Section of Rebacchi's remodeling of
the Augusteo. (Museo di Roma,
B/213)
7
Scheme for the mausoleum and its
periphery: The Piano Regolatore of
1909. (From *Capitolium* 9, 1933, p.
114)

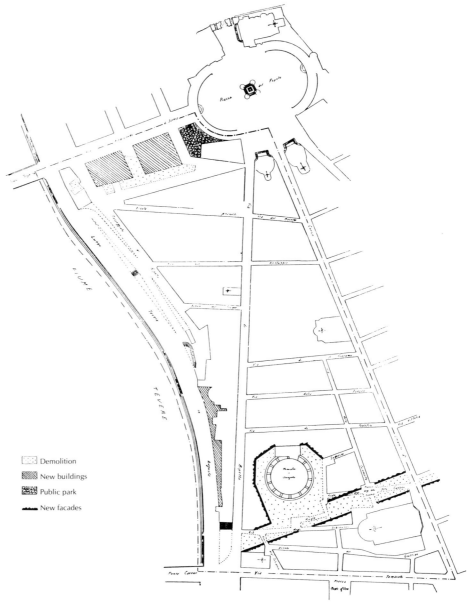

Demolition
New buildings
Public park
New facades

8
Scheme for the mausoleum and its
periphery: the Variante Generale of
1925–1926. (From *Capitolium* 9,
1933, p. 115)

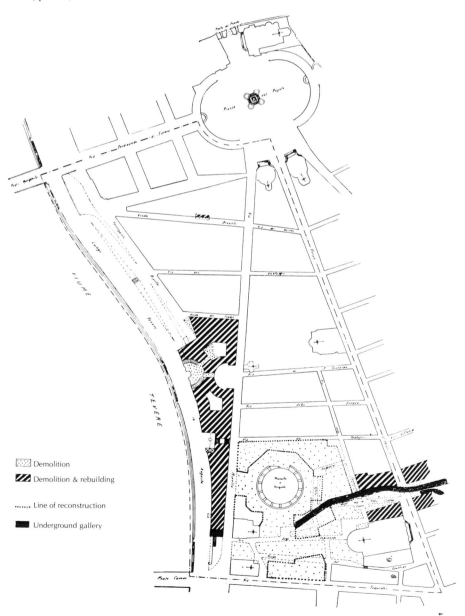

Demolition

Demolition & rebuilding

Line of reconstruction

Underground gallery

two Christian monuments, S. Girolamo degli Schiavoni and S. Carlo al Corso, were also slated for substantial liberation. The proposal of 1909 had left the urban setting of S. Carlo untouched, and with the uncompromising axiality of the new artery it had condoned the shaving off of the southeast corner of S. Rocco. S. Girolamo, on the other side of Via degli Schiavoni, was left with a triangular wedge of construction attached to its northern flank. The Variante Generale of 1925/1926 now proposed that this wedge be removed, that S. Rocco be untouched along the south side, and that the entire west end, the apse or *tribuna,* of S. Carlo be freed so that the splendid cupola by Pietro da Cortona could afford an unobstructed view from the direction of the river. The new avenue would adjust itself to these liberated masses of the three churches.

The Augusteo itself would be kept free of the avenue and the awkward form of its piazza as it appeared in the Piano Regolatore of 1909 improved in two ways: (a) the south side was to be circumscribed more gracefully by means of two corner exedrae, and (b) open space was to be created between the Augusteo and Via di Ripetta, balanced by an appropriate indentation on the eastern side of the piazza between Vicolo Soderini and Via delle Colonnette. In addition, there was to be an underground gallery for trams, starting at Via della Croce and passing north of Piazza degli Otto Cantoni to emerge at the largo to the south of the Augusteo that corresponded to the old Via degli Schiavoni. This was part of an extensive subway system detailed in a supplementary report on traffic submitted along with the Variante Generale.

The conservation-minded commission of the Variante also tried to secure the traditional character of the area around the Augusteo. For the most part, the building fabric dated from the later eighteenth century (Figs. 9a, 9b). It was the result of an effort of reconstruction after the disastrous fire of May 1734, known as the "incendio della Legnara." The residential development of the area had begun in earnest in the early sixteenth century with the opening of Via Leonina, later Via di Ripetta.[8] This was then a semirural zone of orchards and gardens, strewn with the hovels of three fringe groups: prostitutes, the labor force for the simple docking facility called Porto di Ripetta, and Slavic immigrants who had fled to Rome after the invasion of Serbia by the Ottomans in 1389. For these last, known as "the Dalmatian or Illyrian nation," a hospital named after their patron saint Jerome had been built here in 1453 by special dispensation of Pope Nicholas V and the medieval church of Santa Marina iuxta Flumen rededicated as S. Girolamo degli Illirici or degli Schiavoni. This is the origin of one of the three

churches involved in the planning of Piazzale Augusto Imperatore. Another, S. Rocco, was a guild church; it was started in 1499 by the *Università degli Osti e Barcaroli* to replace a much earlier oratory dedicated to St. Martin. The third church in question, S. Carlo al Corso, rose between 1612 and 1672, well after the district had changed from countryside into a suburb primarily of working-class people and aliens. It was to serve as the "national" church of Lombardy in honor of the two great patron saints of Milan—Ambrose and Carlo Borromeo. Later still, in 1703–1706 the now flourishing Porto di Ripetta was made monumental under Clement XI with the famous stairs of Alessandro Specchi (Fig. 10).

The stairs and the adjacent customs house to the north survived the fire of 1734 but succumbed in the late nineteenth century to the new Tiber embankments and the Lungotevere (Fig. 11). The Variante Generale, returning to the idea of a uniform frontage in the Piano Regolatore of 1909, now proposed a grand reconstruction of the riverfront in settecento taste, from Pietro Camporesi's neoclassical Accademia di Belle Arti to the north all the way to Piazza Nicosia.[9] The scheme that was developed included an exedra and stair complex between Via di Ripetta and the river, back to back with the characteristic east horseshoe of the Accademia, and formal palazzi on either side of Ponte Cavour. The palazzi were in fact executed by 1930. Between Ponte Cavour and the Accademia, the designs of Andrea Busiri Vici faithfully reproduced the settecento customs house adjacent to the old Porto di Ripetta, but on a much larger scale.[10] To the south of Ponte Cavour, Felice Nori designed a related building that would harmonize with the neighboring Palazzo Borghese; in front of the north facade of this building, the Palazzo Marescalchi Belli, he set up the Fontana dei Navigatori and the two hydrometric columns of the old port, in storage since the construction of the Lungotevere. This latter ensemble still stands.[11] Busiri Vici's structure would be destroyed shortly, as we shall see, to make room for the Ara Pacis (Fig. 12).

The Variante Generale never became law. Its more sweeping recommendations, among them the notion of a subway system, came under criticism. The city cited cost and technical difficulties in postponing its execution and pushing for four new tramlines for the immediate alleviation of traffic. One of these affected the area around the Augusteo. Reverting to the logic of geometry, the city version asserted once more the expediency of a new artery "in rettifilo," a straight line from the east end of a twenty-meter wide Via della Croce to Ponte Cavour. The tram service would be above ground, and the piazza of the mausoleum was to be given a blunt right-angle form with narrow passage to the Ripetta and Via della Frezza. A different revision of the Variante scheme was offered by the Ufficio Tecnico, the planning office of the city responsible for translating the ideas of the master plan into final working drawings (Fig. 13). The Ufficio brought the shape of the piazza closer to a perfect circle, omitting the south exedrae and reducing the open space toward the Ripetta to a small three-bay portico. The north side of the piazza was to be moved up all the way to Via dei Pontefici. The circle was to be defined by modern buildings that would replace existing run-down tenements.

It was this last provision that formed the central objection to the Ufficio scheme in a report by a special commission of the Federazione Fascista dell'Urbe dated June 1927.[13] Too much of Rome had already been disfigured since 1870 by the speculative instinct and the "stil massonico," the report said. The new buildings were bound to dwarf the mausoleum. What is more, the circular piazza was much too restrictive and marred the visibility of the monument it was supposed to enhance. The commission endorsed instead an alternative project by one of its members, the architect Enrico Del Debbio, that foreclosed any construction of "pompous and inexpressive new palaces" (Figs. 14a, 14b). It was not that Del Debbio prized the settecento character of the area or that he objected to extensive demolition. His piazza would be, to the contrary, considerably larger. It would be entered on the Corso side through a V-shaped forecourt that framed a distant view of the mausoleum from the widened Via della Croce. A diagonal slash from the northwest corner of the piazza to the Lungotevere was meant to ensure the proper flow of traffic—except for trams which would be put underground for the whole length of Via della Croce and up until the Lungotevere. The idea was to create a "zona di silenzio tramviario" and to rid the entire area from Piazza di Spagna to the river of what the report called "contaminazione tramviaria." The phrase is Mussolini's. It appears in the famous speech of 31 December 1925 dealing with the physical future of the city, where he set the goal of ridding the streets from the tracks and noise of trams in favor of newer means of communication.[14]

The report admits that the Del Debbio project would require a total sacrifice of one thousand square meters of buildable land and about thirteen million lire over and above the provisions of the Ufficio Tecnico proposal; but such a signal relic of the Roman empire, the tomb of its founder, surely justified the added expense. According to the report, four criteria should condition the planning of this area: the principle of the exploitation or reevaluation (valorizzazione) of ancient Roman ruins; the optimum visibility of the monuments situated in the area, and their maximum isolation (isolamento); their decorous and impressive arrangement; and the easy flow of traffic. "The commission holds that the problem, because of its high interest for the art, the dignity, and the grandeur of Rome, should be resolved with an ampler vision of the ambience and a concept of maximum refinement and importance. The perspective views [to be created by Del Debbio's project] will make of this zone a monumental center truly worthy of the greatest artistic traditions of Rome's past and its imperial future."[15]

The language of the report and its Fascist sponsorship introduce a new element into the planning history of Piazzale Augusto Imperatore. Earlier projects were motivated by the necessity to improve communication and the attendant benefit of historic preservation. Without denying the demands of traffic, the special report of the Federazione Fascista clearly considers them secondary. Furthermore, it reassesses the issue of preservation and conservation along lines that were becoming the official policy of Fascist Rome with respect to the handling of its ancient ruins. "Maximum isolation" echoes the directive of Mussolini in the 1925 speech just mentioned: "The millennial monuments of our history must loom gigantic in their necessary solitude."[16] Valorizzazione was also becoming a common term. It went beyond excavation and conservation. At issue was the presentation of Roman ruins in the context of the resurgence of the grandezza of ancient Rome under the aegis of the Fascist regime. Filippo Cremonesi, the first appointed governor of Rome after the abolition of the elective rule of the city, stated this concept as part of the program of his administration. "In the present national rebirth, which in the august name of Rome will relead Italy to its imperial destiny, the administration of this city at the Campidoglio feels the gravity of the mission entrusted to it: a mission that not only entails the necessary development of the modern metropolis but also includes the conservation, excavation and interpretation (valorizzazione) of the vestiges of ancient Rome."[17]

Contrary to the generic worth of most Roman ruins in the process of valorizzazione, the Mausoleum of Augustus carried special meaning because of its association with the founder of the empire. The Markets of Trajan, the Colosseum, the Republican temples of Largo Argentina were crucial relics of the grandeur that was Rome; their excavation and systematization afforded visible proof of the intent of the new regime to make contact with the power and ethos of the past as the first step toward

9a
Aerial view of the area around the
mausoleum, about 1915. The monument is in the top left-hand corner, the
church of S. Giacomo in Augusta at
the top right-hand corner, and Via del
Babuino at the bottom right-hand
corner. (Aerofototeca)

9b
Baroque house at the corner of Via
del Corso and Via dei Pontefici; demolished in March 1935.

13
Project of the Ufficio Tecnico, 1926.
(Based on *La sistemazione della zona augustea,* Rome 1927, unnumbered drawing)

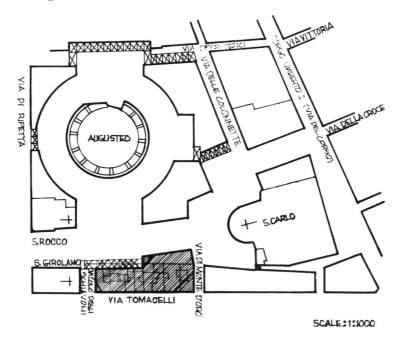

SCALE: 1:1000

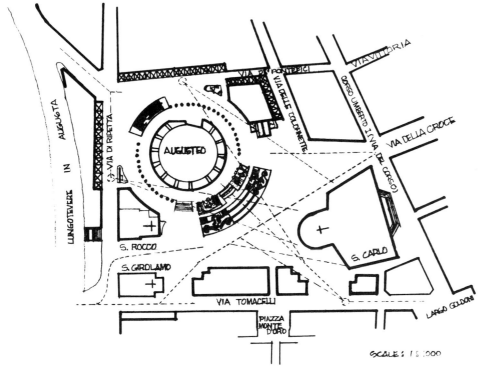

SCALE: 1:1000

14a
Project by Enrico Del Debbio, for the Federazione fascista dell'Urbe, 1927. (Based on *La sistemazione*)
14b
Del Debbio project, view: from Via dei Pontefici looking toward the tribuna of S. Carlo. (Based on *La sistemazione*)

resurrecting them. The specific chronology and patronage of these buildings were not of consequence. To Mussolini ancient Rome meant imperial Rome; and imperial Rome was encapsulated in the name of Augustus. In all his pronouncements and writings it is hard to find reference to any other emperor. In the speech of 31 December 1925, the tone is set for the identification of Mussolini with Augustus. "In five years Rome must appear marvelous to all the people of the world: vast, ordered, powerful as it was in the time of the first emperor Augustus."[18] For the next fifteen years this identification would be enhanced and refined in a two-pronged propaganda campaign: the Duce would emulate the policies of the emperor, and the apologists of his regime would labor parallelisms between it and the Augustan age.

Augustus was, in fact, not an ideal persona. The impulsiveness and vigor of the Duce, the dash of the condottiere that was in him, seemed to find their most suitable echo in the tempestuous career of Julius Caesar, and in the early years of the regime this similarity was often drawn out. The Duce had been born thirty kilometers from the Rubicon, so he could cross it like Caesar and march on Rome.[19] But for all the psychological appropriateness of the Caesar paradigm, at least two historical facts militated against it. Caesar may have been a forerunner of Roman imperium but its official architect was Augustus. And then there was the fact of Caesar's short rule and violent death.

There were three chief monuments in Rome associated with the age and person of Augustus: the Forum of Augustus, the Ara Pacis Augustae, and the mausoleum. Of these, the forum was being exhumed since 1924 under the direction of Corrado Ricci, one of the earliest Fascist excavations of ancient Rome. In drawing up a list of priorities for further excavation, Cremonesi hailed "the happy redemption" of the forum as an auspice.[20] The Ara Pacis and the mausoleum were, of course, on the list. They presented different problems. The precise form of the altar and even its identity had been matters of scholarly dispute since 1879, when F. von Duhn saw the connection among a number of reliefs dispersed in various collections of Florence, Rome, Paris, and Vienna and identified these with the Ara Pacis Augustae set up on the Campus Martius, near Via Flaminia, in 9 B.C. to commemorate Augustus's victorious campaigns in Spain and Gaul.[21] Excavations in 1903 under the Palazzo Peretti-Ottoboni (now Fiano) in Via in Lucina permitted the revision of the first tentative reconstruction of the monument on paper by E. Petersen the year before. The urgent task now was to bring together all the reliefs and assemble the monument in a place suitable to its valorizzazione. Its original site under the Palazzo Fiano was unsatisfactory, both scenographically and programmatically. An early possibility, the site of the demolished Palazzo Piombino across from the Column of Marcus Aurelius, had been preempted by the belated completion of the Galleria Colonna. In 1925 Carlo Cecchelli proposed the Capitoline, and precisely the spot overlooking the Foro Olitorio and the theater of Marcellus where the temple of Jupiter Capitolinus had stood. He published a design for this proposal by the young architect Oriolo Frezzotti, showing the altar under a protective canopy in the form of a *portantina,* an ancient Roman sedan chair.[22] But whatever its destination, there was no doubt about the importance of the altar. Both Cecchelli and Cremonesi use exactly the same language to describe it, clearly repeating an approved text. The Ara Pacis is "the radiant expression of Roman imperium, the record of a conclusive moment when all the decrepit civilizations of the old world became brothers, as it were, and were constrained to renew themselves under the strong impetus of Rome."[23]

The identity and general form of the mausoleum were not a mystery. But it had not been an exposed ruin for centuries, and its continued use had prevented systematic excavation. As late as 1925, M. Piacentini was drawing up designs for the remodeling of the concert hall.[24] It seemed inevitable now that with the prevailing sentiment to isolate the Augusteo, the unsuitability of its modern destination would become apparent. According to early Fascist policy, the reuse of an ancient monument would be tolerated, indeed welcomed, only if the monument were made to serve a function similar to its original one. To have concerts in the Basilica of Maxentius was one thing, to have them over the ashes of the Julio-Claudian dynasty was another. The Augusteo had been the personal memorial of the first emperor and, therefore, a kind of shrine to the Roman empire now being revived. What was more, it had already been used more than once as the platform from which this Fascist renaissance was proclaimed. The Third National Fascist Congress was held in the Augusteo in November 1921. Even if this had been merely a practical convenience, the Augusteo being one of the largest halls in Rome, there was clearly a sense of destiny in the use of this same hall for the Fascist congress of June 1925 when the Duce assured the delegates, to sustained applause, that "the only city that on the coasts of the Mediterranean, fated and magic, has created an empire is Rome."[25]

Mussolini had been making similar pronouncements of the inevitable resurgence of imperial Rome as far back as the speech in Bologna in May 1918.[26] But he was then an adventurous journalist, with hardly any following. He had since risen spectacularly to take charge of Rome, and his prophecies of empire acquired a new authority spoken from the

Capitoline or within the tomb of the first Roman emperor. On 20 April 1926, the birthday of Rome, he listened in the Augusteo to a speech by the Florentine poet F. Valerio Ratti entitled "Rome's Mission in the World." Ratti likened him to Caesar and Augustus. "I am here," Ratti said, "to celebrate with you, Romans, among the live stones of the tomb of Augustus, the resurrection of imperial Rome in the world."[27]

It was now time for the valorizzazione of the mausoleum in this light. The Department of Antiquities of the Governatorato authorized in the same year the excavation of the monument, and the task was assigned to G. Q. Giglioli assisted by A. M. Colini. In two separate campaigns between 1926 and 1930, the burial crypt was systematically explored. Giglioli began to play a significant part in the planning of the area. His name is listed in the report of the special commission of the Federazione Fascista dell'Urbe as a sponsor of the Del Debbio scheme, along with Ricci; another archaeologist, R. Paribeni; and the new governor prince Ludovico Spada Potenziani. In publishing the results of his work, Giglioli harped on the value of the monument for the symbolic structure of the regime. It was he who conceived of a vast all-inclusive exhibition of Roman antiquity to coincide with the bimillennial of the birth of Augustus, a project subsequently approved by Mussolini. The liberation of the mausoleum and the creation of a nonarchitectural piazza for it found in Giglioli an eloquent and authoritative spokesman. In 1930, with the debate still on about the final form of the piazza and no official scheme adopted, he wrote: "We have faith that on 23 September 1938 the Duce of the new Italy could, on the bimillennial of the birth of Augustus, admire the great ruin [of the mausoleum], completely isolated and surrounded anew by those groves that Augustus bequeathed to his good people of Rome."[28]

In 1931 Rome acquired a new Piano Regolatore. Prepared in less than six months under the personal supervision of the Duce, it included the liberation of the mausoleum. The plan was a triumph of Fascist space-lust and the policy of sventramenti, or wholesale urban clearance. The demolition around the mausoleum was to be more extensive than in any previous project, more so even than Del Debbio's (Fig. 15). The circular piazza, as defined by the Ufficio Tecnico and more amply by Del Debbio (Figs. 13–14b), was given up in favor of a generally rectangular piazza circumscribed by Via dei Pontefici to the north; Vicolo del Grottino to the south; the Ripetta to the west, with a block of building between it and the mausoleum, and the newly completed block of Busiri Vici between the Ripetta and the river; and to the east, by a line along the west side of Piazza degli Otto Cantoni.

The eastern approach from Piazza di Spagna was also altered. Instead of Via della Croce, the plan now specified the widening of Via Vittoria further north. In addition, Via delle Carrozze was also to be widened so that it would line up on axis with the Corso facade of S. Carlo—a solution that prefigures the opening of Corso del Rinascimento on axis with Sant' Andrea della Valle. The choice of Via Vittoria over Via della Croce was designed to spare Piazza di Spagna from becoming a main focus of the new traffic pattern being created between the northeastern hills and the river. The new piazza of the mausoleum was not being spared this fate. On the contrary, it was being exposed to the full fury of motor traffic from all directions. The projects of the Piano Regolatore of 1909, the Variante Generale of 1925–1926, and the Ufficio Tecnico (Figs. 7, 8, 13) had shielded the mausoleum by keeping the piazza around it closed and using only the southern avenue for cross-traffic between the Corso and the river. Del Debbio had aired the piazza both toward the northwest and southeast, but the principle aim in this was to secure carefully staged views of the mausoleum (Fig. 14). The main access to the mausoleum, in his project, was to be from the southeast, and the monument was to communicate with the tribuna of S. Carlo across unencumbered space. The diagonal slash from the northwest corner of the piazza out toward Lungotevere in Augusta was of modest width and left the Accademia di Belle Arti building intact.

In the 1931 proposal this slash is prodigious. It starts to the east of the Ripetta where part of the block between Via dei Pontefici and Via della Frezza is cut back for its sake. On the opposite side of the Ripetta the proposed new mass of construction is correspondingly set back. The diagonal avenue pushes up toward Ponte Margherita through the mass of the Accademia. The brashly sacrificed neoclassical building is to be replaced by new construction. Further north the avenue also destroys the green ramps of the Passeggiata di Ripetta and a building block north of the Passeggiata. The width of the Lungotevere in Augusta at Ponte Margherita would thus correspond to that of the Lungotevere Arnaldo da Brescia—the idea being to create an ample approach into the center of town from the north that would bypass the narrow Porta del Popolo, namely, along Via Flaminia, Via Luisa di Savoia, Lungotevere Arnaldo da Brescia and Augusta, and then through the new piazza of the mausoleum to the Corso and Piazza Venezia. The Corso itself would be relieved by an eastern thoroughfare running parallel to it, in line with the present Via Belsiana/Via del Gambero, from Via Vittoria to Piazza San Silvestro. There was still a further approach into and out of the piazza of the mausoleum, from the south. The Piano Regolatore prescribed a substantial cut through the existing

15
Scheme for the Mausoleum and its
periphery: The Piano Regolatore of
1931. (From *Capitolium* 9, 1933, p.
122)

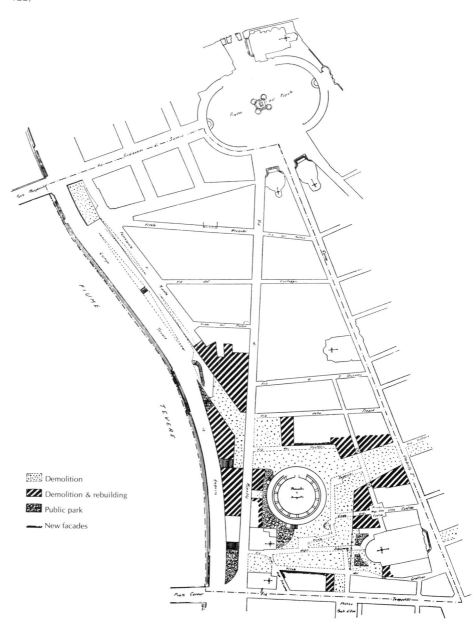

Demolition
Demolition & rebuilding
Public park
New facades

287
The Emperor and
the Duce: The
Planning of
Piazzale Augusto
Imperatore in
Rome

urban fabric to link the piazza with the Parliament building and the Pantheon. It would enter the piazza across from Piazza Monte d'Oro after making a jog to skirt the eastern outline of the Palazzo Borghese.

The central dilemma of Fascist historical planning is well illustrated by the changes that have occurred in the projects involving the mausoleum since 1925. The dictates of valorizzazione and Mussolini's "necessary solitude" doctrine created, at great material and human cost, vast spaces around relics of antiquity; and these vast spaces were seized upon by traffic engineers and transformed into foci for multidirectional traffic. The commission appointed to prepare the Piano Regolatore of 1931 was instructed to reconcile history with the exigencies of modern life, specifically communication needs. Respect for history stopped with "Christian-Renaissance" Rome; it did not apply to the more recent pre-Fascist period of the city's development. But even for the "good" centuries, respect was to be limited to significant buildings and not standard, nonmonumental architecture. In praising the product of the commission, Mussolini dismissed any scruples about the scale of demolition it required by saying that it was encumbent upon his administration to "respect to the highest degree that which represents the living testimony of the glory of old Rome. But monuments, ruins, are one thing; the picturesque and so-called local color, another. . . . All the sordid picturesque is entrusted to His Majesty the pick. All this picturesque is destined to come down and must come down in the name of decency, of health, and, if you wish, the beauty of the Capital."[29] With precepts such as these the commission should not be blamed for the extravagant devastation they prescribed in the periphery of the mausoleum, nor for sacrificing the original parklike environment of the mausoleum, the "sylvae et ambulationes" in Suetonius's description,[30] to the insatiable demands of traffic.

An action plan for the area in agreement with the general layout of the Piano Regolatore was approved by royal decree on 2 May 1932, with only minor revisions (Fig. 16). And it was on the basis of this *piano particolareggiato* that Mussolini initiated the demolition with the speech of 22 October 1934.[31]

But between the action plan and the inaugural picking in Vicolo Soderini, the character of the project underwent new changes. Sometime in 1932, the Duce had approved Giglioli's idea for a spectacular exhibition to commemorate the bimillennial of the birth of Augustus. The celebration was to be an elaborate, year-long pageant that would take advantage of the historical occasion to sing the successes of the regime. Giglioli's Mostra Augustea della Romanità, the central event of the bimillennial, was not intended therefore as a scholarly exhibition but

one of propaganda—a didactic display of the achievements of the Roman empire to bolster national pride in the past and inspire loyalty for the present custodians of this exalted tradition. The Exposition of the Fascist Revolution in 1932, on the occasion of the tenth anniversary of the regime, had been immensely successful. The Mostra Augustea would use the same medium, shifting the focus on antiquity as the first chapter of the same story. The visual power of this paradigmatic historicism had been exploited before in the field of planning. The thrust of Fascist valorizzazione had been urban scenography. Monuments of the past were unencumbered and exposed as major exhibits— backdrops of certified splendor against which modern life could unfold. Projects like Via del Mare and Via dell'Impero were, at one level, open-air museums of live history. The scenographic possibilities of the mausoleum of Augustus had not as yet been fully explored. What it would look like after it had been isolated had not been resolved. Its relation to the three churches that were to be preserved remained vague. Finally, there was no definite agreement on the form and function of the new buildings that were to define the lines of the action plan.

In April 1932 Antonio Muñoz a member of the commission that drafted the Piano Regolatore, was put in charge of the restoration of the mausoleum.[32] Art historian and indefatigable chronicler of Fascist sventramenti, Muñoz had already established himself as a foremost restorer of ancient and medieval monuments. We might mention his work on the so-called temple of Fortuna Virilis, and Santa Sabina on the Aventine. He derived his restoration theory from Camillo Boito and his practical knowledge from his teacher Giovanni Battista Giovenale. According to Boito, the proper handling of a historical building should begin with the stripping from the fabric of any elements extraneous to the original period. The building should then be repaired, not reconstructed, and repaired only where absolutely necessary and in such a way that modern patches can be plainly detected in the masonry.[33] These principles had guided Giovenale in a celebrated case in Rome, the restoration of Santa Maria in Cosmedin undertaken by the Associazione Artistica tra i Cultori di Architettura in 1894–1899. Giovenale had torn off the baroque façade by G. Sardi to reveal the original medieval prospect of the church. On the question of the general setting of restored monuments, especially ancient ruins, Muñoz was incorrigibly romantic. He insisted on parklike landscaping, or at the very least a sprinkling of trees, chiefly evergreens. "I cipressi di Muñoz" became a fond refrain. To him is due the landscaping of Nero's Domus Aurea, the temple of

16
Action plan approved by decree of 2
May 1932. (From *Capitolium* 9, 1933,
p. 123)

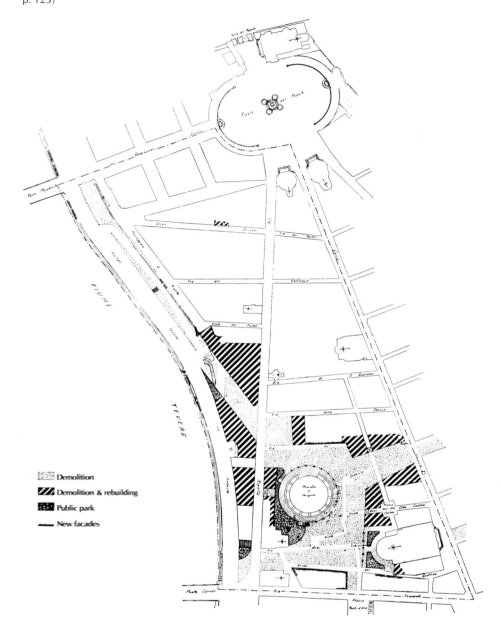

Demolition

Demolition & rebuilding

Public park

New facades

Venus and Rome, the Foro di Largo Argentina, and his crowning work, the isolamento of the Capitoline.

Muñoz studied the spate of reconstructions on paper of the Mausoleum of Augustus, especially those based on the Giglioli excavations. Rejecting the common solution of two superimposed stories with a tumulus on top covered by trees,[34] Muñoz was at first inclined to accept the solution of Giglioli: a one-story plinth carrying the tall cone-shaped tumulus. By 1934, however, he embraced Guglielmo Gatti's version, arrived at independently also by the engineer Massimo Poscetti: a low plinth, then the tree-lined tumulus in the middle of which sits a second story, topped in its turn by trees and the statue of Augustus.[35]

There was of course no thought of reconstructing the building in toto. The Augusteo was now to be gutted as well as isolated externally. The view from the piazza would be of the masonry plinth with its crown of cypresses and bay hedges, and the outer ring of the second story minus the tumulus and the statue. Drawings of this arrangement shown to the Duce during the inaugural ceremony of 22 October 1934 met with approval. Noting the would-be hollow interior of the mausoleum, Muñoz writes, the Duce saw instantly its possibilities as a hypaethral rotunda, some forty-two meters in diameter, "for reunions and celebrations that would assume a grand solemnness from the Latin sanctity of the place."[36] In another visit to the site, on 7 April 1935, the Duce was shown a model of this scheme, and it too was approved.

All suggestions for reusing the rotunda were subsequently turned down. One proposal would convert it into a gallery for contemporary art with movable partitions and a roof of iron and glass invisible from the outside. Cipriano Oppo, writing in *La Tribuna* on 5 August 1936, recommended that a Fascist structure be set up in the hollow of the rotunda as a symbol of the old supporting the new, "the empire resurgent through the work of Fascism"; what he had in mind was a "torre littoria," the triumphal Fascist tower of the kind that was being proposed for a number of Italian cities. The previous year, for example, there had been a competition for such a tower to rise in Piazza del Duomo at Milan.[37] But Muñoz's purism prevailed. The mausoleum that had been in more or less constant use for centuries was transformed, beginning in the spring of 1938, into an authentic Roman ruin. The holes in the Augustan fabric were plugged with off-color bricks that distinguished them as additions to the discerning eye, without marring unduly the general rich tone of the masonry (Figs. 17a, 17b).

Meanwhile, Vittorio Ballio Morpurgo had been entrusted with the final design of the piazza and its new buildings. He was handpicked, it is not clear exactly by whom, some time in 1934. There were frequent competitions for Fascist projects in Rome, some of them announced and judged with great fanfare. But the practice of assigning major architectural and planning programs to trusted architects was also common. Del Debbio had been selected by the administration of the Opera Nazionale Balilla in 1927 for the Foro Mussolini complex. Mussolini himself was credited with having decided on Marcello Piacentini for the ambitious new campus of the University of Rome. Morpurgo's involvement with the formal undertakings of the regime was new. His work to date, conventional in nature, had been mostly private commissions for residential architecture. He was not a stranger, however, to large-scale planning. He had drafted a master plan for the city of Varese exhibited in the first Mostra Nazionale dei Piani Regolatori, held in Rome in 1929. Earlier, in the competition of 1924, his project for the Istituto di S. Spirito and its periphery in the Borgo had been singled out as one of two winning designs, and he was subsequently asked by the Governatorato to collaborate with the other winner, Pietro Aschieri, on the final scheme.[38] But in 1934 Morpurgo joined the front rank of establishment architects with three major projects at once. In the much publicized competition for a Palazzo Littorio, headquarters for the Fascist party and a permanent museum of Fascism, the design he submitted jointly with Arnaldo Foschini and Del Debbio placed first.[39] The building was eventually built at the Foro Mussolini and now serves as the Ministry of Foreign Affairs. In the same year, he was assigned the task of creating a suitable museum for the Roman galleys sensationally dredged out of Lago di Nemi.[40]

Whatever his talents may have been, Morpurgo should not alone be held accountable for the ultimate failure of Piazzale Augusto Imperatore. In apportioning blame it is well to keep in mind that the extent of the demolition, the purpose of the piazzale, the main accesses into it, and the form and setting of the restored mausoleum had all been decided before he came aboard. The idea of collecting other elements of Augustan art about the mausoleum was also prevalent.

Morpurgo's client was a monstrous composite. At the top came Mussolini. He affected the planning of the piazzale in two ways: He felt free to make changes when he was inspired to do so, and his approval had to be obtained at every major stage of the construction. The review occurred during the regular inspection tours of urban projects on ceremonial days such as the birthday of Rome and the anniversary of the Fascist march on Rome. His expertise derived from the fact that it was he, the Duce, "who feels more than anyone else the sanctity of these

17a
The Mausoleum of Augustus as it appears today. (Fototeca Unione, 1076)
17b
Interior view of the mausoleum after the gutting of the concert hall, with the dome of S. Carlo al Corso visible beyond. (Museo di Roma, C/411)

ruins."[41] Next in line was the Governatorato, and its various offices responsible for historic monuments in particular and public works in general. The governor of Rome from 1935 to 1937 was the leading Fascist official Giuseppe Bottai, who moved on to become minister of education; he was succeeded by the princes Piero Colonna and, in 1939, Gian Giacomo Borghese whom Muñoz calls "the faithful interpreter of the will of the Duce."[42] Muñoz himself headed the Department of Antiquities and the Fine Arts. Finally, Morpurgo had to contend with the financial sponsor of the piazzale, the giant organization of social security called Istituto Nazionale Fascista della Previdenza Sociale or INFPS, and its president, Bruno Biagi. The INFPS, in addition to providing social security, selective unemployment benefits, and most forms of insurance, was a major investor in architectural and planning projects in the thirties. A vast endowment fund, built on the surplus of social security contributions from employers and employees, was used in part to commission buildings for the benefit of workers and low-income groups, such as tuberculosis sanatoria, maternity hospitals, convalescence homes, and housing; and in part to support the public works program of the regime, since this program was intimately linked to the rate of unemployment.[43]

Morpurgo prepared a complete first project, published in 1935, which was characterized as "a free architectural interpretation of the outline proposed in the Master Plan [of 1931]." His specific charge was to create a special piazza for the mausoleum within the larger frame of the piazzale and dignify the original entrance, which Giglioli's excavations had shown to be in the south; to connect satisfactorily the mausoleum with the three surrounding churches; and to articulate the formal facades that would define the piazzale, especially on the north and east sides.

The fact that the Corso ran at an angle to the Ripetta posed some additional problems. The action plan of 1932 that Morpurgo inherited was ambivalent on this issue (Fig. 16). Most of the east side of its piazzale was lined up parallel to the Ripetta, but the obliqueness of Via delle Colonnette was preserved and echoed in the jag of the north frontage. In an unpublished plan that seems to be a tentative first attempt to civilize the action plan, Morpurgo suppresses the jag and the stretch of Via delle Colonnette immediately to the south of Via della Frezza and reorders the north block of the piazzale to consist of two unequal parts joined by a galleria that would provide access to Via della Frezza (Fig. 18). The western half is a porticoed building, concave so as to reflect the exterior form of the mausoleum. The

portico is carried over to the other side of the galleria for three bays that provide a formal facade for the southern approach from Piazza di Monte d'Oro. The northwest diagonal in the action plan is now brought into the piazzale by carrying the upper line of this avenue to the east of the Ripetta, where the portico of the northern block of the piazzale starts. At this point of the Ripetta a triangular largo is fashioned, eating into the block between Via della Frezza and Via di S. Giacomo (now Via Antonio Canova). The other major change involves the southern approach of the mausoleum. There is a monumental staircase flanked by a set of propylaea; the western unit is actually the church of S. Rocco and a small block attached to its north flank, the only built elements remaining on this side between the mausoleum and the Ripetta.

The first official Morpurgo project of 1935 had various advantages over this preliminary sketch plan. Its main effect was to tidy up the design and to create firm blocks that would eliminate the chopped up nature of the sketch (Figs. 19–22). On the Via Tomacelli side the westernmost break is closed up and substituted by a galleria within the body of the uniform block that continued the mass of S. Girolamo until the southern approach into the piazzale. There is as yet no indication of what the program of this block might be. The inner face of the block, toward the piazzale, is made oblique to form a ninety-degree angle with the entrance corridor of the mausoleum, which is itself not quite parallel to the line of the Ripetta. A wide and more or less straight street is thereby created that starts between S. Girolamo and S. Rocco and ends up on axis with the tribuna of S. Carlo. The street is defined by the flanks of the two churches, the S. Girolamo block, and the line of the propylaea to the mausoleum. In the middle of the grand staircase of the propylaea going down to the Augustan level stands a statue of the emperor facing in toward the mausoleum. The concept of placing identifying statues of emperors before their monuments had already been applied at Via dell'Impero. The staircase is flanked by two building blocks of unequal size meant to contain archaeological finds of the area. Between these buildings and the mausoleum there were to be evergreens. The project clearly establishes a precise axis from Via Tomacelli to the mausoleum, marked by the galleria, the statue of the emperor at the top of the propylaea stairs, and the entrance corridor of the mausoleum itself. The mausoleum could also be approached directly from the Ripetta by means of two stair ramps, one of which replaced the tiny building attached to the north flank of S. Rocco in the preliminary sketch plan. The Busiri Vici block along the west side of the Ripetta was left intact (Fig. 20).

19
The first Morpurgo project, 1935.
(Based on *Capitolium* 11, 1935, p.
252)
20
Model of the first Morpurgo project,
looking west from the Corso. The
Busiri Vici block can be seen in the
background, to the right of the dome
of S. Rocco. (From *Architettura,* special Christmas issue 1936, p. 89)

18
Preliminary sketch plan by Vittorio
Ballio Morpurgo, 1934.

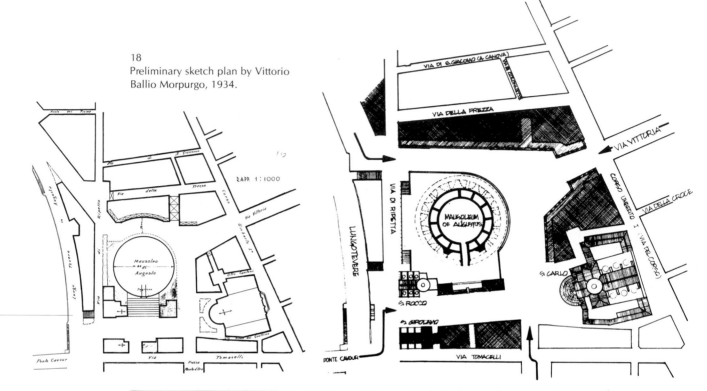

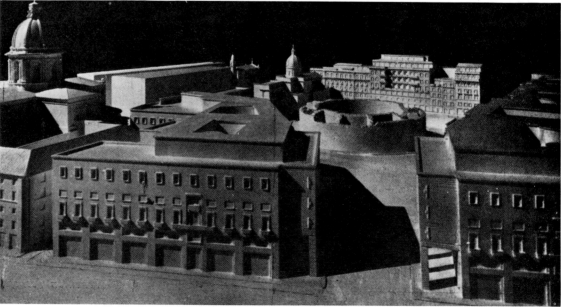

21
Model of the first Morpurgo project
looking north toward Fabbricato *B*,
with the Mausoleum and its proposed
propylaea in the foreground. From *Architettura*, special Christmas issue
1936, p. 89)

22
Rendering of the first Morpurgo project, looking into the piazzale, in the
direction of S. Carlo, from within the
V-shaped forecourt of the Corso side.
From *Architettura*, special Christmas
issue 1936, p. 90)

But the main improvement was the neat definition of the north side of the piazzale by one long porticoed building, labeled Fabbricato B, that stretched from the Ripetta to the Corso (Fig. 21). A hypaethral galleria in marble, entered through a monumental portal, provided passage to Via della Frezza. This galleria now lined up with the southern approach into the piazzale, and the part of the north block to the east of the galleria formed one-half of the V-shaped forecourt on the Corso side, a feature that harked back to the Del Debbio scheme of 1927. The other half of the forecourt was defined by a second building, of irregular shape, called Fabbricato A. It was bounded by the Corso; vestiges of the old street pattern along the south side (Vicolo and Piazza degli Otto Cantoni, and Via della Tribuna); and toward the piazzale, by a porticoed frontage helping to shape the forecourt and to establish the eastern line of the piazzale just beyond the tribuna of S. Carlo.

The two buildings were curtain architecture; their primary purpose in the design of the piazzale was to act as space definers. It would seem that Morpurgo's initial inclination may have been to keep them as low as possible; in an unpublished sketch he compares the effect of low blocks beyond which the picturesque skyline of Via della Frezza and Via Tomacelli might show, with the unrevealing height that the buildings were to assume in actuality (Fig. 23). INFPS could not be expected to finance mere screens on this expensive downtown land. Its president, Biagi, is praised for agreeing to limit the height to three stories above a porticoed ground floor in order to ensure the architectural success of the project as a whole, whereas speculative greed would have pushed lesser men to demand additional stories that would have towered over the mausoleum.[45] At any rate, there was no clear idea what the buildings would contain. Morpurgo's project speaks of shops on the ground floor behind the porticoes and then apartments and offices further up; also a "sala per spettacoli."

On the Corso side, the facades of the two buildings were to be slightly recessed in their entirety from the line of S. Carlo and its wings, known as canonichette (Fig. 20). The entrance into the V-shaped forecourt between these facades was to be twenty meters wide, exactly the new width of Via Vittoria. On either side of the Corso entrance, Morpurgo specified a recessed panel with sculpture in relief. This motif was to be carried within and repeated three times, twice on the north building (Fabbricato B) and once at the south end of the east building (Fabbricato A). The facade of Fabbricato B toward the piazzale, and specifically the part west of the hypaethral galleria, was recessed in the middle to emphasize the axis of the mausoleum, and the sculpture panels were to punctuate this axiality at the inner ends of the projecting four-bay wings (Fig. 21).

Judging from renderings and photographs of the model, the style of these buildings was quite restrained. The inner facades, toward the piazzale, are flat beyond the level of the porticoes, with rows of totally framed windows and no cornice line between stories. Toward the Corso, the piano nobile windows have projecting balconies in deference to the older palazzi on the avenue (Fig. 20). The inner flanks of the Corso entrance are treated differently (Fig. 22). The lines of the porticoes are carried upward to form deep sunken bays that subsume the three stories. The effect is similar to the main entrance of the university that was being completed at about this time. Indeed, the resemblance is more general, and not insignificant. The exclusive use of piers instead of columns for the piazzale porticoes, the sheer planes of the inner facades undivided into stories and unaccentuated for the most part into vertical bays, recall the generic modernism devised by Marcello Piacentini for the Città Universitaria, in answer to the challenge from younger architects eager to display the formal advances of the Modern Movement. Piacentini crushed this uprising of the exponents of "rational architecture" against the traditionalist establishment by assigning individual buildings of the university complex to some among them and then overwhelming their purist efforts with the rhetorical monumentality of travertine piers, giant inscriptions, and inflated art. For a short time after that, piers and smooth surfaces came to denote modernism, and Morpurgo's style in the project of 1935 goes along with this trend. But having embraced the revolt and thereby neutralized it, imperialism of form quickened with the proclamation of the Fascist empire. The stripped planes and nonliterary forms of the International Style came to be ridiculed as "transalpine rationalism"; the column returned. In the final project of the Piazzale the piers are retained, but as executed the porticoes are primarily columnar.

The final Morpurgo project was published in 1936; it was based on a revised action plan made legal through a royal decree dated 1 April 1935.[46] A number of studies by the city's own planning branch, the Uffici Tecnici del Governatorato, intervened between the first and final projects. Their effort of revision produced a scheme including one important feature, namely, the linking of S. Girolamo and S. Rocco at the easternmost point of their flanks by a bridge or cavalcavia (Fig. 24). Beyond this, the scheme suppressed any building between the mausoleum and Via di Ripetta, as well as the propylaea envisaged by the first Morpurgo project. In effect, the mausoleum's immediate periphery on all four sides would consist of landscaping, to the west and south, and of open roadway, with the sole exception of the mass of S. Rocco.

Morpurgo responded with two separate counter-proposals of his own. In one, he defined the Ripetta side with a low line of building, presumably to accord with the porticoed ground story of Fabbricati A and B (Fig. 25). To the immediate south, too, where the propylaea were to be, we now see a deep two-way portico with the statue of the emperor set against its short east side facing the tribuna of S. Carlo. A diagonal cut is introduced into Fabbricato B at the Ripetta corner, with the triangular largo in the manner of the first Morpurgo project. This feature is also present in the official scheme of the Governatorato, but here the largo is repeated in reverse with a corresponding cut into the Ripetta block, thus forming a long and narrow piazzetta at the crossing of the Ripetta and the new diagonal artery. In the second alternative proposal Morpurgo retains the notion of a building line between the mausoleum and the Ripetta, now called Fabbricato C, but he also insists on his propylaea and his southern axis to Via Tomacelli (Fig. 26). The cavalcavia is ignored, and neither the triangular largo nor the doubled version of it figures in the northwestern corner of the piazzale. Instead, the proposed diagonal artery toward the Lungotevere now begins on the west of Via di Ripetta, while both the Via della Frezza/V. di S. Giacomo block and the mass of Fabbricato B are left intact along the eastern line of this street.

By the time of Morpurgo's final project, the caval-cavia between S. Rocco and S. Girolamo found its way back into the design (Figs. 27, 28). It had no function other than that of "connection between the architectonic volume and the building complex [of the churches]," to quote Morpurgo.[47] The provision for the propylaea to which Morpurgo had clung was also abandoned; the two churches were themselves now called propylaea, and the passage through until the tribuna of S. Carlo called a "strada-piazza." In the outer face of the pylon that separated the two lights of the bridge connecting the churches, a fountain called La Botticella that had stood on Via di Ripetta for a hundred and fifty years was now to be reassembled, "as an element of environmental curiosity and topographical reference," again to quote Morpurgo.[48] Above the two lights ran a frieze of sculptural panels interrupted by five windows wider than they were high. A variant showed this feature as a normal one-story corridor unit with balconied windows and no frieze. Statues flanked the grand staircase of the mausoleum. The south building of the strada-piazza was specified as the Collegio degli Illirici, or Collegio Jugoslavo, a monastic structure belonging to S. Girolamo. It was to rise one story higher than the rest of the new buildings to form a kind of loggia containing three mural panels that related to the history of this eastern congregation. The museum function of the discarded propylaea was transferred to an underground museum, the central room of which would exhibit the reconstructed Ara Pacis. It was to be entered by means of ramps flanking the grand staircase and illuminated by skylights set in the level of the strada-piazza. The statue of Augustus stood at the head of the stair associated with two tablets carrying the text of the emperor's testament known as Res Gestae Divi Augusti, a lapidary version of which in both Greek and Latin had survived in the pronaos of the temple of Augustus at Ankara. A cast of this inscription had been made by an Italian mission in 1911. The mausoleum, the Ara Pacis, and the Res Gestae were being brought together in a scenographic arrangement, or rather a historical collage.

But the major impetus for the final project came from Mussolini. At one of his inspection tours after the publication of the first Morpurgo project, the Duce decided that the entire orientation of the piazzale should be shifted forcefully toward the river. Not only was there to be no architectural definition of the piazzale on the Ripetta side, but the block by Busiri Vici erected less than a decade ago between the Ripetta and the river was to be torn down and the slope landscaped. The mausoleum would thus face the Tiber, the literary image to be created being, according to one commentator, "of the flow of centuries before the solid reference point of one name and one immortal idea."[49] This new U-shaped arrangement, fully open toward the west, necessitated the toning down of the Corso approach. The V-shaped forecourt was now replaced by a gentle convex curve that continued the line of Via Vittoria along the main facade of Fabbricato B.

The design of this building was changed slightly. The section of the facade directly opposite the mausoleum was made to project, instead of being recessed as in the 1935 solution; the sculpture panels were set in the fourth bays from the ends of this projecting section. The hypaethral galleria was given up in favor of an auditorium for the Accademia Filarmonica housed in this section of Fabbricato B. A large frontispiece singled out this section of the long facade, with an inscription panel below, then a tall sunken panel of murals, and a sculptural group above the roof line. Entrance to the auditorium and passage to Via della Frezza was to be had from the sides of this frontispiece.

Fabbricato A also underwent revision. Its north facade was noticeably concave to accommodate the curved new shape of Via Vittoria's extension. In plan the east facade shows only the merest projection in the center, but viewed in elevation it presents a

23
Unpublished Morpurgo drawing exploring the effects of keeping the new structures low around the piazzale.

24
Revision by the Uffici Tecnici of the Governatorato of the first Morpurgo project. (From *Capitolium* 12, 1937, p. 146)

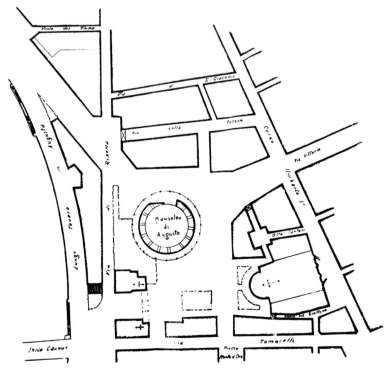

25
Morpurgo counterproposal to the re-
vised version of the Governatorato.
(From *Capitolium* 12, 1937, p. 147)

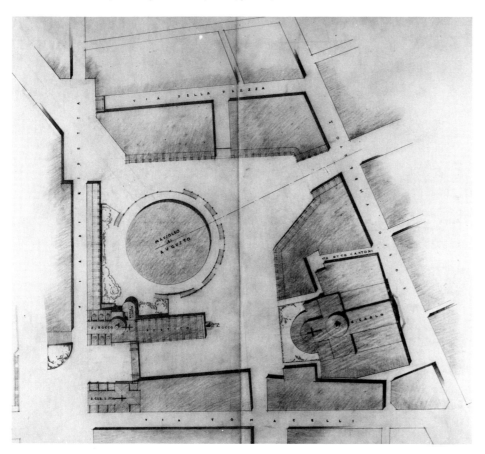

26
Morpurgo variant counterproposal
to the revised version of the Governatorato.

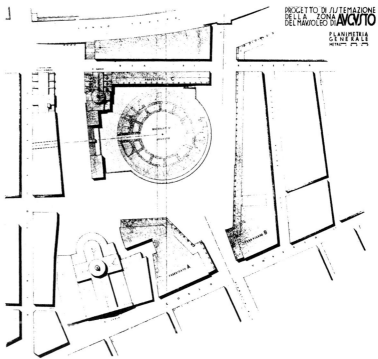

27
Final Morpurgo project, 1936; model
photographed from southwest to
northeast. (From *Architettura*, special
Christmas issue 1936, p. 92)

28
Final Morpurgo project, variant study
for southwest corner of the piazzale;
unpublished drawing. From left to
right: the Collegio degli Illirici, the
cavalcavia, and S. Rocco.

IL NVOVO FORO DI AVGVSTO VARIANTE

one-bay deep setback for this center and a different pattern of fenestration. In effect, the two wings and the continuous portico form one mass behind which sits the main block of the building. The left wing, with the concave northern facade, was to contain a movie theater. Between the two wings, a gallery connected the piazzale with the Corso. The Corso side of this gallery opened up to a small forecourt, the survivor of the V-shaped forecourt in the first Morpurgo project, called Piazzetta di S. Carlo. It was an inset between the mass of S. Carlo and the Corso facade of Fabbricato A, and it obliterated the last remnant of the older fabric, namely, the characteristic small Piazza degli Otto Cantoni and the eastern half of the original Via degli Otto Cantoni. To the left of the inset, that is, to the south of those entering the gallery, a low parapet-wall shielded the change of level between the pavement of the inset and the higher backpath to the tribuna. Unpublished sketches indicate that Morpurgo wanted to have a water cascade on the north face of the parapet-wall, and on top of it a statue of S. Carlo that would dominate the piazzetta (Fig. 29).

On the whole, there was praise for Morpurgo in the press. He was lauded for adhering faithfully to the general pattern of new avenues in the Piano Regolatore of 1931, especially the widened Via Vittoria and the projected southern line to Parliament and the Pantheon. His final scheme responded to his "characteristic largeness of vision in conceiving the monumental ensemble and his aristocratic instinct in working out details."[50] The color of brick and travertine merged the old monuments with the new buildings. Imperial and Fascist Rome came together here, and the three churches were retained as well, as testimony to the historical development of the city. "Here where Christian Rome has set up the religious aspiration of its domes and imperial Rome the manly and secure firmness of its walls, the Rome of Mussolini will provide the unity of composition and atmosphere."[51]

Criticism was directed toward two points. One concerns the mausoleum and pertains to Muñoz's contribution: its restoration is too dry, too archaeological. Ugo Ojetti proposes to ring it with statues of great augustani: Agrippa, Livia, Virgil, Germanicus, Maecenas, Horace, Livy. "The idea of Augustus today is alive, supreme, and tangible: it is not a hole and not a ruin." There is also some worry about the monotony of the new structures. What figure is the mausoleum going to cut, Ojetti asks, "among these angular and shiny giants?" Why not have, instead of these curtain buildings, a major public edifice like a theater or a museum dominate the piazzale? To hide within their unvaried frames a movie theater and an auditorium for the Accademia Filarmonica is not the same thing at all.[52] In 1934

when the demolition of the Augusteo had been decided upon for the sake of exposing the fabric of the mausoleum, a competition was held for a new auditorium to replace it. The site chosen was the corner of Viale Aventino and Viale Guido Bacelli, at the opposite end of Via dei Trionfi from the Arch of Constantine. The jury, which included Piacentini and Muñoz, had selected two projects, by the teams of Guidi/Nervi/Valle and DeRenzi/Libera/Vaccaro. The jury's plans to have a final runoff for the winning design were dropped by 1936, and the site was preempted by the new Ministry of African Affairs.[53] Ojetti wonders why the auditorium could not have been moved to the new Piazzale Augusto Imperatore.

Actually, Morpurgo had investigated this possibility in a number of studies. Since the beginning of his involvement with the piazzale he had been encouraged to consider, for the north of the piazzale and the northwestern triangle between Via di Ripetta and the Lungotevere after the proposed demolition of Camporesi's Accademia di Belle Arti along the path of the new diagonal artery (Fig. 16), an ensemble of buildings dedicated to the arts, especially music. There were two musical institutions of the State that would benefit from such a program: the Reggia Accademia Filarmonica Romana and the Reggia Accademia di Santa Cecilia, the former now housed in the so-called Casina del Valadier on Via Flaminia, the latter in a former convent at the corner of Via Vittoria and the Corso. The northwestern triangle is designated for a "liceo artistico" in the final Morpurgo project. An earlier solution shows it as the seat of the Accademia Filarmonica, the site being defined by the diagonal artery, the Ripetta, and Vicolo del Fiume to the north (Fig. 30). The conservatory of the Accademia di Santa Cecilia is then allotted most of the block between Via di S. Giacomo (A. Canova) and Via del Vantaggio, that is, the site of the present Ospedale di S. Giacomo in Augusta. The Ripetta facade of this latter building preserves the chapel at the south corner of the block and the corresponding neoclassical frontispiece to the north used as end feature by Pietro Camporesi the younger in his redoing of the hospital. Fabbricato B on the piazzale itself would house the auditorium proper. A detailed scheme for it presents two monumental facades, one toward the Ripetta and the other toward the piazzale (Figs. 31a, 31b). Both eschew the tiered arrangement of windows designating the stories of an office building in order to afford unified frontages of a public character. On the Ripetta side the formula is of four tall window-bands linked at the bottom by a continuous balcony; on the piazzale side the facade plane is largely solid above the portico, except for narrow slits along the bottom of

29
Morpurgo study for the Piazzetta di S.
Carlo; unpublished, 1937.

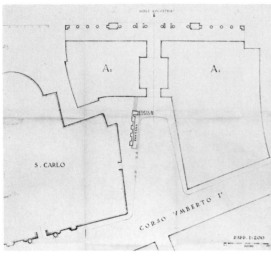

30
Morpurgo project for the area north of
Via di S. Giacomo (A. Canova) and
the corresponding triangle west of Via
di Ripetta; unpublished, 1936[?].

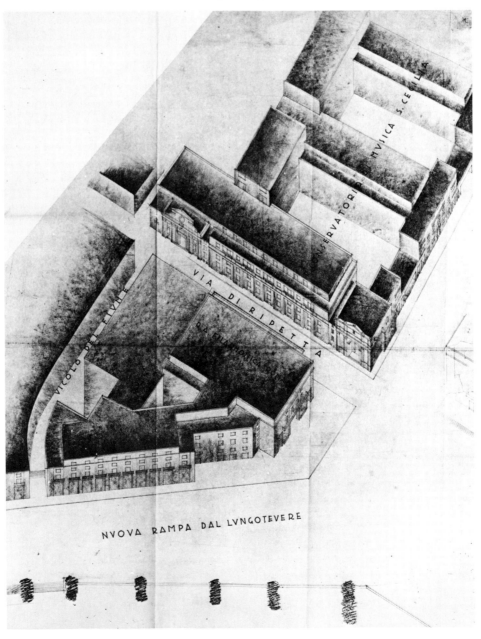

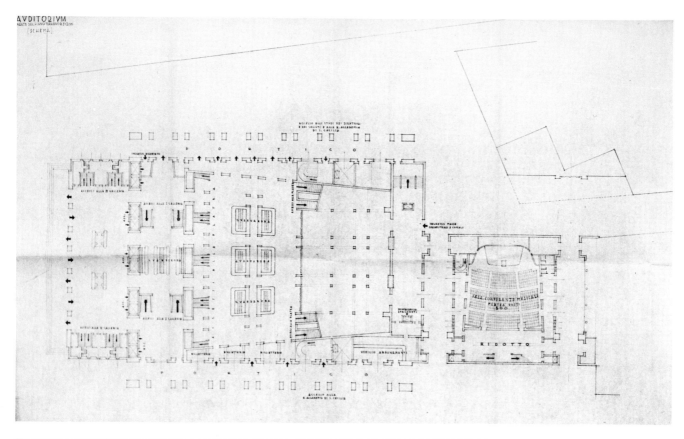

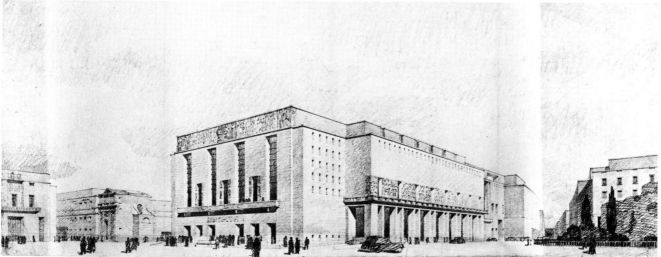

31a
Project for an auditorium building on the north side of the piazzale, plan; Morpurgo, unpublished, 1936[?].

31b
Project for an auditorium building, general view; unpublished. The shorter facade is on the Ripetta, the longer on Via dei Pontefici.

the plane, dividing a broad sculptural frieze, and a band of very small windows along the top. This grandiose program, which would have amplified the scope of the piazzale considerably, remained on the boards.

Two sets of circumstances conspired to bring about fundamental alterations in the final Morpurgo project, and they are evident in the executed version of Piazzale Augusto Imperatore as we have it today. The latter of these is the result of the war; it affected the realization of the new approaches into the piazzale and made a shambles of its circulation rationale. To this point I shall return shortly. The second set of circumstances relates to the political mentality of the Fascist regime during the years when the piazzale was under construction and is reflected in the attempt to imbue this historically suggestive planning scheme with more tangible symbolic content. Valorizzazione, like all other party propaganda, was now becoming dogmatic. The Italian empire had been proclaimed in May 1936. Although the title "Emperor of Abyssinia" had to be conferred upon Victor Emanuel III, no one, and least of all the Duce himself, doubted the identity of its true founder. The act, however postured it may have appeared to outsiders, was prophecy fulfilled. The chief obstacle to the grand comparison, the reality of Augustus's empire, had been removed by the creation of an empire of Mussolini's own. The argument that the Duce of Fascism was the new Augustus had thus been clinched. Propagandists—planners and artists included—derived thereby fresh authority for their labors. The Mostra Augustea della Romanità added impetus to this rejuvenated process of historical parallelism. In hundreds of books and articles, scholars and journalists alike probed into all aspects of the Augustan age. And their concluding thoughts were invariably dedicated to the present.

In two works of these years written by Fascist stalwarts, such elements of similarity were collected and systematized. Of these books, L'Italia d'Augusto e l'Italia d'oggi by Minister of Education G. Bottai is the subtler propaganda.[54] There is, he asserts, no need to draw exact parallels. Augustus and Mussolini are "two great heads of state grappling with many identical or similar or assimilable problems to which they provide, each one, solutions proper to their times."[55] What is important is the unity of concept and method "that makes of Italian politics across the centuries, in the most diverse periods and historical climates, the same politics—unmistakable for its human balance, its harmonious sense of relationships, its live intuition of reality."[56] Nonetheless, Bottai builds on his analysis of the institutions of the Augustan age to conclude his presentation with a list of specific parallels. Both periods had the challenge of resolving the conflict between civil and military

power; both did so with the transformation of party militia into a national guard and the institution of the empire. Both men had the same respect for parliament, a formal respect that led them to keep it, out of deference to the past, but alter substantially its structure and function. The centralization of power in Rome and the system of provincial government subject to central authority—this too they hold in common. "Rome reconstructed . . . veterans and youth called together to support and defend the regime."[57] Finally, the religious and moral policy of these two architects of empire is hailed, the reference being to Augustus's restoration of the state religion and Mussolini's conciliation of state and church, after fifty bitter years of conflict, with the signing of the Lateran Accords in 1929 between his government and Pope Pius XI.

Emilio Balbo's Protagonisti dell'Impero di Roma, Augusto e Mussolini is more explicit—and more fulsome.[58] "The great Artificer," the Duce, is presented as combining in his character the best of Caesar and Augustus: the genius of one, the "solid architecture" of the other.[59] Balbo has a reserved opinion of Augustus. Caesar was greater, but Augustus had the wisdom to surround himself with first-rate men who helped him govern and spread to the masses the essence of his thinking. There were generals who fought his wars, poets who sang paeans to the great Augustan themes of peace and prosperity, health of the body and the spirit, the return to the land. But the price was a corporate image of empire; whereas the Fascist empire, being the handiwork of Mussolini alone, is more harmonious. Augustus and Mussolini are protagonists of the same story, "the Dioscouri of the same constitutional and political crisis."[60] Both men suppressed civil disorders that rent the fiber of Italian society: they recognized the need of the people for authoritarian rule. Pedantically, Balbo goes on to equate Augustus's reconquest of Spain with the Fascist intervention in the Spanish civil war on the side of General Franco. But there is still more. Like Augustus, Mussolini grasped the beneficence of public works; they not only serve to enhance national patrimony but also to provide jobs for the unemployed. The Duce ennobled labor, as had Augustus. He emulated the Augustan policy of population growth by rewarding fecundity and honoring the prolific mother. Now as then, rural Italy is rejuvenated, cities decongested, veterans settled in new country towns such as Aprilia, Littoria, Sabaudia, Pontinia. Rome is bound to have its Virgil again, to rhapsodize the fertile land, the grazing ground. And in the midst of it all, the subject of religion is brought up anew. Where, Balbo asks, did Christianity fit in this great equation of Romanness? The case had been made before, and Balbo repeats it.

Jesus was born in the time of Augustus; Christianity without Rome would never have amounted to much; and just as the birth of the first Roman empire coincided with the birth of Christianity, so in the second empire Mussolini restored the ancestral faith of the people by his conciliation of the Vatican.

If the Church found the association with the mythology of the regime objectionable or distasteful, it did not say so. On the contrary, it accepted publicly the claims of Fascist propaganda and reinforced the symbolic content of this association from its own viewpoint and to its own advantage. The reason Mussolini could revive the Roman empire was precisely that the Church had maintained the universalism of Rome after the close of the pagan era. Mussolini himself, as early as 1922, had declared that "the universalism of the papacy [is] the heir of the universalism of the Roman empire." The Church, furthermore, had no difficulty in condoning the Ethiopian war, since it interpreted Fascist imperialism merely as a different means toward the same end: the subjugation of the world by Rome. In a remarkable speech on 26 February 1937 at Milan's Castello Sforzesco, Cardinal Schuster candidly espoused this theme in presenting the Church's own view of the propinquity between the emperor Augustus and the Duce.[61] ". . . The Eternal City pursues its double mission of civilization and religion; while the august pontiff Pius XI sends missionaries to the ultimate limits of the world to preach Jesus Christ the Universal Savior, the Italian legions, in claiming Ethiopia for civilization and banishing from it slavery and barbarisms, wish to secure for these peoples and the entire civil consortium the double benefit of imperial culture and the Catholic faith that resides in common Roman citizenship." To Schuster, in pagan terms, the Lateran pact was the new Ara Pacis of the resurgent empire, and the Duce the new Augustus. In Christian terms, the pact was the modern equivalent of the Edict of Milan of 313, whereby the Roman State abandoned its persecution of the church and recognized the legitimate authority of Christianity; and in these terms, Mussolini was the new Constantine the Great.

This contrived ideology had found its way into the Mostra Augustea, where it acquired visual force. To the many rooms documenting every aspect of Roman life in antiquity was added a room devoted to early Christianity, the heir of the empire. Beyond this, highlighted by gigantic inscriptions from Dante, Petrarch, Macchiavelli, D'Annunzio, Victor Emanuel III, and of course Mussolini, came a special exhibition dedicated to "The Immortality of the Idea of Rome; The Renaissance of Empire in Fascist Italy." A vast photographic collage along the walls displayed climactic evidence of this immortal idea. Represented, among others, were three triumphal

arches side by side: that of Constantine the Great in Rome, that by Marcello Piacentini at Bolzano, and the Ara dei Dileni in Cirenaica set up in memory of "the triumphal visit of the Duce in Libya" and the inauguration of the imperial highway called Strada Litoranea. THE SERIES HAS BEEN RESUMED, a title announced, and the panorama continued with a triptych consisting of the obelisk Augustus had erected in the Circus Maximus to commemorate the conquest of Egypt, flanked by the obelisk of Axum and the Lion of Judah, trophies of the Fascist conquest of Abyssinia. A modern painting of the offerings of gold by Roman women during the Punic Wars was paired with an image of the queen leading Italian matrons as they turned in their wedding rings for the coffers of the Fascist wars. The conciliation of church and state was illustrated by a photograph that showed the "happily united" flags of Italy and the Vatican in the entrance portico of St. Peter's.[62] One Mussolini dictum proclaimed that "the Italian people is an immortal people that always finds a spring for its hopes, its passion, its grandeur"; the same words that appear on the portico of Fabbricato A in Pazzale Augusto Imperatore, in the midst of a long sculptural frieze by Alfredo Biagini.

What the two books and the Mostra Augustea demonstrate is the literalness with which late Fascism sold its message of revived Roman grandezza, and the labored, highly selective historical revisionism it indulged in. The pairing of the emperor with the Duce and the weaving of the Christian, or rather papal, theme into this impressionistic canvas are both basic to the understanding of the iconography of Piazzale Augusto Imperatore. The precedent of the Bottai-Balbo exegesis and Giglioli's bimillennial exposition supply the interpretive tools. Material evidence in the piazzale itself includes the monuments, the inscriptions, and the art.

After the publication of Morpurgo's final project in 1936, a new monument was added to the major four, the mausoleum and the churches, that had been the historic elements in the planning of the piazzale until then. The monument was the Ara Pacis, and the decision to set it up by the river, between the Lungotevere and the Ripetta, was once again Mussolini's (Fig. 32). From the start of Morpurgo's involvement with this program, the intention had been present to relate this masterpiece of Augustan art to the mausoleum. Initially, the reliefs that comprised it, those among them that belonged to or could be acquired by the state, were to be housed in the museum planned for the propylaea block of the mausoleum. In the final Morpurgo project, when the museum was put underground, a scheme was worked out to mount these reliefs in the central room in a way that would approximate the original form of the altar. "It seems clear," the official literature said, "that the topographic connection of the museum with the ruins will increase the interest of both and help further developments for the glory of the great Emperor whose name the zone bears."[63] But the glory, as every one associated with this enterprise knew, was to be shared by the Duce. Both in terms of urban scenography and symbolic impact, therefore, the underground arrangement was unsatisfactory. A recent Mussolini directive, embraced by the final Morpurgo project, had already brought about the clearing of buildings between the Piazzale and the Lungotevere in an effort to reorient the entire composition toward the Tiber. Now, sometime in 1937, the Duce gave the order to utilize this space for the Ara Pacis, to be set up on axis, laterally, with the mausoleum.

In the same year new excavations were undertaken at the original site of the Ara Pacis at the corner of Via in Lucina and the Corso. This delicate operation below the Palazzo Fiano was masterminded by the hydraulic engineer Giovanni Rodio and involved the freezing of the soil to permit excavation. Simultaneously a campaign was launched to bring together the disjecta membra of the altar. The greater part of the reliefs were in the custody of the Museo delle Terme in Rome and the Uffizi in Florence. These presented no problem. The church was the owner of two related pieces of the senator frieze. One was in the Vatican museums; the other had been used, upside down, as a tombstone for Monsignor Sebastiano Poggi, bishop of Ripa, in the Gesù since 1628, and its true identity was not established until 1899. These too were eventually assimilated, the Vatican fragment not until 1954 when it was donated to the state by Pope Pius XII. Several pieces, including two rinceau pilasters, immured in the garden facade of the Villa Medici, the seat of the French Academy in Rome, were foreign property, and in the end had to be reproduced in plaster. A handsome fragment that belonged to the procession panels was also in French hands. In their effort to appease Mussolini and forestall his threatened attack on France the authorities were willing to allow its transfer to Rome, but Ambassador André François-Poncet's offer to this effect in May 1939 was turned down. Mussolini is quoted as saying, "Had I accepted the fragment of the Ara Pacis, the whole French press would have said that I would have to be satisfied with a few stones instead of Tunisia or Corsica."[64]

During 1938 the Ara Pacis Augustae was assembled in its new location under a protective shell designed by Morpurgo; the archaeological director was G. Moretti. At least two solutions for this shell had been proposed (Figs. 33, 34). One utilized a peripteral colonnade; the other consisted of walled-in short ends with entrance doors from north and south, and for the long sides toward the river and the Ripetta, a system of double piers and floor-to-ceiling glazing. In the end, the latter scheme was adopted with some changes. The system of the long sides was carried all around the building, and the plain piers were redesigned to echo abstractly the pilasters of the altar itself (Figs. 35a, 35b). The tall base of the building on the Ripetta side was used to inscribe the text of the Res Gestae (Fig. 36). As reconstructed, the Ara Pacis lost its original east-west axis and was turned around ninety degrees to line up with the Ripetta. But it managed in its reincarnation to expose the themes and words of the Augustan age as a foil for Fascist response.

At the Mostra Augustea, the Res Gestae had been prominently displayed as part of the reconstruction of the pronaos of the temple of Augustus in Ankara. This spare recital of the emperor's accomplishments had been inscribed, in accordance with his wishes and at the instigation of his successor Tiberius, upon two bronze tablets set up at the entrance to the mausoleum. Morpurgo's final project provided for the recreation of this arrangement. The subsequent reordering of the piazzale along an east-west axis no doubt influenced the decision to relegate the text to the Ripetta frontage of the reconstructed Ara Pacis. Its language, especially the parts dealing with the emperor's construction and repair of public buildings, was now echoed in the main commemorative inscription of the piazzale, on the ground-story level of the frontispiece of Fabbricato B that culminated the axis of the southern approach (Figs. 37, 38). It is in Latin and refers specifically to the "extraction of the mausoleum from the shadows of the centuries," the remaking of the Ara Pacis, and the erasing of the extant congestion for the greater splendor of streets, buildings, and churches. The year: 1940, the eighteenth of the Fascist era.[65]

The inscription is flanked by two winged victories holding up fasces. Further up, beyond the presentation balcony, there is a mosaic triptych. The river Tiber stands up in his waters holding the infant twins, Romulus and Remus, with the she-wolf at his feet. The Sun rises out of the sea holding on to his horses; he is accompanied by two divinities [?]. The narrow side panels below this trio show heroic figures representative of various labors: drawing water, reaping, planting trees. Rome set out from such modest beginnings, the inscription over the window says, in seeming reference both to the fateful infants and to these heraldic personifications of pastoralism: HIS AB EXIGVIS PROFECTA INITIIS ROMA. The tripartite composition recalls that of the cuirass in the Augustus of Prima Porta, flattened out—the central, culminating scene topped by a celestial motif

32
Revised plan of the piazzale, 1938.
The Ara Pacis is shown in place, and
the space in front of the tribuna of S.
Carlo has been redesigned.

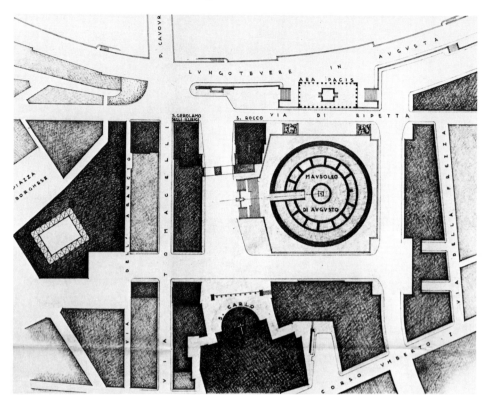

33
Model of one Morpurgo solution for
the Ara Pacis building, 1938. (Vasari)
34
Model of an alternative Morpurgo solution for the building of the Ara
Pacis. (Vasari)

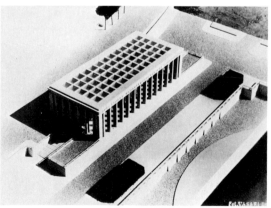

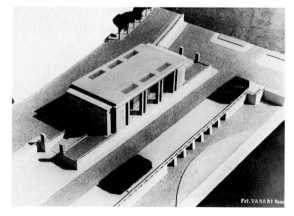

35a
The Ara Pacis building, final solution.
The photograph is taken after 1971
when the building was restored on the
initiative of the Rotary Club. (M.
Treib)

35b
The interior of the Ara Pacis building,
just after construction, 1939. (Vasari)

36
Podium of the Ara Pacis building, Via di Ripetta; detail of the Res Gestae text. (M. Treib)
37
Piazzale Augusto Imperatore from the southeast; to the right, the Fabbricato A. (R. Tobias)

The frontispiece of Fabbricato *B*. (M
Treib)

and flanked by supportive images. The sentiment is an evocation of continuity and the virtues of the simple life. The style is unmistakably of the thirties.

On this same facade, in the fourth bay from each end of the projecting central portion, two inset panels contain reliefs that illustrate the kinship of Roman imperial and Fascist arms (Figs. 39–40b). The western panel is composed of Classical military motifs disposed around the windows: helmets, shields, bows and arrows, musical instruments, and so forth (Fig. 40a). Below, in raised letters, the Christian date: A. MCMXL POST CHRISTUM NATUM. The other panel shows muskets, cannon, gas masks, and contemporary Italian uniforms (Fig. 40b). The corresponding Fascist date below this panel was subsequently chiseled out. To Fascist interpreters, as we have seen, the Ara Pacis was a monument eloquent of military strength, the symbol of Roman dominion over "all the decrepit civilizations of the old world." The martial aspect of the Augustan age was increasingly insisted upon after 1935 when Fascist policy became openly aggressive.

Other Augustan themes singled out in contemporary Fascist accounts of the altar were: "la glorificazione viva della famiglia," evident, according to this view, in the presence of numerous children who accompany the marching dignitaries in the great procession panels; and the flowering of agriculture and husbandry, with the consequent abundance of the land, as portrayed in the allegory of the Tellus relief[66] (Fig. 41). The appropriateness of these latter themes to Fascist iconography should be clear from our discussion of the books by Bottai and Balbo. They constitute the subject matter of the long frieze by Alfredo Biagini on Fabbricato A across the piazzale from the Ara Pacis (Figs. 42–43c). Motifs of the Tellus relief—the goddess with the full breasts holding healthy babies in her lap, the grazing sheep and lazing cow, the plants and fruits and flowers— are given here a contemporary reading, interspersed with related neo-Augustan concerns, in forty-two near life-size figures on either side of the Mussolini aphorism on the immortality of the Italian people. It is a Virgilian idyl in Carrara marble: shepherd boys tending their flocks, robust peasant mothers dangling Fascist babies, young girls carrying baskets of fruit or husks of grain, the hoeing and tilling of the land, the pressing of the grape, the noble laborer hoisting his spade and pick like standards of battle. These images of Fascist prosperity are not irrelevant to the social security concerns of the corporate client that commissioned the building, but subjects more directly representative of the program of the INFPS are contained in tiny terracotta reliefs above the top-story windows of this central section of Fabbricato A (Fig. 44).

Christian content is tied in with this double golden age of empire, Augustus's and Mussolini's, by means of various devices. First comes the presence of the three churches on the piazzale, which allows Mussolini, in his commemorative inscription on Fabbricato B, to refer to AEDES, the word used repeatedly in the Res Gestae in the inventory of the many temples repaired or rebuilt by Augustus during his reign. Illirici and Schiavoni, attached to the name of S. Girolamo, have the ring of titles of conquest that formed a string of epithets identifying a specific Roman emperor. Here and there around the piazzale, representations in relief of the Madonna with the Christ Child, and once also the infant St. John, provide the Christian equivalent of Tellus and the Fascist mother.

The Christian thread is also helpful in the introduction of the theme of peace which, above all others, characterizes the achievement of Augustus and is the chief justification for the existence of the Ara Pacis. Between 1937 and 1940, when the piazzale was under construction, it would have been too incredible even for Romans to represent Fascist Italy as peaceful. To be sure, party rhetoric maintained that the recent adventures of aggression were for the sake of peace. In the speech of 9 May 1936 proclaiming the founding of the Fascist empire, the Duce described it as "the empire of peace, because Italy wants peace for herself and everyone else";[67] and this passage was included as one of the inscriptions of the hall dedicated to The Immortality of the Idea of Rome in the great Augustan exposition of the following year. But by 1940 peace was an improbable addition to the parallelisms between the ages of Augustus and Mussolini. The emperor's championship of peace is echoed instead by Christ. In the central one of three mosaic panels that decorate the top story of the Collegio degli Illirici, facing toward the Mausoleum and the Ara Pacis, Christ is celebrated as PRINCEPS PACIS (Fig. 45). The lateral panels deal with subjects of local importance for this alien congregation. To the left, the Byzantine emperor Heraclius baptizing Croatians with the assistance of priests invited from Rome; to the right, Demetrius (Swonimir), duke of Dalmatia and Croatia, being raised by Pope Gregory VII to the rank of king and becoming the vassal of St. Peter, an event that occurred in 1076.[68]

In addition to Augustus and Christ, there is present on the piazzale a third prince of peace. He is Pope Pius XI, whose adopted motto read "Pax Christi in regno Christi." Achille Ratti was elevated to the seat of Peter as Pius XI in 1922, the year of the Fascist march on Rome; he died in 1939 when the deterioration of the regime had set in irreversibly.[69] In the parallel lives of the emperor and the Duce, the role of Pius XI was a mediating one; or so at least

39
Facade of Fabbricato *B* along Via dei
Pontefici, showing the arms panels.
(R. Tobias)

40a
Fabbricato *B*: Roman arms. (M. Treib)

40b
Fabbricato *B*: Fascist arms. (M. Treib)

41
Ara Pacis, the so-called Tellus relief;
detail.

42
Fabbricato *A*, along the east side of
the piazzale. (R. Tobias)

43a
Sculptural frieze of Fabbricato *A,* by
A. Biagini, 1940; detail

43b
Sculptural frieze of Fabbricato *A*;
detail.

43c
Sculptural frieze of Fabbricato *A*;
detail.

44
Fabbricato *A*, facade toward the piazzale; small reliefs just below the main cornice line representing accidents insured by INFPS.

45
The Collegio degli Illirici, facade toward the piazzale. (R. Tobias)

Fascist commentary would have it. It was his agreement to the Lateran accords of 1929 that had endowed Mussolini's reputation as protector of the ancestral faith, a policy much exploited by Augustus. This unwitting assistance of Pius in the marriage of the two empiremakers is quite naturally introduced into the iconography of the piazzale through the presence of the church of S. Carlo. At the time Achille Ratti was elected pope, he had been archbishop of Milan, and S. Carlo as the "national" church of Lombardy had been specifically associated with him. It was here in this church, furthermore, that Ratti said his first mass on 21 December 1879, the day after he had been ordained priest in the Lateran. This fact is recorded in one of two plaques affixed to the tribuna of S. Carlo, the other being devoted to the conciliation of church and state through the Lateran accords. Pius is described as an "advocate of concord among peoples" who, in the name of justice and peace, restored Italy to God and God to Italy.[70]

A cobbled platform distinguishes the level of the tribuna from that of the rest of the piazzale. The small semi-independent piazzetta that is thus formed is further isolated from the main space by means of a low stone fence with roundheaded posts, very commonly used in the Fascist period. The two ends of the fence are punctuated by life-size statues of S. Ambrogio and S. Carlo, by Arturo Dazzi and Attilio Selva respectively (Fig. 46). The earlier notion of Morpurgo's to have the single statue of S. Carlo dominating the piazzetta at the Corso entrance to the piazzale with an adjacent cascade-fountain had been discarded in favor of this new arrangement.

Today the only sculptural decoration for this piazzetta is four small travertine panels over the entrance proper, consisting of a heraldic interweaving of all three threads—pagan, Christian, and Fascist (Figs. 47–48b). The point here is to demonstrate the mutual dependence of church and state in antiquity and in the present, a familiar theme of Fascist propaganda. "Every religion, in order to accomplish its mission of the care of the spirit, is in need of the support of the state," to quote Balbo.[71] The left-hand panels represent the state as a composite of arms and the arts (Fig. 48a). The top relief blends the Roman eagle, shield, and crown of victory with a Classical capital. For the Fascist equivalent, there is the fasces and an open book crossed with a gun, the ideogram for Mussolini's famous maxim, inscribed on the entrance of the new University: "Libro e moschetto, Fascista perfetto" (the book and the musket make the perfect Fascist). The right-hand panels represent Roman religion with an emblem of such symbols as the hourglass and the sacrificial axe, while below, Catholicism is evoked with the

cross, the miter, the staff, and the chalice (Fig. 48b). A panel over the door of the northern facade of the piazzetta has been defaced, except for a crown; it probably represented the crest of the House of Savoy, to which Victor Emanuel III belonged.

Augustus died an old and venerated man. The political system he nurtured was passed on peaceably to the care of his successor. Mussolini's end came about differently: the grand comparison foundered. His work was renounced, his plans for the future abandoned, projects of grandezza in progress at his fall were left unfinished. Some small signs of the damnatio memoriae he suffered are here and there noticeable around Piazzale Augusto Imperatore, but the effort clearly was not thorough. His words and the imagery of his age remain unmolested. Even his name is only half expunged in the Latin inscription of Fabbricato B (Fig. 38). If this vast and graceless square fails to excite today, as urban space or as conceit, it is not because its purpose has been maimed posthumously. Nor is it true that the work, when arrested by the collapse of the regime, was too incomplete to register its full impact. With the exception of some sculpture—the statue of Augustus at the entrance to his mausoleum, for example, the reliefs of the cavalcavia between S. Girolamo and S. Rocco, the group atop the frontispiece of Fabbricato B, and perhaps one or two others—the piazzale had been finished by 1941, the nineteenth of the Fascist era (Fig. 49). The blame, in large measure, is inherent.

To be just, one element of failure should be ascribed to adversity. The original conception of this grandiloquent Fascist project was wedded to a broad system of circulation. Without arguing the wisdom or folly in the constant philosophy of sventramenti, it must be admitted that the futility of the square is attributable, at one level, to the fact that the fast new arteries prescribed by the master plan of 1931, which the square was designed to accommodate, did not in fact materialize. The traffic route from the periphery of Piazza Colonna to the extramural north was aborted because the proposed slash that would lead to the piazzale from the Pantheon and the Parliament building remained on paper (Fig. 50). Similarly, the flow of traffic from Piazza di Spagna to the right bank could not be effectuated without the widening of Via Vittoria. After the war, an attempt was made to set straight this latter problem. In October 1951 the city council voted approval of a proposal that revived the idea of a new road and tunnel along Via Vittoria, but the vehement outcry in the press convinced the Ministry of Public Works to veto the proposal.[72] Rome had had enough of demolition.

Yet even with the intended traffic scheme fully in operation, the inefficacy of the piazzale would not have disappeared. The basic conflict of the project was between the traditional concept of a piazza, which assumes enclosure, and a major traffic interchange dependent upon open flow. By insisting upon both of these, the coherence of the project was inevitably prejudiced. In the end, the design stumbled into an unadmitted compromise—a piazza within a piazza, with the traffic interchange fitted between the two.

The inner piazza was preordained. Once the decision had been made to isolate the mausoleum and reveal its original frame, a well around it would have to result, with a grade difference of about five meters (15 ft.) between the Augustan level and the modern street level. This well, properly circumscribed, could serve as a natural piazza with a main southern approach where the entrance to the mausoleum had been.

Now Fascist planners were never very successful in the handling of these archaeological wells. The disposition of the Largo Argentina temple complex is a case in point. The method by which visitors would reach the ancient ground level was not adequately resolved here, largely because of the speedy traffic lanes established on all four sides and also because of the considerable lateral spread of the ruins that discouraged axial approaches. The fence at the modern street level strengthens the sense of separation, so that the visitor looks down upon the temples today as at some fixed attraction in a pit. But the mausoleum was a single strong form with a definite axis. The extent of the sanctioned demolition afforded room enough to negotiate the change of level less abruptly. In the Muñoz/Morpurgo collaboration a solution was developed that recognized these two facts by availing itself of landscaped slopes all around and a grand staircase to mark the south axis (Figs. 19, 27, 28).

This, however, was not to be the real piazza. It was turned instead into the central feature of an encompassing piazzale whose own defining lines were pushed further and further out, partly to match the scale and importance of this monument with the size of the space created for it and partly because of the demands of the new traffic arteries, which were directed hitherward. Isolated in its own archaeological setting and surrounded by fast traffic lanes, the relation between the mausoleum and its vast piazzale became obscure. What is more, the main approach of the mausoleum from the south, which supplied a clear axis for the inner piazza, was now in open conflict with the vacillating orientation of the piazzale itself. The inner axis could not be continued directly southward beyond Via Tomacelli. The design favored a main statement on the Corso side at first; then, at Mussolini's direction, the Piazzale was opened toward the Tiber; finally, this new axis was awkwardly blocked by the mass of the Ara Pacis building.

Beyond the unreconciled tensions of axis and congruity between the mausoleum and its immediate periphery on the one hand and the expansive piazzale on the other, other elements of the design add to the confusion. The actual height of the enclosing modern buildings, for one thing, appears to have been a poor choice. It manages to screen the surrounding urban fabric so completely that the piazzale, at least from within, becomes totally detached from its historic context. The scale is so out of tune with the prevailing spatial organization of this zone that it is a surprise to come upon this modern square in the thick of the Piazza del Popolo trident or to walk out of its untidy vastness in any direction but the west (Fig. 51). Outsized urban spaces were not new to Rome. Indeed, to Fascist thinking they were another throwback to the age of Augustus, whose forum in Rome, excavated by the regime in the twenties, was viewed as an example of the imperial program, started under Julius Caesar, "to create in the urban fabric vast open spaces."[73] The contrast of passage from a dense network of streets into such explosive openness had been successfully cultivated in Rome, both then and later, notably in the baroque period, for its dramatic possibilities. The drama is absent in the case at hand for two reasons. Most of the approaches into the piazzale are themselves too ample to induce the desired excitement of release from a state of constriction; and secondly, the mausoleum itself so massively dominates the space that it is hard to believe that the piazzale is indeed larger than Piazza del Popolo to the north. In absolute volume, yes; but at Piazza del Popolo the vast oval space, for one thing, is unencumbered except for the obelisk in the middle that focuses it. The experience, therefore, coming up the Corso or the Ripetta or Via del Babuino, is of approaching the beacon of the obelisk, sensing the openness it signifies, and at the end stepping into this anticipated openness. The only meaningful constriction at the edges of the piazzale is the entrance gallery from the Corso. But the view one has ahead as he crosses it is of a tree-topped mass thoroughly obstructing any sense of ampleness beyond (Fig. 52).

What this discussion suggests is that the enclosing buildings of the piazzale, to engender some kind of positive experience, should have been either lower or taller than they are. The former possibility, toyed with by Morpurgo, would have exposed the irregular and picturesque skyline of the older fabric at least toward Via Tomacelli and Via della Frezza, and this in turn would have established the urban context of this project (Fig. 23). Fascist planners and architects were often inclined to contrive physical connections between their work and neighboring structures of

47
Corso entrance to Piazzale Augusto
Imperatore. (M. Treib)

46
Statue of S. Carlo Borromeo, by A.
Selva, 1940. (M. Treib)

48a
Corso entrance; detail of emblems of
state. (M. Treib)
48b
Corso entrance; detail of emblems of
church. (M. Treib)

49
Pier of cavalcavia between flanks of S.
Girolamo and S. Rocco; inner face
toward piazzale, detail with date. (M.
Treib)

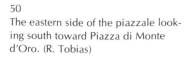

The eastern side of the piazzale looking south toward Piazza di Monte
d'Oro. (R. Tobias)

51
Aerial view of the area between
Piazza del Popolo at the top and the
piazzale at bottom left. The photo-
graph was taken in December 1942.
(Courtesy of E. Nash)
52
The inner portico of Fabbricato A, on
axis with the Corso entrance. (M.
Treib)

older periods. Sometimes the device consisted of nothing more than the mechanical repetition of single motifs or of facade articulation. In the exterior frontages of the piazzale, especially on the Corso and on Via Tomacelli, the practice holds. We have already noted the piano nobile balconies of the Corso facade as one such accommodation. On the Tomacelli side, the main cornice between the travertine and brick sections of the Collegio degli Illirici facade, as well as the height of the building when viewed from the street, were conditioned by string courses along the flank of the adjacent church of S. Girolamo. But these were worthy links because the parent buildings, the older palazzi on Via del Corso and S. Girolamo respectively, as high-style architecture, merited respect. Within, the thought of looking out toward a ring of older construction as a gesture of physical continuity through the ages had no appeal precisely because of the picturesque character of the roofscape, disparageable, according to no less a person than Mussolini, as mere local color. As far as the interior of the piazzale is concerned, the only concession made to the zone's physical past is to compose the buildings in a combination of brick and travertine, the formula adopted generally by Fascist architects on the grounds that these were the commonest materials of Roman monuments since antiquity.

The second alternative, making the modern buildings of the piazzale higher than they are, would also have been effective, in a different way. It would have produced a definite contrast of height between the mausoleum and its built periphery, so that the distinction so obvious in plan or in air views between the circle of the monument and the rectangular frame of the piazzale could register within. As it is, there is little difference today between the full height of the mausoleum and that of Fabbricati A and B. The cylinder of the mausoleum rises twelve meters (36 ft.) above the modern street level; *i cipressi di Muñoz* upon the structure, taller since the thirties, lift the mass up to the roofline of the Fabbricati. The so-called Sedia del Diavolo in Piazza Elio Callistio off Via Nomentana, a rectangular Roman tomb of imperial date, is much better served by the modern highrise apartment houses that surround it, accentuating its own scale and at the same time making them appear as an extension of it.

The question of how successful Piazzale Augusto Imperatore was as propaganda is harder to resolve. There is no doubt that the medium of urban planning was not the most direct for this kind of historical confrontation between the emperor and the Duce. The contrived similarities of their rules could have been more graphically and economically projected in a poster, say, or a mural, which would be easier to read. The techniques of the Mostra Augustea also produced more compact and impressive statements than are possible, perhaps, in the complex framework of large-scale urban design. Once again, however, we recall that there are superb examples in Rome where a new piazza or spatial sequence is burdened with political meaning and still succeeds as urban architecture. Baroque concetti were no less complicated than the neo-Augustan iconography of the piazzale.

One obvious point in this regard is that Morpurgo was not Bernini. Leaving aside the question of abilities, Morpurgo's control of his design was anything but total. But whatever the circumstances of its creation, the piazzale is not a good example of political art. Its aim is diffuse, both because the iconographic content to be broadcast was diffuse and also because the design of the piazzale, as it finally emerged, was diffuse. That the message was read at its time with varying degrees of understanding should not be in question. Romans were already cognizant of this kind of historical associationism through the full range of propaganda machinery used by the regime. What is doubtful is that the piazzale could sharpen the familiar message or add to it a new dimension of meaning.

And if for its time the piazzale was routine political art, for us today it is without impact. The precise relevance of art in the service of politics is not binding on posterity: But such art, if it is forceful, will not fail to engage posterity despite the detachment from its object. Piazzale Augusto Imperatore lacked conviction in its own terms; as a consequence, it is unable to impress us today. Its aim as political art had been to use relics of the Augustan age to lend authority to Fascist achievement. The contest, at least in the visual sense, was never really joined. The Fascist side of the balance is too weak: what we are conscious of is the Augustan substance. Our opinion of Augustus is not affected by his association with Mussolini, and our opinion of Mussolini is not enhanced. The Duce yields to the emperor and is lost. The piazzale, in the end, remains a colossal mistake.

Notes

This paper was started during a long stay in Rome in 1968 made possible by a Humanities Research Fellowship from the University of California, Berkeley; the work was subsequently supported by grants from the University's Committee on Research. The results were briefly summarized in the larger context of my recent book, *The Third Rome, 1870–1950: Traffic and Glory* (Berkeley, 1973), especially pp. 36–37 and 68–69. Papers of Vittorio Ballio Morpurgo dealing with the subject are now in the possession of his nephew, the architect Giorgio Santoro. Figures 12, 18, 23, 26, 28, 29, 30, 31a, and 31b are published here through his courtesy. I have also had the assistance of Meredith Clausen during the last phases of the research, and George Kunihiro and James Hong in the preparation of the illustrative material.

323
The Emperor and
the Duce: The
Planning of
Piazzale Augusto
Imperatore in
Rome

1
The text of this speech is given in *Scritti e discorsi di Benito Mussolini,* Hoepli edition, vol. IX (Milan, 1935): 137–138.

2
Mussolini's exact words are: "Ho ordinato che siano raccolte in grandi album moltissime fotografie degli esterni ed interni da demolire. . . ." I have been unable to locate any such large albums. The Museo di Roma has numerous volumes of photographs that record Fascist clearance projects of the twenties and thirties; one only, volume 7, is concerned with the mausoleum. In addition, the Museo di Roma has a series of drawings by Lucilio Cartocci, two of which are relevant. One shows an entire elevation of Vicolo Soderini before its demolition (Inventory no. 1194, ink on tracing paper, 34 cm high by 168.3 cm long, dated August 1935). The other is a ground-story elevation of the west side of the Corso, from Via degli Otto Cantoni to Via Pontefici, prior to the erection of Morpurgo's buildings (no. 14208, 34 by ca. 300 cm, dated 1935).

3
Ezio Bacino in *Gazzetta del Popolo,* 23 February 1937, p. 3.

4
The post-Antique history of the Mausoleum of Augustus is discussed in the following: Emilio Calvi, "L'Augusteo (Il teatro Corea)," *Nuova antologia di lettere, scienze ed arti,* series V, vol. 134, (1908): 103–109; V. Gardthausen, "Das Mausoleum Augusti," *Mittheilungen des deutschen archäologischen Instituts, römische Abteilung,* 36–37 (1921–1922), cols. 111–114; Antonio M. Colini, "Il Mausoleo d'Augusto," *Capitolium* 4 (1928): 11–22.

5
See Attilio La Padula, *Roma e la regione nell'epoca napoleonica* (Rome, 1969), p. 131 and pl. LXXXIX.

6
General planning histories of modern Rome that can be consulted for this and other details include: Marcello Piacentini (with F. Guidi), *Le vicende edilizie di Roma dal 1870 ad oggi,* (Rome, 1952); *Roma, città e piani* (Rome, 1959); Italo Insolera, *Roma moderna, un secolo di storia urbanistica,* Rome, 1971 (rev. ed.); Spiro Kostof, *The Third Rome, 1870–1950: Traffic and Glory* (Berkeley, 1973).

7
For the 1909 and subsequent official projects until 1932, see Virgilio Testa, "Attuazione del Piano Regolatore di Roma, piani particolareggiati di esecuzione: la zona del Augusteo," *Capitolium* 9 (1933): 107–128.

8
A recent account of the street is F. Bilancia and Salvatore Polito, "Via Ripetta," *Controspazio* 5 (1973), 18–47. For the history of this region in general, see Ermanno Ponti, "Come sorse e come scompare il quartiere attorno al Mausoleo di Augusto," *Capitolium* 11 (1935): 235–250; and Tod A. Marder, "The Porto di Ripetta in Rome," unpublished manuscript (1976; originally a Columbia University dissertation, 1975).

9
See: "Sistemazione del Lungotevere in Augusta," *Capitolium* 2 (1926): 102–104; and Carlo Cecchelli, "Fra Roma vecchia e nuova: artistiche sistemazioni all'antico Porto di Ripetta," *Capitolium* 4 (1928): 173–179.

10
Cecchelli, ibid., attributed the building to engineer Carlo Grazioli, but Andrea Busiri Vici recently claimed it as his own (*Capitolium* 40 [1965], 495 ff.).

11
On this north facade, there is the following inscription: QUO LOCO AD MAUSOLEUM AUGUSTI/CLEMENS XI/ FLUVIALEM PORTUM EXTRUXERAT/EIUS LOCI DECORI ATQUE AMOENITATI/AEDIBUS EXCITATIS ET VETERE FONTE RESTITUTO/ PRIVATO SUMPTU PROVISUM/ AD MCMXXIX/ GIACOMO MARESCALCHI BELLI FECIT. The paved space in front of the facade, containing the fountain and the columns, is called Piazzetta del Porto di Ripetta.

12
See: "Il riordinamento della circolazione tramviaria," *Capitolium* 1 (1925): 486 ff., esp. 491–493.

13
Federazione Fascista dell'Urbe, Commissione di studio problemi cittadini, *La sistemazione della zona augustea* (Rome, 1927); the report is addressed to the Governor, prince Ludovico Spada Potenziani, and is signed by G. Ceccarelli, president; M. Baratelli; E. Del Debbio; T. Mora; and P. Santamaria.

14
Scritti e discorsi, V (Milan, 1934): 245: "Voi toglierete la stolta contaminazione tranviaria che ingombra le strade di Roma . . ."

15
La sistemazione . . . augustea, pp. 20–22.

16
"I monumenti millenari della nostra storia debbono giganteggiare nella necessaria solitudine," *Scritti e discorsi,* V: 245.

17
Capitolium 1, (1925): 394.

18
Literally, "the first empire of Augustus." The text is as follows: "Tra cinque anni Roma deve apparire meravigliosa a tutte le genti del mondo; vasta, ordinata, potente, come fu ai tempi del primo impero di Augusto." *Scritti e discorsi,* V: 244.

19
Mussolini himself encouraged the comparison. He collaborated with Giovacchino Forzano on the play called *Cesare,* in which the case is made so heavyhandedly that it offended Mussolini's son-in-law and foreign minister, count Galeazzo Ciano. "Adulation is an art which one must practice with control. Forzano evidently goes too far in identifying the Duce with Caesar." [H. Gibson, ed., *The Ciano Diaries, 1939–1943* (New York 1949), p. 71.].

20
Capitolium 1 (1925): 402.

21
For a full bibliography on the Ara Pacis, see Ernest Nash, *Pictorial Dictionary of Ancient Rome,* 2d ed. (New York/ Washington, 1968), p. 63; full illustration in G. Moretti, *Ara Pacis Augustae* (Rome, 1948).

22
"L'Ara della Pace sul Campidoglio," *Capitolium* 1 (1925): 65–71.

23
Cf. *Capitolium* 1 (1925): 59, 394.

24
"La trasformazione dell' Augusteo," *Capitolium* 1 (1925): 24–27.

25
"L'unica città che nelle rive del Mediterraneo, fatale e fatato, abbia creato l'impero è Roma." *Scritti e discorsi,* V: 112.

26
For these early utterances, see Alessandro Bacchiani, "Roma nel pensiero di Benito Mussolini," *Capitolium* 1 (1925): 387–392.

27
The speech is published in full in *Capitolium* 2 (1926): 33–43.

28
Capitolium 6 (1930): 567.

29
Speech of 18 March 1932, in *Scritti e discorsi,* VIII: 30.

30
Aug. 100.

31
Several alternative projects to the piano particolareggiato were privately proposed between 1932 and 1934. One, by the Sicilian team of Rende-Nicotra, adds to the widened Via Vittoria a second transverse axis running from the facade of S. Carlo to Pietro Bernini's Barcaccia fountain in Piazza di Spagna. The eastern half of the piazza of the mausoleum, according to this scheme, is defined by a hemicycle, with the two transverse axes radiating out from it. [It is this Rende-Nicotra project of about 1933 that is illustrated in *Roma, città e piani* (n. 6 above), p. 139, fig. 159, where it is labeled as a "progetto anonimo e senza data."] A second project, by M. Zocca, accepts the action plan of 1932 but prolongs the new Via Vittoria, by means of a tunnel underneath Trinità dei Monti, until Via V. Veneto. For these and two other projects that do not affect the piazza of the mausoleum, see Pablo Rossi De Paoli, "L'isolamento dell'Augusteo e la sistemazione del traffico est-ovest a Roma," *Urbanistica* 4 (1935): 32–39.

32
See his own account, "La sistemazione del Mausoleo di Augusto," *Capitolium* 13 (1938): 491–508.

33
See Boito's *Questioni pratiche di belle arti* (Milan, 1893): 4 ff.

34
For a version of this scheme, see R. A. Cordingley and I. A. Richmond, "The Mausoleum of Augustus," *Papers of the British School at Rome* 10 (1927): 23 ff.

35
See Gatti, "Il Mausoleo di Augusto, studio di ricostruzione," *Capitolium* 10 (1934): 457–464. For the Poscetti version, see the 14 November 1934 issue of *Giornale d'Italia.*

36
Capitolium 13 (1938): 503.

37
See Ferdinando Reggiori, "Il concorso per la torre littoria sull'area della 'Manica lunga' di Palazzo Reale in Piazza del Duomo a Milano," *Architettura* 14 (1935): 475–486.

38
See *Architettura e arti decorative* 9 (1929/1930): 215, for the Varese master plan; 236 ff., for a boarding school by Morpurgo at Varese; and 365 ff., for the S. Spirito project.

39
For this competition, see special issue of *Architettura* (1934).

40
See *Architettura* 19 (1940): 371–376.

41
Ugo Ojetti in *Corriere della sera,* 26 November 1936.

42
Dedication page of A. Muñoz, *L'isolamento del Colle Capitolino* (Rome, 1943).

43
For INFPS, see the pamphlet in English, *Work of the National Fascist Institute of Social Insurance* (Rome, 1935).

44
See *Architettura,* special Christmas issue (1936), entitled "Urbanistica della Roma Mussoliniana," p. 79. For this first project, see also: "L'isolamento del mausoleo di Augusto," *L'Ingegnere* 9 (June 1935); "La sistemazione del Mausoleo di Augusto," *Capitolium* 11 (1935): 251–255.

45
Architettura, special Christmas issue (1936), p. 80.

46
See: Q. R., "La sistemazione della zona circostante l'Augusteo," ibid., 79–102, with English version on pp. 83–85; and V. Morpurgo, "La sistemazione augustea," *Capitolium* 12, 193, 145–158. For the action plan of 1 April 1935, see ibid., after p. 512.

47
Cited in R. L., "Lo sviluppo dei lavori nella zona dell'Augusteo," *Il Popolo di Roma,* 10 January 1937.

48
Ibid.

49
Ojetti in *Corriere della sera,* 26 November 1936.

50
Architettura, special Christmas issue (1936), p. 85. The English is theirs.

51
E. Bacino, "Il Mausoleo di Augusto nella nuova sistemazione dell' Urbe fascista," *Gazzetta del Popolo,* 23 February 1937.

52
See n. 49.

53
See: "Concorso nazionale per il progetto dell'auditorium in Roma," *Architettura* 13, (1934), Supplemento sindacale p. 63; also Mario Paniconi, "Concorso per l'auditorium di Roma," *Architettura* 14, (1935): 671–691; and note on the abandoned runoff in *Architettura* 15 (1936): 45.

54
The book was the first in a series of papers called Quaderni Augustei issued by the Istituto di studi romani to coincide with the bimillennial of the birth of Augustus.

55
Bottai, *L'Italia d'Augusto,* p. 23.

56
Ibid., p. 24.

57
Ibid., p. 24.

58
The book was published in 1941, but written in 1937.

59
Protagonisti, p. 13.

60
Ibid., p. 14.

61
See Giulio De' Rossi dell' Arno, *Pio XI e Mussolini* (Rome, 1954), 134–138.

325
The Emperor and
the Duce: The
Planning of
Piazzale Augusto
Imperatore in
Rome

62
For these details of the Augustan exposition, see the
catalog, *Mostra augustea della Romanità* (Rome, 1938):
436–437.

63
Architettura, special Christmas issue (1936), p. 85.

64
The Ciano Diaries, p. 90.

65
The inscription reads: HUNC LOCUM UBI AUGUSTI
MANES VOLITANT PER AURAS/POSTQUAM IM-
PERATORIS MAUSOLEUM EX SAECULORUM TENEBRIS/
EST EXTRACTUM ARAEQUE PACIS DISIECTA MEMBRA
REFECTA/ MUSSO [LINI DUX] VETERIBUS ANGUSTIIS
DELETIS SPLENDIDIORIBUS/ VIIS AEDIFICIIS AEDIBUS
AD HUMANITATIS MORES APTIS/ ORNANDUM CEN-
SUIT ANNO MDCCCXL [AE. F. XVIII].

66
See, for example, the interpretation of Domenico Mustilli,
''Le imprese e la politica di Augusto nell'arte del suo
tempo,'' *L'Urbe* (May 1937): 2–10, esp. 5–6.

67
''Impero Fascista perchè porta i segni indistruttibili della
volontà e della potenza del Littorio romano. Impero di
pace perchè l'Italia vuole la pace per se e per tutti . . .''
Scritti e discorsi, X (Milan, 1936): 118.

68
See J. W. Bowden, *The Life and Pontificate of Gregory the
Seventh,* vol. 2 (London, 1840): 159–160

69
On the life and times of Pius XI, see most recently *Pio XI
nel trentesimo della morte* (Milan, 1969), with ample
bibliography.

70
The inscriptions on the plaques read: (a) CONCORDIAE
INTER GENTES ADSERTOR/ AUSPICE CHARITATE/
DUCTU JUSTITIAE ET PACIS SUASU/ LATERANENSIBUS
PACTIONIBUS/ ITALIAE DEUM RESTITUIT/ DEOQUE
ITALIAM/ PIUS XI PONT. MAX./ QUI FIDE PIETATE
SAPIENTIA/ REBUS GESTIS/ URBI ET ORBI ADMIRAN-
DUS/ ANTECESSORES LONGE AEQUAVIT/ MAGNA SUA
PRO RELIGIONE/ IN FULGIDA ECCLESIAE LUMINA/
DIVOS AMBROSIUM ET CAROLUM/ SAECULARI CUL-
TOS CELEBRITATE/ AD CIVIUM DECUS ET EXEMPLIUM/
ROMANIS LOMBARDISQUE SOCIATIS/ MARMOREA UT
HAEC SIGNA/ PUBLICE EXSTARENT PRAESTITUIT. (b) IN
CONTINENTIBUS AEDIBUS/ SACRORUM ALUMNIS/ IN-
SUBRIBUS OLIM INSTITUENDIS/ ANIMUM AD STUDIA
REFERENS/ IN PRINCIPE ECCLESIARUM BASILICA/ SAC-
ERDOTI AUCTUS/ ACHILLEUS RATTI/ MEDIOLANENSIS
GREGIS/ QUILISQUE CHRISTI UNIVERSI/ SUMMUS
FUTURUS PASTOR/ VIRTUTIS ORDINIS DOCTRINAE/
HUMANAE AC DIVINAE SCIENTIAE/ CULTO ET AUCTOR
MUNIFICUS/ NOVORUM INVENTORUM FAUTOR/
PRAECLARO HOC IN TEMPLO/ PATRIO DEVICTUS OB-
SEQUIO/ CORAM BORROMAEI CORDE/ ID. XXI M. DEC.
A. MDCCCLXXIX/ PRIMUM SACRUM FECIT.

71
Protagonisti, p. 104.

72
Roma, città e piani, (Turin, 1958), pp. 210–215; Robert C.
Fried, *Planning the Eternal City, Roman Politics and Planning since World War II* (New Haven and London, 1973),
pp. 41 ff.

73
L'Urbe, May 1937, p. 9.

15
Some New Towns in Italy in the 1930s

Henry A. Millon

The 1930s saw new sectors of cities and new towns being built or projected in many parts of the world. From this decade came the enlargements to Amsterdam (van Eesteren, 1935–), Paris, Lyon, and Berlin, the new "green" towns of the United States (Greenbelt, Maryland; Greendale, Wisconsin; and Greenhills, Ohio) and among the many projects those for Algiers (Le Corbusier, 1933–), Tractorstroi, Magnitogorsk, Stalingrad, Autostroy, and Broadacre City. To my knowledge the new Fascist government in Italy built at least seven new towns in the thirties.

Mussolini's town building began in western Sardinia with the construction of Mussolinea (now called Arborea), inaugurated in the fall of 1928. Two of the seven were specialized towns. One, Carbonia, in southern Sardinia, was for workers who were to mine coal in the region. The other, Guidonia, was to be the principal military aviation training center near Rome. Although built in the late 1930s, they will not be examined in this chapter. Instead, I would like to draw your attention to the five remaining new towns built between 1932 and 1939, for I think they illustrate the effect changing political conditions had on architecture and urban planning.

These five towns lie in an area south of Rome in the province of Lazio. Three of them are built on new land reclaimed from the Pontine marshes that existed there since ancient Roman times. Two others are built near the sea between these reclaimed lands and the Ostian plain. All were begun during Mussolini's tenure as prime minister, and he officiated at the foundation ceremonies of all five. Mussolini and King Victor Emmanuel III were both present at the inauguration of Sabaudia, the second of the towns.

All the Pontine towns, as well as the other new towns founded by Mussolini, were important to his internal programs. In his desire to found the new Roman-Italian empire, Mussolini strove first to emulate, then to surpass the emperors of ancient Rome. At the inauguration of the first of these towns, Littoria (Latina, today), he said "What was tried in vain during the passing of twenty-five centuries, today we are translating into a living reality,"[1] emphasizing thereby that the draining of the marshes planned by Julius Caesar and only partially accomplished over the intervening centuries was finally achieved by the Fascist state under his leadership. The draining of these marshes and, similarly, the earlier draining of the Terralban marshes in western Sardinia provided new land for farming, as did the land reclamation projects in barren, hilly, and semimountainous areas. In a law promulgated on 20 December 1928 Mussolini said "redeem the earth; and with the earth, man; and with men, the race."[2] The new land was to be treated as an internal colony with colonists resettled (veterans from the Veneto in the Pontine area) on the reclaimed land.

The relationship of the Pontine towns to the policies of the state should be examined, but first we should see something of the region—the town plans and buildings, the relationship between the towns, and the relationship between the towns and the land. In each case I would like to direct your attention to the constituent elements, their placement and arrangement in the town, and the building forms chosen.

Work was begun on the reclamation of the Pontine marshland in 1930. The area of reclaimed land was about 750 square kilometers. Lying between the Lepine Mountains, the Alban Hills, and the Tyrrhenian Sea, in geological times the area was a shallow bay stretching from Terracina to the Alban foothills north and east of Anzio, with Monte Circeo, a lone island, at the south. The marshland was formed as the coast warped up more rapidly than the inland area, trapping water in the lower land (some of it remains today below sea level). The runoff from the Alban Hills and Lepine Mountains also collects in the area. The area is today divided topographically into three zones:

1. The coastal zone—dunes up to twenty to twenty-five meters high with coastal lagoons behind, as at Sabaudia, with the largest lagoon.
2. The inland regions close to sea—heights twenty to forty meters.
3. The interior up to the base of Monte Lepini—marshlands watered by rivers from bases of mountains (the one at Ninfa is a good example). Other rivers include the Amaseno, issuing from the center of the Lepine Mountains.

Until the land reclamation projects, there was virtually no cultivation of the land—some was used for grazing—only clearings in thickets and woods. Buildings existed only along the Via Appia and some along the shore. For the most part conditions were extremely primitive, with endemic malaria.

With land reclamation and the end of malaria, cultivation began. The entire project was turned over to the Opera Nazionale per i Combattenti (ONC—Italian veterans of World War I) and, within a year of the inauguration of Littoria and eight months after the inauguration of Sabaudia, the new province of Littoria was created on 18 December 1934. The next day the third town, Pontinia, was founded. The province of Littoria was carved out of part of the southeast section of Lazio and the northwest section of Naples, and Littoria was made the provincial capital. Sixteen months later Aprilia, the fourth Pontine town, was founded, and twenty-four months after it, on 25 April 1938, Pomezia, the fifth of the new towns, was begun. Pomezia was not within the confines of the province of Littoria. It was founded to be an agricultural center for the reclaimed, but formerly largely barren, rolling land to

the northwest of Aprilia. The new farmers and townspeople were veterans from the north of Italy who were to be "colonists."

With the exception of Littoria and Pontinia, the other three town plans were chosen in open competition. The composition of the juries and their official statements would make an interesting topic in itself. The statements chronicle the alteration in political attitude over the six-year period. We will instead examine the towns and their plans. The design of Littoria was given to the architect Orolo Frezzotti in April 1932 (Fig. 1). As stated in an article in *Architettura* the following year, "in a few days the respective designs were ready: the following 30 June the foundation stone of the Palazzo Comunale was laid."[3]

Undoubtedly design continued while other parts were under construction, but the city plan was in large measure determined in less than ninety days. By the time of the inauguration six months later, the article goes on to say, "at least the principal body of its buildings were complete." Clearly, in time to make a May 1933 deadline for the publication of the magazine, the railroad station, post office, and Fascist party headquarters were completed and photographs of them reproduced. The September issue illustrated the completed stadium, church, water tower, town hall (Fig. 2), Caserma of the Milizia, the agricultural office of the Veteran's Administration, the Gymnasium of the Balilla Group (Fig. 3), some housing (Fig. 4), market and shops. The article makes it clear other buildings were also complete and occupied. The town was capable of housing some population and of functioning in an elapsed time of sixteen months.

Meanwhile, on 21 April 1933, the competition for the design of Sabaudia had been announced. The drawings were due on 25 May, that is, thirty-three days were allowed to prepare and submit the design. The winner was announced in June, and Mussolini laid the cornerstone of the Town Hall on 5 August. Also constructed with alacrity, Sabaudia was inaugurated by King Victor Emmanuel III on 15 April of the next year, 1934 (Fig. 5).

Pontinia, the third town (Fig. 6), was founded on 19 December 1934 and inaugurated one year later (18 December 1935). In contrast to the other four towns, growth has been minimal until recently.

The designs of Aprilia and Pomezia were both won in a competition two years apart by the architects Petrucci and Tufaroli and engineers Paolini and Silenzi. The cities were founded by Mussolini on 25 April of 1936 and 1938 respectively. Although smaller than Littoria and Sabaudia, they took relatively longer to build—each exactly eighteen months and five days.

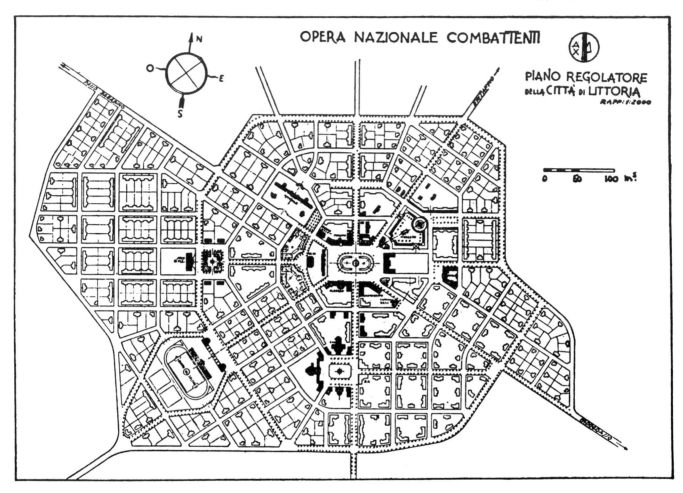

1
Littoria/Latina. Master plan. Frezzotti, architect-planner, 1932. (Photo: *Town Planning Review,* Vol. XVII, No. 1, June 1936, p. 45)

2
Littoria/Latina. Town hall. Frezotti, architect, 1932. (Photo: ENIT, Rome)
3
Littoria/Latina. St. Mark's square with the Gymnasium of Balilla facing on the square. O. Frezzotti(?), architect, 1932. (Photo: ENIT, Rome)

4
Littoria/Latina. Housing to north of
main square. O. Frezzotti(?), architect,
1932. (Photo: ENIT, Rome)

5
Sabaudia. Master plan. G. Cancellotti,
E. Montuori, L. Piccinato, and A.
Scalpelli, architects and planners,
1933. (Photo: *Town Planning Review,*
Vol. XVII, No. 1, June 1936, p. 47)

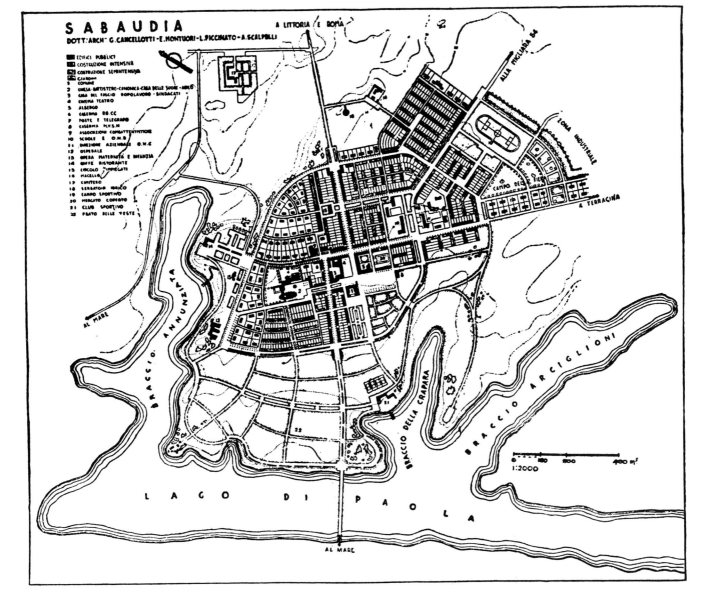

6
Pontinia. Air view, 1934. (Photo:
Fotocielo, Rome)

7
Borgo Vodice. View of main square
and church, mid-1930s. (Photo:
Neville Powers, 1971)

Littoria was expected to become the largest urban aggregation in the region and was to serve as the administrative center for the region. The other urban centers, Sabaudia, Pontinia, Aprilia and Pomezia, were to be smaller but with all the necessities of political and social life. At a smaller scale of organization were to be the *borghi,* or villages, which contained only a chapel, medical dispensary, provisions store, office of the agricultural arm of the ONC to provide technical assistance, an elementary school, and a post office. The smallest organizational unit was the farm itself.

Borgo Vodice, one of the borghi built during the first few years, contains the constituent elements distributed around a rather large central open space. All the buildings (today there are also some residential buildings that were not part of the original intention) were placed to one side of a T intersection of the new road system. The chapel centered on one side of the open space (Fig. 7). The ONC shed for agricultural machinery was to the left. The provisions store was opposite and the post office to the right of the church. Behind the church was the school. In the center of the open space a monument was erected. It commemorated the war dead of the 1914–1919 war who came from this farming area. Since the area was swamp and marshland at that time, the monument can only commemorate the dead who were relatives of the colonists who moved to the south when the marshes were drained. The monument provided, therefore, a bit of instant history for the families in the surroundings, and perhaps was intended to provide a sense of belonging, a sense of place and continuity that would otherwise have been absent.

There are differences in architectural and city plan character among Littoria, Sabaudia, and Pontinia, and a noticeable change in building form in Aprilia and Pomezia from the earlier towns. This change parallels, I believe, an alteration in official policy that can be traced in Italian architectural publications.

In the spring of 1934, during and after the competition for Sabaudia, architectural design became the subject of acrimonious national debate in both houses of parliament. The debate was well publicized and focused on the newly announced competition for the Palazzo del Littorio in Rome, but the designs for Sabaudia and the new Railroad Station in Florence received severe attacks, because they were neither Italian nor Roman. Phrases such as "we have had enough of Sabaudia" and "the station in Florence: think of it and be ashamed" were shouted in the Camera dei Deputati. Construction in the heart of Rome "should not be architectural construction of a German nature; we do not want that because it is far away and contrary to our sentiment." Even more,

"we do not want a Bolshevik architecture. No hybrid compromise, no conspiracy between Bolshevik and Japanese art: we want our own architecture."[4] Statements such as these were received with general applause.

The debate caused concern in many places. Mussolini invited the designers of the Florence Railroad Station (Michelucci, Berardi, Gamberini, Baroni and Lausanna) and of Sabaudia (Luigi Piccinato, Eugenio Montuori, Gino Canalloti, and Alfredo Scalpelli) to Rome to be reassured and to hear his comments. In the presence of the Secretary of the Fascist party Mussolini said:

I have called you because, after what has been said in the two houses of parliament, I would not wish you to believe that they were also my ideas. None of it: I wish to clarify in an unequivocal way that I am for modern architecture, for that of our time. . . . It would be absurd to think that we, today, were not able to have our architectural thought; it is absurd not to wish a rational and functional architecture of our time. Each age has given its functional architecture: even the monuments of Rome, that we are excavating today, responded to their function. . . . Tell the young architects who come out from the schools to make my motto theirs: "don't be afraid to have courage". . . . It is not possible to remake the ancient, nor is it possible to copy it. . . . I will give orders to all the agencies, to all the ministers, to all the offices, to make constructions of our time. I do not wish to see Balilla centers or Fascist party quarters in the architecture of the time of De Pretis. Tell them this and make it known to everyone.[5]

In the June 1934 issue of *Architettura* Marcello Piacentini, the most influential architect in governmental circles, wrote an article praising the planning and architectural qualities of Sabaudia, noting the integration of open green spaces within the town and their continuity with the green space outside the town (Fig. 8). He also praised the placement of the tall elements as orientation points in relation to entering roads and the neatness and sobriety of the architecture as well adapted to the simple, rural character of the place.

Time has agreed with Piacentini's and Mussolini's views of 1934. Both the Florence station and Sabaudia continue even today to be singled out as examples of progressive modern architecture of the mid-1930s in Italy by such authors as Bruno Zevi and Nicholas Pevsner, to name only two, while Littoria is today criticized for its "empty grandiloquence" and Pontinia, Aprilia, and Pomezia for their false imitative folklore."[6]

But Piacentini was, in Zevi's words, to become "the official bureaucratic architect," and indeed he served on all juries and wrote and spoke prolifically. Because, among other things, he had spoken out early (in the 1920s) for rationalist architecture and had in the early 1930s supported the railroad station in Florence (he was on the jury) and Sabaudia, he was able to present himself as progressive (and probably was at the time). As the thirties advanced, he became more influenced by Austrian neoclassicism and various types of Italian and Roman pseudorevivals. By May 1936, in his published criticism of the plan for Aprilia in *Architettura* (Gustavo Giovannoni was on the jury),[7] he was well on the way toward assuming the kind of nationalist chauvinism that characterized his years of greatest influence and that has been discussed in the book by Giulia Veronese, *Difficoltà politiche dell'architettura in Italia 1920–1940* (Milan, 1953) and Chapter V in Zevi's *Storia dell'architettura moderna* (Turin, 1950).

Piacentini had become critical of the basic planning tenets of the program for Aprilia. He argued that the program should have called for a regional plan, and that the original conception of a region with a small number of rural urban centers the size of Sabaudia and Aprilia should have been altered to have a larger number of still smaller centers. He thought Littoria should be increased in importance and the other smaller centers decreased in size. Littoria had initially been planned for 4,000 but was intended to grow. Sabaudia was planned for 5,000 with no further growth to occur. Pontinia, Aprilia, and Pomezia were to be about 3,000 each with little growth envisaged, and each was to have about 9,000 farmers depending on and contributing to it.

According to Piacentini the experience with Sabaudia had shown that some of the public facilities provided were not being used. He did not explain what he meant, and I have not yet found out what he may have had in mind.

Piacentini cited, as an example of the kind of center he envisaged for the region, the village of S. Maria di Galeria, and he included an illustration of its plan (Fig. 9). S. M. di Galeria is little more than a large farm complex with two courtyards. One courtyard (with a fountain) is surrounded primarily by various farm structures for the storing of farm animals, equipment, grain, and forage. The second, smaller courtyard contains a small residential nucleus, a chapel, and a dispensary.

Such a center is very much like the twelve borghi founded as an integral part of Mussolini's program for the Pontine region. The borghi were to contain, as we have seen and shall read in Piccinato's own words in a moment, many of the elements cited by Piacentini. What praise Piacentini has for Aprilia is that the architecture is "sober and pleasing" and that the whole complex is "balanced and harmonious." He adds, however, that it does not represent a step forward from Sabaudia.

It is my belief that Piacentini's new position, harking back to the rural S. Maria di Galeria type, is based on specific policies that are part of an integrated view of the city and the countryside and the production and consumption promulgated by the Italian state. The use of specific indigenous architectural forms was due to a significant change in the internal economy of the Italian state in response to a sharply altered international situation.

Before examining these policies and their consequence we should go back two years to 1932 to see what the designer of Sabaudia wrote about the program for Sabaudia and the territory for which it was to be the center. I think the ideas that led to Piacentini's position were sown much earlier, and some appear in Piccinato's statements made in *Urbanistica* in January 1934, while Sabaudia was under construction but before it was inaugurated.

Piccinato's theme is decentralization. He argues that mass transportation and industrial organization, which made concentration possible, will now be able to serve decentralization with the fruits of the industrial production spread by new scientific applications to the entire countryside. Examples cited of the first tentative steps toward urban decentralization are the regional agricultural and industrial plans of England and Germany, the urban mining centers of the Ruhr, and the Russian industrial city of Autostroy. Littoria and Sabaudia, however, are, according to Piccinato, fundamentally new steps toward the new urban life.

They are not just a new building form, like the "famous German Siedlungen for the unemployed," but instead a new vision of collective life. Littoria and Sabaudia have their own functional imperatives as communal agricultural centers, tied to their territory and to the productive land. They are, he says, inconceivable outside the agricultural organization that supports them and that they support. They emerge to serve the reclaimed land and not to enjoy or exploit the fruits of the land and are, therefore, functionally the opposite of traditional towns.[8]

Piccinato cites the "American architect Frank Lloyd" as one who has had the courage to examine fully the world urban situation in a "series of recent talks." He may be referring to the first appearance of an outline of Broadacre City in the publication of the *Disappearing City* in 1932. I have yet to trace the series of lectures to which Piccinato refers. "Broadacre City: A New Community Plan," was not completely published until the April 1935 issue of *Architectural Record,* a year and four months after the publication of Piccinato's statements. Piccinato praises Wright for examining the city, not through formal expressions, but in the light of recent significant (presumably economic) crises.

Piccinato states that economic forces will cause the dissolution of the city into minor communal centers, each responding to its own productive function. The future will see, according to his view, only

8
Sabaudia. Plan showing green areas.
G. Cancellotti, E. Montuori, L. Piccinato, and L. Scalpelli, architects and
planners, 1933. (Photo: *L'architecture
d'aujourd'hui,* No. 7, September
1934, p. 19)

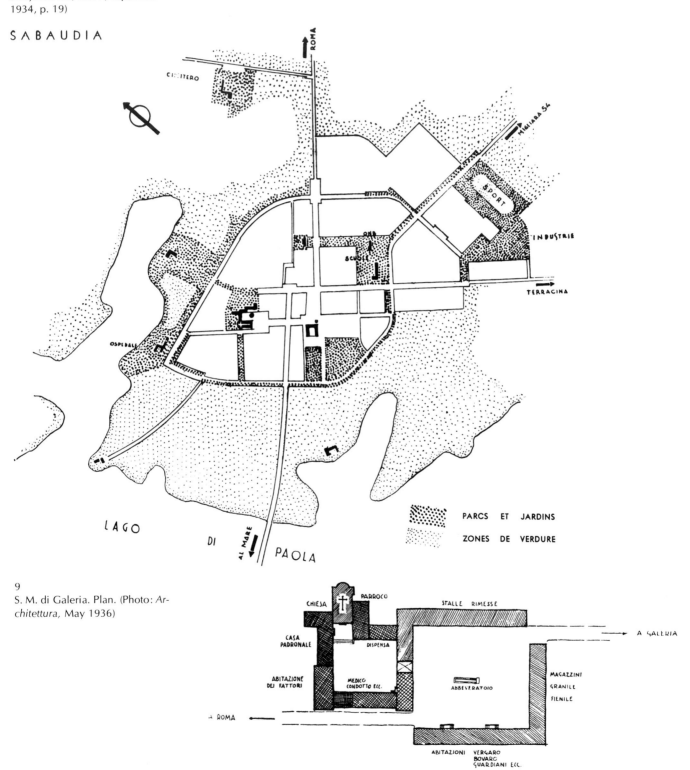

SABAUDIA

PARCS ET JARDINS

ZONES DE VERDURE

9
S. M. di Galeria. Plan. (Photo: *Architettura,* May 1936)

a few city types: industrial centers, artistic centers, educational-cultural centers, mining centers, and agricultural centers. No longer should we "talk about the city but instead it must be seen as the regional city, the provincial city, the national city."[9]

Sabaudia, in responding to this view, is the nucleus of a group of farms. According to Piccinato:

To each farm will be given a plot of land varying from fifteen to thirty hectares (37–75 acres). The size will be different in accord with the crop to be grown and the economic potential of the colonist.

Each group of farms has a 'Borgo' (the elemental urban unit) as their head, in which there was to be an office of the Agricultural Concern of the Opera Nazionale per i Combattenti, chapel, first aid station, school, post office, and grocery store. The office of the Agricultural Concern was to oversee the direction, administration, and assistance of their respective group of farms.[10]

The various concerns (businesses) of the Borghi (including that of Sabaudia) report directly to Rome to the headquarters of the Opera Nazionale per i Combattenti. For matters concerning their urban life (commerce, exchange, political and administrative life) the farmers were to come to the communal center of Sabaudia.

The integrated scheme for the functioning of the reclamation agricultural center demonstrates, therefore, how the agricultural life of the farm develops independently from its political and administrative activity, which takes place in the communal center. The latter (communal center) combines in itself all the institutions necessary to life: communal offices, Fascist party headquarters, church, hotel, market, theater, schools, gymnasium of the Opera Nazionale del Balilla, hospital, lying-in and infant care, playing fields, cemetery [see Fig. 10].

The building of these institutions should be proportioned to the needs of the entire agricultural center and not only to those of the communal town center itself: this explains the apparent disproportion between the size of the public buildings and the number of houses that, together with the public buildings, comprise the true and characteristic urban aggregate: naturally, one should not tire of repeating it, Sabaudia is seen comprehensively in its territory, or rather as a strongly decentralized building pattern that has its center in a large central district.[11]

Sabaudia was, therefore, in Piccinato's view merely one element in a plan that, if fulfilled, would see the depopulation of the urban centers of Italy, the creation of towns with specialized purposes, and the integration of all towns, industries, villages, and agricultural centers into a coherent, mutually supportive whole. Thus Sabaudia was both prototype and paradigm for one level of urban aggregation.

For Piccinato the architecture and urban plan of Sabaudia displayed a new vision of a portion of an integrated agricultural and industrial state. The architectural forms were contemporary, progressive, and restrained (Fig. 11). Contemporary European conceptions of the relation between green areas and urban centers, the orientation, height, and spacing of buildings, the reinforcement gained by the grouping of similar activities, and the arrangement of the plan to capture some of the qualities of the site brought it immediately much favorable international notice.

Littoria had, by comparison, not fared so well. Elements within the nearly radial plan (Fig. 1) were more evenly distributed, producing a more uniform whole, and the major individual public structures within it (with a few notable exceptions) were more grandiloquently conceived and immodestly rhetorical (Figs. 2, 12). Pontinia was a mixture of the sententious (the Palazzo Comunale) and the sober (Fig. 13).

Aprilia and Pomezia are, however, quite rural in character by comparison (Fig. 14). The rustic quality is achieved not only by the use of hipped tile roofs (as opposed to the flat roofs of Sabaudia and Pontinia) and arcuated loggias and windows (where strict trabeated loggias were used in all three previous towns) but also the size of the public open spaces (Fig. 15). In Aprilia, for example, the main square with its casa (not palazzo) comunale, Fascist party headquarters, the military police headquarters, office of the ONS and parish church all fronting on it is, perhaps, half the size of the piazza in Borgo Vodice and one quarter the size of that in Sabaudia. Some of the reasons for the rustic, indigenous character can be traced in Italian economic and political theory of the period.

Piccinato's program (it is also Mussolini's program) for decentralization has political overtones that merge with colonization and rural policies of the state. The development of the policies may be easily traced, for our purposes, through comparisons of the changes and additions made to historical and descriptive articles in the *Encyclopedia Italiana* from its first edition published over a period of six years (1929–1935) to the *Appendices,* the first of which came out in 1938 with an extensive article on *Bonifica* (land reclamation) and with a revised article on Italy by Virginio Gayda, the editor of the chief Fascist newspaper, *Giornale d'Italia.*

Gayda, speaking about internal colonization and the relation to "Integral Reclamation," cites Mussolini's laws of 1928 and 1933 as legislation that "consecrates the new type of reclamation, transforming it from a merely hygenic to a demographic, economic, and social play." He continues to explain that "In its high economic and social value this [policy] expresses also one of the vital principles of the Fascist regime: the defense and development of agrarian [life] for national balance against the excesses and delusions of industrial urbanism." Gayda cites the reclamation of the Agro Pontina as the most expressive synthesis of reclamation.[12] Prof. Arrigo Serpieri, writing about the goals of land reclamation and improvement in the entry "Bonifica," delineates the virtues of rural life and states that the degree of rurality should be measured not so much by the percentage of the total that is made up of agricultural

10
Sabaudia. Air view from northwest. G. Cancellotti, E. Montuori, L. Piccinato, and A. Scalpelli, architects and planners, 1933. (Photo: Fotocielo, Rome)

11
Sabaudia. View of parish church looking northwest from tower of town hall.
G. Cancellotti, E. Montouri, L. Piccinato, and A. Scalpelli, architects and
planners, 1933. (Photo: ENIT, Rome)

12
Littoria/Latina. View looking west
through east portico of main square.
O. Frezzotti, architect, 1932. (Photo:
ENIT, Rome)

13
Pontinia. View looking north from
main square to parish church. (Photo:
ENIT, Rome)

14
Aprilia. View of main square. Petrucci
and Tufaroli, architects; Paolini and
Silenzi, engineers, 1936. (Fascist party
headquarters building at tbe left and
shops behind arcade). (Photo: ENIT,
Rome)

15
Aprilia. View of main square with
church of St. Michael. Petrucci and
Tufaroli, architects; Paolini and
Silenzi, engineers, 1936. (Photo:
ENIT, Rome)

population, but by the percentage of the agricultural population that is in colonial status. That is, "peasants tied to the soil with stable rapports, the continuity of work—which has for the fascist doctrine fundamental importance." Rural inhabitants thus understood, he adds, represent in the national complex a factor of cohesion, of order of discipline, of sober habits, of high family sentiment. Rural life, Serpieri says, is a sure guaranty of the continuation of the lineage: and further that certain degenerative phenomenon of capitalistic civilization are of the world of the city, of industry, of traffic, and not of the rural world. The restless and insatiable search for more enjoyment is not of the rural world. He concludes this section saying: "A people over-deruralized [over-urbanized] resembles an army with many generals, but without a disciplined mass of soldiers that follow and obey: it is a people devoted to defeat, in the grand and perpetual battle of which history is woven."[13]

This is not the place to trace the evolution of these views nor the way they came to be connected with similar policies and views in Germany. I would only call your attention here to Barbara Lane's treatment of the subject in her *Architecture and Politics in Germany, 1918–1945* (Cambridge, Massachusetts, 1968), in which she discusses the views promulgated by Richard Darré in Germany in two books that appeared in 1929 and 1930. Although their extreme statements never gained full party support, they caricature the Italian views just recorded.

In the earlier of the two, *The Peasantry as the Life Source of the Nordic Race* (1929), Darré differentiates between settlers and nomads. Settlers produced warriors and aristocrats and spawned the Nordic race. The nomads, because of their hard life, were always materialistic. They became Europe's tradesmen, without any respect for property, and thus have a tendency to communism. Nomads are sophists in philosophy and uncreative in art, since they never see the true reality of things. Settlers, on the other hand, with true peasant thought, perceive the essence of reality and the process of growth and change. A peasant stays on his property tending his corn and pigs. In Darré's view the peasant people have produced both German idealism and natural philosophy.

Darré's next book, *Nauadel aus Blut und Boden* (Munich, 1930) was more explicit about the relationship to modern technology and the modern city. The Nordic race has never been successful in founding cities, Darré said, since separation from the land was foreign to them. Nomads, however, could spread their cultural values in cities, since they do not need to provide for the future. The Nordic race propagates in the soil, and the modern city, therefore, is an infertility machine. He saw the

nineteenth-century industrialization as destroying the Nordic race and said its only hope lay in repatriation of new generations of racially pure Nordic peasants to the soil.

At this point the two attitudes are clearly parallel. Both Darré and the Italians are arguing for repatriation—both for colonization of the soil, both for the stability that comes from attachment to the soil, both for the honest day's work.

It is in light of these theoretical bases that we must see arguments for the return to simple indigenous italic forms desired by men like Piacentini. The formal manifestations have political and social content that was intended to be explicit.

In addition, the economic sanctions placed on Italy by the League of Nations, which began on 18 November 1935 as the result of Italy's invasion of Ethiopia on 3 October 1935, drew a sharp nationalistic reaction. The sanctions were described as putting Italy in a state of seige and led to the institution of a policy of autarchy or economic self-sufficiency. Several journals devoted to the economic and commercial consequences were founded as Italy strove to survive and flourish without the importation of goods witheld because of the sanctions.[14] Although the sanctions were never decisive economically (they never included petroleum products and were at any rate terminated in July 1936, after the war ended in Ethiopia), they seem to have served to redirect the architectural aims of the period toward indigenous medieval forms for rural architecture and toward classical ancient Roman and Renaissance forms for public architecture in the larger urban centers. The literature of 1936–1940 is explicit about steel and concrete not being Italian or Roman while brick, terra cotta, and stone were in the tradition of the people of the Italic peninsula. (Nervi was prompted to write a piece at this time explaining that reinforced concrete served the purposes of autarchy best because it used a minimum of steel and was, therefore, the most economical material.)

In the light of these political and social attitudes Littoria, Sabaudia, Pontinia, Aprilia, and Pomezia seem to bear greater significance than N. Pevsner accorded them when he said that the buildings ". . . in the new towns of Littoria and Sabaudia . . . will one day once more come into their own. They all combine a convincing rectangularity with fine shows of shining marbles inside and out."[15]

Notes

1
Quoted in Carlo Cecchelli, "La metropoli dell'agro Pontino; Littoria", *Emporium*, 78 (October 1933), p. 252. For a general survey of what the draining of the Pontine Marshes meant to some Italians of the period as a technical, economic, political, and national achievement, see the collection of lectures by various authors in the *Corsi Superiori di*

Studi Romani during the academic year 1933–1934, published as *La Bonifica delle Paludi Pontine* (Rome, 1935).

2
Quoted in entry "Bonifica" by Arrigo Serpieri found in Appendix I, *Encyclopedia Italiana* (1938), p. 299.

3
Architettura (Dec. 1933), p. 583.

4
Quoted in Giulia Veronese, *Difficolta' politiche dell'architettura in Italia, 1920–1940* (Milan, 1953), p. 72.

5
Antonio Muñoz, *Roma di Mussolini* (Rome, 1934), p. 445.

6
Bruno Zevi, *Storia dell'Architettura Moderna* (Turin, 1961), 4th ed., pp. 277 ff.

7
For Gustavo Giovannoni's part as an architectural historian furthering the expansionist aims of the Fascist nation see the author's "The Role of History of Architecture in Fascist Italy," *JSAH* XXIV (1965), pp. 53–59.

8
Luigi Piccinato, "Sabaudia," *Urbanistica,* I (1934), pp. 10–12.

9
Ibid., p. 13.

10
Ibid., p. 14.

11
Ibid., pp. 14–15.

12
Virginio Gayda, *Encyclopedia Italiana,* Appendix I, p. 751.

13
Serpieri, *Encyclopedia Italiana,* Appendix I, p. 299.

14
For example: *Autarchia: Rivista di Studi economici,* (Turin, 1939); and *Autarchia e commercio: giornale dei commercianti destinati ai consumatori* (Roma, 1939–1943).

15
Nikolaus Pevsner, *Outline of European Architecture* (Jubilee edition) (Baltimore, 1960), p. 611.

16
Philip Guston and
Political Humanism

Francis V. O'Connor

Philip Guston is known chiefly as an abstract expressionist. He is, however, the only member of that movement who began his career with, and has returned to, an art of social concern. Thus his abstract expressionist phase from the late 1940s through the 1960s is preceded by a decade in which he explores a wide range of themes concerned with the place of man in his world and is followed in 1970 by a sudden return to similar, if more deeply ironic themes. This chapter discusses the roots of what I shall call Guston's "political humanism" and outlines the unity within an apparently inconsistent stylistic development.[1]

Post-Surrealism

Born in Montreal in 1913, Philip Guston moved to Los Angeles in 1919. During the late 1920s he studied for a time at Manual Arts High School and later, ca. 1930, for a few months at the Otis Art Institute. He was also active in the local John Reed Club. During 1934 he was employed on the first New Deal work-relief program for artists, the Public Works of Art Project (PWAP), and after he left it in March, he visited Mexico to study the work of that country's distinguished muralists. He returned to Los Angeles in 1935.

His circle of friends at this time—almost all fledgling artists—included Jackson Pollock and his brothers, Manuel Tolegian, Leonard Stark, Donald Brown, and the future art critic, Jules Langsner. He also came within the orbit of the painter Lorser Feitelson (then in his early thirties) who had founded a movement known as neo-classicism (after its European counterpart) during the late 1920s. This evolved in the early 1930s into what Feitelson called post-surrealism.[2] His fellow artists in this movement were Reuben Kadish, Knud Merrild, Grace Clements, Lucien Labaudt, Elizabeth Mills, Helen Klokke, and Feitelson's future wife, Helen Lundeberg. The post-surrealists exposed Guston to the spatial and anatomical mastery of Renaissance muralists, especially Piero della Francesca, Paolo Uccello, Luca Signorelli, and Andrea Montegna, and to the symbolic potential of divergent scales and juxtaposed images to be found in Salvador Dali and the surrealists.

Since I believe the aesthetic of post-surrealism was crucial to Guston's formation as an artist and to his later development, it would be useful at this point to explore its major tenets. Feitelson, in a radio interview with Arthur Millier, the art critic for the *Los Angeles Times* who did the most to promote post-surrealism, stated:

We Post-Surrealists thoroughly agree with our predecessors, the Surrealists, that the vague, half-formed ideas and images which we all experience, whether asleep or awake, are at least as important as the things we see with our eyes. We believe that the very term "artist" still implies one who imposes *order* upon the images of either the outside world or the inner world. We believe that the wonders of the cerebral world are not only as marvelous as the fantasy of the subconscious world of basic sensual memories, but that their intellectual manipulations have incomparably profound possibilities. . . . Now, we Post-Surrealists contend that the shock experience stimulated by the erotic and sadistic symbolism [of the Surrealists] does *not* in itself constitute an aesthetic experience. All great achievement in the fields of aesthetics, science, and philosophy has been eternally recognized by the rare quality of the creator's intellectual ingenuity. . . . We are building idea-making machines. . . . The various parts of a machine must be *exactly* the right size and shape to fit and balance each other. Just so must the parts of a picture fit together. . . . We Post-Surrealists recognize that the observer wants *meaning* in art. We regard the aesthetic (the *harmony* part, in other words) as a method of creating meaning. . . . We agree . . . about the necessity of art being individual expression, but the art we are interested in making is not just a picture on canvas, but *a picture in the other fellow's mind.* Now such a picture is really an *idea—* or, if you like, a sequence of ideas. Our business is to arouse and guide that sequence or *pattern of ideas.* [3]

A major exhibition of the post-surrealists took place during the summer of 1936 at the Brooklyn Museum, with Feitelson, Lundeberg, Clements, Klokke, Labaudt, and Merrild showing thirty-five works. The mimeographed catalog of the show contains the following description of the movement, quoting from Millier's articles:

All the modern movements, according to Feitelson, whether they painted fresh eggs on a plate or went "abstract" and pictured "planes" which look to the general public like so many dislocated shingles, have used the old aesthetics of visual color harmony and "lines of beauty." . . . Instead, [the post-surrealists] choose a color or line or tone only because it aids the idea an object or group of objects is intended to arouse in the mind of the beholder. The length or size of an object depicted is not determined, as in the prevalent mode of composition, by the space in the picture it has to fill or by naturalistic proportions, but by the object's psychological importance in the whole picture, both as it affects the spectator and as it relates to the other idea-conveying objects in the picture. This method of composing will, Feitelson believes, evolve its own aesthetic. But you will no longer see a picture as a decorative arrangement on a wall. Instead you will stand in front of it and enjoy a sequence of optically apprehended thoughts which total up to a universal idea. [4]

The March 1936 issue of *Art Front* contains an essay titled "New Content—New Form," by one of the participants in the Brooklyn show, Grace Clements. In it she states that the post-surrealists desired "an art which subjectively will express the social aspirations of today, while in technical effort it will cerebrally parallel the scientific and psychological contributions of our time." [5] Noting that there is a "paucity of vital revolutionary art in America" despite the increasing social consciousness of artists, she asks why and points, in answer, to the static "*fixed* point of view" of the great perspectival tradition of occidental art and to the lack of subject matter and aesthetic unity respectively in the twentieth century's two dominant movements, abstractionism and surrealism. What then "will be the forms in which the new content may be expressed?" she asks. Merely to picture a bread line does not convey the social and economic reasons for its existence. Clements feels the answer lies in rationalizing surrealism's pictorial devices. "We, too, must deal with subjective associative ideas, but ideas of extreme complexity, which must be controlled by the *head* no matter how much fire the *heart* may contain. It will be a cerebral art rather than an emotional one; that is, an art *calculated* in its organization. Because we must observe the limitations of our medium, we must convey ideas which can be optically apprehended." [6] In order to achieve this, she concludes by suggesting that the montage techniques of cinema, the surrealist juxtaposition of disparate objects, and their symbolic variation in size, shape, and importance to express psychological or subjective value, along with the abstractionist's use of multiple viewpoints and applied tactile materials, can all contribute to a universal and timeless art of social content founded on fundamental human experience and answering a fundamental human need.

It is clear from these statements that Philip Guston was exposed at an early age to a complex of aesthetic attitudes that rejected "art for art's sake" for a more directly communicative and socially committed art that would go beyond "social realism" to reveal the causes and motives of social realities in plastic terms rather than merely represent their consequences. The means to this end would be a conscious exploitation of the time- and space-transcending potentialities of modernist styles in order to present a visually legible and psychologically effective commentary on the political situation. In short, traditional pictorial narration was rejected as bankrupt, modernist styles in themselves were seen as disengaged from existential realities, and only a bold reformulation of modernist devices could communicate the artist's social concern to the viewer.

The "optical apprehension" referred to in both the Brooklyn Museum catalog and Clement's essay is of a generalized rather than a specific situation. There is little evidence that the short-lived post-surrealist movement dealt too consistently with gut political issues. Indeed, in reviewing the 1936 exhibition, the editor in chief of *Art Front,* the painter Joseph Solman, noted a definite split within the movement, with Clements and Merrild giving "concrete expression" to social content while Lucien Labaudt, Lundeberg (to be Feitelson's wife), and the founder himself were almost totally lacking in concern for the "great class struggle." For Solman, Feitelson is "floundering among outworn pictorial trappings and the usual grandiose symbols of Genesis, Conjugation, and Death." He concludes: "This manifestation on the part of painters to weld together critical thinking with a modern plastic approach is sufficiently superior to the commonplace proletarian 'snapshot' to merit some real attention. But they might be reminded that just as Post-Impressionism rebelled against the romantic confetti of its father movement by means of flat surface areas and vigorous contours so Post-Surrealism must reject the hallowed spaces of surrealism and replace its dead symbols with living ones."[7]

While these polemics were appearing in New York on the occasion of the Brooklyn Museum show, the young Philip Guston was busy at work on one of the most impressive monuments of the post-surrealist movement—and his second mural. This work, until now obscure (Fig. 1), was painted in collaboration with Reuben Kadish while both were employed on the WPA Federal Art Project from August 1935 to July 1936 in what is presently the lobby of the Scientific/Medical Arts building in the City of Hope National Medical Center at Durate, just outside Los Angeles.[8]

Extending across the entrance wall, it depicts an elaborate surrealist fantasy of the cycle of human life from birth to death and consists of over forty dramatically modeled figures posed in an architectural setting. This remarkable mural—remarkable for the youth of its creators (Kadish, like Guston, was in his early twenties) and for the elegance and variety with which the difficult fresco medium is employed—is crowned by an illusionistically painted lintel bearing grisaille portrait medallions of Renaissance masters such as Piero, Michelangelo, and Massaccio.

The grandiose theme of the life cycle, influenced no doubt by Feitelson's taste for similar subjects, can be read from left to right. It begins with a child emerging from a shell at the bottom left and proceeds through various maternal, adolescent, and mature figures, most shown with symbols of the arts and sciences. At the right the theme of old age and death is summed up in the image of a green corpse whose golden head-shroud enfolds a shattered sphere. The work abounds in quotations from the whole range of Italian quattrocento muralists, in tromp-l'oeil architectural renderings, and in heroic gesticulation and foreshortening. It also abounds in many of those devices recommended by Clements, including a tactile differentiation between the roughly surfaced architectural elements and the smooth plaster planes of the figures.

The mural's social content—given some ambiguities of iconography—is certainly on the side of the "universal and timeless" example rather than the "class struggle" precept. Fundamental human experiences are dealt with and there is no overt attempt to relate man's journey through life to specific social or economic impediments. The artists' conception of a humanist ideal is shown—an eloquent rebuke to the political and social circumstances of the times.

I would like to suggest that these attitudes, born of the post-surrealist ambience and embodied in this impressive mural, would inform not only Guston's subsequent career but also most of the best art of "social content" created during the 1930s. The blunt depiction of bread lines, strikers, or misery in general, seldom raised "social realism" above the level of traditional genre painting. Indeed, if one analyzes the 150-odd art works reproduced in *Art Front* between 1934 and 1937, one finds, even in that hotbed of social and aesthetic radicalism, that 29 percent of the works are basically semiabstract and/or surreal in one of the senses described by Clements; 27 percent depict some aspect of political, social, or economic misery and injustice; 20 percent are traditional still life, interiors, or genre; 16 percent social satire (usually cartoons); 3 percent nonobjective, and the remaining 5 percent posters or other designs dependent on verbal slogans. If the depictions of misery and injustice are added to the satires, 43 percent of the work illustrated can be said to reflect the policy of the magazine in respect to the function of art. But by far the most visually interesting and stylistically advanced art attempts to transcend the bounds of traditional verisimilitude the better to make pictorial points in the human cause. The post-surrealist point of view, therefore, seems in retrospect a more mature approach to the problem of expressing social concern in the visual arts, since it recognized that obsession with overt social content reduces art to the function of propaganda. In all his subsequent works, Guston would seek out means to express positive concern for humanity's social situation—or the artist's. I think this tendency is best called "political humanism" rather than "social realism."

The social orientation of surrealist-influenced art in America during the 1930s has not been studied in detail. In New York an amorphously organized group has been recognized and named "social surrealists." This group was made up of David Smith, Peter Blume, Louis Guglielmi, Robert Gwathmy, Walter Quirt, and Philip Evergood. Quirt especially was so identified at the time. I would add to the list artists such as Arshile Gorky, William Baziotes, Boris Margo, James Guy, Joseph Vogel, and Julio Diego, as well as the post-surrealists of Los Angeles, and name the entire group "political humanists" despite their diverse styles, in order to avoid confusion with the European Dali-dominated movement they were for the most part rejecting aesthetically and to provide a consistent name for what was a national, not just a New York, phenomenon.[9]

In 1936, after finishing his collaborative WPA mural at Durate, Guston moved to New York. Thereafter through the early 1940s he would work on a succession of Treasury Section commissions and WPA Federal Art Project mural projects. In 1941, having left the New York WPA/FAP the year before, he went to teach at the State University of Iowa, where he finished his last Section commissions. For clarity, his murals can be listed as follows:

ca. 1937–1938
(Section) Mural for Commerce, Georgia Post Office, entitled *Early Mail Service and Construction of Railroads.*

ca. 1938
(WPA/FAP) Studies for unexecuted mural for waiting room of Nurses Home at Kings County Hospital.

1938–1939
(WPA/FAP) Mural for WPA Building at the New York World's Fair, entitled *Maintaining America's Skills* (Fig. 2).

1940
(WPA/FAP) Mural for lobby of Community Building at Queensborough Housing Project.

1940–1942
(Section) Mural for auditorium of Social Security Building at Washington, D.C., entitled *Reconstruction and the Well-Being of the Family* (Fig. 3).

1942
(Section) Mural in U.S. Forestry Building, Laconia N.H.[10]

These works were among the nearly 4,000 murals designed and executed under the Treasury Department and WPA art programs between 1933 and 1943. Nearly all dealt with apolitical regional or historical subject matter, as did Guston's Post Office and Forestry Service walls for the Treasury Section. While such murals today constitute a vast cultural history in images of the Roosevelt era, they were not created to serve overt propagandistic purposes. Indeed, both sponsoring agencies tended to avoid any hint of such activity. There were, however, two mural cycles created toward the end of the 1930s that were conceived to promote the temporary and long-range social welfare policies of the New Deal, and Guston contributed a wall to each.

The WPA Building at the New York World's Fair was decorated by a group of artists from the New York City Federal Art Project with themes glorifying the emergency work-relief programs of the Works Progress Administration. These works were created by Anton Refregier, Seymour Fogel, Eric Mose, Ryah Ludins, Guston, and others. Guston painted the

theme mural on the facade, Fogel executed an interior mural officially described as "showing how people can be raised from starvation and hopelessness to self-support and self-reliance," and Refregier completed a series of tall panels symbolizing the cultural projects of the WPA.[11]

In Washington several years later, the new Social Security Building (now HEW) was decorated by the Treasury Section with murals by Ben Shahn, Seymour Fogel, and Guston depicting the benefits of the new social security legislation. Fogel's two murals were entitled *The Security of the Family* and *The Wealth of the Nation.* Shahn's program, entitled *The Meaning of Social Security,* was based on FDR's message to Congress on the legislation.

An analysis of the thematic material in these two mural cycles reveals the New Deal's official policy toward the controversial area of social welfare. The WPA murals emphasize employment and the preservation of individual skills at a time of economic crisis. The dominant image is that of the worker—conceived to include both laborer and scientist, secretary and artist. The main point is the government's unflagging versatility in providing honest, useful work for all citizens—a point doubly important in 1939, when the WPA was fast losing its capacity to achieve those goals because of an increasingly conservative Congress. The Social Security murals were concerned with the more universal theme of the family (which appears in all the murals) and the government's obligation to secure its members' right to employment, education, recreation, a wholesome environment, and a dignified old age. In both programs the equality of the races, sexes, and professions is stressed and the basic American virtues of diligence, thrift, self-reliance, and family solidarity are extolled. There is ample evidence that the artists involved expressed these themes with deeply felt enthusiasm. Shahn, for instance, stated in a letter to the Section that he had been probing for a decade the issues that were "the background and substance of Social Security."[12] Perhaps the best insight into the attitudes of the artists involved in the WPA murals is to be found in the diary Anton Refregier kept while working on his panels:

October 1938—There are six of us doing work for this project. Guston, Fogel, Ryah Ludins, Eric Mose, and Lou Ross. I am raised to the rank of Assistant Supervisor. This means a few more dollars to live on. From the present check of $23.86, I will receive $34.00 a week. This helps.
November 1938—The other night the Project was discussed at the Artists' Union. It was felt we have a great opportunity to counteract the reactionary attacks and charges of "boondoggling" and "leaning on a shovel."
December 1938—Yesterday I went to Brooklyn with . . . , Harry Knight and the sculptor David Smith, who is in charge of the Technical Unit of the Art Project, to see the place that is going to be our

Philip Guston and Reuben Kadish, mural at City of Hope National Medical Center, Durate, California. WPA Federal Art Project, 1935–1936. (Photo: Courtesy City of Hope National Medical Center)

2
Philip Guston, *Maintaining America's
Skills*. Exterior mural for WPA Build-
ing at New York World's Fair, 1939.
(New York City WPA Art Project;
photo: Archives of American Art,
Smithsonian Institution)

Philip Guston, *Reconstruction and the Well-Being of the Family*. Mural for the auditorium of the Social Security Building, Washington, D.C. (now HEW), 1940–1942; installed 1943. (Public Buildings Service; photo: National Archives)

workshop. It's the shell of an old church. The Project carpenters are putting in a floor, staircase, and an arrangement for the moveable panels so that we can work on a thirty-foot stretcher without climbing the scaffolding.

January 1939—The work is going full swing. The workshop is the closest to the Renaissance of anything, I am sure, that has ever happened before in the States. My assistants and I have the central part of the studio. On the left, Philip Guston is working on the full-size drawings for the mural he is going to do for the outdoor wall of the building. In front of us, Sy Fogel is working on a large canvas. In back Eric Mose with his assistants. Other artists are working elsewhere. Every person here is dedicated to the Project. Everyone feels and knows that we must do our utmost. We know that there are a bunch of commercial mural painters preparing murals for the different buildings of the Fair—Hildreth Mière and others. They are making at least ten times more money than we are. But they can have it. Theirs will be the usual commercial crap. They are not moved as we are by our content—by our search for creative and contemporary design—by our concern for people. WE are the mural painters. We hope we are catching up with our great fellow artists of Mexico. We will show what mural painting can be!!

April 1939—The Fair is about to open. Today I was in Flushing Meadow to watch the installation of the murals. I have a feeling of tremendous satisfaction. . . . The work . . . of Guston, Ludins—is superb. Our building is a gem and millions of people will see it.

Mid-summer 1939—. . . a day was set aside at the initiative of the National Society of Mural Painters for a popular vote on all the murals. On entering the Fair that morning, the people were given a ballot. The result: Philip Guston's outdoor mural, first prize; and my indoor mural, second.

Fall 1940—Now the Fair is dismantled. Burgoyne Diller, the head of the Mural Project, tried unsuccessfully to find a permanent place for my murals—offering them to high school auditoriums. But nothing came of this. The murals were destroyed.[13]

Guston's prizewinning mural (Fig. 2) was also destroyed. It depicted three monumental construction workers grouped around a woman holding a microscope. In terms of the national image of the WPA and its budgetary realities (over 75 percent of its funding went to its Division of Engineering and Construction) this was a totally accurate statement of where the New Deal's work-relief programs had their greatest impact. If the female scientist holding her window to the mysteries of life and death seems protected by the male laborers, this too is an accurate picturing of the WPA's expeditiousness in justifying support to esoteric research (including the arts) by massively subsidizing the unskilled common man's primary need for remunerative labor. Thus this mural, one of the great monuments of American social humanism, symbolizes the social and economic aspirations of the day: honest employment for both blue and white collar workers. And it does so in a simple visual vocabulary of montage devices, shifting space planes, and strong, flat, legible shapes.

Guston's triptych in the auditorium (Fig. 3) of the Social Security Building in Washington, D.C., is his most impressive extant mural and, like that at the World's Fair, supports a controversial and far-reaching government policy with tact and skill.

It was painted in oil on canvas applied to three moveable screens on the auditorium stage, each 11'10" high. The central panel depicts a family picnic; the left, workers engaged in irrigation and forestry; the right, an urban construction team made up of a Negro and white working together. Like the murals by Shahn and Fogel outside the auditorium, the theme of the family made secure by the fruits of honest labor dominates Guston's work. The rural and urban experience of America are mediated by the recreational park.

Given an intimate environment for his work, Guston carefully balanced the tonal range of his painting with the bleached walnut paneling and gold draperies of the handsome auditorium. He was also conscious of the decorative aspect of this work. In a letter to the Section, he states that "the design was conceived directly in color and it is in tapestrylike color patterns. . . . The problem of decorating a moveable screen on a stage rather than an architectural mural space certainly intrigued me. The delicate balance between a strong realism and an all-over decorative pattern is what I'm after."[14] This perhaps explains the somewhat hieratic postures of the figures and the well-handled interludes of starkly detailed stone walls and stripes accenting the generally quiet surface. The figures are heavily modeled in a sculptural mode reminiscent of the "classic" Picasso and the Mexicans. The overall figure composition suggests that the artist, faced with a triptych, had studied the work of Max Beckmann. This is especially evident in the scale of the figures in the side panels and the use of walls and piles of wood and stone to mask the lower legs, as Beckmann does in the right panel of his famous *Departure* triptych of 1932–1933.

When the mural was installed in 1943, *Art News* printed a full-page reproduction and quoted the artist as saying, "I would rather be a poet than a pamphleteer." This is certainly a precise description of his stance as a New Deal muralist and a good prophecy of the future development of his social humanism. His origins as an artist were rooted in the epic vision of the post-surrealists and especially the sensibility of its founder, Feitelson. His taste was for the big theme, and all his means were devoted to its forceful and elegant expression.

With his last Section mural commissions completed, Guston turned to easel painting, exhibiting his work in several one-man shows and winning the first prize at the Carnegie in 1946. His paintings of this period, such as *Ceremony* and *If This Be Not I* (Fig. 4), are strongly influenced by Beckmann in their treatment of figures, though Guston's emphasis on children playing in urban settings is quite different from the atrocities and obscure rituals depicted by the German master. His world is one of make-believe, though the many masked faces suggest a sinister dimension to the innocents depicted. Indeed, from the Durate mural through the end of his representational paintings in the late 1940s, the image of the masked, averted, or partially obscured face is often found in his work. The specific threats of the time are not depicted—only our adaptation (such as it is) to them. And the terrible dimensions of the universal confusion and fear are dramatized by making children in the fantasy of their play—rather than adults—hide their faces.

Guston's 1970 Exhibition of "Hoods"

With this background it is not too surprising that Guston's most recent paintings are dominated by hooded figures in urban settings whose seemingly antisocial behavior is as discreetly handled as the social content of his earlier humanist works. Indeed, an easel work of the early 1930s, Conspirators (Fig. 5), shows three hooded Ku Klux Klansmen huddled together while holding a whip, a spiked stick, and a wooden cross with a lynching rope hanging from it. These sinister figures are set in the stark architectural setting favored by the post-surrealists and painted in dramatic chiaroscuro.[15]

Guston's exhibition (Fig. 6) at the Marlborough Gallery in October 1970[16] came as a shock to an art world that was habituated to his abstract expressionist style and ignorant, or only dimly aware, of such early works. This was due in part to the irresponsible curatorial custom of mounting "retrospective" exhibitions which ignore an artist's early work if seemingly irrelevant to, or compromising of, his current, more marketable, productions.[17] The show was greeted with stammers and invective. Hilton Kramer wrote a harsh review in the Sunday New York Times, entitled "A Mandarin Pretending to be a Stumblebum."[18] He had previously called DeKooning's similarly difficult, later paintings "pompier." Kramer's conclusion was that Guston was faltering and out of touch, a view shared by other critics. Only Harold Rosenberg, in the New Yorker, came to the artist's defense, asserting that Guston had "returned to picture-making; that is, to an art able to get along without words." Conscious that Guston was reacting against the frivolity of pop art and the overintellectualized techniques of minimal painting and sculpture during the 1960s—a decade of unprecedented social and political upheaval—Rosenberg saw clearly that the "scandal" of the Marlborough show was ironically not "that this leading Abstract Expressionist has introduced narration and social comment but that he has done his utmost to make problems of painting seem secondary."[19]

The new paintings depicted a vacuous urban world filled with strange, bloated creatures whose heads, while generally interpreted in terms of Ku Klux Klan masks and the precedent of the early easel work, can also be recognized as bent and battered bullet or rocket cones with rivetlike rows of dots delineating jointures or patches. The historical, technological—and perhaps even phallic—connotations of these rather shabby heads are best summed up with the word hood in the sense derived from hoodlum; the resulting verbal/visual pun captures the mood of the works.

Guston's hoods are sinister, underground personages, ham-handed cigar smokers who patrol city streets, inhabit bare rooms, and do antisocial things such as carrying nail-studded sticks, collecting old shoes (occasionally attached to disembodied legs), huddling together and pointing fingers—though at times even larger fingers point at them. These works are painted predominantly in tones of pink, white, and black with occasional touches of yellow and cool colors. They present a surface texture of such unrelieved aesthetic awkwardness as to make the practitioners of pop and funk art (with whom Guston has, I think, been too facilely compared) kindred to Hals and Fragonard!

Indeed, for an art world long committed to defining "quality" in terms of large-scale formal elegance and immaculate purity and precision of technique, Guston's new, small easel paintings, with their raw colors, ragged paint, and gross subject matter, must have seemed comparable to the Art Workers Coalition's infamous box of cockroaches dumped amid the Metropolitan's trustees at banquet! The reaction of disdain and the judgment of faltering decline were both predictable and seemingly deserved. Yet an artist of Guston's stature cannot be so easily dismissed, especially when his new work, however "difficult" (as these problems are called before they are solved by historical perspective), is firmly rooted both in his own past development and in evolving artistic tendencies.

The 1970 show returns Guston full circle to his artistic origins in the post-surrealist movement of the 1930s in Los Angeles. Just as Feitelson and his followers rejected the psychotic imagery of a Dali for a rational and universal commentary on generalized humanistic themes, Guston, in his recent work, generalized—and satirized—the coteries of malefaction in society by reducing the political and psychological similarities of the street gang/Mafia/government bureaucracy/secret police/Weathermen/Minutemen to the common denominator of hood. As in his New Deal murals, Guston does not narrate the social conditions that nurture hoods—rather he chooses to illustrate the repulsive milieu of their minds. Rosenberg states:

Guston's temperament is not a political one. His natural bent is toward sensitivity and elegance, toward the artistic, though with a conscious, strongminded resolve to resist facility and seductive painting. In the social-realist thirties, Guston's paintings touched politics only at a tangent; they avoided picket lines and dust bowls and translated combat into myth. I suspect that it is for refreshment as an artist, rather than as a partisan of social ideals, that he has abandoned his Abstract Expressionist experiments, which had become increasingly austere. . . . In the last analysis, Guston's exhibition is political by way of art and does more for art than for politics. It comes at the beginning of a decade in which a pressing need has arisen for a new outlook on art— one that will end its isolation from the crises of the time.[20]

Here, however, Rosenberg is confusing the "art world" with the "real world" in seeing Guston's latest departures as only relevant to the situation of recent coterie art in New York. Rather Guston is making a general commentary on both, realizing that there has been all too much of the corruption of the real world in the art world and that the politics of both are now pretty much identical. His hoods anticipate the moral squalor of Watergate as much as the less dangerous trangressions of "the Art Crowd."

Nor is Guston alone in generalizing—or mythologizing, to use Rosenberg's term— the corruption in the social order. A small group of artists have dealt with humanist moral values in their creations since the 1930s and have worked parallel to and in the shadow of the popularized movements of the last three decades. Thus the artists brought together in the "New Images of Man" exhibition organized by Peter Selz at the Museum of Modern Art in 1959 attempted to dramatize, primarily through expressionist means, the alienation of man in the modern world. More recently, another group, led by the poet and activist Barry Schwartz, has continued this tradition.[21] While Guston is not, and probably would not want to be, a member of this humanist movement, his work is certainly more closely related to its sensibility than to the cynical satire of the pop or funk artists, who glamorize the physical and moral squalor their art purportedly derides. While Guston's painterly grossness is, in essence, the tour de force of an experienced and sophisticated artist, the painterly slovenliness of many of those associated with Schwartz's group can only bring it discredit on the level of the political medium it has chosen: art. The problem has been trenchantly articulated by Parker Tyler, and his remarks, while directed at Schwartz's group, apply equally to Guston:

The power of some of the most passionate and pyrotechnic obsessions made visible here is the power of disaster *as disaster,* emotional disturbance *as emotional disturbance,* extremism *as extremism:* none of these things, primarily, *as art.* I wonder— and to me this is the true pathos of the Humanist crisis—if we have to sacrifice the image of human perfection (which is what art *as such* means) in order to shock humanity into its own true existence![22]

We probably do, and there is a certain aesthetic legitimacy in the violations of canon and sensibility necessary to effect the shock. But one wonders at the extent of the prophylactic value of violence— and what it does ultimately to its idealistic perpetrators—especially an artist such as Guston. And one wonders even more at the effect of rejecting the value of perfection—especially on those younger artists who have yet to attain it.

Guston and Abstract Expressionism

I have left a discussion of Philip Guston's abstract expressionist phase until last because it can now be considered in the context of his development to date.

Of all the artists associated with Guston in the abstract expressionist enterprise, only he makes public the facture of his paintings with such clarity. Unlike any of his peers, he openly pushes his medium about until a structure or image of sorts emerges from the primordial "mud." The dominant grayish halftone background in his paintings is the result of that intermixture—or, as he calls it, "erasure,"—of colors every art student recognizes with despair. To Guston's credit, his mud tends to a freshness and vitality bespeaking his technical professionalism— but mud it remains. His total process remains visible on the surface of his canvas. Unlike Pollock or De-Kooning, it does not consist in clearly discernible stratifications revealed beneath an ultimately resolved surface; unlike Kline or Still, it does not merely contribute to the achieved surface. It simply remains for the eye to see: the trampled arena of the painter's physical and psychological struggle to resolve the absence of literal subject matter of any kind.

Thus, to look at one of his early abstract expressionist masterpieces, *Painting* (Fig. 7) at the Museum of Modern Art, is to see a work of overall pinkish coloration with a broad central area of crosshatchings of bright reds accented with touches of violet, green, and peach. The effect of the almost pretty color alludes to the late Monet; the building up of small, roughly brushed rectangles of pigment, to the plus-minus structures of the early Mondrian. But there is no image other than this open building up of colored paint, thin at the edges and dense at the center. The artist's paintings of the early and mid 1960s provide greater contrast of forms and more broadly painted and at times more dramatically colored compositions. Yet the imagey is as anomalous as the facture is overpowering.[23]

Among his peers, Guston paints the most nakedly. The viewer of the results, however aesthetically unsophisticated or kinesthetically ignorant of paint

4
Philip Guston, *If This Be Not I,* 1945.
Oil on canvas, 41½ × 54½ in. Col-
lection, Washington University, St.
Louis, Missouri. (Photo: Washington
University)
5
Philip Guston, *Conspirators,* early
1930s. Oil on canvas, 50 × 36 in.
Whereabouts unknown. (Photo: Cour-
tesy of the artist)

6
Philip Guston, *Dawn,* 1970. Oil on
canvas, 67¼ × 108 in. Collection of
the artist. (Photo: O. E. Nelson)

7
Philip Guston, *Painting,* 1954. Oil on
canvas, 63¼ × 60⅛ in. Collection,
the Museum of Modern Art, New
York. Gift of Philip Johnson. (Photo:
Museum of Modern Art, New York)

manipulation, cannot avoid the nervousness, the tentativeness, the hesitancy, the groping, the fierce desperation of the process by which Guston's paintings are crafted. Indeed, this visible struggle is the artist's only subject matter, and its public openness, more than its formal and coloristic resolutions, is in perfect congruence with his great social murals of the 1930s or his recent return to pictorial content.

From another viewpoint, Guston, rather than Pollock, is the classic "action painter," for if abstract expressionism took surrealist psychic automatism to its logical conclusion, then Guston did so on the most elementary level: the stark application of pigment. This is his great virtue as a painter during the 1950s and 1960s—and his greatest fault as an artist. His work, except for an occasional vague image, is iconographically empty. It does not go beyond the tensions its facture reports. It is propaganda for the plight of the struggling artist, who has succeeded the struggling worker of the 1930s and here precedes the struggling citizen of the 1970s. For all its coloristic and formal elegance, Guston's art is still dedicated to that rationalizing process the post-surrealists applied to the iconography of Dali, or that Guston himself has recently applied to the imagery of popular culture. It is dedicated to the post-surrealists' "optical apprehension" of ideas rather than to the abstract expressionist ideal of psychic apprehension of the icons underlying its formal complexities and painterly pyrotechnics. Pollock's subject matter: the animal, the eye, the totem, sex, and the hierarchies and intricacies of the natural world—or De Kooning's women—are basically apolitical. They transcend situation and, for whatever reasons, are recognized as universally valid and meaningful. Guston's humanism is of another order, basically a political one. He wishes to encounter within the process of his art the social and moral tensions of his day as if he were the first—or last—painter.[24] It doesn't matter whether they are the economic lacks of the depression, the loneliness of the abstract expressionist milieu, or the technological turpitude of the present. Just as the post-surrealists decided this could only be done by making art directly and explicitly communicative of ideas, however generalized or idealized, so also Guston has chosen to follow a similar literalist aesthetic in each of the three phases of his career. The import of the art he created as an abstract expressionist is the same as his early murals and recent hoods. It is rooted in his lifelong political humanism—a humanism that has never accepted the political implications of mankind's collective psychic unity but has always recognized the artist's function in society as prophet and promulgator of human values.

Notes

1
For general information about Guston I have consulted Dore Ashton, *Philip Guston* (New York: Grove Press, 1960), and her *Yes, but . . . A Critical Study of Philip Guston* (New York: The Viking Press, 1976), the catalog of the Solomon R. Guggenheim's 1962 retrospective exhibition, the Jewish Museum's exhibition, "Philip Guston: Recent Paintings and Drawings" of 1966, and Marlborough, New York's show of recent paintings in October 1970. I also interviewed the artist on August 26, 1970, at Woodstock, New York.

2
For the history and aesthetic of post-surrealism, I have relied on the papers of Lorser Feitelson and Helen Lundeberg in the Smithsonian's Archives of American Art, the press clippings and other materials on those artists and Reuben Kadish preserved in the Ferdinand Perret Research Library at the Smithsonian's National Collection of Fine Arts, and on Jules Langsner, "Permanence and Change in the Art of Lorser Feitelson," *Art International,* Vol. VII, No. 7 (September 25, 1963), pp. 73–76.

3
The interview, undated, seems to be about 1936 and is preserved in the Perret Library.

4
A copy of this catalog can be found in the library of the Brooklyn Museum.

5
Art Front (March 1936), p. 8.

6
Ibid., p. 9.

7
"The Post Surrealists of California," *Art Front* (June 1936), p. 12.

8
Guston's first mural was done in collaboration with Reuben Kadish in the University at Mrelia, Michoacán, Mexico, ca. 1934. In my interview with Guston, he pointed out that this work, as well as that at Durate, were both created in collaboration, and that it would be difficult today to distinguish his contribution to them. See *California Arts and Architecture* (April 1941) on Kadish and for illustrations of the Durate murals. One must note, however, that the mural is signed "Phillip Goldstein/Reuben Kadish/August 1935–July 1936," thus giving Guston (he changed his name in 1937) precedence and that certain of his other works, such as the now destroyed *Conspirators* of the early 1930s, were conceived in the same style. Guston's beginnings as an artist are rooted in post-surrealism and his subsequent aesthetic attitudes, if not his style, reflect those origins.

9
See Stanley Meltzoff, "David Smith and Social Surrealism," *Magazine of Art,* Vol. 39, No. 3 (March 1946), pp. 98–101. For a useful survey of this whole area, see also Jeffrey Wechsler, *Surrealism and American Art: 1931–1947,* exhibition catalog (Rutgers University Art Gallery, March 5 to April 1–24, 1977).

10
The files on Guston's Section murals are preserved in Record Group 121, Records of the Public Buildings Service, at the National Archives, Washington, D.C. I am indebted to Dr. Belisario R. Contreras for making copies of these available to me. Information about the Kings County Hospital sketches is preserved in the files of the New York City

Art Commission at City Hall, New York, and a photograph of the sketch for the Queensborough Housing Project can be found in the Photograph Archive of the Museum of Modern Art.

11
See Olive Lyford Gavert, "The WPA Federal Art Project and the New York World's Fair, 1939–40" in Francis V. O'Connor, ed., *The New Deal Art Projects: An Anthology of Memoirs* (Washington, D.C.: Smithsonian Institution Press, 1972), pp. 247–267.

12
Shahn to Edward Rowan, November 7, 1940.

13
Quotes from a transcript of Refregier's unpublished diary made available to the author.

14
Guston to Rowan, June 2, 1942.

15
This destroyed work is illustrated in Dore Ashton, *The New York School* (New York: Viking, 1973), Fig. 8, p. 39.

16
The gallery put out a well-illustrated catalog at the time of the show in October 1970.

17
The earliest work in the Guggenheim's 1962 retrospective was dated 1941.

18
October 25, 1970. A rebuttal by Guston's daughter appeared on December 6, 1970, entitled "A Personal Vendetta Against Guston?"

19
Harold Rosenberg, "Liberation From Detachment," *New Yorker,* November 7, 1970, p. 136.

20
Ibid., p. 138–139.

21
See Barry Schwartz, *The New Humanism: Art in a Time of Change* (New York: Praeger Publishers, 1974).

22
Parker Tyler, "What Price Humanism?" *Arts in Society,* Vol. 10, No. 1, Spring-Summer 1973, p. 56. This entire issue is devoted to the New Humanism.

23
The best critical discussion of Guston's work of this period is to be found in Lawrence Alloway, "Notes on Guston," *The Art Journal,* Vol. XXII, No. 1, Fall 1962, pp. 8–11.

24
See dialogue in Jewish Museum catalog between Rosenberg and Guston.

17
Art of the New Chile: Mural, Poster, and Comic Book in a "Revolutionary Process"

David Kunzle

Introductory Note

The following chapter was completed early in 1973 and reflects some of the euphoria with which I returned from my 1972 visit to Chile. It was written in a spirit of optimism transmitted not only by the works of art themselves but also by the artists and critics I spoke to. With the terrible counterrevolution of 11 September 1973, innocence has been shattered, and joy has turned to rage.

A chapter intended to be timely in the fullest sense, that is, not only deriving from our contemporary situation but also written in hopes of changing it, would appear to demand radical revision, or at least a new framework, in order to incorporate the transformed political scene in Chile. The conventions of scholarship, indeed, might insist that the "new evidence" facilitating a really up-to-the-minute reevaluation of the material here uncovered (and now proved to be "politically naive," "misdirected," or even objectively a "failure"[1]) be applied in order to give the proper historical dimension, such as only the art of a closed, past epoch, and not an art in progress, can enjoy. The benefits of hindsight here are tremendous.

I have chosen not to revise this chapter beyond adding a few footnotes. I have chosen not to turn present tenses into past tenses; let them evoke a "continuous present" which stands for a future. As I was dolorously considering the necessity of making some changes, a new cultural venture thrust itself upon us, one which in the new circumstances seemed more politically cogent. In the months immediately following September 11, we made a film called *Chile: with Poems and Guns* (now distributed by Tricontinental Films) about the counterrevolution, United States imperialism in Chile, and the socialist achievements they have temporarily destroyed. This film, which used much of the visual material presented here, was the collective, low-budget enterprise of a group of cinematographic neophytes formed for the purpose, who discovered the value of the pooling and fusion of experience, ideas, and labor, of transcending individual talents and traditional divisions of labor, and of concerting goals. This was done in a spirit akin, we hoped, to that we had witnessed in Chile under the Popular Unity government, in the cultural as well as economic sectors.

The murals, posters, and comic books described here, like all the cultural products of the Popular Unity (UP) regime, have been subject to systematic destruction by the fascist junta. In the company of socialist literature of all kinds, posters and comic books have been publicly burned in the streets (Figs. 1, 2); murals have been whitewashed and cleaned off (Fig. 3). The freedom of the press guaranteed under the UP has now been totally destroyed;

mere possession of a UP poster can mean imprisonment and death. Seldom in recent history have workers and their expression, artists and their art, been subject to so cruel a repression.

This situation places a new responsibility upon the critics and historians who hope to revitalize the art they write about. It would be a gross critical misuse of Chilean revolutionary art merely to laud it and quietly deplore its repression without simultaneously urging the necessity of turning all available energies toward the active rescue of that art and the ideas it embodies.[2] Such a rescue can only be achieved through the total defeat of Chilean fascism and the U.S. economic interests that sustain it. The enemies of Chilean art, and of the people who made that art, sit in the highest offices of the U.S. government, the CIA, and the Pentagon, as in those of the great multinational corporations such as the Kennecott and the International Telephone and Telegraph Companies. Chilean art is an exhortation to action; discussion of Chilean art must be the same.

Background

Chile is unique among Latin American countries for the manner in which socialism has made a successful bid for power through "democratic" electoral and legal mechanisms set up by bourgeois regimes. Chile is indeed undergoing what the Chileans call a "revolutionary process." Standing at the threshhold of a gradual process of transformation from capitalism to socialism. Chileans recognize that a cultural transformation must go hand in hand with the necessary economic changes.

The Unidad Popular, the Popular Unity government of Salvador Allende, governs but does not control Chile. In effecting its program of popular reform, it has to contend with a seditious army, a majority opposition in the legislature, a judiciary inherited intact from the previous bourgeois regime, and entrenched monopolistic economic interests. All these aim to sabotage the economy and create a climate of psychological terror sufficient to topple the Popular Unity regime, presumably through military intervention. Of overriding significance for our present study is the fact that the right-wing opposition still controls much of the educational media and many of the best-selling newspapers and magazines. The purpose of this chapter is to show how, in opposition to a majority press, in the face of great psychological and physical terrorism, Allende's government has gained the support of an army of cultural workers who have devised various alternative channels of communication. As far as the pictorial media are concerned, they are of three principal kinds: mural, poster, and comic strip.

It is no accident that these are among the major media that have emerged in the United States as harbingers of a counterculture and protest opposed to capitalist, bourgeois values. But to compare the anarchist ideology and techniques of the Poster of Protest or a Zap comic book, or even an angry ghetto mural, to their Chilean counterparts is to reveal how very different are the circumstances in which they arose and the purposes they serve.

The Popular Unity government was voted in, with a slender majority, against the massive opposition of the capitalist-controlled press and a propaganda campaign that has been described as "immense, absolutely overwhelming."[3] Publicity for Jorge Alessandri, Allende's opponent on the Right, employed the grossest scare tactics. Marxism (or Communism) was presented in posters and radio advertisements as the system that would bring Russian tanks into the main square of Santiago, exchange the schoolboy's textbook for a gun, and send him off, according to the whim of international Communism, to Cuba or Moscow. A radio spot featured the rat-tat-tat of a machine gun, followed by a woman's scream. "They've got him, they've got my son!" "Who?" "The Russians!" The "campaign of terror" was, as a Chilean Congressional investigation verified, financed by the U.S.-owned Anaconda Copper Company and was the brainchild of a U.S. advertising agency.

The Chileans are avid readers of newspapers; literacy is about the highest in Latin America (85 percent). Eleven major national dailies have a combined circulation of 853,000; among an adult population of five million, counting several readers per newspaper, one may conclude that most Chileans read at least one paper. Two years after the UP victory the majority of the press is still against the government. Circulation figures published in July 1972 by the Office of Information and Radio showed that progovernment dailies sold 312,000 copies per issue, antigovernment dailies 541,000.[4] In the Sunday papers the proportion is similar. Revenues from capitalist advertising continue to underpin the opposition press. The major chain of opposition newspapers, the Mercurio chain, is controlled by Agustin Edwards, scion of an old patrician family, living (since the UP took power) in Miami, and International Vice-President of Pepsi-Cola. The distortions and lies of that most outwardly respectable of the conservative papers, the *Mercurio,* have been exposed time and again yet continue unabated. Indeed, as the UP government has strengthened its hold upon popular opinion, the hysteria of the opposition press has increased.

Idealists on the Left have tended to assume that the truth will out, that actions speak louder than words. The fallacies of this attitude are stressed in a

1
Silkscreen poster: "America Despierta" (America awakens).

2
Junta troops burn Popular Unity government literature, including poster
reproduced in Figure 1. (Photograph
published over the international wire
services in September 1973)

3
Junta sympathizer cleans off pro-UP
government mural slogan. (Photograph published over international
wire services in September 1973)

pamphlet on the problems of publicity published in February 1972 by Volodia Teitelboim, distinguished writer, senator, and member of the political commission of the Chilean Communist party. It is not enough, warns Teitelboim, to do things well for everything to be well. "Absolutely false. If the people do not know, if public opinion does not know, it is as if they (the Left, the government) had not done it, or done it badly. . . ."[5] The opposition press fabricates an atmosphere of total governmental failure, of imminent catastrophe, providing the emotional premise for a military coup on the pretext of avoiding civil war. The right-wing press tries to throw the country into neurosis, push people into panic terror, into the dark forest of collective fears. They unleash prejudice and frustration, they exploit all the emotional fissures of popular insecurity.

Let us take just one example of the Chilean right-wing press in action. With the approach of the Fiesta Patria, the national holidays of 18 September 1972, and against a mounting political tension, the opposition fomented rumors of an intended army coup. The tabloid *La Tribuna* carried a front page featuring photographs of serried rows of military heads and hats, and the enormous headline, occupying fully two-thirds of the page, appeared to say: THERE'S RATTLING OF SABERS. Closer inspection, however, revealed the words "but not" sandwiched in very small print in between, so that technically the headline read: "THERE'S RATTLING but not OF SABERS."

To counter journalistic lies (repeated as fact by the U.S. press) Teitelboim exhorts the communications media sympathetic to the UP to join in the primordial "battle for the truth," to defend it and diffuse it at the base, with "simple, compact, limpid images," and "legitimate, convincing, categorical messages."[6]

To enable the people to take over their own ideological self-defense, an extensive network of centers for popular culture has been proposed by the National Cultural Commission of the Communist party. These will combat illiteracy by means of "brigadas de alfabetizadors," form libraries, conduct educational programs on social problems, promote folklore, workers' theater, chorales, musical groups, and art workshops. People's theater under the aegis of the Amalgamated Labor Union (CUT) is already in action in the factories and countryside, but on the whole it is yet premature to speculate upon the potential of such centers in Chile. It is, however, opportune to examine the manner in which existing cultural vehicles are being converted to the dissemination of a new imagery and new ideas.

The Art Institution

At a meeting on Latin American figurative art held at the Casa de las Americas, La Havana, 27 May 1972,

the following manifesto, signed by thirty-four artists and art critics (several of them Chileans), was published. It took the form of a poster to be placed in any exhibition of Latin American art throughout the continent. In Chile it was circulated widely. The manifesto was worded thus (with some condensation):

CALL TO THE PLASTIC ARTISTS OF LATIN AMERICA
Every Latin American artist with a revolutionary consciousness must contribute to the resuscitation and growth of our values, in order to shape an art that shall constitute the patrimony of the people and the genuine expression of our America. Revolutionary art transcends elitist aesthetic limitations, opposes imperialism, rejects the values of the dominant bourgeoisie. The Revolution liberates art from the iron mechanism of supply and demand as it operates in bourgeois society. Revolutionary art proposes no model, establishes no predetermined style, but is imbued, as Marx says, with the tendentiousness of true creativity, to the extent that it affirms and defines the personality of a people and a culture.

The Latin American artist cannot declare himself neutral, nor can he abstract his role as an artist from his duties as a man. Revolutionary consciousness springs, in an artist, from the recognition of the alienation and mutilation he suffers in the exercise of his creative gifts, which he overcomes when he commits himself actively to the revolutionary struggle, waging it from within and with the arms of his creativity. For this reason the militant attitude of the Latin American artist is as important as his work. The one is identified with the other. This attitude is measured by his ability to invent the necessary instruments for communicating with the people and to resist all forms of imperialist penetration. He must denounce, reject, and destroy (always according to the specific peculiarities of the struggle in each country) all the manifestations of cultural oppression on the part of imperialism, be it via protests, abstentions, boycotts, or whatever tactic may be appropriate, including where necessary the violent response to the colonialist violence of the system. The Revolution is a process that begins long before the seizure of power and continues far beyond it. By engaging himself in the struggle, the artist not only contributes to the realization of that seizure of power but helps afterwards to activate an authentically revolutionary cultural program leading to the formation of the new man.

We thus denounce the existence of:
imperialist ideological penetration in Latin America, whereby culture is used as an alienating weapon;
artistic dependence on the international centers that propagate bourgeois ideology:
exploitation of art by local bourgeoisies, transforming it into one or more means of oppression of the people;
the so-called neutrality of art;
the dependence of the artist on the rigid mechanism of the commercial market, on the imposition of fashions and the aestheticism emanating from them;
the so-called aesthetic revolutions presented as substitutes for social revolution;
the manipulation of so-called cultural organizations to the profit of bourgeois ideology;
the cultural support certain artists offer to governments maintaining the capitalist system;

4

"El Arte de America Latina es la Revo-
lucion" (The Art of Latin America is
Revolution), silkscreened cover for se-
ries published by Latin American Art
Institute (*Cuadernos de Arte Latino
Americano*), 1973.

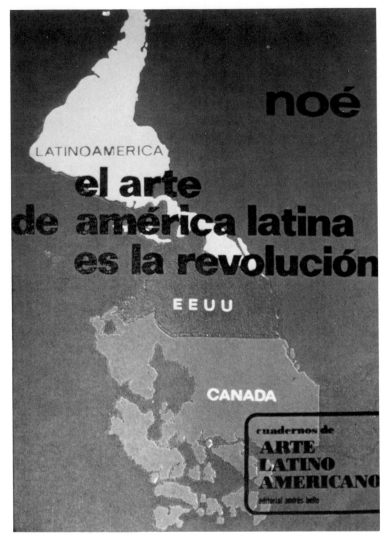

5
Poster reproducing Joan Miró painting
done especially for and donated by artist to the Museo de Solidaridad Chile
(Museum of Chilean Solidarity). The
poster is for a preliminary exhibition
of donated works.

the individual competition to which the artist is subjected as he searches for personal triumphs; the use of art as a liberal screen to conceal the exploitation and repression of the people.

It was with such ideals in mind that Chilean artists, art critics and art teachers united to found, under the aegis of the Faculty of Fine Arts of the University of Chile, on 29 December 1970 (a few months after the UP took power), the Instituto de Arte Latinoamericano (IAL). In its studies of Latin American art, in its publications, the IAL analyzes the problems of cultural dependency upon the European and North American traditions (Fig. 4). It is a remarkable fact that there existed hitherto not a single specialized magazine devoted to the study of Latin American art; no museum dedicated to the preservation of its history; no society or institution concerned with its promotion; not even a specialized library. The IAL has attracted the critics and professors Mario Pedrosa, ex-director of the Saõ Paolo Museum, and Aldo Pellegrini from the Argentine; it hopes to win the collaboration of many other specialists. A library is in the making, including photographs, slides, films, and taped interviews that will cover not only Latin American art and artists but also foreign art dealing with Latin American themes (upon the history of which the IAL Director, Miguel Rojas Mix, is an expert).[7]

The IAL is destined to become a center for round-table discussion, with facilities for lectures and seminars. Among its various extension activities will be mobile poster exhibits (two of which have already circulated), the promotion of archeological expeditions, mural painting, and the improvement of urban and environmental planning. The IAL should become a focal point for the social activity of artists, architects, sociologists, and educators in their common endeavors to raise the cultural level of the people.

A permanent major collection is envisaged under the name of Museum of Latin American Art, which has already sponsored several exhibitions held in halls now drawn under the wing of the IAL: the Museum of Contemporary Art, the Museum of Popular Art, and the University Gallery. "American, I do not invoke your name in vain" was the title of the first exhibition, held in the Museum of Contemporary Art and restricted for practical reasons to Chilean artists. "Homage to the Triumph of the People" included the participation of major Argentine and Uruguayan artists, as well as Chileans; the Ramona Parra Brigades commemorated the new mural art. Less obviously political in inspiration was the exhibition of "Abstracts, Geometrics, and Kinetics."

Respectful of the power of a mass medium neglected by bourgeois art and academic institutions, the IAL is launching a seminar and contest for the Latin American comic strip and in so doing is attempting to overcome the obvious difficulties of putting under one harness specialists from the many different fields comic strips touch (or should touch): mass-communications, sociology, pedagogy, art criticism, and so on. There is, however, agreement on one point, which is the starting point for the necessary transformation of a medium hitherto so closely identified with bourgeois interests: exposure of the U.S. and U.S.-inspired comics as one of the most potent "hidden" arms of imperialism.

Another museum, the Museo de Solidaridad Chile, is designed with an entirely novel purpose: to attract donations from artists all over the world. So far, it is the Latin American artists who have rallied to the call in the greatest numerical strength: already, eighty-two Mexican, fifteen Cuban, seven Argentine, seven Brazilian, and one each of Venezuelan and Uruguayan artists are represented. Among the Europeans, we find twenty-eight Spanish artists, (including Miró, who made a painting specially, Fig. 5), twenty-four French (including Lurçat and Vasarely), two Italians, one Dutch, one Portuguese, and one Rumanian. From the United States only four artists have as yet sent work: Ritch Miller, Pablo O'Higgins, J. Petlin, and Angela von Neumann. Philip Guston, Robert Motherwell, Frank Stella, Adja Yunker, and Philip Youngerman have promised to donate, as have Francis Bacon, David Hockney, Philip King, Henry Moore, Ben Nicholson, Eduardo Paolozzi, and Bridget Riley, from England.

The International Committee of Artistic Solidarity with Chile, the "patrons" of the museum, is comprised of the following distinguished names: Louis Aragon, the poet; Jean Leymarie, Director of the Museum of Modern Art in Paris; Giulio Alberti, the Spanish poet; Carlo Levi, the Italian senator, painter, and writer; José Maria Moreno Galvan, Spanish art critic; Aldo Pellegrini, Argentine writer and art critic; Julius Starzynski, Polish professor and art critic; Mariano Rodriguez, painter and vice-director of the Casa de las Americas in Cuba, Mario Pedrosa, vice-president of the International Association of Art Critics; and Danilo Trelles, cineast and consultant to the Fine Arts Department of UNESCO.

"The museum exists. There is no building. But there are donations of works of art, which have arrived and continue to arrive." Thus the museum director, Mario Pedrosa, a refugee from political persecution in Brazil where he was director of the musem at Saõ Paolo toasted the election of Allende from the Chilean Embassy where he was hiding. In his speech of 26 April 1972, thanking President Allende for his patronage of the museum and for the role the government played, via its embassies, in

361
Art of the New
Chile: Mural,
Poster, and
Comic Book in a
"Revolutionary
Process"

providing transport and so forth, Pedrosa stressed the uniqueness of a museum founded on the concept of solidarity and fraternity: here were artists from various countries of the world, of various political persuasions (although none of course from the Right), spontaneously moved to give art to the people of a small, poor country on the periphery of the earth, at this critical moment in its history.

The museum is for the people, for factory worker, miner, and peasant to consider as part of their patrimony. At the first showing of donated work in the new United National Conference on Trade and Development (UNCTAD) building, 35,000 people attended in ten days. The original home intended for the museum, the UNCTAD building, has been found unsuitable, and a permanent, specially designed site is being sought elsewhere in Santiago; but parts of the collection will be perpetually on the move, so as to reach the whole country.[8]

Murals: the Ramona Parra Brigades

But the true museum—and newspaper—of the people is in the street. In every city, once-empty walls have been seized by UP political parties. For two years now the slogans of the Communists, always the most propaganda-conscious of the Chilean Left parties, have dominated, through the work of the Ramona Parra Brigades.[9]

The origin of these well-known guerrilla muralists, as they call themselves, dates back to a march held in September 1969, from Valparaiso to Santiago, denouncing capitalism and imperialism. Youths from the Juventudes Comunistas, Communist Youth (JJCC) prepared the way by painting messages of support on banners and walls along the route. Later, as the election campaigns got under way, they formed groups working in support of Allende's candidacy. They called themselves the Ramona Parra Brigades (BRP) after a militant young working girl martyred in 1949. [There are other muralist brigades attached to other parties—Movimiento de Accion Popular Unido (MAPU) and the Socialist, but they are far less numerous and tend to confine themselves to verbal slogans.] The Ramona Parra Brigades during the election period restricted themselves to utilitarian political messages. They worked in a clandestine fashion, usually by night and as fast as possible in order to get the job done before the arrival of the police or slogan painters from rival political parties. There were frequent cases of arrests and rough handling from both the law (on the pretext that they were defacing public and private property), and from right-wing groups. It was thought useful then to adopt noms-de-guerre and the hard hats worn by construction workers; both are

still retained, although since the establishment of the Popular Government the police are unable to intervene.

A brigade is composed of a maximum of twelve persons—workers and high school and college students. A dozen is about as many as their transportation (battered old pickup trucks) can hold, including their equipment (huge fifty-gallon vats of paint), and about as many as can conveniently work on a single wall simultaneously. The *brigadistas* tend to be very young, of both sexes, average age about seventeen, with many in their very early teens. They elect a leader who is charged with political and cultural education and liaison with the Party for instruction on the current political tasks. All the brigades stand under the aegis of the Comisión Nacional de Propaganda. Each expedition or *rallado* is carefully planned beforehand, especially as regards place (due consideration being taken of visibility and public access) and content (choice of theme, wording of slogan, type of visual design from existing repertory). Group self-criticism follows when the job is complete.

Chile abounds in walls suited to slogan-painting, in the city centers, suburbs, villages, and countryside, and along the roads. The BRP have seized walls originally built to demarcate the rights of private property, restored them, as it were, to the people who built them, and made them into the ramparts of revolution. The brigades do not, however, paint schools, hospitals, or churches. Nor do they choose to paint over the arrogant, U.S.-style commercial billboards, the ubiquitous reminder of bourgeois power. They respect the legal norms in the strictest sense. In the cities, universities and factories their work is largely welcome, but in the villages and suburbs the brigades find it indispensable to explain to the locals what they are about and to reassure them that they are not going to "dirty their walls," as the opposition press claims they do. (A comic-book style pamphlet published by the right-wing Partido Nacional shows a decent girl, thinking of joining the Party, and horrified by the filthy behavior of the BRP, who splash "Death to all . . ." on the walls, and scream "hurry up comrades, we have to scrawl all over the houses of those wretched 'momios' (mummies, reactionaries)."

The mural painters work according to a division of labor akin to that of the medieval craft, with an altogether modern emphasis on speed and efficiency. The *trazador* traces the outlines of the letters (or image) with a sure and practiced hand, never faltering even on the huge scale of eight to ten feet high. His is the most difficult role, the one to which each brigadista aspires. Then comes the *rellenador*, who fills in the letters (or image); then the *fondeador*, who adds the background. To these three principal roles are joined, as the design requires, that of the *filetador,* who adds thin outlines or contours, and the *retocador,* who touches up. The paint used is cheap house paint with a casein base, which does not weather as well as the more expensive paints used for murals in the United States; much time is necessarily spent in repairing old murals, when they are not simply painted over with a fresh slogan or design.

The work is fast, dirty, and rough. The wall surface itself is usually uneven, with relief variations in the cement and stone of up to two and three inches, necessitating jabbing, thrusting, and twisting, as well as stroking with the brush. The brigade cannot afford the expense of a spray gun and spray paint, which would be ideal for this kind of surface. To reach the top of the design one has to stand on tiptoe; to deal with the bottom, one crouches, splashing grass and ground as well.[10] Getting dirty seems to be sensed as part of the game; in this context, it makes the school kid feel like a manual worker. As they work shoulder to shoulder, weaving in and out, meshing their gestures, the joy and energy of their teamwork expresses the very spirit of the message they paint. Participating in the great march, 800,000 strong, in celebration of the second anniversary of the electoral triumph, I observed the BRP truck suddenly pull up, apparently out of nowhere, and disgorge its dozen guerrillas, who launched themselves, amidst a cheering crowd, against an enemy position: the wall opposite the neo-Fascist (U.S.-supported) Patria y Libertad offices. In a moment, the crypto-swastika PL symbol was covered over with a progovernment slogan (Fig. 9).

The verbal slogans of the BRP are always basic, but they are of differing kinds. Most frequent is the phrase that has become the BRP motto: LUCHAR, TRABAJAR, ESTUDIAR PARA LA PATRIA Y LA REVOLUCION ("struggle, work, study for the fatherland and the revolution"). The straight newspaper headline: Y SE NACIONALISARON LAS MINAS ("and the mines were nationalized"); or the promise for the future: Y HABRA TRABAJO PARA TODOS ("and there will be work for all") appear in lapidary monumentality, as does the verse from Pablo Neruda, who has been absorbed into the national consciousness: ME HAS DADO LA PATRIA COMO UN NACIMIENTO ("you have given me the fatherland like a birth"). The phrase LOS NINOS NACEN PARA SER FELICES ("children are born to be happy") was the invention, it seems, of an eleven-year-old working with the brigades. Anti U.S. slogans are in a minority (LIBERTAD PARA ANGELA DAVIS, NIXON[11] ASESINO). The BRP believe they have turned the street into *las pizarras del pueblo,* "the chalkboards of the people." Among other

things, those immense slogans may be considered a new incentive to literacy, for an illiterate peasant with any consciousness of his cultural deprivation can hardly pass daily by those huge letters without eventually learning to decipher their meaning.

Immediately after the election of Allende, the BRP added images to their slogans. They painted their first pictorial mural two days after the day of victory. Whereas previously the task was to proclaim a name or a party, they now aim to express the programs, ideas, and spirit of the Popular Government—the revolutionary process itself. Illustrating the slogans and using pictorial designs on their own, the BRP can convey a richer message in an immediately appealing form. The brigades would not have grown so phenomenally over the last two years (150 spread over the whole of Chile) and come to command the respect of Chileans of all kinds, had they not found a form of imagery that could be understood and accepted by all classes and relatively easily duplicated by fledgling brigades. At first, they worked with designs they subsequently decided were too abstract. To reach the artistically uneducated, they draw upon an archetypal symbology, a language of the simplest and most universal images, suggestive of peace, work, and collective strength: doves, flowers, hands, fists, faces, flags, stars, an ear of corn, a factory chimney, a hammer, a sickle (and of course a hammer-and-sickle, which seems, in this context, so much more than a mere political symbol). In their use of symbolism rather than social-realist illustration, the brigades have confirmed that the Cuban poster-artists were asserting in the late sixties: uncultured people can (still) respond to symbolic art (Figs. 6–8). The imagery seems to be of hybrid origin: besides the obvious debt to Picasso, Léger, the European poster and avant-garde Western graphics (pop art and so on) there are evident references to Rivera and especially Siqueiros, and via them, perhaps, back to pre-Columbian art.[12] At its best, BRP work attains a homogeneous blend, with something of Siqueiros's dynamic elasticity and something of Rivera's granite compactness. (One of Siqueiros's best murals may be seen in the library of the Escuela Mexico in Chillan, Chile.) The BRP work has something of the heroic scale of the great Mexican murals if not their sophistication, something of their symbolic strength if not their emotional range. It also realizes an ambition of Siqueiros never realized by that artist, that is, the creation of a work of art legible by a spectator passing at a speed of sixty miles per hour. But there is a difference: the Mexicans created works of art intended to last, whereas the art of the BRP is essentially expendable, in the sense that it is intended to be immediately functional. The brigadistas and their sympathizers call this work "contingent art," meaning that it lives and dies with the particular social circumstances that called it into being. It

6
Ramona Parra Brigades. Poster for exhibition at Museum of Contemporary Art, April/May 1971.

7
Ramona Parra Brigades. Mural on Rio Mapocho, Santiago, detail. (Photo: Deena Metzger)

8
Ramona Parra Brigades mural. ". . . Y
Habra trabajo para todos" (And there
Will Be Work for All). (Photo: Monin
Mendez)

9
Ramona Parra Brigades at work during
annual demonstration in support of
UP government, 4 September 1972.
(Photo: Deena Metzger)

may be painted over as those circumstances change, or it may be left to deteriorate in the wind and rain.

The BRP mural may not last forever but while it lasts reaches out almost infinitely into space. The interior walls painted by the Mexican fill only the space those walls enclose. It is an architecturally conditioned space. The exterior walls painted by the BRP fill a space limited only by the physiology of the eye. The 400-foot Rio Mapocho mural, which involved thirty workers for fifteen days, can be seen from almost a mile off. Closer to it, one can recognize another dimension of its essential "murality": the forms echo and exploit the shape and even the texture of the rough stone with which the wall was built (Figs. 6–7).

The Mexican muralists claimed in their manifestos and often tried in their practice to work as a collective. Yet their murals are with few exceptions the individual conceptions of single exceptional artists. The only signature on the Chilean murals is the initials BRP, sometimes followed by the letters JJCC (Communist Youth), the family name. Even the really outstanding designs—those of the Rio Mapocho, near the State Technical University, at the Yarur textile factory, and in Quilloto—are presented as the result of a collective artistic effort.

Matta

There is an internationally famous artist who is Chilean by birth: Roberta Matta, born in Santiago in 1912, living in Paris and Italy since 1933, an important surrealist painter with a longstanding sympathy for socialism. Detached from the mother country, which could not support his kind of art, he has nevertheless followed political events there closely and returned to Chile in order to affirm his solidarity with Allende's new government. In November 1971 he addressed the students of the Fine Art School: "Now I have tried to ennoble materials which seemed vulgar, like mud, for instance . . . let us paint in brigades using primary colors, big brushes, on the houses of peasants, on factories. This is what the brigades have done, with their almost adolescent art."[13]

The veteran artist joined the adolescent workers of the brigades. Together they painted a swimming pool in La Granja, a working-class suburb of Santiago. The mural is signed BRP, but the design is unmistakably Matta's: absurd little figurines, anthropomorphic worms, all arms and legs, knotted into and growing out of each other; comical, coital, playfully Boschian, self-conscious gnomes left stranded by the receding waters of the unconscious (Fig. 10). "A vencer": are they celebrating a sexual or political victory, or both?

Matta and the brigades do appear to represent incompatible elements: the great individualist, dealing with intensely personal imagery,[14] and the collective of worker-painters, dealing with strictly social imagery. United in the substance of their political beliefs, they share no common ground in the form of their expression. And yet, in its very different way, Matta's art shares some of the adolescent joy he admired in the brigades.

The Posters

The muralists share the walls of Chile with the postermakers, whose work they have often helped to paste up. The new political poster, like the mural, aims to seize control of the streets from commercial advertising. Before the electoral campaign, the Left had used little beyond the cheapest, most utilitarian form of poster, and even during the campaign they did not try to rival the saturation advertising of their opponents. But having won the election and control of the Zig-Zag offset lithographic press, the UP has invested heavily in posters as a means of spreading the spirit and character of its programs among the people.

The Chileans use three different words for poster, each of which connotes a different origin and function. The word cartel is the broadest, referring basically to the informational type of poster; the French affiche is used for the more artistic (traditionally, French) kind; and poster has recently been introduced into Latin America, as into the continent of Europe, to describe the U.S. type of imaginative, psychedelic, humorous pop poster. The new political poster contains elements of all three types.

That the poster is a medium suited to the needs of the new Chile is widely recognized among cultural organizations, artists, and critics. The role of the revolutionary poster has been underlined by exhibitions from various countries. In the month of September 1972 alone there were to be seen, in Santiago, exhibitions of Cuban posters (in the UNCTAD building), U.S. posters of protest, posters from liberated Vietnam (both in the Museum of Fine Arts), and over one hundred Chilean political posters (Centro de Arte).[15] The Cuban example (now world-famous)[15] could hardly have failed to inspire the Chileans, who have not, however, tried to imitate it formally.

A few weeks before the election, around mid-August 1970, an exhibition was assembled of a series of thirty-six posters, all donated by different artists, many of whom had never used the silkscreen medium or a political theme before. The series was shown simultaneously as a group in eighty different places all over Chile, and individual posters were sold (at a low price) in order to raise funds for the electoral campaign. The first edition of 500 copies was quickly exhausted, and up to 3,000 copies of a single poster were eventually printed, in order to reach homes that had never possessed an original work of art before.

It is unfortunate that opponents of the UP regime are extremely assiduous in defacing and tearing down the government program posters. The serried ranks in which they appear on walls and hoardings are so rapidly thinned that even the most inoffensive and unprogrammatic examples (and especially, for some reason, those celebrating childhood) have difficulty in surviving for long.

Since a new government or Left party-sponsored poster appears each week, the otherwise rather drab streets of Chile constantly show new faces. Not unlike the murals in style and content, but (as the work of trained artists) rather more sophisticated, the posters are designed to reassure the public at an unstable period and to arouse simple optimism and national rather than class solidarity. Unlike the more utilitarian posters of the Movement of the Revolutionary Left (an extraparliamentary party), these posters show no recognition of the possibility of an armed confrontation with the Right. (The murals are also implicit testimony to the belief in the peaceful road to socialism.) The concept of revolutionary class struggle on an international scale, so prominent in the Cuban posters, is largely absent.

Some of the best posters celebrate the nationalization of copper on what has come to be known as the "Second Independence Day" in 1971 (copper constitutes about 80 percent of Chilean foreign exchange and before nationalization was controlled by the U.S. companies). Below a thesaural definition by Neruda, the broadest cross section of Chilean society stands in serene unity of purpose upon bars of copper (Fig. 11). The theme here is unity; in another (Fig. 12) it is maturity ("Chile goes into long pants—now copper is Chile's") where Chile sees itself as a political adolescent attaining the maturity only economic independence can bring. The theme of childhood—the joys and privileges to which younger children have a right, the responsibilities falling on the shoulders of the older ones—runs deep through the new Chilean art. "The happiness of Chile begins with the children" (Fig. 13) is a frequent slogan on both posters and murals asserting a simple, childlike joy in bright color and form.

The same simplicity characterizes some otherwise sophisticated posters summoning the privileged, older youth to voluntary work, to commit themselves to the nation as a whole, presenting the concept that play, like education, should not be the prerogative of a single class. The very playfulness of these designs tends to expose the falsity of the bourgeois dichotomy between work and play. Since 1970, the voluntary work programs, largely staffed by students, have helped to build homes for the poor

and playgrounds for children and to repair earthquake damage (Fig. 14). The earthquake is interpreted allegorically, not just as a natural disaster but as the spirit of the new Chile breaking through the barren rocks of the past (Fig. 15). In another telling image, the necessity of work, and the beauty of cooperative effort are conveyed by a pair of birds building a nest (Fig. 11).

These posters are made by a tremendously prolific team of artists, who have also revolutionized record-sleeve design and the film poster.[16] The new Chilean folksong and a burgeoning film industry dealing with themes of topical and social interest have already driven a deep wedge into the public cultural consciousness, hitherto dominated by U.S. and European imports.

Most of the larger, government-sponsored posters are printed at the offset lithographic press of Quimantú. The State Technical University (UTE) has its own offset press, used to publicize its cultural events, summer schools, further education programs, and other government efforts to draw the working classes into the educational and cultural life of the nation. The UTE posters tend to be smaller, quiet, and witty; more "Cuban," perhaps, in their tone. Among the best are images suggesting that economic and cultural production are somehow equal, sharing the same goals and status; the industrial or agricultural worker is not to be considered inferior, or even essentially different from, the intellectual and artistic worker. In this spirit, symbols of manual labor are deftly converted into and equated with symbols of culture—and nature. The cog of the machine becomes the rising sun, the wrench is like a guitar (Fig. 16), the pick is like a book.

Chile is as yet far from generating a working-class art, and it may be some time before the proletariat can overcome their cultural deprivation and the false bourgeois ideals thrust upon them for so long. A pointer to the future may be found in the work of A. R., whose silkscreen designs of the Chilean peasantry and fisherfolk have won the respect of the Chilean intelligentsia. His art has the simplicity and humor of a Posada print, combined at times with a certain oriental ornamentality (Fig. 17).

The posters sponsored by government agencies are, naturally, directed toward national issues; posters produced by individual artists as the expression of their personal commitment to socialism are often conceived in an internationalist spirit and draw stylistically on the pop art and other avant-garde movements that have also furnished styles and images to the protest graphics of Western capitalist countries (Figs. 18a, 18b). The Chilean artists also use the gun as the politico-cultural symbol of capitalist oppression. Believers in the peaceful road

10
Roberto Matta and Ramona Parra
Brigades. Detail from a swimming
pool at La Granja, near Santiago. The
figures say: "the loveliest star is the
hand of the worker," "let's win," "run
so that I can catch you," "half way
round and slowly." (Photo: Deena
Metzger)

11
Poster celebrating nationalization of
copper: "Chilean Copper: you are the
fatherland, the pampa, and people,
the sand, clay, school, home resurrection, fist, offensive, order, parade, attack, wheat, struggle, grandeur, resistance." (Neruda)

12
Poster celebrating the nationalization of copper: "Chile goes into long pants. Now copper is Chile's!!"

13
Poster: "The happiness of Chile begins with the children."
14
Poster: "To work! Voluntary Work summer '72."

15
Poster: "Through reconstruction, life is reborn. Reconstruction of the earthquake-shattered zones."

16
Poster for Fourth Conference of Young Workers: "La llave de la cultura es de los jovenes trabajadores" (the key [or wrench—pun] to culture is with the young workers).
17
Silkscreen print: Fisherman with fish.

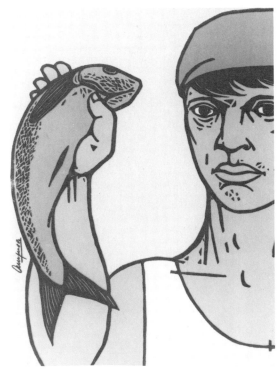

18a
JUSTICIA " 'Secret' graphic revelation of CIA covert activities against Chile."

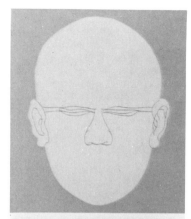

TE ES EL ENEMIGO. CUIDADO, TIENE MUCHAS CARAS. ¡A DERROTARLO

18b
"This is the Enemy: he has many faces. Defeat him!"

to socialism, they do not see it, as do the Cubans, as a symbol of popular revolutionary power, although they have been quick to identify with the Cuban revolution. Perhaps the best-known expression of commitment to Latin American solidarity, prominently displayed in the Peña Parra where the famous Parras[17] sing, is the huge, bipartite silkscreen called *America Despierta*. (Figs. 1 and 2). This fine cartographical allegory presents Latin America as a restless interlock of hopes and agonies, symbols of the old jostling symbols of the new, a continent caught between the fires of fascism and revolution.

It should be noted, in passing, that the face of Allende himself is relatively little in evidence. One of the new president's first actions on taking office was to stop the printing of the thousands of portrait posters of himself; such posters are normally sent out to hang in public buildings throughout the land whenever a new president is elected. It is the socialist idea, not the individual personality, that matters.

Comic Books

Nowhere has the cultural dependence upon the United States presented itself in a more garish light than in the domain of the comic strip and comic book, whose social influence causes Chilean intellectuals much anxiety. Throughout Latin America, U.S. comics saturate the market. The empire of Disney in particular has strengthened its hold over the past decade, at a time when his comics have lost their ground in the domestic market.

The true message of Disney to the third world, its fundamentally insulting, bourgeois, and imperialist character, has been exposed by two young Chilean intellectuals: Ariel Dorfman, a literary critic and novelist from the University of Chile, and Armand Mattelart, a sociologist from the Catholic University, both of whom have worked as advisers to Quimantú, the publishing house responsible for the new Chilean comics.[18]

The Disney and other U.S.-style comics were published by the huge Zig-Zag publishing corporation, which served the interests of the ruling Democratic-Christian party until that party lost to Allende in 1970. When the Popular Unity came into power, the Zig-Zag employees, who had long been dissatisfied with the firm's operations, arranged for it to go bankrupt. This allowed for an easy government takeover and for a potentially massive instrument of public education to pass to the Left. Under the new, Mapuche Indian name of Quimantú, it became a major cultural enterprise of the UP government, publishing various magazines and cheap paperbacks concerned with the new Chile. The head of the comics section (a longtime Marxist with twenty years experience at Zig-Zag) remembers how around the

changeover date, 12 March 1971, he and his team worked day and night to transform the existing bourgeois comics without interrupting the regular flow to the magazine kiosks. Artists were reoriented, new story-writers engaged, fresh scenarios, characters, and locales invented in order to express the new socialist ideals. The transformation was, of course, incomplete, affecting principally the content; drawing styles and compositional techniques remained (with some notable exceptions) traditional. Quimantú's success at presenting the new ideas to the old readership may be gauged from the circulation figures, around 150,000 total per issue, plus about two-thirds of that figure in foreign (Latin American) sales.[19]

We may properly begin with *Cabro Chico* (Little Kid), along with *La Firme* the most remarkable of the Quimantú comics, and like *La Firme* an entirely new publication (the other titles treated here are conversions from existing formats). Designed for children up to about eleven years and conceived in cooperation with the University of Chile's Department of Preschool Education, *Cabro Chico* spearheads the movement to break the Disney monopoly. The mix of picture puzzles, short stories, paper cut-out toys, and miscellaneous pictorial and educational matter is more familiar to Europeans than Americans. The standard of drawing is consistently high.

Among the Cabro Chico comic strips, the most startlingly innovative experiment is one that testifies more to naive enthusiasm for socialist doctrine than to realistic appraisal of the difficulties of drawing children (and parents) out of their Disneyland fantasies. At its inception, *Cabro Chico* set about the task of instant conversion of hallowed fairy tales to the use of a new Chilean society. Parody of fairy tales and folk myths as a convenient means of satirizing contemporary conventions in thought and behavior is an old literary device (Rabelais, Swift, and so on). The exploitation of this mode in a magazine directed specifically at younger children is sufficiently novel to warrant some examination.

Cinderella in *Cabro Chico* is the spoiled younger sister, a Lolita type who complains she is unable to attend a party because she hasn't a thing to wear. Wandering disconsolate about town, she is suddenly invited to participate in a TV contest, which she wins. She is showered with luxurious clothes and other gifts, only to discover that these "prizes" are not her property but a publicity gimmick of the TV sponsors. Cinderella's tears are softened, however, by her being allowed to keep her finery on until midnight. She goes to the party, is a great success, and dances with the nightclub owner until midnight. A phone call at this moment suddenly reminds her of her promise to return the apparatus of seduction.

She rushes off in such haste that she leaves behind a boot (which she had removed after accidentally spilling wine into it). When the nightclub owner arrives at her home the next day with the missing boot, Cinderella identifies herself as the wearer and offers to marry the Prince Charming, who, however, casually declines, since he already has a girl friend. Collapse of Cinderella.

In Snow White and the Seven Dwarfs, Snow White is the capricious bourgeois daughter, spoiled by her father. Her stepmother sees her problem, and following the advice of her mirror, sends her for a bracing walk in the forest with a hunter. Snow White escapes and comes upon the house of the seven dwarfs, where she soon finds herself earning her keep by working, for the first time in her life, at domestic tasks. Checking out a rumor of a hard-working girl living with the seven dwarfs, the stepmother disguises herself as an old hag, is overjoyed to observe her daughter converted to the virtues of labor, and leaves her a basket of apples as a reward. Sick from a surfeit of apples, Snow White is lying in bed when a prince passes by, is instantly smitten with her beauty, and declares his love and desire to marry her. Snow White tells him off smartly for being so stupid as to propose to an unknown person, and the seven dwarfs (arriving on the scene) peremptorily demand to know who the stranger is, where he works, or what he studies—questions most embarrassing to this idle scion of capitalist wealth (Fig. 19). His illusions destroyed, he jumps on his horse in a huff but is invited by Snow White to take her home to her parents. In the last picture he is seen with the elated parents and daughter, as boyfriend rather than lover or husband, paying the dwarfs the first of the promised weekly visits. Thus is the bourgeoisie gently converted to socialist values.

Pictorially the imitation of Disney is slick and complete, although tinged with parody. Snow White is distinguished from her original by the humorously degenerate pout and the Prince Charming by his vacuous aristocratic expression.

As parody, the Cabro Chico fairy tales show obvious signs of strain in their attempt to preserve characteristic detail (Cinderella's boot, Snow White's apples), the symbolic nature of which is inevitably lost; they are also very incomplete. The task of transforming an entire content while preserving familiar formal elements is, arguably, an impossible one. The new social values and satirical flashes sit heavily upon the story line. As was expected by the editors, the experiment was attacked by the bourgeois press as an attempt to brainwash children; less expected were the sudden slump in sales and other evidence that the readers (the children) were simply turned off. It is of course doubtful that any

kind of satire on this relatively sophisticated and intellectual level could succeed with preteen children; it might conceivably appeal to the alienated offspring of the educated bourgeoisie, who are, however, not Cabro Chico's primary audience and are not as numerous as in the United States. In this country, cultural alienation is so strong and begins so early that an advanced ten- or twelve-year-old can enjoy the parody of Mad magazine. The comic fairy tale à la Mad, poised somewhere between Grimm-Disney and the TV commercial, the parodistic western, and the travesty of the newspaper strip, is achieving something of the status of a genre in the United States. This can happen only in a society where the consciousness of oversaturation and manipulation by the mass media is high; in Chile it is not.

Under heavy fire from the bourgeois press and bourgeois readers, the editors of Cabro Chico unequivocally state their belief that the traditional fairy tale contains values that (whatever their historical role) can only be harmful when transplanted to a Third World culture at this period of its development. In one of the adult supplements normally occupying the center pages of the magazine (Cabro Chico 5), there is a series of juxtapositions of drawings and texts, those of the traditional fairy tale and those of the new Cabro Chico version. The villainous stepmother of Snow White, who tries to have her child cruelly murdered, is contrasted to the sympathetic stepmother of the new version; the rich, blond prince arriving—and accepted in marriage—out of the blue, is contrasted as an ideal for the young girl with the young man who is taught that work is the normal condition of life and that mutual knowledge is the basis for marriage. The "hero" Puss-in-Boots who lies, betrays, murders, and threatens the peasantry in order to enrich his master is contrasted with the Cabro Chico hero Pedro, who denounces the wicked cat. The cruelty and sadism of the fairy tale, often defended as necessary food for the childish imagination, are denounced by Cabro Chico as the lamentable byproduct of bourgeois competitiveness. What is the point, asks Cabro Chico, of showing a wolf (not a class of animal we need to fear nowadays) physically devouring innocent grandmothers and little girls and then being killed and slit open; why not try winning him over with tea and cookies?[20] The gruesome imagery of the old fairy tale is identified as the parent of the far more realistic, far more horrible, and even more dangerous mythology of Superman and the U.S. horror comics.

After half a dozen issues, Cabro Chico abandoned the demystification of the fairy tale in favor of simpler and more positive—if less intellectually diverting—approaches. The incorporation of socialist ideals is best studied in the serial called "Estos

Cabros" (Those Kids), which has a realistic and flexible framework of everyday life in village and suburb. Life here is not dominated by individualism and competition, nor is it governed by supernatural forces; the values presented are those of collective enterprise, fraternal affection, and commonsense ingenuity as applied to the solution of practical problems. In a typical episode (Fig. 16), the Cabros defend the bit of municipal land that they are using as a playground (having no other) but that is destined for commercial use. They organize against bureaucratic attempts to expel them, putting up signs saying "WE HAVE SEZED [sic] THE TREES" (Fig. 20). The Kids win, after a direct and collective confrontation with the authorities (shown to be stuffy rather than evil), during which the courageous intervention of a little girl among them plays a critical role; at the end, they have the cooperation of some openminded neighbors.

In most bourgeois children's strips, the spaceadventure provides a context of passivity, in which the young heroes undergo the miracles of technology or learn to manipulate quasi-supernatural powers. In *Cabro Chico* the child is taught the value of creativity. An openly doctrinal but very amusing episode of "Año 2,200" (*Cabro Chico* 5) shows the earthling children on a strange planet, returning to their spaceship to find that it has been dismantled by a band of primitive beings armed only with an (un)screwdriver (*destornillador*), given to them by scientists who had previously landed on the planet and taught them how to dismantle machines. The stranded children take the native beings to the remnants of their spaceship, hand them a similar instrument called a screw(together)driver (*atornillador,* a term peculiar to South America), and teach them to do the operation in reverse "and go on to new and better things." "I get it," says a spaceling, "we have to create." Which might be the motto of *Cabro Chico*. The quasi-pun around the word *tornillador* reveals a respect for the verbal—a respect that is rare in children's comics.

There is hardly a strip in *Cabro Chico* without touches of humor—humor tending more to nuances than in the Disney animal slapstick from which it derives. Humor is predominant in the only continuing serial with an out-and-out evil character. In "Martin y Kano" (characters also being popularized in televised and animated film form), with its stereotyped formula of the evil being from outer space aiming to conquer the earth, humor is used to deactivate what is assumed to be essentially pernicious and false to reality, that is, the manichaen segregation of life forces into good and evil. The figure of Lunatic is always ridiculous and pathetic rather than malevolent, and his antics and the mode of his defeat represent a simple social farce; he has

to be avoided, managed, and foiled by the young, rather like a crotchety old misanthropic neighbor.

Purely pictorial values predominate in "Zipi in the Musical Planet," which aims to render, in graphic, quasi-psychedelic imagery, the joy and beauty of music. Like the story, the art is reminiscent of the *Yellow Submarine* film cartoon. The denizens of the Planet of Love are being robbed of their music, their sole means of subsistence, by the denizens of the Silent Planet, which cannot bear music. But unlike the typically bourgeois solution proposed in the *Yellow Submarine,* where irredeemably evil forces have to be physically destroyed, *Cabro Chico* brings about a negotiated settlement between the antagonists, with faults recognized and concessions made on both sides.

Cabro Chico is not only for children. Each issue contains a black-and-white "parents' supplement" relating to hygiene, health, household, and child care. Not only class boundaries but generational boundaries must be crossed. This device (not used, so far as I know, in the bourgeois West) draws the adult into the literature and therefore into the fantasy world of the child; it simultaneously draws the older child into adult problems. Adults and children share the learning experience. *Cabro Chico* shows that learning, whether from comics or in the schoolroom, can be fun. One issue (*Cabro Chico* 25) is even devoted to satirizing and exposing the unnecessary petty tyranny and pedantry of the old school system, in order to overcome fears traditionally inculcated in the poor and illiterate.

There are six adult action comics in the Quimantú stable, all of which try in some way to dismantle the U.S. concept of the superhero. They have succeeded, to varying degrees, in bringing the adventure story closer to Chilean reality, to the life of the Chilean people. "Los Cinco de la Aurora" (in *El Manque* comic) concerns the life of the fisherman and deals with the antisocial effects of drunkenness (in *El Manque* 234 a professional diver is nearly killed through the negligence of his drunken comrades). *El Manque* 235 shows how a case of homicidal insanity is handled by community rather than institutional justice. *Guerra* 161 contains a lesson in fraternal internationalism—criminals who exploit a quarrel between visiting Norwegians and local Chilean sailors in order to rob and murder one of the former, are tracked down by the exertions of the latter. The criminals are here unidentified as a class, and the police play their traditional role, but in another episode (*Guerra* 156) the criminals are squarely defined as agents of monopoly capitalism whose sabotage is foiled by the people of a new government-supported fishing center.

19

Cabro Chico comic, version of Snow
White and the Seven Dwarfs: the
Prince is rejected by Snow White.

20

Cabro Chico comic, "Estos Cabros":
the Kids defend their playground by
putting up signs saying: "We have
sezed [sic] the trees."

One serial in *Guerra* comic deals exclusively with the paramilitary operations of the Comando Operacional Naval Unido (CONU), a composite of Chilean navy, coast guard and customs officers, who are often engaged in the suppression of smuggling. Since the CONU is so clearly playing the role of good guys and protectors of the people, the serial may be regarded as an attempt to win over to the revolution a sector of the armed forces at a time when their loyalty appears uncertain. In "The Plunderers," unpatriotic villains smuggle automobile spares to Argentina; they are foiled by the CONU, tipped off,—significantly—by a "humble electrician."

Smuggling, like hoarding, is one of the economic plagues bourgeois obstructionism has visited upon Chile; both are forms of theft. In the Quimantú comics theft takes on various aspects, all related to the concept that property is communal rather than individual. The thief is the monopolist, the capitalist, foreign or domestic, draining off the natural resources of the country (in *Delito* 122 with uranium, secreted in a remote mountain lair, standing for Chilean copper); but he is also (in the same issue of *Delito*) the petty pickpocket who thoughtlessly inflicts suffering on members of his own class. The uranium monopolist was destroyed by the professional detective; the pickpockets are unmasked by the people of their own community, fellow *pobladores*.

The bourgeois stereotype of the lone detective single-handedly thwarting evil still survives (Ricardo Santana in *Delito*'s "Espia 13"), as does that of the lone adventurer (El Manque, in the comic of that title). But El Manque finds himself (more by accident than design) involved in what is essentially the class struggle: thus he helps, as one individual among many others of like convictions, to smash a *latifundista* who has hired thugs to terrorize the peasants (*El Manque* 234). The loneliness of El Manque is that of a man alienated from his class, partly (in his intellectual consciousness) the drop-out from the bourgeoisie, and partly (in his working-class solidarity) the *afuerino*, the migrant worker suffering from economic dislocation.

The adventure strips are mostly conceived within the revolutionary process as the Chilean experience has defined the term. If they appear on occasion to stand outside of it, they are never opposed to it. The vigorously drawn *Guerrillero* presents episodes of the cunning and courage of the Independence patriot Manuel Rodriguez, who (by this showing) achieved great ends without resorting to much violence. But "Mizomba" is hardly a guerrilla figure, as the comic title suggests; he is a cousin of Tarzan who was converted for a while into a clothed Chilean character but rejected as such by the readership.

White, blond, and naked, he lives among African natives, but not as a Savior figure; attempts are made to mitigate the racist potential of a heroic white individual in a society of primitives. Visually rather dazzling, the appeal of Mizomba is that of the exotic rather than the violent.

The fantasy figure of Mizomba may be contrasted with the white guerrillas in *Jungla*, clearly set in the jungles of contemporary Brazil. Gruesome incidents are based on press reports (such as the tapping of the blood of captured guerrillas, in order to sell it for profit on the markets of Taiwan and Haiti). Note, however, that the Indians on whose behalf the guerrillas are operating (usually in other ways than with armed defense) have apparently no leadership or organization of their own. There is no Indian patriot-hero in the Quimantú comics.[21]

The most important war strip is set in Vietnam and called "Corresponsal de Guerra" (War Correspondent, in *Guerra* magazine). The editorial philosophy of war is stated in an interview with (real-life) Chilean journalist Fernando Bellet (*Guerra* 157), who participated in the Normandy landings in 1944: war is the degradation of mankind and fear the impulse behind what we have been taught to regard as heroism . . . "but there are wars and wars, and one must distinguish the just from the unjust. One cannot compare the liberation movement of Spartacus with the horrible war Hitler brought to the world. Some men cherish the monster of war in their hearts. Our task is to destroy it forever, and that can be done only when all men are equal and have the same opportunities . . ."

The equation, implicit within the context of the comic, of the United States with the Nazis, and the whole reversal of roles (brave orientals versus vicious North Americans) is designed to jolt Chileans, the overwhelming majority of whom are Caucasians who have been conditioned by the U.S. media to regard (white) North Americans as crusaders for freedom and civilization in the non-white world. A typical cover of *Guerra* seeks to epitomize the injustice of a war conducted by machines against defenseless civilians (Fig. 21), and the story line usually stresses the suffering of the Vietnamese (without, however, ignoring their armed resistance) and the callousness and cruelty of the U.S. command. The responsibility of the press (that is, world opinion) is dramatized in the way the war correspondents (a veteran Republican Spaniard and a young Chilean) intervene physically against the wanton burning, killing, and rape.

The air war over the north is the subject of *Guerra* 158, in which the U.S. crew and the correspondents (permitted on board by the same kind of administrative error that allows them to observe the true

377
Art of the New
Chile: Mural,
Poster, and
Comic Book in a
"Revolutionary
Process"

character of ground combat) parachute out and are captured. They are taken on a tour (as real-life POWs were) of the terrible destruction wrought by the bombing, including that on the dike-system (this episode appeared some months before it became common knowledge that the United States was deliberately aiming at the dikes). Observing the efforts of the people to down planes, the young Chilean photographer has occasion to befriend a Vietnamese girl, a schoolteacher and militia leader, whose beauty and heroism arouse his lust and the reader's expectations of romance. But there is to be no sexual imperialism here, and the last the Chilean sees of his Vietnamese friend is her drowning as she rescues one of her little pupils from the flood caused by a breaking dike.

A moral distinction is maintained between the U.S. officers in charge and the common soldiers, who are shown capable, on occasion, of disobeying orders. There are degrees of individual responsibility and of victimization. In *Guerra* 160 ("Yerba Mortal"), an entire combat unit is shown to be drugged as it executes the scorched-earth policy and engages thereafter in insane forms of fratricidal vengeance. The U.S. black soldier is represented as a relatively innocent victim and a potential subversive. The blacks keep their distance from the whites and despise the Uncle Tom who suffers every indignity at the hands (and feet) of the white racist officers in his ambition to become a real American. This he believes he has achieved by shooting up some Cong civilians—only to be returned to his habitual latrine cleaning (Fig. 22).

The Quimantú comics cautiously lay down the ideological groundwork for a new society. There remains one group to consider—a group that aims to give the public a crash course in what it means to move from a capitalist to a socialist way of life. Under the name *La Firme* (which literally means "constant" or "steadfast" and colloquially, "upfront"), conceived and executed by a team of three artist-writers whose styles are distinguishable but perfectly harmonized; the series has been published biweekly ever since the UP government came to power. About 50,000 copies of each issue are sold on the kiosks and distributed free to poor housewives, workers, and schoolchildren. Their themes are as wide-ranging and far-reaching as the political and economic problems of Chile today: copper, energy, food-production, retail distribution, democratic liberties, education, the media, and so on (Fig. 23). *La Firme,* the most directly political and didactic comic, is also (perhaps paradoxically) the most consistently amusing, the most truly comic in its style. In conception it is (along with *Cabro Chico*) the most original of all the Quimantú comics, blending political and social problems into a framework of humor, fantasy, and fairy tale.

The dialectic of capitalist versus socialist ideas is not merely presented but acted out in real-life situations—factory, store, and street.[22] In this way the ideological confrontation with capitalism and the bourgeoisie is vividly and intricately woven into the existing fabric of Chilean reality, and the Chilean learns, as from satirical theatrical skits, to overcome social prejudices and irrational fears of change. The magazine is also truly Chilean in its liberal use of Chilean slang, puns, and double meanings.[23]

We may select for analysis *Supercauro en el Misterio de las JAP,* which contains not only a simplified, pungent, and witty exposition of a major national problem (the shortages and inflation caused by bourgeois obstruction of UP programs) but also a critique, enjoyable by children and adults alike, of the manic individualism underlying the whole U.S. Superman syndrome.

Harmonious in its dual purpose as political comic and cultural anticomic, *Supercauro* fuses the political and cultural revolutions into one. *Superkid in the Mystery of the JAPs* parodies the Superman comic within the context of political activism. Superkid is a gutsy youngster who has acquired supernatural powers by dint of his diet of fish and milk (significant UP government innovations include the promotion of the native fishing industries, as reliance upon Argentine beef imports is reduced, and the guarantee that each Chilean schoolchild shall be given a free pint of milk a day.) Hearing housewives complain about a lack of certain foodstuffs in the shops, Superkid determines to seek out and destroy the Evil Cause of the shortage. He zooms around zapping the poor retailers and other persons low on the distribution hierarchy (Fig. 24). Recognizing his errors and leaving himself scarcely time to apologize to them, Superkid flies on until he reaches the true culprits, the big distributors—crooks whose bullets bounce off the armor of his virtue. Virtuous he is, but ignorant. A housewife, engaged in organizing the neighborhood JAPs (Committees on Supplies and Price-control) explains patiently to the young firebrand that "the problem of shortages, speculation, and hoarding is very delicate . . . it's no use one person, even a superhero, trying to solve it personally . . . a solution lies in the cooperative effort of all consumers and small retailers, organized in the JAP."

Perplexed at first as to how his superheroic personality can fit into all this, Superkid determines to investigate the JAPs, eventually discovering all he—and the Chilean housewife or retailer—needs to know. After more hair-raising adventures, during which he is exposed to the insidious propaganda against the JAPs put out by opposition press and radio, and during which he shatters various windowpanes (for which he has to pay out of his own

21
Cover of *Guerra* comic (original artwork). U.S. soldier in Vietnam aims at Vietnamese woman in fields.

22
Guerra comic: the U.S. black soldier hopes to impress his white superiors by shooting defenseless Vietnamese, but is returned to his habitual latrine cleaning.

23
La Firme comic: further education
program, during which Pepe learns to
drive a tractor but graduates with a
less good grade than his horse.

24
La Firme comic: Supercauro (Superkid) investigates the cause of food
shortages and mistakenly goes around
zapping the retailers.

pocket), he returns at last to normal life and school (where he is mildly punished for his unexplained absence). Superkid is left sadly reflecting: "I don't want to complain, but it *is* difficult being a Superhero and studying at the same time . . . I bet this doesn't happen to Batman and Superman." Indeed it doesn't—but then they don't live in Chile.

Notes

1
As suggested by a participant in the symposium on which this volume is based.

2
An artist can be politically active in a thousand ways; but as an example of artistic activism that preserves the medium and injects political content by the provision of a new context, we may cite an example that could hardly be more germane to the substance of this chapter. A group of New York artists recently painted a copy of the Santiago Rio Mapocho mural (described below) publicly in the street, on panels eight by one hundred feet, and set them up outside the Chilean airline offices on Fifth Avenue (*Art Workers News,* published by the National Art Workers Community, Vol. 3, No. 8, November 1973, p. 1).

There exists now (since 1976) a Center for the Defense of Chilean Culture, which coordinates cultural activities of exile groups working against the Junta. It is based in Paris, but reaches out all over Europe, Latin America and the U.S.

3
Richard Feinberg: *The Triumph of Allende, Chile's Legal Revolution* (Mentor Book from the New American Library, 1972, p. 91). This is an excellent introduction to contemporary Chile. On p. 93 Feinberg gives the circulation figures and political allegiance of all the major newspapers and magazines.

4
Printed in *Chile Hoy,* An. 1, n. 4, Julio 7–13.

5
Volodia Teitelboim, *Sobre el problema de la publicidad,* Cuadernillo de Propaganda No. 1, Impresora Horizonte (1972), pp. 6 and 18.

6
Teitelboim, pp. 23–24.

7
See *La Imagen Artistica de Chile,* just published by the IAL, in which Rojas Mix analyzes the stereotypical distortions the Chilean native reality has suffered at the hands of European artists and travelwriters. The aims of the IAL were outlined for me in the course of many conversations I was fortunate enough to have with its director. These aims were also formulated in the *Annales de la Universidad de Chile,* Nueva Serie Abril–Junio 1970, Año 129, No. 1.

8
During the coup, when the military, as they bombed the presidential palace, made the UNCTAD building their headquarters, the works of art temporarily stored in the basement were thrown into the street. There is now (1975) an international movement to recall them and set up a Museum of Solidarity in exile.

9
For information on the history and procedure of the BRP, I am indebted to "Mono" González who lent me his unpublished manuscript on the subject, gave me posters and

slides, and provided me with an opportunity to observe and participate in the work of the brigade. A very particular debt is owed to Deena Metzger, the compañera with whom I had many provocative and fertile discussions on Chilean art and who offered many valuable criticisms of this article.

10
Problems with scaffolding, so familiar to American popular muralists, simply do not arise: it is too cumbersome and expensive. The typical BRP mural is long and low.

11
Usually in the international Left spelling with a swastika replacing the "x."

12
It should be noted, however, that there is in Chile, unlike Mexico, virtually no indigenous artistic tradition upon which a muralist can draw.

13
Adapted from the transcription in Ernesto Saul, *Pintura Social en Chile,* Colección Nosotros Los Chilenos, Empresa Editora Nacional Quimantu, Santiago 1972, p. 89. This useful work is chiefly concerned with the realistic murals of the postwar era.

14
Much of Matta's painting in recent years has, however, carried plainspoken political connotations, discernible in such a series-title as "Desastres del Imperialismo Americano."

15
See David Kunzle, "Uses of the Portrait: The Che poster" in *Art in America* September-October 1975, vol. 63, no. 5, pp. 66–73; and Kunzie, "Public Graphics in Cuba: A Very Cuban Form of Internationalist Art," in *Latin American Perspectives,* Special Issue, Cuba: La Revolución en Marcha, Issue 7, Supplement 1975, Vol. II, No. 4, pp. 89–110.

16
I have eliminated their names, as well as those of other well-known artists I had originally identified personally, because their present fate is unknown to me. I can, however, cite Guillermo Nuñez, an internationally known artist working in avant-garde styles, recently (1976) released into exile from prison where he was tortured.

17
Angel Parra, originally sentenced by the Fascist junta to thirty years hard labor, has been released into exile because of international pressure.

18
Para leer al Pato Donald, Ediciones Universitarias de Valparaiso, 1971. There are many other Latin American editions. There are also editions in European languages, and an English language edition, prepared by David Kunzle was published by International General (P.O. Box 350, New York 10013) in 1975, and on sale in the U.S. 1976, after twelve months of detention by U.S. Customs acting on behalf of Disney.

19
This figure lies, however, well below the total sales figure of the various Disney magazines, which sell over a million a month. It is one of the paradoxes of a society trying to blend socialism into existing capitalist structures that Quimantú cannot afford to discontinue printing the Disney comics on the basis of the contract they inherited from Zig-Zag.

20
Critics to the left of the UP, denying the feasibility of a "peaceful road to socialism," have in effect asked where

381
Art of the New
Chile: Mural,
Poster, and
Comic Book in a
"Revolutionary
Process"

and when was the capitalist wolf ever won over by tea and cookies? In post-coup retrospect, one becomes more conscious of elements of pacifist as well as socialist ideology in the UP propaganda and publications. *Cabro Chico's* pacifist transformation of the fairy tale is particularly ironic because many favorite fairy tales originated in a historical (broadly medieval) folk consciousness which saw and imagined class conflict as cruel but inevitable (cf. Jack Zipes, "Breaking the magic spell: The politics of the Fairy Tale," *New German Critique,* No. 6, Fall 1975, pp. 116–135.

21
To compare, for instance, with Cuba's "Tupac Amaru" (in *C Linea*).

22
A comparison may be made with the admirable political comics of the Mexican caricaturist and writer Rius (*Los Agachados,* and others), where despite an amusing drawing style, the political information comes over in a more stolidly didactic, more theoretical way. (There is, of course, no comparable "revolutionary process" in Mexico today.) The Cubans, who are very conscious of the uses of the political and didactic comic and of the problems of creating such a comic of any quality, have voiced their admiration for *La Firme* (see Prensa Latin's anti-comic, *C Linea, Revista Latino americana de Estudio de la Historieta*).

23
For integral reproduction, in translation, with brief content analysis of a *La Firme* story of worker exploitation, see David Kunzle, "The Chilean Worker as Mythic Hero: The 'Shanks of Juan'," in *Praxis* no. 2, January 1976, pp. 199–200; and for the role of a multinational corporation and U.S.-controlled communications media, the same author's "*Chile's La Firme* versus I. T. T.," in *Latin American Perspectives,* issue 16, Winter 1978, Vol. V, No. 1, pp. 114–133.

Contributors

John E. Bowlt is an associate professor in the Department of Slavic Languages and Literature at the University of Texas. He has written many articles on various aspects of modern Russian art and has co-organized a number of art exhibitions in Europe and the United States. One of his latest publications is *Russian Art of the Avant-Garde: Theory and Criticism 1902–34* (Viking Press, 1976).

Ruth Butler is chairman of the Art Department at the University of Massachusetts, Boston, and is an authority on nineteenth-century sculpture.

Stanton L. Catlin is professor of art, director of the Graduate Program in Museology, and director of exhibitions at the Lowe Art Gallery in the College of Visual and Performing Arts at Syracuse University.

Carol Duncan is an associate professor in the School of Contemporary Arts at Ramapo College of New Jersey.

Paula Hays Harper's interest in art and politics began with her M.A. thesis on the role played by printed pictures during the Reformation and continued with an exhibition and catalog of a group of propaganda posters from the Hoover Institution at Stanford University (*War, Revolution and Peace*, Stanford Museum, 1971). Her interest was applied to contemporary politics with an exhibition of graphic art protesting the Vietnam War (*Against the Madness: Art from California Campuses*, Washington, D.C., 17–27 June 1970). She received a Ph.D. in art history from Stanford University, has taught at the University of New Mexico and California Institute of the Arts, and is currently working on a biography of Camille Pissarro with coauthor Ralph Sikes.

Alison Hilton is the author of a dissertation on "Russian Art in Transition: Realism and Its Aftermath, 1870–1900" (Columbia University) and articles on Russian and European art.

Spiro Kostof is a professor of architectural history at the University of California, Berkeley.

Max Kozloff is a former editor of *Artforum*. His publications include *Renderings*, *Cubism/Futurism*, and *Jasper Johns*, as well as numerous articles on art and on photography.

David Kunzle has written on popular, political, and revolutionary art. His major book is *The Early Comic Strip: Picture Stories in the European Broadsheet c. 1450–1826*, History of the Comic Strip, vol. I. He is Associate Professor of the History of Art at the University of California at Los Angeles.

Henry A. Millon is professor of history of architecture at the Massachusetts Institute of Technology.

Francis V. O'Connor is an authority on American art and has published *Federal Support for the Visual Arts: The New Deal and Now* (New York Graphic Society, 1969), *The New Deal Art Projects: An Anthology of Memoirs* (Smithsonian Institution Press, 1972), and *Art for the Millions* (New York Graphic Society, 1973). At present he is coediting, with Eugene Victor Thaw, a catalogue raisonné of the work of Jackson Pollock, which will be published by the Yale University Press in 1977. He is also publishing a quarterly newsletter entitled *Federal Art Patronage Notes*.

Eberhard Schroeter has studied at the universities of Berlin, Vienna, and Rome, specializing in Italian nineteenth- and twentieth-century architecture and city planning with a dissertation on Roman architecture under the Fascist regime for Heinrich Thelen, Freie Universität Berlin. In 1975 he received an M.B.A. from The European Institute of Business Administration (INSEAD). He is now living in Rome.

Helen Searing, associate professor of art history at Smith College, is a specialist in the field of modern architecture.

Ralph E. Shikes is the author of *The Indignant Eye: The Author as Social Critic in Prints and Drawings from the Fifteenth Century to Picasso* (Beacon Press, 1969), and is coauthor with Dr. Paula Hays Harper of a forthcoming biography of Camille Pissarro.

Richard Stapleford is teaching at Hunter College, City University of New York.

Carroll William Westfall is associate professor of the history of architecture and art at the University of Illinois at Chicago Circle.

Stanislaus von Moos, art historian, taught at Harvard University and at the Architectural Association School in London. He is at present the editor of *werk archithese* and teaches art history at the University of Berne, Switzerland.